Data Structures Through 'C' Language

OTHER TITLES OF INTEREST

Getting Skilled with **Java**
ISBN: 9789391392499

Java
ISBN: 9789388176507

Software Design Patterns
for **Java Developers**
ISBN: 9789391392475

Java 8 to **21**
ISBN: 9789355513922

Let Us **Java** - 7th Edition
ISBN: 9789355517555

Java Professional
Interview Guide
ISBN: 9789391030056

Web Development Toolkit
for **Java Developers**
ISBN: 9789355510341

Jakarta EE for
Java Developers
ISBN: 9789355510082

Core Java Made Simple
ISBN: 9789386551979

Java for **Web Development**
ISBN: 9789355511430

Mastering Java
Persistence API (JPA)
ISBN: 9789355511263

Java Programming
Simplified
ISBN: 9789389845143

Decoding JavaScript
ISBN: 9789390684816

100+ Solutions in **Java** –
2nd Edition
ISBN: 9789389845600

Java in Depth
ISBN: 9789386551573

Selenium with **Java**
A Beginners Guide
ISBN: 9789391392680

Data Structures Through

Language

DOEACC SOCIETY
(An Autonomous Body of Ministry of Information Technology, Government of India)

Developed for DOEACC SOCIETY by
Samiran Chattopadhyay
Debabrata Ghosh Dastidar
Matangini Chattopadhyay

www.bpbonline.com

REPRINT 2026

FIRST EDITION 2001

ISBN-10: 81-7656-375-7
ISBN-13: 978-8-17-656375-8

Distributors:

BPB PUBLICATIONS
20, Ansari Road, Darya Ganj
New Delhi-110002
Ph: 23254990/23254991

DECCAN AGENCIES
4-3-329, Bank Street,
Hyderabad-500195
Ph: 24756967/24756400

MICRO MEDIA
Shop No. 5, Mahendra Chambers,
150 DN Rd. Next to Capital Cinema,
V.T. (C.S.T.) Station, MUMBAI-400 001
Ph: 22078296/22078297

Published by Manish Jain for BPB Publications, 20 Ansari Road, Darya Ganj, New Delhi-110002 and Printed by him at Manipal Technologies, Manipal

www.bpbonline.com

To Our Beloved Parents

Preface

Approach

Algorithms are central to the study of Computer Science. Data Structures play an important role in the design of algorithms. It is mandatory for an expert software professional to have a thorough understanding of the basic data structures. This book describes several data structures, their usefulness and applications, and algorithms involving them.

Data structures are abstract notions and thus, they can be specified using a very formal language and algorithms for these data structures may be developed in any language including structured English. A standard programming language appears to be a natural choice for describing data structures and algorithms, as such languages are unambiguous. We have been guided to choose "C" programming language for this purpose because of well known versatility of 'C' language and the fact that "C" is known to a vast majority of the intended readers and thus, it does not add unnecessary complexity for learning data structures.

The book is primarily intended to be used by undergraduate students who are familiar with the concepts of programming and "C" programming language. The topics chosen are centered around a standard data structures syllabus for any undergraduate curriculum. The book also covers the syllabi of the paper "Data structure" for "A" and "B" level courses of DOEACC. Our presentation style is based on our belief in progressing from the concrete to the abstract. We have taken special care while introducing new concepts and while proceeding from simple to more complex ideas. Examples are numerous and they have been selected carefully. Each chapter ends with a collection of all the ideas introduced and developed there-in. Exercises are exhaustive and they have varied complexities. A large collection of various objective type questions (with answers) has been provided in the Appendix A.

Outline of the book

As an introduction to data structures, Chapter 1 develops the basic ideas of algorithm design, specification and analysis. This chapter introduces the definition of data structures and Abstract Data Type (ADT) with a number of examples. The mathematical notions used for analyzing algorithms have also been developed in this chapter. The basic idea of verification of algorithms has been introduced.

Any student familiar with "C" programming language would know about array as a built-in type. However, Chapter 2 treats arrays from a different perspective and explains implementing an ordered list by an array. Examples involving arrays include matrix manipulation, polynomial and large integer arithmetic, transposition of sparse matrix etc. All these examples are presented in an exhaustive manner guiding the reader from simplest to more complex issues. Representation of multi-dimensional arrays has also been dealt with in this chapter.

Linked list, one of the most commonly used data structure, has been discussed in Chapter 3. Chapter 3 covers all kinds of lists – singly connected, doubly connected and circular. Each operation on lists has been discussed in detail. Advanced concepts such as array implementation of linked lists and dynamic memory allocation are introduced and fully developed. Chapter 3 also deals with generalized lists. Many examples have also been provided.

Two important types of lists, stacks and queues are the topics described in Chapter 4. Both array and linked list implementation of these data structures have been discussed. Expression evaluation and topological sort are chosen as applications of stacks and queues respectively. Representation of multiple stacks and queues has also been explained.

Chapter 5 deals with strings. Apart from simple operations on strings, string matching is explained elaborately. Algorithms like Knuth-Morris-Pratt, Boyer-Moore and Rabin Karp have been described in great detail in as lucid language as possible. Recursion is an important mathematical notion that is extremely helpful in solving complex problems and in understanding advanced data structures. A complete chapter, Chapter 6, deals with recursion. It also develops concepts such as recursion tree, analysis of recursive algorithms, and removal of recursion.

Tree is probably the most important non-linear data structure. Two chapters are devoted for explaining the tree data structure. Chapter 7 explains basics of trees and describes binary trees, threaded binary trees and binary search trees. Recursive and non-recursive algorithms for traversal of trees, insertion, deletion and search on every type of tree have been explained in a very intuitive manner. More advanced trees such as AVL trees, 2-3 trees, B-trees and priority queues are discussed in chapter 8. Set representation using trees is also explored in this chapter.

Searching and sorting are discussed in Chapter 9. Several searching and sorting methods such as linear search, binary search, insertion sort, shuttle sort, shell sort, bubble sort, selection sort, merge sort, quick sort, heap sort etc. have been described. All methods are analyzed fully and compared with one another. Hashing is also discussed in detail.

Chapter 10 introduces the graph data structure and all related terminology. Various graph representations, graph traversal techniques are discussed. Algorithms are described and analyzed for two typical problems, namely, shortest path and minimal spanning tree of a graph.

Appendix A contains a large collection of a variety of objective type questions with answers.

Appendix B deals with two advance topics, namely, Garbage Collection and Game Tree.

Acknowledgement

Completing an assignment such as writing a text book is an arduous task which can never become successful without active participation of a large number of people. We like to thank Mr. Prasanta Banerjee for patiently typing the entire manuscript. We are also grateful to Ms. Siuli Roy and Ms. Chhanda Roy for helping us in testing some of the programs written in this book. The effort could not be successfully completed without incessant assistance by the people in DOEACC Society, a society under the Ministry of Information Technology. Especially, we are thankful to Late T. C. Gupta and Mr. Basab Dasgupta. We are also grateful to Dr. P. N. Gupta, the Executive Director of the DOEACC Society. More information about DOEACC may be found in Appendix C. Acknowledgement is also due to anonymous referees who provided many effective suggestions. We are grateful to our family, friends and colleagues for providing continuous encouragement and useful inputs.

Contents

OTHER TITLES OF INTEREST

Python Networking
Solutions Guide
ISBN: 9789355513571

Programming
In **Python**
ISBN: 9789386551276

Basic **Core Python**
Programming
ISBN: 9789390684953

Advance **Core Python**
Programming
ISBN: 9789390684069

Basics of
Python Programming
ISBN: 9789388511803

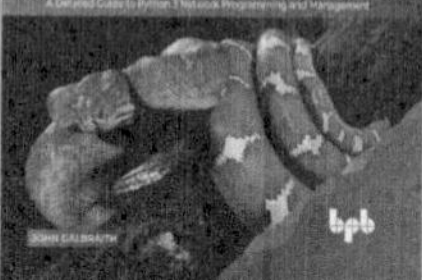

Network Programming
in **Python**: The Basic
ISBN: 9789355512574

An Introduction to **Python**
Programming: A Practical Approach
ISBN: 9789391392062

Programming Techniques
using **Python**
ISBN: 9789389845891

Python GUI Programming
with **PAGE**
ISBN: 9789355518378

Data Structures
with **Python**
ISBN: 9789355513304

Enterprise Automation
with **Python**
ISBN: 9789355511379

IoT Data Analytics
using **Python**
ISBN: 9789355515759

Python for **Everyone**
ISBN: 9789355518170

Python
for **Professionals**
ISBN: 9789389423754

Web Data Mining
with **Python**
ISBN: 9789355513632

Python
Quick Interview Guide
ISBN: 9789389423303

Edge Computing
with **Python**
ISBN: 9789355512000

Chapter 1

Introduction

1.1 Introduction to Algorithms

The field of computer science centres around writing programs to solve several problems in a variety of domains. As Nicholas Wirth has brilliantly expressed, a program is a combination of algorithms and data structures. This chapter attempts to clarify the basic concepts of these two terms. The notion of algorithm is so fundamental to problem solving using a computer that study of algorithms often appears to be synonymous to the study of computer science. Loosely speaking, an algorithm is a description of steps or instructions required to solve a given problem. An algorithm also specifies the sequence in which the steps are to be performed. Once these steps described in an algorithm are performed on a sample data representing an instance of the problem, the expected result (which is also known formally as output data) is obtained. Take the problem of finding the Greatest Common Divisor (GCD) of two positive integers as an example. The inputs to an algorithm that solves the given problem are two positive integers. The output is also a positive integer which is the GCD of the integers given as input. There are many ways to solve the above problem. One such solution is the famous Euclid's algorithm which is presented in the following. The algorithm is described as a series of steps, which are to be performed in the same sequence as they are written. Each step of the algorithm is also labelled. The labels are shown in italics.

Algorithm FindGCD

Step 1. Read two positive integers "x" and "y".

Step 2. Divide "x" by "y". Let the remainder be "r" and let the quotient be "q".

Step 3. If "r" is zero then jump to step 8

Step 4. If "r" is not zero then follow the steps 5 through 7

Step 5. Assign "y" to "x"

Step 6. Assign "r" to "y"

Step 7. Go to step 2.

Step 8. "y" is the required GCD

Step 9. print "y".

Step 10. Stop.

The steps, which are mentioned in the above algorithm, are so simple that anyone carrying out these steps precisely knows what to do in each step. While carrying out the steps of an algorithm on some input data, one must encounter some step containing a statement like "stop" after a finite number of steps. From the above example, it can be said that an algorithm is a sequence of instructions which act on some input data to produce some output within a finite number of steps. More formally, an algorithm must have the following properties:

- Input: There are some (possibly empty) input data which are externally supplied to the algorithm.
- Output: At least one output is the result.
- Finiteness: If the instructions or steps of an algorithm are carried out then, for all possible combinations of input data, the algorithm must terminate after a finite number of steps. An algorithm is said to terminate if the step being carried out contains a statement like "Halt" or "Stop".
- Definiteness: The steps must be clear and unambiguous.
- Effectiveness: The steps of an algorithm must be very basic. By "basic", it is meant that if a person wishes to carry out a step, one should be able to mechanically do that using a pencil and a paper and without applying any intelligence. Thus, following step is not effective.

Select a number so that the sum of its digits is equal to the product of the digits.

Note that the first three properties listed above apply to an algorithm as a whole while the last two talks about the properties which each step in the algorithm must possess. Also note that while an algorithm must terminate in a finite number of steps, not all programs terminate. The most typical example of an indefinitely running program is the Operating System. It waits for events in an infinite loop and terminates only when the computer is switched off. Technically, such programs are referred to as procedures. Otherwise, the words program and algorithm can be used interchangeably.

Various issues and directions of study arise out of the above definition of algorithms. These are briefly touched upon in the following:

i. Expressing an algorithm: "Definiteness" property of an algorithm demands that each step in an algorithm must be clearly and unambiguously specified. Thus, expressing these steps in a natural language (like English) becomes difficult due to intrinsic ambiguities of such languages. Pictorial description of an algorithm is also possible through "flowcharts". But flowcharts are difficult to write and manage for large problems. The flowchart for the algorithm "FindGCD" is shown in Figure 1.1. Programming Languages are probably the best languages to express algorithms as far as "definiteness" property is concerned. But, syntax of a programming language often becomes a burden while designing an algorithm as the focus tends to shift from designing to expressing the algorithm. In this book, "C" language has been chosen to describe most of the algorithms.

ii. Designing an algorithm: Problem solving still remains a work of art and therefore, creating an algorithm for solving a problem is mostly an innovative exercise. Thus, there is no methodology, which may be used to automatically generate algorithms for a given problem. However, new techniques and strategies have evolved over time which have been proved to yield good algorithms in restricted domains of application. Studying these strategies, one may gain useful ideas which may be applied to devise an algorithm for a new problem. At this point, it must be said that design of an efficient or a good algorithm depends heavily on the organization of the data on which the algorithm operates. This point will be further elaborated latter in this section.

iii. Analyzing an algorithm: Once an algorithm is designed, there are two issues which are to be properly dealt with. One issue is validation of the algorithm and the other issue is evaluating the complexity of the algorithm. It is necessary to show that the designed algorithm yields correct output for all possible combinations of input values. This is also called "program proving" or "program verification". Although this is a very important task, formal methods to accomplish this task are prohibitively complex. Hence, most often, program testing remains the only practical way to ensure the correctness of a program. The other aspect of analysis is equally challenging. When a program is executed, it uses resources of a computing system such as central processing unit, memory etc. One important topic in the study of algorithms is to determine the amount of time and storage an algorithm may require for execution. These results are useful for comparing algorithms and for predicting the performance of the algorithm in the best, worst and average case. More on this aspect of analysis of algorithms will be discussed in section 3 of this chapter.

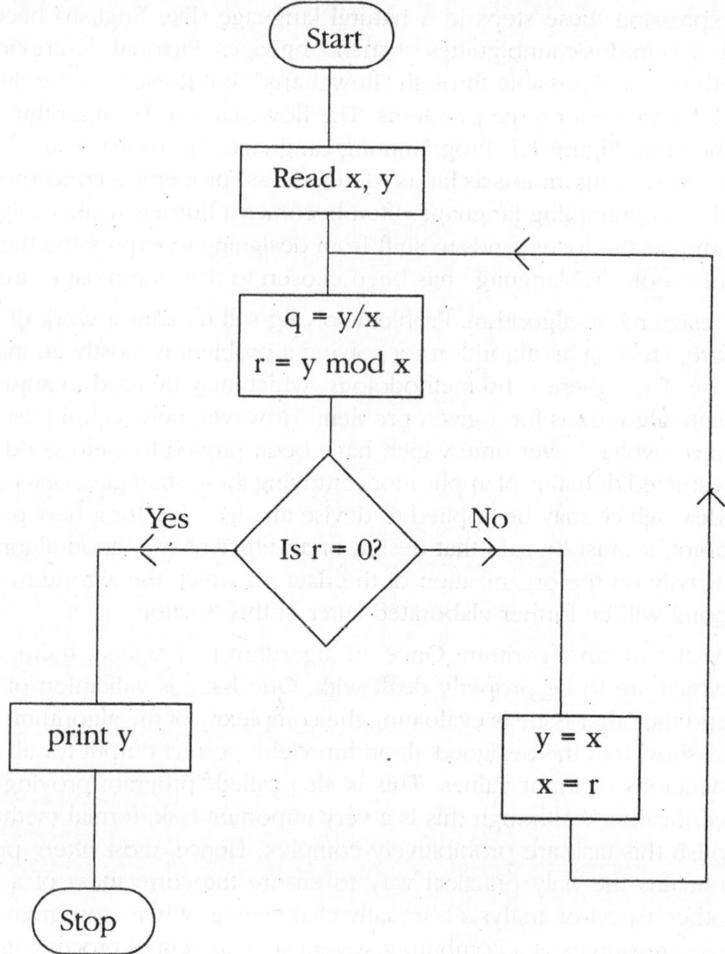

Figure 1.1 Flow chart of the algorithm "FindGCD"

An algorithm may be viewed as a function which transforms the input data to the output data. In the process of this transformation, an algorithm makes use of several variables to store and manipulate intermediate results arising out of intermediate computations. It is important to understand that the organization of "data" on which an algorithm works influences the very design of that algorithm in a great way. To appreciate this point further, consider an example. Suppose that it is required to write a program that will store the words of a dictionary so that if some word is given as input to the program then the program tells whether that word exists in the dictionary or not. In one approach to solve this problem, words of the dictionary may be stored in an array in any arbitrary manner. To search for given a word in this case involves searching the entire array unless a match is found or the array is exhausted. In another approach, the words of the dictionary may be stored in alphabetical order similar to the manner in which words are found in the dictionary itself. In this approach, searching becomes easier because it can exploit the ordering of the words in the array. Specifically, one can go to the middle of the array and by comparing the given word and the word at middle one can choose only one half of the array for further inspection. This process can be continued until the middle word matches with the given word or the array is exhausted by the process of halving the array. Comparing these two approaches, it is clear that the search algorithm is fundamentally different in these two approaches. Consequently, complexity of the algorithms is also different. In yet another approach, in addition to keep the words arranged alphabetically, another list is maintained to remember the position of the first word starting with a specific letter. That is, the second list maintains the position of the first word starting with 'A', 'B', 'C' and so on. This approach is called "indexing". The search algorithm can find out the first letter of the given word and find the part of the first array of all words starting with that letter. On this part of the array search may proceed in the way outlined in the second approach. The third approach may be efficient in many cases but it uses more space to do so. The extra space is required for storing the second list. The above discussion explains that the design of the "search" procedure is dependent on the organization of the data on which "search" works. So, it is clear that the design of an algorithm is greatly influenced by the organization of the data on which the algorithm operates.

Thus, data, its representation, organization, and operations on data are equally critical to the study of computer science as crucial the study of algorithm is. One objective of this book is to study many different types of organizations of data. For each such organization, some relevant operations will also be explored. Algorithms to implement such operations will be discussed and often the complexity of these algorithms will be computed. After understanding the topics discussed in this book, the reader should be confident on the usage and implementation of the standard organizations of data. More importantly, the reader should be able to devise new organizations of data for different applications so that the problem at hand can be solved in a more efficient way.

1.2. Abstract Data Type (ADT) and Data Structure

"Type" or "data type" is a common terminology in mathematics and in programming languages. Variables are declared to be of a particular "data type". These declarations mean that the variables can assume values only from a particular set. The type of the variable determines this set. Thus, "type" may be defined as a set of values. (However, this definition is not complete as will be seen in the sequel). There are plenty of examples of "data type" in programming languages. In languages like FORTRAN, Pascal, C, the standard built-in types include integers, real numbers, characters and so on. Variables declared of type integer may assume any integral value. However, depending on the machine, there is a limit to the range of integers that can be properly used in any programming language. Hence, there is a subtle distinction between "type" in mathematics and "type" in computers. For example, the type "integer" is definitely a finite set in any programming language. This distinction is more pronounced for real numbers. Since each number is to be finally represented in a finite number of bits in a computer, the continuity property of real numbers in mathematics is lost in the corresponding type in a programming language. In fact the set of real numbers in mathematics does not have a one to one mapping to the set of real numbers in a programming language. Moreover, a type is not just a set of values. A "type" also determines the set of operations applicable to the set of values that the said "type" represents. Note that the operations are defined while "type" itself is being defined. In other words, to define a type, the set of values and the set of operations are defined. Any object of that type can assume the values defined for that type and the operations defined on that type may be applied on the object of that type. Thus, for type "integer", the operations such as addition, subtraction, multiplication etc. are defined. These operations are defined to be binary and they are defined on two objects of type integers. So, two variables of type integer can be added. But, two variables of type character can not be, usually, added or multiplied. Although most programming languages support some standard "data types", they are not enough for most of the applications. So, programming languages usually support creating new data types in terms of "Structured types". A "Structured type" is made up of several components each of which are either an atomic type or another "Structured type". This can be accomplished in "C" language by defining a "struct". However, just by defining a structured type, the operations applicable to objects of that type can not be specified. This is why the concept of an Abstract Data Type (ADT) is required.

An ADT is defined to be a mathematical model of a user-defined type along with a collection of all primitive operations on that model. To illustrate this notion, define a new data type "SET", which denotes a set of entities. An object of type "SET" is defined to be a collection of "N" otherwise unrelated entities. If the type of each entity is represented by a set of values "D" then an object of type "SET" having "n" entities may assume any value from the set D(i.e. D X D X D X ... X D) where multiplication in this context means set multiplication. The primitive operations that may be defined for this ADT are given in the following:

1. Assign (SET A, SET B)

   This operation assigns the set identified by "B" to "A".

2. Null (SET A)

   This operation assigns null (an empty set) to "A".

3. SET Union (SET A, SET B)

This operation creates a new set which is the "union" of the sets identified by "A" and "B". This operation returns the new set.

4. int Find (ENTITY x, SET A)

   This operation searches the set "A" to check whether an entity "x" is a member of the set "A". If "x" is a member of the set "A" then the operation returns a value "1"; otherwise the operation returns a value "0".

5. SET Intersection (SET A, SET B)

   This procedure returns a new set which is the intersection of the sets identified by "A" and "B".

6. int Cardinality (SET A)

   This operation returns an integer which is the number of members in the set identified by "A".

It is possible to go on adding more operations to the list of operations applicable to sets. The operations described here should be taken as a representative set of operations on the ADT concerned. The actual number of operations will depend on the requirements of the application at hand. Also note that while defining the operations on an ADT, the aspect of implementation is not paid attention to. After understanding the operations and the set of values for an ADT, one thinks of the organization of the data of an ADT and then the implementation of the operations are considered. Further note that the operations are only defined. The algorithms or procedures to carry out these operations are not mentioned at all. It must also be borne in mind that the definition of the ADT's must be precise. Hence, usually the language of choice is not a natural language but a formal one. For the sake of simplicity and easy readability, the operations of the ADT "SET" are defined in the way "C" functions are defined and these operations are explained using simple English. Moreover, all those operations are defined in terms of known set operations (like intersection, union etc.) which are already accurately defined in mathematics. For a more precise definition of an ADT consider the next example. Suppose an ADT for natural numbers is to be defined for addition operation alone. The data set D = {0, 1, 2, 3, ..., ∞}. Let there be the following operations as defined next.

1. IsZero

   "IsZero" is a function whose domain is the set "D" and whose range is the set "Boolean" = {True, False}. The definition of "IsZero" is as follows:

   IsZero (x) = True, if x = 0

   = False, otherwise.

2. Successor

   "Successor" is a function whose domain and range are "D". The function is defined as follows:

Successor (x) = x + 1 for all xεD.

3. Add

"Add" is a function whose domain is D X D and range is "D". This function is defined as follows:

Add (x, y) = y if x = 0
= Successor (Add (z, y)) if Successor (z) = x

With the help of "Successor" function and the element '0', all elements of "D" can be accessed. For example, 1 = Successor (0), 2 = Successor (Successor (0)), 3 = Successor (Successor (Successor (0))) and so on. Similarly, Add (3, 4) may be computed as:

Add (3, 4)
= Add (Successor (Successor (Successor (0))),
Successor (Successor (Successor (Successor(0)))))

= Successor (Add (Successor (Successor(0)),
Successor (Successor (Successor (Successor(0))))))
= Successor (Successor (Add (Successor (0),
Successor (Successor (Successor (Successor(0)))))))

= Successor (Successor (Successor (Add (0,
Successor (Successor (Successor (Successor(0))))))))

= Successor (Successor (Successor (
Successor (Successor (Successor (Successor(0)))))))
= 7

Observe that the definition of "Add" operation is intentionally made cryptic. The operation is defined in terms of "Successor" operation. Probably "Add" will never be implemented in this fashion. But any implementation of "Add" must conform to the given definition. It is to be emphasized again that defining an ADT implies defining the operations (and not efficient algorithms to implement them) in precise terms. In fact, an ADT is formally defined to be a triplet (D, F, A) where "D" stands for a set of Domains, "F" denotes the set of operations and "A" represents the axioms defining the functions in "F".

Formally, a data structure is merely an instance of an ADT. Therefore, in order to define a data structure, an ADT has to be defined. This is the reason why the triplet that defines the underlying ADT most often characterizes a data structure itself. However, the term data structure refers to the structural relationship present within data and thus should be viewed as a 2-tuple (N, R) where "N" is a finite set of nodes representing the data elements and "R" is a set of relationship among those nodes. For example think of a tree data structure where nodes are related to each other by "Branching" relationship. As a data structure is a lively object, representation and manipulation of such relationship is to be properly understood as well.

1.3 Analysis of Algorithms

Most often there will be many different algorithms for solving the same problem. In the course of discussing data structures it will be seen that a data structure can be represented in a number of ways and there may be a number of algorithms to implement an operation on the said data structure. In such situations, it is required to compare two algorithms to implement an operation on the said data structure. In such a situation, it is required to compare two algorithms and choose the better one. This is one of the most important motivation to analyze an algorithm.

Analyzing an algorithm should typically reveal some quantitative metrics about the requirement of computing resources by the algorithm during its execution. Most important of these resources are computer time and memory. Consequently, analysis of algorithms focuses on computation of space and time complexity. Space in this context means storage required in addition to the space required to store the input data. Computer time, an algorithm might require for its execution, would usually depend on the "size" of the input. Thus time complexity of an algorithm is often a function of input size, "n". Moreover, the same algorithm may take different time to execute for different inputs having the same size. The different types of time complexity that researchers are interested in are the best case, the worst case and the average case time complexity. Best case time complexity of an algorithm is a measure of minimum time that an algorithm will require for an input of size, "n". Similarly, the worst case time complexity of an algorithm is a measure of maximum time that an algorithm will require for an input of size "n". The time that an algorithm will require to execute a typical input data of size "n" is known as its average case time complexity. Computation of average case time complexity of an algorithm requires some assumptions of statistical distribution of the input data and often turns out to be complex mathematical problem.

It is very difficult, however, to compute the exact time taken by an algorithm for its execution. There are several important factors which influence the time required by an algorithm. Many of these factors are outside the domain of a programmer. For example, programs are translated into machine code for a given computer and it is a challenging task to compute how long, even one "C" statement might take to execute in an environment where resources are being shared. This is why time analysis implies defining a function f(n) that gives an estimate of the volume of work done by an algorithm for its execution on an input of size "n". An important step in the analysis of an algorithm is to identify the abstract operations on which an algorithm is based. For example, in a program to compute the maximum element in an array of "n" elements, the primary operation that an algorithm performs is the comparison operation. If the program to sort an array of "n" elements is considered, then one more operation other then comparison becomes important which is exchange operation. This step of identifying the primary operations of an algorithm helps us in separating the analysis of an algorithm from its implementation.

Before discussing the mathematical notation useful for computing the complexity of an algorithm, some discussions on frequency analysis of a few algorithms will not be out of place. Consider the following function, for example.

```
void oneAssignment()
{
    int x, y, z;
    z = x + y;
}
```

The most important operation that the above function performs is addition. The number of additions that it performs is 1. Consider the next function:

```
void nestedLoop(int n)
{
    int i, j;
    int x, y, z;
    for (i = 0; i< n; i++)
        for (j = 0; j < n; j++)
            z = x + y;
}
```

The number of assignment operations the function "nestedLoop" performs is

$$\Sigma_{i=1,n} (\Sigma_{j=1,n} (1)) = \Sigma_{i=1,n} (n) = n^2$$

Now, consider another function with a nested loop:

```
void anotherNestedLoop(int n)
{
    int i, j;
    int x, y, z;
    for (i = 0; i < n; i++)
        for (j = i; j < n; j++)
        {
```

```
            if (j %2 == 0)
                  break;
            z = x + y;
      }
}
```

When control enters into the inner loop then the value of "i" is either even or odd. Consequently either an even or an odd value initializes "j". If "j" is initialized to an even value then the assignment is performed. But, before the next iteration "j" is incremented and so "j" becomes an even number. Hence, the loop is broken. If "j" is initialized to an odd value then, the assignment operation is not performed at all. Although the above function contains a nested loop, the number of times the assignment operation is executed is n/2+1.

Now, consider the following versions of functions computing the n-th element in the Fibonacci sequence. A Fibonacci sequence is a series of positive integers as given in the following:

0, 1, 1, 2, 3, 5, 8, 13, 21, ...

Thus, the 0th Fibonacci number is 0, the fifth Fibonacci number is 5 and so on. For a given "i", if i > 1 then, the i-th Fibonacci number is given by the sum of (i-1)-th Fibonacci number, and the (i-2)-th. Fibonacci number. Thus, the fourth Fibonacci number is the sum of the second and the third Fibonacci numbers. The 0th and 1st Fibonacci numbers are "0" and "1" by definition. A simple iterative function computing the n-th Fibonacci number is given in the following.

```
int findFibo(int n)
{
      int i;
      int curr, prev=1, lastprev=0;
      if (n==0) return 0;
      if (n==1) return 1;
      for (i = 2; i <= n; i++)
      {
            curr = prev + lastprev;
            lastprev = prev;
            prev = curr;
      }
      return curr;
}
```

The operation that is important for this algorithm is the addition in the statement which has been shown in boldfaced letter. It is easy to see that this statement is executed (n-1) times for any n > 1. Next consider a recursive algorithm which serves the same purpose as "findFibo".

```
int recursiveFibo(int n)
{
        if (n==0) return 0;
        if (n==1) return 1;
        return (recursiveFibo(n-1) + recursiveFibo(n-2));
}
```

It is interesting to find out the number of addition operations this algorithm performs. Let S(n) denote the number of addition operations that is required by the algorithm "recursiveFibo" when invoked for "n". Then, according to the algorithm "recursiveFibo",

$$S(n) = S(n-1) + S(n-2) + 1, \text{ for } n > 1$$

while S(0) = S(1) = 0.

Therefore, the following holds.

$S(2) = S(1) + S(0) + 1 = 1$

$S(3) = S(2) + S(1) + 1 = 2$

$S(4) = S(3) + S(2) + 1 = 4$

$S(5) = S(4) + S(3) + 1 = 7$

$S(6) = S(5) + S(4) + 1 = 12$

It can be proved by mathematical induction that S(n) = F(n+1) – 1 for n > 1 where F(n) denotes the n-th element in the Fibonacci series.

To prove the induction base note that S(2) = F(3) – 1 = 2 – 1 = 1. By induction hypothesis, assume that the result holds for all "k" when k < m. Now it has to be proved that the result also holds for S(m).

By definition of S(n), S(m) = S(m-1) + S(m-2) + 1.

By using induction hypothesis, S(m-1) = F(m) – 1 and S(m-2) = F(m-1) – 1.

Hence, S(m) = F(m) – 1 + F(m-1) – 1 + 1

That is, S(m) = F(m) + F(m-1) –1

But F(m) + F(m-1) = F(m+1) and thus, S(m) = F(m+1) – 1. Hence the result follows.

Although the number of additions required by the function is obtained, this function is not a known function as a polynomial of degree "n" or an exponential function. The exact value of F(n) is difficult to calculate. But it can be shown that the value of F(n) is upper bounded by ϕ^n for some constant ϕ. Let ϕ be the root of the equation $x^2 - x - 1$

= 0. Then it can be shown by induction that $F(n) \leq \phi^{n-1}$ for n > 0.

The induction base is true as $F(1) = 1 \leq \phi^0$. By induction hypothesis assume that the result $F(n) \leq \phi^n$ for all "k", k < m. To prove the result for k = m, note that

$F(m) = F(m-1) + F(m-2)$

That is, $F(m) \leq \phi^{m-2} + \phi^{m-3}$ (By applying induction hypothesis on F(m-1) & F(m-2)).

That is, $F(m) \leq \phi^{m-3} (\phi + 1)$

That is, $F(m) \leq \phi^{m-3}.\phi^2$

That is, $F(m) \leq \phi^{m-1}$.

Hence $F(n) \leq \phi^{n-1}$ for n > 0.

Two points have been highlighted in the analysis of the above algorithms. First, the algorithm in its entirety is not taken up for complexity analysis. Instead, some key operations, which will reveal the computational complexity of the algorithm, are considered. Second, many mathematical tools including mathematical induction are to be rigorously used to carry out the complexity analysis of algorithms.

1.4. Asymptotic Notation

It has already been mentioned that the function to measure time complexity of an algorithm is meant to be independent of machine architecture or programming language. The focus of such metrics should solely be on the order of magnitude of the frequency of execution of statements. O-notation is one of the very famous mathematical tools available for this purpose.

f (n) = O(g(n)) (should be read as "f of n is equal to big-oh of g of n") if and only if there are two positive constants "c" and "n" so that the following inequality holds for all $n \geq n_0$

$$|f(n)| \leq c|g(n)|$$

Try to understand the meaning of f(n). Assume that f(n) stands for computing time of some algorithm when the algorithm is run on an input of size "n". And g(n) be a known standard function like n^2, n^3, nlogn etc. That is, the behaviour of g(n) is known before the time complexity of the algorithm is computed. If analysis leads to the result f(n) = O(g(n)) then it means that if the algorithm is run on some computer on some input data for sufficiently large values of "n" then the resulting time will be less than some constant times |g(n)|.

The O-notation has been extremely useful to classify algorithms by their performances. This notation also helps designers to search for the "best" algorithms for some problems. If it can be shown that the complexity of an algorithm is O(f(n)) and there does not exist any algorithm with complexity O(g(n)) such that g(n) is weaker than f(n) then, the algorithm is said to be of optimal complexity. However, the results expressed using O-notation must be interpreted very carefully. The following points must be kept in mind in this context.

- Complexity expressed in O-notation is only an upper bound and the actual complexity may be much lower.
- This complexity can almost be treated as worst case complexity. But the input that causes the worst case may be unlikely to occur in practice.
- The constant c is unknown and is not necessarily small.
- Similarly the constant n_0 is unknown and may not be small.

It is obvious that merely stating that the complexity of an algorithm is O(f(n)) does not mean that the algorithm ever takes that long time. It just means that the analysis proves that the algorithm does not take a longer time. Actual running time required in practice might be much lower. This calls for developing better notation where it is also known that there is some input for which the algorithm actually takes O(f(n)) time.

Worst case complexity is not always very helpful as well. It may so happen that although the worst case complexity is O(f(n)), typical input data is never like that. Therefore, the average case complexity of the algorithm is much less than its worst case complexity. A very classic example is the "Quick Sort" algorithm. Although its worst case complexity is $O(n^2)$, its average case complexity is O(nlogn).

The constants "c" and "n_0" implicit in the O-notation hide the details of implementation. But these constants are actually important when the algorithms are executed in practice. See the following figure for an illustration. Although $O(n^{3/2})$ will be assumed to be larger than $O(n\log^2 n)$, that is not the case for small values of "n". Even when "n" runs into thousands, $n\log^2 n$ is more than $n^{3/2}$. This remains the case until "n" runs into tens of thousands. See Figure 1.2.

n	**¼ nlogn**	**½ nlogn**	**$n\log^2 n$**	**$n^{3/2}$**
10	22	45	90	30
100	900	1800	3600	1000
1000	20250	40500	81000	31000
10000	422500	845000	1690000	1000000
100000	6400000	12800000	25600000	31600000
1000000	90250000	180500000	361000000	1000000000

Figure 1.2 Effect of constants on f(n).

It is extremely difficult to derive the complete formula for time complexity. Most often only the leading term is calculated. Thus, in most cases, the order of magnitude of complexity is the only result that can be achieved. The values of the constants are not known at that time. It is not usual to calculate the values of the constant times unless they greatly influence the behaviour of the algorithm.

The most common computing times of algorithms are

$$O(1) < O(\log n) < O(n) < O(n\log n) < O(n^2) < O(n^3) < O(2^n)$$

logn If the time complixity of an algorithm is logn, then the algorithm is said to be logarithmic. When a program is logarithmic, the program becomes slightly slower as "n" increases. This time complexity usually occurs in algorithms which solves big-problems by transforming it into smaller ones and thereby cutting the size of the input by some fraction. It is also interesting to note that a change in the base of the logarithm results in a change in the constant term of the complexity and that change is also very small. When "n" is 1000, logn is 3 if the base is 10 and logn is approximately 10, if the base is 2. When n is a million, logn is doubled. Whenever n becomes two-fold, logn only increases by a constant.

n When the time complexity of an algorithm is "n", then the algorithm is said to be linear. Usually this is the case, when some processing or the other has to be carried out on each individual element of the input. Naturally the time required by an algorithm is linearly proportional to "n". Thus, if "n" is doubled, the processing time of the algorithm is also doubled. This is the complexity of the optional solution for an algorithm if the algorithm must process all "n" inputs or must produce "n" outputs.

nlogn If an algorithm solves a problem by breaking it up into smaller sub-problems and solving these sub-problems independently and finally combining the solutions to the sub-problems then, the time complexity of such algorithms turns out to be nlogn.

n^2 If time complexity of an algorithm is n^2, then the algorithm is said to be quadratic. Since n^2 increases very rapidly with an increase in "n", quadratic algorithms are practically useful only for relatively small problems. When an algorithm processes all pairs of data item then, the time complexity of the algorithm turns out to be quadratic.

n^3 If an algorithm processes triplets of data items, the complexity of the algorithm becomes cubic and can not be practically useful.

2^n Algorithms with exponential running time are not suitable for practical use. Usually these algorithms arise as brute force solution to the problems. Most often several innovative heuristics are to be applied to such algorithms so that the average case complexity of the algorithms become much less than exponential.

Figure 1.3 indicates the relative sizes of some of these functions.

n	logn	√n	nlogn	nlog²n	n²
10	3	3	30	90	100
100	6	10	600	3600	10,000
1000	9	31	9,000	81,000	1,000,000
10,000	13	100	130,000	1,690,000	100,000,000
100,000	16	316	1,600,000	25,600,000	ten billion
1,000,000	19	1,000	19,000,000	361,000,000	one trillion

Figure 1.3

Often the results of a mathematical analysis are not exact but approximate. The result may be an expression having a sequence of decreasing terms. In such a case, the largest term (which is also called the leading term) is the most important one. In fact, O-notation is developed precisely for such experience so that by using this notation concise statements can be made.

Suppose that an algorithm consists of three blocks. The first block is for initialization and takes a constant amount of time, say "c". The next block is a simple iteration whose time complexity is c.n. The last block has a time complexity of c(nlogn). The overall time complexity of the algorithm is

$$c + cn + cnlogn$$

$$\text{i.e., } cnlogn + O(n) = O(nlogn)$$

Note that, as far as analysis of algorithms is concerned, the exact value of "c" is not important because the analysis attempts to reach an approximate result only. Whenever f(n) is asymptotically large compared to another function g(n), f(n) + O(g(n)) typically means "approximately f(n)". The following observation can be applied to an algorithm consisting of several blocks where time complexities of these blocks are O(n), $O(n^2)$,.., $O(n^m)$ respectively.

Observation

If $A(n) = a_m n^m + \ldots + a_1 n + a_0$ is a polynomial of degree m then $A(n) = O(n^m)$.

Proof

The proof is based on a simple inequality

$$|A(n)| \leq |a_m| n^m + \ldots + |a_1| n + |a_0|$$
$$\leq (|a_m| + |a_{m-1}|/n + \ldots + |a_0|/ n^m) n^m$$
$$\leq (|a_m| + \ldots + |a_0|) n^m \text{ for } n — 1$$

If c is made equal to $|a_m| + \ldots + |a_0|$ and $n_0 = 1$ then, $|A(n)| \leq c| n^m|$ for all $n \geq n_0$.

Hence, $A(n) = O(n^m)$.

Like any mathematical formalism, O-notation has a set of rules of manipulation. For example,

$$n^m = O(n^p) \text{ when } p \geq m \qquad \text{.........................(1)}$$

$$O(f(n)) + O(g(n)) = O(|f(n)|+|g(n)|) \qquad \text{.........................(2)}$$

Thus, $n^3/3 + n^2/2 + n/6 = O(n^3) + O(n^3) + O(n^3) = O(n^3)$

Some more rules for O-notation are given in the following:

$f(n) = O(f(n))$ .... (3)

$C.\ O(f(n)) = O(f(n))$ if C is a constant .... (4)

$O(O(f(n)) = O(f(n))$ .... (5)

$O(f(n)\ O(g(n)) = O(f(n)\ g(n))$ .... (6)

$O(f(n)g(n)) = f(n)O(g(n))$ .... (7)

There are notation other than O-notation for describing an algorithm's performance. O-notation is seen to be particularly useful for expressing upper bounds (i.e., worst case) for complexities of algorithms. There are mathematical notation for expressing a formula for stating lower bounds also.

$f(n) = \Omega(g(n))$ (to be read as " f of n is equal to omega of n") if and only if there exist positive constants c and n_0 so that for all $n > n_0$, the following holds:

$$|f(n)| \geq c\ |g(n)|$$

If the time complexity of an algorithm is f(n) such that $f(n) = \Omega(g(n))$ then, the best case time complexity of the algorithm is g(n). If it can also be shown that $f(n) = O(g(n))$ then both the best and worst case complexities of the algorithm is the same amount within a constant factor. In these circumstances, the following notation is used.

$f(n) = \theta(g(n))$ (to be read as " f of n is equal to theta of n") if and only if there exist positive constants c_1, c_2 and n_0 so that for all $n > n_0$, the following holds:

$$c_2\ |g(n)| \geq |f(n)| \geq c_1\ |g(n)|$$

An even stronger mathematical notation is defined in the following.

$f(n) \sim o(g(n))$ ("f(n) is asymptotic to g(n)") if and only if

$$\text{limit}_{n \to \infty} (f(n)/g(n)) \to 1.$$

Since f(n) becomes g(n) as "n" increases, these terms should agree even closer than by a constant factor.

1.5 Verification of algorithms

In this section a simple example is taken up to bring out few fundamental ideas behind verification of algorithms in a lucid manner. Consider the simple function to find out the index of the minimum element of "n" integers stored in an array.

```
int findMin(int a[], int n)
{
        int i, min;
        min = 0;
        for (i = 1; i < n; i++)
                if (a[i] < a[min])
                min = i;
        return (min);
}
```

It is required to prove that the function actually returns the index of the minimum value in the array "a". See that the claim is justified if the array contains just one element. Because, in this case, the only element in the array is the desired minimum. The function sets "min" to 0 and if "n" is 1 (which is the case now) then the "for"-loop will not be entered. Thus 0 will be returned which is the index of the minimum element of the array with a single element.

To prove the claim for any general "n", the "for" loop needs to be carefully examined. It is required to make an assertion about the "for"-loop which is true whenever the body of the "for"-loop is executed. The assertion must be suitable for our proof. For instance, "i>0 && i < n" is an assertion which is true about the "for"-loop. The assertion that is desirable in this context could be:

i >0 && i < n && "a[min] is the minimum in the part of the array from a[0] to a[i]"

It is to be proved that this assertion is valid whenever execution of the body of the "for"-loop is complete. The proof is based on induction on "i". It is easy to see that the assertion is valid when the body of the "for"-loop is executed for the first time (i.e., when i = 1). So, the induction base is proved. By induction hypothesis, assume that the claim is valid for some i = j. It is to be proved that the claim is valid for j+1 as well. As j > 0 so is j+1. If j+1 == n then by hypothesis, a[min] is minimum in the part of the array from a[0] to a[n–1]. So, in this case, the "for"-loop will not be entered and the value of "min" will be returned. The only case left to be considered is j+1 < n. By hypothesis, a[min] is minimum in the part of the array from a[0] to a[j]. In side the loop, a[min] is compared to a[j+1] and if a[j+1] < a[min] then, "min" is updated to j+1. If a[j+1] < a[min] then, that means a[j+1] is less than all elements from a[0] to a[j]. So a[j+1] is also the minimum for all elements from a[0] to a[j+1]. Hence before the next iteration of the loop, "min" either remains or is assigned to the index of the minimum element of the array from a[0] to a[j+1].

Thus, the following two observations are proved:

(i) the assertion is valid for i = 1 and

(ii) if the assertion is valid for i = j the it remains valid for i = j+1.

Combining them, it can be said that after the body of the "for"-loop is executed for i = n-1, the part of the assertion "a[min] is the minimum in the part of the array from a[0] to a[n-1]" will be true. The next iteration of the "for"-loop will not be carried out as "i" will become equal to "n" and the program will return the correct value of "n".

The readers should be able to appreciate the kind of mathematical rigour that is required to prove the correctness of an algorithm. Most often, this is impractical for any complex algorithm and the task of "verification" is replaced by "testing". However, exhaustive "testing" is also a formidable task in itself and so programmers have to fall back on "pseudo-exhaustive" testing only.

1.6 Conclusions

This chapter is devoted to clarify the basic concepts of data structures and algorithms. The concept of Abstract Data Type (ADT) has been explained before the concept of data structure is formalized. Basic motivations for analysis of algorithms are discussed and fundamental principles of analysis of algorithms have been explained. Mathematical tool like O-notation is described for the purpose of analyzing algorithms. Based on this foundation, the remaining chapters are developed. In the latter chapters, various data structures along with their operations will be discussed. Most of the algorithms will be analyzed for computing their time complexities. Thus, this introductory chapter lays the foundation stone for the remaining chapters.

Exercises

1. Consider the following "C" function.

```
int F(int x)
{
    if (x % 2 = = 0)
            return x/2;
    else
            return F(F (3*x + 1));
}
```

   Prove that F(x) terminates for all integers x.

2. Let $P(x) = c_0 + c_1x + c_2x^2 + .. + c_mx^m$. If $x \geq r$ then show that $P(x) = O(x^m)$. Is $P(x) = O(x^m)$ true when x>0?

3. Prove the following identities.

   i. $f(x) = O(f(x))$

ii. c. O(f(x) = O(f(x)) if "c" is a constant

iii. O(f(x)) + O(f(x)) = O(f(x))

iv. O(O(f(x)) = O(f(x))

v. O(f(x)) O(g(x)) = O(f(x)g(x))

vi. O(f(x)g(x)) = f(x)O(g(x)).

4. Prove the following:

i. $n^a = O(n^b)$ if and only if $a \leq b$

ii. $n^a = O(b^n)$ for all "a" and all "b", b>1 but $b^n = O(n^a)$ for b>1

iii. If f(x) = O(g(x)) then f(x)h(x) = O(g(x)h(x)) for any nonzero function h(x)

iv. log log n = $O((\log n))^{1/2}$

v. If 0<x<y then $n^x = O(n^y)$ but $n^y \neq O(n^x)$

5. Prove that $\log_a n = O(\log_b n)$ for all real values of "a" and "b" such that a>1 and b>1. This result shows that the logarithmic time does not depend on the logarithmic base chosen.

6. Which function grows faster ?

i. $\sqrt{n}$ or logn ?

ii. $n^{\log n}$ or $\log n^n$?

Prove your claim.

7. Prove or disprove the following:

i. cosO(x) = 1 + $O(x^2)$ for all real numbers x.

ii. $O(x^2 + y^2) = O(x^2) + O(y^2)$

iii. O(f(x) + g(x)) = f(x) +O(g(x)) if f(x), g(x) > 0 for all x.

8. Consider the following argument:

Since n = O(n), 2n = O(n) and so on hence,

$\Sigma_{i=1,n}$ i.n $=\Sigma_{i=1,n}$O(n) = $O(n^2)$

Is the argument sound?

9. Write a function "Power" which is used to evaluate x^n given values of "x" and "n" for "n" for $n \geq 0$. Thus, the prototype of the function is declared as follows.

```
double power (double x, int n);
```

A simple way to compute x^n (where "n" is an integer and $n \geq 1$) will require (n – 1) multiplications. But if "n" is represented as a sum of "k" integers where each integer is a power if 2 then much less number of multiplications are required. For example, if "n" is 100 then "n" can be written as 64 + 32 + 4. So, x^{100} can be computed in the following steps.

```
t1 = x*x; /* t1 = x² */
```

```
t2 = t1*t1; /* t2 = x^4 */
t3 = t2*t2; /* t3 = x^8 */
t4 = t3*t3; /* t4 = x^16 */
t5 = t4*t4; /* t5 = x^32 */
t6 = t5*t5; /* t6 = x^64 */
t7 = t5*t6; /* t7 = x^96 */
t7 = t7*t2
```

t7 stores the result. Only 8 multiplications are required for this purpose. One way to break "n" as a sum of integers which are powers of 2 can be achieved by finding the binary representation of "n". The 1's in the binary representation of "n" indicates the terms, which can be added to produce "n". Write a "C" function "Power" as described, and compute its worst case time complexity.

Chapter 2

Arrays

2.1 Introduction

Arrays are the simplest and, in many programming languages (e.g., FORTRAN), the only means of structuring data. Informally, an array is an ordered collection of items, all of which are of the same type. So, a line of text can be represented by an array of characters, an n-dimensional vector may be represented by an array of "n" real numbers and so on. In C, an array "a" of 10 integers may be defined as

```
int a[10];
```

The above definition in C implies that any number between 0 to 9 is a valid index of the array "a". Thus, a[0] means the 0-th element of "a", a[5] represents the 5-th element and so on. However, a[11] does not represent a valid component of "a" because the index (i.e., 11) is beyond the range of indices specified in the definition. For the same reason, a[-1] is not correct. It is important to note that the range of valid indices is specified differently in different programming languages. For example, an array of 10 integers may be defined as "a[2..11] : integer" in Pascal. This definition in Pascal implies that the range of valid indices is all integers from 2 to 11. In general an one dimensional array "a" may be declared as a[l..u] where "l" and "u" represent the lower and upper limits of the indices of "a". Precisely, an array is a set of pairs – index and value. For each valid index of the array, there is an associated value. The index set, in general, is finite and therefore can be mapped to a finite subset of the set of positive integers. "Retrieve" and "Store" are primary operations which are performed on array data structure. Retrieve takes an array name and an index as inputs and returns the appropriate value or an error. "Store" is used to modify the value associated with an index of an array. Implementation-wise, an array is usually allocated a consecutive set of memory locations. However, this is not always true and more importantly, it must be mentioned that the issue of the internal representation of an array should not confuse our logical view about the array as a data structure.

An array such as described above is called a one-dimensional array. The array "b" as declared in the following is a two-dimensional array of integers.

```
int b[10][5];
```

The index set of the array "b" can be mapped to all tuples (i, j) where $0 \le i < 10$ and $0 \le j < 5$. If (i, j) is a valid tuple then, b[i][j] is a valid element in "b". Similarly a 5-dimensional array may be defined in "C" as

```
int c[10][5][6][9][20];
```

c[i][j][k][l][m] is a valid item if $0 \le i < 10$, $0 \le j < 5$, $0 \le k < 6$, $0 \le l < 9$, $0 \le m < 20$. In general, an m-dimensional array, "A" may be logically defined as:

A: <u>ARRAY</u> [l_1.. u_1, l_2.. u_2, ..., l_m.. u_m] of item, where A is the name of an m-dimensional array; the set of indices is all m-tuples (i_1, i_2, i_3, ..., i_m) such that $l_j \le i_j \le u_j$ for all j = 1 to m and item is the type of the value associated with some index (which is an m-tuple) of the array. Therefore, all operations defined on variables of type "item" are equally valid on A [i_1, i_2, i_3, ..., i_m]. Moreover, by means of a proper addressing mechanism it is assumed that any element of an array can be accessed in a constant amount of time.

It is easy to see that any ordered list (a_0, a_1, a_2, a_3, ..., a_{n-1}) of "n" numbers can be most conveniently represented by a one-dimensional array where the list element a_i is associated with the index "i" of the array.

2.2 Ordered List and Arrays

Besides the basic operations, such as "Retrieve" and "Store", a number of operations are also performed on ordered lists. Important among them are given in the following:

i. Computing the length of a list.

ii. Searching for a given element in a list.

iii. Inserting a new element at a specified position "i", $0 \le i \le n-1$ where "n" is the length of the list.

iv. Deletion of an element at a given position, "i", in a list of "n" elements.

v. Reversing a list.

vi. Sorting a list.

In a latter chapter, the topic of sorting a list will be separately dealt with in detail. In this chapter, algorithms implementing some of the said operations will be discussed. Before describing "C" functions for these operations, it is important to note that an additional variable "n" is required to represent an ordered list by an array. "n" will store the number of elements in the list. In all functions describing these operations, an array "A" and an integer "n" will denote an ordered list. To simplify further, it is always assumed that only an ordered list of integers is considered. To start with, the problem of searching in an array "A" for a given element "k" is taken up. The function returns an integer, i, so that A[i] = k if a match is found; if no match is found then the function returns –1. As a first step, the 0-th element of "A" is compared with the given element "k". If the elements compared are same then the function returns 0. Otherwise, the comparison is performed between "k" and the next element in the array. Once again, if a match is found after comparison then the function returns the index of the current element. If comparison does not yield a match then the comparison is continued. So, the algorithm consists of a loop in which these comparisons are repeatedly carried out until either the list is exhausted or a match is found. If the list is exhausted then the function "Search" returns -1;

```
int Search (int A[], int n, int k)
{
        int i = 0;
        for (i = 0; i < n; i++)
                if (A[i] == k)
                        break;
                if (i == n)
                        return –1;
                else
                        return i;
}
```

For an unsuccessful search, the number of comparisons required to establish that "k" is not equal to any of the n elements of the array "A" is "n". When search is unsuccessful, its time complexity is O(n). If search is successful, the number of comparisons required is one more than the index of the element of "A" with which "k" is found to be equal. Thus, the number of comparisons can be 1, 2, 3, ... or "n" depending on the element being found to be equal to "k".

Assuming that each of these cases is equally likely for a successful search, the average behavior of the algorithm is

$$(1+2+3+\ldots+n)/n = (n+1)/2 = O(n).$$

For both successful and unsuccessful search, it can be said that search has O(n) complexity in the average case. It is also easy to see that search has O(n) complexity even in the worst case.

Next consider the problem of inserting an element, "k", in the i-th position of an ordered list of "n" elements. In this case, the elements to the right of the i-th element of the array have to be shifted towards right. To avoid the problem of overwriting, first shift A[n-1] to A[n], then A[n-2] to A[n-1] and so on until A[i] is moved to A[i+1]. Only then, A[i] can be rewritten by the new element "k". Note that if the shifting operation is done from the i-th position to the n-th position of the array then all A[j]s will become A[i] for $i+1 \leq j \leq n$. The insertion of an element has been illustrated in the Figure 2.1. The array initially contains seven elements. An integer 7 is inserted at the 3rd position.

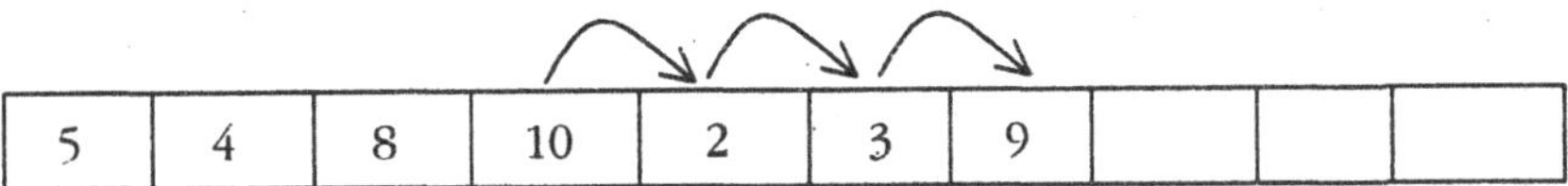

Figure 2.1 (a) The original array; curved arrows show the shifting of the elements to the right.

5	4	8	10	10	2	3	9		

Figure 2.1 (b) The array after the shifting operation is complete.

5	4	8	7	10	2	3	9		

Figure 2.1 (c) The final array after inserting 7 at the 3rd position.

Figure 2.1. Insertion of an element in an array.

```
void Insert (int A[], int n, int i, int k)
{
        int j;
        for(j = n-1; j >=i; j—){
                A[j+1] = A[j];
        }
        A[j] = k;
}
```

Like insertion, deletion also involves shifting of array elements. In the case of deletion of the i-th element of the array, all elements from the (i+1)-th position are to be shifted to its left by one position. The deletion procedure is illustrated in Figure 2.2 where the third element is to be deleted from the array.

5	4	8	10	2	3	9			

(a) The original array; curved arrows show the shifting of the elements to the left.

5	4	8	2	3	9				

(b) The array after the shifting operation is complete.

Figure 2.2. Deletion of an element in an array.

The function for deleting the i-th entry may be written as follows:

```
void Delete (int A[], int n, int i)
{
    int j;
        for (j = i+1; j < n; j++)
            A[j-1] = A[j];
}
```

To complete our discussion on basic operations on one dimensional arrays, the problem of reversing an array "A" is discussed. If it is allowed to use another array "B", then setting B[i] by A[n-i-1] for all i, $0 \le i \le n-1$ followed by copying all elements of "B" back to "A" could be a suitable algorithm. However, it is not necessary to use a second array "B" for this purpose. In figure 2.3, an array of nine elements is reversed. The steps to do so include exchanging A[0] with A[8], A[1] with A[7], A[2] with A[6] & A[3] with A[5]. Hence, by swapping the contents of A[i] and A[n-i-1] for $0 \le i \le n/2$, the array "A" can be reversed. Also note that such swapping should continue only n/2 times irrespective of whether n is even or odd. If, by mistake the exchange of contents is done n times, the array does not change as it is reversed twice.

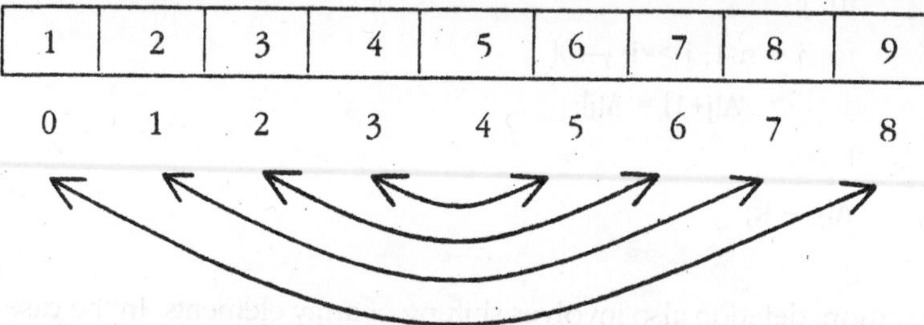

Figure 2.3. Reversing an array; the curved arrows indicate required exchange operations.

```
void reverse (int A [], int n)
{
        int i, t;
```

```
        for (i = 0; i < n/2; i++)
        {
                t = A[i];
                A[i] = A[n-i-1];
                A[n-i-1] = t;
        }
}
```

Consider another simple problem involving one dimensional arrays of integers. The problem at hand is to find out the maximum (or the minimum) of the elements in an array say "A". Assume that the array "A" contains "n" integers from A[0] to A[n-1]. The algorithm for finding the maximum may be stated as follows. Let "max" be a variable which will hold the maximum of the array as the array is being scanned from 0 to (n-1). To begin with, "max" is set to A[0]. Then "max" is compared with A[1]. If A[1] > max then "max" is modified and is set to A[1]. The process of comparison and suitably updating "max", if required, continues for all A[j] for j = 1 to n-1. The "C" function to find out the maximum is as given in the following.

```
int findMax (int A[], int n)
{
        int max, i;
        max = A[0];
        for (i=1; i<n; i++)
                if (A[i] > max)
                        max = A[i];
        return max;
}
```

A minor modification to the above function will make it compute the minimum element in the array "A". In particular, the comparison in the "if" statement of the above function is to be reversed so that the above function returns the minimum element in the array. The function for finding for finding the minimum in an array of "n" elements is described next.

```
int findMin (int A[], int n)
{
        int min, i;
        min = A[0];
        for (i=1; i<n; i++)
                if (A[i] < min)
```

```
            min = A[i];
        return min;
}
```

Both the functions "findMax" and "findMin" will make (n-1) comparisons to obtain the result. A more interesting problem would be to write a function that will evaluate the maximum and the minimum elements of an array. From our earlier discussions, the following function "simpleMaxMin" results.

```
void simpleMaxMin (int A[], int n, int *max, int *min)
{
        int i;
        *max = *min = A[0];
        for (i=1; i<n; i++)
                if (A[i] > *max)
                        *max = A[i];
        for (i=1; i<n; i++)
                if (A[i] < *min)
                        *min = A[i];
        return;
}
```

It is obvious that the function "simpleMaxMin" requires 2(n-1) number of comparisons in the best, worst and average cases. The most rudimentary way to improve the performance of the above function is possible by checking the condition A[i]<(*min) only when the result of the condition A[i]> (*max) is false. Hence, the new function is :

```
void maxMin (int A[], int n, int *max, int *min)
{
        int i;
        *max = *min = A[0];
        for (i=1; i<n; i++)
                if (A[i] > *max)
                        *max = A[i];
                else if (A[i] < *min)
                        *min = A[i];
        return;
```

Consider an array "A" of 7 elements where "A" is as shown in Figure 2.4.

-5	0	9	15	21	22	25

Figure 2.4. The array "A" of 7 elements.

Basically the elements in "A" are already arranged in an increasing order. In this case, the value of (*max) is initialized to –5. Since, in each iteration in the for loop, A[i] is greater than the current value of (*max), the second comparison (A[i] <(*min)) never takes place. Hence, number of comparisons that "maxMin" requires is clearly just (n-1). However, if all elements in "A" are arranged in descending order then, both comparisons are required in the above function. Consequently, in such cases, number of comparisons required would be 2(n-1). Average number of comparisons will be definitely less than 2(n-1). On the average, the first comparison will be "true" half the time and therefore the total number of comparisons is n-1 + (n-1)/2 i.e. (3n-1)/2.

An interesting solution to the problem may be obtained if it is formulated recursively. Let "recursiveMaxMin" be the name of the recursive function to find the maximum and the minimum element of an array "A". The function divides the array "A" into two halves and calls the same function on each half to obtain their minimum and maximum. These two maximum values (minimum values) of these two halves are compared to calculate the overall maximum (minimum). Recursion stops if there are less than two elements in the array. This algorithm is the basis of the "C" function that is presented next. To simplify, the array "A" is assumed to be global.

```
void recursiveMaxMin (int i, int j, int *max, int *min)
{
        int lmax, lmin, umax, umin, mid;
        if (i == j)
                *max = *min = A[i];
        else if (i == j -1)
        {
                if (A[i] < A[j])
                {
                        *max =  A[j];
                        *min = A[i];
                }
                else
```

```
        {
            *max =  A[i];
            *min =  A[j];
        }
    }
    else
    {
        mid = (i + j)/2;
        recursiveMaxMin (i, mid, &lmax, &lmin);
        recursiveMaxMin (mid + 1, j, &umax, &umin);
        *max = lmax > umax ? lmax : umax;
        *min = lmin < umin ? lmin : umin;
    }
    return;
}
```

If T(n) is the number of comparisons required by "recursiveMaxMin" for an array of n elements then, by definition of the function, T(n) can be described as follows.

$$T(n) = \begin{cases} T(n/2) + T(n/2) + 2 & , n > 2 \\ 1 & , n = 2 \\ 0 & , n = 1 \end{cases}$$

If $n = 2^m$ for some "m" then,

$$\begin{aligned} T(n) &= 2T(n/2) + 2 \\ &= 2\,(2T(n/4) + 2) + 2 \\ &= 2^2\,T(n/2^2) + 2^2 + 2 \\ &\;\;\vdots \\ &= 2^{m-1}\,T(n/2^{m-1}) + \Sigma_{i=1,\,m-1}\,(2^i) \\ &= 2^{m-1} + 2^m - 2 \\ &= n/2 + n - 2 \\ &= 3n/2 - 2 \end{aligned}$$

Note that 3n/2 –2 is the best, worst and average case time complexities when "n" is a power of 2.

2.3. Matrix as a 2-Dimensional Array

Mathematically, a matrix, "A", is a collection of elements "$a_{i,j}$" for all i, j's such that $0 \le i < m$ and $0 \le j < n$. The matrix "A" is said to be of order m x n. Pictorially a matrix can be described as shown in Figure 2.5. The matrix "A" is also said to consist of "m" number of rows and "n" columns. The element $a_{i,j}$ is the element positioned at the i-th row and the j-th column in Figure 2.2. The elements $a_{i,i}$ for all "i" are called diagonal elements of "A". If m = n (i.e. number of rows and number of columns are equal) then, the matrix "A" is called a square matrix. Each row or column of a matrix is also known as its row vector or column vector respectively. Primitive matrix operations are (i) addition of two matrices, (ii) multiplication of two matrices, (iii) transposition of given matrix, (iv) evaluation of the determinant of a square matrix etc.

$$\begin{pmatrix} a_{0,0} & a_{0,1} & a \ldots\ldots & a_{0,n-1} \\ a_{1,0} & a_{1,1} & a \ldots\ldots & a_{1,n-1} \\ a_{2,0} & a_{2,1} & a \ldots\ldots & a_{2,n-1} \\ .. & & & \\ .. & & & \\ a_{m-2,0} & a_{m-2,1} & a \ldots\ldots & a_{m-2,n-1} \\ a_{m-1,0} & a_{m-1,1} & a \ldots\ldots & a_{m-1,n-1} \end{pmatrix}$$

Figure 2.5. Pictorial representation of a mxn matrix.

A matrix can be conveniently represented by a two-dimensional array. Moreover, the arithmetic computations involving matrices can be easily translated into algorithms using two-dimensional arrays. In the following, "C" functions are discussed to compute the sum and product of two matrices and to compute the transpose of a square matrix.

Let A & B be two 3 X 4 matrices as given in the following:

$$A = \begin{vmatrix} 1 & 2 & 3 & 4 \\ 5 & 6 & 7 & 8 \\ 9 & 10 & 11 & 12 \end{vmatrix} \qquad B = \begin{vmatrix} 9 & 1 & 0 & -5 \\ 6 & 2 & 10 & 0 \\ 9 & -15 & 5 & 9 \end{vmatrix}$$

$$C = A + B = \begin{vmatrix} 1+9 & 2+1 & 3+0 & 4+(-5) \\ 5+6 & 6+2 & 7+10 & 8+0 \\ 9+9 & 10+(-15) & 11+5 & 12+9 \end{vmatrix}$$

Note that $c_{i,j} = a_{i,j} + b_{i,j}$ for all i and j such that $0 \leq i < 3$ and $0 \leq j < 4$.
The following function "MAdd" adds two matrices "A" and "B" to produce a matrix "C". The order of all the matrices "A", "B" and "C" is m x n.

```
void MAdd (int A[10][10], int B[10][10], int C[10][10], int m, int n)
{
        int i,j;
        for (i = 0; i<m; i++)
                for (j = 0; j < n; j++)
                        C[i][j] = A[i][j] + B[i][j];
}
```

The product of two matrices "A" and "B" is defined only when the number of columns of "A" is equal to the number of rows in "B". In that case, the (i, j)-th element of the product "C", $c_{i,j}$ is the dot product of the i-th row vector of "A" and the j-th column vector of "B".
Dot product of a vector $X = (x_1, x_2, \ldots, x_m)$ and $Y = (y_1, y_2, \ldots, y_m)$ is defined as

$$X.Y = (x_1y_1 + x_2y_2 + x_3y_3 + \ldots + x_my_m)$$

If C = AXB then,

$$c_{i,j} = \Sigma_{k=0,n-1}\ a_{i,k} \cdot b_{k,j}$$ where "n" is the number of columns of "A".

Let A and B be 3 X 4 and 4 X 3 matrices respectively. Suppose A and B are given as follows:

$$A = \begin{vmatrix} 9 & 1 & 0 & -5 \\ 6 & 2 & 10 & 0 \\ 9 & -15 & 5 & 9 \end{vmatrix} \qquad B = \begin{vmatrix} 1 & 2 & 3 \\ 4 & 5 & 6 \\ 7 & 8 & 9 \\ 10 & 11 & 12 \end{vmatrix}$$

Then, "C" becomes

$$\begin{vmatrix} -37 & -32 & -27 \\ 84 & 102 & 120 \\ 74 & 82 & 90 \end{vmatrix}$$

Note that

$$= 9*1 + 1*4 + 0*7 + (-5)*10$$
$$= 9 + 4 + 0 - 50 = -37$$

Let "A" be a mxn matrix and "B" be a nxp matrix. From the earlier discussions, it follows that for a given i, j, C[i][j] may be computed by evaluating the sum of a series of k terms where each term is A[i][k]*B[k][j]. Clearly, "k" varies from 0 to (n-1). C[i][j] itself, has to be computed for all i, j, 0≤i<m and 0≤j<p. The "C" function for computing

the product of two matrices is given in the following. The arrays "A", "B", "C" storing the matrices A, B and C are to be passed as parameters. In addition, three integers m, n, p are also to be provided so that the order of the matrices A and B are known to the function. The function assumes that the matrices in "A" and "B" are order m x n and n x p respectively.

```
void matrixMult( int A[10][10], int B[10][10], int C[10][10], int m, int n, int p)
{
        int i, j, k;
        for (i = 0; i < m; i++)
              for (j = 0; j < p; j++)
              {
                    C[i][j] = 0;
                    for (k = 0; k < n; k++)
                          C[i][j] +=  A[i][k]*B[k][j];
              }
}
```

The complexity of the algorithm "matrixMult" is O(mnp) because of three nested loops.

Next, consider the computation of the transpose of a square matrix "A". Transpose of an n X n square matrix A is a matrix B such that an element $b_{i,j}$ of B is equal to the element $a_{j,i}$ of A for $0 \le i,j < n$. For example, if A is given as in the following:

$$A = \begin{vmatrix} 9 & 1 & 0 \\ 6 & 2 & 10 \\ 9 & -15 & 5 \end{vmatrix}$$

Then B, the transpose of A is given by

$$B = \begin{vmatrix} 9 & 6 & 9 \\ 1 & 2 & -15 \\ 0 & 10 & 5 \end{vmatrix}$$

So, a straightforward function to compute the transpose of a square matrix may be written as follows :

```
void transposeMatrix (int A[10][10], int B[10][10], int n)
{
        int i, j;
        for (i=0; i<n; i++)
              for (j=0; j<n; j++)
```

```
            B[i][j] = A[j][i];
    return;
}
```

It is not necessary, however, to use the additional two-dimensional array B for computing the transpose of a matrix. Observe that if the values A[i][j] and A[j][i] are exchanged once for all "i" and "j" then, the final array "A" is the transpose of the original "A". As in the problem of the reversal of an array, we have to be cautious so that we do not exchange the contents of A[i][j] and A[j][i] twice. That is why, only elements to the right of the diagonal elements are exchanged with their counter parts. The function for transposing a matrix "A" is described next.

```
void transposeMatrix2 (int A[10][], int m, int n)
{
        int i, j; int t;
        for (i=0; i<m; i++)
                for (j=i+1; j<n; j++)
                {
                        t = A[i][j];
                        A[i][j] = A[j][i];
                        A[j][i] = t;
                }
}
```

2.4 Representation of polynomials using arrays

A polynomial, P(x) of degree "n" is defined as the following expression

$$P(x) = a_0 + a_1x + a_2x^n + \ldots\ldots + a_nx^n$$

where "a" is any real number and "n" is an integer.

Thus, $1 + 2x^2 - 3x^5$ is a polynomial of degree 5 and $x + 3x^2 - 4x^3 + 9x^5 + x^6$ is a polynomial of degree 6. Often a polynomial of degree "n" is thought of as a sum of (n+1) terms where each term is a tuple (a, i) representing $a_i.x^i$. It is interesting to treat polynomial as an ADT. If a polynomial is treated as an ADT then, common operations will include all arithmetic operations like addition, multiplication etc. But in addition to arithmetic operations some other operations will also be required. Most important among them are initialization and copy operation. Initialization of a polynomial, P, means assigning an empty polynomial to P. The implementation of definitions is dependent on its representation. "Copy(Q, P)" means copying a polynomial P to Q term by term. Addition and multiplication of polynomials are fairly common and often one needs to write programs involving these operations. In this section, some algorithms for these operations will be discussed in detail. To start with, recall the addition and multiplication of polynomials. If the polynomials $1 + 2x^2 - 3x^5$ and $x + 3x^2 - 4x^3 + 9x^5 + x^6$ are added then the sum is another polynomial that is given by:

$$1 + x + 5x^2 - 4x^3 + 6x^5 + x^6$$

If these two polynomials are multiplied, the product

$$(1 + 2x^2 - 3x^5)(x + 3x^2 - 4x^3 + 9x^5 + x^6) \text{ is given by}$$

$$x + 3x^2 - 2x^3 + 6x^4 + x^5 - 2x^6 + 9x^7 + 14x^8 - 27x^{10} - 3x^{11}$$

Suppose that a function is to be written to add two polynomials. The first step towards a solution is to properly represent a polynomial. The simplest way to represent a polynomial of degree "n" is to store the coefficient of (n+ 1) terms of the polynomial (many of which could be zero) in an array. Thus, the polynomial $1 + 2x^2 - 3x^5$ (i.e., $1 + 0.x + 2.x^2 + 0.x^3 + 0.x^4 + (-3).x^5$) is to be stored in an array 'A' of 6 real numbers as shown below

Coefficient:

1	0	2	0	0	-3	....

Consequently, a polynomial may be defined as the following structure

```
typedef struct polynomial
{
        float coefficients [1000];
        int degree;
} polynomial;
```

This representation of a polynomial puts a limit to the maximum degree (in this case, 1000) of the polynomial that may be stored.

Addition of two polynomials represented in this manner is straight forward. Elements of the "coefficients" array of the polynomials are just to be added. The "addPoly" function described next performs this addition.

```
void addPoly (polynomial *p1, polynomial *p2, polynomial *p3)
{
        int i, m, n;
        m = p1->degree < p2->degree ? p1->degree : p2->degree;
        for (i = 0; i <= m; i++)
                p3->coefficients[i] = p1->coefficients[i] + p2->coefficients[i];
        if(p1->degree > m)
```

```
        for(i = 1+m; i <= p1->degree; i++)
                p3->coefficients[i] = p1->coefficients[i];
    else
        for(i = 1+m; i <= p2->degree; i++)
                p3->coefficients[i] = p2->coefficients[i];
        p3->degree = m;
}
```

Although these algorithms are conceptually simple, there is a serious drawback of such representations. Suppose that the polynomial $1 + x^{100}$ is to be stored. The "coefficients" array will contain 101 real numbers. 99 of which are zero. This is a wasteful representation if there are many zero terms in the given polynomial. This difficulty may be overcome if only the non-zero terms are chosen to be stored. Each non-zero terms $a_i x^i$ is represented by a tuple (i, a_i) where a is the coefficient part and x^i is the exponent part of that term. Thus, a polynomial is defined as:

```
typedef struct termType
{
        int coefficient, exponent;
} termType;

typedef struct poly
{
        termType terms [1000];
        int noOfTerms;
} poly;
```

It is always wise to arrange the array "terms" in some fashion. Most commonly, this array is arranged in order of increasing value of the "exponent" part of the terms. Let "P" be the polynomial $5 - 2x^2 + 9x^4$ represented as an array of structure as shown in the following figure.

5, 0	-2, 2	9, 4	.....

Let "P" be another polynomial $6x - 7x^2 + 10x^3$, which is represented by an array as shown in the following.

6, 1	-7, 2	10, 3	.....

The addition function of two polynomials becomes more interesting now. If p1 and p2 are two polynomials to be added to compute the sum p3 then, the terms of p1 and p2 are examined one by one. If the "exponent" part of these terms are the same then a new term for p3 is created. The coefficient of this new term in p3 is sum of "coefficient" part of the current terms in p1 and p2. Then the process continues with the next terms of p1 and p2. If the "exponent" of the terms of p1 and p2 are not the same then, let the term in p1 be the term with lesser exponent. The term of p1 is then copied to p3. The process continues with the next term of p1 and current term of p2. If the exponent part of the term of p2 is less then, this term is copied to p3 and the next term in p2 is processed. This entire process is explained in the following example.

When polynomials P_1 and P_2 are added, addition begins with examining the first term of the polynomials P_1 and P_2. Since the exponent part of the first term of P_1 is less than that of P_2, these terms can not be added. The term with lesser exponent (that is, the first term of P_1) is copied to P_3 and the next term of P_1 is taken up in the next phase. The result after this step is shown in Figure 2.6(a). The terms to be processed after this phase are pointed to by arrows.

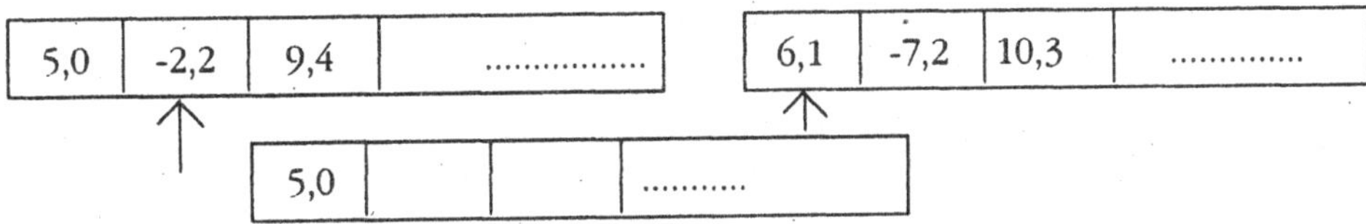

Figure 2.6(a) Adding two polynomials represented by two arrays of doublets.

As can be seen in the above diagram, the second term of P_1 and the first term of P_2 are currently selected for comparison. As the exponent part of the term in P_2 is less then that of P_1, this term is copied and inserted to P_3 and the next term of P_2 is taken up for further consideration. The result after this step is shown in Figure 2.6(b).

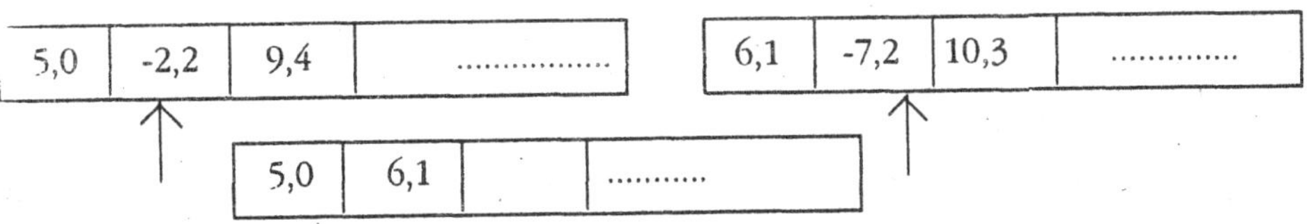

Figure 2.6(b) Adding two polynomials represented by two arrays of doublets (Contd.)

The current terms of P_1 and P_2 have same exponent. Hence, the coefficients of these terms are added. This sum becomes the coefficient of a new term. The exponent of the new term is same as exponent of the current term of either P_1 or P_2. This new term is then copied to P_3. As both the terms of P_1 and P_2 are used, the next iteration makes use of the next terms of P_1 and P_2. The result of this step is shown in the next diagram.

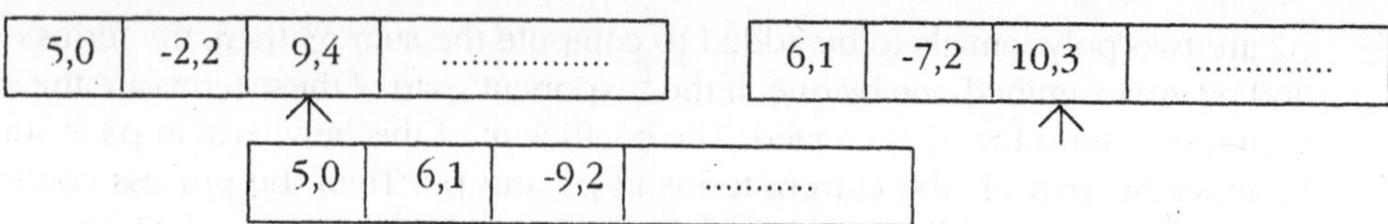

Figure 2.6(c) Adding two polynomials represented by two arrays of doublets (Contd.)

The following figure shows the situation after completion of another step in this procedure.

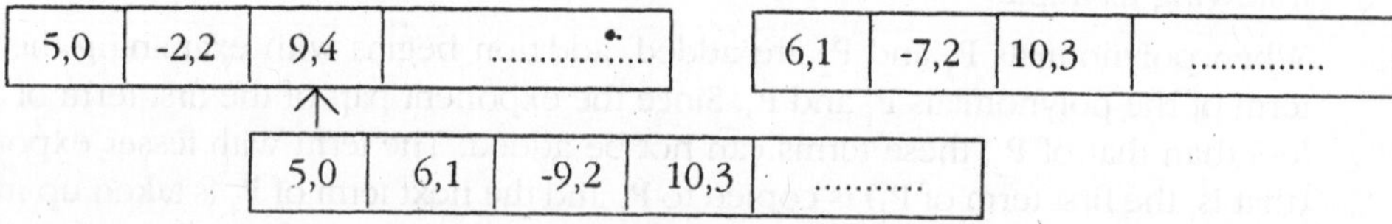

Figure 2.6(d) Adding two polynomials represented by two arrays of doublets (Contd.)

Now, P_2 is exhausted. So, the remaining terms of P_1 (in this case only one) are copied to P_3.

The key step in the procedure consists of three sub-steps: i) comparison of the current terms of P_1 and P_2, ii) copying a new term to P_3 and iii) advancing to the next terms of P_1 and P_2 as governed by the result of the comparison. This step is repeated as long as there are terms in both P_1 and P_2. Once the list of terms in one of these polynomials is exhausted, the remaining terms in the other polynomial is just copied. This scheme is the base of the function "addPoly2" described next. The "addPoly2" function adds the polynomials pointed by p1 and p2 and stores the sum in a polynomial pointed by p3.

```
void addPoly2 (poly *p1, poly *p2, poly **p4)
{
    int i, j, k, l;
    poly *p3 = *p4;
    for (i = 0, j = 0, k = 0; ((i < p1->noOfTerms) && (j < p2->noOfTerms)); k++)
    {
        if(p1->terms[i].exponent == p2->terms[j].exponent)
        {
            p3->terms[k].coefficient = p1->terms[i].coefficient +
                                       p2->terms[j].coefficient;
            p3->terms[k].exponent = p1->terms[i].exponent;
            i++; j++;
```

```
        }
        else if (p1->terms[i].exponent < p2->terms[j].exponent)
        {
                p3->terms[k].coefficient = p1->terms[i].coefficient;
                p3->terms[k].exponent = p1->terms[i].exponent;
                i++;
        }
        else
        {
                p3->terms[k].coefficient = p2->terms[j].coefficient;
                p3->terms[k].exponent = p2->terms[j].exponent;
                j++;
        }
    }
    if (i < p1->noOfTerms)
        for (l = i; l < p1->noOfTerms; l++, k++)
        {
                p3->terms[k].coefficient = p1->terms[l].coefficient;
                p3->terms[k].exponent = p1->terms[l].exponent;
        }
    else
        for (l = j; l < p2->noOfTerms; l++, k++)
        {
                p3->terms[k].coefficient = p2->terms[l].coefficient;
                p3->terms[k].exponent = p2->terms[l].exponent;
        }
    p3->noOfTerms = k;
}
```

The time complexity of the above algorithm is O(n+m) where "n" and "m" are the degrees of the polynomials.

2.4.1 Evaluation of a polynomial

Let P(x) be a polynomial where $P(x) = 2 + 3x^2 + 5x^4$. Often it is required to evaluate the value of P(x) when a particular value of "x" is specified. For instance P(1) = 2 + 3.1 + 5.1 = 10. The function to evaluate the polynomial for a given value of "x" is simple. For each term (c, e), compute x^e and multiply that value with "c". Then, accumulate the sum of the terms in a "for loop". The following function "evaluate" computes the value of the polynomial pointed to by "p" using the second parameter "d" as the value of "x" and returns the computed value of the polynomial.

```
double evaluate (poly *p, double d)
{
        int i, j;
        double term, result = 0;
        for (i = 0; i < p->noOfTerms; i++)
        {
                term = 1;
                for (j = 1; j <= p->terms[i].exponent; j++)
                        term *= d;
                term *= p->terms[i].coefficient;
                result += term;
        }
        return(result);
}
```

The complexity of the above algorithm can be computed as follows. The inner "for-loop" continues for (e_i - 1) times if the exponent of the i-th term is e_i. Now, the outer "for-loop" continues for "p" times where "p" is the number of non-zero terms of the polynomial. Hence, total complexity of the algorithm is $\Sigma_{i=1,p}$ (i-1)+k for some constant "k". In the worst case, for a polynomial of degree n, $P(x) = \Sigma\, a_i x^i$ where all a_i are non-zero. In such cases, p = n. Thus, the worst case complexity becomes

$$\Sigma_{i=1,p}\ (i-1)+k = n(n-1)/2 + k.n = O\ (n^2).$$

It is easy to see that if the terms are ordered in increasing values of their exponent parts then the time complexity of the above algorithm can be reduced. Note that e_i (the exponent of the i-th term) $\geq e_j$ for i > j. Hence, to compute x^i knowing x^j only (i-j) number of additional multiplications are required. This fact is used in the next algorithm.

```
double evaluate2 (poly *p, double d)
{
        int i, j;
        double result = 0;
        double term;
        term = 1;
        for (i = 1; i <= p->terms[0].exponent; i++)
```

```
        term *= d;
    result += term* p->terms[0].coefficient;
    for (i = 1; i < p->noOfTerms; i++)
    {
        for(j = 1+p->terms[i-1].exponent; j <= p->terms[i].exponent; j++)
            term *= d;
        result += term* p->terms[i].coefficient;
    }
    return result;
}
```

2.4.2 Multiplication of polynomials

If P_1 and P_2 are two polynomials $1 + 4x^2 + x^4$ and $2x^2 + x$ then multiplication of these two polynomials is carried out in the manner as explained in the following.

$$(1 + 4x^2 + x^4)\,(2x^2 + x^4)$$

$$= 1.(\,2x^2 + x^4) + 4x^2.(2x^2 + x^4) + x^4.(2x^2 + x^4)$$

$$= 2x^2 + x^4 + 8x^4 + 4x^6 + 2x^6 + x^8$$

$$= 2x^2 + 9x^4 + 6x^6 + x^8$$

As explained above, multiplication of P_1 and P_2 involves multiplying P_2 by each term of P_1 and adding these sub-products. The following algorithm serves this purpose. The algorithm "multPoly" is written using structured English instead of "C" language. Writing the algorithm in "C" is left as an exercise.

```
void multPoly(poly p1, poly p2, poly p3)
{
    Initialize polynomials p4, p5, p6;
    for(each term t of p1)
    {
        Initialize polynomial p6.
        Let p4 be the polynomial obtained by multiplying p2 by t.
        Add p4 and p5 to obtain p6.
        copy p6 to p5.
    }
    copy p5 to p3.
}
```

The "multPoly" algorithm needs addition of two polynomials and copying one polynomial. It has been seen that the worst case time complexity of addition of two polynomials and the copying one polynomial is O(n) if n is the degree of the polynomials being added. The worst case complexity of multiplication is $\Sigma_{i=1,p} O(n)$ where p is the number of terms in the polynomial p2 . As there could be a maximum of n+1 non-zero terms in a polynomial of degree "n" therefore, the worst case complexity of "multPoly" algorithm is $O(n^2)$.

To improve upon the simple multiplication algorithm, the polynomials can be split into two halves, multiplication can be performed on those halves and then the sub-products can be added.

If $p(x) = a_0 + a_1x + \ldots\ldots + a_{n-1}x^{n-1}$ then let it be split to two polynomials $p_h(x)$ and $p_l(x)$ where,

$$p_h(x) = a_0 + a_1x + \ldots\ldots + a_{n/2-1}\, x^{n/2-1} \text{ and}$$

$$p_l(x) = a_{n/2}x + \ldots\ldots + a_{n-1}x^{n/2-1}$$

so that $p(x) = p_h(x) + x^{n/2}.\ p_l(x)$

Similarly, q(x) is split into $q_h(x)$ and $q_l(x)$ so that $q(x) = q_h(x) + x^{n/2}.\ q_l(x)$.

Now, the multiplication of p(x) and q(x) may be given by:

$$p(x)q(x) = (p_h(x) + x^{n/2}.\ p_l(x)\ ).(q_h(x) + x^{n/2}.\ q_l(x))$$
$$= p_h(x)\ q_h(x) + x^{n/2}(p_l(x)\ q_h(x) + p_h(x)\ q_l(x)) + x^n.\ p_l(x)\ q_l(x)$$

An intelligent trick can reduce the number of polynomial multiplication required to compute p(x)q(x). If three polynomial multiplication are done to compute $r_1 = p_l(x)q_l(x)$, $r_2 = p_h(x)\ q_h(x)$ and $r_3 = (p_l(x) + p_h(x)\ )(\ q_l(x) + q_h(x))$ then , p(x)q(x) can be re-written as :

$$p(x)q(x) = r_1 + (r_3 - r_1 - r_2)\ x^{n/2} + r_2\ x^n$$

Thus, if T(n) is the number of multiplication required to multiply two polynomials of degree "n" then, by the above scheme,

$$T(n) = T(n/2) + T(n/2) + T(n/2) = 3T(n/2)$$

If $n = 2^m$ for some "m" then,

$$T(2^m) = 3T(2^{m-1})$$
$$= 3^2\ T(2^{m-2})$$
$$= 3^3\ T(2^{m-3})$$
$$\vdots$$
$$= 3\ T(2^0)$$
$$= 3$$

As $m = \log_2 n$, $3^m = (2^x)^y = (2^y)^x = n^x = n^{1.59}$ where $x = \log_2 3$ and $y = \log_2 n$.

Clearly, number of multiplications using this scheme is significantly less than the number of multiplications required by the "multPoly" function. It can also be proved that the total overall time complexity of the recursive algorithm is actually $O(n^{1.59})$ for any n. See exercises.

2.4.3 Large integer arithmetic

In some specialized applications, it may be required to manipulate very very large integers which can not be stored in variables of type "int" or "long" in "C" programming language. For example, suppose that 64 digit numbers are to be represented. Value of such integers is larger than the maximum number which can be stored in a variable of type "long". So, a different representation scheme is required for large integers. Note that a number can always be considered to be a special type of polynomial. For instance, a number such as 1024 can be denoted by the following expression.

$$1x10^3 + 0x10^2 + 2x10^1 + 4x10^0$$

Clearly, the expression is the value of $P(x) = x^3 + 2x + 4$ when $x = 10$. In fact, any decimal integer of "n" digits can be thought of as the value of a (n-1)degree polynomial $P(x) = \Sigma_{i=0,n-1}\, a_i x^i$ for $x = 10$ where each a_i represents a digit of the number. As a_i denotes a digit, $0 \leq a_i \leq 9$. Thus, a number, N, can be represented as a polynomial in which each term in the polynomial represents a non-zero digit and its position from the right end of the number. So, the following 30-digit number

410596400003007000000008020010

can be represented as shown in the following.

1,1	2,4	8,6	7,15	3,18	4,23	6,24	9,25	5,26	1,28	4,29

Addition of two large integers represented in this manner is very similar to addition of two polynomials. The only difference is that although the "coefficient" part of the "digits" is between 0 and 9 for the integers to be added, after being added the coefficient part of a digit may become more than 9. In such a case, the new digit is "olddigit % 10" and another digit ("olddigit/10, oldexponent + 1") is to be imported for addition. The details of addition procedure is left as an exercise.

2.5. Sparse Matrix Representation

A sparse matrix is one where most of its elements are zero. For example, the following 6X6 matrix A is a sparse matrix.

$$A = \begin{pmatrix} 0 & 0 & 9 & 0 & 0 & 0 \\ 5 & 0 & 0 & 1 & 0 & 8 \\ 0 & 2 & 0 & 0 & 4 & 0 \\ 0 & 1 & 19 & 0 & 0 & 0 \\ 1 & 5 & 0 & 0 & 6 & 0 \\ 0 & 0 & -1 & 0 & 0 & 0 \end{pmatrix}$$

Such a matrix may be represented more economically (in terms of space) if conventional two-dimensional array representation of matrices is not used. The idea is, it is possible to store informations regarding non-zero elements only. If this is done, then the matrix may be thought of as an ordered list of non-zero elements only. Information about a non-zero element has three parts : (i) an integer representing its row, (ii) an integer representing its column and (iii) the data associated with this element. Such a 3-tuple can be implemented by structures in "C" in the following manner:

```
typedef struct element
{
        int row, col, val;
} element;
```

Then, a sparse matrix may be defined as

```
typedef struct spmat
{
        int no_of_elements;
        int no_of_rows, no_of_columns;
        element data[100];
}spmat;
```

Thus, the 6X6 matrix, "A" may be described as a one-dimensional array, "a", such that a.no_of_elements is 12, a.no_of_columns is 6, a.no_of_rows is 6 and the array a.data may be depicted as shown in Figure 2.7.

0,2,9	1,0,5	1,3,1	1,5,8	2,1,2	2,4,4	3,1,1	3,2,19	4,0,1	4,1,5	4,4,6	5,2,-1

Figure 2.7. Representing sparse matrix using array of structures.

Since each element in the array is a 3-tuple, the contents of the array is pictorially shown by means of three integers separated by commas. To find out the saving in space that could be achieved by such a representation, consider the space required for storing a mXn integer matrix in a two dimensional array. Naturally, the size required for the array is m*n*(size of an integer) number of bytes. In the representation using one dimensional array, an array of size "p" is required where p = number of non-zero elements in the matrix. Each element in "p" needs room to store 3 integers. Hence, the total space required is 3p*(size of an integer). Clearly, the second representation becomes advantageous if

3p*(size of an integer) < mn*(size of an integer)

i.e. p < mn/3

In other words, if number of non-zero elements is less than one third of the total number of elements in the matrix then the "array of structure" representation is better in terms of space.

Although the non-zero elements may be stored in the array "data" in any order, keeping them ordered in some fashion may be advantageous for further processing. Note that in the example, a.data is arranged in increasing order of the row number of non-zero elements. Moreover, for elements with same row number, the array is arranged in order of increasing column number. If a function is to be written to compute total number of elements in each row of the matrix, then such a function would traverse the array only once to get the result.

However, if someone wants to know the number of elements in each column, a straight forward function would take $O(mn^2)$ time to find that out. As the array "data" is not ordered in increasing order of column number, the entire array is to be searched to find which elements belong to a given column number. The "C" function for finding number of elements in each column is given in the following.

```
void find(spmat *a)
{
        int j, i;
        int count = 0;
        for (i = 0; i < a->no_of_columns; i++)
        {
                count = 0;
                for (j = 0; j < a->no_of_elements; j++)
                        if (a->data[j].col == i)
                                count++;
                printf ("number of element in column %d is %d", i, count);
        }
}
```

Clearly, the number of comparisons is p*n (where "p" is number of non-zero elements in the matrix represented by "a") and p = O(mn) in the worst case. Hence, the time complexity of the above function is $O(mn^2)$. However, a function for the same may be written for a mXn matrix represented conventionally using a two-dimensional matrix which will work in O(mn) time. It is natural, therefore, to ask whether the saving in space achieved by our representation is responsible for such poor performance in processing. A closer inspection, however, reveals that the complexity of the above function may be improved by using a programming trick. Let an array "col" be declared as int col[n] so that col[i] stores the number of elements in the i-th column. The algorithm is as follows. col[i] is initialized to 0 for all i, $0 \le i < n$.

If "a" is the sparse matrix declared as "spmat a" then, the elements of the array a.data is scanned one by one. If a.data[j].col is "i" for some "j" then col[i] is incremented. This step is repeated for all j. The following function uses this algorithm.

```
void colelements(spmat *a)
{
        int i, j;
        int col[100];
        for (i = 0; i < a->no_of_columns; i++)
                col[i] = 0;
        for (i = 0; i < a->no_of_elements; i++)
        {
                j = a->data[i].col;
                col[j] += 1;
        }
        for (i = 0; i < a->no_of_columns; i++)
                printf ("no. of elements in column %d is %d", i, col[i]);
}
```

The first and third "for-loop" make "n" iterations while the number of iterations in the second "for-loop" is "p" where "n" is the number of columns and "p" is the number of non-zero elements of the sparse matrix. The time complexity of the above function is O(n+n+p). In the worst case p = O(mn). Then, the complexity becomes O(n+n+O(mn)) = O(mn). Also, observe that this time-efficient function needs an additional space in the form of array "col".

The next problem to be dealt with is computing the transpose of a sparse matrix defined as "spmat *a". On the surface, this might seem to be an easy problem with a straight forward algorithm as follows.

```
void simpleTranspose (spmat *a, spmat *b)
{
        int i;
        b->no_of_rows = a->no_of_columns;
        b->no_of_columns = a->no_of_rows;
        b->no_of_elements = a->no_of_elements;
                for (i = 0; i < a->no_of_elements; i++)
                {
```

```
            b-> data[i].row = a-> data[i].col;
            b-> data[i].col = a->data[i].row;
            b-> data[i]. val = a->data[i].val;
        }
}
```

If this function is executed on the matrix in Figure 2.7, then the transposed matrix becomes:

2,0,9	0,1,5	3,1,1	5,1,8	1,2,2	4,2,4	1,3,1	2,3,19	0,4,1	1,4,5	4,4,6	2,5,-1

Figure 2.8. The transpose of the matrix of Figure 2.7.

Although the algorithm "simpleTranspose" runs in O(mn) time in the worst case and the transpose is properly computed, the matrix pointed to by "b" suffers from a serious drawback. The array "b->data" is not arranged in the way "a->data" was. Therefore, the function "simpleTranspose" turns out to be unsatisfactory. The next function overcomes this problem by finding out elements in the original matrix for columns starting from 0 to n-1.

```
void transpose (spmat *a, spmat *b)
{
        int i, j, k = 0;
        b->no_of_rows = a->no_of_columns;
        b->no_of_columns = a->no_of_rows;
        b->no_of_elements = a->no_of_elements;
        for (i = 0; i < a->no_of_columns; i++)
                for (j = 0; j < a->no_of_elements; j++)
                {
                        if (a->data[j].col== i)
                        {
                                b->data[k].row = i;
                                b->data[k].col=a->data[j].row;
                                b->data[k].val = a->data[j].val;
                                k++;
                        }
                }
}
```

For an mxn sparse matrix with "p" non-zero elements, the function "transpose" runs in O(mn^2) time. Observe that, the major problem in this function is that for a given "j", the index in b-> data where a->data[j] is to be stored is not known. Also, note that the columns in "a" becomes rows in "b". Let the number of elements with row number as "i" in "b" be denoted by r_i. Then, r_i is equal to the number of elements with column number as "i" in "a". The index in b->data from where elements of the k-th row in "b" are to be stored is $\Sigma_{i=0,k-1} r_i$.

That is, b->data[0] contains information about the elements whose row number is 0 (Assume there are some non-zero elements in 0th row). b->data[0+number of elements in 0th row] contains the first non-zero element of the next row. In other words, b->data contains the first non-zero element of the first row. Similarly b->[r_0+r_1] contains the first non-zero element in the 2nd row and so on. r in "b" is nothing but col[0] as computed in the function "colelements". Then,

$r_2 = r_1 + col[1]$

$r_3 = r_2 + col[2]$

Once r_i is computed, this information can be used to store the elements of a->data to corresponding elements b-> data.

```
void fastTranspose (spmat *a, spmat *b)
{
        int i, j;
        int S[100],col[100];
        for (i = 0; i < a->no_of_columns; i++)
                col[i] = 0;
        for (i = 0; i < a->no_of_elements; i++)
                col[a->data[i].col] += 1;
        S[0] = 0;
        for (i = 1; i < a->no_of_columns; i++)
                S[i] = S[i-1] + col[i-1];
        for (i = 0; i < a->no_of_elements; i++)
        {
                j = a->data[i].col;
                b->data[S[j]].row = a->data[i].col;
                b->data[S[j]].col = a->data[i].row;
                b->data[S[j]].val = a->data[i].val;
                S[j] += 1;
        }
        b-> no_of_rows = a->no_of_columns;
```

```
        b-> no_of_columns = a->no_of_rows ;
        b-> no_of_elements = a->no_of_elements;
}
```

2.6. Representation of a multi-dimensional array in a one-dimensional array.

Although programmers writing in a high level language (like C, Pascal, FORTRAN etc.) certainly use multidimensional arrays, computer memory (from where such arrays would be allocated) is conceptually only one-dimensional. That is, physically, computer memory can only be viewed as consecutive units of memory. In high level languages like "C", abstraction is provided so that a programmer can view data objects as a multidimensional array. But, a programmer writing programs in assembly level language can not define or use multi-dimensional arrays. In assembly language, usually memory can be reserved for a chunk of bytes or words or of such known units. Thus, even for programmers using high level languages, it is important to know how multi-dimensional arrays may be represented using one dimensional arrays,. Consider the following "C" definition for a five-dimensional array of integers.

```
int a[10][5][12][9][7];
```

Clearly, the maximum number of integers that can be stores in the array is

$$10*5*12*9*7 = 37800$$

Moreover, five indices are required to access any individual element of the array. If these indices are denoted by i_1, i_2, i_3, i_4 and i_5 then according to the definition of "C" language, the following inequalities must hold.

$0 \leq i_1 < 10$,

$0 \leq i_2 < 5$,

$0 \leq i_3 < 12$,

$0 \leq i_4 < 9$ and

$0 \leq i_5 < 7$

In other words if the indices i_1, i_2, i_3, i_4, i_5 are valid for the defined array then, the 5-tuple $(i_1, i_2, i_3, i_4, i_5)$ must belong to the following set:

$$[0..9] \times [0..4] \times [0..11] \times [0..8] \times [0..6]$$

Where $[i..j]$ represents the set $\{k \mid k$ is an integer and $i \leq k \leq j\}$.

As has been discussed, a general "m" dimensional array may be defined as

item $a[l_1..u_1][l_2..u_2]....[l_m..u_m]$ where, for every j, the index i_j satisfies the following criterion:

$$l_i \le i_i \le u_i$$

The total amount of space that is required for the array a may be given by

$$(\pi_{j=1,m} (u_j - l_j + 1))*(\text{sizeof (item)})$$

Thus, it should be clear that from the definition of an m-dimensional array, the total space that is required to represent it using a one-dimensional array could be calculated. It is also clear that, space-wise, all the elements of the array

```
int a[10][5][12][9][7];
```

may be stored in the following array.

```
int b[37800];
```

However, it is not easy to say which element in "b" contains a particular element of "a". For example, if the programmer wishes to access a[1][1][1][1][1] then the question is which element of "b" contains that element? Formally, assume that an m-dimensional array "a" is represented using a one-dimensional array "b". Then each index of "a", which is an m-tuple has to be uniquely mapped to an index (which is an integer) of "b". More precisely, a mapping between the sets "A" and "B" has to be established where the set "A" is given by

$$A = \pi_{i=1,m} [0..u_i]$$

and the set B is given by

$$B = [0..\ \pi_{i=1,m} (u_i) - 1]$$

Naturally, the mapping has to be one to one (i.e. bijective).

The crux of the problem is, therefore, to find out such a mapping scheme. First, consider representing a two-dimensional array defined as "int a[m][n];" using a one-dimensional array "int b[m*n];" . Assume that m, n are integer constants. The two-dimensional array "a" may be regarded as a matrix as shown in Figure 2.9 (a). Pictorially, each row of the matrix may be stored one after another in the array "b". See Figure 2.9 (b).

	0	**1**	**2**	**......**	**j**	**......**	**n-3**	**n-2**	**n-1**
0	X	X	X	......	X	......	X	X	X
1	X	X	X	......	X	......	X	X	X
2	X	X	X	......	X	......	X	X	X
.	.	.	.	......	X	......	.	.	.
i	X	X	X	......	X	......	X	X	X
.	.	.	.	......	X	......	.	.	.
m-2	X	X	X	......	X	......	X	X	X
m-1	X	X	X	......	X	......	X	X	X

Figure. 2.9 (a) A two dimensional array seen as a matrix

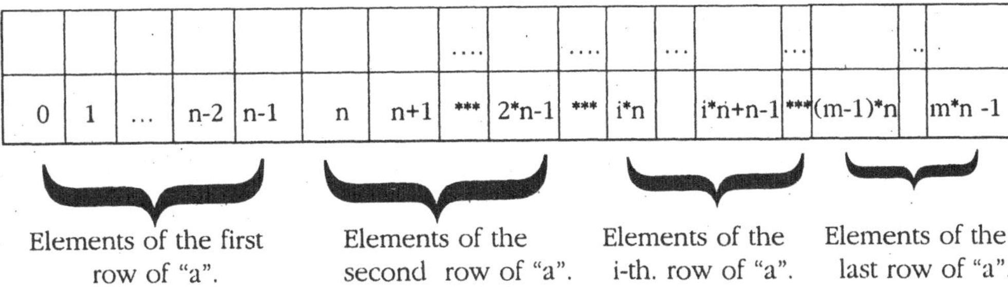

Figure. 2.9 (b) Representation of "a" in a one dimensional array.

From the figure, it can be said that a[i][j] is the element $a_{i,j}$ in the matrix as shown in Figure 2.9(a). And the element $a_{i,j}$ in the matrix may be mapped to the ((i*n) + j)-th element in "b". Thus, the mapping function becomes (i*n + j) from the set [0..m-1] X [0..n – 1] to [0..m*n-1]. It should not be assumed that this is the only possible mapping scheme. A simple variant to the above scheme may be obtained by storing the matrix in Figure 2.9(a) column by column (instead of row by row) in the one-dimensional matrix, "b". In the new scheme, the mapping function naturally becomes different. The first scheme where the two-dimensional array "a" is stored row by row is also known as row-major ordering. The second scheme is similarly called column-major ordering.

Generalize the idea of row-major ordering for finding out a mapping scheme to store a three-dimensional array "a[m][n][p]"in a one-dimensional array. The basic principle of row-major ordering is that the indices are arranged in increasing order of the decimal numbers the indices may denote. Consider the array int a[2][4][3]. The row-major ordering of the set of indices will imply the following arrangement.

(0,0,0), (0,0,1), (0,0,2), (0,1,0), (0,1,1), (0,1,2),
(0,2,0), (0,2,1), (0,2,2), (0,3,0), (0,3,1), (0,3,2),
(1,0,0), (1,0,1), (1,0,2), (1,1,0), (1,1,1), (1,1,2),
(1,2,0), (1,2,1), (1,2,2), (1,3,0), (1,3,1), (1,3,2)

The index of the array is a 3-tuple as shown by (i, j, k). The number represented by such a tuple is 100*i+10*j+k. Observe that the above sequence of indices is arranged in increasing order of the numbers represented by the 3-tuple. Moreover, the right most element of a tuple is incremented most frequently. When the rightmost component of a tuple reaches its maximum, then it is set to its least value and the component to its left is selected as a candidate for increment operation. Similarly if this component has also reached its maximum then, it is set to its minimum and the component to its left is chosen to be incremented. This process continues until the leftmost component of the tuple reaches its maximum. Therefore, to reach an element a[i][j][k], first go to the element a[i][0][0]. Number of elements between a[0][0][0] and a[i][0][0] is the number of elements in the (i-1) two-dimensional arrays if the array declared like c[n][p] i.e. i*n*p. Next a[j][j][0] is to be reached. Number of elements between a[i][0][0] and a[i][j][0] is j*p. Number of elements between a[i][j][0] to a[i][j][k] is k. Thus the mapping function is f(i, j, k) = i*n*p + j*p + k.

The same conclusion can be reached if the three-dimensional array is viewed pictorially as shown in Figure 2.10.

Figure 2.10 illustrates that row major ordering of a three-dimensional array may be viewed as a collection of "m" two dimensional arrays of order nxp for i = 0 to m-1. So the element a[i][0][0] is placed after placing all (i-1) arrays of n*p elements. Subsequently use Figure 2.9(b) to find out the position of a[i][j][k] in a two dimensional array of order nxp.

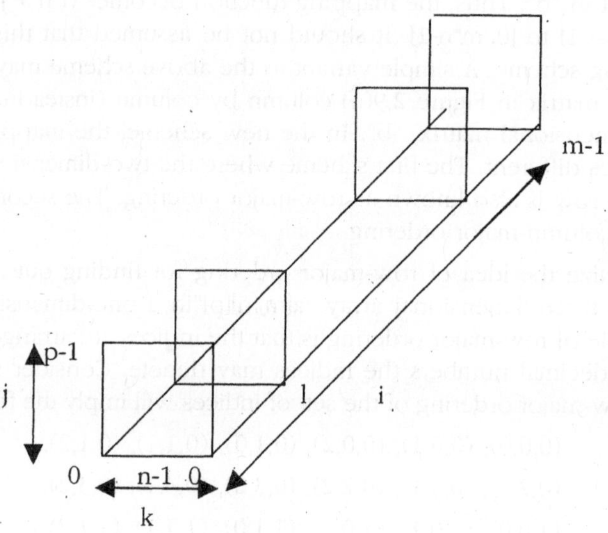

Figure 2.10. Depiction of a three dimensional array as a collection of two dimensional arrays.

Now, consider the m-dimensional array as defined in the following

$$\text{int } a[u_0][u_1][u_2]\ldots[u_{m-1}];$$

where each "u_i" is an integer constant. Location of $a[i_0][i_1][i_1]\ldots[i_{m-1}]$ may be found out by first finding the position of $a[i_0][0][0]..[0]$. As before, number of elements between a[0][0]..[0][0] to $a[i_0][0][0]..[0]$ is i_0*number of elements in the (m-1)-dimensional array of order u_1x u_2x....x u_{m-1}; i.e,

$$i_0 * u_1 * u_2 * \ldots * u_{m-1} = i_0 * \pi_{i=1,m-1}(u_i)$$

Similarly, number of elements between $a[i_0][0][0]..[0]$ and $a[i_0][i_1][0]..[0]$ is

$$i_1 * \pi_{i=2,m-1} (u_i)$$ and so on.

Thus the position of $a[i_0][i_1][i_2]....[i_{m-1}]$ is given by the following formula.

$$i_0 * \pi_{i=1,m-1} (u_i) + i_1 * \pi_{i=2,m-1} (u_i) + ..$$
$$+ \ i_{m-2} * \pi_{i=m-1,m-1} (u_i) + i_{m-1}$$
$$= \Sigma_{j=0,m-2} (i_j * \pi_{i=j+1,m-1} (u_i)) + i_{m-1}$$

In fact, the system allocates memory for any m-dimensional array from a large single dimensional array only and therefore the compiler changes any reference to an element of the array using one such mapping scheme only. This technique is quite powerful in the sense that it helps us to store several special matrices in a one-dimensional array. Some such cases have been explored in the exercises.

2.7 Points to be remembered

- In this chapter, array data structure has been explained in depth.
- The concept of an ordered list is introduced and an array representation of an ordered list is exhaustively discussed.
- Many interesting and important operations on ordered lists are considered and algorithms to implement these operations are described. In particular, algorithms for insertion into an ordered list, deletion from an ordered list and reversal of an ordered list are described. It is noted that shifting of elements may be necessary for insertion and deletion operations on an ordered list.
- Two-dimensional arrays are discussed with special reference to matrix arithmetic. Algorithms for computing addition, multiplication of two matrices and computing the transpose of a given matrix are described.
- Arrays of records have been illustrated by taking up two important applications involving polynomial and sparse matrix manipulations. In both of them, special programming tricks have been discussed in detail to reveal the art of designing efficient algorithms.
- Finally, the technique of representing a multi-dimensional array using a one-dimensional array has been fully described. Row major and column major representations of multi-dimensional arrays have also been discussed.

Exercises

1. Write a "C" function to find out the maximum and the second maximum values in an array of integers. What is the time complexity of your function?
2. Write a "C" function to compute the determinant of a square matrix of real numbers. Analyze the time complexity of your function.

3. Define polynomial as an Abstract Data Type. Write a "C" function to multiply two polynomials and to return the product. Analyze the time complexity.

4. Write a recursive "C" function to multiply two polynomials using the scheme which has been discussed in this chapter.

5. Write "C" functions to add and multiply two large integers, which can not be represented by built-in types.

6. Write a "C" function to compute the product "C" of two sparse matrices "A" and "B" represented as ordered lists instead of two-dimensional arrays. To compute one element in "C", dot product of one row of "A" and one column of "B" is to be evaluated. As has been discussed in this chapter, it is difficult to obtain the elements of a particular column in "B". But, the transpose of "B" can be computed efficiently in B′. Now, each row in B′ corresponds to a column in "B". B′ can be used for efficient multiplication. Use these observations to write an efficient function for multiplication. Your function should not exceed O(mnp) for multiplying a m x n matrix by a n x p matrix.

7. A complex valued matrix "A" can be represented by a pair of matrices "B" and "C" where elements in "B" and "C" are real numbers. Write a function to multiply two complex valued matrix X and Y. Note that if X = B+iC and Y = D+iE then,

   X*Y = (B+iC)*(D+iE) = (B*D-C*E) +i(C*D+B*E)

   Compute the number of addition and multiplication operations required by your function.

8. Write a "C" function to find out whether there is an element "$a_{i,j}$" in a m x n matrix "A" of numbers such that "$a_{i,j}$", is the smallest value in the i-th row and the largest value in the j-th column. How many comparisons does your function make?

9. Suppose an array is declared as follows.

   char $A[u_1][u_2] \ldots [u_m]$

   If this array is stored in a column major fashion then what is the addressing formula for the element $A[i_1][i_2] \ldots [i_m]$?

10. When all elements above the diagonal of a square matrix are zero then such a matrix is called a lower triangular matrix. A 5x5 triangular matrix is shown in the following figure.

```
| X               |
| X X      zero   |
| X X X           |
| X X X X         |
| X X X X X       |
```

The elements marked 'X' may be nonzero,ones and all other elements are zero. The maximum number of nonzero elements in a n x n square matrix is the sum of the number of nonzero terms in each row. The i-th row contains "i" number of nonzero elements. So, the maximum number of nonzero terms is $\Sigma_{i=1,n}(i)$ = n(n+1)/2. For large n, n(n+1)/2 will be significantly less than "n^2". So, it may be useful to store such a matrix "A" in a one dimensional matrix "B" of size n(n+1)/ 2. If this is done then some addressing mechanism must be provided so that an element a of "A" can be uniquely stored in and returned from the array "B". Find out this addressing scheme as a function of i and j.

11. Do exercise 10 for an upper triangular matrix. An upper triangular matrix is a square matrix where all elements below the diagonal are zero. A 5x5 upper triangular matrix is shown in the following.

```
| X X X X X |
|   X X X X |
|     X X X |
| zero  X X |
|         X |
```

12. How many additions and multiplications are necessary and sufficient to store an m-dimensional array in a row major fashion?
13. How many multiplications and additions are required to access the element $A[i_1]. [i_2] \ldots [i_m]$ in an m-dimensional array represented in a row major manner?
14. An important special case of a sparse matrix arises often in a numeriacal analysis is the tridiagonal matrix. This is a square matrix where all elements other than the ones on the main diagonal and on the diagonals immediately below and above the main diagonal are necessarily zero. A tridiagonal matrix is shown in the following. All elements not marked as 'X' are zero.

```
| X X                       |
| X X X                     |
|   X X X          Zero     |
|     X X X                 |
|         X . .             |
|                 . . .     |
|                   . . .   |
| Zero              X X X   |
|                   X X X   |
|                     X X   |
```

The nonzero elements can be conveniently stored in a one dimensional array by choosing an appropriate addressing scheme to map an element of the tri-diagonal matrix to a unique element of the one dimensional array. Find a proper addressing mechanism.

15. Generalize the concept of a tri-diagonal matrix to a band matrix. In a band matrix, all nonzero elements must lie on the main diagonal or on one of the (a-1) diagonals below and above the main diagonal, as shown in the following figure.

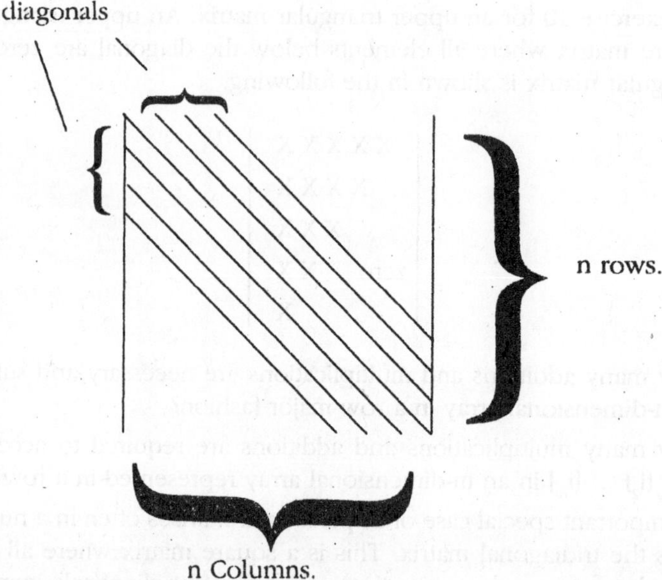

Represent such a matrix in a one dimensional array by appropriately choosing an addressing mechanism.

16. Write a "C" function to compute the median of a list of odd number of distinct integers stored in an array. The median of a list of integers is one element in the list such that the number of elements less than the median is the same as the number of elements greater than the median. For example, suppose that the list of integers is given by L as follows.

L = (10, 5, 1, 2, 6, 100, 51, 17, 19)

The median of L is 10 as there are four elements in the list (i.e. 1, 2, 5, 6) which are less than 10 and there are four elements in the list (i.e. 17, 19, 51, 100) which are greater than 10. Do not sort the array for this purpose.

Chapter 3

Linked Lists

3.1 Introduction

Array data structure has some simple and beautiful characteristics. It is simple to understand; time to access any element from an array is constant. But some severe limitations can also be attributed to its simple structure. First, the size of an array has to be defined when the program is being written and its space is reserved during compilation of the program. This means that the programmer has to decide on the maximum size of data, which is expected and accordingly define the size of the array. During execution of the program, it may so happen that the actual size is less than the defined size and so, a good amount of space is wasted. The opposite phenomenon could also happen. While executing with larger sample, the size of actual data may potentially exceed the limits of the defined size producing undesirable results. More annoying is the fact that such "overflow" occurred not because of unavailability of memory in the computing system but because the array was defined to be too small. Even when one array is defined large enough, overflow can still happen. This is because, different lists grow and shrink during execution of a program and overflow may occur for one array while the space of other arrays may remain relatively unused.

The second problem that arises in list implementation using arrays is that of insertions and deletions. It has been mentioned that during insertion operation, the nodes after the inserted node have to be shifted one position to the right. Similarly, during deletion, all nodes to the right of the deleted node have to be shifted to left. This means that number of shifting for insertion and deletion is O(n) for a list of "n" nodes in the average case. If individual elements of an array are huge records then such shifting will actually become prohibitively time-consuming. In this chapter, a new data structure is discussed in which these shortcomings are overcome.

An elegant solution to the problem of data movements which occurs in arrays can be achieved through "linked" representation of lists. Array representation of lists was made possible through indices. The i-th element of the list was stored in the i-th index of some array. This is also known as "sequential" representation of a list. In "linked" representation, each element of a list is stored in a node where a node contains two pieces of information. The first part of the node is the data item of the element of the list. The second part of the node is a "link reference" to the node holding the next element of the ordered list. This reference can definitely be the run-time address of the next node but it must be borne in mind that it is not necessary for a reference to contain physical address of the memory where the next node is stored. The basic point is, one must be able to access the node representing the next element of the ordered list from a given node by using a reference of a node representing an ordered list. Representation of an ordered list of integers given by L = (10, -5, 0,99) using links may be depicted as shown in Figure 3.1.

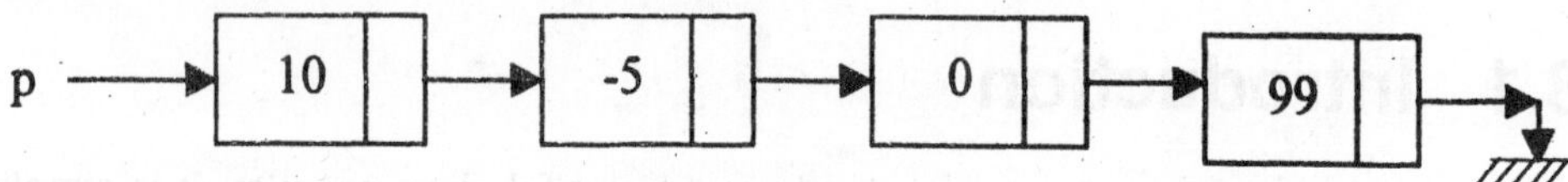

Figure 3.1 Representation of an ordered list of integers

Note that each node typically contains a "data" field and a "link" field. Arrows in Figure 3.1 show the "link" fields. The reference to the next node is always kept in the "link" field of a given node. Observe the "link" field of the last node. Since this node does not have any node as its next node, the "link" field is typically set to a default value, which indicates the end of the list. The list is identified by a reference to the first node, which has been shown by an arrow to the first node.

Another difference must be noted between array and linked representations of ordered lists. In arrays, almost always the elements in the ordered list are stored in contiguous memory locations. However there is no such need if ordered lists are represented using links. It is possible that actual address of the second node is less (numerically) than the actual address of the first node.

In "C" programming language pointers are an automatic choice for implementing linked list data structure. Clearly, pointers hold actual address during run-time and therefore, they are natural choice for implementing reference. More importantly, it must be said that "linked" representation alone does not solve the problem of overflow or fixed size, which occur in array representation. To overcome these problems, programming languages must provide facilities for

- acquiring memory for storage during run-time.
- dividing the memory into two parts like "data" part and "link" part.
- freeing memory during execution of the program once the need for the acquired memory is over.

In "C" programming language, the first and the third task may be performed using standard library calls such as "malloc" and "free". The second task involves declaring self-referential structure, which has been discussed in the next section. The standard library call "malloc" is a function that needs an integer as its argument. If a call is made as "malloc(80)" then a chunk of eighty bytes is acquired and a pointer to the first byte of the acquired chunk is returned. It may be pointed out here that if "malloc" can not acquire the amount of storage asked for (most probably because the system runs out of memory) then, "malloc" returns a pointer the value of which is "NULL". So, every call to "malloc" should be checked to determine the value of what has been returned. This detail has been omitted in most of the functions described in this chapter. Since "malloc" is the function to dynamically acquire memory from the system, it will not usually fail if the system has enough memory to be acquired. Thus, the problem of overflow occurs only if there is real shortage in space in the computing system which can not be helped during execution of a program. The library call "free" is used to return the chunk of bytes (that is no longer needed for program execution) to the system. Ideally, every chunk of space that is acquired using "malloc" must be returned using "free" in a given program. A few more points about "malloc" and "free" would not be out of place. When a program is executed, a process is created. Every process is associated with a "stack" and a "heap". The stack is used for the storage of automatic variables. Whatever space is reserved through "malloc", it is acquired from the heap. And that space remains available to the program throughout its execution unless the space is made available or returned to the system by an explicit call to "free". It would be proper for the reader to understand the basic principles of pointers and the working of "malloc" and "free" to completely comprehend the topics in this chapter.

3.2 Implementation of linked list data structure using pointer data types

It has already been pointed out that each node in a linked list consists of two logical parts: (i) the data (i.e., the information) associated with this node and (ii) an address (not necessarily physical) pointing to the next node in the list. Such a node can be declared in C using self-referential structures. Assume that the type of data to be stored in each node is a pre-defined data type "data". Then, the declaration of a node in a simple linked list is as follows:

```
typedef struct node
{
        data item;
        struct node *next;
} node;
```

Note that each variable of type "node" contains a member "next" which is of type pointer to "node". This member is used to store the address of the next node in the list.

The first operation that will be discussed is creation of a linked list of "n" nodes. For simplicity, it is assumed that the "data" part of each node is an integer. It is further assumed that the "next" member of the last node of the list is set to "NULL". Recall that a pointer to the first node of the list identifies a linked list. A linked list, "p" of four numbers with data parts as 10, -5, 0 and 99 is already pictorially described in Figure 3.1.

The following "C" function creates a linked list of "n" nodes (each node contains an integer) and returns the pointer to the first node in the list. The type declaration of the nodes is as follows:

```
typedef struct intnode
{
        int element;
        struct intnode *next;
} intnode;
intnode * create(int n)
{
        intnode *p, *q, *r;
        int i;

        /* get the first node */
        p = (intnode *) malloc(sizeof(intnode));

        /* read the integer to be stored in this node */
        scanf("%d", &(p->element));

        /* set next of p to NULL */
        p->next = NULL;

        /* assign p to q */
        q = p;

        /* In a for loop create all other nodes */
        for(i = 0; i < n-1; i++)
```

```
    {
        /* get pointer to next node */
        r = (intnode *) malloc (sizeof(intnode));
        scanf("%d", &(r->element));
        r->next = NULL;
        /* q points to the last element in the already  created list. Set
next  of                    q to r */
        q->next = r;
        /* Now the node pointed to by r is a part of the list. Reset q so
that it                     still points to the last element of the list. */
        q = r;
    }
    return p;
}
```

To see how the "create" function works, trace its steps manually. Assume "create(4)" is called and the data supplied at input are 10, -5, 0 and 99 respectively. The result of first four executable statements in the function may be pictorially described in Figure 3.2.

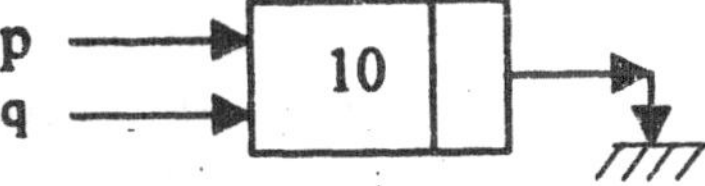

Figure 3.2. The linked list after the execution of first four statements.

In the first iteration of the for loop, the result of exeution of first three statements is shown in the next Figure 3.3 (a).

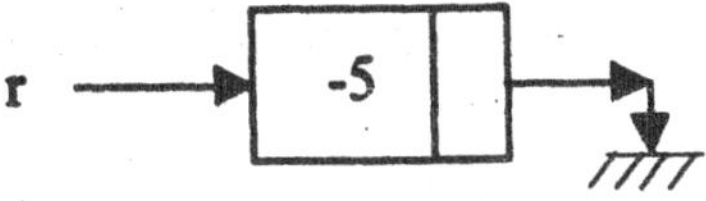

Figure 3.3(a). Execution of the first three statements in the first iteration of the "for" loop.

Once the last two statements of the for loop are executed, the result is as shown in Figure 3.3(b).

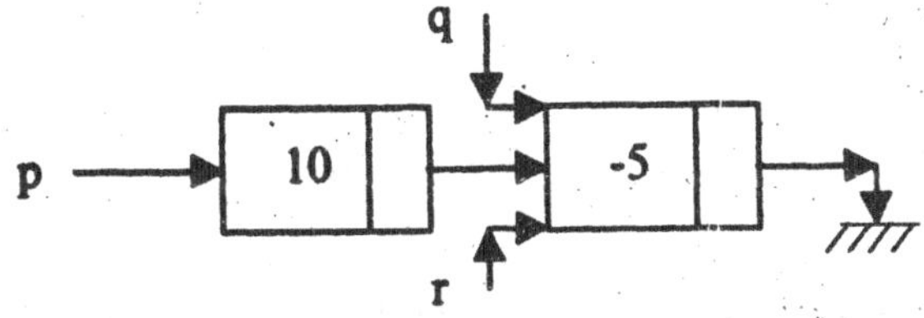

Figure 3.3(b). The status of linked list after the execution of the last two statements.

Note that "q" advances to point to the next element. At the end of the second iteration, the linked list looks like the one as shown in Figure 3.3(c).

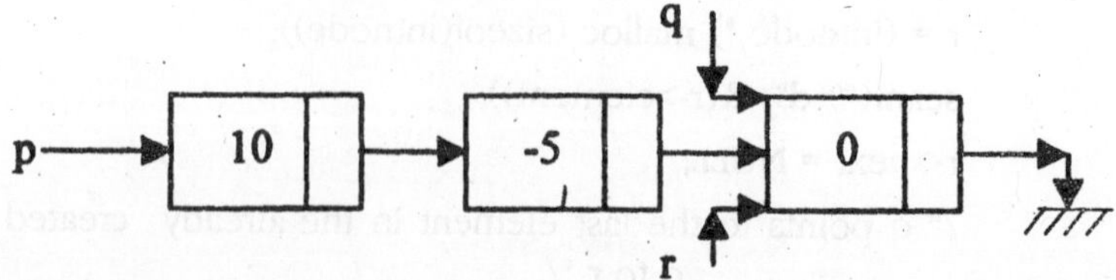

Figure 3.3(c). Linked list after the end of the next iteration.

At the end of the third and final iteration, the linked list is as shown in Figure 3.3(d).

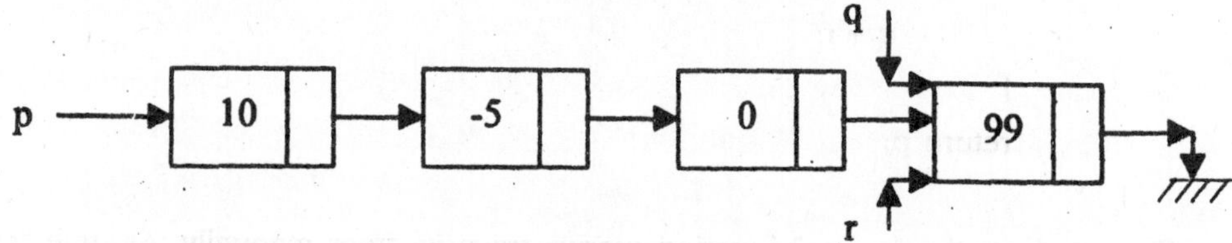

Figure 3.3(d). Link list after the end of the final iteration.

In order to traverse a linked list, "p", it is sufficient to assign "p" to p-> next in a loop as long as "p" is not equal to NULL. It is necessary to save "p" to a temporary variable "t" because otherwise, the pointer to the list would be destroyed.

The following "C" function prints the integers associated with the nodes of a linked list of type "intnode".

```
void printlist (intnode *p)
{
    intnode *t
        t = p;              /* save p */
        while (p ! = NULL)
        {
            printf ("%d ", p-> element);
            p = p-> next;
        }
        printf ("\n");
        p = t;              /* restore p */
}
```

The next operation that will be considered is insertion to a list. Consider the linked list of integers as shown in the Figure 3.4.

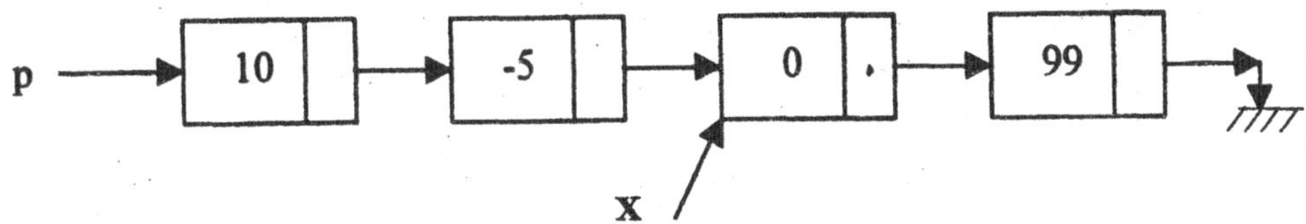

Figure 3.4. A link list.

Assume that "X" is another pointer which points the third node in the list. For the time being, do not bother to know how the value of the pointer variable "X" is set so that "X" is able to point to that element. Suppose that one more node, as shown in the Figure 3.5 (being pointed to by "t"), is to be inserted into the list "p" after the node pointed to by "X".

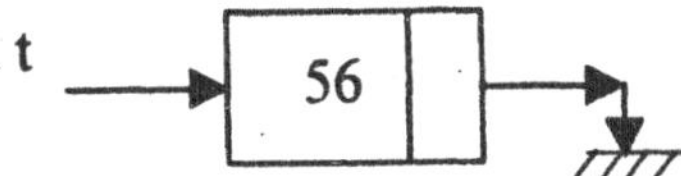

Figure 3.5 A node of a linked list.

Naturally, (X -> next) and (t -> next) have to be updated so that after the insertion the linked list may be depicted as shown in the Figure 3.6.

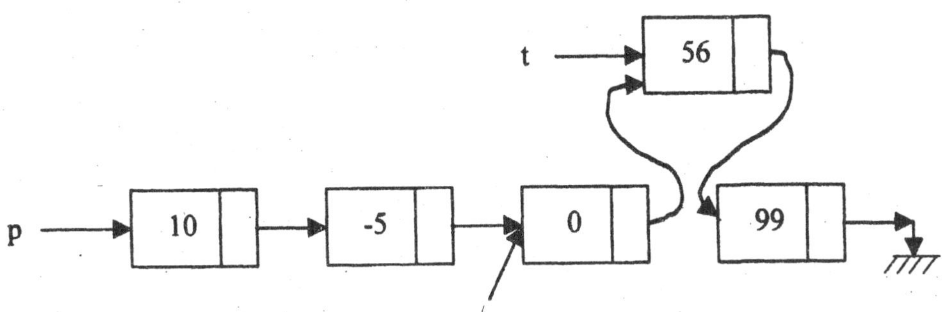

Figure 3.6. The linked list after the insertion of the node shown in Figure 3.5.

That is, "next" of "t" should point to what "next" of "X" was pointing to before insertion. And then, "next" of "X" should point to the node that is being pointed to by "t". More specifically "t->next" has to be assigned the value of "X->next" and subsequently "X-> next" has to be assigned the value of "t".

In many situations, the insertion operation on a linked list specifies the position of the node exactly where insertion is to be made. Formally, the prototype of such a function "insertList" is:

```
void insertlist (intnode**p, int i, intnode t)
```

The above prototype implies the node pointed to by " t" is to be inserted at the i-th position (i.e. after the (i - 1)-th node) of the list "*p". Thus the pointer "X" as discussed earlier should point to the (i - 1)-th node of the list and has to be computed by traversing the first (i-1) nodes of the list. This leads to the following "insertlist" function. It is assumed that the first element in the list occupies the 0-th position.

```
void insertlist (intnode**p, int i, intnode *t)
{
    int j;
    intnode *q, *x;
    if (i==0)
    {
        t->next = (*p);
        (*p) = t;
        return;
    }
    q = *p;
    for (j = 1; (j < i)  && (q != NULL); j++)
        q = q -> next;
    if ((q ==  NULL) && (i > 0)) return;
    x = q;
    t->next = x->next;
    x -> next=t;
    return;
}
```

See that the for loop is terminated if either the list is exhausted or "j" becomes equal to (i-1). In the first case, insertion is not possible and so, the function immediately returns. Insertion at the 0th position of a list (i.e., insertion at the beginning of a list) is always treated specially because such insertion implies modification to the pointer which points to the beginning of the list. This is tackled in the above function by modifying (*p) if the value of "i" is zero.

Next, consider the deletion operation. Let the operation be deletion of the i-th node in a linked list. Once again, consider the linked list as shown in Figure 3.7(a) in which the node pointed to by "X" is to be deleted. The node that is affected by this deletion is the node which precedes the node pointed to by "X". Therefore, to perform delete operation, the pointer to the node preceding the node to be deleted is required to be found out. Let "Y" be the pointer to the node preceding the node pointed to by "X". After deletion, the "next" of the node pointed to by "Y" is to be set to the next node of the node pointed to by "X" (before deletion). In the Figure 3.7 (a), next of "Y" should be the node containing 99 after deleting the node pointed to by "X".

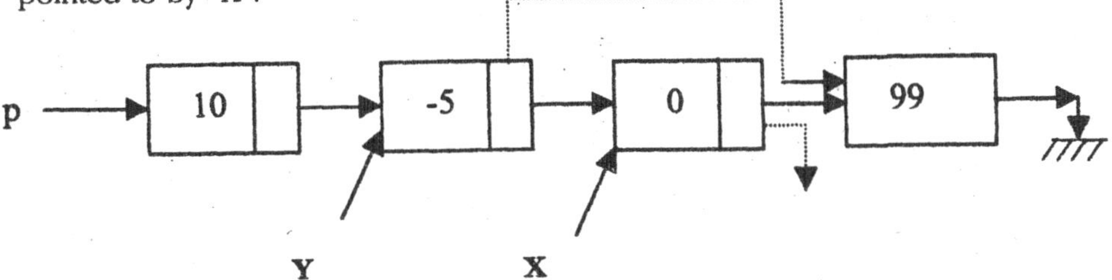

Figure 3.7 (a) The list "p" where the node pointed to by "X" is to be deleted.

"Y" points to the node preceding the node pointed to by "X". The deletion operation implies that the "next" of node pointed by "Y" is to be modified as shown by the dotted lines. Also, the next of the node pointed to by "X" has to be made NULL. The resultant list after deletion operation is performed is shown in Figure 3.7 (b).

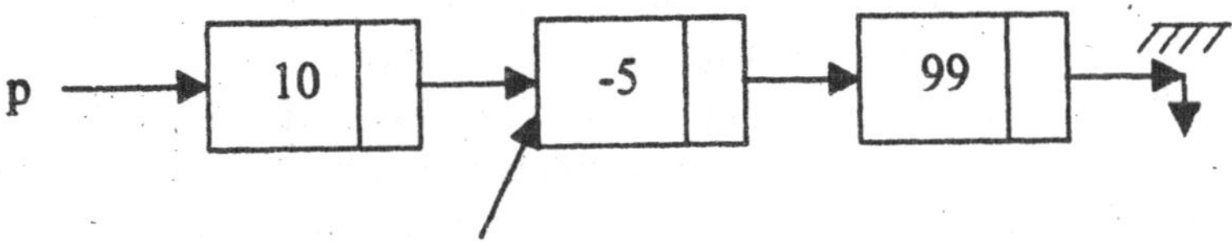

Figure 3.7 (b) The list "p" after deletion.

The "C" function to delete the i-th node in a list "p" is presented next.

```
void deletelist (intnode **p, int i)
{
        intnode * y, *x;
        int j;
        y = *p;
        if (i == 0)       /* the first node is to be deleted */
        {
                *p = (*p)->next;
                free (y);
                return;
```

```
    }
    x = y->next;
    for (j = 1; j < i && (x != NULL); j++)
    {
        y = x;
        x = x->next;
    }
    if ((x == NULL) && (i >0))
        return;
    y -> next = x -> next;
    x -> next = NULL;
    free (x);
    return;
}
```

Deletion of the 0th node of a list is to be treated specially like insertion at the beginning of a list. When the 0th node is deleted, the pointer pointing to the start of the list has to be advanced and the 0th node is to be freed.

From the earlier discussions, it should be clear that one can proceed only in one direction from one node in a linked list to another following the "next" field in the nodes. That is, all (i – 1) nodes in a list must be traversed to reach the i-th node in the list. If the pointer to the i-th node is known, that does not help us to compute the pointer to the (i–1)-th node. Therefore, if it is required to print the integers in a list of integers in the reversed order (without using an additional list) then, a straight forward function is not very efficient. A straightforward function has to traverse the entire list "p" to obtain the last element in the list and may set a pointer "X" to the last element. Then, once again, the list has to be scanned from the beginning till it reaches the node pointed to by "X". This process has to continue as long as "X" does not become equal to "p", the beginning of the list.

```
void Reverseprint (intnode *p)
{
    intnode *x, *q;
    if (p == NULL) return;
    x = NULL;
    while (x != p)
    {
        q = p;
```

```
        while (q->next != x)
        q = q -> next;
        printf ("% d ", q->item);
        x = q;
    }
}
```

To see how this function works on a list, consider the following example. Let the list of integers be as shown in Figure 3.1.

Initially x ¹ p. In the outer while loop, "q" is initialized to "p" as shown in Figure 3.8 (a).

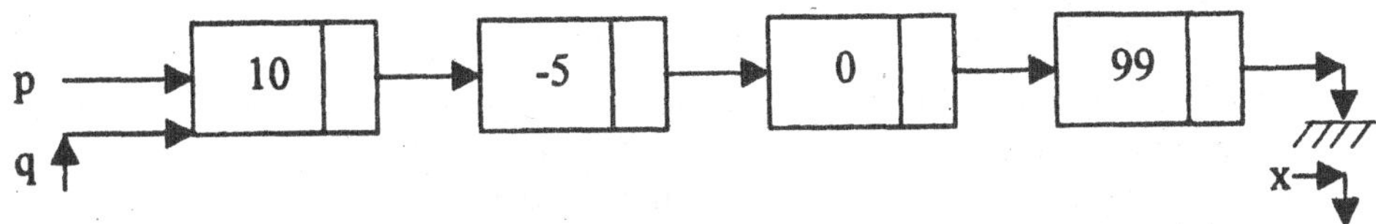

Figure 3.8. (a)

After the inner while loop terminates, the pointer "q" will point to the last element. "x" is also set to "q" as shown in Figure 3.8 (b).

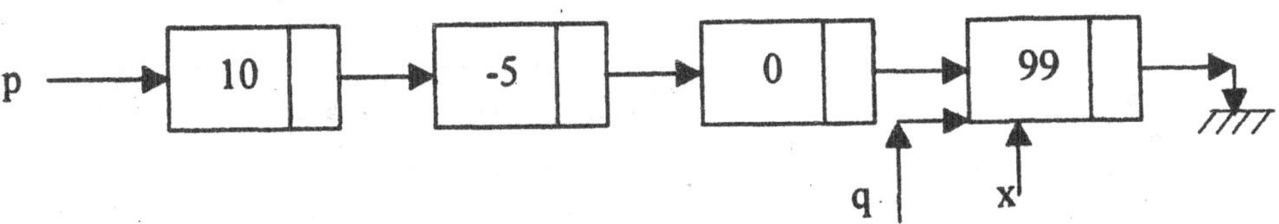

Figure 3.8. (b)

In the next iteration of the outer while loop, "q" is once again reset to "p". And "q" advances till "next" field of "q" points to the node which is also pointed to by "x".

So, after the second iteration of the outer while loop, the pointers "q" and "x" will be set to point to the third element from the beginning as shown in Figure 3.8 (c).

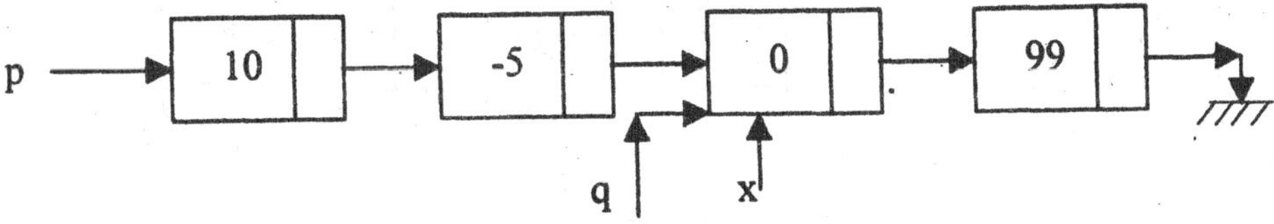

Figure 3.8. (c)

After the fourth iteration, the pointers "q" and "x" will be set to point to the first element as shown in Figure 3.8 (d).

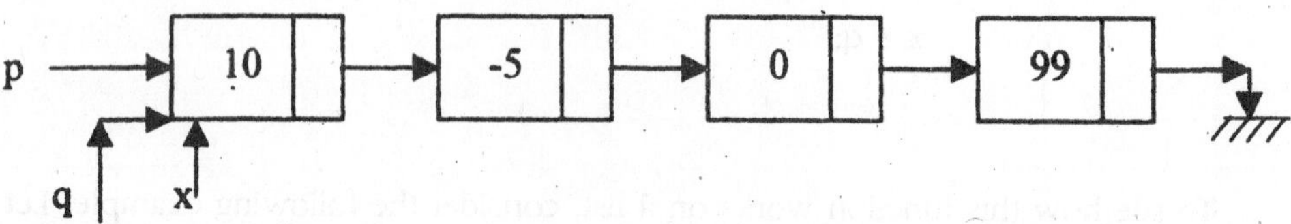

Figure 3.8. (d)

Since, "p == x" is true now, the outer while loop also terminates.

The time complexity of the above algorithm may be computed as follows. In a list of "n" nodes, the last node is scanned after visiting "n" nodes. The data in the second last node is printed after visiting another (n – 1) nodes. So, the total number of times the nodes are visited is equal to $\Sigma_{i=1,n}(i)$ which is n(n + 1)/2. Clearly, this is not desirable, because the same list could be printed in reverse order if the list was represented using an array.

In search of an improved algorithm see that it would be nicer if the links of a list could be reversed as the list is traversed from left to right. Then, printing the list in reverse can be done just by scanning the new list. For instance, consider the list in Figure 3.1. After reversing the links of that list the new linked list becomes the one as shown in Figure 3.9.

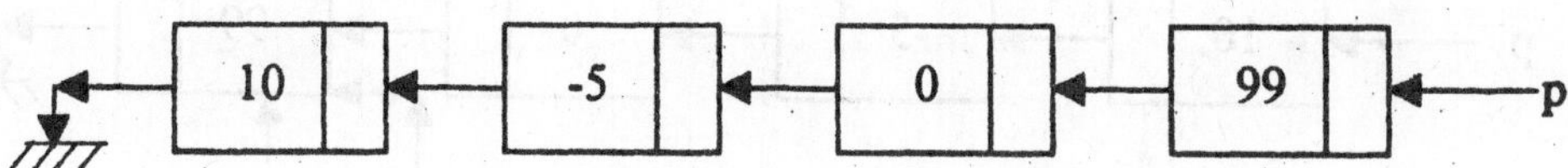

Figure 3.9. The linked list of Figure 3.1 after reversing the links.

Now the list in Figure 3.9 can be traversed and printed. One way to reverse the pointer of a given node in a linked list is to use three pointers: one pointer pointing to a given node, one pointing to the preceding node and another one pointing to the next node in the list as shown in Figure 3.10 (a).

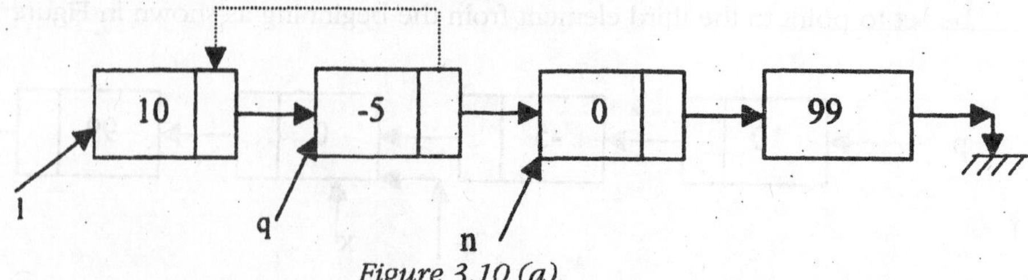

Figure 3.10 (a).

In this figure, "q" points to any particular node. "l" points to the node which precedes the node pointed to by "q" and "n" points to the node which is next to the node pointed to by "q". Now, if "q -> next" is reset to "l" as shown by dotted arrow then, the link between the first two nodes are reversed. But there is no way to reach the node "n" from the node "q". That is why, the pointer to the node next to the one whose link is being reversed is stored in "n" so that one can go to the "next" node after reversing the link of a node and can continue the reversal process. Subsequently, advance "l", "q" and "n" in the following manner.

```
l = q;
q = n ;
n = q -> next;
```

After these assignments, the list with the pointers is shown in Figure 3.10 (b).

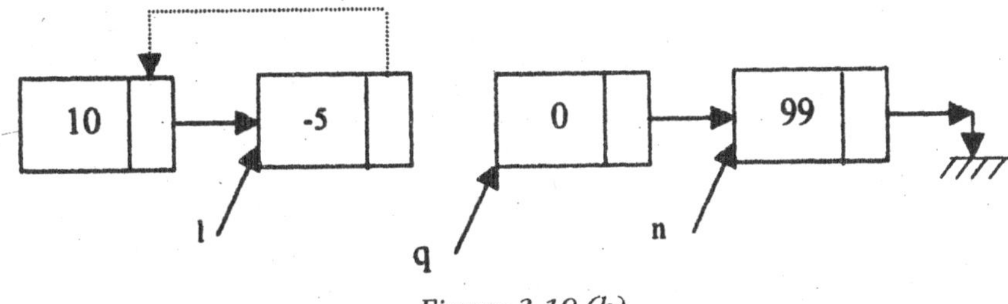

Figure 3.10 (b).

If the same process is applied on the node pointed to by "q", the list may be depicted as shown in Figure 3.10 (c).

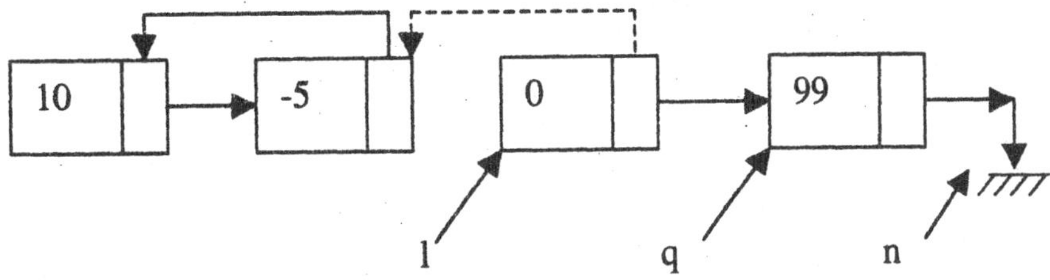

Figure 3.10 (c).

To apply this process on the first node, set "l" to NULL. "q" should point to the first node and "n" should point to the second node. See Figure 3.11 (a). Then, perform the same operations.

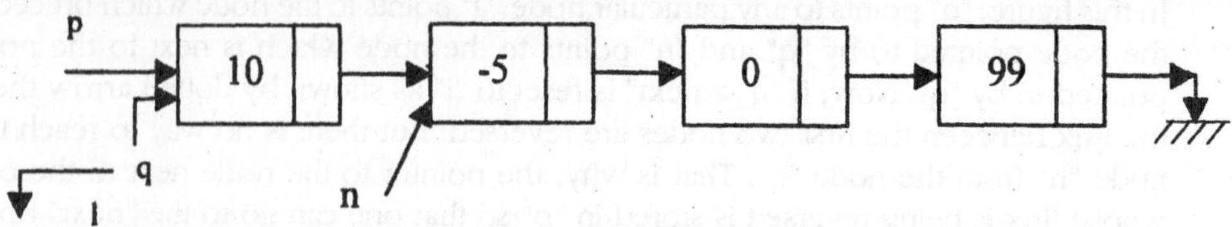

Figure 3.11 (a).

The resultant list is shown in Figure 3.11 (b).

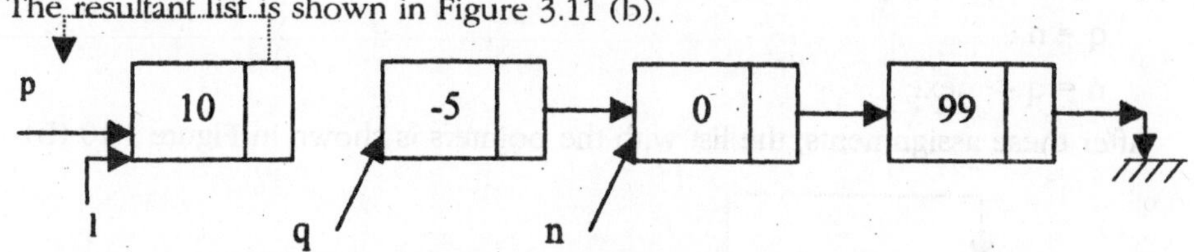

Figure 3.11 (b).

The "C" function to reverse a list is as follows. The pointer "l" is initialized to NULL. "q" is set to the beginning of the list. "n" is initialized to the second (may be NULL) node of the list. Subsequently, link of each individual element is reversed until the end of the list is encountered.

```
intnode * reverselist (intnode *p)
{
    intnode *l, *q, *n;
    q = p;
    l = NULL;
    n = q -> next;
    while (q->next != NULL)
    {
        q->next = l;
        l = q;
        q = n;
        n = q -> next;
    }
    q->next=l;
    return q;
}
```

Two more relatively simple operations on strings will be discussed now. The first operation is concatenation of two NULL terminated linked lists given by "p" and "q". After concatenation, "p" will point to the concatenated list. The algorithm is straight forward. The first list is scanned to get hold of a pointer to the last node. The "next" field of the last node is then modified so that it points to the second list "q". The function to concatenate two linked lists "p" and "q" of integers is presented next.

```
intnode * concatenate (intnode *p, intnode *q)
{
    intnode *r;
    if (p ==  NULL)
            p = q;
    else
    {
            r = p;
            while (r->next != NULL)
                    r = r -> next;
            r->next = q;
    }
    return p;
}
```

The last operation to be discussed is appending a node to a linked list "p". This function is actually the same as concatenation if we assume "q" to be a list of just one node.

3.3 Doubly linked lists

Linked lists that have been considered so far contain only one link field, which points to another node in the list. This is why these lists are also referred to as singly connected linked lists. It has been pointed out that such lists, sometimes, are too restrictive. For example, it has been seen that in order to delete a node pointed to by "p", another pointer "q", pointing to the preceding node is required to be known. One way to find out "q" is to start from the beginning of the list and traverse the list to the node whose "next" field is equal to "p". This pointer "q" would not have been necessary if another link field pointing to the previous node is maintained with every node in the list. In that case every node will have two link fields: previous and next. Then, it would be easy to move to either left or right from any given node.

If the links are implemented through pointers then two pointers are to be introduced to each node of the list instead of one pointer. One of these two pointers will point to the next node to its right and the other pointer will point to the preceding node to its left. The type declaration for such a node containing integers is as follows.

```
typedef stuct intdnode
{
    int data;
    struct intdnode *right, *left;
}intdnode;
```

Pictorially, each node may be depicted as Figure 3.12.

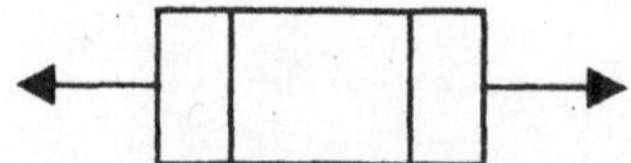

Figure 3.12. A node in a doubly connected list.

Thus, a doubly connected list of integers may look like the one as shown in Figure 3.13.

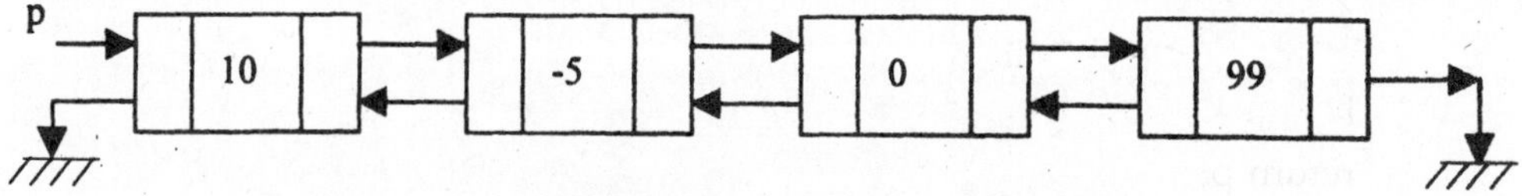

Figure 3.13. A doubly connected list of integers.

Observe that the left link of the first node and right pointer of the last node are set to NULL.

Insertion and deletion are two basic operations on such lists. As before, consider that a new node pointed to by "t" is to be inserted after the node pointed to by "X" in a doubly connected linked list "p" as shown in the figure 3.14 (a). Suppose that the pointer to the node next to "X" be "Y"

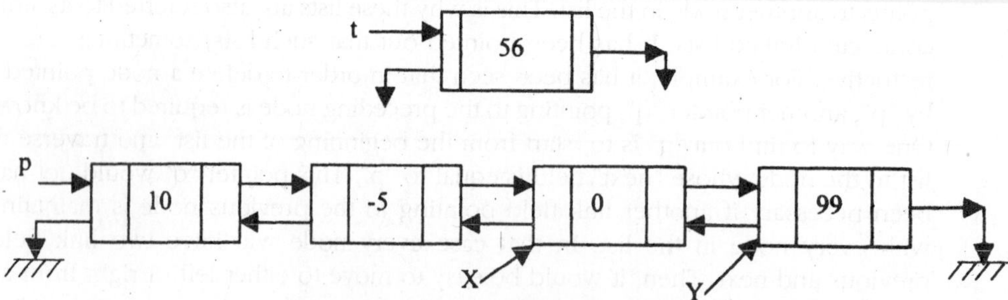

Figure 3.14 (a). Insertion of a node in a doubly connected list.

Two nodes that are affected by the insertion are the nodes pointed to by "X" and "Y". In the Figure 3.14 (a), the last two nodes are the ones that are affected by the insertion. First of all, the "right" pointer of the node pointed to by "t" is to be set to "Y". The "left" pointer of the newly inserted node is to be assigned the value of "X" and left pointer of the node pointed to by "Y" is to be assigned the value of "t". These pointer manipulations are shown in the Figure 3.14 (b), where modifications required for "insertion" are indicated by dotted lines.

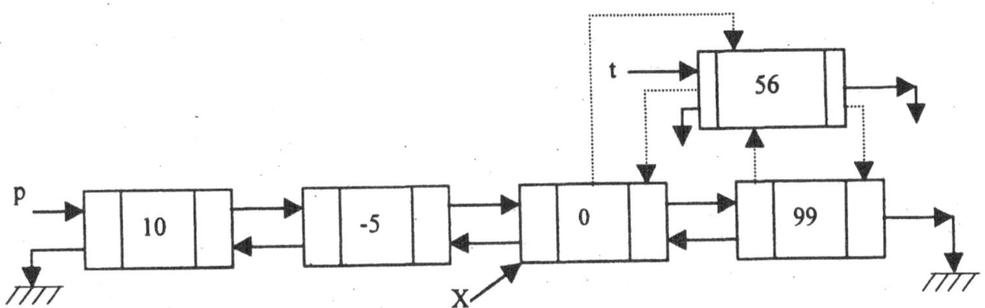

Figure 3.14 (b). A doubly linked list after the insertion of the node.

The "C" function for inserting a node pointed to by "t" in a doubly linked list (*p) after a node pointed to by "x" is presented next.

```
void doubleinsert (intdnode **p, intdnode *x, intdnode *t)
{
    t->right = x->right;
    t->left = x;
x->right = t;
    if (x->right != NULL)            /* Inserting at the end */
            x -> right -> left = t;
}
```

Note that right pointer of "x" could be NULL in which case insertion is actually being done after the last node. Hence, in that case, the question of modifying the "left" pointer of the node "x->right" does not arise.

Deletion of a node in doubly connected list is also similar. Let the node pointed to by "X" is to be deleted in the doubly connected linked list as shown in the Figure 3.15(a).

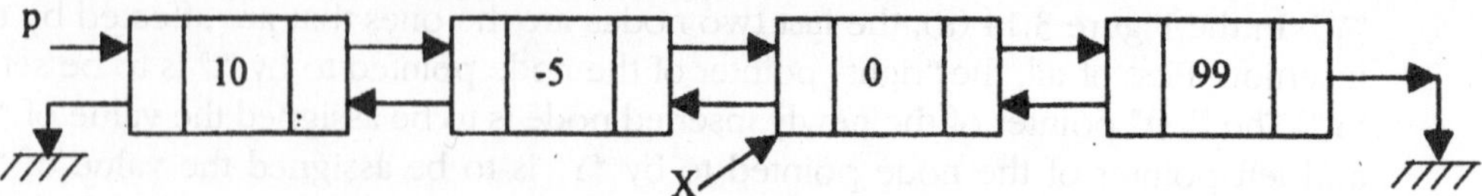

Figure 3.15 (a) A doubly connected linked list.

Let the nodes immediately to the left and right of "X" be "Y" and "Z" respectively. As discussed in case of deletion from a singly connected linked list, the "right" link of the node "Y" has to be modified. Moreover, in the case of doubly connected linked lists, the "left" link of "Z" also needs to be updated.

Figures 3.15 (b) and 3.15 (c) illustrate the deletion operation where the dotted lines denote the modified pointers. Also, the pointers that have been struck out will not be present after deletion operation.

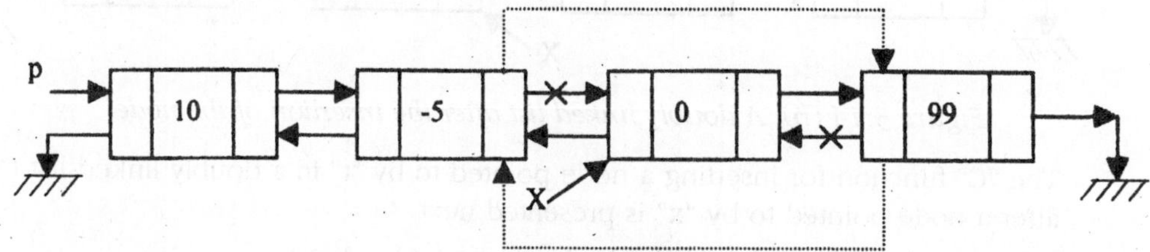

Figure 3.15 (b)

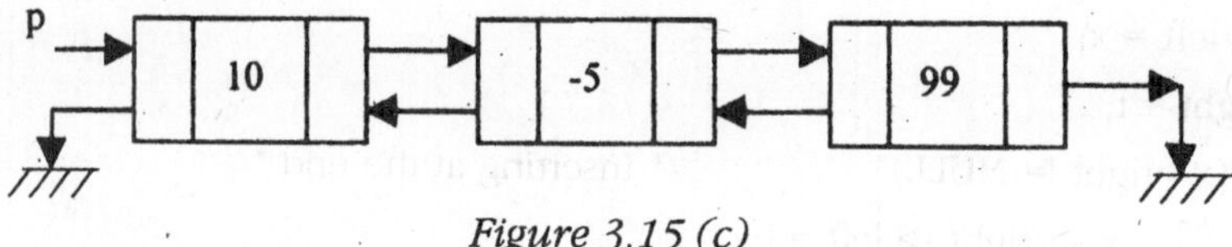

Figure 3.15 (c)

The "C" function to delete a node pointed to by "x" in a doubly connected linked list "**p" is described next.

```
void doubledelete (intdnode **p, intdnode *x)
{
    if (x != *p)
            x->left->right = x->right;
    else                /* deleting the first node */
            *p = x->right;
    if (x->right != NULL)     /* deleting the last node */
```

```
        x->right->left = x->left;
    free (x);
    x = NULL;
}
```

Once again (as in the "doubleinsert"), special care has to be taken to delete the first or the last node. If the node to be deleted is the first node then the pointer to the list is to be advanced. If the node to be deleted is the last node then there is no node to its right. Also note that it is easy to access the node to the left of the node to be deleted as every node has a "left" and a "right" pointer.

Reversing the links of a list has already been discussed for singly connected linked lists. In case of doubly connected linked lists, reversing technique is a little different. The reverse list of the list in Figure 3.13 is shown in Figure 3.16 (a).

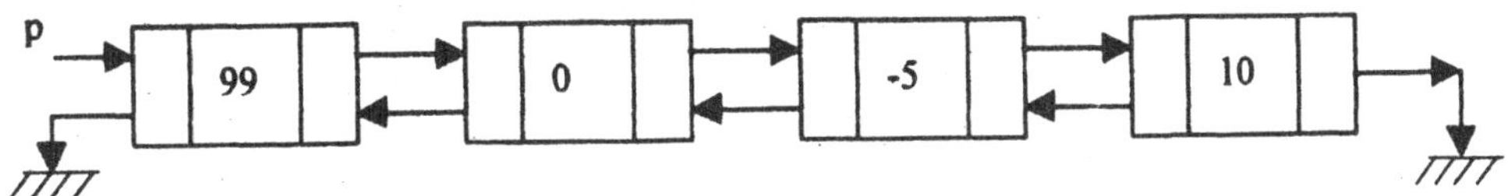

Figure 3.16 (a) The reverse list of the list in Figure 3.13.

Such a reversal may involve manipulation of both the "right" and "left" pointers of each node. Instead, it is also possible to swap the data items of the nodes equidistant from the front and the lack. This algorithm is like the one that was used in reversing the elements of an array. To do so, first traverse the entire doubly connected list so that a pointer to the last node is obtained. Let this pointer be stored in "q". Now, "p" points to the first node and "q" points to the last node. The data (e.g., integer) contained in these nodes may be swapped.

Subsequently, "p" may be advanced using the "right" pointer of the node "p" was pointing to and "q" may be advanced using the "left" pointer of the node to which "q" was initially pointing. After these movements, "p" points to the second node and "q" points to the second last node. The data part of these nodes are swapped. The process continues till "q" and "p" coincide with each other. The function for this purpose is described next followed by Figures 3.16 (b) and 3.16 (c) illustrating the steps of the algorithm.

```
intdnode* doublereverse (intdnote *p)
{
    intdnode *q;
    q = p;
    /* Move "q" to the last node */
    while (q->right != NULL)
```

```
    q = q->right;
    while (p != q)              /* As long as nodes "p" and "q" are not the same */
    {
        int t;
        t = p->data;
        p->data = q->data;
        q->data = t;
        p = p->right;
        if (p == q)     /* Takes care if the list contains even number of nodes. */
            break;
        q = q -> left;
    }
}
```

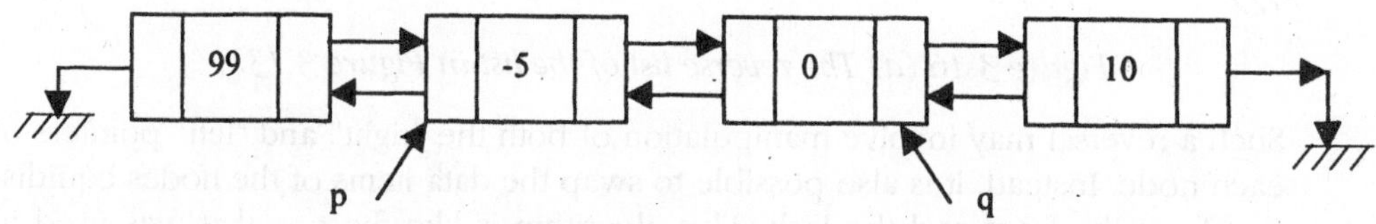

Figure 3.16 (b) After the first iteration of the second while loop.

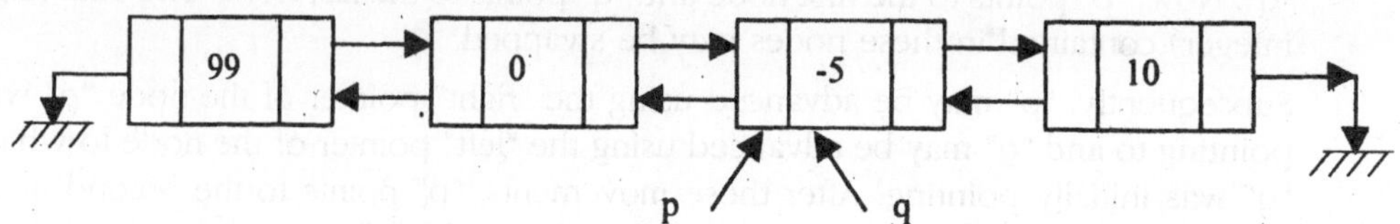

Figure 3.16 (c) At the end of the second iteration of the second while loop.

3.4 Circular lists

In some applications, it may be more convenient if the link field of the last node in a singly connected linked list points back to the first node of the list. Such a list is called a circular linked list as shown in Figure 3.17.

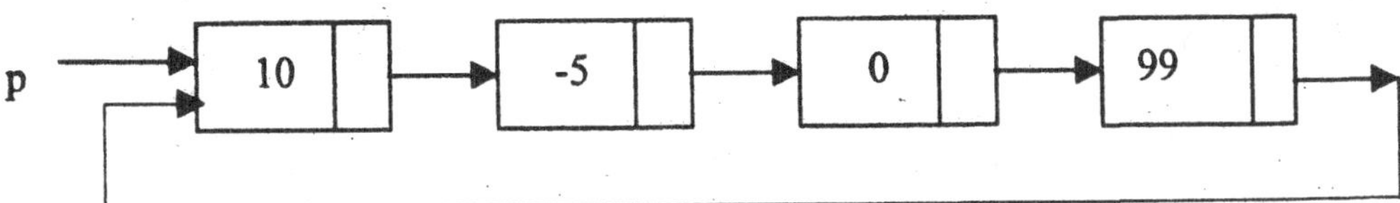

Figure 3.17 Example of a circular linked list.

Algorithm for traversing a circular list is slightly different than the same algorithm for a singly connected linked list because "NULL" is not encountered as the link field for any node in a circular list. For traversing a circular list, one needs to save the starting pointer and traverse as long as the link field of a node becomes equal to the saved pointer. Sometimes it is advantageous to identify a circular list by the pointer to the last node in the list as shown in Figure 3.18.

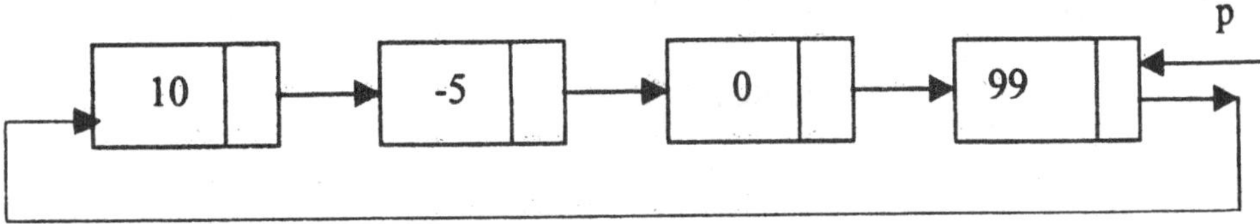

Figure. 3.18 Example of a circular linked list identified by a pointer to the tail of the list.

Particularly, insertion of a node at the start or end of a circular list identified by a pointer to the last node of the list takes a constant amount of time irrespective of the number of nodes in the list. Similar benefit is also enjoyed when two circular lists are concatenated. The algorithms for the problems mentioned are left as exercises.

Doubly connected linked lists may also be circular. Sometimes a head node is introduced to distinguish between an empty and a non-empty list. The head node is like any other node except that the data field of the head node is not relevant. The head node provides symmetry to the nodes in a circular list. Consider Figure 3.19 where a head node is introduced to a circular doubly linked list.

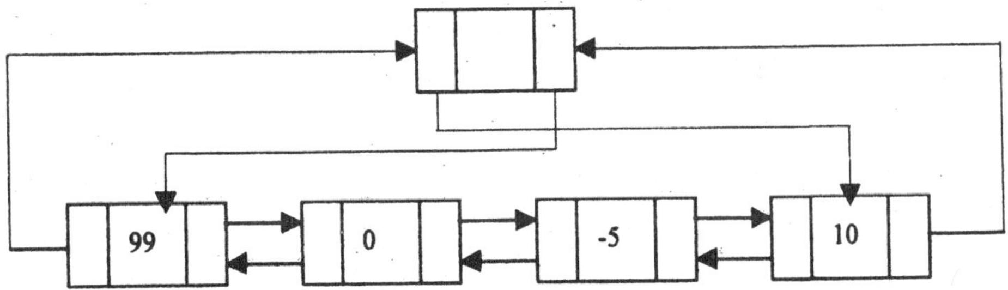

Figure 3.19 Doubly linked circular list with a head node.

Now, suppose that "p" points to any node in the list in Figure 3.19. The following observations are true about "p".

right link of left link of "p" is "p".

left link of right link of "p" is "p".

Without the head node, the above observations are not true for the nodes at either extremes. With the inclusion of a head node, an empty list is not really empty as it definitely contains a head node as shown in the following.

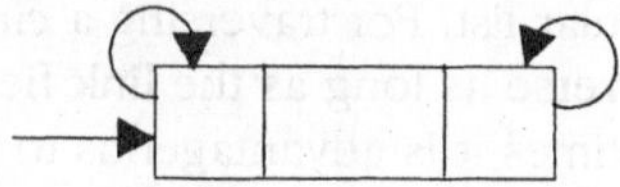

3.5 Application of Linked Lists

3.5.1 Polynomials as linked lists

Representation of polynomials has already been discussed in the previous chapter. It is mentioned that polynomials can be thought of as an ordered list of non-zero terms. Each non-zero term is a 2-tuple containing two pieces of information: (i) the exponent part and (ii) the coefficient part.

Thus, the polynomial $2x^4-5x^2+6$ is represented as:
((0,6), (2, -5), (4,2))

The first tuple indicates the term $6.x^0$, i.e., 6; the second tuple indicates $-5.x^2$ and the last tuple denotes $2x^4$. The tuples are arranged in increasing order of their exponent part. That means the first tuple contains the non-zero term with the least power of "x" and the last tuple contains the non-zero term with the highest power of "x". The linked list representation of the said polynomial is shown in Figure 3.20.

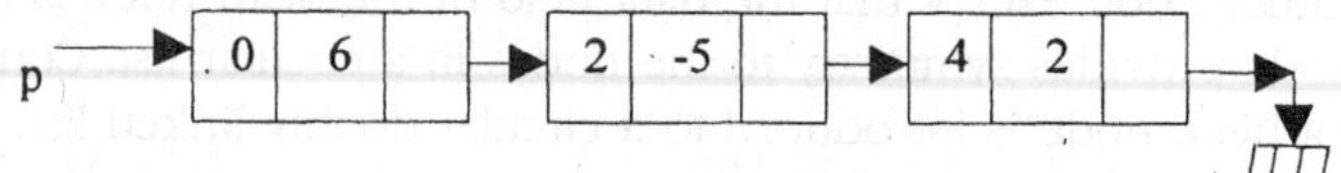

Figure 3.20 Representing a polynomial as a linked list.

Each term in the polynomial can be defined as the following struct.

```
typedef struct polynode
{
    int coefficient;
    int power;
    struct polynode *nextnode;
```

```
} polynode;
```

The algorithm to add two polynomials denoted by "p" and "q" is similar to that described for array representation of polynomials. Both the lists are scanned term by term. Whenever the "powers" of the current terms of "p" and "q" are same, their coefficients are added to obtain the coefficient of the term of the new polynomial. The exponent part of this term is the same as that of the current term of either of "p" or "q". Subsequently, both pointers pointing to the current nodes are advanced to point to the next node. If the "power" part of one polynomial, say "p", is less then a new node is created which is a copy of the term of "p" and this new node is added to the resultant list. When one of the lists of "p" and "q" is exhausted then the remaining nodes of the other list is simply copied to the resultant list.

```
void polyadd (polynode *poly1, polynode *poly2, polynode **polysum)
{
   polynode *p, *q, *r, *s;
   int newcoefficient, newpower;
   p = poly1;
   q = poly2;
   r = NULL;
   while((p!= NULL) && (q != NULL))
   {
         if (p->power == q->power)
         {
               newcoefficient = p->coefficient + q->coefficient;
               newpower = p->power;
               p=p->nextnode;
               q = q->nextnode;
         }
         else if (p->power > q->power)
         {
               newcoefficient = q->coefficient;
               newpower = q->power;
               q = q->nextnode;
         }
         else
         {
               newcoefficient = p->coefficient;
```

```
                newpower = p->power;
                p = p->nextnode;
            }
            if (newcoefficient != 0)
            {
                /* Insert this term to the resultant list */
                s = (polynode *) malloc (sizeof (polynode));
                s->coefficient = newcoefficient;
                s->power = newpower;
                if (r == null)
                        *polysum = s;
                else
                        r->nextnode = s;
                r = s;
                s->nextnode = NULL;
            }
    }/* while ((p!= NULL) && (q != null)) */
    if (p == null)
    {
            while (q != NULL)
            {
                s = (polynode *) malloc (sizeof (polynode));
                s->coefficient = q-> coefficient;
                s->power = q->power;
                if (r == NULL)
                        *polysum = s;
                else
                        r->nextnode = s;
                r = s;
                s->nextnode = NULL;
                q = q->nextnode;
            }
    } else
```

```
{
        while (p != NULL)
        {
                s = (polynode *) malloc (sizeof (polynode));
                s->coefficient = p->coefficient;
                s->power = p->power;
                if (r == NULL)
                        *polysum = s;
                else
                        r->nextnode = s;
                r = s;
                s->nextnode = NULL;
                p = p->nextnode;
        }
}
}
```

3.5.2 Josephus problem

There is an interesting programming problem known in the literature as Josephus problem. The problem can be stated as follows. Suppose there are "n" children standing in a circle playing a game. Arbitrarily one of them is designated as number 1 and others are numbered in a clockwise fashion starting from the child with number 1. Then they choose a lucky number, say "m". Immediately after, they start counting from the child designated number 1 and counting proceeds in a clockwise manner until the m-th child is identified. Then, the m-th child is eliminated from the circle and as a result the circle shrinks. Counting for the next round begins from the child next to the eliminated one and proceeds until the m-th child is identified. This child is then eliminated and the circle shrinks further. Thus, in each round of counting, one child gets eliminated. Consequently, after some round of counting only one child will be left and this child is declared the winner of the game.

It is required to write a program to identify the winner in the game described above. Inputs to this program are two integers "n" and "m" and the output is the integer identifying the winner. From a programming point of view, the problem can be tackled easily if we represent the children in a circular linked list. There will be no special head node but a pointer to the node representing the child from where the counting begins in each round. Each node for a child contains an integer specifying its number in the original circle and a pointer to the next child in the current circle. The major operation involved in this algorithm is deletion from a circular linked list. The structure of the "child" is shown below.

```
typedef struct child
{
    int originalPosition;
    struct child *nextChild;
}child;
```

Algorithm for identifying the winner is shown next.

```
int findwinner (int n, int m)
{
    create the circular linked list with n children.
    let p be a pointer to the beginning of the list;
    while (the list contains more then one element)
    {
            Set a counter to zero;
            Go to the next node and increment counter as long as counter
            is less than m;
            Delete the current node;
    }
    Get the original position of the only node present and
    return the original position;
}
```

The " C" function of the above algorithm is described in the following:

```
int findwinner (int n, int m)
{
    int i, counter;
    child *p, *q, *r;
/* Initializing the circular linked list */
    p = (child*) malloc (sizeof (child));
    p->originalPosition = 1;
    p->nextChild = p;
    q = p;
    for (i = 2; i <= n; i ++)
```

```
    {
        r = (child *)malloc (sizeof (child));
        r->originalPosition = i;
        r->nextChild = p;
        q->nextChild = r;
        q = r;
    }
    /* Starting the game */
    while (p->nextChild != p)
    {
        q = p;
        r = q;
        for (counter = 1; counter < m; counter ++)
        {
            r = q;
            q = q->nextChild;
        }
        r->nextChild = q->nextChild;
        p = r->nextChild;
        q->nextChild = NULL;
        free (q);
        q = NULL;
    }
    return (p->originalPosition);
}
```

3.5.3 Sparse Matrix

Representation of a sparse matrix has already been discussed in the previous chapter. In this chapter, a linked list representation of sparse matrices is considered. As before, an element of a sparse matrix is assumed to consist of three integers: (i) its row number, i, (ii) its column number, j and (iii) its value, val. Unlike array representation, the matrix is not thought of as a chain of such triplets. Instead, consider "head" nodes for each row and each column pointing to the elements in a particular row or column. A head node for a row contains three parts as shown below:

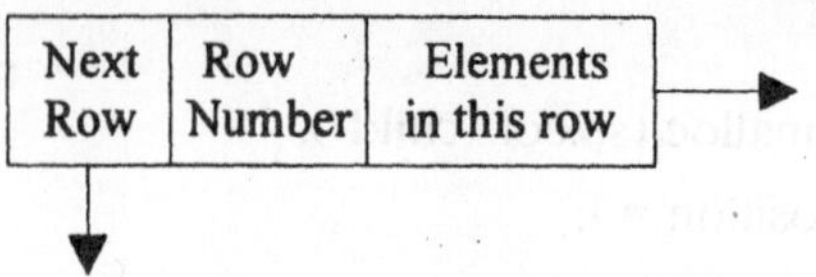

"Row number" indicates the row to which this "head" node is pointing to by the component "Element". This "head" node also points to another "head" node for the next row. Thus a "row" is defined as follows:

```
typedef struct row
{
    int row_number
    Element *right;
    struct row *nextRow;
} row;
```

Similar a "column" consists of its column number, a pointer pointing to the next column and a pointer to elements in that column A "column" is defined as:

```
typedef struct column
{
        int column_number;
        Element *down;
        struct column *nextColumn;
}column;
```

An element is defined as:

```
typedef struct Element
{
        int i, j, val;
        struct Element *right;
        struct Element *down;
}Element;
```

The structure of one element is pictorially illustrated in the following figure.

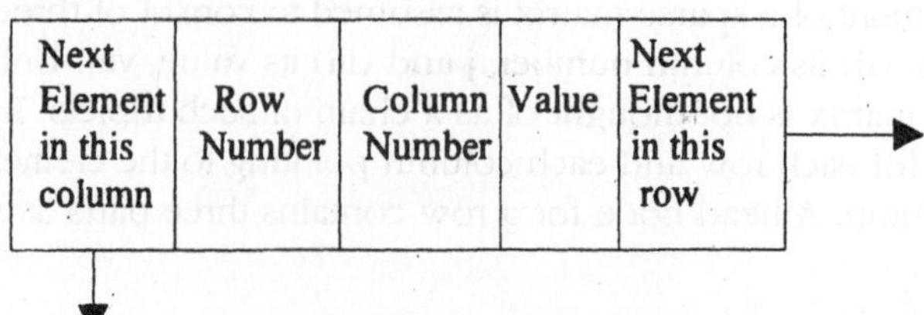

A sparse matrix, therefore, can be defined as a node having two pointers one pointing to the list of rows and the other pointing to the list of columns. In addition, this node should contain two integers specifying the number of rows and the number of columns. Thus, such a node can be depicted as follows:

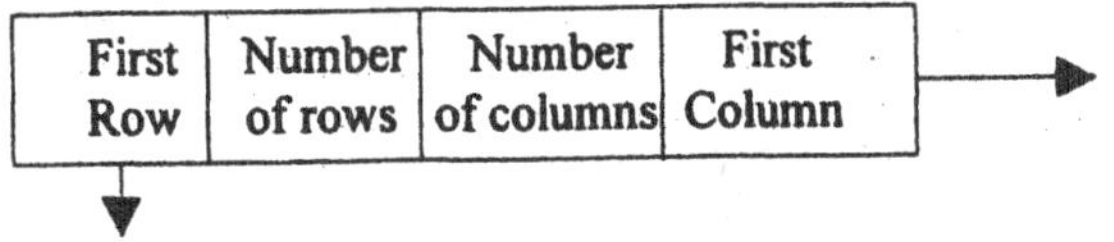

The type "spmat" may be defined as the following structure:

```
typedef struct spmat
{
        row * firstrow;
        column * firstcolumn;
        int no_of_rows, no_of_columns;
} spmat;
```

The initial configuration of a 3 X 3 matrix is shown in Figure 3.21. If A be a 3 X 3 matrix as given below:

$$A = \begin{vmatrix} 0 & 5 & 0 \\ 9 & 0 & 7 \\ 1 & 2 & 3 \end{vmatrix}$$

Then its list representation is shown in Figure 3.22.

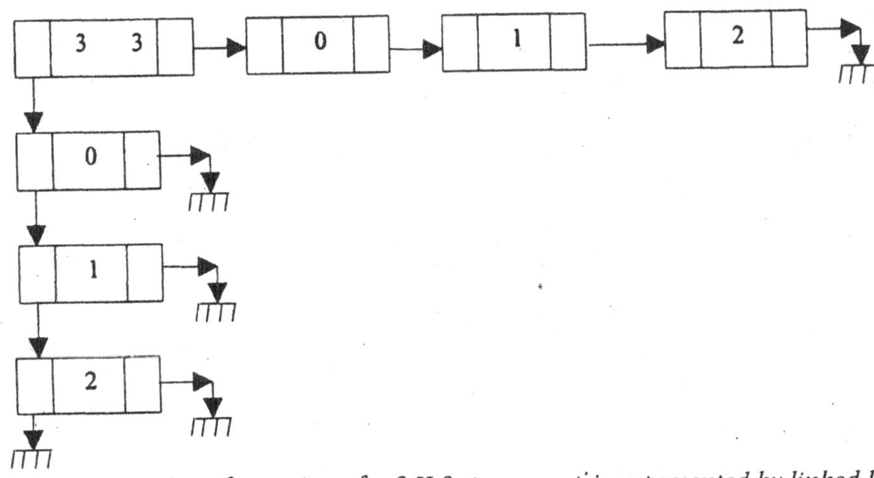

Figure 3.21 Initial configuration of a 3 X 3 sparse matrix represented by linked lists.

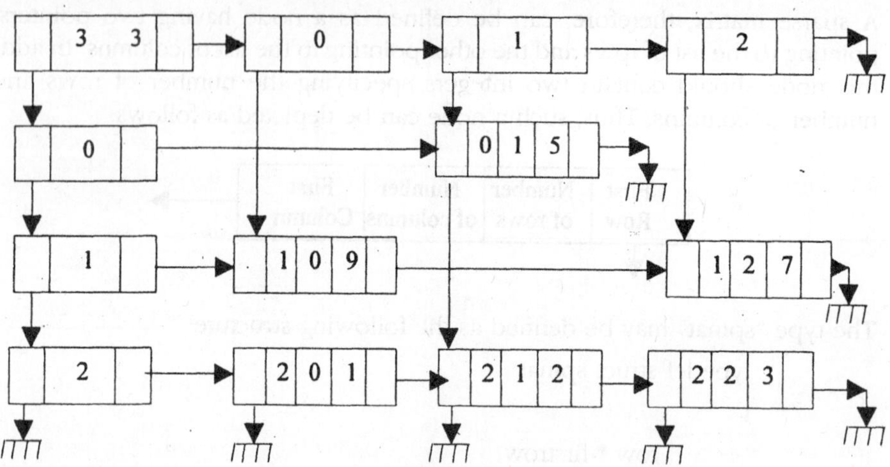

Figure 3.22 The linked list representation of the sparse matrix "A".

Observe that the elements in each row are arranged in increasing order of their column numbers. Similarly, the elements in each column are arranged in increasing order of their row numbers.

In order to create a linked list version of a sparse matrix, the elements of the matrix represented as triplets of (row, column, value) must be inserted repeatedly to a partially constructed sparse matrix by linked list. In the following, a function "insert" is written which inserts an element of a sparse matrix into a partially constructed sparse matrix pointed to by "a". It is assumed that the matrix (*a) is already initialized.

```
void insert (spmat *a, int val, int rowno, int colno)
{
   int i;
   Element *p, *q, *s;
   row *r; column *c;          /* First allocate memory for Element and fill up its fields
*/
   p = (Element *) malloc (sizeof (Element));
   p->val = val;
   p->i = rowno;
   p->j = colno;
   /* Find the row pointer, "r", where this element has to be added */
   r = a->firstrow;
   for (i = 0; i < rowno; i ++)
```

```
    r = r->nextRow;
    /* Now add this element in a proper position in this row, "r" */
  q = r->right;
  if (q == NULL)
  /* This row, "r", may not have any element as yet */
  {
    r->right = p;
    p->right = NULL;
  }
  else
  {
  /* Elements in a row are sorted on its column number. The current element p is,
  therefore, properly inserted in the list so that the list remains sorted after the inser-
  tion. */
    while ((q != NULL) && (q->j < colno))
    {
            s = q;
            q = q->right;
    }
    s->right = p;
    p->right = q;
  }
  /* Element p is to be added to a column as well. */
    c = a->firstcolumn;
    for (i = 0; i < colno; i++)
            c = c->nextColumn;
    q = c->down;
    if (q == NULL)
    /* This column, q, may be empty. */
    {
            c->down = p;
            p->down = NULL;
    }
  else
```

```
{ /* Elements in a column are sorted on its row number. The current element p is
to be properly inserted so that the list remains sorted after insertion. */
        while ((q!= NULL) && (q->i < rowno))
        {
                s = q;
                q = q->down;
        }
        s->down = p;
        p->down = q;
    }
}
```

Next, consider adding two sparse matrices pointed to by "a" and "b" respectively to produce a third matrix pointed to by "c". First, the resultant matrix pointed to by "c" is to be initialized. Then, the elements in matrices represented by "a" and "b" are taken up row by row. If the column numbers of the elements in "a" and "b" match then the values of these elements are added and a new element is inserted in the matrix "c". If the column numbers of the elements concerned are not the same then the element with lesser column number is inserted to "c". Note the striking similarity of this routine with the function to add two polynomials.

```
spmat* addmatrix (spmat *a, spmat *b)
{
    int i, v,j;
    row *r1, *r2;
    Element *p, *q;
    spmat *c;
    initialize(&c, a-> no_of_rows, a->no_of_columns);
    r1 = a->firstrow;
    r2 = b->firstrow;
    for (i = 0; i < c->no_of_rows; i ++)
    {
        p = r1->right;
        q = r2->right;
        while ((p!= NULL) && (q != NULL))
        {
            if (p->j == q->j)
            {
```

```
                    insert (c, p->val+q->val, i, p->j);
                    p = p->right;
                    q = q->right;
                }
                else if (p->j < q->j)
                {
                    insert (c, p->val, i, p->j);
                    p = p->right;
                }
                else
                {
                    insert (c, q->val, i, q->j);
                    q = q->right;
                }
            }
            /* Copy the remaining elements from the row which is not exhausted */
            while (p != NULL)
            {
                insert (c, p->val, i, p->j);
                p = p->right;
            }
            while (q != NULL)
            {
                insert (c, q->val, i, q->j);
                q = q->right;
            }
            r1=r1->nextRow;
            r2=r2->nextRow;
        }
    }
```

3.6 Array Representation of linked lists

It has been repeatedly emphasized that linked lists may be implemented even without using pointers. In this section, representation of linked lists using arrays will be explained. For simplicity and ease of explanation, linked lists of integers will be considered only. Also, "struct" in "C" will not be used to make the discussion applicable to other programming languages like FORTRAN. To begin with, consider the ordered list of integers as given by L = (10, -5,0, 99). This list can easily be stored in an array, say "Elements". To implement the concept of "link", another array "next" is to be used. No longer, the i-th element of "L" is guaranteed to be stored in the i-th index of the array "Element". It has been discussed that every node in linked representation of lists contains two parts: "data" and "link". These two parts of a node are split and stored in two arrays "Element" and "Next". If Element[i] represents the data part of a node then Next[i] denotes the "link" part of that node. In this case, "link" does not mean actual physical address. Rather Next[i] is an integer and if Next[i] is "j" then the node next to the one represented by the i-th index of "Element" and "Next" is the node represented by the j-th index of "Element" and "Next". Further, if Next[i] = -1 then, the node under consideration is assumed to be the last node. Initially, these arrays are unused and so, a variable "free" is set to 0. "free" keeps track of the available part in the arrays "Element" and "Next". Figure 3.23 illustrates this initial situation.

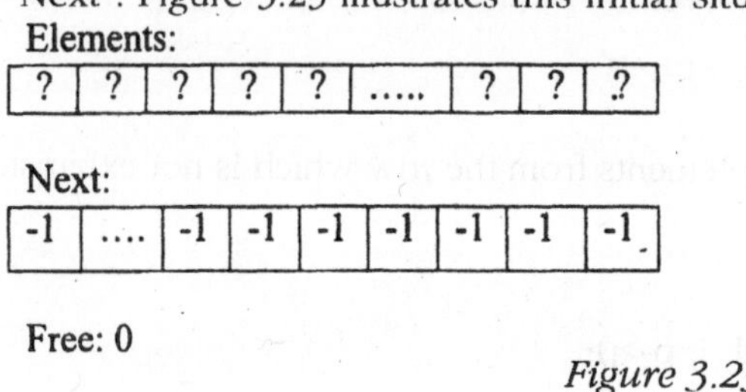

Figure 3.23

The moment the first element of the list "L" is added, Element[0] contains 10, Next[0] remains –1, "free" becomes one (because the arrays are available from index 1 onwards) and a new variable "Start" is required to remember which index in these arrays represent the first node in the list. This is shown in Figure 3.24 (a).

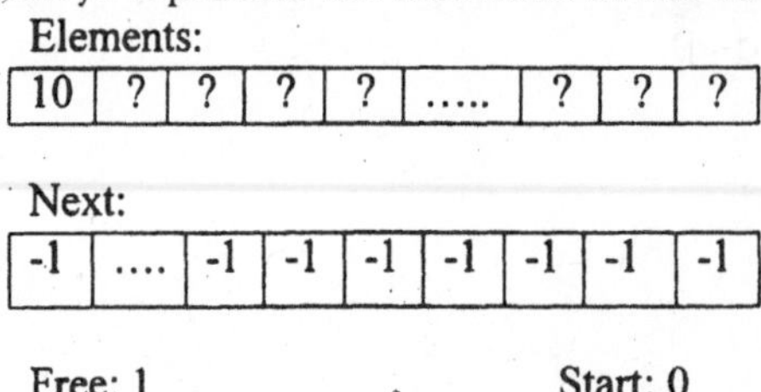

Figure 3.24(a) Adding first node to the list.

Once attempt is made to add the second element of "L", the already existing list is traversed from "Start". First, find out the index of the first node by seeing the value of "Start". In this case this value is 0. Go to Next [0]. Since Next [0] is – 1, this is the end of the list. So, the new node has to be appended after this node. Index of the arrays "Elements" and "Next" where the new node may be stored is found by inspecting "free". Next[0] is updated by the current value of "free". Subsequently, "free" is also incremented. See Figure 3.24 (b), which illustrates this appending operation to the list.

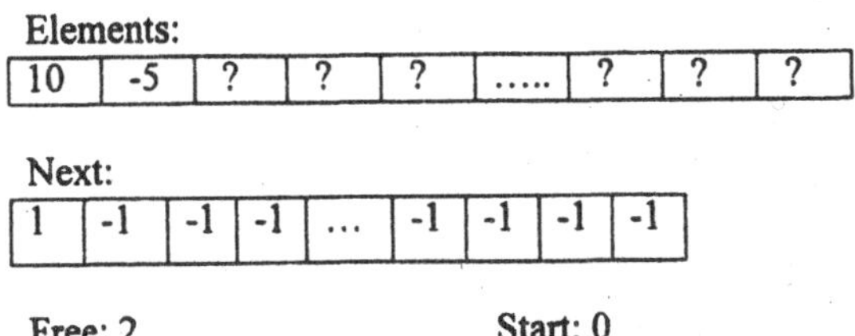

Figure 3.24(b) Adding second node to the list.

Note that Elements[1] is set to –5, Next[0] is set to 1 and Next[1] is set to –1.

Another addition to this list implies traversing the list from "Start". As of now, "Start" = 0. As, Next[0] is 1, the next node can be found in index 1 of the arrays "Elements" and "Next". Visiting Next[1], it is found that the value is –1. That is, this is the last node. As before, Next[1] is set to the current value of "free". Elements[free] is set to the new data and Next[free] is set to –1. "free" is then incremented. The following two figures (Figures 3.24 (c) and 3.24 (d)) illustrate the addition of the third and the fourth element of L.

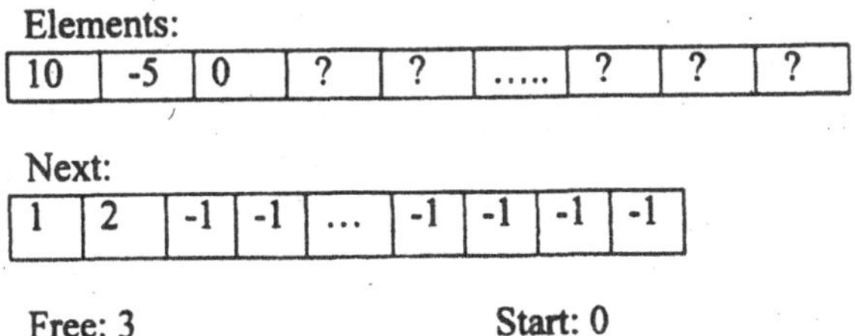

Figure 3.24(c). Adding third node to the list.

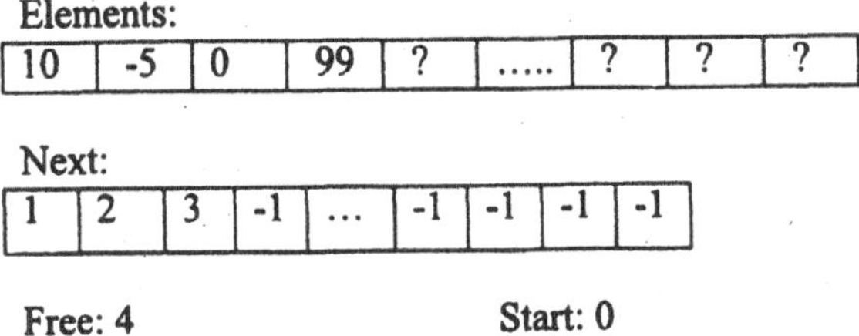

Figure 3.24 (d). Adding fourth node to the list.

Consider that the second node in the linked list so obtained is to be deleted. Naturally, the "link" field of the first node has to be changed to the "link" field of the second node. The resultant array is shown in Figure 3.25.

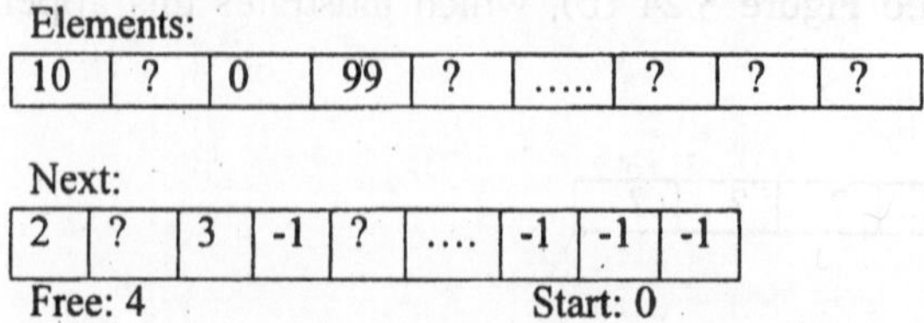

Figure 3.25 Deletion of the second node from the list.

Note that no shifting of elements are performed in either of the arrays. Only the "Next" array is updated. Figure 3.26 illustrates the contents of the arrays if a new element with value 56 is appended to the list at this point.

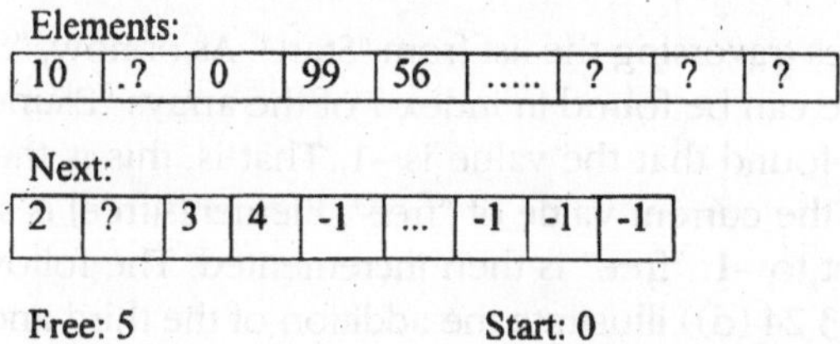

Figure 3.26 Adding another node to the list.

Observe that, due to simplicity of memory acquiring mechanism, the unused node 2 (i.e. the element with index 1 in the arrays "Elements" and "Next") could not be reused. Recall that the simple way a new node is acquired is by inspecting the value of the variable "free". Since "free" can not keep track of the dynamic scenario, it increases monotonically and does not pay attention to unused nodes, which were allocated earlier. Figure 3.27, in this context, illustrates deletion of the first node in the list. The value of the "Next" array with index "Start" has to be made the new value of "Start". In this example, "Start" = 0. And, Next[0] = 2 before deletion. So, the new value of "Start" becomes 2 and Next[0] becomes undefined after deletion.

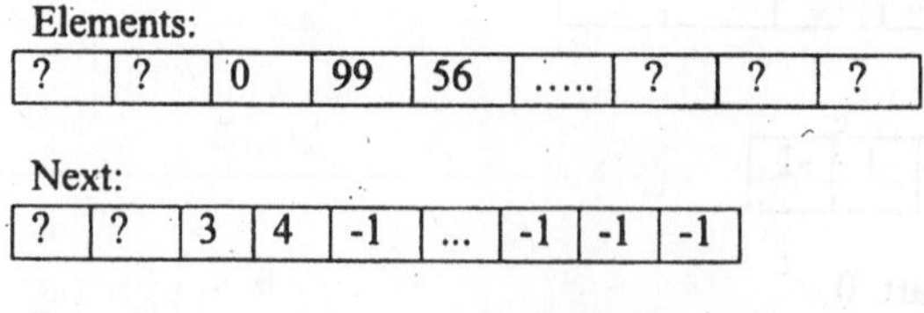

Figure 3.27 Deletion of the first node from the list.

The operations that have been discussed so far on linked lists implemented through arrays are as follows:

Traversal of a list

Insertion at a given position

Deletion of a node specified by its position from a list.

The functions for these operations are presented next. In all these functions, the variables as defined in the following are assumed to be global.

```
int Elements[100];
int Next[100];
int free = 0;
int Start = -1;              /* empty list. */
```

The following function prints the values of the nodes while traversing through them.

```
void traverselist (int startIndex)
{
    int i = startIndex;
    while (Next[i] != -1)
    {
            printf("%d ", Elements[i]);
            i = Next[i];
    }
    printf("%d", Elements[i]);
}
void insertlist (int *startIndex, int position, int value)
{
    int i, k;
    /* First acquire memory */
    Elements[free] = value;
    /* Insertion at the beginning */
    if (position == 0)
    {
            Next[free] = *startIndex;
            *startIndex = free;
            free++;
            return;
```

```
    }
    /* Traverse the list to get hold of the (position-1)-th node */
    k = *startIndex;
    for(i = 0; i < position-1; i++)
            k = Next[k];
    Next[free] = Next[k];
    Next[k] = free;
    free++;
}
```

Deletion of a node is similar and is left as an exercise. It has already been pointed out that the deleted nodes are not returned to the available part of the array. In fact, the scheme to acquire a node from the "buffer" is also very naïve. A more sophisticated scheme for acquiring and freeing chunks of bytes from a single dimensional array has been discussed later in this chapter.

3.7 Dynamic Memory Management

Think of an application, which dynamically allocates chunks of memory from an array of bytes and frees unused blocks previously allocated to the same array. More explicitly, the application would call a function getNode(numberOfBytes) to get a pointer to a chunk of memory whose size is at least the "number of Bytes" provided as the actual parameter. Correspondingly, the application would call a function free (anAddress) to put a previously allocated chunk of memory back to the pool of available memory. This section deals with the issues of writing the functions "getNode" and "free". The array of bytes from where allocations are to be made and to which free nodes are to be returned will be assumed to be global. The functions "getNode" and "free" have to use this global array only, to keep track of free and used blocks in the array. Suppose that the name of the array be "buffer" and initially it contains "M" bytes, all of which are available. Assume that three calls to "getNode" are issued after some time as getNode (100), getNode (50), getNode (150). Pictorially the "buffer" would look like the following.

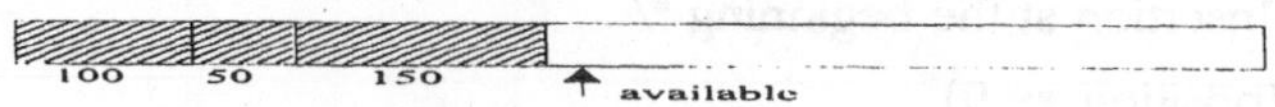

The shaded portions indicate "used" blocks. The available part of the block is pointed to by "available". Now assume that the second allocated block is freed. Now the array looks like the following.

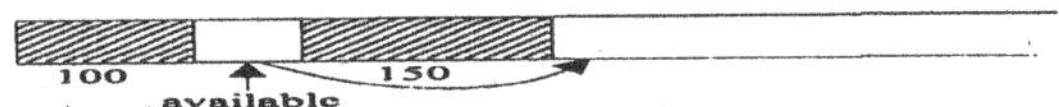

The available part of the buffer now becomes non-contiguous and therefore, these separate available portions must be linked by some mechanism which is shown by arrows in the above diagram. Suppose another "getNode" is issued at this point for allocating 30 bytes. The available list must be traversed to find a free block of at least that size so that the address of such a block can be returned. So, the algorithm for the function "getNode" is simple to understand. Before describing this function, some more points are to be addressed for understanding the available list.

It should already be understood that a random sequence of calls to functions "getNode" and "free" will divide the buffers to non-contiguous used and available segments. A singly connected linked list may be one way to keep track of these available segments. The pointer "available" points to the beginning of this list. Each segment is a chunk or block of bytes. It is now necessary to differentiate between a used block and an available or a free block in the buffer. If a block is free, one pre-determined portion of the block must contain a pointer to the next available block. Similarly, the size information of a free or used block has to be maintained as well. So, every block in the buffer will contain three pieces of information: (i) flag to indicate whether the block is free or used; (ii) size indicating total number of bytes in the block; and (iii) an index pointing to next free block in the list. The last component is particularly required if the flag is set to "FREE". Note that the link to the next node is not physical address but is implemented as an integer denoting an array index. If the link field is –1, the list is assumed to be exhausted. The structure of a block is shown in the following diagram.The function "getNode" is described next.

Flag (unsigned char)	Size (integer)	Link (integer)	block of "size" number of bytes.

```
char * getNode (int size)
{
   int p, x, headerSize;
   p = available;
   headerSize = 1+2*sizeof(int);
   while (p != -1)
   {
          if ( *((int *)(buffer +p + 1)) >= (size + 2*headerSize))
          {
```

```
            *((int *)(buffer + p + 1)) = *(int*)(buffer + p + 1) – size-1 - 2 *
            sizeof(int);
            x = (p + 1 + sizeof(int)* 2 + *((int *)(buffer + p + 1)));
            buffer[x] = USED;
            *((int *)(buffer + x + 1))= size;
            x += 1 + 2 *(sizeof (int));
            return (buffer + x);
        }
            p = *((int *)(buffer + p + 1 + sizeof (int)));
    }
    return NULL;
}
```

The above function is a little complicated. Study the body of the "while"-loop carefully. As "p" is initially set to the index of the first free segment in buffer, buffer [p] is the beginning of the first free block. So, "buffer[p]" contains the "flag" component; buffer[p + 1] contains the first byte of the integer denoting size; buffer[p + 1 + size of (int)] contains the first byte denoting the index of the next free segment. The first line inside the while loop is an "if" statement. Since "buffer + p + 1" is the address where the "size" of the free block is stored, that information is extracted by a proper type casting and the available size of that segment is compared with the required size. If the available size is more then allocation is possible from this free block. The block is allocated from the end of the free segment. Before obtaining the index of the buffer from where allocation can be made, the size of the free block is reduced by subtracting the required size from the available size. Once the available size is reduced, the block beginning at buffer[p + 1 + 2 * size of (int) + available size] may be allocated. The header information for this block is to be properly set. Then the address of the first byte of the block beyond the header is to be returned. If the required size is more than the available size of this free block then the next free segment is to be considered. The index of the next free segment is retrieved from buffer[p + 1 + size of(int)]. So, "p" is updated by that value and the "while" loop continues.

The algorithm of "free" is equally interesting. A pointer to a character is passed to "free" as an actual parameter. Understandably, this character pointer, "p", is pointing to some element of the buffer. That is p = &(buffer[k]) for some k. Now &(buffer[k]) = buffer + k. So, k = p – buffer. This is how, from the character pointer, the starting index of the block of the buffer which is to be freed can be calculated. Once this is done, the new segment can be inserted before the first block of the available list. The function to free a block is described next. First the start index "k" is calculated which indicates the beginning of the block to be freed. Then "k" is decremented so that the index of the header of this block is found. The header precedes the allocated block and the header contains one character and two integers.

```
void free (char * anAddress)
{
    int k, p;
    k = anAddress – buffer;
    k -= (2 * size of(int) + 1);
    buffer[k] = FREE;
    p = available;
    *((int *)(buffer + k+1 + sizeof(int))) = p;
    available = k;
}
```

So, the amount by which "k" is to be reduced is 2 * sizeof(int) + 1. Now, information in the header is to be modified. The flag component has to be set to "FREE". Then, the size information need not be changed. But the available list must be updated. As this block is inserted in the beginning of the available list, the link field of this block is to be set by the index of the first block of the available list. Then the head of the available list is to be changed to point to this newly freed block.

The two algorithms discussed so far are the most rudimentary versions of dynamic storage management. Although these algorithms are conceptually simple, there are some practical problems associated with them. The first problem is referred to as fragmentation. It is experimentally observed that if blocks of exactly required size are returned by the "getNode" function then eventually, the sizes of the free blocks at the beginning of the list are reduced to a minimum. In such an event, the size of these free blocks are not suitable for further allocation. But these blocks increase the overhead of searching for a free block to allocate. The second problem is that such small sized free blocks tend to appear only at the beginning of the available list. So in every call to the "getNode" function these blocks are to be unnecessarily traversed.

As one solution to the above problems, the "getNode" function may be changed in the following way. If the required size is slightly more than the available size then the free block is allocated as a whole without sub-dividing it further. As another improvement, the available list may be implemented as a circular list instead of a chain. The advantage is that the search for a free block may start from anywhere and thus allocation can be attempted from different parts of the list unlike the present case when allocation is always attempted from the beginning of the list. The final improvement that may be suggested is coalescing the free blocks. Once a block is freed its immediate left and right neighbours may be examined to check whether these blocks are free as well. If either or both of these neighbours are free then the adjacent free blocks may be combined to one free block of larger size. This improvement needs easy and efficient access to left and right neighbours from any given block. This is possible if the available list is maintained as a doubly connected linked list with a header.

The structure of a block now contains a header having four fields: flag, size, left link and right link. As before if "flag" is equal to zero then the block is free; otherwise, the block is used. For convenience, a trailer is also added to each block. The trailer contains the same flag and a link to the beginning of the same block as shown in the following figure.

flag	size	left	right	....	flag	self

With this structure, the revised functions of "getNode" and "free" are described next.

The function "getNode" first checks whether there is a large enough block in any node in the "available" list. If such a block is found then either an entire block or a part of it is allocated. The allocation is done from the rear end of the block. Each allocation needs additional space for a header and a trailer for the new block. At the outset, the complete one-dimensional array is organized as shown in the following figure.

The beginning and the end blocks are "used" blocks of size 0. These blocks are shown by shaded rectangles. The blank rectangles represent free blocks connected in a circular list. The size of the first free block is 0. The used blocks act as sentinel blocks and help us in avoiding checking of boundary conditions in the function "free". The free block with size 0 acts as a header to the available list.

```
char *getNode (int size)
{
   int p, diff;
   int blockSize, leftBlockIndex, rightBlockIndex, availableSize;
   int headerSize, trailerSize;
   p = available;
   headerSize = 1 + 3*sizeof(int);
   trailerSize = 1 + sizeof(int);
```

```
do
{
        diff = (*(int*)(buffer + p + 1)) - (size + headerSize + trailerSize);
        if (diff > 0)
        {
                blockSize = *(( int*)(buffer + p + 1));
                if (diff < 10)
                {
                        leftBlockIndex = *((int*)(buffer +p+1+ sizeof(int)));
                        rightBlockIndex = *((int * )(buffer +p+1+2*sizeof(int)));
                        *((int*) (buffer + leftBlockIndex +1+2* sizeof(int))) =
                                        rightBlockIndex;
                        *(int *)(buffer + rightBlockIndex +1+sizeof(int)) =
                                        leftBlockIndex;
                        *(buffer +p) = USED;
                        *(int *)(buffer + p+1+3*sizeof(int)+blockSize) = USED;
                        available = leftBlockIndex;
                        return(buffer + p+headerSize);
                }
                *((int *)(buffer + p+1)) = diff;
                *((int *)(buffer + p+1+3*sizeof(int)+diff)) = FREE;
                *((int *)(buffer + p+1+3*sizeof(int)+diff+1)) = p;
                available = p;
                p = p + *((int*)(buffer + p+1))+trailerSize+headerSize;
                *(buffer + p) = USED;
                *((int*)(buffer + p+1)) = availableSize =
                                blockSize-diff-headerSize-trailerSize;
                *(int*)(buffer + p+headerSize+availableSize) = USED;
                *(int*)(buffer + p + headerSize+size+1) = p;
                return (buffer + p+headerSize);
        }
        p = * ((int *)(buffer + p + 1 + 2*sizeof(int)));
 } while (p != available);
}
```

```
void free (char *k)
{
    int headerSize, trailerSize, p;
    int endofPreviousBlock, beginOfNextBlock, blockSize;
    char prevBlockStatus, nextBlockStatus;
    int leftBlock, leftOfRight, rightOfRight, currentSize;
    int nextBlockSize, beginOfPrevBlock, prevBlockSize, nextP;
    int size;

    headerSize = 1 + 3*sizeof(int);
    trailerSize = 1 + sizeof(int);
    p = k - buffer;
    p -= headerSize;
    blockSize = *((int *)(buffer + p+1));
    endofPreviousBlock = p - trailerSize;
    beginOfNextBlock = p + headerSize+blockSize+trailerSize;
    prevBlockStatus = *(buffer + endofPreviousBlock);
    nextBlockStatus = *(buffer + beginOfNextBlock);
    if((prevBlockStatus == USED) && (nextBlockStatus == USED))
    {
            /* both adjacent block are in use; */
            /* Set a free block and put it in the list */
            leftBlock = (*(int*)(buffer + available+1+sizeof(int)));
            *((int *)(buffer + p+1+ 2*sizeof(int))) = available;
            *((int*)(buffer + p+1+sizeof(int))) = *((int*)(buffer +
                                    available+1+sizeof(int)));
            *(int*)(buffer + available+1+sizeof(int)) = p;
            *((int*)(buffer + leftBlock+1+2*sizeof(int))) = p;
            available = p;
            *(buffer+p) = FREE;
            return;
    }
    else if((prevBlockStatus == USED) &&(nextBlockStatus == FREE))
```

```
{
        currentSize = *((int *) (buffer + beginOfNextBlock + 1));
        leftOfRight = *((int*)(buffer + beginOfNextBlock+1+sizeof(int)));
        *((int*)(buffer + leftOfRight+1+2*sizeof(int))) = p;
        rightOfRight =*((int*)(buffer + beginOfNextBlock+1+2*sizeof(int)));
        *((int*)(buffer + rightOfRight+1+sizeof(int))) = p;
        *((int*)(buffer + p+1+sizeof(int))) = leftOfRight;
        *((int*)(buffer + p+1+2*sizeof(int))) = rightOfRight;
        *((int*)(buffer + p+1)) += *((int*)(buffer + beginOfNextBlock+1)) +
                        headerSize + trailerSize;
        *((int*)(buffer + beginOfNextBlock+headerSize+currentSize+1)) = p;
        *(buffer + p) = FREE;
        *((int *)(buffer + beginOfNextBlock + headerSize + currentSize)) = FREE;
        available = p;
        return;
}
else if((prevBlockStatus == FREE) &&(nextBlockStatus == USED))
{

        int totalSize;
        beginOfPrevBlock = *((int *)(buffer + endofPreviousBlock+1));
        prevBlockSize = *(int *) (buffer + beginOfPrevBlock + 1);
        currentSize = *((int *) (buffer + p + 1));
        totalSize = *((int*)(buffer + beginOfPrevBlock+1)) +
                        currentSize+headerSize+ trailerSize;
        *((int*)(buffer + beginOfPrevBlock+1)) = totalSize;
        *((int *)(buffer+beginOfPrevBlock+headerSize+totalSize)) = FREE;
        *((int *)(buffer+beginOfPrevBlock+headerSize+totalSize+1)) =
                        beginOfPrevBlock;
        available = beginOfPrevBlock;
}
else
{
        nextBlockSize = *((int *) (buffer + beginOfNextBlock + 1));
        beginOfPrevBlock = *((int *)(buffer + endofPreviousBlock+1));
```

```
        prevBlockSize = *(int *) (buffer + beginOfPrevBlock + 1);
        leftOfRight = *((int*)(buffer + beginOfNextBlock+1+sizeof(int)));
        rightOfRight =*((int*)(buffer + beginOfNextBlock+1+2*sizeof(int)));
        *((int*)(buffer + leftOfRight+1+2*sizeof(int))) = rightOfRight;
        *((int*)(buffer + rightOfRight+1+sizeof(int))) = leftOfRight;
        nextP = *((int*)(buffer + endofPreviousBlock+1));
        size = blockSize+prevBlockSize+nextBlockSize+
        2*headerSize+2*trailerSize;
        *((int*)(buffer + p+2* headerSize+blockSize+trailerSize
                        +nextBlockSize+1)) = nextP;
        p = nextP;
        *(buffer + p )= FREE;
        *((int *) (buffer + p+1)) = size;
        *(buffer + p+headerSize+size) = FREE;
        available = nextP;
        return;
    }
}
```

Study the function "free" in more detail. The three conditions in the function body correspond to the following three cases. The first case is that both the adjacent blocks are used as shown in Figure 3.28.

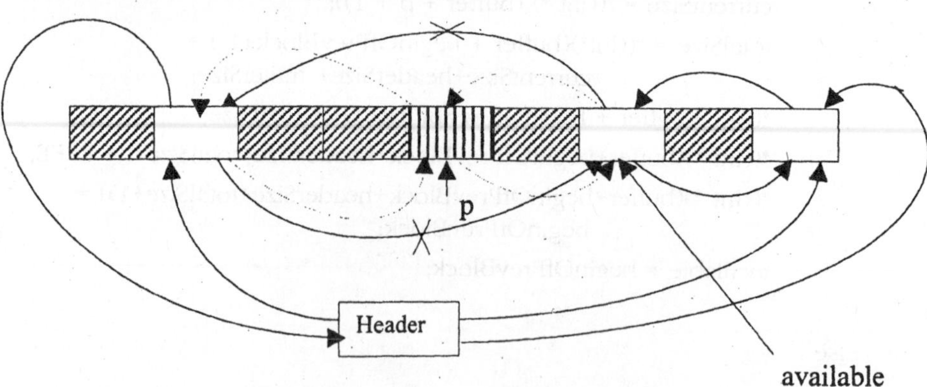

Figure 3.28 Freeing a block both adjacent blocks of which are used.

The diagonally shaded regions are used currently; the blank rectangles are currently available. The vertically shaded block is the one, which is going to be freed; "available" points to a block in the available list. Once the block indexed by "p" is freed, it is inserted before the node pointed to by "available". To facilitate this task, the "left" of "p" must be set to the "left" of the node currently indexed by "available". The "right" of "p" must be set to "available". The "left" of the block currently indexed by "available" has to be setto "p". The "right" of "left" of "p" (which is already been assigned) has to be reset to "p". The dotted lines in Figure 3.28 indicate the new links to be incorporated and the links marked by "cross" in the same figure will no longer be valid. These address manipulations are actually performed in the corresponding body of the condition block in the function "free". Finally, "available" is set to "p".

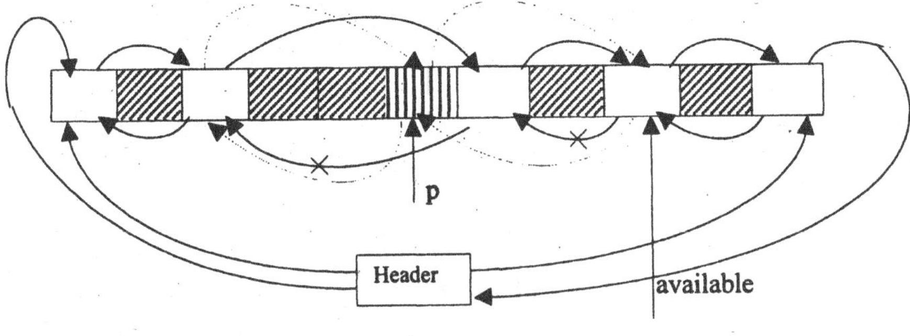

Figure 3.29

Figure 3.29 illustrates the second case where the right neighbour of the block, which is to be freed is already a free block. So, while freeing the block indexed by "p", this block and its right neighbour must be combined. To do so, the following four link manipulations are required. The "left" of "right" neighbour of "p" is set to the "left" of "p". The "right" of current "left"(after the previous assignment) of "p" has to be set to "p". The "left" link of the "right" link of "right" neighbour of "p" has to be set to "p". The "right" link of "right" neighbour has to be current value of right of "p". The size information of the combined block is to be stored in the header of the combined block. Similarly, the "flag" fields of the "header" and "trailer" are to be properly adjusted. The self link in the "trailer"(The self link is not shown in the figures) has to be set to "p" (which is originally set to the right neighbour of "p").

Figure 3.30 illustrates the last case where both the "right" and "left" neighbours of the block to be freed are already free.

In this case, the required link manipulations are as follows.

The "left" link of "right" link of right neighbour of "p" is to be set to the "left" link of right neighbour of "p".

The "right" link of "left" link of right neighbour of "p" is to be set to "right" link of right neighbour of "p".

As before, the size of the combined block has to be increased. This further implies that the "header" of the "left" neighbour of "p" has to be updated. The "trailer" of the "right" neighbour of "p" is also to be updated because the self-link in this trailer will now point to the "left" neighbour of "p".

Also note that the "free" algorithm takes a constant amount of time independent of the number of free blocks.

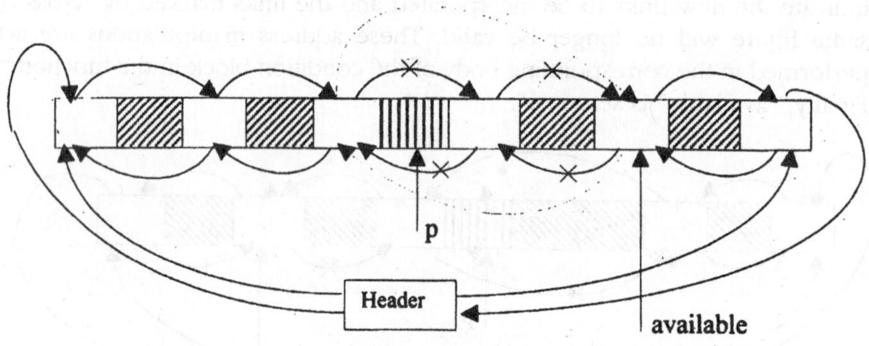

Figure 3.30

3.8 Generalized Lists

A linear list may be defined as a finite sequence of n > 0 elements, $a_0, a_1, \ldots, a_n$, which is denoted by $A = (a_0, a_1, \ldots, a_n)$. The elements of a linear list are restricted to be atoms and thus the only structural property a linear list used to have is the one of position. It is sometimes useful to relax this restriction on the elements of a list, permitting them to have a structure of their own. This leads to the notion of a generalized list in which the elements a_i, $0 \le i \le n$, may be either atoms or lists.

A generalized list, A, is finite sequence of $n \ge 0$ elements, $a_0, a_1, \ldots, a_n$ where each a_i is either an atom or a list.

If $n \ge 1$, then a_0 is said to be the head of "A" while $(a_1, \ldots, a_n)$ is called the tail of "A".

Note that the above definition is a recursive definition and so one should study it carefully. The definition is recursive because within our description of what a list is, we use the notion of a list. This may appear to be circular, but it is not. It is a compact way of describing a potentially large and varied structure. We will see more such definitions in later chapters. Some examples of generalized lists are:

A = ( )

A = (a, (b, c))

In the first example "A" is null or an empty list and its length is zero. In the second example "A" is a list of length two. Its first element is the atom 'a' and its second element is the linear list (b, c).

3.8.1 Representation of generalized lists using arrays

It has already been pointed out that a generalized list is a sequence of entities each of which is either atomic or a list by itself. Suppose an atomic entity in a list is simply an integer. To represent a sequence of entities, a link field is required in each entity so that the next entity in the sequence may be reached. Such singly connected linked lists are discussed in depth in previous sections of this chapter. In case of a generalized list, the entities are not the same. Thus, there must be a field to identify the type of an entity under consideration. Suppose this field is called the "flag" field. The second information in the generalized list is either an integer or a link depending on its "flag" part. The third field represents the next entity in the list. Consider the list

A = (1, (2, (3, 4)), 5)

Its linked list representation is shown in Figure 3.31.

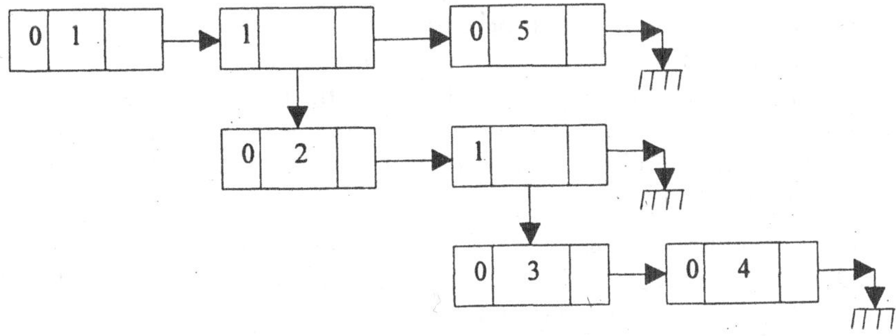

Figure 3.31 Linked list representation of the list "A"

It is assumed that if "flag" is set to 0 then the entity is atomic; if "flag" is set to 1 then the entity is a list. If the linked list is implemented using arrays then such an entity can be defined by the following structure.

```
typedef struct node
{
        int flag;
        union {
```

```
                int data;
                int subList;
        }dataOrSulList;
        int next;
    }node;
```

The links "next" and "subList" are of type integer because they represent indices to an array "buffer". The following function "countAtom" counts the number of atomic nodes in a list identified by "p".

```
int countAtom (int p)
{
    if (p == -1)
            return 0;
    if (buffer [p].flag == 0)
            return (1+countAtom(buffer[p].next));
        return (countAtom (buffer[p].dataOrSubList.subList)+countAtom
        (buffer[p].next));
}
```

Notice that the recursive definition of the data structure can be very conveniently exploited in the algorithm manipulating the data structure. The function "countAtom" can be expressed as follows. If the current entity is an atom then total number of atoms is one plus number of atoms present in the list starting from the next entity in the sequence. If current entity is a list itself then the number of atoms in this list plus the number of atoms in the list beginning from the next position in the sequence gives the required number. If the current node is NULL (i.e., - 1) then there is zero number of elements in this list.

The next function in this discussion finds out whether two lists given by "p" and "q" are equal or not. Once again, the function is recursive and the logic of recursion is very similar to the function "countAtom".

```
int Equal (int p, int q)
{
    if(((p == -1) && (q != -1)) || ((q == - 1) && (p != - 1)))
            return 0;
    if((p == -1) && (q == -1)) return 1;
    if (buffer[p].flag != buffer[q].flag)
            return 0;
    if (buffer[p].flag == 0)
```

```
        if (buffer[p].dataOrSubList.data == buffer[q].dataOrSubList.data)
                return (Equal(buffer[p].next, buffer[q].next));
        else
                return 0;
        else
                return (Equal(buffer[p].next, buffer[q].next) &&
                Equal (buffer[p].dataOrSubList.subList,
                buffer[q].dataOrSubList.subList));
}
```

The issue of forming a generalized list is consciously avoided as that requires some allocation strategy from the array "buffer". It is interesting to note that some version of "getNode" and "free" is required for implementing allocation and de-allocation from the "buffer". Interested readers are encouraged to write these routines for generalized lists.

3.8.2 Shared and Recursive Lists

Till now a generalized list is defined only in terms of its members which, in turn, may be lists. But consider the following instances of generalized lists:

A = (1, (2, (3)), 4)

B = (A, 5)

See that the generalized list "B" is defined in terms of another generalized list "A" so that the list "B" becomes ((1, (2, (3)), 4), 5) upon expansion. In many occasions, such definition of one list in terms of another is desirable as such definitions definitely take less space during implementation. This is because the sub-lists, which are shared by more than one list need not be repeatedly stored in memory. So, the lists "A" and "B" may be represented as shown in Figure 3.32.

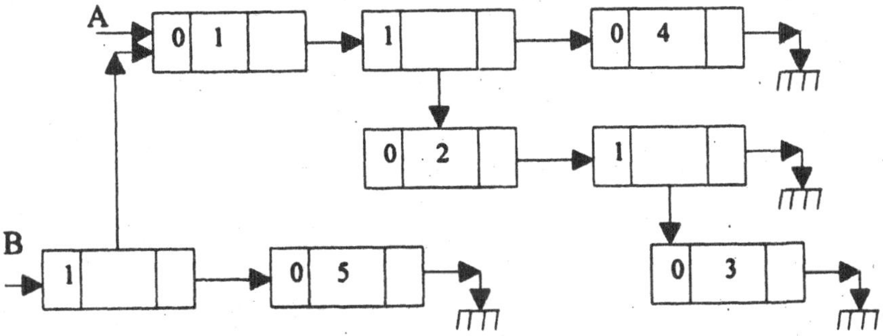

Figure 3.32 Linked list representation of the shared list B.

But, there are certain problems associated with such a space-efficient representation. Suppose that the first element in "A" is to be deleted at this point. Now, links of all other lists, which are referring to "A" are affected and all of them are required to be updated. This becomes a very difficult task, as there is no table available which can identify all other lists, which are sharing the list "A". To overcome this difficulty, a header is associated with every generalized list so that the first node of a generalized list is a header. However, the connotation of "flag" and "data" fields in the header should be different. As such "flag" field of a header is not important. And the "data" field in the header may contain the number of elements in the list.

Deletion of a list poses one more problem in connection with shared lists. As before, assume that B = (A, 5) where "A" is another list. Now even if "A" is deleted, the nodes of "A" can not be returned to available pool as "B" is also sharing the list "A". In such case, a mechanism is required to determine whether the nodes in a list can be physically returned to the storage pool. This mechanism is provided through maintaining a "reference count" in the header of a list. The idea is to use the "data" field in the header in a different sense. The value stored in "data" field of the header will be equal to the number of lists referring to this list. Whenever a list is created, this count is set to one as at least one list uses this header. And whenever some other list "B" refers to a list "A", the reference count of the header of "A" is incremented. In the new scenario, the structure of the list in Figure 3.32 is redrawn in Figure 3.33. Note that a header is incorporated for every sub-list as well.

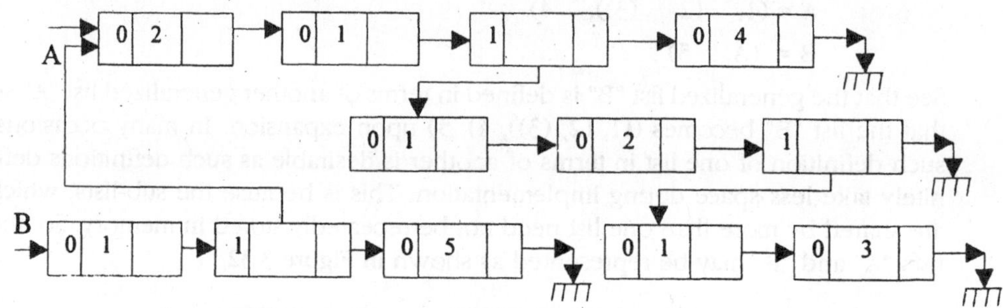

Figure 3.33 The list of Figure 3.32 after incorporation of head node with reference count for each list.

Now, consider a function "delete" which is used to erase a list. The first step in "delete" is to decrement the reference count of the list. If this count (after decrementing) is greater than zero then nothing more can be done. If the count is zero than this list is to be physically returned to the memory. This is done easily for all atomic nodes in the list. For sub-lists, this function has to be recursively called. The exact function is not written and is left as an exercise.

Observe that shared list opens up another potential problem. Consider the list as defined in the following:

A = (a, b, A)

Such a list is defined in terms of itself and thus, such lists are referred to as recursive lists. Also consider the following definition, which introduces recursion in an indirect manner:

B = (A)

A = (b, B)

Deletion of a list is particularly difficult in case of recursive lists – direct or indirect. Actually, reference count never becomes zero even when all the lists accessing them are deleted. Freeing the nodes of a generalized list in these circumstances is very difficult and requires a strategy known as garbage collection and compaction.

3.9 Points to be remembered

- Linked list is the simplest and one of the most important data structures.
- Singly connected linked lists are conceptually the simplest ones. Such linked lists may be represented using pointer data types and self-referential structures.
- Ordered lists may be represented using arrays or singly connected linked lists. Several operations like creation, insertion, deletion, etc. on ordered lists are elaborately explained. It may be mentioned here that insertion and deletion operations become simple link manipulations and these operations do not involve any shifting of data elements. However, as far as random access of any element is concerned, arrays are superior to linked lists, as linked list is basically a sequential organization of data.
- Singly connected linked lists can not be traversed in the backward manner with the same ease as forward traversal. To overcome this problem, doubly connected linked lists are used where every node contains links to its left and right neighbours.
- Typically, the link field of the last node in a singly connected linked list is set to a default value (such as NULL) to denote the end of the list. This NULL link may be set to the beginning of the list and the resulting list is called circular linked list. They are advantageous in certain applications.
- It is repeatedly mentioned that pointers are not the only mechanism to implement a linked list. To illustrate this further, implementation of a simple linked list using arrays has been exhaustively discussed. The implementation discussed makes use of two arrays "data" and "link" to store the nodes of the lists. Instead, an array of records may be used for the same purpose.
- Several applications of linked lists have been described. They include manipulations of polynomials, finding the winner in the famous Joshephus'

problem and manipulations involving sparse matrices.

- Dynamic memory management is an involved topic. The basic idea is to allocate space from a huge chunk of memory at the run time and to manage that space efficiently. The method described to do so involve maintaining special headers and trailers with each block, allocated or unallocated. The headers are also known as tags and hence, this method is known as "boundary tag".
- A list contains entities, which, usually, are atomic. Generalized lists contain entities which are either atomic or lists themselves. Such lists can be implemented using pointers or arrays.

Exercise

1. Write a "C" function to combine two singly connected linked lists in the following manner. Suppose, one list is "L" which can be given by L = (l_0, l_1, ..., l_m) and the other list is "M" where "M" can be expressed as M = (m_0, m_1, ..., m_n) where each l_i, m_i represents one node in the respective lists. For simplicity, you may assume that each node contains an integer as the data. After combining them, the combined list should be (l_0, m_0, l_1, m_1, ...,). Do not use any additional node for writing the function.
2. Write a "C" function to split a given list of integers represented by a singly connected linked list into two lists in the following way. Let the list be L = (l_0, l_1, ..., l_n). The resultant lists would be R_1 = (l_0, l_2, l_4, ...) and R_2 = (l_1, l_3, l_5, ...). As in the previous exercise, do not use any additional node.
3. Write a "C" function to insert a node "t" before a node pronted to by "X" in a singly connected linked list "L". Note that the algorithm for insertion described in the chapter inserts a node after a node "X" in a list.
4. Write a "C" function to delete a node pointed to by "p" from a singly connected list "L". Note that both the formal parameters for the function "delete" are two pointers. So, the pointer to the node preceding the node pointed by "p" has to be properly computed.
5. Suppose that an ordered list L = (l_1, l_2, ..., l_n) is represented by a singly connected linked list. It is required to append the list L′ = (l_n, l_1, l_2, ..., l_n) after another ordered list M represented by a singly connected linked list. What is the time complexity of your algorithm?
6. Do exercise 3 for the case of a circularly linked list.
7. Do exercise 3 for the case of a doubly connected linked list.
8. Write a "C" function to concatenate two circular linked lists producing another circular linked list. As it has been pointed out in the chapter assume that a circular linked list is identified by a pointer to its tail.
9. Suppose that there is an array, "A" where each element in the array is an

ordered list of integers. For example, a sample array may be described as given below.

A[0] : (1, 2, 5)

A[1] : (2, 3, 9)

A[2] : ( )

A[3] : (1, 9)

10. Suppose the lists are represented as singly connected linked lists. It is required to find out the lists (identified by indices of the array "A") in which the integers occur. In the example, "1" occurs in the lists A[0] and A[3], "2" occurs in A[0] and A[1] and so on. The following array needs to be produced. Each element in the resultant array contains an integer "k", and an ordered list of integers. If "i" is an integer in the list, the list in A[i] contains "K". The resultant list in this example is:

    B[0] : 1, (0, 3)

    B[1] : 2, (0, 1)

    B[2] : 5, (0)

    B[3] : 3, (1)

    B[4] : 9, (1, 3)

    Write a "C" function to accomplish this task. Compute the time complexity of your algorithm.

11. Write "C" function to compute the following operations on polynomials represented as singly connected linked lists of nonzero terms.

    i. Evaluation of a polynomial

    ii. Multiplication of two polynomials.

12. It is not necessary to store two pointers in a doubly connected linked lists. From a given node "p" in a doubly connected linked list, the preceding and the following nodes must be accessed. If the addresses of these two nodes are "X" and "Y" then "X⊕Y" is stored in the node "p" where ⊕ denotes the "exclusive-or" operation. The list is identified by the pointer to the first node. In the first node let "X" be 0 and hence X⊕Y becomes only "Y". So, while traversing the list, the second node may be reached. Now, once the address of the preceding node "X" (the first node in this case) is known, compute X⊕ (X⊕Y), (X⊕Y) is already stored in the second node), X⊕ (X⊕Y) = Y. So, pointer to the third node is known. If (X⊕Y) ⊕Y is computed then (X⊕Y) ⊕Y = X is also obtained. On reaching the second node, both "X" and "Y" can be computed. The same logic can be applied to all the nodes. Write "C" functions to:

    a. create a doubly connected linked list of n integers where each node contains a "data" and a "link" field.

b. traverse the list created in (a) from left to right

c. traverse the list created in (a) from right to left.

13. Write a "C" function "initialize(spmat *a, int m, int n)" to initialize an empty sparse matrix having "m" rows and "n" columns. The idea of initializing a sparse matrix represented by linked lists has been fully explained in this chapter. Show that the time complexity of the algorithm "initialize" is O(n+m).

14. Write a "C" function to read a sparse matrix and compute its linked list representation. You can achieve this by initializing the sparse matrix (Exercise 12) and then repeatedly calling "insert" (See this chapter) to insert the non-zero elements of the sparse matrix. Show that even when the non-zero elements of the sparse matrix is provided at the input in a row major fashion, the worst case time complexity of your "read" function is more than O(mn) where "m" and "n" are the number of rows and columns of the sparse matrix respectively. Modify the "insert" function so that the worst case time complexity of the "read" function becomes O(mn).

15. Write a "C" function to print a sparse matrix, each row in one line of output and properly formatted, with zero being printed in place of zero elements. Input to your function is "spmat *a" (i.e., a pointer to a linked list representation of a sparse matrix).

16. Write a "C" function to compute the transpose of an mXn sparse matrix represented by linked list. The prototype of the function "transpose" may be as follows:

    spmat *transpose(spmat *a);

    Compute the worst case time complexity of the function "transpose". The worst case time complexity should not be more than O(mn).

17. Write "C" functions to

    i. add two mXn sparse matrices and

    ii. multiply two mXn sparse matrices.

    where all sparse matrices are to be represented by linked lists. The worst case time complexity of the "add" and "multiply" functions should be $O(n^2)$ and $O(n^3)$ respectively.

18. Consider representing a linked list of integers using arrays as has been discussed in this chapter. Write a "C" function "delete (int i)" to delete the i-th node from the list.

19. Consider non-recursive and non-intrusive (i.e., not sharable) generalized lists as discussed in this chapter. Write "C" functions to

    i. reverse a list;

    ii. find the maximum level of nesting of a list;

iii. copy one list to another.

20. Consider non-recursive but sharable generalized lists as discussed in this chapter. Write a procedure to delete such a list and return the acquired memory to the system.

21. Represent a polynomial by a circular linked list. Rewrite the "C" function to add two polynomials using this representation. How do you represent the zero polynomial? If you introduce a head node and set the "power" field of the head node to a negative number, do you get any benefit in terms of coding?

22. Consider a circular list with a pointer pointing to its tail. Write "C" functions to

    i. insert a node to the front of the list;

    ii. insert a node to the rear of the list;

    iii. find the length of the list.

    See that the algorithms for the first two operations take a constant amount of time.

Chapter 4

Stacks and Queues

4.1 Introduction

Stacks and queues are special kinds of linear lists. It may be recalled that a linear list is an ordered collection of a number of items of the same type. A linear list, L, of "n" elements is usually denoted by $L = (a_1, a_2, \ldots, a_n)$ where "a_i" represents the i-th element of the list. Two operations that are frequently performed on a linear list are insertion into and deletion from a list. In the case of an ordinary linear list, these two operations may be performed at any position in the list. Thus, insertion before the fifth element or deletion of the tenth element of a list are perfectly valid operations as long as the list contains the required number of elements. A stack is a linear list where all insertions and deletions are permitted only at one end of the list. Thus, if elements are continuously inserted into a stack then, it grows at one end. And if an element is deleted from a stack then it shrinks at the same end. Figure 4.1 depicts this expansion and shrinking of a stack. Initially the stack is empty. As the elements A, B, C, D, E are inserted into it, the stack grows continually upward. And if two elements are deleted from the stack then, the elements E and D are removed from the stack. From the very nature of a stack, it is clear that the element that is removed from a stack has been the last element inserted into the stack. For example, the first element deleted from the stack in Figure 4.1 was E, which had been the last element to be inserted into the stack. This is why a stack is often called a "Last In First Out (LIFO)" list.

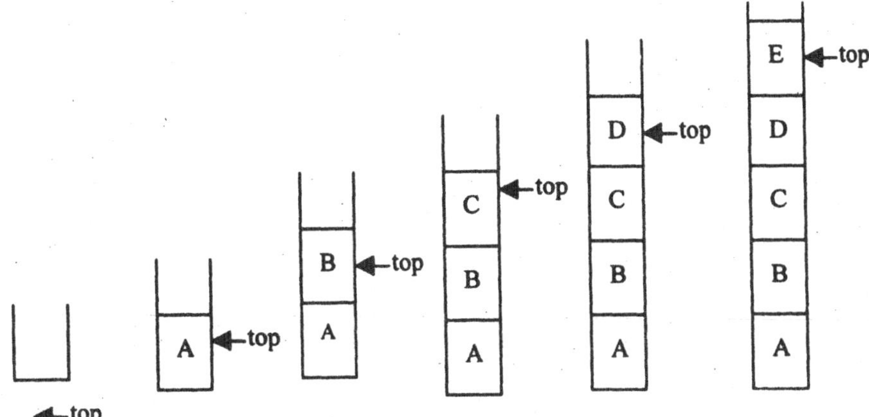

Figure 4.1(a) Insertions into a Stack.

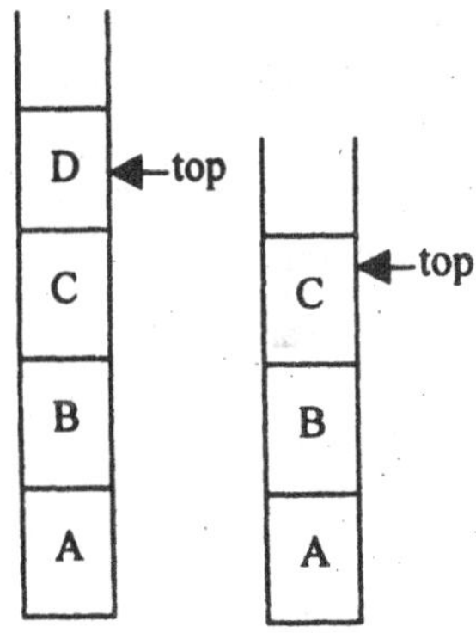

Figure 4.1(b) Two deletions from the Stack of Figure 4.1(a).

A queue, like a stack, is another special type of ordered list. A queue is an ordered list where insertions are permitted at one end of the list and deletion is permitted at the other end of the list. By convention, the end where insertions are performed is called the "rear" of the list and the other end from where deletions are done is called the "front" of the list. The names of the ends are so chosen that the queue data structure resembles the queues in every day life. In Figure 4.2, addition to a queue is explained. The queue is initially empty. Elements 'A', "B', 'C', 'D' are added to the queue one by one and the queue grows to the right. Naturally, the "rear" end of the queue also shifts towards right but the "front" end remains at the current first element 'A'. If an element is removed from the queue, the element at the front (i.e., 'A') will be removed and "front" end shifts to the next element in the queue. See that the first element removed is the first element added to the queue. Hence, a queue is often called First In First Out(FIFO) list.

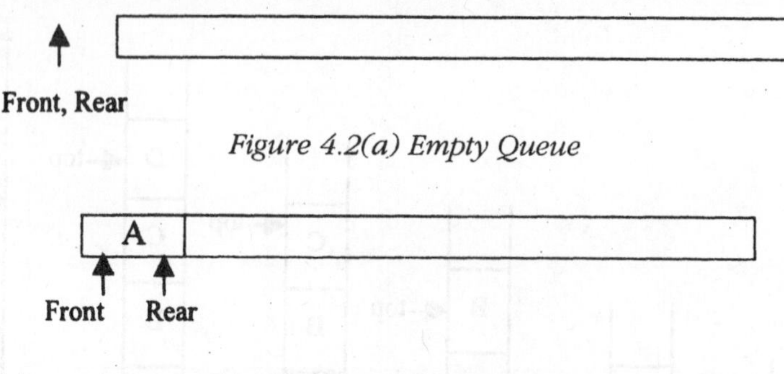

Figure 4.2(a) Empty Queue

Figure 4.2 (b) The queue after insertion of 'A'

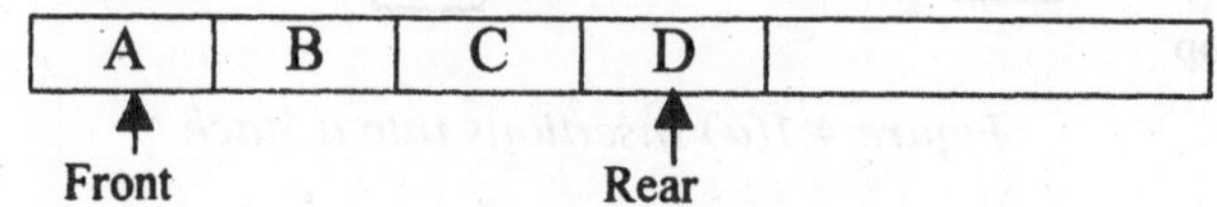

Figure 4.2 (c) The queue after insertion of 'B', 'C', 'D'

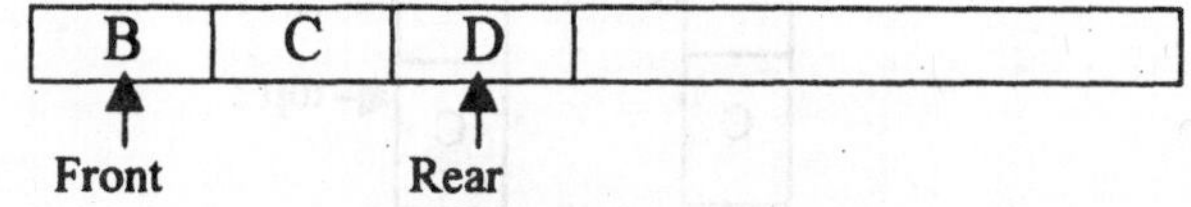

Figure 4.2 (d) The queue after deletion of 'A'

Figure 4.2 Operations on a queue

Stacks and queues can also be defined as Abstract Data Types (ADTs). A stack of elements of type T is a finite sequence of elements of T together with the following operations.

a. **Initialize** a stack as an empty stack.
b. Determine if a stack is **empty** or not.
c. Determine if a stack is **full** or not.
d. If a stack is not full, then **push** a new node at one end of the stack, called its top.
e. If a stack is not empty, then retrieve the node at its top.
f. If a stack is not empty, then **pop** the node at its top.
g. Copy one stack to another stack.

A queue of elements of type T is a finite sequence of elements of T together with the following operations.

a. Initialize a queue to be empty.
b. Determine if a queue is empty or not.
c. Determine if a queue is full or not.
d. Add a new node after the last node in a queue (i.e., at the "rear" end of the queue) if it is not full.
e. Retrieve the first node of a queue, if it is not empty.
f. Remove the first node in a queue (i.e., at the "front" end of the queue), if it is not empty.

4.2. Array representation

The most primitive representation of a stack can be done by using a one-dimensional array of data records. In addition to the one-dimensional array, which is used to hold the elements of the stack, another variable "top" is required to keep track of the index of the last inserted element (i.e. the topmost element). Formally, a stack may be defined as follows:

```
typedef struct stack {
        dataType AnArray[MAX_STACK_SIZE];
        int top;
}stack;
stack aStack;
```

Type of each element in the stack is assumed to be "dataType", a predefined type. There must exist an upper limit of the number of elements which may be stored in the stack. In the given declaration, the upper limit is assumed to be MAX_STACK_SIZE, a predefined constant. In this case, "aStack" is a variable of type "stack" and aStack.AnArray[top] is the topmost element. When "aStack" is initialized, aStack.top is set to –1. After each insertion (deletion) aStack.top increases (decreases) by 1. Therefore, to check whether a stack is empty or not one can simply compare aStack.top with –1. If aStack.top is equal to –1 then the stack is empty; otherwise, the stack is non-empty. "C" functions for pushing into or popping from a stack are presented next.

```
int push (dataType a, stack *x)
{
        if (x->top == MAX_STACK_SIZE)
                return 0;
        else
        {
                x->top += 1;
                x->AnArray[x->top] = a;
```

```
                return 1;
        }
}
int pop (stack *x, dataType *a)
{
        if (x->top == -1)
                return 0;
        else
        {
                *a = x->AnArray [x->top];
                x->top  = x->top - 1;
                return 1;
        }
}
```

The above functions take a constant amount of time, being independent of the number of elements of the stack.

Similar to a stack, a queue may also be conveniently represented by a one-dimensional array which may hold the data items. Two other variables "front" and "rear" are also required to point to the beginning and end of the queue. A queue data type may be defined formally as follows.

```
typedef struct queue {
        dataType Elements[MAX_QUEUE_SIZE+1];
        int front, rear;
}queue;
```

During the initialization of a queue, Q, its "front" and "rear" are set to (-1). On each addition to a queue, which logically takes place at the rear end of the queue, "rear" is incremented by one. On the other hand, after each removal operation, "front" is incremented by one. It has to be mentioned here that addition must not be done if the queue is full and similarly removal should not be done if the queue is empty. Therefore, conditions for empty queue and full queue have to be carefully formulated. The following points have to be observed in this context.

i. if the queue is non-empty then, "front" always denotes one less than the index of the beginning of the queue.

ii. the length of the queue is ("rear"-"front"), and

iii. If the condition ("front" == "rear") is TRUE then the queue is empty.

First confirm that the above observations hold for an initialized queue which is obviously empty as well. Whenever an item is added then "rear" is increased by one and "front" does not get affected. Thus, length of the queue increases by one as length = "rear"-"front" which is correct. Whenever an item is deleted, "front" is incremented. Length of the queue decreases by one. If the new "front" becomes equal to "rear" then the queue becomes empty.

"C" functions for adding an element to a queue and removing an element from a queue are presented next.

```
int addq (dataType item, queue *q)
{
        if (q->rear == MAX_QUEUE_SIZE)
                return 0;
        else
        {
                q->rear += 1;
                q->Elements [q->rear] = item;
                return 1;
        }
}
int deleteq (dataType *data, queue *q)
{
        if (q->front  != q->rear)
        {
                (*data) =  q->Elements [ ++ (q->front)];
                return 1;
        }
        return 0;
}
```

If insertions and deletions are implemented as above then a particular problem is encountered. Consider the operations "addq" and "deleteq" being repeatedly performed on a queue in the sequence as shown in Figure 4.3.

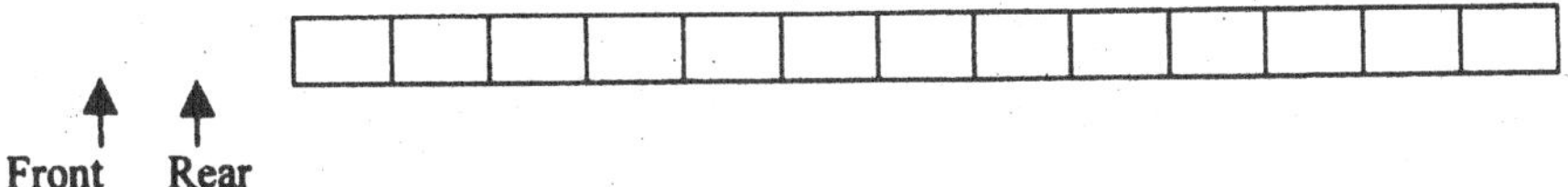

Figure 4.3 (a) An empty queue

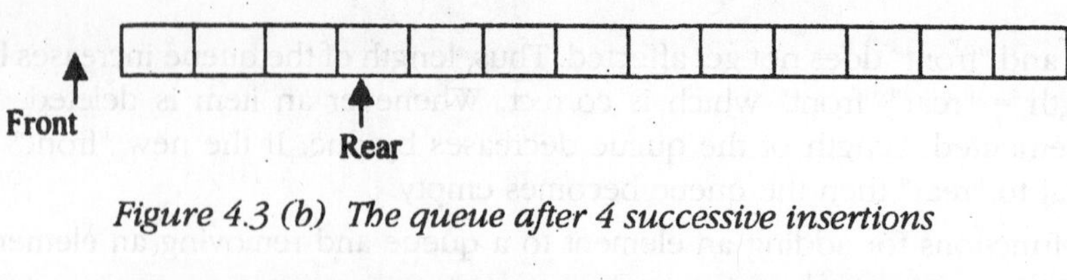

Figure 4.3 (b) The queue after 4 successive insertions

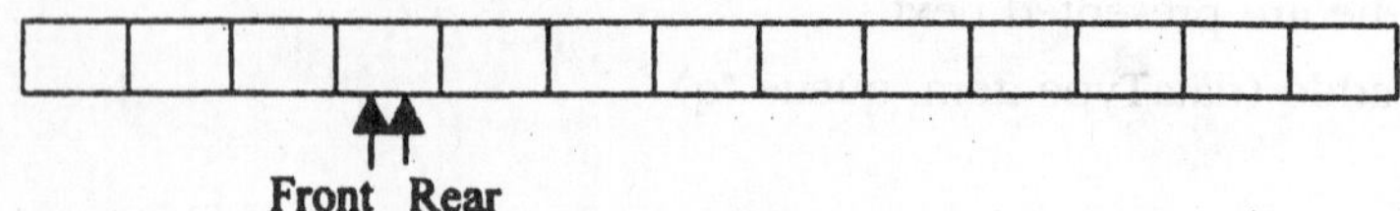

Figure 4.3 (c) The queue after 4 successive deletions

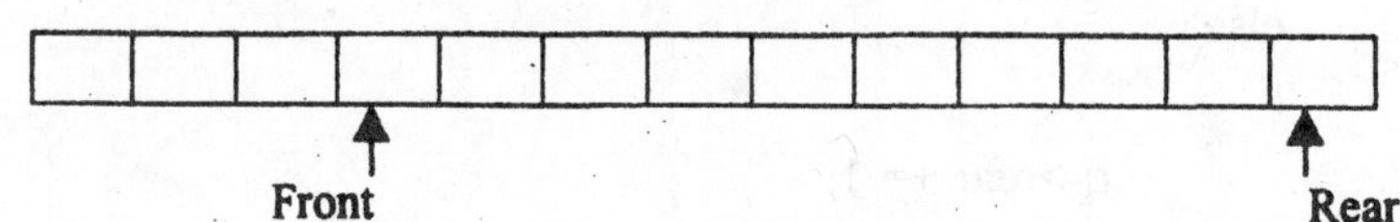

Figure 4.3 (d) The queue after 9 successive insertions

One more insertion at this point will become impossible as the "rear" has attained MAX_QUEUE_SIZE –1, although there are four empty spaces in the queue. Also note that the queue tends to shift towards the right end as "front" always tries to catch up with the "rear" of the queue. One simple way to overcome this problem is possible by resetting the "front" and "rear" to -1 once the queue is found to be empty. This can be achieved by rewriting the "deleteq" function in the following way.

```
int deleteq (queue *q, dataType *data)
{
        if (q->front ==  q->rear)
        {
                printf ("Queue is empty \n");
                q->front = -1;
                q->rear = -1;
                data = NULL;
                return 0;
        }
        (q -> front) += 1:
        (*data) = q->Elements [q->front];
        return 1;
}
```

Even with this version of "deleteq" function, it is quite possible that "addq" function does not add an item to the queue because of queue-full condition although there is some room in the queue. To overcome this problem, one may shift the "Elements" array towards left whenever "rear" is seen to be equal to "MAX_QUEUE_SIZE-1". But such a solution is certainly time consuming especially if the number of elements in a queue is large at the time when "queue_full" condition is fulfilled.

A more efficient queue representation using arrays is achieved by regarding the array of elements of a queue to be circular. Assume that the index of the array increases in clockwise direction except the index MAX_QUEUE_SIZE-1. Every element in the array has one clockwise and one anti-clockwise neighbour. The indices of the clockwise and the anti-clockwise neighbours of the i-th element of the array are (i+1)%MAX_QUEUE_SIZE and (i-1)%MAX_QUEUE_SIZE respectively. As before, "rear" points to the element which is at the rear end of the queue and "front" points to anti-clockwise neighbour of the beginning of the queue. Initially, let "front" and "rear" be initialized to zero. In this case also, "front" is equal to "rear" if and only if the queue is empty. Figure 4.4 shows a circular queue with four elements where front = 1 and rear = 5. Every insertion implies that "rear" of the queue increases by one except when rear = MAX_QUEUE_SIZE-1. If "rear" is equal to MAX_QUEUE_SIZE-1 then after one more insertion "rear" is made zero provided the queue is not yet full.

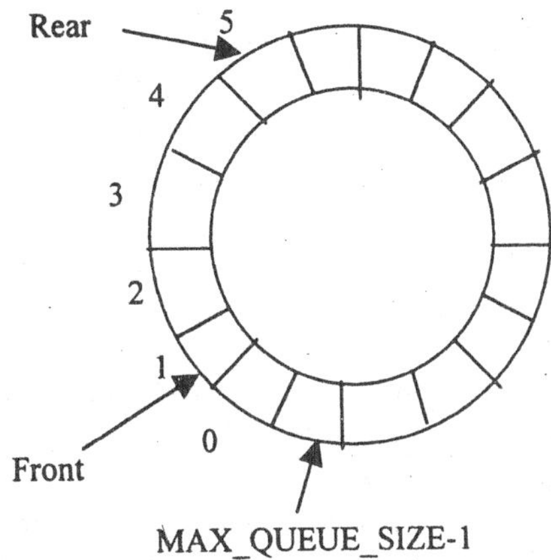

Figure 4.4. An example of a circular queue

The modified versions of the addition and deletion functions are given in the following.

```
int addToCircq (dataType item, queue *q)
{
        int t;
```

```
        t = (q->rear + 1)% MAX_QUEUE_SIZE;
        if (t == q->front)
                return 0;
        q->rear = t;
        q->Elements [q->rear] = item;
        return 1;
}
int deleteCircq (dataType *item, queue *q)
{
        if (q->front == q->rear)
        {
                printf ("Queue is empty. \n");
                item = NULL;
                return 0;
        }
        else
        {
                q->front = (q -> front +1)% MAX_QUEUE_SIZE;
                *item =  (q->Elements [q->front]);
                return 1;
        }
}
```

It is interesting to note that apparently the conditions for "queue_full" and "queue_empty" are the same. But there is a subtle difference. During addition, the condition (q->front == q->rear) is checked after incrementing q->rear. This further means that all the available MAX_QUEUE_SIZE number of elements are not used in this implementation. In fact, the total capacity of the queue is now rendered one less than MAX_QUEUE_SIZE. In order to use all of the MAX_QUEUE_SIZE entries, a special variable "count" may be maintained for each queue to keep track of the number of elements in a queue. "count" may be made a component of the data type queue and "count" should be set to zero when a queue is initialized. During addition, "count" is checked against MAX_QUEUE_SIZE to determine whether the queue is full. Similarly, if "count" is zero then it implies that the queue is empty. Writing algorithm for addition and deletion operations on a circular queue using "count" is left as an exercise.

4.3 Linked list representation of stacks and queues

An alternative and efficient representation of stacks and queues is possible by using linked lists instead of arrays for storing their data elements. The advantages of such representations over array representation are similar to those of linked lists over arrays in general. Specifically, in such cases, the stack or queue is never full as long as the system has enough space for dynamic memory allocation. A stack can be simply represented by a singly connected linked list as shown in Figure 4.5. The pointer to the beginning of the list can serve the purpose of the "top" of the stack. To initialize a stack, one can simply set its "top" to NULL.

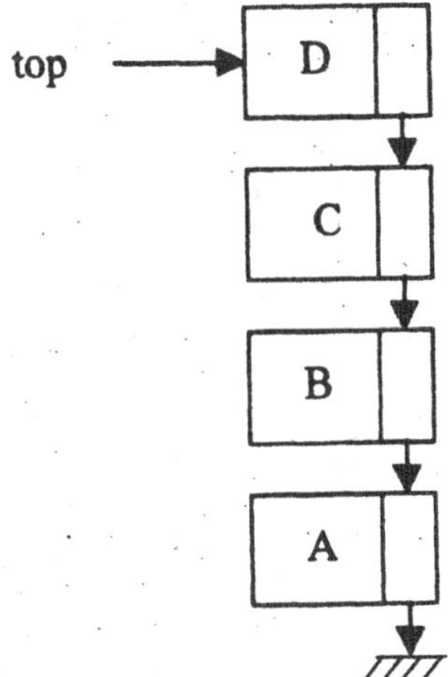

Figure 4.5. Linked list representation of a stack after 'A', 'B', 'C', 'D' have been pushed onto it in that order.

A stack can be defined as the following structure.

```
typedef struct stackElements {
        dataType item;
        struct stackElements *next;
}stackElements;
typedef struct stack {
        stackElements *top;
}stack;
```

If "s" is a variable of type "stack", then "s.top" points to the top of the stack "s". Push and pop operations on such a stack will typically involve manipulation of this "top" pointer. The functions for "push" and "pop" operations are described next.

```
void push (dataType a, stack *s)
{
        stackElements *x;
        x = (stackElements *) malloc (sizeof(stackElements));
        x->item = a;
        x->next = s->top;
        s->top = x;
}
int pop (dataType *a, stack *s)
{
        stackElements *t;
        if(s->top == NULL)
        {
                printf("Queue is empty \n");
                a = NULL;
                return 0;
        }
        *a = s->top->item;
        t = s->top;
        s->top = s->top->next;
        free(t);
        return 1;
}
```

Note that there is no question of stack overflow in this case.

A queue can be similarly represented by a singly connected linked list of queue elements. In addition to the list, two more pointer variables "front" and "rear" are also required to represent a queue. "front" and "rear" point to the elements at two extreme ends of the queue as shown in Figure 4.6.

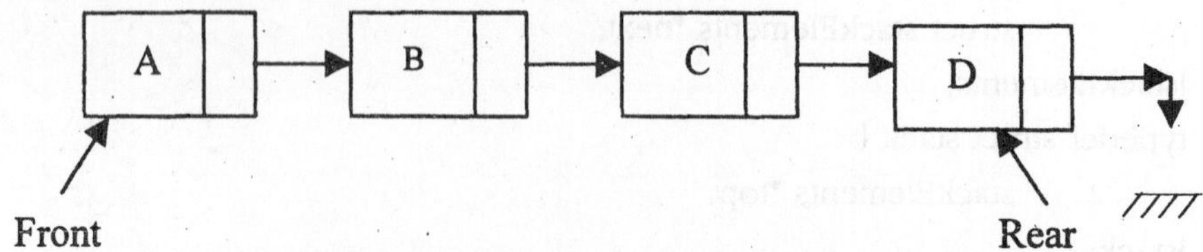

Figure 4.6. Linked list representation of a queue.

When a queue is initialized, both its pointers "front" and "rear" should be set to

NULL. The declaration of a queue using linked list is as follows.

```
typedef struct queueElements {
        dataType item;
        struct queueElements *next;
}queueElements;
typedef struct queue {
        queueElements *front;
        queueElements *rear;
}queue;
void addq(queue *q, dataType x)
{
        queueElements *t;
        t = (queueElements *) malloc (sizeof(queueElements));
        t->item = x;
        t->next = NULL;
        if(q->front == NULL)
        {
                q->front = t;
                q->rear = t;
                return;
        }
        q->rear->next = t;
        q->rear = t;
}
```

Note that special care has to be taken for insertion into an empty queue. In this case, "front" pointer has to be initialized to point to this first item in the queue. At the same time, "rear" pointer has to be updated also to point to the newly added item. Similar care is also necessary for deletion from a queue if the queue contains exactly one element, which is being pointed to simultaneously by "front" and "rear" pointers. The function for deletion operation is presented in the following.

```
int deleteq(queue *q, dataType *a)
{
        queueElements *t;
        if(q->front == NULL)
        {
                printf("Queue is empty \n");
```

```
            a = NULL;
            return 0;
        }
        t = q->front;
        q->front = q->front->next;
        *a = t->item;
        if(q->rear == t)
            q->rear = NULL;
        free(t);
        return 1;
}
```

4.4 Application of Stacks

There are numerous applications of stacks in computer algorithms. Some important uses of stacks will also be discussed in subsequent chapters. To begin with, consider the problem of checking whether a string of opening and closing parentheses is a well formed expression of parentheses or not. For example, the following strings are well formed.

(())(()())

((()))

(()(())()()((()))()))

But the following strings are not well formed.

(()

)()(

(())(

A very simple algorithm based on stack can be formulated for solving the above problem. The algorithm is as follows. Scan the string from left to right. Whenever an opening parenthesis is found, push it into the stack and whenever a closing parenthesis is found, pop the stack once. If the stack is found empty when a pop operation is performed on the stack then it must be an error as it means that one closing parenthesis does not have a corresponding opening parenthesis. Once the string is exhausted, the stack must become empty as well because otherwise, there must be unmatched opening parenthesis. The algorithm is presented next. Input to the algorithm is a string of '(' and ')'. The output is +1 if the input is well formed; otherwise, the output is –1.

Algorithm checkParenthesis

Get the next character of the input string and assign it to x;

assign FALSE to error;

```
while((the input is not exhausted) && (not error))
{
        switch(x)
        {
                case '(':
                        push x into the stack;
                        break;
                case ')':
                        if the popped element is NULL
                                error = TRUE;
                        break;
        }
        Get the next character of the input string and assign it to x;
}
if(not error)
        if(stack is empty)
                return 1;
        else
                return -1;
return -1;
```

4.4.1 Evaluation of arithmetic expression

An arithmetic expression consists of operands and operators. The basic set of operations include addition, subtraction, multiplication, division and exponentiation. The symbols of the operators representing these operations are +, -, *, / and ^ respectively. The operands are either numeric constants or numeric variables. In the ensuing discussion, only numeric constants are taken into consideration as operands. For example,

9 + 5*7 – 6^2 + 15/3 ...... (1)

is a valid arithmetic expression. In order to evaluate an expression, standard precedence rules for arithmetic expression are applied. For example, the exponentiation operation has the highest priority or precedence. This means that the exponentiation operations are carried out first in an arithmetic expression. So, in order to evaluate the expression (1), 6^2 is to be computed first. Hence, the resultant expression becomes

9 + 5*7 – 36 + 15/3 ...... (2)

The priorities of multiplication and division operations are the same and this priority is less than that of exponentiation but more than those of addition or subtraction. In the expression (2), there is a multiplication and a division operation. These two operations are to be carried out next. Consequently the expression becomes

9 + 35 – 36 + 5 ...... (3)

The priorities of addition and subtraction operations are the same and therefore, these operations are carried out at the end. Hence, the result after computation of the above expression is 13. Default priority of an operation can be changed by enclosing the operation within parenthesis. The expression 1 + 2*3 will normally evaluate to 1 + 6 i.e. 7. But (1 + 2) *3 will evaluate to 3*3 i.e. 9. By enclosing the addition operation within parenthesis, priority of the operation becomes highest and hence, the operation is computed first. In general, if a sub-expression is enclosed within opening and closing parenthesis, the priority of the sub-expression becomes highest. In the following table, the priorities of different arithmetic operators are specified.

Operator	Priority
( )	4
^	3
*, /	2
+, -	1

In all expressions mentioned so far, the binary operators always appear between its operands. For example, if an expression is 2 + 3, then 2 and 3 are the operands of the operator +. Such expressions are known as infix expressions. Note that, in an infix expression, the unary operator always precedes its operand. As it has been already discussed, evaluation of an infix expression by a computer is not straight forward because the priorities of the operators involved are not explicit in such expressions. Only when an infix expression is fully parenthesized, the priorities of the operations are explicitly revealed. For example, consider the following expression.

4 + 2 * 3 ^ 2 + 9/3 – 1*8

The sequence of evaluation of the individual operations in the given arithmetic expression can be obtained only after applying rules relating to the priorities and precedences of the arithmetic operators involved in the expression. Applying these rules, the sequence of evaluation of the above expression can be explicitly stated as shown in the following.

(((4 + (2 * (3 ^ 2))) + (9 / 3)) – (1*8))

Another form of expression known as postfix expression is more amenable to mechanical evaluation. In a postfix expression the operators always appear after its operands. So, the infix expression "3 +2" becomes "3, 2 +" in its postfix form. The postfix form of "3 + 5 * 6 – 1" is "3, 5, 6, *, +, 1, -". If a postfix expression is to be evaluated, the expression is scanned from left to right. As soon as an operator is encountered, the last two operands are used to perform the operation and the result is remembered. If the expression is "3, 5, 6, *, +, 1, -" then 3, 5, 6 are scanned and the operator '*' is encountered. The last two operands which are 5 and 6 are fetched and multiplication is performed and the result, 30, is stored. So the resultant expression becomes "3, 30, +, 1, -". Continuing the same procedure, 3 and 30 are scanned and the '+' operator is encountered. The result, 33 is stored. Consequently the expression becomes "33, 1, -". In the final scan, 33 and 1 become the operands for the subtraction operation and the result becomes 32. Although it may appear that repeated scans from the beginning of the expression are required, use of a stack may eliminate that need. Suppose the elements of the expression are scanned from left to right. If the element is a numeric value then it is pushed into a stack of integers. As soon as an operator is encountered the required number of integers are popped out from the stack, the operation is performed and the result is pushed back to the stack. Then, once again, elements are scanned from the remaining expression and the same process is continued. The following figure illustrates this procedure by showing the content of the stack and the remaining expression. Let the postfix expression be "3, 5, 6, *, +, 1, -". Initially the stack is empty as shown below.

Stack content	Remaining expression
NIL	3, 5, 6, *, +, 1, -

Next, 3 is scanned and pushed into the stack.

Stack content	Remaining expression
3	5, 6, *, +, 1, -

In the same way, 5, 6 are scanned and pushed into the stack.

Stack content	Remaining expression
3, 5, 6	*, +, 1, -

Now, the operator '*' is scanned. As '*' is a binary operator, the stack is popped twice to fetch its operands. So, 5, 6 are popped and then they are multiplied and the result, 30 is pushed into the stack.

Stack content	Remaining expression
3, 30	+, 1, -

The next element being scanned is '+'. As before, 30 and 3 are popped out and added. The result 33 is pushed back to stack. Condition of stack after the operation is shown in the following.

Stack content	Remaining expression
33	1, -

Next, '1' is scanned and pushed into the stack resulting in the configuration as shown in the following.

Stack content	Remaining expression
33, 1	-

The current element being scanned is '-'. 1 and 33 are taken out and subtraction operation is performed. The result 32 is pushed into the stack. Now the expression is exhausted. Therefore, the item popped up from the stack is the result of the evaluation of the expression. The condition of stack is shown in the following.

Stack content	Remaining expression
32	NIL

The algorithm for the postfix expression evaluation is described next. The input to the algorithm is an expression having operands and operators. The output is the result after evaluating the expression. The last element of the expression is denoted by a special symbol, say a '$'.

```
Algorithm evaluatePostfixExpression
Initialize a stack of real numbers.
Get the next element from the expression.
while the element obtained from the expression is not '$'
{
        if the element represents a numeric value
                push the numeric value to the stack.
        else if the element represents an operator
        {
```

pop the operands from the stack.

Perform the operation denoted by the operator to get a result.

Push the result to the stack

}

Get the next element from the expression.

}

The next problem to be tackled is that of converting an infix expression to a postfix one. The trick involves exposing the priorities of the operators in the infix expression. The simplest way to do so is by fully parenthesizing the infix expression. By complete parenthesization, it is meant that every operation in the expression its to be suitably enclosed within parentheses so that the desired priorities of these operations are accurately expressed. For instance, let the expression be :

4 + 3 * 10/6 + 7 – 4/2 + 5^3

After complete parenthesization, the above expression will look like as the following.

((((4+ ((3 * 10)/6)) + 7) – (4/2) + (5^3))

As the priorities are properly set, the operators can now be moved after the operands. Since every operation is enclosed within parentheses, any operator along with its operands is also within a unique pair of parentheses. The right end of the unique parentheses is the near most right parentheses enclosing an operator. If the operators are now moved to the right ends of their corresponding parentheses then the postfix expression obtained is as shown in the following.

((((4 + ((3 * 10) / 6)) + 7) – (4 / 2)) + (5 ^ 3))

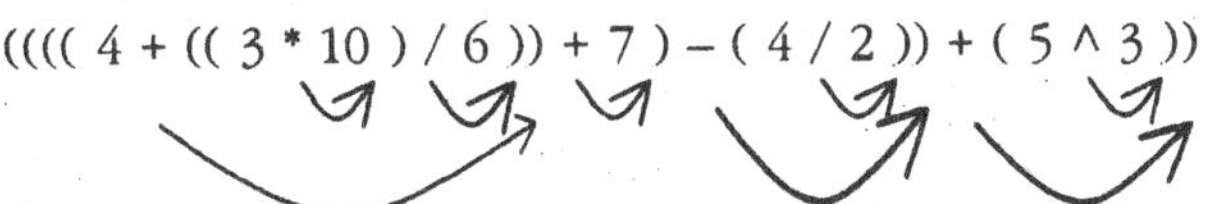

After these two steps, if the expression is written with the operators placed at their respective right parentheses then, the expression becomes an equivalent postfix expression. The postfix form of the above expression thus becomes:

4, 3, 10, *, 6, /, +, 7, +, 4, 2, /, -, 5, 3, ^, +

Note that in the process of transforming an infix-expression to its postfix from the relative positions of the operands (i.e. the numeric constants) do not undergo any change. Only the operators are displaced in the process. To identify the basic step, consider the transformation of a simple expression, 3 * 2 + 6, to its postfix. When the expression is scanned element by element then the first element scanned is the numeric constant "3". Since, this element is an operand and relative positions of the operands do not change, "3" will be appended to the resultant postfix expression. Next element scanned is "*", an operator. It is now known that "*" can not be processed before seeing the next operator. So, "*" needs to be stored somewhere. Let "*" be stored in a stack. The next element to be stored is "2", which can be immediately appended to the resultant postfix expression. Then "+" is scanned. As operation denoted by "+" has a lesser priority than that of "*" (the operator on the top of the stack) therefore, computation of "*" must be precede the computation of "+". So, if the priority of the operator at the top of the stack is greater than or equal to the priority of the operator being scanned then the operator at the top of the stack should be popped and the same must be appended to the resultant postfix expression. Popping must continue as long as the stack top contains an operator whose priority is greater than or equal to the priority of the operator scanned. When no more pop operation can be done, the currently scanned operator is pushed into the stack. So, the stack of operators grows in such a manner that the operators in it from the bottom to the top are arranged in non-decreasing order of priority. The said process continues till the input is exhausted. Once there is no more input, the operators inside the stack are popped one by one and appended to the postfix expression.

A particular problem arises if the priority of the operator at the top of the stack is the same as that of the operator being currently scanned. Typical example is the expression 3 + 3 – 5 when the "-" operator is scanned. This issue is resolved theoretically by assuming the operations to be either left associative or right associative. For example, "+", "-", "*" and "/" are said to be left associative and "^" is assumed to be right associative. Another example of a right associative operator is "(". If the operators are left associative then the scheme discussed earlier works correctly. But consider 3^2^3 is to be evaluated and the current operator is the second "^" operator. Now the top of the stack also contains the operator "^". Since the priorities of both these operators are the same hence, according to the logic of the scheme described earlier, the operator at the top of the stack will be appended to the prefix expression. So, the postfix of 3^2^3 becomes 3, 2, ^, 3, ^ which is incorrect. In order to overcome this problem, each operator is provided a pair of priorities: (i) in stack priority (isp) and (ii) input priority (ip). Once the operators are pushed into the stack, the priorities of the operators imply their in-stack priorities. If they appear in the input, their priorities mean their input priorities. For left associative operators, both these priorities could be set to the same value. For right associative operators, the input priority must be more than its in-stack priority. The following table shows the in-stack and input priorities for some common operators.

Operator	In-stack Priority	Input Priority
+, -	1	1
*, /	2	2
^	3	4
(	0	4

The action to be taken if the current operator is ")" is worth mentioning. If the current operator is ")" then the corresponding "("must be the last "(" stored in the stack. All operators in the stack from top to this "(" operator are enclosed in parenthesis in the infix expression. And these operators are arranged inside the stack from the top in non-descending order of their priorities. Once ")" is encountered as the current operator, all operators in the stack from the top to the first "(" operator are to be popped one by one and appended to the postfix expression. The algorithm "convertToPostfix" is presented next. The input to the algorithm is an infix expression E, consisting of operands, operators and the delimiter "$". The output is a postfix expression.

Algorithm convertToPostfix.

Initialize a stack, s, of operators (that is s.Elements[i] is an operator for i = 0 to s.top-1)

```
While 'next' element in "E" is not the delimiter, '$'
{
        get the next element of "E" and assign it to "x".
        switch (x)
        {
                case operand:
                        Append "x" to the output postfix expression.
                        break.
                case operator:
                        if "x" is not ")" or "(" operator {
                        while ((ip (x) ≤ isp(operator at the top of the stack)) &&
                                        (not stack underflow))
                                {
                                Pop the stack "s" and assign it to "y"
                                Append "y" to the output.
                                }
                        Push "x" to "s"
                        }
                        else if operator is "("
                                Push "x" to "s"
                        else
                        {
                        while ((operator at the top of the stack is not "(" ) &&
```

```
                        (not stack underflow))
            {
                        Pop the stack "s" and assign it to "y"
                        Append "y" to the output.
            }
            Pop the "(" operator from the stack
        }
    }
}
```

Take the example of 4 + 3 * 10/6 + 7 – 4/2 + 5^3 as an infix expression and trace the steps of the algorithm "convertToPostfix". The content of the stack from bottom to top is shown from left to right in the following figure.

Content of the stack	isp(top of the stack)	ip (current element)	Output	Remaining input string
NIL	-	-	-	4+3*10/6+7-4/2+5^3
NIL	-	-	4	+3*10/6+7-4/2+5^3
NIL	-	1	4	3*10/6+7-4/2+5^3
+	1	-	4,3	*10/6+7-4/2+5^3
+	1	2	4,3	10/6+7-4/2+5^3
+,*	2	-	4,3	10/6+7-4/2+5^3
+,*	2	2	4,3,10	/6+7-4/2+5^3
+,/	2	-	4,3,10,*	6+7-4/2+5^3
+,/	2		4,3,10,*,6	+7-4/2+5^3
+	1	1	4,3,10,*,6,/,+	7-4/2+5^3
+	1	1	4,3,10,*,6,/,+,7	-4/2+5^3
-	-	-	4,3,10,*,6,/,+,7,+	4/2+5^3
-	-	2	4,3,10,*,6,/,+,7,+,4	/2+5^3
-,/	2	-	4,3,10,*,6,/,+,7,+,4	2+5^3
-,/	2	1	4,3,10,*,6,/,+,7,+,4,2	+5^3
+	1	-	4,3,10,*,6,/,+,7,+,4,2,/,-	5^3
+	1	4	4,3,10,*,6,/,+,7,+,4,2,/,-,5	^3
+,^	3	-	4,3,10,*,6,/,+,7,+,4,2,/,-,5	3
NIL	-	-	4,3,10,*,6,/,+,7,+,4,2,/,-,5,3,^,+	

4.5 Application of a queue : Topological Sort

Think of an application, which is often required for task scheduling. Very often, tasks required to be performed can be ordered. Suppose that one large software application is to be written. There are many subtasks associated with writing a software application, which are listed below.

- Requirement analysis
- Design specification
- Coding
- Unit Testing
- Integration Testing
- System Testing

The tasks listed above are to be carried out in that order for successful completion. Suppose that the entire application can be divided into four major modules - M_1, M_2, M_3 and M_4. Out of these four modules, M_1 and M_2 are closely related and so are M_3 and M_4. First, the requirement analysis of the entire application, which is task numbered 1, is done. Once this task is complete, design of the four modules M_1, M_2, M_3 and M_4 may be initiated. Let design of the modules M_1, M_2, M_3 and M_4 be designated tasks numbered 2, 3, 4, 5 respectively. These tasks can be concurrently executed and once all of them are complete, review of the design of the entire application, task numbered 6, may start. After this review is complete, coding of the individual module can begin. Coding of the modules M_1, M_2, M_3 and M_4 be designated tasks numbered 7, 8, 9, 10 respectively. After the coding of one module is complete, unit testing of that module may begin. The tasks of unit testing of the modules M_1, M_2, M_3 and M_4 be numbered 11, 12, 13, 14 respectively. Once unit testing of M_1 and M_2 are complete, integration testing of these two modules, tasks numbered 15, can start. Similarly, integration testing of M_3 and M_4, task numbered 16, can start after the unit testing of these two modules are complete. Once these two integration testing is done, system testing of the entire application may start. Graphically the dependency of these tasks may be presented as shown in Figure 4.7.

Each circle in Figure 4.7 represents a task as explained. An arrow from one task numbered "i" to another task numbered "j" implies that the task numbered "i" must be finished before the task numbered "j" can begin. In other words, the task numbered "i" precedes the task numbered "j". For a simplified view of a job, the diagram is manageable. But in most real life situations, the diagram becomes unmanageably complex. The precedence information between tasks comes in as input and the diagram is to be built to sort the tasks in ascending order of their precedence. Such an ordering is called topological ordering of the tasks. Consider the problem of sorting these tasks in the order mentioned, if the precedence information of the tasks is provided at the input. For simplicity, assume that the tasks are identified by integers. Notationally, let i<j denotes that the task numbered "i" precedes the task numbered "j". The function "topologicallySort" will be fed a list of duplets (i, j) which denotes i<j. To preserve the precedence information, the function is required to have a structure. Suppose the structure is declared as follows.

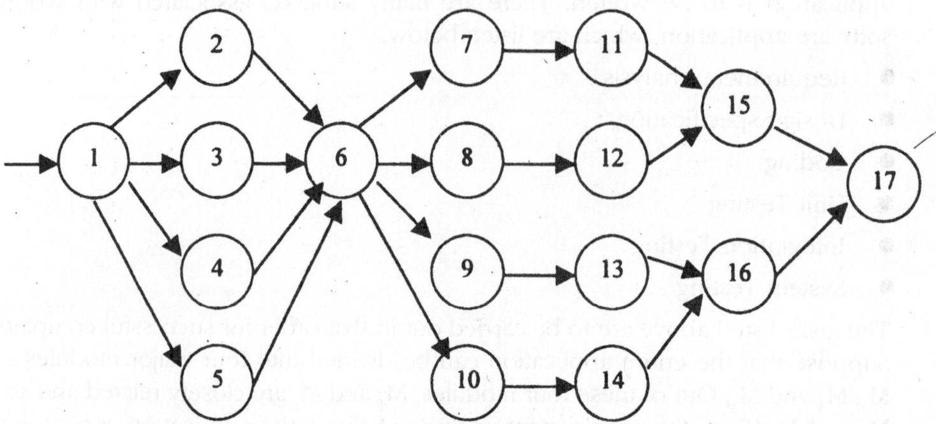

Figure 4.7 Dependency among tasks. An arrow from circle i to circle j indicates that the task j is dependent on the task i.

```
typedef struct list
{
        int count;
        intnode *dependents;
} list;
list taskInfo[100];
```

Each i-th element in the taskInfo array contains a "count" which indicates the number of the immediate predecessors of the task numbered "i". In Figure 4.7, taskInfo[1].count should be zero and taskInfo[6].count should be four. In addition to "count", taskInfo[i].dependants points to the list of tasks (identified by integers) which are directly dependent on the completion of the i-th task. In other words, the i-th task precedes the tasks given in the list pointed to by taskInfo[i].dependants. The algorithm exploits this memory layout. The algorithm merely prints the tasks whose "count" field is zero and then decrements the "count" field for all tasks which are pointed to by the "dependant" field of that task. Searching repeatedly for all tasks with "count" zero, can be avoided by keeping them in a queue which are processed one by one. The queue may be a simple queue of integers where these integers identify the tasks. The algorithm "topologicallySort" is presented next.

Algorithm topologicallySort

```
Read n, number of tasks;
for(i = 0; i < n; i++)
{
        taskInfo[i].count = 0;
        taskInfo[i].dependents = NULL;
}
Read N, number of relations;
for(i = 0; i < N; i++)
{
        Read the doublet (j, k) suggesting j < k;
        taskInfo[k].count += 1;
        Insert a node with data part as j in the list taskInfo[k].dependents;
}
for(i = 0; i < N; i++)
{
        if(taskInfo[i].count == 0)
                add i to a queue QInt of integers;
        while(remove from QInt is successful)
        {
                Let the removed element be r;
                print r; x = taskInfo[r].dependents;
                while(x != NULL)
                {
                        k = x->element;
                        taskInfo[k].count = 1;
                        if(taskInfo[k].count == 0)
                                add k to QInt;
                        x = x->next;
                }
        }
```

The complexity of the above algorithm can be proved to be O(n+N). The actual proof is left as an exercise.

4.6 Representation of multiple stacks in a single array.

In many applications and algorithms, several stacks and queus are required. Sometimes, these data structures are to be allocated from a single array, say, A. Suppose that "A" is an array of "M" data items and declared as

dataType A[M]

where "dataType" is a predefined type and "M" is defined as a constant integer. Further suppose that "N" number of stacks of the said "data" items are to be accommodated in "A". One simple way to achieve this objective is to divide the array "A" in "N" nearly equal parts where the i-th stack will be housed in "A" from the index (i)*⌊M/N⌋ to the index (i*⌊M/N⌋) -1 as shown in Figure 4.8. If T[i] and B[i] represent the indices of "A" which contains the topmost and the bottommost elements of the i-th stack respectively then initially T[i] and B[i] are given as follows:

T[i] = B[i] = (i)*⌊M/N⌋ for i = 0,...., N-1

B[N] = M

Although the N-th stack does not exist, B[N] has been defined to simplify the "push" operation as will be clear when the function "push" is described.

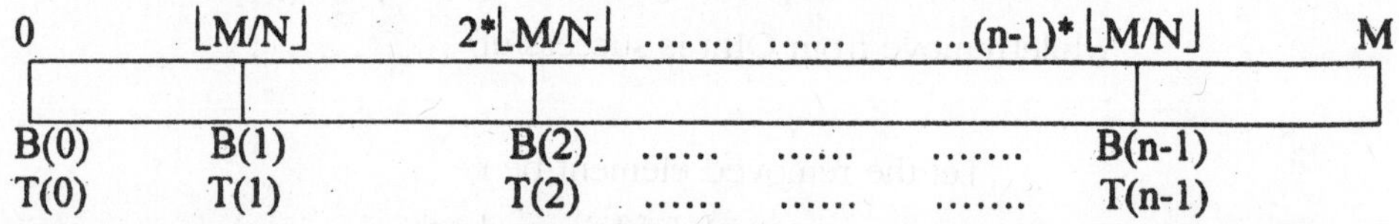

0	⌊M/N⌋	2*⌊M/N⌋	...(n-1)* ⌊M/N⌋	M
B(0)	B(1)	B(2)	B(n-1)	
T(0)	T(1)	T(2)	T(n-1)	

Figure 4.8 Representing multiple stacks in a single array. Initial values of B(i) and T(i) are indicated.

As a consequence of the above representation, "Push" and "Pop" operations on the stack undergo slight changes. In the following, these operations are described for the i-th stack. The list of arguments to these routines includes an integer i, to identify the stack. The other argument to the function "push" is the data which has to be pushed into the respective stack. The function returns a negative number if overflow occurs.

```
int push (int i, dataType  x)
{
        if ((T[i] +1) == B[i+1])
                return -1;
        else
```

```
        {
            T[i] = T[i] +1;
            A[T[i]] = x;
        }
        return 1;
}
```

The function for "Pop" operation is similar. It returns a data item that is being popped. If the return value is NULL then it implies that popping has been attempted on an empty stack.

```
int pop (int i, dataType *a)
{
    if (T[i] == B[i])
    {
        a = NULL;
        return -1;
    }
    *a = A[T[i]];
    T[i] = T[i] - 1;
    return 1;
}
```

It is interesting to observe that overflow may occur while pushing onto the i-th stack for some "i" but there may be enough room in the array "A", which houses all N stacks. Whenever an overflow is encountered while pushing into the i-th stack, there could be three possibilities as outlined in the following.

a. There may exist a stack to the right of the i-th stack where some space is available. Try to find out such a stack. Formally, find the smallest "k" for which i<k≤n and T[k]<B[k+1] if any such k exists. Then all stacks numbered (i+1) to k may be moved right by one position to avoid the overflow. That is, A[j] is to be shifted to A[j+1] for all j, T[k]≥j>B[i+1]. Next set B[j] to B[j]+1 and T[j] to T[j]+1 for all j, i<j≤k.

b. There may exist a stack to the left of the i-th stack where some space is available. Try to find out such a stack. If no "k" can be found as in (a). Formally, find the largest "k", for which 1≤k<i where T[k]<B[k+1]. Move all elements of "A" left by one position for all elements in the stacks numbered K- 1 to i. Then set the bottom and top elements of these stacks by the following assignments.

B[j] = B[j]-1, T[j] = T[j]-1 for all j, k<j≤i.

c. There is no space either to the right or to the left of the i-th stack. So, an "overflow" is unavoidable.

Analysis of performance in such cases is very complicated and not completely done. Similar representation of multiple queues in a single one-dimensional array is considered in the exercises.

4.7 Points to be remembered

- Some specialized versions of linear lists are very important in many applications. A stack is such a special linear list where insertion and deletion can take place only at one end. This end is typically called the top of the list. It can be easily seen that the last element inserted in such a list is the first one to be deleted. That is why, stacks are often referred to as Last In First Out (LIFO data structure.
- Queues are also special linear lists where insertion are permitted at one end called "rear" end of the list and deletions are permitted at the other end of the list called "front". In a queue, the elements are inserted and deleted in a First In First Out (FIFO) manner.
- Stacks and queues can be easily implemented using array data structure. The special cases of overflow and underflow are to be handled if stacks and queues are implemented as arrays. If a queue is implemented using an array then a typical problem may occur. After a sequence of add and remove operations on a queue, the queue tends to move to the right and becomes full even when there is some unutilized space in the array storing the elements of the queue. To overcome this problem, circular queues are introduced.
- Stacks and queues may be represented by linked lists as well. If they are so represented and linked lists are implemented through pointers and run-time memory allocation then the problem of "overflow" becomes less relevant.
- Stacks and queues are heavily used in many applications. In fact, the mechanism of sub-routine calls and returns are implemented through stacks. In the ensuing chapters, lots of such applications will be discussed. In this chapter, a very interesting problem of evaluation of an infix expression has been taken up. First, the in-fix expression is converted to its postfix equivalent and then the postfix expression is computed. In both these processing, stacks become a very convenient data structure to organize data.
- Queue data structure is also used in many applications like event simulation, job scheduling etc. In this chapter, the use of queue is illustrated by applying it to solve the problem of topological sorting of a graph.
- Sometimes, it becomes necessary to accommodate a number of stacks in a single large array. The large array is divided into small equal-sized segments to house individual stacks. But, in that case, it may be possible that overflow occurs for one stack while there are empty spaces in many other stacks.

Exercise

1. Define a structure for a circular queue using an array but do not have a "count" field which determines the number of elements in the queue. Instead, have a boolean variable "full" or "empty" which is FALSE, if the queue is empty and TRUE, if the queue is full. Write the functions for "add" and "delete" for such a circular queue. Make sure that no space is wasted in the array.
2. A double-ended queue (deque) is a linear list where additions and deletions can be performed at either end. Represent a deque using an array to store the elements of the list and write the "C" functions for additions and deletions.
3. Repeat exercise 2 by representing a deque using linked list.
4. Write a "C" function to copy one stack to another assuming
   i. the stack is implemented using array;
   ii. the stack is implemented using linked list.
5. Repeat exercise 4 for a queue.
6. In a circular queue represented by an array, how can one specify the number of elements in the queue in terms of "front", "rear" and MAX_QUEUE_SIZE? Write a "C" function to delete the K-th element from the "front" of a circular queue.
7. Can a queue be represented by a circular linked list with only one pointer pointing to the tail of the queue? Write "C" functions for the "add" and "delete" operations on such a queue.
8. Write a "C" function to test whether a string of opening and closing parenthesis is well formed or not.
9. Write a "C" program to read an arithmetic expression comprising of numeric constants and operators and to evaluate the expression at the input.
10. Like postfix expressions, prefix expressions can also be defined. In such a prefix expression, an operator is immediately followed by its operands. For example, prefix expression of "9+3*4-5/6" is "+,9,-,*,3,4,/,5,6". Write algorithms to-
    i. evaluate a prefix expression;
    ii. convert an infix expression to its prefix form.
11. Write an algorithm to construct a fully parenthesized infix expression from its postfix equivalent. Write a "C" function for your algorithm.
12. How can one convert a postfix expression to its prefix equivalent and vice-versa?
13. Represent N queues in a single one-dimensional array. Write functions for "add" and "delete" operations on the i-th queue.
14. Represent a stack and a queue in a single one-dimensional array. Write functions for "push", "pop" operations on the stack and "add", "delete" functions on the queue.

Chapter 5

Strings

5.1 Introduction

A wide variety of applications from different domains such as word processing, computer graphics etc. involve manipulation of texts. Text is nothing but a stream of symbols and often referred to as strings. Therefore efficient representation and handling of strings play an important role in data structure. Informally, a string is a sequence of symbols where the symbols are chosen from a pre-specified set which is also known as the alphabet set. This set of symbols could be the set of alphanumeric characters on a keyboard. Then, "abc25x", "p5(10(a,)mkw5)" are examples of strings. Formally, strings over a set of symbols, Σ, are recursively defined as follows.

1. If a symbol "a"∈ Σ then "a" is a string.
2. If "x" and "y" are two strings then "xy" is a string.
3. Nothing else is a string.

For example, let Σ = {a, b, c}. By clause (1) of the above definition, "a", "b" and "c" are strings. Since "a", "b" are strings, "ab" is also another string by clause (2) of the definition. Similarly, as "c" and "ab" are strings, "cab" is also a string. It can be easily seen that "aabb", "abcabccbb", "ccccc" are also strings whereas "abdcb"is not a string.

The rule stated in clause (2) of the definition of strings is called concatenation, which essentially appends the second string "y" to the end of the first string "x". So, the result of concatenation of two strings "acb" and "cbb" is "acbcbb".

The number of symbols occurring in a string is known as its length. For example, the length of "acbcb" is five whereas the length of "aaca" is four. Occasionally, a special string with length zero becomes very useful. Such a special string is known as the null string or the empty string which is typically denoted by "φ". Concatenation of "φ" with any string "x" results in the string "x" itself. Therefore, "φx" = "xφ" = "x". The empty string neither occurs in Σ nor follows from the definition of string over Σ as stated earlier. The general definition of string over Σ after incorporating the notion of a null string is given in the following.

1. A null string of length zero, often denoted by "φ"is a string.
2. If "a" ∈ Σ then "a" is a string.
3. If "x" and "y" are two strings then concatenation of "x" and "y" written as "xy" is a string.
4. Nothing else is a string.

The above definition does not restrict strings to be of finite length only. However, in practice, only finite strings (i.e. strings of a finite length) are usually dealt with.

String as an ADT

There are several operations, which typically arise in the context of string manipulation. Few important such operations are outlined below. Each operation is denoted by a "C" function declaration which is followed by a brief description.

IsEmpty (string s)

This operation checks whether a string "s" is null. The result of the operation is set to "1" if "s" is null; otherwise, the result is "0".

StringLength (string s)

This operation computes the length of a string "s", which is produced as the result.

string StringConcatenate (string s1, string s2)

This oiperation concatenates two strings "s1" and "s2" to produce another string.

StringCopy (string s1, string s2)

This operation copies a string "s2" to "s1". Naturally, the original content of "s1" (if any) is lost. This operation becomes useful whenever one string is to be assigned to another srtring.

int StringCompare (string s1, string s2)

This operation compares two strings "s1" and "s2" and finds out whether they are identical. For example, the strings "abcabbac" and "abcabbac" are identical but "abcab" and "abab" are not. When two strings are not identical, this operation may determine which string is less if the relationship "less than" is defined on such strings.

int StringSearch (string s1, string s2)

This operation tests whether a given string "s2" occurs in another given string "s1". For example, "abab" occurs in "baababaabba" but "baaa" does not occur in "baababaabba". This problem is commonly known as the string searching problem where "s2" is called the pattern and "s1" is called the text. This problem occurs frequently in text processing and word processing applications and hence an efficient solution to this problem is extremely useful. Efficient algorithms for this problem will be discussed in depth in subsequent sections.

void StringSubstitute (string s1, string s2, string s3)

This operation substitutes a string "s3" for the first occurrence (if any) of a string "s2" in another string "s1". For example the result of substituting "abcab" in place of "abab" in "abbabababbbc" is "abbabcababbbc". Note that only the first occurrence of "abab" has been replaced without altering its other occurrences. This problem can also be generalized to replace each occurrence of "s3" in "s1" by "s2". Text substitution is also useful in editing applications.

5.2 Representation of strings

A string may be represented by an array or a linked list. A string of characters having length "n" can be implemented by a one dimensional array of "n" elements where the i-th element of the array stores the i-th element of the string. Type declaration for such a string would be as follows.

```
typedef struct string
{
   int length;
   char str[1000];
}string;
```

In such a representation, there must be a maximum length of the strings to be manipulated. The actual length of a string varies and can only be known during execution. But, in this representation, the maximum length has to be specified a-priori. If the maximum length is too big then substantial wastage of memory occurs; on the other hand, if maximum length is small then it will not be possible to store strings with length more than the specified maximum. The advantage of such a representation is that the array elements may be directly accessed and this could speed up several operations on strings. An alternative representation of strings can be done by using linked lists. A string represented by a linked list is identified by a pointer to the linked list. Each node in the list contains a symbol and a pointer to the next symbol in the string. The pointer of the node containing the last symbol in the string is set to null. Thus, the string points to its first symbol and the list is to be traversed to get all of its symbols. In this case, a string may be declared as:

```
typedef struct string
{
    char symbol;
    struct string *next;
}string;
```

Consider the string "abbbcabca". Figure 5.1(a) shows the array representation of the above string (MAX_LENGTH assumed to be 15), while Figure 5.1(b) illustrates linked list representation of the same string.

str:

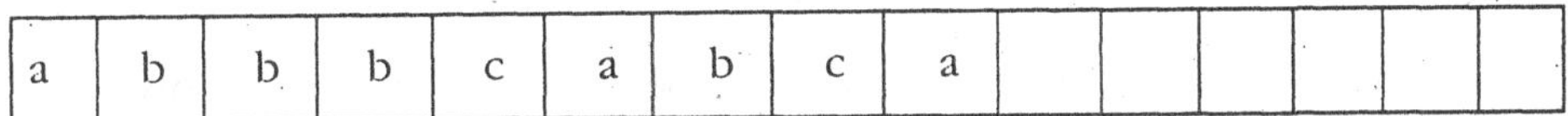

length: 9

Figure 5.1(a): Array Representation of a string

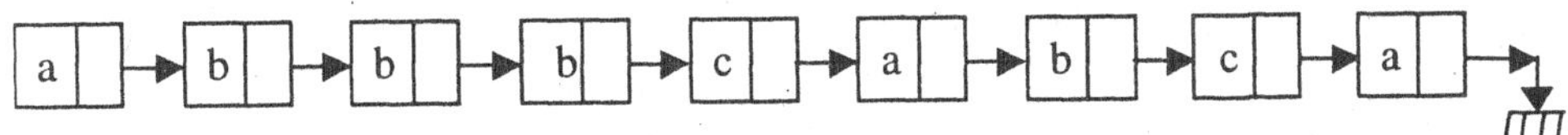

Figure 5.1(b): Linked List Representation of a string

In practice, array representations of strings are most commonly used although the array is created dynamically (using "malloc" library call) and destroyed (using "free" library call) whenever the string is no longer necessary. Sometimes the length of a string is not explicitly mentioned (as in C) even when it is represented by an array. However, most operations on strings require information of its length. In such cases, a special symbol (that is, a symbol which does not belong to Σ) is appended to the end of the string. The special symbol serves as the end marker of the string.

str:

a	b	b	b	c	a	b	c	a	\0					

Figure 5.2. Array Representation of null terminated strings. The last character is '\0' which acts as the end-marker of the string

In "C" programming language, this end marker is the null character ('\0'). That is why these strings are often referred to as null terminated strings. If the null character itself is a part of the string then null terminated strings can not be used. Type declaration of such a string of characters would simply be declaring the string as an array of characters or as a pointer to a character.

Several operations that were discussed in the earlier section can be easily implemented for null terminated strings. For example, the length of a string can be easily calculated by counting the number of characters before the null character is encountered. "C" functions for several operations on strings are presented in the following.

```
int stringLength(char *s)
{
    int i;
    for (i=0; s[i] != '\0'; i++);
    return i;
}
```

The function to copy a string "s2" to another string "s1" is also straightforward. The string "s2" is copied into "s1" one by one as long as the null character is not encountered in "s2". Note that the space for the string "s1" is not allocated inside the function. It is assumed that the caller of this function will reserve enough space for "s1" before calling this function.

```
void stringCopy(char *s1, char *s2)
{
    int i = 0;
    while(s2[i] != '\0')
    {
            s1[i] = s2[i];
            i++;
    }
    s1[i] = '\0';
}
```

The function to compare two strings checks whether the characters in both the strings are identical. This comparison continues as long as the characters are identical or the smaller string is exhausted. Once this happens, the difference between the next characters of the strings is returned. The function returns "0" if both the strings are same. If the first string ("s1") is greater then the function returns a positive number; otherwise, the function returns a negative numebr.

```
int stringCompare(char *s1, char *s2)
{
    int i = 0, j;
    int m,n;
    m = stringLength(s1);
    n = stringLength(s2);
    j = m < n ? m : n;
    while ((s1[i] == s2[i]) && (i<j))
    i++;
    return(s1[i] - s2[i]);
}
```

5.3 String searching algorithms

Finding out the occurrence of a smaller string (often referred to as "pattern") in a larger string (also called the "text") is a significant problem. More specifically, consider the problem of finding the beginning of the first occurrence of a given pattern in a text. The problem is, therefore, to construct an algorithm, which takes two arguments – a pattern "p" and a text "s" and returns an integer "i" such that "i" is the minimum index in "s" from which position a match is found. If "p" does not occur in "s", the function returns a negative number, say -1. For example, let "s" be "abaababbababba" and p be "abb". The function should return 5. If "p" occurs twice in the text "s" even then the starting position of the first match will be returned. If "p" is "aabb" and "s" is "aabaababab" then the function returns -1 as "p" is non-existent in the given string "s". Both the strings (pattern or text) are assumed to be implemented as one-dimensional arrays of characters terminated by NULL characters. Assume that "m" and "n" denote the lengths of the pattern and string respectively. Till date, many string searching algorithms have been developed. There are simple algorithms which are easy to comprehend and easy to implement but these algorithms are costly in terms of execution time. On the other hand, the sophisticated algorithms are very efficient but their operations are considerably involved. It will be seen that the overall performances of these algorithms are, to a great extent, application dependent. That is, the nature of the string and the pattern considerably influence the efficiency of these algorithms. Four pattern matching algorithms will be discussed in this chapter starting with conceptually simple brute force algorithm followed by more sophisticated algorithms.

Brute Force algorithm

This is the most rudimentary algorithm for string searching. It starts by scanning the text from its 0th index and checks whether the pattern matches the text from that position. To check whether a match occurs or not, all the first "m" characters in the string from its 0th position are compared one by one to all "m" characters of the pattern. During these comparisons, if (0+k)-th character of the text is not the same as the k-th character of the pattern ($0 \le k < m$) then a match can not occur from the 0th position of the string. Then, it becomes necessary to find a match starting with the 1st position (or index) of the string. This process continues until a match is found starting from the i-th position of the text or the text is exhausted. The latter case indicates that the pattern is non-existent in the text. The following "C" function is based on the described algorithm. The parameters "s" and "p" are declared to be arrays of characters. "s" denotes the text and "p" denotes the pattern.

```
int bruteStringSearch (char *s, char *p)
{
    int i, j, k,m,n;
    n = strlen (s);
    m = strlen (p);
    for ( i = 0; i <= n-m; i++)
    {       j =0;
            k = i;
            while ((s[k] == p[j]) && (j < m))
            {
                    k++;
                    j++;
            }
            if (j == m)
            return i;
    }
    return (-1)
}
```

The outer "for" loop may have to be executed at most (n-m+1) times. The worst-case complexity of the inner "while" loop is also O(m). Thus, the worst-case complexity of the algorithm "bruteStringSearch" is O(mn).

Consider that s = "xxxxxxx" and "p" be "xxxy". It is clear that starting from any position of the text, one has to make all four character comparisons to detect a mismatch. This is because the mismatch is detected only after the last character of the pattern is compared to the corresponding character of the string. In this example, exactly (n-m+1)*m number of comparisons are required where "n" and "m" are lengths of the text and the pattern respectively. In practice, however, a mismatch will be detected much earlier than all "m" comparisons, which will reduce the average case complexity of this algorithm. The average performance of the algorithm will be much better if the alphabet set, Σ, contains larger number of symbols. Due to this reason and because of the simplicity of the algorithm, this algorithm is very often implemented in practice for string searching applications.

5.4 Knuth Morris Pratt Algorithm for string searching

Knuth and Pratt developed another algorithm for string searching in 1976. Morris also independently developed the same algorithm. Their algorithm is known as Knuth-Morris-Pratt algorithm, KMP in short. The KMP algorithm runs in O(n+m) worst case time which is much better than the worst case complexity of the brute force algorithm.

KMP algorithm may be viewed as an improvement over the brute force method as it successfully avoids many redundant comparisons, which the brute force algorithm would have performed. Consider the string "xyyyyyx" and the pattern "xyyxy". At first, the brute force method tries to match the pattern "xyyxy" with the text beginning from the 0th index. The comparison between s[3] and p[3] results in a mismatch. Once this mismatch occurs, the brute force algorithm would blindly proceed to check for a possible match starting from the index one of the text. So, the next comparison to be performed by the brute force method is between the 0th character of the pattern (i.e., "x") and the 1st character of the string (i.e., "y"). Considering the available information at the end of the 0th trial (starting from the 0th index of the text), this comparison becomes unnecessary. After the comparisons made in the initial trial it is already known that the first three characters of the pattern are the same as the first three characters of the string (as the fourth comparison resulted in a mismatch). Moreover, since the pattern is known, it is also known that the first two characters in it ("x" and "y" respectively) are distinct. Using this knowledge about the pattern and the knowledge that the first three characters of the text have matched with those of the pattern, it can be safely concluded that the first two characters in the string must be distinct (as they are "x" & "y" respectively). So the 0th character in the pattern must be distinct from the 1st character of the text. Therefore, without making any more character comparison, it can be concluded that the trial starting from the 1st position of the text is bound to result in a mismatch. The brute force algorithm does not attempt to make use of such acquired knowledge. It would blindly go for a trial from the index one of the text and will detect a mismatch only after making at least one comparison (between the 1st character of the string and the 0th character of the pattern). This comparison could be avoided because the result of this comparison can be inferred from the available information. Consider another example where "s"="xxxxxyyxzy" and "p" = "xxxy". During the 0th trial of the brute force algorithm a mismatch will be detected as s[3]

≠ p[3] after the fourth comparison. But this necessarily means s[0] = p[0], s[1] = p[1], s[2] = p[2]. It is also known that p[0] = p[1] = "x" and p[1] = p[2] = "x". It follows that p[0] = s[1] and p[1] = s[2]. These results of the comparisons between p[0] and s[1] and p[1] and s[2] are known from the experience of the 0th trial and from the nature of the pattern. So, in the 1st trial, the first comparison could be between s[3] and p[2]. The brute force algorithm, however, would have ignored the knowledge accquired in the 0th trial and would compare p[0] and s[1] to begin the 1st trial – a comparison which is redundant. This discussion reveals that it is possible to avoid a large number of redundant comparisons if the peculiarities of the pattern under consideration are analyzed. The KMP algorithm attempts to do so to the maximum possible extent and thereby achieving higher efficiency.

Let the i-th trial of the algorithm be defined as the process of checking whether the pattern matches with the text starting from its i-th index. Thus, the i-th trial compares s[i] with p[0], s[i+1] and p[1] and so on until the comparison results in a mismatch or the pattern is exhausted. The i-th trial is a success if s[i+j] is equal to p[j] for all j, 0 ≤j <m.. Otherwise, the i-th trial is said to yield a failure. In the i-th trial, as long as s[i+k]==p[k], k=0,1,2,.. ,m-1 the algorithm proceeds to compare s[i+k] with p[k] for the next value of k. In this sequence, for some k = j, if s[i+j] is not equal to p[j] for the first time then one must know the next trial to look for a match. Note that it is now known that the i-th trial is a failure. At that point it is to be decided whether the (i+1)-th trial is necessary to be considered at all. Recall the example where s = "xyyyyx" and p = "xyyxy", it could be inferred that the 1st trial must result in a failure. Therefore, the (i+1)-th trial can be skipped completely if its outcome can be predicted to yield failure given the result of the i-th trial. The other point to note is the following. It may so happen that for the trial to be considered, results of first few comparisons are already known. This point was highlighted in the example where s = "xxxxxyyxzy" and p = "xxxy". In that example, the 1st trial does not start by comparing s[1] and p[0]. Instead, the first comparison in that trial is between s[3] and p[2]. In some other example, it may so happen that when a new trial is to be initiated, the first three characters of the text in that trial are known to be matching.

In general, as long as s[i] is equal to p[j], the next comparison to be made is between s[i+1] and p[j+1] provided j < m. If it is found that s[i] ≠ p[j] in some trial then it implies that s[i-j] = p[0], s[i-j+1] = p[1], …., s[i-1] = p[j-1]. Next trial, normally, should be the (i-j+1)-th trial. But, if it is known that the string obtained by concatenating p[0], p[1], …,p[j-2] is not the same as the string obtained by concatenating p[1], p[2], …,p[j-1] then the part of the text s[i-j+1], s[i-j+2], …, s[i-1] will not match with p[0], p[1], …,p[j-2]. Thus, examining the left portion of j-th character in a pattern it is possible to say whether (i-j+1)-th trial should be initiated at all, knowing that (i-j)-th trial yielded a failure. And if this trial is initiated, the first comparison is to be made between s[i] and p[j-1]. If it is seen that (i-j+1)-th trial should be abandoned then compare the strings "p[2], …, p[j-1]" and "p[0], …, p[j-

3]". If these strings are not the same then (i-j+2)-th trial should be abandoned. Otherwise, the (i-j+2)-th trial starts by comparing s[i] with p[j-2]. In general, if s[i] ≠ p[j] and the string "p[0], p[1], ...,p[k-1]" matches with "p[j-k], .., p[j-1]" then the string "s[i-k], ..., s[i-1]" definitely matches with "p[0], p[1], ...,p[k-1]". Hence, the next comparison should be between s[i] and p[k]. This analysis can be made by looking at the pattern "p" only.

From the earlier discussion, it should be clear that whenever s[i] is not equal to p[j] then it is necessary to decide whether to compare s[i] with p[j] (i < j) or to compare s[i+1] with p[0]. The decision to compare s[i] with p[k] corresponds to deciding whether one or more trials can be skipped. And the decision to compare s[i+1] with p[0] corresponds to initiate the (i-j+1)-th trial. Moreover, it also indicates the number of the first few characters in the pattern which must be matching with the corresponding characters for the trial match to be considered next.

To facilitate this processing, assume a table "next" of "m" entries. Suppose at some stage it is detected that s[i] is not equal to p[j] as discussed above. next [j] (= r, say) now gives the indication about the next comparison. If r ≥ 0 then the next comparison is between s[i] and p[r]. If r is equal to -1 then the next comparison is made between s[i+1] and p[0]. The logic of computing the "next" table for any given pattern is more involved and will be discussed subsequently. For the time being, assume the availability of this table and see how KMP algorithm works.

```
int KMP (char *s, char *p)
{
   int i, j, m, n;
   n = strlen(s);
   m = strlen(p);
   for (i = 0, j = 0; i < n && j < m; i++, j++)
         while ((j >= 0) && (s[i] != p[j]))
         j = next [j];
   if (j == m)
         return i-m;
   else
   return -1;
}
```

Consider an example where s = "ababbaabababababb" and p = "abababb". First, think of the next table for the pattern "p". The "next" table is shown in the following.

Next[i]	-1	0	0	1	2	3	4
i	0	1	2	3	4	5	6

By definition, Next[0] is set to –1 as there are no characters in "p" to the left of the 0th character of "p". To compute next[1], note that the only character in "p" to its left is the same as the character from the beginning of "p" to the 1st character (excluding itself). Hence, Next[1] is also always set to 0. To find "next[2]" note that there is no repetitive sub-pattern in "ab" the part of "p" to the left of the 2nd character in "p". However, the part of "p" to the left of the 3rd character in "p" is "aba". The sub-pattern "a" occurs in the beginning and at the end of the sub-pattern "aba". Hence, next[3] is 1. Now, look at the left of the 4th character in "p", which is "abab". Clearly the sub-pattern "ab" occurs in the beginning and at the end of the sub-pattern "abab". Thus, next[4] is 2. In this way the computation of the next table may be completed.

The Table 5.1 gives a trace of the algorithm "KMP". The values of "i", "j", s[i], p[j] are listed in each row of the table.

i	j	s[i]	p[j]	Remarks
0	0	a	a	
1	1	b	b	
2	2	a	a	
3	3	b	b	
4	4	b	a	Till this point, s[i] was equal to p[j]. Thus the body of the inner while loop was not being executed. Now as s[i] ¹ p[j], the body of the inner while loop will be executed and j will be computed as next[j].
4	2	b	a	
4	0	b	a	
4	-1	-	-	
5	0	a	a	
6	1	a	b	
6	0	a	a	
7	1	b	b	
8	2	a	a	
9	3	b	b	
10	4	a	a	
11	5	b	b	
12	6	a	b	
12	4	a	a	
13	5	b	b	
14	6	b	b	

Table 5.1 Trace of the KMP algorithm where s = "ababbaabababababb" and p = "abababb".

Construction of the "next" table is more involved and interesting. Suppose that in some trial s[i] is found not to be equal to p[j]. Necessarily the first j characters of "p" must have matched with corresponding characters of "s". That is s[i-1] = p[j-1] ... s[i-j] = p[0]. In general, s[i-v] = p[j-v] for 1 ≤v ≤ j. Now concentrate on the pattern. According to our notation the current trial is (i-j)-th trial which results in failure. Suppose, there is some "k" (k < j) such that p[0] = p[j-k], p[1] = p[j-k+1],..., p[k-1] = p[j-1]. See Figure 5.3. In other words, the part in "p" between indices "0" and "k-1" repeats itself from index (j-k) to index (j-1) in "p" as shown in the figure. Combining the two sets of equations the following can be concluded.

p[0] = p[j-k] = s[i-k]

p[1] = p[j-k++1] = s[i-k+1]

p[k-1] = p[j-1] = s[i-1]

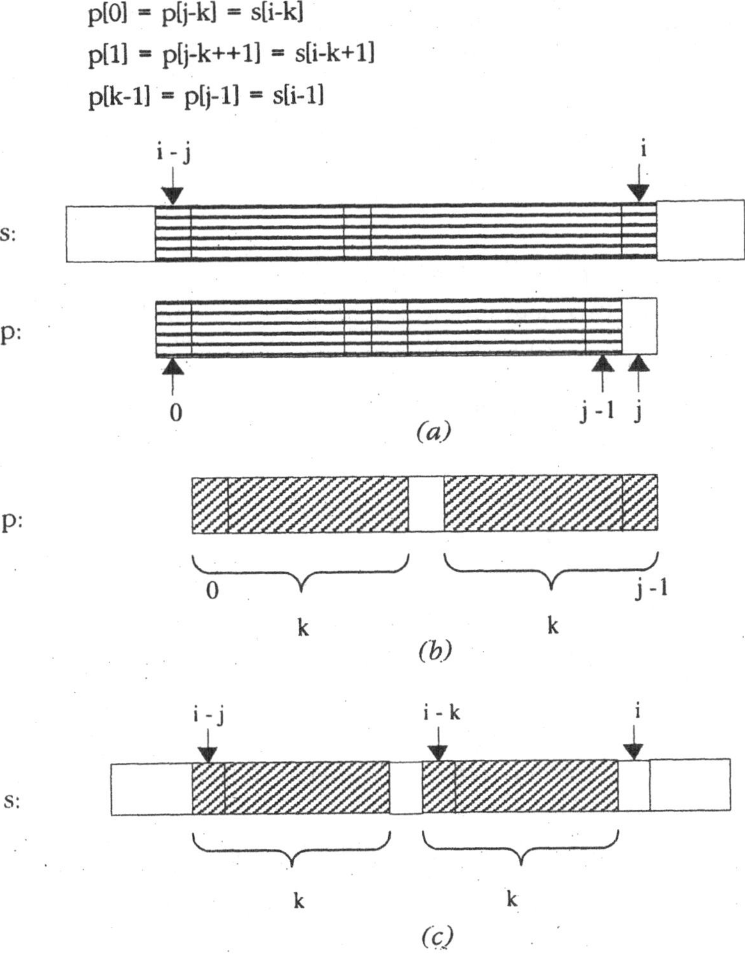

Figure 5.3. Illustration of next calculation. (a) suggests that in the (i-j)-th trial, a mismatch is detected when s[i] ≠ p[j]. All characters in "p" to the left of index "j" are same as the characters in the text. This is shown by the horizontal lines.

"p" is such that p[0] = p[j-k], p[1] = p[j-k+1], ..., p[k-1] = p[j-1]. Diagonal lines in Figure 5.3 (b) show this fact.

Due to Figure 5.3 (a), p[0] to p[j-1] of "p" can fit in the portion s[i-j] to s[i-1] in "s". Due to Figure 5.3 (b), s[i-(j-k)] = p[0]. s[i-(j-k)+1] = p[1] and so on. Thus a new trial may begin from (i-j+k)-th position of "s" by comparing s[i] with p[k]. This is shown in Figure 5.3 (c).

Therefore, the (i-k)-th trial may be attempted when the (i-j)-th trial ends in a failure. The advantage is that the first "k" characters of the pattern are known to match for the (i-k)-th trial. So, if it is decided to try the (i-k)-th trial then the first "k" characters need not be compared again. After the failure of the (i-j)-th trial, one can straightway jump to verify the (i-k)-th trial only if it can be proved that no trial starting from index (i-j+1), (i-j+2),...,(i-k-1) of the text can result in a success. In fact (j-k) number of trials are skipped by this jump. To ensure that no trial between (i-j+1) to (i-k-1) can result in success, the jump should be reduced to a minimum. For this purpose the largest k satisfying the following two properties is chosen.

1. k < j and
2. p[0] = p[j-k], p[1] = p[j-k+1], .., p[k-1]=p[j-1].

To see this, consider two values of "k", namely "k_1", "k_2" which satisfy these properties. Suppose $k_1 > k_2$. As discussed, the trial corresponding to k_2 would have ignored the trial corresponding to k_1, which might lead to a success. Formally, next[j] for any j, $0 \le j < m$ is defined as follows.

next[j] = -1, if j = 0

= max { k | p[0] = p[j-k],
p[1] = p[j-k+1],
:
p[k-1] = p[j-1] }
if such a k, $1 \le k < j$, exists.

= 0, otherwise.

That is, except for j=0, next [j] is the maximum "k" such that the first "k" characters of the pattern "p" match with the last "k" characters immediately preceding the j-th character in "p".

For example, consider the next table shown for the pattern "xxyyxxyx". To obtain next[7], observe that the first three characters of the pattern match with the last three characters immediately preceding the seventh character. Thus, next[7] = 3.

The above definition immediately suggests an algorithm for constructing the "next" table for a given pattern. A brute force algorithm can do this. Such an algorithm will try to find a value of "k" from the set of all possible values of k (k=1,2 ..., j-1) which satisfies the said property and then selects the maximum value of "k". Clearly, this method would become time consuming. The KMP algorithm suggests one technique for constructing this table very efficiently. In this approach the next[j] is constructed in the ascending order of j i.e., for j=0,1,2,.., m-1. next[0] is known by definition. next[1] is also trivially seen to be zero. Suppose the value of next[k] is to be computed for k=2,..., m-1. Assume safely that for all j, j<k, next[j] has already been computed. Suppose, next[j-1] = n_1 (See Figure 5.4). If p[n_1]=p[j-1] then clearly, next[j] = n_1+1. If p[n]≠p[j-1] then, suppose next[n_1] = n_2 (See Figure 5.4).

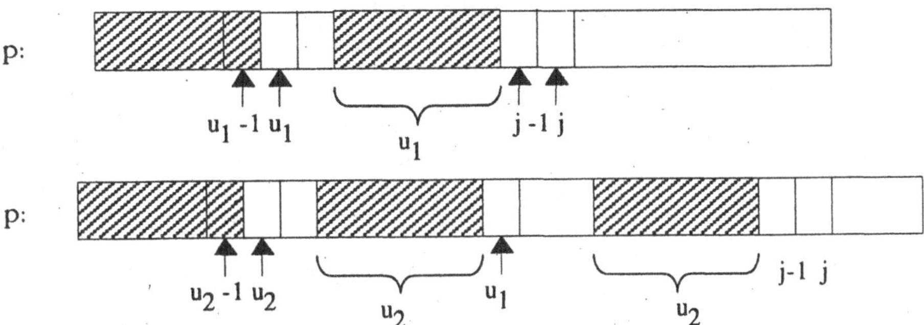

Figure 5.4: Computation of next. next[j-1] = u_1. Therefore, the shaded portions in the pattern "p" are equal. Now, concentrate on next[u_1]. If next[u_1] = u_2 then the shaded portions in the figure are also the same signifying that if p[u_2] = =p[j-1] then next[j] = u_2+1.

If p[n_2] = p[j-1] then next[j] =n_2+1. If p[n] ≠ p[j-1] and next[n_2] = n_3 then compare p[n_3] with p[j-1]. If they match, next[j] can be set to n_3 + 1 and so on. This process is continued till some "r" is reached such that (n_r= -1 or (n_r≥ 0 and p[j-1] = p[n_r])) in which case next[j] is set to n_r+1. In the former case, next[j] is set to zero. Therefore, in any case, next[j] is set to n_r+1. The function "getNext" is presented which constructs the "next" table for a given pattern "p". For ease of future explanation, the steps of the function are labelled.

```
void getNext (char *p, int next[])
1. {
2.         int i,j;
3.         int m =strlen (p);
4.         next[0] = -1;
5.         for (j=1; j<m; j++)
6.         {
7.                 i = next[j-1];
8.                 while ((i >= 0) && (p[j-1] != p[i]))
9.                         i = next[i];
10.                next[j] = i+1;
```

11. }
12. }

First, apply the algorithm to construct the "next" table for the pattern "abababb". The Table 5.2 shows a trace of the algorithm by listing the values of "j" at each iteration of the "for" loop. For each iteration of the "for" loop, the values of "i" (after being calculated in that iteration of the for-loop), and the values of p[j-1], p[i] and "next[j]" in each iteration of the while loop are also listed.

j	i	next[j]	p[j-1]	p[i]	Remarks
0	0	-1	-	-	Does bot enter into the for-loop.
1	-1	0	-	-	Does not enter into the while-loop.
2	0	-	b	a	Control goes to the body of the while loop. "i" changes as shown in the next row.
2	-1	0	-	-	
3	0	1	a	a	Condition in the while-loop is false. Hence next[j] is computed by incrementing "i".
4	1	2	b	b	"
5	2	3	a	a	"
6	3	4	b	b	"

Table 5.2 The trace of the algorithm "getNext" for a pattern "abababb".

Consider the construction of the "next" table for another pattern "ababbaaa". The trace of the algorithm is shown in Table 5.3.

j	i	next[j]	p[j-1]	p[i]
0	-	-1	-	
1	-1	0	-	-
2	0		b	a
2	-1	0	-	-
3	0	1	a	a
4	1	2	b	b
5	2	-	b	a
5	0	-	b	a
5	-1	0	-	-
6	0	1	a	a
7	1	-	a	b
7	0	1	a	a

Table 5.3 The trace of the algorithm "getNext" for a pattern "ababbaaa".

The proof to show that the function "getNext" computes the "next" table correctly (i.e., according to its definition) is based on induction. Clearly, "getNext" sets next[0] to -1. So, the induction base is proved. Suppose the induction hypothesis is true for all k<j. Note that "getNext" first compares p[j-1] with p[next[j-1]]. There could be two possibilities giving rise to the following two cases.

Case 1:

Suppose p[j-1] is equal to p[next[j-1]]. The inner while loop will terminate immediately and next[j] is set to next[j-1]+1. Since it is obvious that next[r] cannot exceed next[r-1] by more than one, next[j] is correctly computed.

Case 2:

Suppose p[j-1] ≠ p[next[j-1]]. In this case, the largest "k" such that p[0] = p[j-k], p[1] = p[j-k+1],...p[k-2] = p[j-2] and p[k-1] = p[j-1] must be found out if such a value of "k" (0<k<j) exists. If no such "k" exists, then next[j] has to be set to zero. These two possibilities are separately dealt with in the following two sub-cases.

Case 2.1

Suppose no such "k" exists. The while loop is terminated only when "i" becomes -1 at line 9, (Note that i will indeed become -1 in a finite number of iterations as the value of "i" decreases (by definition next[i]<i) after each execution of line 9. Consequently, next[j] becomes zero once line 8 is executed. The computation of next[j] is thus correct for this subcase.

Case 2.2

Suppose such a "k" exists. Let $u_1, u_2, \ldots, u_k$ be values of i, 1< i < j, such that

p[0] = p[j-i+1], p[1] = p [j-i+2], .., p[i-1] = p[j-2] .... (1)

Assume that $u_1, \ldots, u_k$ are arranged in descending order. According to the definition of "next",

u_1= next[j-1].

Now, p[0] = p[j- u_1+1], p[1] = p[j- u_1+2], ..., p[u_1–2] = p[j-3], p[u_1–1] = p[j-2]

Also, p[0] = p[j- u_2+1]

So, p[u_1–1] = p[u_2–1], p[u_1–2] = p[u_2–2], ..., p[0] = p[u_1- u_2]

At line 9, "i" gets the values u_1, u_2, in succession. The while loop continues until p[u_i] = p[j-1] for some i or next[u_i] = -1. Assume that the while loop terminates with i = u_k. At step 10, next[j] will be set to u_k+1. From the set of equalities as mentioned in (1), it follows that next[j] is u_k+1. Hence, next[u_1] = u_2. Similarly next[u_2] = u_3.

Thus, "getNext" correctly computes the next table.

Next, consider the time complexity of computing the "next" table. The type of analysis being done for this algorithm is different than the other analyses. This analysis is known as "amortized" complexity analysis.

Note that "i" is initially 0. From the definition of "next", it follows that "i" can never become negative. Therefore, the total decrement in "i" during the course of the algorithm cannot exceed the total increment in "i". The only way in which "i" may get incremented is by means of executing the first and the last statement of the body of the "for" loop. Note that, in each iteration of the "for" loop, the last statement stores (i+1) to next[j]. Immediately thereafter, index of the "for" loop becomes j+1. Consequently, (i+1) is assigned to "i" as the first statement in the next iteration of the "for" loop. Thus, "i" can increase by at most 1 in every iteration of the "for" loop and thus, the maximum possible total increment in "i" is (m-2).

Now, consider the process of decrementation of "i" in the algorithm. The only way to decrement "i" is by executing the assignment statement of line 9 (because next[i] < i). However, line 9 defines the body of the "while" loop. So, the total number of times line 9 is executed define the complexity of the "while" loop. Since total decrement of "i" can not exceed total increment in "i", the complexity of the "while" loop can not be more than (m-2).

It now follows that the total complexity of both the "for" loop and the "while" loop are O(m). Consequently, the complexity of the function "getNext" is O(m) + O(m) = O(m). As a corollary, it follows that the total number of character comparisons performed in line 8 does not exceed 2m-3. This is so because the number of comparisons in which "p[j-1] == p[i]" holds (which would terminate the "while" loop) is no more than m-1, the number of times the "for" loop is iterated. On the other hand, the number of comparisons where "p[j-1] != p[i]" holds is no more than (m-2), the number of times line 9 is executed. (Note that this analysis necessitates the comparison(p[j-1]!=p[i]) in evaluating the condition of the while loop. The assumption can always be fulfilled by a trivial rewriting of the "while" loop).

The complexity analysis of the KMP algorithm is the same. It can also be shown that the worst case complexity of the KMP algorithm is O(m).

5.5 Boyer-Moore Algorithm

The KMP algorithm makes a significant amount of study of the pattern to construct its "next" table. But it does not explicitly consider the text string while analyzing any mismatch. However, if a mismatch occurs while comparing s[i] with p[j] for some "i" and some "j" then the information s[i] can also be utilized in the following way. Assume "s" to be "xyxxyzxyyzyxyyxyxyy" and "p" be "yxyxyy". As before, let "m" and "n" denote the lengths of "p" and "s" respectively. So, m = 6 and n = 19. The first deviation from earlier pattern matching algorithms is that, the occurrence of a pattern will now be searched from right to left. Thus, the 0th trial match that checks whether the pattern occurs in the text from its 0th index starts by comparing p[m-1] with s[m-1] and continues to the left until the comparison fails or p[0] becomes equal to s[0]. In the latter case, the pattern is actually found in the text. In the current example, the 0th trial begins by comparing s[5] with p[5] as m = 5. As s[5] = "z" and p[5] = "y", the comparison fails. Not only this comparison fails, but it can also be seen that s[5] = "z" and "z" does not occur in "p". Hence, all trials starting from index "0" to index "5" of "s" are bound to fail and the next trial should begin only from the 6th element of "s". It must be noted that these conclusions could be derived without even scanning s[0], s[1], s[2], s[3] and s[4]. Consider the next trial which checks whether "p" occurs from the 6th position of "s". As this is a right to left search, the first comparison in this trial takes place between s[11] and p[5]. Clearly, s[11] ≠ p[5]. But, s[11] is "x" and "x" occurs in "p". Naturally s[11] has to be equal to some p[j], 0 ≤ j ≤ m, for a match. In fact p[1] = p[3] = s[11]. Once again, note that the 7th trial need not be attempted because if the 7th trial (trial beginning from the 7th element of "s") has to yield a match then s[11] must be the same as p[4] and it is known that s[11] ≠ p[4]. Thus, s[11] must be aligned either with p[1] or with p[3]. If p[1] is aligned with s[11] then the attempt is to check whether the pattern exists from the 10th element of "s" and aligning p[3] with s[11] attempts to check whether "p" occurs from the 8th element of "s". Since the risk of overlooking a possible match can not be taken, p[3] is to be aligned with s[11] initiating a trial from the 8th element of "s". In fact, whenever s[i] ≠ p[m - 1], the next trial is governed by the largest "j" for which p[j] is equal to s[i]. In this example, the next trial to be considered is the 8th trial, which starts by comparing s[13] and p[5]. This trial continues by comparing s[13] and p[5], s[12] with p[4], s[11] and p[3], s[10] and p[2] stops after comparing s[9] and p[1]. Once again, s[9] ≠ p[1] and s[9] is "z" which does not occur in "p". Thus the next trial (the10[th] trial) begins to check a match from the 10th element of "s". This trial starts with the comparison between s[10+5] and p[5]. As s[15] is equal to p[5], next comparison is made between s[14] and p[4] and it is found that s[14] ≠ p[4]. As s[14] = x, and p[1] = p[3] = x, s[14] is aligned with p[3] indicating that the next trial should be the 11th trial. As the first comparison in this trial between s[16] and p[5] yields a mismatch and s[16] = "x", p[3] is once again aligned with s[16] to initiate the 13th trial. As one can verify, this trial ends with a success. The complete procedure discussed above is illustrated in Figure 5.5. The trial number being attempted is shown at the left column. The comparisons performed are underlined

```
Trial No.       s = x y x x y z x y y z y x y y y x y x y y
   0                y x y x y y
   6                            y x y x y y
   8                                y x y x y y
  10                                    y x y x y y
  11                                      y x y x y y
  13                                          y x y x y y
```

Figure 5.5 Working of a right to left string searching algorithm with appropriately shifting the pattern to the right after a mismatch.

The scheme discussed so far is merely a modification to the brute force algorithm for pattern matching. The modifications are two-fold. First, in any trial, the pattern is searched from right to left. The second improvement is shifting the pattern to the right whenever a mismatch is encountered. This shifting operation may allow the function to avoid a few trials. It has also been discussed that the amount of shift depends on the character of the text at the time of a mismatch. More precisely, if s[i] ≠ p[j] in some trial then the amount of shift depends on s[i]. In our example, if s[i] is "z" then the amount of shift is equal to the length of the pattern. If s[i] ≠ p[m-1] and s[i] is "x" then the amount of shift is (m-1-k) where "k" is the largest index such that p[k] is "x". It should be clear by now that a table like the "Next" table is to be constructed that will help to compute the amount of right shift of the pattern whenever a mismatch occurs while comparing s[i] and p[j]. Call this table the "shift" table. The meaning of the shift table is as follows. Let shift[k] = j and "k" is any symbol which may occur in the text. This signifies that if p[m-1] ≠ s[i] at some point of time and s[i] is "k" then the amount of possible shift is (m-j-1). Note that this array is indexed by "k", a symbol. This is not syntactically possible in a programming language, as "k" is not an integer. So, the symbols of the text are associated with a unique integer known as its index. If the set of symbols used in the text is {x, y, z} then it may be said that index("x") = 0, index("y") = 1 and index ("z") = 2. The "shift" array is indexed by the indices of the symbols. The algorithm for constructing the "shift" array is outlined in the following.

```
void constructShift(char * p)
{
    int i, j;
    char x;
    for each character "x" in the set of symbols
    {
        if "x" does not belong to "p"
```

```
        shift[index(x)] = m;
    }
    for(i = 0; i < m; i++)
    shift[index(p[i])] = m-i-1;
}
```

Let the alphabet set be {x, y, z} and the index function be defined as follows.

index(x) = 0

index(y) = 1

index(z) = 2

Let p be "yxyxyy" and m = 6. Then, once the first "for" loop is executed, shift[2] becomes "6". The trace of the second "for" loop is shown in the Table 5.4.

i	p[i]	index(p[i])	shift[0]	shift[1]
0	y	1	-	5
1	x	0	4	5
2	y	1	4	3
3	x	0	2	3
4	y	1	2	1
5	y	1	2	0

Table 5.4 Trace of the second "for" loop of the algorithm "constructShift" for a pattern "yxyxyy"

Note that the given definition of "shift" allows the pattern matching function to decide about the amount of shift whenever s[i] ≠ p[m-1]. But, in general, a mismatch might occur while comparing s[i] with p[j], 0 ≤ j < m. The amount of shift is to be calculated in that situation also. Let s[i] ≠ p[j] for some "j" and shift[index(s[i])] = t. This means p[m-t-1] = s[i] and for any k, m > k > (m-t), p[k] ≠ s[i]. Now (m-t-1) could be greater than or less than "j", giving rise to the following two cases.

Case 1: (m-t-1) < j

This corresponds to the Figure 5.5(a). In this case, it is possible to align p[m-t-1] with s[i] shifting the pattern towards right by(j- m + t+1) positions. The next trial becomes the (i-j+j-m+t+1)-th i.e. the (i-m+t+1)-th trial and the next comparison has to be made between s[i-m+t+m-1+1] and p[m-1], i.e. between s[i+t] and p[m-1].

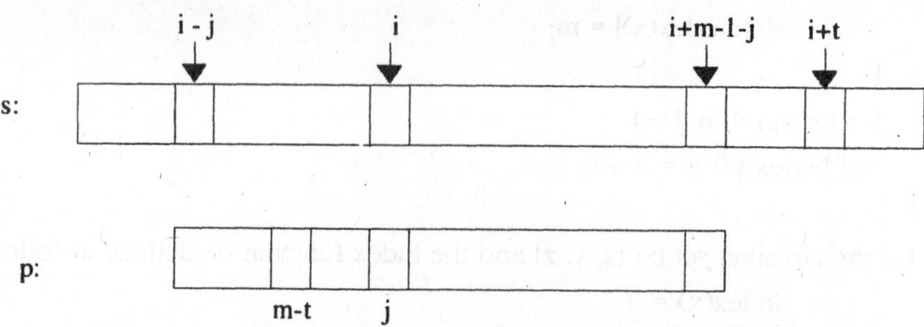

Figure 5.5(a) In the (i-j)-th trial, "p" is compared with "s" from right to left. That is, the first comparison is between p[m-1] and s[i+j+m-1]. A mismatch is detected when s[i] is compared with p[j]. If shift[index(s[i])] = t then s[i] = p[m-t-1].As (m-t-1) < j, the pattern may be shifted by an amount (j-m+t+1) to the right. Thus the next trial to try is the (i-m+t+1)-th trial.

Case 2: m-t-1 > j.

From Figure 5.5(b), it can be easily seen that the pattern can not be shifted right to align p[m-t-1] with s[i]. So, this mismatch does not allow the pattern matching function to skip any trial. The next trial is the (i-j+1)-th trial and the next comparison is to be performed between s[i-j+1+m-1] and p[m-1], i.e. between s[i-j+m] and p[m-1].

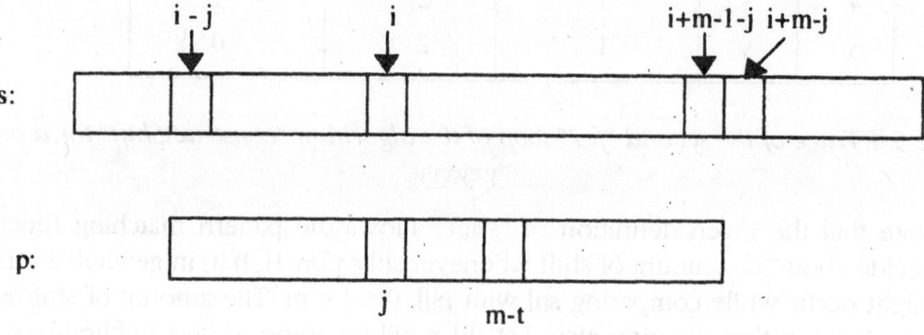

Figure 5.5(b) In the (i-j)-th trial, "p" is compared with "s" from right to left. That is, the first comparison is between p[m-1] and s[i+j+m-1]. A mismatch is detected when s[i] is compared with p[j]. If shift[index(s[i])] = t then s[i] = p[m-t-1].As (m-t-1) > j, the pattern may only be shifted by one to the right.

These ideas lead to the following algorithm.

```
int rightLeftScan(char * s, char * p)
{
    int i, j, m, n, skip;
```

```
    m = strlen(p);
    n = strlen(s);
    for(i = m-1; j = m-1; j > 0; i —, j —)
    {
            while(s[i] != p[j])
            {
                    skip = shift[index(s[i])];
                    i += ((m-j) > skip) ? m-j : skip;
                    if(i >= n)
                    return (-1);
                    j = m-1;
            }
    }
    return i;
}
```

Let "s" be "xyxxyzxyyzyxyyxyxyy" and "p" be "yxyxyy". The shift table has already been constructed. The trace of execution of the algorithm "rightLeftScan" for finding a match of "p" in "s" is presented in the Table 5.5.

In the worst case, the algorithm "rightLeftScan" behaves as a brute force algorithm that works with a right to left order of comparing the characters of the pattern with those of the text. This happens when all entries in the "shift" table are zeros. However, such is not the case in general. In fact, on an average, it is observed that "s" contains many characters not in the pattern, and, therefore, quite often the amount of skip will be "m". This happens especially when the alphabet set is large and "m" is small. In these cases, the algorithm "rightLeftScan" tends to make only about O(n/m) character comparisons.

i	j	s[i]	p[j]	shift[index(s[i])]	Remarks
5	5	z	y	6	Enters into the while-loop.
11	5	x	y	2	Inside the while-loop.
13	5	y	y	-	Does not enter the while-loop.
12	4	y	y	-	
11	3	x	x	-	
10	2	y	y	-	
9	1	z	x	6	Enters the while-loop.
15	5	y	y	0	
14	4	x	y	2	Does not enter the while-loop.
16	5	x	y	2	Enters the while-loop.
18	5	y	y	-	
17	4	y	y	-	
16	3	x	x	-	
15	2	y	y	-	
14	1	x	x	-	
13	0	y	y	-	Pattern is found in the text.

Table 5.5 Trace of the algorithm "rightLeftScan" where s = "xyxxyzxyyzyxyyxyxyy" and p = "yxyxyy".

At this point, it is important to note the similarity of the approaches taken by the algorithms KMP and the "rightLeftScan". Both the algorithms attempt to skip one or more trials which are guaranteed to be unsuccessful based on the mismatch detected in the current trial. However, the amount of this "skip" may be different in these algorithms. Another difference is that the KMP algorithm starts a trial by comparing the pattern with the text from left to right whereas the "rightLeftScan" algorithm uses a right to left comparison technique. This difference is artificial as the KMP algorithm can be rewritten so that it also works for a right to left comparison scheme. Now think of combining the KMP algorithm based on a right to left comparison and the "rightLeftScan" algorithm just described. Suppose that at any stage of computation, a mismatch occurs as s[i] ≠ p[j]. The "next" table as generated by the KMP algorithm suggests an effective skip of "p" consecutive trials and the "shift" table of the "rightLeftScan" algorithm suggests a skip of "q" trials. Since both the algorithms are correct, "k", which is maximum of "p" and "q" consecutive trials can be skipped. The resulting algorithm then will enjoy its worst case complexity no worse than that of the KMP algorithm and at the same time its average complexity will be as good as that of the "rightLeftScan" algorithm. Boyer-Moore algorithm does exactly this. The detailed coding of the algorithm is left as an exercise. Also recall that the worst case complexity of the KMP algorithm is O(n+m). It now follows that Boyer-Moore algorithm makes O(n+m) character comparisons in the worst case and only about O(n/m) comparisons on an average. The algorithm is, therefore, very efficient in practice.

5.6 Rabin Karp Algorithm for pattern matching

The last algorithm to be discussed in this context is named after its inventors Rabin and Karp. Their algorithm, is based on the idea of hashing and the readers would appreciate the algorithm better after they understand the concept of hashing which is discussed in depth in Chapter 9. The problem of pattern matching is essentially searching whether "p" is equal to the (n-m+1) strings of length "m" where these strings start at s[i] for i = 0 to n-m. That is, pattern matching may be thought to be a problem of searching "p" in the strings "s[0], s[1], ..., s[m-1]", "s[1], s[2], s[3], ..., s[m]", ..., "s[n-m], s[n-m+1], ..., s[n-1]". The way searching is done using hashing is as follows. A hash function "f" is applied on the entities (stored in an array, say A) in which search is to be done and the results are remembered. The same "f" is applied on the key "k" which is to be searched. f(k) is compared with the results of applying "f" on the available data set "A". If f(k) is not the same as f(A[i]) then A[i] can never be equal to "k". However, it may be possible that f(k) and f(A[i]) are the same but "k" and A[i] are not. Thus, whenever f(k) and f(A[i]) are the same, "k" and A[i] are to be examined element by element to see whether "k" and A[i] are equal. In the present context, "k" is the pattern "p" and A[i]'s are the sub-strings of "s" of length "m" starting from the index "i" of "s" where i = 0, 1, ..., n-m. First, the hash function "f" is to be properly chosen. A standard hash function converts a string to a number according to the following formula. Suppose, "x" is a string of length "m" and each character of "x" may be denoted by x[i] for i = 0 to m-1. Then,

$$f(x) = (x_0 d + x_1 d + .. + x_{m-2} d + x_{m-1}) \bmod Q$$

where "d" is an integer and "Q" is a large prime number and x_m denotes some number equivalent to the character x[m].

Consider an example where s = "2 1 7 9 3 5 9 1 4 1 9 9" and p = "1 4 1 9 9". Note that all symbols used to build the text and the pattern are characters "0" to "9". It can be said that "p" is to be searched in an array of eight strings. These strings are termed as s_i for i = 0 to 7 where s_i denotes the string of "s" starting from its i-th index. Therefore, s_0 is "21793", s_1 is "17935", s_2 is "79359", s_3 is "93591" and so on. Let the hash function "f " be defined for a string "x" as given in the following.

$$f(x) = \Sigma_{(i=0,m-1)}((x[m]-'0')d^i) \bmod Q$$

where (x[j]-'0') denotes the the number equivalent to the digit x[j]. Thus, f(p) = f("14199") = 59 where d = 10 and Q = 101. The values of $f(s_i)$ for various values of "i" are listed in the following.

$f(s_0)$ = f("21793") = 78
$f(s_1)$ = f("17935") = 58
$f(s_2)$ = f("79359") = 74
$f(s_3)$ = f("93591") = 65
$f(s_4)$ = f("35914") = 59
$f(s_5)$ = f("59141") = 56
$f(s_6)$ = f("91419") = 14
$f(s_7)$ = f("14199") = 59

The algorithm first computes f(p) and then compares f(p) with $f(s_0)$. Since f(p) ≠ $f(s_0)$, the algorithm proceeds to compare f(p) with $f(s_1)$. As long as f(p) ≠ $f(s_i)$ the algorithm goes on to compare f(p) with $f(s_{i+1})$ in the next iteration. When f(p) becomes equal to $f(s_i)$ for some "i" then "p" and s_i are compared element by element. In this example f(p) is equal to $f(s_4)$. So "p" and s_4 are compared element by element and it is found that p ≠ s_4. Therefore, the algorithm proceeds until f(p) matches with $f(s_7)$ and it is found that "p" is actually equal to s_7.

It is also interesting to note that if $f(s_i)$ is known then $f(s_{i+1})$ can be computed in one step as given in the following.

$$f(s_{i+1}) = (d(f(s_i)\text{-}s[i].(d^{m-1} \bmod Q)) + s[i+m]) \bmod Q$$

To understand the above expression assume that n_i be given by the following.

$$n_i = d^{m-1}s[i] + d^{m-2}s[i+1] + d^{m-3}s[i+2] + \ldots + s[i+m-1]$$

Clearly, $f(s_i) = n_i \bmod Q$

$$n_{i+1} = d^{m-1}s[i+1] + d^{m-2}s[i+2] + \ldots + d\,s[i+m-1] + s[i+m]$$

So, $n_{i+1} - d(n_i - s[i]\,d^{m-1}) + s[i+m] = 0$

i.e., $n_{i+1} = d(n_i - s[i]\,d^{m-1}) + s[i+m]$

i.e., $f(s_{i+1}) = (d(n_i - s[i]\,d^{m-1}) + s[i+m]) \bmod Q$

Only problem with this equation is that the number (n – s[i] d) may become too large to be accommodated in computer memory. Following modulus operations may be used to restrict these numbers:

(a + b) mod Q = (a mod Q + b) mod Q

(a.b) mod Q = (a. (b mod Q)) mod Q

Then,

$f(s_{i+1})$ = $(d(n_i - s[i]\,d^{m-1}) \bmod Q + s[i+m]) \bmod Q$

$= (d(n_i - s[i] (d^{m-1} \bmod Q) + s[i+m]) \bmod Q$

Rabin- Karp algorithm first computes f(p) for the pattern "p". It also computes the expression (d mod Q) and f(s). Subsequently, the values of f(s) are computed for i = 0 to (n-m) and these values are compared against f(p). If, for some "i", f(s) is equal to f(p) then the pattern might occur in the sub-string of "s" starting from index "i". To check whether this is the case, the pattern "p" is compared with the sub-string of "s" starting from its i-th element one by one. This leads to the following algorithm. In the following algorithm, it is assumed that the characters occurring in "s" and "p" represent digits. That is, s[i] or p[i] contains any character between '0' and '9'. In a general case, s[i] or p[i] may contain any character. The algorithm needs to be modified for the general case.

```
int RobinKarp(char * s, char * p)
{
    int d = 10, Q = 101;
    int h = 1, key = 0, t = 0, i,j,k;
    int m = strlen(p);
    int n = strlen(s);
    for(i = 1; i < m; i++)
            h = (d * h) % Q;
    for(i = 0; i < m; i++)
    {
            key = (key * d+(int)(p[i]-'0')) % Q;
            t = (t * d+(int)(s[i]-'0')) % Q;
    }
    for(i = 0; i < n-m+1; i++)
    {
            if(t == key)
            {
                    for(k = i, j = 0; j < m; k++, j++)
                    if (s[k] != p[j])
                            break;
                    if(j == m)
                            return i;
            }
            t = (t - (int)(s[i]-'0')) * h) % Q;
            t = (t * d + (int)(s[i+m]-'0')) % Q;
    }
```

```
return -1;
}
```

It can be easily seen that the worst case time complexity of Rabin-Karp algorithm is O(nm). But if "Q" is larger than the length of the string then the average case complexity of the algorithm becomes O(n+m).

In general, "d" represents the number of symbols occurring in "s" or "p". All symbols belonging to Σ are assigned unique integers from "0" to (d-1). For computing "key" or "t", these unique numbers are considered which represent s[i] or d[i].

5.7 Points to be remembered

- String is an important data structure in various applications like word processing. As an abstract data structure, several operations that can be applied on a string include finding its length, copying a string into another, comparing two strings, concatenation of a string after another and searching for a pattern in a text.
- Strings may be implemented by arrays or linked lists. Array representation is almost always preferred.
- An important subclass of strings are known as null terminated strings which are used in "C" programming language. Operations on null terminated strings can easily be implemented in "C" language.
- Searching for a pattern in a text is an important and a significant problem. The simplest brute force algorithm accomplishing this task is computationally expensive. If "m" and "n" are lengths of the pattern and the text respectively then the time complexity of a brute force string searching algorithm is O(mn).
- Knuth Morris Pratt (KMP) Algorithm examines the pattern to exploit periodicity of the sub-strings in the pattern. This algorithm first computes a "Next" table and then uses this table to search the pattern in a text. Time complexity of KMP algorithm is O(m+n).
- A significant improvement of performance may be achieved if the pattern is matched against the string from right to left. On a mismatch, the pattern may be shifted right possibly skipping a few trials. This idea leads to a right to left brute force string searching algorithm. Combining this algorithm with a right to left version of KMP algorithm yields a much better algorithm known as Boyer-Moore algorithm. Although the worst case time complexity of Boyer-Moore algorithm O(m+n), its average complexity is O(n/m).
- Rabin and Karp invented yet another string searching algorithm based on hashing.. The worst case time complexity of their algorithm is as bad as O(nm) but its average case complexity is O(n+m).

Exercises

1. Rewrite the "C" function "bruteStringSearch"to search for a pattern in a text where the text is scanned from right to left.
2. Construct the "next" tables for the following patterns.

   (a) abababba (b) ababbbba (c) aaaaa

   (d) abcdefgh (e) aaabbbabab (f) abracadabra

   (g) abaabaabb (h) ababaab
3. Construct the "shift" table for the following patterns

   (a) aaaaa (b) abcdef (c)abdabdab

   (d) aedcdea (e) abcabcaab (f) aababbcabab
4. Write a "C" function to implement the KMP algorithm where the text is scanned from right to left for the pattern.
5. Write a "C" function which has two strings "x" and "y" as formal parameters. The function finds out the first symbol of "x" which does not occur in "y".
6. It is required to find the occurrences of a pattern, "p", in a text, "s". Suppose that the "next" table is constructed for the string obtained by concatenating "s" after "p". How can this "next" table help in finding a match of "p" in "s"?
7. Let one problem be finding whether any one of "k" patterns occur in a string "s". Modify Rabin Karp algorithm to solve this problem.

Chapter 6

Recursion

6. 1 Introduction

Recursion is a fundamental concept in mathematics and in computer science. Functions in mathematics and subprograms in a program are often defined recursively. In many programming languages (including "C") subprograms are called functions. From the perspective of a programming language, a function is called recursive if the function calls itself. This feature of calling the same function from itself was not supported in older programming languages like Fortran-77, or GW-Basic. But almost all modern programming languages do support recursion. The reason why recursion has become more popular among computer scientists is that it is easier to define algorithms recursively. Such definitions are sometimes elegant and are more amenable to mathematical manipulations for the purpose of verification and analysis. However, it must be borne in mind that recursive definition of an algorithm does not always provide the most efficient solution. In fact, it may be noted that all recursive algorithms can be converted to an equivalent non-recursive version and often the non-recursive versions are preferred because of reasons related to performance.

Understandably, if a function calls itself unconditionally, then no function after being called would ever be able to return and an infinite sequence of calls to the same function would be produced. Such functions will not terminate. Hence recursive functions usually calls itself on a condition. On some other conditions (known as terminating conditions) the recursive functions terminate enabling its caller to proceed. A useful class of algorithms known as divide and conquer algorithms has been evolved which exploits the concept of recursion.

Recursive algorithms have already been developed in previous chapters of this book. This chapter introduces concepts and tools for designing and analyzing the basic structures of recursive algorithms. In doing so, several illustrative problems and their solutions have been explained in detail. This chapter also deals with techniques to remove recursion and ways to analyze recursive algorithms.

6.2 Simple Recursion and Recursion Tree

Most of the readers are familiar with recursive functions for problems like computing the factorial of an integer or finding the n-th number of a Fibonacci series. Consider the definition of the factorial of a positive integer "n" as given in the following.

$$\text{Factorial}(n) = \begin{cases} 1, & \text{if } n = 0 \\ n*\text{Factorial}(n-1), & \text{if } n > 0 \end{cases}$$

Note that the function "Factorial" is defined in terms of itself for n > 0. This is why the function "Factorial" is said to be defined recursively. Converting recursive definition of a function to an algorithm is often straightforward. The function "Factorial" can easily be converted to the following algorithm.

```
int factorial (int n)
{
    if (n == 0)
            return 1;
    return (n*factorial (n – 1));
}
```

It is easy to verify that the number of multiplications required by the function "factorial" for an integer "n" is "n". Also note that a simple iterative (non-recursive) function can be written for computing the factorial which is presented in the following.

```
int iterativeFactorial (int n)
{
    int i, fac = 1;
    for (i = 0; i<n; i++)
            fac *= (i+1);
    return fac;
}
```

If the function "factorial" is invoked with an actual parameter 5 then, as a result, factorial (4) is invoked. Once "factorial(4)" is called, "factorial(3)" is called and so on. This process continues until "factorial(0)" is called which returns immediately without calling any other function. The sequence of calls can be depicted pictorially as shown in Figure 6.1. Each node in the diagram represents a call to factorial and the label of the node denotes the value of the actual parameter.

An edge from a node "x" to another node "y" in Figure 6.1 signifies the fact that the call to "factorial" represented by node "x" necessitates another call to "factorial" represented by node "y". Once the call to "factorial(0)" is over, control goes to the caller function which is the suspended function "factorial(1)" in this case. The curved arrows in Figure 6.1 denote the return of a call to the "factorial" function. The number labeling a curved arrow denotes the value returned by the called function. The necessary tasks (a multiplication in this case) are performed and the function "factorial(1)" returns the value "1" to its caller, "factorial(2)". In "factorial(2)", "2" is multiplied with the value returned by "factorial(1)" (i.e., 1) and the result "2" is returned to its caller "factorial(3)". This process continues until control returns to "factorial(5)" where 5 is multiplied with the value returned by "factorial(4)" and the result is returned to the caller.

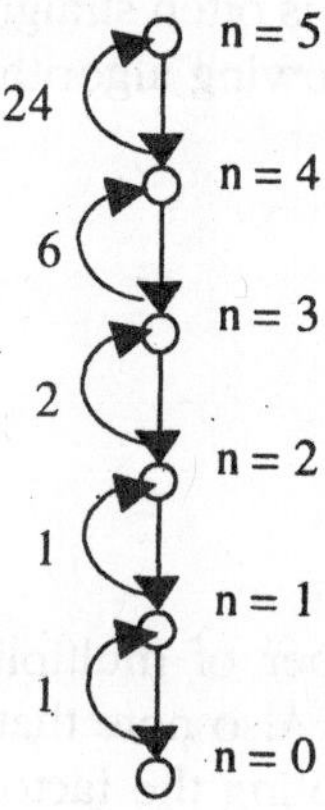

Figure 6.1 Sequence of recursive calls generated when "factorial (5)" is called. The circles denote processing of one particular call to "factorial". The value of the parameter "n" as passed to this call is labelled against each circle. The arrows denote a call to "factorial" from within the function "factorial" itself. Such a diagram is often referred to as a "recursion tree".

Note that time complexities of both the iterative and recursive algorithms for computing the factorial of an integer are the same. At a first glance, it may appear that the function "iterativeFactorial" requires more space for execution than the function "factorial" because the iterative function requires space to store values of an integer "i". However, this observation is not true. Recall that a call to "factorial(5)" gave rise to five successive calls to the same function "factorial". Whenever a subroutine is called, the context of the caller at the point of the call must be remembered so that when control comes back to the caller, the caller can smoothly resume its operations. Moreover, in each call to a function, space for all local variables (including the formal parameters) has to be reserved. Therefore, to execute a call to "factorial(5)", space is to be reserved for "n" for all functions which are called. Consequently, it is not true that the function "factorial" is not using any space other than the space required to store the value of "n". In fact, a call to "factorial(5)" requires space for storing five integers, each one being used for storing the actual parameter needed to recursively call the function "factorial". More surprisingly, the actual time taken by the recursive algorithm is considerably greater than that of the iterative algorithm although the time complexities of both these algorithms are the same. Thus, it may not be easy to say that a recursive algorithm always performs better. This is further elaborated in the following example.

The notion of Fibonacci Sequence of integers has already been discussed in Chapter 1. A recursive algorithm for finding the n-th integer in the Fibonacci Sequence has also been described. Recall the algorithm in the present context.

```
int Fibo (int n)
   {
          if (n ==0)
                 return 0;
          if (n ==1)
                 return 1;
          return (Fibo (n-1) + Fibo (n-2));
   }
```

Assume that "Fibo(5)" is invoked. To evaluate "Fibo(5)", "Fibo(4)" and "Fibo(3)" are to be invoked. The sequence of calls to the function "Fib)" may be depicted in the same way as the sequence of calls to the function "factorial" was shown in Figure 6.1.

In fact, it is possible to draw a diagram such as Figure 6.2 for depicting sequence of recursive calls for any recursive function. Such pictorial representation of calls to recursive functions is called a "recursion tree", which is very useful in analyzing recursive algorithms.

As it was the case in Figure 6.1, each node in the Figure 6.2 represents a call to the function "Fibo". Each node is labelled with the value of "n", which is the actual parameter for this call. As before, an edge from a node "x" to nodes "y_1", "y_2" signifies that a call to "Fibo" corresponding to node "x" recursively calls "Fibo" corresponding to "y_1" and "y_2". Moreover, the edges are ordered from left to right so that a call represented by the left most edge is made first and then the call represented by right edge is made. For example, to complete a call to "Fibo(5)", a call to Fibo(4) is made first and then a call to Fibo(3) is made.

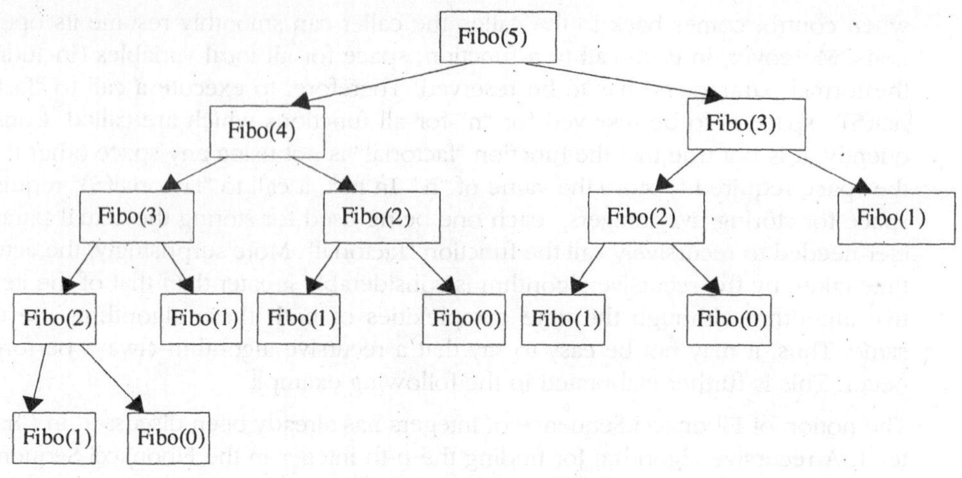

Figure 6.2 Recursion tree for the function "fibo" when called with an actual parameter "5".

The structure of the recursion tree highlights important characteristics of the underlying recursion. For example, it is evident from the figure that the function "Fibo" is called several times with the same actual parameter. Note that, "Fibo(3)" is called twice and "Fibo(2)" is called three times. It would be probably more efficient if the values of "Fibo(n)" are remembered and reused without reevaluating it for a number of times. This observation actually points out why the recursive algorithm is far less efficient than an iterative solution to the same problem. Recall that the time complexity of the algorithm "Fibo" is $O(\phi^n)$ for a constant ϕ while the time complexity of a simple iterative solution (as given in Chapter 1) is just O(n).

6.3 Divide and Conquer

Divide and conquer class of algorithms have already been discussed in Chapter 3 in the context of polynomial multiplication. The basic idea behind this class of problems may be summarized in the following.

DivideAndConquer (problem, "p", of size "n")

{

if the size "n" is small enough

Solve the problem and return.

Split the problem to sub-problems p_0, p_1, ..., p_{m-1} so that size of each p_i is less than "n".

For each i (from "0" to "m-1")

Call DivideAndConquer(p_i) to obtain a solution s_i.

Extend solutions s_0, s_1, ..., s_{m-1} to obtain the overall solution.

}

The words printed in *italics* in the above description represent non-trivial operations. In fact, designing a divide and conquer algorithm often boils down to defining these actions. Many algorithms arising in the domain of sorting and searching belong to this class. They are described in Chapter 9. Various tree and graph algorithms also belong to this class. They are described in Chapter 7 and Chapter 10 respectively.

6.4 Tower of Hanoi Problem

A French mathematician Edouard Lucas invented a cute puzzle called the "Tower of Hanoi" in 1883. The problem is as follows. A tower of eight disks is initially stacked in decreasing size on one of three available pegs as shown in the Figure 6.3. The goal is to transfer the entire tower of disks from one peg (say, "A") to another peg (say, "B") using the third available peg (say, "C") so that only one disk can be transferred at one time and a smaller disk can never be placed on a larger disk during this process of transfer. In fact Lucas attached a legend with his puzzle by associating it with the famous temple of Brahma. The tower of Brahma contains 64 golden disks placed on one of three diamond needles. Lucas said that at the time of creation of the universe God placed the disks on the first needle and subsequently asked some priests to move the disks from the first to the third needle using the second needle subject to the two conditions already mentioned.. It was believed that the day priests would finish the task, the world would come to an end.

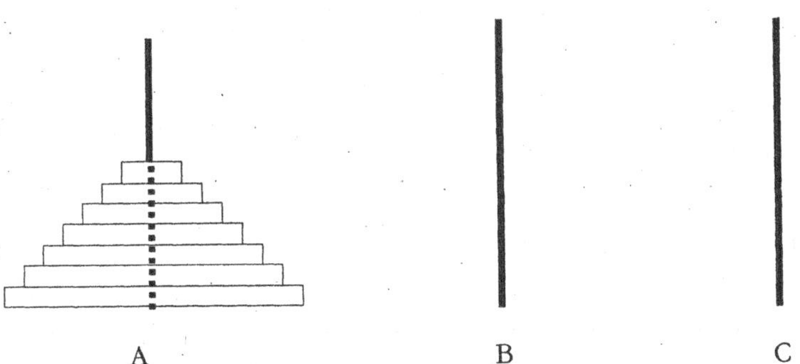

Figure 6.3 The Tower Of Hanoi problem. A number of disks are stacked on Peg "A" in decreasing order of size. They are to be transferred to Peg "C" using Peg "B" satisfying two conditions mentioned in the text.

Consider that the problem is to write a program to find out the moves required to transfer "n" disks from peg "1" to peg "3" using peg "2". Note that the problem is trivial if "n" is "1". Then, the disk is moved directly from peg "1" to peg "3". Assume that a solution to the problem of transferring (n-1) disks from one peg to another using a third auxiliary peg is known to us. In other words, the solution is assumed for a smaller value of n. Then, the upper (n-1) disks may be assumed to be moved from peg "1" to peg "2" using peg "3". The largest disk which is remaining on peg "1" can be directly moved to peg "3". Once this is done, the (n-1) disks can be moved from peg "2" to peg "3" using peg "1". Note that the above description extends a solution for transferring (n-1) disks to a solution for transferring "n" disks. Thus, a recursive definition of the problem is obtained. Let move (n, s, d, u) denote moving "n" disks from peg numbered "s" to peg "d" using peg "u". Then "move" function can be recursively defined as follows.

$$\text{move}(n, s, d, u) = \begin{cases} \text{move}(n-1, s, u, d) \text{ and} \\ \text{move the n-th disk from peg "s" to peg "d" and} \\ \text{move}(n-1, u, d, s) & \text{,if } n>1 \\ \text{move the disk from peg "s" to peg "d"} & \text{,if } n=1 \end{cases}$$

The "C" function for this problem is described next.

```
void move (int n, int s, int d, int u)
    {
        if (n == 1)
        {
                printf ("move the disk from %d to %d\n", s, d);
                return;
        }
        move (n-1, s, u, d);
        printf ("move the disk from %d to %d\n", s, d);

        move (n-1, u, d, s);
    }
```

Note that a non-recursive formulation of the above problem is not at all easy. Recursion is particularly suitable for a problem like this. To analyze the time complexity of function "move", note that a call to "move" results in two calls to the same function and some fixed task (like printing a line). If T(n) denotes the time required by "move" if it is called with an actual parameter "n" then T(n) can be expressed recursively as follows.

$$T(n) = \begin{cases} T(n-1) + C + T(n-1) & ,\text{if } n > 1 \\ C & ,\text{if } n = 1 \end{cases}$$

where C is a constant.

Thus, $T(n) = 2T(n-1) + C$ for $n > 1$

$$= 2(2T(n-2) + C) + C$$

$$= 2^2T(n-2) + C(1 + 2)$$

$$= 2^3T(n-3) + C(1 + 2 + 2^2)$$

.

.

.

$$= 2^{n-1}T(n - n + 1) + C(1 + 2 + 2^2 + \ldots + 2^{n-2})$$

$$= 2^{n-1}C + C\ (1 + 2 + \ldots + 2^{n-2})$$

$$= C.2^n$$

$$= O(2^n)$$

Consider the trace of the algorithm when three disks are initially placed on peg "1" and these disks are to be moved to peg "3" using peg "2". That is, "move(3, 1, 3, 2)" is called. See the recursion tree as shown in Figure 6.4(a). In turn, a call is made to "move(2, 1, 2, 3)". Subsequently, a call is made to "move (1, 1, 3, 2)". Consequently, the first line of the output of Figure 6.4(b) is generated and the function call returns to the caller (i.e. in the function call "move(2, 1, 2, 3)"). The second line of output is produced and the call "move(1, 3, 2, 1)" is made. This call returns to its caller (which is the suspended function "move (2, 1, 2, 3)") after printing the third line of the output as shown in Figure 6.4(b). The function "move(2, 1, 2, 3)" is now complete and it returns to its caller which is the function "move(3, 1, 3, 2)". This process continues until the function "move(3, 1, 3, 2)" returns. Readers are encouraged to trace the remaining flow of control through the recursion tree and to verify that the output generated by a call to move(3, 1, 3, 2) is in deed as given in Figure 6.4(b).

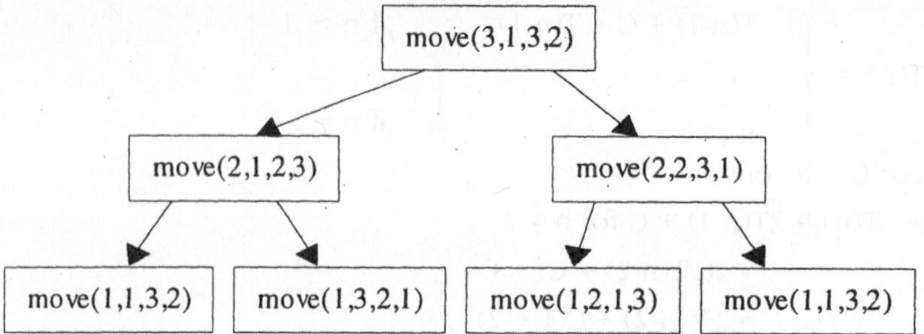

Figure 6.4 (a) Recursion tree for the function "move".

move the disk from 1 to 3
" " " " 1 to 2
" " " " 3 to 2
" " " " 1 to 3
" " " " 2 to 1
" " " " 2 to 3
" " " " 1 to 3

Figure 6.4(b) The lines of output generated by a call to "move(3, 1, 3, 2)".

6.5 The Permutation generation

Consider another interesting problem of printing all possible permutations of integers 1, 2,..., n. Clearly, there are n! such permutations. To illustrate the idea of recursively generating permutations, carefully study the diagram in Figure 6.5. This diagram is a tree where the top node represents the permutations of a set of integers containing only one element, "1". Each node in the tree represents a permutation. The tree may be horizontally divided into four levels as shown in the figure. The nodes at the i-th level represent permutations of integers 1, 2,..., i. Assume that the generation of permutations start from the level 1 of the tree. There is only one node at level "1". This node represents the only permutation possible with one integer "1". That permutation is denoted by (1). To obtain the nodes in the next level, just insert "2" to all possible positions of the permutation represented by its parent node. Each permutation obtained by such insertion is represented by nodes in the 2nd level. For example "2" can be placed in two positions in the list (1) producing the lists (1, 2) and (2, 1). These two permutations are the two nodes in level 2 and they are the possible permutations of integers 1 and 2. Take all the nodes from the second level one by one. Put "3" in all possible positions of the permutation represented by the node currently taken. The resultant permutations are the ones achievable from the set of integers 1, 2, 3. Thus, the tree provides a systematic way of generating permutations which can be formally summarized as follows. Consider a function "Permutation(k)" which generates the list of all permutations of the set of integers {1, 2, 3,..., k}.

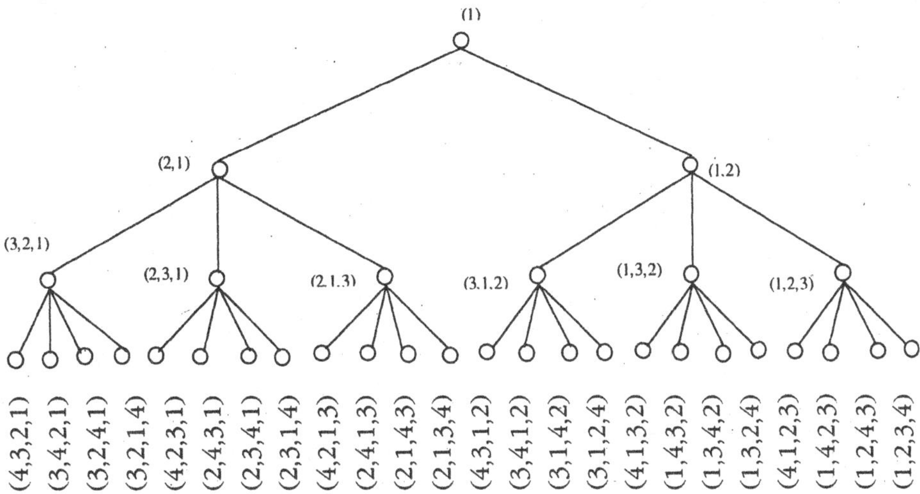

Figure 6.5 Tree for generating permutations

Permutation(1) is obvious and it returns the list (1). Permutation(k) can be defined in terms of Permutation(k-1) in the following way. Let "L" be the list generated by Permutation(k-1). Each element of "L" is a permutation. So, an element in "L" is once again a list of all integers from 1 to k-1. Insert "k" at all possible positions to each element in "L". Note that the elements in "L" contain all integers from 1 to k-1 and hence insertion of k increases the size of these elements. "k" can be inserted to such a list in "k" different positions. So, from each element of "L", a new set of "k" elements is generated. Moreover, as the elements in "L" are distinct, the resultant elements after insertion of "k" also remain distinct. To illustrate these ideas, assume that Permutation(2) is given and Permutation(3) is to be generated. That is, k = 3, L = ((1, 2), (2, 1)). So, "L" contains two elements (1, 2) and (2, 1) each of which is a list. Take the element (1, 2). Insert "3" in all possible positions of (1, 2). There are "3" positions and 3 new elements are generated from (1, 2) which are (3, 1, 2), (1, 3, 2) and (1, 2, 3). Take the other element of "L" which is (2, 1). "3" may be inserted in three different positions of (2, 1) yielding (3, 2, 1), (2, 3, 1) and (2, 1, 3).

These ideas can be easily translated to the following recursive algorithm. However, there is a problem of finding an appropriate return data type for the function. In the definition of "Permutation", it is assumed that the result of the function is a list of permutations, i.e. a list of list. Moreover, the definition freely expands the permutations which are lists themselves. To eliminate the burden of passing a list of list to each function call, a global list is maintained. As the permutation generation process starts with "1" and continues indefinitely, a termination condition is required. A global integer "n" is kept for this purpose. If "k" is equal to "n" then recursion is terminated. The algorithm is presented next.

```
Algorithm PrintPermutations(int k)
{
    /* Let L denote one permutation of the set of integers 1, 2,..., k-1. */
        for each possible position in "L"
        {
            insert "k" to "L"
            /* Naturally, size of L grows */
            if(k == n)
                print "L";                  /* reursion terminates */
            else
                PrintPermutations(k+1);         /* recursive call */
            remove "k" from "L"
        }
}
```

If all permutations of integers 1, 2,..., 10 is required to be printed then "PrintPermutations(1)" is to be called after assigning 10 to "n" and "L" is initialized to NULL. Trace the algorithm when it is called with k = 1 and the value of the global integer "n" is 4. As, "L" is empty, there is only one place to insert. So, "L" becomes (1) after inserting "1" to an empty list. As k ≠ n, the same function is called with k = 2.

When "PrintPermutations(2)" is called with L = (1), there are two positions in "L" where "k", i.e., 2, can be inserted. For the first position, when "2" is inserted to "L", "L" becomes(2, 1). Once again, as "k"(i.e., 2) is not equal to "n"(i.e., 4), "PrintPermutations (3)" is called. Only after this call returns, this iteration of the for loop will be finished and the next iteration will start. The sequence of calls till now is shown in Figure 6.6(a).

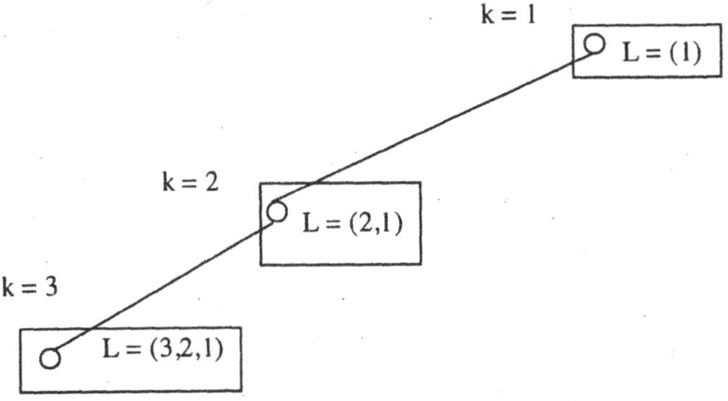

Figure 6.6(a). In this recursion tree, each box represents one instance of a call to printPermutations. The value of "k" is written against each box. Inside a call (i.e., a box), each iteration is shown as a circle. The value of "L" at the time of entering into the "for" loop is shown against each circle.

Now, "PrintPermutations(3)" is called with L = (2, 1) There are three possible positions to insert "3" into "L". The first possibility is to add "3" to the beginning of "L". In the first iteration of the "for" loop, "L" becomes (3, 2, 1). As k ≠ n, the same function is once again called with k = 4 suspending the remaining task in this "for" loop.

When "PrintPermutations(4)" is called with L = (3, 2, 1), there are four possible positions to insert "4". In the for loop, insertion of "4" to "L" is done. As the condition (k == n) becomes true now, no more recursive call results. Instead, "L" is being printed in each iteration of the for loop. Consequently, the following four lines would be printed as a result of this call to "PrintPermutations(4)".

4, 3, 2, 1
3, 4, 2, 1
3, 2, 4, 1
3, 2, 1, 4

At the end of each iteration, "4" is removed from the expanded "L" and so, this call returns to its caller with "L" remaining as (3, 2, 1). Once the control comes back to the previous instance of the call "PrintPermutation(3)" the suspended iteration of the for loop of this function becomes complete after removing "3" from "L". In the next iteration, "3" is inserted in the next position so that "L" becomes (2, 3, 1). The sequence of calls at this stage is shown in Figure 6.6(b). Once again "PrintPermutation(4)" is called with this "L". As k == n in the call "PrintPermutation(4)", the following outputs will be generated.

4, 2, 3, 1
2, 4, 3, 1
2, 3, 4, 1
2, 3, 1, 4

Once "PrintPermutations(4)" has been called from all three iterations of the for loop of the current instance of the call "PrintPermutations(3)" with L = (2, 1) control goes back to the call of instance of "PrintPermutations(2)" with L = (1).

Once control comes back to the call "PrintPermutations(2)" witl L = (1), the first iteration of the for loop can be completed and the next iteration begins. In the next iteration "L" becomes (1,2) after inserting "2" to "L". The recursion tree upto this point has been drawn in Figure 6.6(c). Once again, "PrintPermutation(3)" is called with this "L". And the process continues. Readers are encouraged to manually complete this process of constructing the recursion tree.

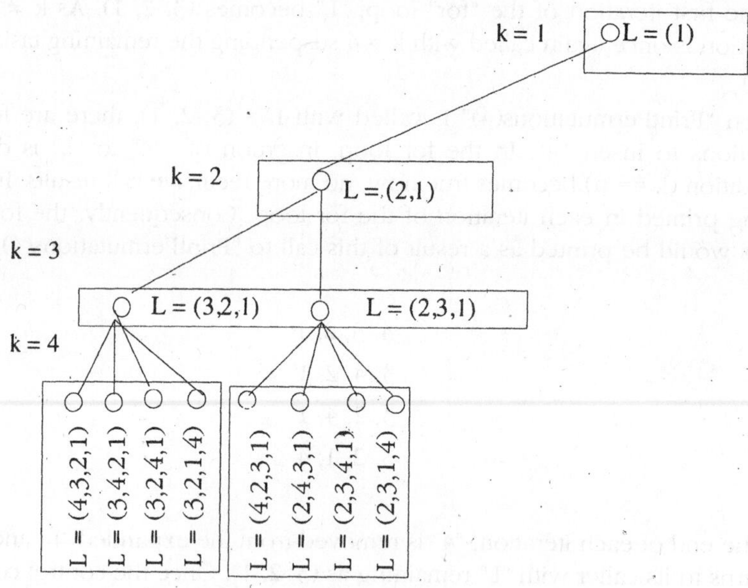

Figure 6.6(b) Partial Recursion tree where each box represents a call to the function "printPermutataions" and each circle inside a box represents one iteration inside a call as explained in Figure 6.6 (a). The second iteration in the call "PrintPermutations(2) is complete at this stage.

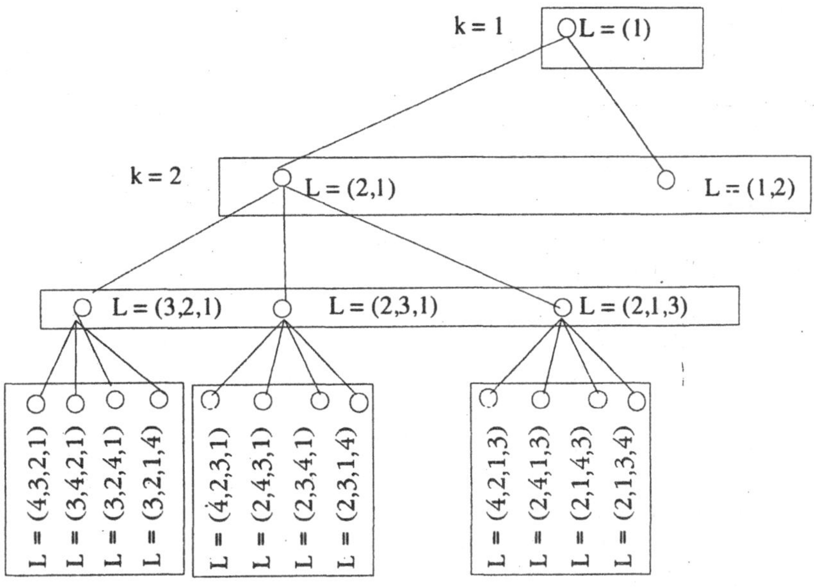

Figure 6.6(c) Partial Recursion tree where each box represents a call to the function "PrintPermutataions" and each circle inside a box represents one iteration inside a call as explained in Figure 6.6(a). The first iteration in the call PrintPermuutations(2) is complete and the second iteration has just begun at this stage.

"C" Function for Permutation

The only non-trivial part of converting the algorithm "PrintPermutations" to a "C" function is deciding upon a data structure of the global list "L" and writing "insert" and "delete" routines for that list. If the list is implemented using an array then the insertions and deletions become inefficient. So, a linked representation of "L" becomes an automatic choice. However, an additional advantage in this case is that the maximum length of the list is known, which is "n". Since this length of the list "L" is known a priori, the linked list representation may be conveniently implemented using arrays. Recall that one step of the algorithm involves insertion of "k" to "L" in all possible positions. This implies that "k" is to be inserted at the beginning (i.e. before the first node) of the list and as well as "k" has to be inserted after every node of "L". To make things uniform it is better to have a dummy node in "L" so that "k" is always inserted after some node.

Array implementation of linked lists has been discussed in Chapter 3. Such an implementation typically requires two arrays: one for storing the data and the other to maintain the links. In this case, however, two arrays are not required. Interestingly, both the data and the links can be managed in one array "Link". The trick is to use the indices of the array as data elements and the contents of the array as links. Thus, the list (0, 3, 2, 1) can be represented as shown.

3	0	1	2							

By default, the first index of the array is "0" which is its first data element. This is correct because "0" acts as the first dummy element of every list. Link to the next element is found in Link[0] which is "3". Since the value of the index is the value of the data, the data of the second element is "3". Link to the next element is to be found in Link[3] which is "2". Once again, the third element in the list is "2". This process continues until Link[k] becomes "0" for some "k".

In such a representation, adding "k" after the node "p" can be done by setting Link[k] to Link[p] and then setting Link[p] to "k". Deletion of "k" which occurs after "p" is also straightforward. Just set Link[p] to Link[k] and the original link from "p" to "k" vanishes. With this background, the "C" function of the algorithm "PrintPermutations" is easy to obtain.

```
void PrintPermutations(int k)
{
   int p = 0;
   do
   {
         Link[k] = Link[p];                    /* inserting k */
         Link[p] = k;
         if (k == n)
               print();
         else
               PrintPermutations(k+1);
         Link[p] = Link[k];                    /* deleting k */
         p = Link[p];
   }     while(p != 0);        /* the loop to insert k in al positions of L */
}
```

Before this function is called, the array "Link" has to be defined globally as

```
int Link [20];
```

and "Link" must be initialized to contain just the dummy element "0" by the following assignment.

```
Link [0] = 0;
```

"Print" is a simple function to traverse the list and print its elements as given in the following.

```
void print( )
{
        int k = 0;
        while(Link[k] != 0)
        {
                printf("%d", Link[k]);
                k = Link[k];
        }
        printf("\n");
}
```

6.6 Backtracking: Eight Queens problem

This is a very famous puzzle in which eight queens are to be placed on a 8X8 chessboard so that no two queens may attack each other. Note that a queen can attack another piece if they lie on the same horizontal or vertical line or on the same diagonal in either direction. This is not a very easy problem to solve because there are so many ways to place the queens that an exhaustive computation is not humanly possible. The diagram in Figure 6.7 illustrates one configuration of the chess board where eight queens are placed in non-attacking positions. However, it must be stated that this is not the only solution configuration for eight queens" problem.

Analyze the problem a little closely. A chess board may be represented by a matrix (i.e., a two dimensional array) "chess" so that each cell in the chess board may be represented by an element of the matrix. All elements of the array may be initialized to zero. An element of the array could be set to "1" whenever a queen is placed on the corresponding cell.

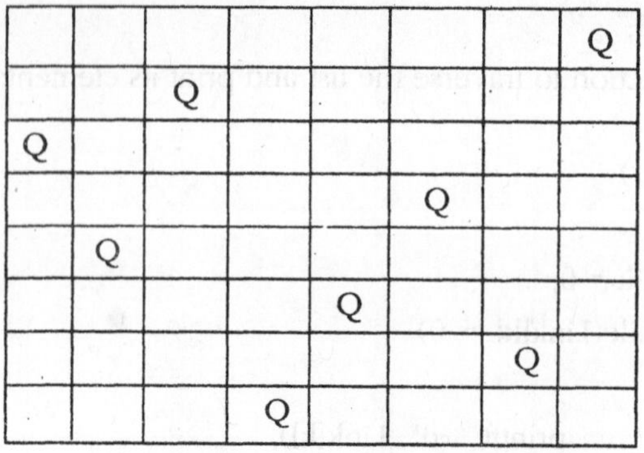

							Q
		Q					
Q							
					Q		
	Q						
				Q			
						Q	
			Q				

Figure 6.7 A solution configuration where eight queens are placed on a chessboard so that they can not attack each other.

That is, if chess[i][j] = 1 then, it is understood that a queen is placed on the j-th column of the i-th row of the chess board. It can be easily seen that two queens can not be placed on the same row in a solution configuration because, in that case, they would be in an attacking position with respect to each other. Thus, it is known that each row in the array contains exactly one queen in the solution configuration. However, the column number where the queen for the i-th row is going to be placed is not known. Thus a one-dimensional array "column" is sufficient as a suitable data structure. If column[i] = "j" then it is understood that the queen of the i-th row is placed on the j-th column. With this information, try to think of the algorithm. First, put the queen at the first row. That is, set column[1] to "1". Now, the queen at the second row can not be placed on the first or second column. So, set column[2] to "3". Next, column[3] can not be set to 1, 2, 3, 4. It can only be set to "5". column[4] may be set to "2". column[5] may be set to "4". Now, it is impossible to place the queen in the 6-th row in a non-attacking cell. This situation is shown in Figure 6.8.

So, it is required to revisit the placement of queen in the 5-th row and put it to a new column. This means that a back tracking is needed to solve this puzzle. So, a first description of the algorithm may be described as follows.

```
NonattackingQueens( )
{
   int columnNo;
   row++;
   for(columnNo = 1; columnNo <= 8; columnNo++)
   {
   if no queen placed in rows from 1 to (row-1) is attacking the position(row,
   columnNo)
```

```
            {
                column[row] = columnNo; /* place the queen on this row. */
                if(row == 8)       /* All queens have been successfully placed. */
                {
                    print the board configuration;
                    return;
                }
                NonattackingQueens( );  /*place another queen in */
                                              /* the next row. */
            }
        }
    }
    row—;
}
```

Q							
X	X	Q					
X	X	X	X	Q			
X	Q						
X	X	X	Q				
X	X	X	X	X	X	X	X

Figure 6.8 The configuration according to the previous description. "Q" is written to indicate that a queen in placed in that cell. "X" is marked to indicate that no queen can be placed in that cell as some other queen in previous rows would have attacked a piece in this cell. Note that a queen could not be placed on the 6th row so that the queens already placed in the first five rows do not attack it.

The function is called by setting the global variable "row" to "0". The function finds out a column where the queen in the current row may be placed. Such a column must be between 1 and 8. If such a column is found, the next queen is placed using the same function. If such a column is not found then the queen in the previous row must be placed on a different column. This is done by returning the current call to its caller after decrementing "row". It is not difficult to check, whether a given position(r, c) is non-attacking for queens in rows from 1 to row-1. The positions of those queens can be retrieved by examining the array "column" for indices 1 to row – 1. Note that a queen in the i-th. row can attack another queen placed at cell (i, j) of the board if any of the two following conditions is true.

(i) The queens are placed on the same column. That is, column[i] is equal to "c".

(ii) The queens are placed on the same diagonal. That is, the magnitude of (r-i) is the same as the magnitude of (c – column[i]).

Writing a "C" function for eight queens problem is left as an exercise. The algorithm "NonAttackingQueens" can easily be generalized to n-queens problem where "n" queens are to be placed in a nXn chessboard so that no two queens attack each other. It is also instructive to draw the recursion tree of this algorithm for n = 4. At each node of the recursion tree the board configuration should be drawn to understand the algorithm better. This problem serves as an example of a class of problems which are solved by the method of trial and error. Whenever a dead end is reached, the algorithm backtracks by undoing the last step and tries to make a new attempt. As it was the case with other problems, backtracking can also be solved in a non-recursive manner.

6.7 Removal of Recursion

It has already been argued that some problems can be easily solved in a recursive manner and it is easier to prove the correctness of recursive algorithms. But it is also said that recursion involves space and time due to function calls. Moreover, some programming languages do not support recursion. Even in such circumstances. the advantages of using recursion may be obtained. One can write the algorithm recursively and prove its correctness. Subsequently, the recursive algorithm may be translated into a non-recursive version by applying certain rules mechanically. Fortunately, any recursive procedure can be converted to a non-recursive procedure.

Any call to a subprogram (recursive or non-recursive) requires that the subprogram has a storage area of its own where it can store its local variables and its actual parameters. Moreover, return address to the calling procedure must also be preserved before the call is made. These tasks are performed by the compiler and thus, they are usually transparent to the programmer. If a recursive call is to be replaced by a jump to the beginning of the function then appropriate care must be taken to preserve local variables and to remember the return address. Otherwise, each call will use the same area for local variables and destroy the values in the storage space for the outer call and the outer call cannot be completed successfully. Thus, any translation must clearly understand the beginning of a recursive call and the end of that call. When a recursive call begins, the values of local variables, parameters and the return address at the time of the call must be remembered. The end of a recursive call is indicated by a "return" statement. At that point of time the previous outer call must be recalled with resetting of the local variables and actions must resume from where it was suspended.

As the execution of subroutine calls work in a Last In First Out (LIFO) manner, local variables, calling parameters and the return address for each call should be stored in a stack. These items, viz. the local variables, actual parameters and the return address actually define the activation record for an activation of a recursive procedure. After the innermost call is finished via one "return" statement, the stack will be popped to recover the return address and all the local variables for the immediate outer call. When the outermost call completes its work, the stack is exhausted.

The above ideas are used for converting a recursive algorithm to a non-recursive one. The rules are given in the following.

Initialization

1. Declare a stack that will hold the activation records consisting of all local variables, parameters called by value and labels to specify where the function is recursively called(if it calls itself from several places).

   The non-recursive function for a recursive function starts with an initialization block which initializes the stack to be empty.

   The stack and the stack top pointer are defined as global variables.

2. To enable each recursive call to start at the beginning of the original function, its first executable statement after the stack initialization block is associated with a label.

The following steps should be done at each place inside the function where it is recursively called.

3. Push all local variables and parameters called by value into the stack.
4. Push an integer "i" into the stack if this is the i-th place from where the function is called recursively (On return, this integer "i" will indicate the part of the code from where to resume. See rule 7.)
5. Set the formal parameters called by value to the values given in the new call to the recursive function.
6. Replace the call to the recursive function with a "goto" to the statement which is the first statement after the stack-initialization block. A label is associated to this statement in rule 2.
7. Make a new statement label Li (if this is the i-th place where the function is called recursively) and attach the label to the first statement after the call to the same function(so that a return can be made to this label).

At the end of the recursive function or whenever the function returns to the calling program, the following steps should be performed.

8. If the stack is empty, then the recursion has finished; make a normal return.
9. Otherwise, pop the stack to restore the values of all local variables and parameters called by value.

10. Pop the integer "i" from the stack and use this to go to the statement labelled by Li.

Try the above rules to convert the function "move" which solves the "Tower of Hanoi" problem to an equivalent non-recursive version. The corresponding non-recursive version is presented in the following. The rules applied are commented appropriately. Observe that a cute and simple recursive algorithm turns into an ugly, complicated non-recursive version. This is partly because the rules were applied mechanically. The non-recursive version can be made more attractive by applying more thought and intelligence as will be described later.

```
void moveNonRecursive(int n, int s, int d, int u)
{
    int t,i;
    stackOfIntegers s1;                     /* rule 1 */
    initialize(&s1);                        /* rule 1 */
    label0:                                 /* rule 2 */
    if(n == 1)
    {
            printf("Move the disk from %d to %d \n", s, d);
            if (isempty(s1))                /* rule 8 */
                    return;
            i = pop(&s1);                   /* rule 9 */
            t = pop(&s1);
            u = pop(&s1);
            d = pop(&s1);
            s = pop(&s1);
            n = pop(&s1);
            if(i == 1)                      /* rule 10 */
                    goto label1;
            else
                    goto label2;
    }
    push(&s1, n);                           /* rule 3 */
    push(&s1, s);
    push(&s1, d);
    push(&s1, u);
```

```
    push(&s1, t);
    push(&s1, 1);                              /* rule 4 */
    n = n-1;                                   /* rule 5 */
    t = d;
    d = u;
    u = t;
    goto label0;                               /* rule 6 */
    label1:                                    /* rule 7 */
    printf("Move the disk from %d to %d \n", s, d);
    push(&s1, n);                              /* rule 3 */
    push(&s1, s);
    push(&s1, d);
    push(&s1, u);
    push(&s1, t);
    push(&s1, 2);                              /* rule 4 */
    n = n-1;                                   /* rule 5 */
    t = s;
    s = u;
    u= t;
    goto label0;                               /* rule 6 */
label2:                                        /* rule 7 */
if (isempty(s1))                               /* rule 8 */
    return;
    i = pop(&s1);                              /* rule 9 */
    t = pop(&s1);
    u = pop(&s1);
    d = pop(&s1);
    s = pop(&s1);
    n = pop(&s1);
    if(i == 1)                                 /* rule 10 */
            goto label1;
    else
            goto label2;
```

```
}
```

The above function uses a user defined type "stackOfIntegers" and four auxiliary functions "initialize", "push", "pop" and "isEmpty". These are defined in the following.

```
        typedef struct stackOfIntegers
        {
                int top;
                int Elements[1000];
        }stackOfIntegers;
void push(stackOfIntegers* s, int x)
{
    s->top++
    s->elements[s->top] = x;
}
int pop(stackOfIntegers* s)
{
    int x;
    x = s->elements[s->top];
    s->top —;
    return x;
}
int isEmpty(stackOfIntegers s)
{
    return((s.top == -1)? 1 : 0);
}
void initialize(stackOfIntegers* s)
{
    s->top = -1;
}
```

Readers must have noticed that once recursion is removed by applying the described set of rules, the algorithm becomes a mess of goto's. Further simplification of the procedure to remove recursion is possible if the recursive call occurs once inside a function. Note that the recursion tree in such a case becomes a chain as shown in Figure 6.1. Consider the following algorithm, which is a general description of a recursive function that includes only one call to itself.

```
void f (parameters)
{
   while (not termination condition of recursion)
   {
         A;
         f (actual parameters);
         B;
   }
   C;
}
```

In the above algorithm, blocks "A", "B", "C" stand for any block of statements. Before applying the rules to remove recursion, note that the rule 10 is useless in this context, as there is no ambiguity for the return address. The simplest non-recursive version is presented next.

```
void fNR (parameters)
{
   initialize stack s;
   label0:
   while (not termination condition of recursion)
   {
         A;
         push parameters into stack s;
         goto label0;
   label1:
   B;
   }
   C;
   if(! isEmpty(s))
   {
         pop data from s;
         goto label1;
   }
}
```

Note that the statement "goto label0" is unnecessary if the body of the while loop does not include the block "B". But then, once block "B" is done, control must go to the beginning of the "while" loop. This can be accomplished by enclosing the while loop inside a do-while loop. Moreover, "goto label1" may be avoided by directly executing Block "B" at that place. As a final point, note that the stack will be empty in the beginning. The next version utilizes these ideas to get rid of "goto" statements and labels.

```
void fNR1(parameters)
{
    intilize stack s;
    do
    {
        if(! isEmpty(s))
        {
            pop data from s;
            B;
        }
        while(not termination condition of recursion)
        {
            A;
            push data to s;
            change parameters;
        }
        C;
    } while(! isEmpty(s));
}
```

Tail Recursion

The general recursion removal technique described earlier, pushes actual parameters, local variables and the return address to the stack before initiating a recursive call. In the return statement (i.e. when the call terminates) values of all the local variables are popped from the stack so that the local variables are reset with these values. Suppose that, as a special case, the last executed statement of a function is a recursive call to itself. This special case is called tail recursion. According to rules 3, 4, 5, 6, 7, the call is replaced by a number of push operations Since this is also the last statement of the function, the immediate "return" is replaced by a number of "pop" operations according to rules 8, 9 and 10. In such circumstances it is pointless to do the push and pop operations mindlessly on the stack. In fact, there is not even any need to use the stack. Instead, the actual parameters used to call the function recursively may be assigned to their new values and then a branch to the beginning of the function is all that is needed to eliminate recursion. The process of transformation can be viewed pictorially in Figure 6.9.

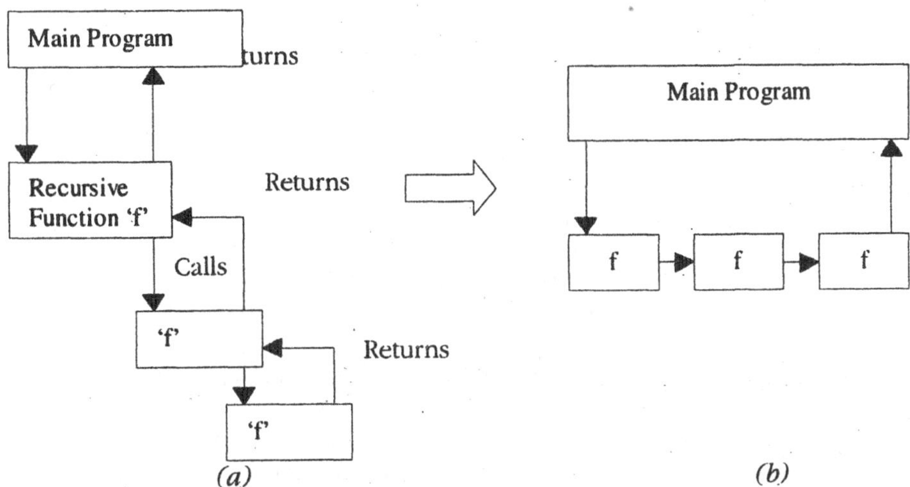

Figure 6.9 Illustration of removing tail recursion. The diagram in (a) shows calls to a tail recursive program. The same sequence of calls can be redrawn as a series of calls as shown in the diagram (b).

Observe that the function "move" to solve the "Tower Of Hanoi" problem is an example of tail recursive function because the last action in "move" is a call to itself.

To remove tail recursion, note that the values of actual parameters "u" and "s" in the last recursive call to "move" are the values of "s" and "u" in the previous call. Thus these values are to be swapped before branching to the beginning of the function after eliminating recursion.

```
void move(int n, int s, int d, int u)
{
    int t;
    l:
    if(n == 1)
    {
            printf("move the disk from %d to %d\n", s, d);
    }
    else
```

```
                move(n-1, s, u, d);
                printf(("move the disk from %d to %d\n", s, d);
                n = n-1;
                t = u;
                u = s;
                s = t;
                goto l;
        }
    }
```

Note that once tail recursion is removed, the recursion tree of the function "move" becomes a chain. More about recursion removal will be discussed in the context of tree traversal algorithms in Chapter 7.

6.8 Analysis of recursive algorithms

In this chapter and in the previous chapters, a number of recursive algorithms have been developed. It has already been mentioned that the basic principle in these algorithms is to decompose a problem into smaller sub-problems, to solve the sub-problems and finally to combine the solutions of the sub-problems into a solution of the original problem. In this section, some basic results on analyzing such algorithms are looked into. Understanding the mathematical properties of the formulas in this section may provide insight into the performance properties of algorithms discussed in the book.

If a recursive function looks through the input of size "n" to eliminate one of them then its time complexity, T(n), follows the following recurrence relation.

$$T(n) = T(n-1)+k.n \text{ where k is a constant.}$$

In this case $T(n) = O(n^2)$ if $T(1) = k'$, a constant

$$\begin{aligned} T(n) &= T(n - 1) + k.n \\ &= T(n - 2) + k(n-1) + k.n \\ &\;\;\vdots \\ &= T(n - n + 1) + k(n + (n - 1) + \dots + 1) \\ &= T(1) + k(1 + 2 + 3 + \dots + n - 1 + n) \\ &= k' + k(n(n + 1) / 2) \end{aligned}$$

If a recursive function halves the input in one step and works only in one half after that step then its time complesity satisfies the following recurrence relation.

$$T(n) = T(n/2) + k$$

If $n = 2^m$ for some "m" then $T(n) = O(\log_2 n)$ provided $T(1) = k'$

$$\begin{aligned} T(n) &= T(n/2) + k \\ &= T(n/4) + k + k \\ &\quad . \\ &\quad . \\ &\quad . \\ &= T(n/2^m) + k.m \\ &= k' + k.\log_2 n \end{aligned}$$

If a recursive function halves the input into two and has to make a linear pass through the input before, during or after the input is split into two halves then the time complexity satisfies the following recurrence relation.

$$T(n) = 2T(n/2) + k.n \text{ for a constant "k".}$$

If $n = 2^m$ then $T(n) = O(n \log n)$

$$\begin{aligned} T(2) &= 2T(2^{m-1}) + k2^m \\ &= 2(2T(2^{m-2}) + k2^{m-1}) + k.2^m \\ &= 2^2T(2^{m-2}) + k.2^m(1 + 1) \\ &\quad . \\ &\quad . \\ &\quad . \\ &= 2^{m-1}T(2^{m-m+1}) + kn(1 + 1 + 1 + \ldots + 1) \\ &= (n/2)k' - k.n + k.n.m \\ &= O(n \log n) \end{aligned}$$

A general recurrence relation can be written as

$$T(n) = aT(n/b) + f(n)$$

where a 3 1 and $b > 1$ are constants and f(n) is a positive function. This relation describes a recursive algorithm which decomposes a problem of size "n" to "a" number of subproblems of size n/b. The total cost of decomposition and the cost of combinations of the results of the subproblems is given by f(n). In this case, T(n) may be expressed as

$$T(n) = \begin{cases} k & \text{if } n = 1 \\ aT(n/b) + f(n) & \text{if } n = b^i \end{cases}$$

where "i" is a positive integer. Then,

$$T(n) = kn^{\log_b a} + \Sigma_{(j=0,\ \log_b n-1)}(a^j f(n/b^j))$$

This result can be easily seen by unfolding the recurrence.

$$\begin{aligned} T(n) &= f(n) + aT(n/b) \\ &= f(n) + af(n/b) + a^2\, T(n/\, b^2) \\ &= f(n) + af(n/b) + a^2\, T(n/\, b^2) + \ldots \\ &\quad a^{\log_b n - 1} f(n/b^{\log_b n - 1}) + a^{\log_b n}\, T(1) \end{aligned}$$

Since, $a^{\log_b n} = n^{\log_a b}$, the result follows.

Let $g(n) = \Sigma_{(j=0,\ \log_b n-1)}(a^j f(n/b^j))$.

Depending on f(n), g(n) can be bounded asymptotically for exact powers of "b" as follows.

1. If $f(n) = O(n^{\log_b a - \epsilon})$ for some constant $\epsilon > 0$ then $g(n) = O(n^{\log_b a})$.
2. If $f(n) = \theta(n^{\log_b a})$ then $g(n) = \theta(n^{\log_b a}.\log n)$
3. If $af(n/b) \leq cf(n)$ for some constant $c < 1$ and $n \geq b$ then $g(n) = \theta(f(n))$.

It can also be shown that T(n) = g(n) for all threes cases mentioned here. The proof for these results are left as an exercise.

6.9 Recursion versus iteration

It is already discussed that recursion implicitly uses a stack in which activation records of recursive calls are pushed. These activation records are popped when a call to a function returns to its caller. Thus, any call to a sub-routine is a time consuming operation during execution of a program and therefore, recursive functions perform better only after eliminating recursion, using rules that were outlined in a previous section. In addition to this, some more points have also been observed. It was argued that recursion should not be used for the computation of the factorial of an integer or computation of the n-th Fibonacci number. Time complexity of a recursive algorithm to compute the n-th Fibonacci number was seen to be too large as compared to an iterative solution. On the other hand, recursion was seen to be the natural choice for solving the "Tower of Hanoi" problem and for generating permutations. Thus, it is important to find out the fundamental characteristics of a problem to decide whether a recursive or a non-recursive solution would be better. Construction of a recursion tree helps in making such decisions as it provides much useful information about the nature of the underlying recursion.

If the recursion tree is a chain then each call to the function results in another call to the same function. For example, the recursion tree for the function "factorial" is a chain. In such a situation, if the recursion tree is generated in a bottom up fashion then the need for recursion is no longer present. It is interesting to note that recursion is inherently a top-down approach in solving a problem. When a recursion tree reduces to a chain then converting a recursive function to an iterative function is often easy and will result in a saving of both space and time.

Now, consider the recursion tree for the solution to find out the n-th Fibnacci number. There are many nodes in the tree representing same tasks done repeatedly. Since recursion implicitly uses a stack data structure, results once obtained are popped and not remembered thereafter. This is why "Fibo(2)" is called so many times. If some data structure other than the stack could be used then results once obtained might be preserved for future references. An automatic choice is an ordered list(represented by an array) to store the intermediate results. The iterative version of the solution for computing the n-th. Fibonacci number is a little tricky because it does not involve an array. But a straight forward bottom-up solution to this problem is found at once if an array is used to store the Fibonacci numbers computed upto any given point as shown below.

```
int Fibo(int n)
{
    int i;
    int Fibonacci[1000];
    Fibonacci[0] = 0
    Fibonacci[1] = 1;
    for(i = 2; i <= n; i++)
            Fibonacci[i] = Fibonacci[i-1] + Fibonacci[i-2];
    return(Fibonacci[n]);
}
```

The above function can not be used to compute Fibo(n) for n≥1000. This function is also a little general in the sense that the same technique can be applied to compute a series of positive integers as defined in the following.

$$G(0) = 0;\ G(1) = 1;\ G(n) = G(n-1) + G(n/2);$$

Note that the trick used in Chapter 1 for the solution of finding the n-th Fibonacci number can not be used for computing the series G as described now.

Sometimes, the symmetry of a recursion tree can also be exploited to avoid recursion. This trick is used to remove recursion from an important sorting algorithm called "merge sort" and is discussed in Chapter 9. As a final comment, it must be mentioned that while any recursion can be replaced by a stack and iteration, any iteration with a stack can also be replaced by recursion. The programmer should first find out which approach leads to a more natural and efficient solution before attempting to improve it.

6.10 Points to be remembered

- Recursion is a powerful mathematical tool to express ideas and functions. Most modern programming languages support recursive function calls. Recursion often offers elegant solutions to difficult problems.
- Recursion tree illustrates the sequence in which calls are made to the same function. Recursion tree is particularly helpful in finding out peculiarities of the underlying recursion.
- A significant class of problems which are solved by recursion is classified as "divide and conquer" problem. Such problems are first decomposed into smaller sub-problems. Recursion is used to solve the smaller problems. Then, these solutions are combined to obtain the overall solution. Several sorting algorithms(e.g. merge sort, quick sort) and binary search algorithm to be discussed in chapter 9 are classical examples of this class of problems.
- Two illustrative problems, namely the "Tower of Hanoi" problem and the problem of generation of permutations are studied in detail to bring out the feature of recursive programming.
- Another class of problems where recursion is useful involves backtracking. These are problems which are solved by trial and error. One illustrative problem of this class is known as eight queens problem which has been studied to show the use of recursion in solving backtracking problems.
- Recursive programs are usually more time consuming because of the overhead of calling functions repeatedly. Thus, it is instructive to convert a recursive algorithm to non-recursive one. There are a set of rules which may mechanically applied for the conversion. The conversion essentially utilizes a stack for this purpose.
- If the recursion tree is just like a chain or the recursion is tail recursion then the set of rules to convert recursive algorithms to non-recursive can be further simplified.
- Analysis of recursive algorithms boils down to solving recurrence relations.

Exercises

1. The binominal co-efficient C is defined as follows.

$$^{n}C_{m} = \frac{n!}{m!(n-m)!}$$

The same can be recursively defined as given below.

$$^{n}C_{m} = {}^{n-1}C_{m} + {}^{n-1}C_{m-1}$$

$$\text{and } {}^{n}C_{0} = {}^{n}C_{n} = 1.$$

Write a recursive function to compute $^{n}C_{m}$. Analyze the time complexity of your function.

2. Ackermann's function A(m, n) is defined as follows.

   A(m, n) = n+1, if m = 0

   = A(m-1, 1) , if n = 0

   = A(m-1, A(m, n-1)) , otherwise.

   Write a recursive function to compute A(m, n).

3. Let "S" be a set of n elements such that S ={1, 2, 3,...., n}. A power set of "S" is the set of all possible sub-sets of "S". For example, if n = 3, S = {1, 2, 3}. Power set of S = {{ }, {1}, {2}, {3}, {1, 2}, {1,3}, {2, 3}, {1, 2, 3}. Write a recursive function to compute the power set of "S".

4. Write a recursive function to solve the "Josephus" problem as discussed in Chapter 3.

5. Write a recursive function to compute the greatest common divisor of two positive numbers using Euclid's Algorithm. See Chapter 1 for a discussion on the Euclid's algorithm.

6. Write a complete "C" program to solve the eight queen's problem as discussed in this chapter.

7. Let T(n) be defined as follows.

$$T(n) = \begin{cases} k & \text{if } n = 1 \\ aT(n/b) + f(n) & \text{if } n = b^i \end{cases}$$

   Prove that

   (i) If $f(n) = O(n^{\log_b a-\epsilon})$ for some constant $\epsilon > 0$ then $T(n) = O(n^{\log_b a})$.

   (ii) If $f(n) = \theta(n^{\log_b a})$ then $T(n) = \theta(n^{\log_b a}.\log n)$

   (iii) If $af(n/b) \le cf(n)$ for some constant $c < 1$ and $n \ge b$ then $T(n) = \theta(f(n))$.

8. Write a recursive function to compute the largest integer less than $\log_2 n$.

9. Remove recursion from the algorithms developed for Exercises 1, 2, 3, 4 and 5 and then optimize the non-recursive versions.

10. Draw a recursion tree for the algorithm for the n-queens problem where n = 4.

11. Write a non-recursive "C" function for solving the n-queens problem.

12. Remove recursion from the "C" function that prints permutation of "n" integers.

13. Remove recursion from the algorithm "move" without tail recursion so that the non-recursive version does not have a "goto" statement.

Chapter 7

Trees

7.1 Introduction

"Tree" is one of the most important nonlinear data structures in computer algorithms. A tree structure depicts a hierarchical relationship among the nodes of the tree. "Parent-child" relationship is a typical hierarchical relationship. Consider representing parent-child relationship among persons in a family. A hypothetical family tree is shown in Figure 7.1.

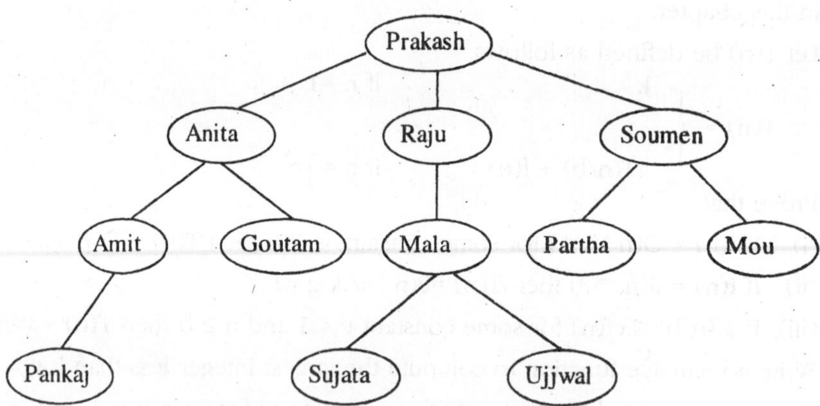

Figure 7.1 A Hypothetical family tree.

In Figure 7.1, each node represents a person whose name is written against that node as its label. Each line connecting two nodes in the figure denotes a relation, namely "parent-child" relation between the connected nodes. If a node "X" is connected to a node "Y" and "X" is above "Y" in the tree then "X" is a parent of "Y" and "Y" is a child of "X". For instance, the node labelled "Prakash" is a parent of nodes labelled "Anita", "Raju" and "Soumen". Similarly, the nodes labelled by "Partha" and "Mou" are children of the node labelled by "Soumen". Often a node is represented or identified by its label and this convention will be used in the remaining part of this book. It is to be noted that the tree originates from a unique node. For example, "Prakash" is the label of the top-most node in the family tree as shown in Figure 7.1. Such a node which does not have any parent is called the "root" node. Also note that the tree can be horizontally divided into several levels. Nodes in the same level may also enjoy a relationship. In this case, the relationship is the "sibling" relationship. For instance, Anita is a sister of Raju and Soumen. Raju and Soumen are brothers of Anita. There may even exist a relationship among nodes which are not directly connected. In Figure 7.1, Mala is a granddaughter of Prakash and Prakash is the grandfather of Mala. So, it should not be assumed that there is no relationship between nodes which are not connected.

Consider another simple example which further illustrates the idea of representing hierarchical relationships by means of trees. Consider simple "reporting to" relationship among employees in an organization. A simplified version of the employee hierarchy in a typical software organization is shown in Figure 7.2.

In Figure 7.2, each node represents a designated person. A line connecting two nodes represents a reporting relationship. From Figure 7.2, it is seen that the node

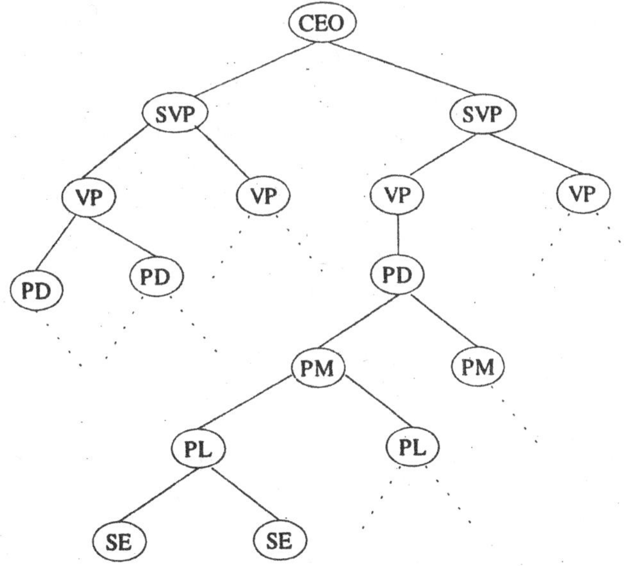

Figure 7.2 Company Tree Structure. The dotted lines represent incomplete subtrees. The following abbreviations are used for the designations labelling the nodes. SVP ≡ Senior Vice-President; PD ≡ Project Director; PM ≡ Project Manager; PL ≡ Project Leader; SE ≡ Software Engineer.

'CEO' is above the node 'SVP' (Senior Vice-President) and these two nodes are connected. This implies that a senior vice-president reports to the CEO. Similarly, a PL (Project Leader) reports to a PM (Project Manager). It should be noted that there is no reporting relationship between nodes in the same level. This tree originates from a unique node, 'CEO' which is the root node of this tree.

7.2 Definition of trees

A tree may be defined as a finite set "T" of one or more nodes such that: (a) there is a specially designated node called the root of the tree, (b) the remaining nodes (excluding the root) are partitioned into $n \geq 0$ disjoint sets $T_1, T_2, \ldots, T_n$ and each of these sets is a tree in turn. The trees $T_1, T_2, \ldots, T_n$ are called the sub-trees (or children) of the root. Note that the definition is recursive as the children of the root of a tree are trees once again.

In Figure 7.1, the root of the family tree is "Prakash". It has three sub-trees or children, rooted at "Anita", "Raju" and "Soumen". As the sub-trees are disjoint sets by definition, the sub-trees rooted at "Anita", "Raju" and "Soumen" in Figure 7.1 are independent and the nodes in these trees are not anyway connected to one another. It can also be said that every node in a tree is the root of some sub-tree. Therefore, Soumen is the root of a sub-tree of Prakash which has two sub-trees Partha and Mou. A node may also have an empty sub-tree as one of its child. For example, Goutam is a root of a tree with no sub-trees. Such nodes which do not have any children are called leaf or terminal nodes.

If a line is drawn from the node "Goutam" to the node "Raju" then both the nodes "Raju" and "Anita" become the parents of "Goutam". That is, more than one node becomes the parent of another node. Moreover, a cycle is formed containing four nodes – Prakash, Anita, Goutam and Raju. This scenario is depicted in Figure 7.3.

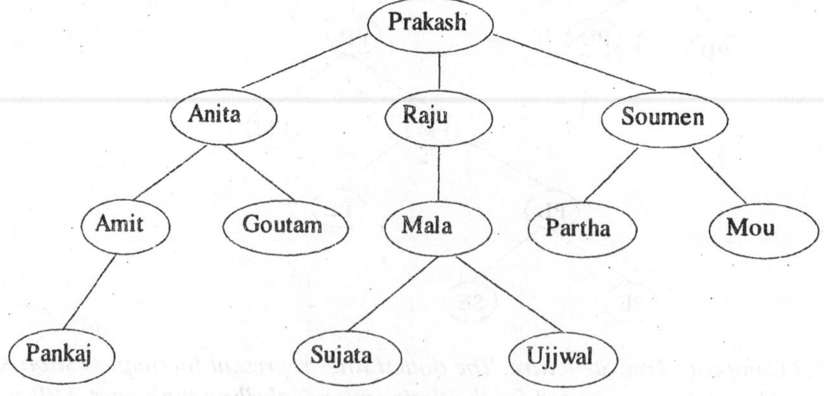

Figure 7.3 The family tree with a cycle.

Obviously, both the sub-trees rooted at "Anita" and "Raju" contain the same node "Goutam" and therefore, these sub-trees are not disjoint. According to the definition of a tree, these sub-trees must be disjoint. So, the diagram in Figure 7.3 does not represent a tree.

Generally, it is a convention to draw the root node at the top and to let the tree grow downwards. This convention is followed while drawing trees in Figures 7.1 and 7.2. However, this is merely a convention and it is not mandatory to follow this convention.

Number of nodes connected by links to a given node "n" is called the degree of the node "n". For example, degree of the node "SVP" in Figure 7.2 is 3 and degree of the node "SE" is 1. Degree of a leaf node or a terminal node is always 1. Some examples of general trees are shown in Figure 7.4.

The level of a node is recursively defined as follows. The level of the root node is defined as 0. The level of any other node is one more than the level of its parent. In Figure 7.4(b), the level of the node "D" is 2 (i.e., one higher then the level of its parent "B" which is 1).

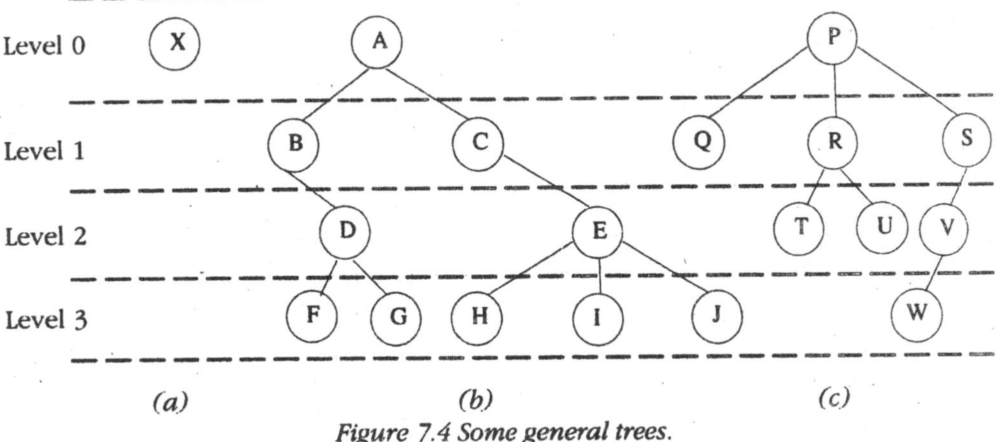

Figure 7.4 Some general trees.

If a node "y" is a child of another node "x" then "x" is said to be the parent of "y". For example, the parent of the node "E" in the tree of Figure 7.4(b) is the node "C". The links between a parent and its children are also referred to as edges or branches. An edge may be defined as a tuple (x, y) which denotes the link between the node "x" and its child "y". A collection of edges connecting one node to another is often termed as a path. For example, the collection of edges {(V, S), (S, P), (P, R), (R, U)} denotes a path from the node "V" to the node "U" in the tree of Figure 7.4(c). All nodes occurring in the path from a given node "n" to the root of a tree are called ancestors of "n".

7.3 Binary Tree

Binary tree is an important class of tree data structure in which a node can have at most two children (which are sub-trees). Moreover, children (or the sub-trees) of a node of a binary tree are ordered. One child is called the "left" child and the other is called the "right" child. An example of a binary tree is shown in Figure 7.5.

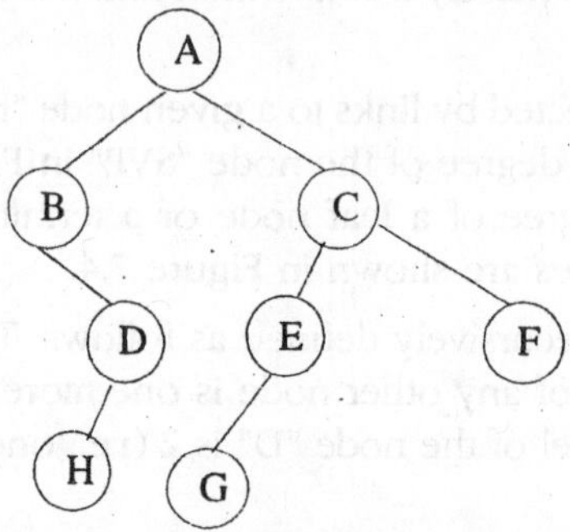

Figure 7.5 A binary tree.

In Figure 7.5, the node "A" (which is the root node) has two children "B" and "C". Similarly, each of the nodes "B", "D" and "E" has only one child "D", "H" and "G" respectively. As every node in a tree is the root of some other sub-tree, "B" and "C" are the roots of the sub-trees of the node "A". In Figure 7.5, the node "E" has a left sub-tree rooted at "G" and the node "B" has a right sub-tree rooted at "D" only. The nodes "H", "G" and "F" have no sub-trees and they are leaf nodes in this tree.

Similar to a tree, a binary tree may also be defined recursively as follows.

i) An empty tree is a binary tree.

ii) A binary tree consists of a node called "root", a left sub-tree and a right sub-tree both of which are binary trees once again.

It should be clear that, by definition, any non-empty binary tree is a tree as well. Examples of some binary trees are shown in Figure 7.6.

Note that, binary trees drawn in Figures 7.6 (ii) and 7.6 (iii) are distinct since the root of the binary tree of Figure 7.6 (ii) has an empty right sub-tree while the root of the binary tree of Figure 7.6 (iii) has an empty left sub-tree. But, the trees of Figures 7.6 (ii) & (iii) are identical, as the ordering of the sub-trees of the root is not significant for trees. Thus, it must be noted that there are fundamental differences between a binary tree and a tree.

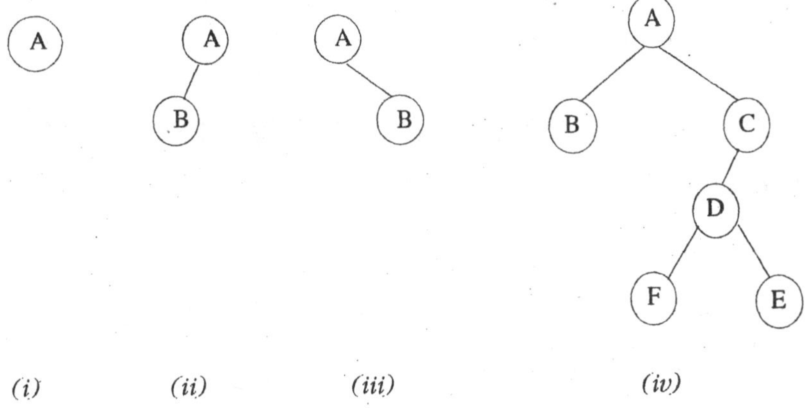

Figure 7.6 Examples of binary trees.

Level of a node in a binary tree is defined in the same way as level is defined for nodes of a general tree. For example, the level of the node "D" of the tree of Figure 7.6(iv), is one higher than the level of node "C" (which is the parent of node "D"). The root node "A" has a level 0. Therefore, the level of "C" is 1 and level of "D" is 2.

Height of a binary tree

The height of a binary tree "T", denoted by height(T), is defined as follows.

height(T) = maximum level of any node of a binary tree "T".

Consider the binary tree of Figure 7.6(iv). The maximum level of any node in this tree is 4. Therefore, height of this tree is 4.

If all non-leaf nodes of a binary tree have exactly two non-empty children and the levels of all leaf nodes of a binary tree are the same then the tree is called a complete or a full binary tree. The tree shown in Figure 7.6(iv) is not a full binary

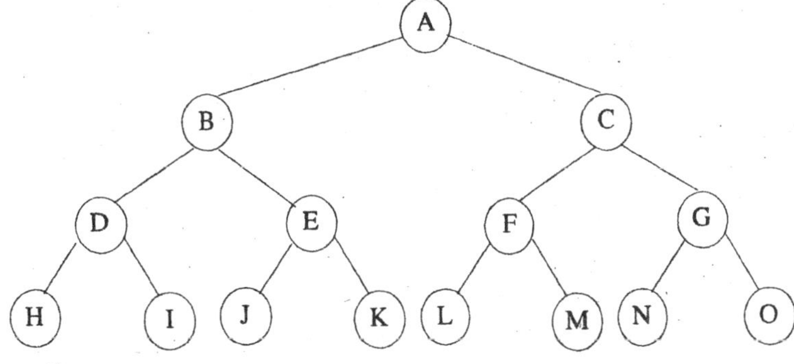

Figure 7.7 A complete binary tree of height 3.

tree as the levels of the leaf nodes "B" and "D" are not the same and there is a node "C" which has only one non-empty child. An example of a full binary tree is shown in Figure 7.7.

7.4 Representation of a Binary Tree using pointers

A non-empty binary tree consists of a root and two children which are binary trees once again. Since the definition of this data structure is recursive, an appropriate representation could be self-referential structures. Each node of the tree is represented by a structure. Each node contains two links to the same structure – "left" and "right" as shown in Figure 7.8 (b). The linked list representation of the tree of Figure 7.8 (a) is shown in Figure 7.8 (c). A straight forward implementation of this representation can be done by using pointers to implement the links. Let "T" be the link to the root node of a tree. If "T" is null, then the tree is empty; otherwise "T" points to the root node of the tree, "left" link points to the left sub-tree of "T" and the right link points to the right sub-tree of "T".

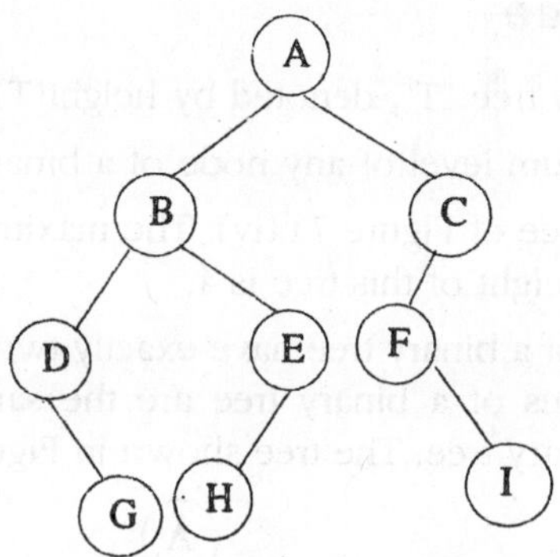

(a) A Sample binary tree

left link	data	right link

(b) Representation of a node in a binary tree.

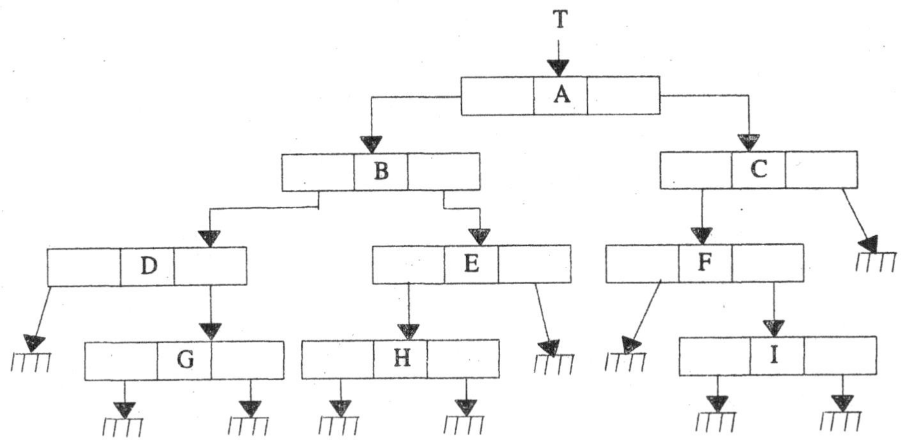

(c) linked list representation of the binary tree of Figure 7.8(a).

Figure 7.8 Pointer representation of a binary tree.

In "C" language, the following structure can be defined to represent one node of a binary tree. It is assumed that the nodes contain just one character as its information.

```
typedef struct bNode {
        char data;
        struct bNode *left;
        struct bNode *right;
} bNode;
```

The following "C" program can be used to construct the binary tree of Figure 7.8(a) using pointers.

```
main( )
{
        bNode  *T;   /* T is the pointer to the root node 'A' */
        bNode *p, *q;
        T = NULL;
        p = (bNode *) malloc(sizeof(bNode));
        p->data = 'A';
        p->left = NULL;
        p->right = NULL;
```

```
T = p; /* T now points to the root node of the tree */
q = T;
p = (bNode *)malloc(sizeof(bNode));
p->data = 'B';
p->left = p->right = NULL;
q->left = p;
q = p;

p = (bNode *)malloc(sizeof(bNode));
p->data = 'D';
p->left = p->right = NULL;
q->left = p;
q = p;

p = (bNode *)malloc(sizeof(bNode));
p->data = 'G';
p->left = p->right = NULL;
q->right = p;
q = T->left; /* q now points to the node 'B' */

p = (bNode *)malloc(sizeof(bNode));
p->data = 'E';
p->left = p->right = NULL;
q->right = p;
q = p;

p = (bNode *)malloc(sizeof(bNode));
p->data = 'H';
p->left = p->right = NULL;
q->left = p;
q = p;
q = T; /* q now points to the root node 'A' */
```

```
p = (bNode *)malloc(sizeof(bNode));
p->data = 'C';
p->left = p->right = NULL;
q->right = p;
q = p;

p = (bNode *)malloc(sizeof(bNode));
p->data = 'F';
p->left = p->right = NULL;
q->left = p;
q = p;

p = (bNode *)malloc(sizeof(bNode));
p->data = 'I';
p->left = p->right = NULL;
q->right = p;
}
```

7.5 Array representation

In Chapter 3, array implementation of linked lists has been discussed in detail. A similar scheme may be used to represent a binary tree using arrays. Consider the binary tree of Figure 7.8(a). Let the "data" fields of the nodes of this tree are stored in an array, "data", in the following way.

data:

A	B	C	D	E	F	G	H	I										

Two more arrays of integers (say, "leftChild" and "rightChild") are required to represent the links of the nodes. If data[i] denotes the data field of a node "n" and leftChild[i] is "j" then data[j] contains data of the left child of "n". Similarly, if rightChild[i] is "k" then data[k] contains the right child of "n". If leftChild[i] (or rightChild[i]) is equal to "-1" then it is implied that the left (or the right) child of "n" is empty. If these conventions are followed then arrays "leftChild" and "rightChild" would look as follows.

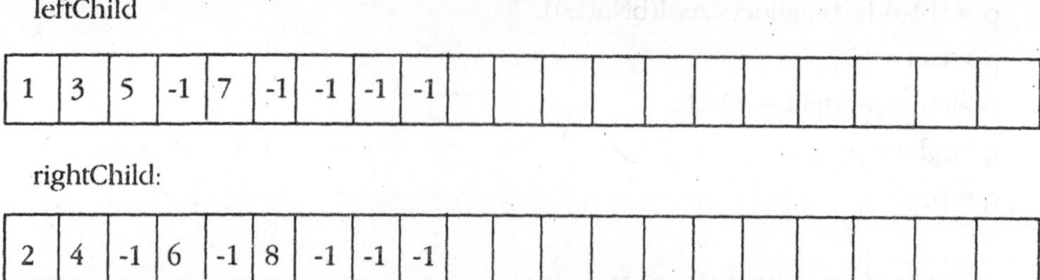

leftChild

1	3	5	-1	7	-1	-1	-1	-1

rightChild:

2	4	-1	6	-1	8	-1	-1	-1

It is known that each node in a binary tree contains three pieces of information: data, link to its left child and link to its right child. In the scheme presented here, these three pieces of information of the i-th node is distributed in the elements of three arrays which are data[i], leftChild[i] and rightChild[i]. For example, data[0] = 'A', leftChild[0] = 1 and rightChild[1] = 2. This signifies that the 0th node contains 'A' as its data; the left child of the 0th node is the node indexed by "1" in these three arrays and the right child of the 0th node is the node indexed by "2" in these three arrays. Assume that, by convention, the root node is always obtained at an index "0" in these arrays.

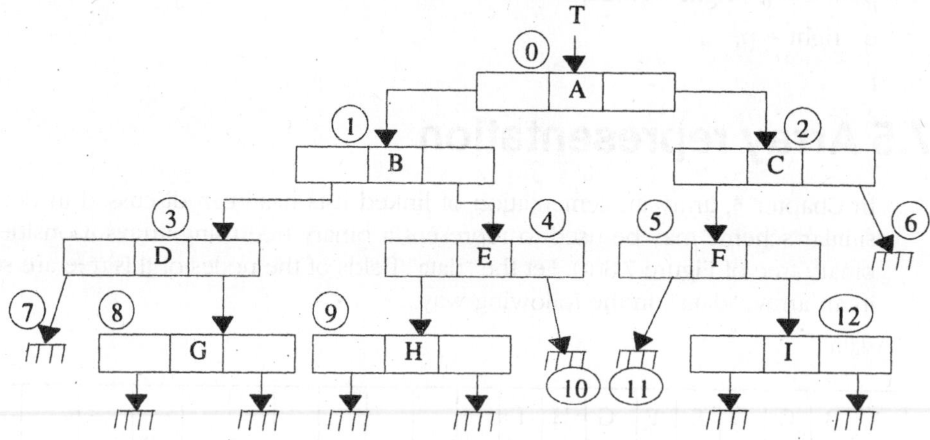

Figure 7.9 Level-wise numbering of the nodes of the tree of Figure 7.8 (a). Some number enclosed in a circle is associated with each and every node of the tree (including NULL or empty nodes).

It is also possible to represent a binary tree using a single array. Consider the same tree of Figure 7.8(a). In order to represent this tree in a single one-dimensional array, the nodes are numbered sequentially level by level. Nodes in the same level are numbered from left to right. The tree of Figure 7.8 (a) is redrawn in Figure 7.9 after labelling every node with a number as mentioned. Note that even the empty nodes are numbered. The numbers are enclosed in circular or elliptical figures. It is interesting to note that if the number appearing against one node "n" is "i" then the numbers appearing against the left and right children of "n" are "2i+1" and "2i+2" respectively. If the nodes of this tree are accommodated in an array, "A", then the numbers appearing against the nodes may act as indices of the nodes in this array. That is, if the number "i" appears against a node "n" then A[i] contains the "data" of the node "n". If the node is "NULL" then its information is assumed to be some unknown constant, (may be '\0') which will not occur as the data. Array representation of the binary tree of Figure 7.9 is shown in Figure 7.10.

A:

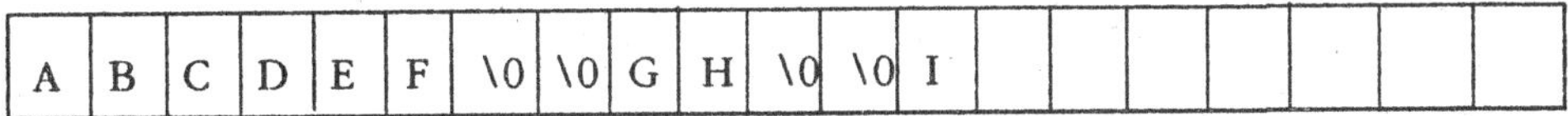

Figure 7.10 Representing the tree of Figure 7.8 (a) using a one-dimensional array.

It is clear from Figure 7.10 that a number of elements of the array will contain just "\0", if the tree is not a complete binary tree. So, such a representation will not always be efficient in terms of space.

7.6 Binary Tree Traversal

Traversal of a binary tree is one of the most important operations required to be done on a binary tree. Many other operations involving binary tree data structure often need to traverse or walk through a given tree. Traversing is a process of visiting every node in the tree exactly once. Therefore, a complete traversal of a binary tree implies visiting the nodes of a tree in some linear sequence. Since a binary tree is defined in a recursive manner, its traversal can necessarily be defined in an identical recursive fashion. For example, to traverse a binary tree, one may first visit the root, then traverse the left sub-tree and finally traverse the right sub-tree. Traversing a binary tree in this manner will produce a particular sequence of visits to the nodes. One may traverse the tree in a different manner (e.g., first traverse the left sub-tree then visit the root and finally traverse the right sub-tree) and a different sequence of visits to the nodes will be produced. It is easy to verify that six such different combinations are possible. If it is conventionally assumed that visiting the left sub-tree always precedes visiting the right sub-tree then only three different combinations remain which are known as Inorder, Preorder and Postorder tree traversal. In the following, these three kinds of traversal techniques are explained along with the necessary algorithms.

7.6.1 Inorder Traversal

If a tree "T", is traversed in an "inorder" fashion then the left sub-tree of "T" is traversed first, then the root node of "T" is visited and then the right sub-tree of "T" is traversed. Quite understandably, the left (as well as the right) sub-tree of "T" could be another binary tree and therefore, traversing the left (or right) sub-tree of "T" is to be carried out in the same fashion as traversing is to be done on "T". In case "T" is empty, then traversal of "T" involves doing nothing. The "C" function for inorder traversal of a tree is as follows. It is assumed that the type of each node in the tree is "bNode" as described earlier . Each node contains a character as its information and it is also assumed that visiting each node involves printing the information associated with that node.

```
void Inorder (bNode *T)
{
        if (T != NULL)
        {
                Inorder (T->left);
                printf ("%c ", T->data);
                Inorder (T->right);
        }
        return;
}
```

If this function is executed on the tree of Figure 7.8(a) then the following output would be produced.

D G B H E A F I C

7.6.2 Preorder Traversal

If a tree, "T", is traversed in "preorder" fashion then the root node of "T" is visited first and then the left sub-tree of "T" is traversed and finally the right sub-tree of "T" is traversed. As before, if T is NULL then traversal of "T" involves doing nothing. Translating these ideas, the following "C" function for Preorder traversal is obtained.

```
void Preorder (bNode *T)
{
        if (T != NULL)
        {
                printf ("%c ", T->data);
                Preorder (T->left);
                Preorder (T->right);
        }
        return;
}
```

If the binary tree of Figure 7.8(a) is traversed in Preorder manner, then the following output would be generated.

A B D G E H C F I

7.6.3 Postorder Traversal

If a tree, "T", is traversed in "postorder" manner, then the left sub-tree of "T" is traversed first, then the right sub-tree of "T" is traversed and finally the root node of "T" is visited. For an empty tree, the traversal implies doing nothing. The "C" function for Postorder traversal of the tree, T, is presented below.

```
void Postorder (bNode *T)
{
        if (T != NULL)
        {
                Postorder (T->left);
                Postorder (T->right);
                printf ("%c ", T->data);
        }
        return;
}
```

The Postorder traversal of the binary tree of Figure 7.8(a) produces the following output.

G D H E B I F C A

7.6.4 Non-recursive Traversal of a binary tree

In the previous chapter, techniques to remove recursion using a stack have been discussed. In this section, this technique will be applied to the recursive traversal algorithms to convert them to equivalent non-recursive ones. Improvements on these non-recursive algorithms will also be attempted and discussed. First, consider transformation of the recursive function "inorder" which is used to traverse a binary tree in an "inorder" manner. The rules discussed in Chapter 6 are applied to the function "Inorder" to obtain the following non-recursive version.

```
void nonRecursiveInorder(bNode * T)
{
    int i;
    bNodeStack s;
    initialize(&s);
    L1: if(T != NULL)
```

```
    {
            pushTree(&s, T);
            pushAddress(&s, 1);
            T = T->left;
            goto L1;
    L2:     printf("%c ", T->data);
            pushTree(&s, T);
            pushAddress(&s, 2);
            T = T->right;
            goto L1;
    }
    L3: if( !isEmpty(s))
    {
            i = popAddress(&s);
            T = popTree(&s);
            if(i ==1)
                    goto L2;
            else
                    goto L3;
    }
}
```

The function "nonRecursiveInorder" assumes definitions of some user-defined types and a few functions implementing a stack. The stack contains either a pointer to a tree or an integer (representing a return address). Further, it is assumed that overflow does not occur and hence error checking due to overflow has not been incorporated.

The type declaration for bNodeStack is as follows.

```
typedef struct bNodeStack
{
   int top;
   treeOrAddress Elements[100];
}bNodeStack;
```

The type of the contents of the stack is either a pointer to a tree or a label as described in the following.

```
typedef union treeOrAddress
{
    bNode * t;
    int label;
}treeOrAddress;
```

The operations to be done on such a stack include initialization, push and pop. These operations are described next.

```
initialize(bNodeStack *s)
{
    s->top = -1;
}

void pushTree(bNodeStack *s, bNode * tree)
{
    s->top += 1;
    (s->Elements[s->top]).t = tree;
}

bNode * popTree(bNodeStack *s)
{
    bNode *x;
    x = (s->Elements[s->top]).t;
    s->top -= 1;
    return x;
}

pushAddress(bNodeStack *s, int x)
{
    s->top += 1;
    (s->Elements[s-> top]).label = x;
}
int popAddress(bNodeStack *s)
{
    int x;
```

```
    x = (s->Elements[s->top]).label;
    s->top -= 1;
    return x;
}
int isEmpty(bNodeStack s)
{
return((s.top == -1)? 1: 0);
}
```

A closer inspection of the recursive function "Inorder" reveals that it is tail recursive. Hence, its tail recursion can be immediately removed and the resultant algorithm is described next.

```
void Inorder1(bNode * T)
{
L1:if (T != NULL)
    {
            Inorder1(T->left);
            printf("%c", T->data);
            T = T->right;
            goto L1;
    }
    return;
}
```

The function "Inorder1" is still recursive. A non-recursive version of the function "Inorder1" is presented next.

```
void nonRecursiveInorder1(bNode * T)
{
    int i;
    bNodeStack s;
    initialize(&s);
    L1:     if (T != NULL)
    {
            pushTree(&s, T);
            pushAddress(&s, 1);
            T = T->left;
            goto L1;
```

```
L2:         printf("%c ", T->data);
            T = T->right;
            goto L1;
    }
    if(!isEmptyStack(s))
    {
            i = popAddress(&s);
            T=popTree(&s);
            if(i == 1)
                    goto L2;
    }
}
```

It is interesting to note that only one label (i.e., '1') is always pushed as an address in the previous function. Therefore, the value of the address being popped out is always "1". Thus, there is no need to push the address into the stack or pop it out. The mesh of goto's can also be easily removed by having two loops one nested in another. Observe that the first part of the algorithm (from the label "L1" upto the start of "L2") can be enclosed in a while-loop. The statement "goto L2" may be avoided by replacing it with the statements starting from the label "L2" and yielding control to the beginning of the while loop just described. The function to traverse a tree in an inorder manner without "goto" statements is described in the following.

```
void nonRecursiveInorder2(bNode * T)
{
    bNodeStack s;
    initialize(&s);
    while(1)
    {
            while(T != NULL)
            {
                    pushTree(&s, T),
                    T = T->left;
            }
            if (isEmpty(s))
                    return;
            T = popTree(&s);
```

```
            printf("%c ", T->data);
            T = T->right;
        }
    }
```

Next, consider the recursive preorder traversal algorithm for a tree as described in the function "Preorder" earlier in the section. This function is also tail recursive. Eliminating tail recursion in a straight forward way, the following algorithm is produced.

```
void nonRecursivePreorder1(bNode * T)
{
L1:if(T !=NULL)
        {
                printf("%c ", T->data);
                nonRecursivePreorder1(T->left);
                T = T->right;
                goto L1;
        }
        return;
}
```

Now, removing recursion from the function "nonRecursivePreorder1" in the standard way, the next non-recursive algorithm can be written.

```
void nonRecursivePreorder2(bNode * T)
{
    bNodeStack s;
    initialize(&s);
    L1: if(T != NULL)
    {
            printf("%c ", T->data);
            pushTree(&T);
            T = T->left;
            goto L1;
    L2:     T = T->right;
            goto L1;
    }
```

```
    if(!isEmpty(s))
    {
            T = popTree(&s);
            goto L2;
    }
}
```

As usual, the algorithm contains a mesh of "goto"s after removal of recursion. In this case also, a closer inspection of this algorithm may enable the reader to eliminate the "goto" statements using "while" loops. The problem of making the algorithm structured is left as an exercise.

In all non-recursive algorithms described in this section, a stack is used. However, it may not be necessary to use the stack if the pointers are properly manipulated. One such interesting case will be discussed in the section of "threaded" binary trees.

Reconstruction of a binary tree from its inorder and preorder traversal

It has already been discussed that postorder traversal of different binary trees may produce the same sequence of nodes. Similarly, inorder or preorder traversal of different binary trees may result in same sequence of nodes. As a result, the original tree can not be reconstructed, given its inorder or preorder or postorder traversal alone. However, if sequences of nodes produced by inorder and preorder traversals of a binary tree are provided then a unique binary tree can be reconstructed. Consider the following example which illustrates the reconstruction of a binary tree given its inorder and preorder traversal.

Let inorder and preorder traversals of a binary tree produce the following sequences of nodes.

Inorder Sequence: D, G, B, H, E, A, F, I, C

Preorder Sequence: A, B, D, G, E, H, C, F, I

Since the first node visited in a preorder traversal of a binary tree is the root, the root of the binary tree becomes 'A'. It is also known that the root node is visited after traversing the left sub-tree in an inorder traversal of a binary tree. Therefore, the nodes to the left of "A" in the given inorder sequence belong to the left sub-tree and the nodes to the right of "A" belong to the right sub-tree of the tree. Moreover, the order in which the nodes to the left of "A" occur in the given inorder sequence is the same as the inorder sequence of the left sub-tree. Let the number of nodes to the left of "A" in inorder sequence by "n". The first "n" nodes beyond "A" in the preorder sequence become the preorder sequence of the left sub-tree. The diagram in Figure 7.11(a) depicts these observations.

Now, the same scheme outlined earlier can be applied to both the left and right sub-trees once again. Consider the left sub-tree of Figure 7.11(a). From the preorder sequence, the root of this sub-tree is "B". The position of "B" in the inorder sequence determines the inorder sequence of the left and the right sub-trees of the sub-tree rooted at "B". The inorder sequence of the left and right sub-trees of the sub-tree rooted at "B" are D, G and H, E respectively. If the preorder sequence is examined with this information, then the preorder sequence of the left and right sub-trees of this sub-tree become D, G, and E, H respectively. Results of further applying these operations produce a tree which is shown in Figure 7.11(b).

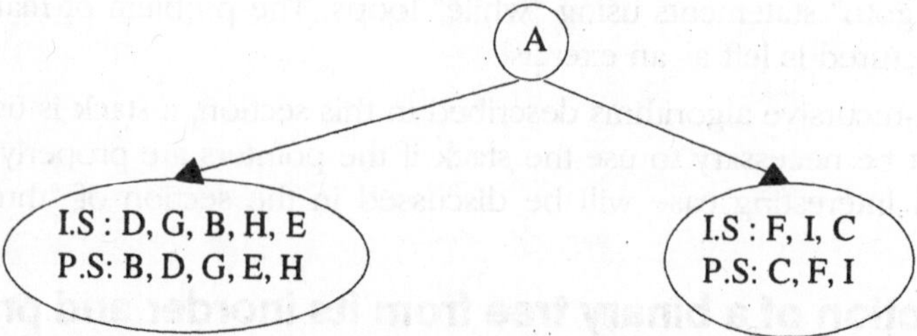

Figure 7.11(a) Illustration of the algorithm to reconstruct a binary tree from its preorder and inorder traversals. In all diagrams of Figures 7.11, "P.S" stands for "Predorder Sequence" and "I.S" stands for "Inorder Sequence"

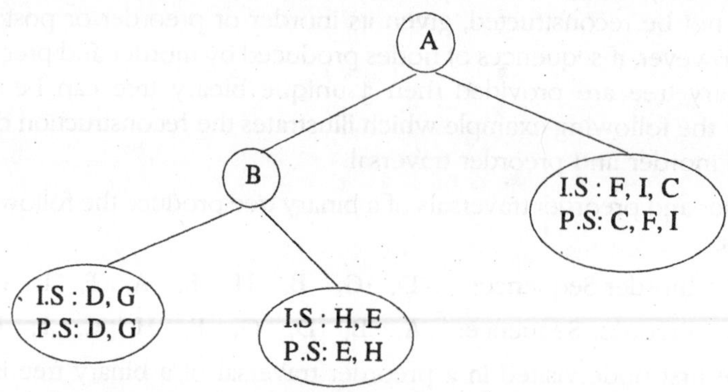

Figure 7.11 (b)

Continuing the same set of operations in each sub-tree, the tree can be constructed. The diagrams in Figures 7.11(c) – 7.11(e) further illustrate the process of reconstruction of the binary tree. Readers are encouraged to trace the next few steps to appreciate the process of complete reconstruction of a binary tree from its inorder and preorder traversal. It is also important to understand that a similar method of reconstruction can be formalized if the iinorder and the postorder traversals of a binary tree is provided. However, a binary tree can not be uniquely reconstructed if its preorder and postorder traversals are provided.

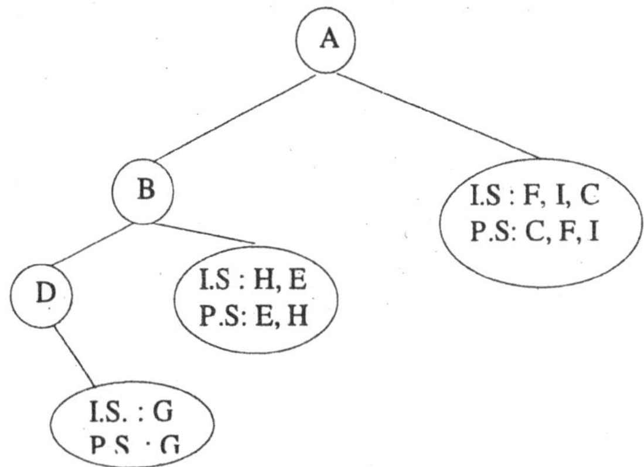

Figure 7.11 (c)

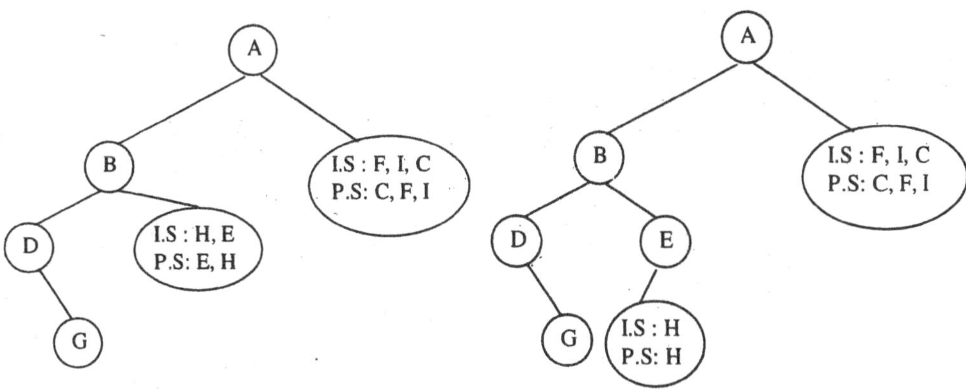

Figure 7.11 (d) *Figure 7.11 (e)*

The reconstruction method which has been discussed in this section to construct a binary tree given its inorder and preorder traversals immediately leads us to the following algorithm, "Reconstruct".

```
bNode *Reconstruct (char inorder[ ], char preorder [ ], int noOfNodes)
{
    bNode *left, *right;
    char tmpInorder [100]; char tmpPreorder [100];
```

```
    if(noOfNodes == 0)
            return NULL;
    Create a node, "Node", of type bNode;
    Node->data = preorder[0];
    Node->left  = NULL;
    Node->right = NULL;
    if(noOfNodes == 1)
            return Node;
    find the index "i" in "inorder" so that inorder[i] = preorder[0];
    if (i > 0) {
            copy the first i elements of "inorder" to "tmpInOrder";
            copy the first i elements "preorder" from index "1"
            to "tmpPreOrder";
    }
    left = Reconstruct (tmpInOrder, tmpPreorder, i);
    Node->left = left;
    if (i < noOfNodes - 1) {
            copy the nodes from index "i+1" to "noOfNodes-1" of "inorder"
            to tmpInorder;
            copy (noOfNodes - i - 1) nodes from index (i+1) to "noOfNodes–1" of
            "preorder" to indices "0" to "noOfNodes-i–1" of "tmpPreorder";
    }
    right = Reconstruct (tmpInOrder, tmpPreorder, noOfNodes-i-1);
    Node->right = right;
    return Node;
}
```

7.7 Some properties of a binary tree

There are a vast number of properties available in the literature regarding trees in general and binary trees in particular. Only a few of them are being considered in this section because they are relevant for different algorithms concerning binary tree data structure.

Property 1. A tree with "n" nodes has exactly (n-1) edges or branches.

This property can be proved by induction on the number of nodes in a tree. If n = 0 then the tree contains only one node and the number of edges or branches is 0. Therefore, the induction base is proved.

Consider any tree with "n" nodes. It must have a root and the root must have "k" children (k > 0). Let n_i denote the number of nodes in the i-th child for i = 0 to (k-1). Naturally, $n = 1 + \Sigma_{i=0,k-1}(n_i)$. Each child is itself a tree with fewer than "n" nodes. Hence, the induction hypothesis can be assumed to be valid for these trees. Therefore, the number of branches in the i-th child of the root is (n_i-1). Total number of branches in all the children of the root is $\Sigma_{i=0,k-1}(n_i-1)$. The original tree contains another "k" branches from the root to its "k" children. The total number of branches in the tree is,

$$\Sigma_{i=0,k-1}(n_i-1) + k$$

i.e., $\Sigma_{i=0,k-1}(n_i) - k + k$

i.e., $n - 1$

Thus, the said property is proved for any tree.

Property 2. In a tree, every node except the root has exactly one parent (and the root node does not have a parent).

This is a direct consequence of the earlier property and the proof is left as an exercise. The next property is stated without any proof. It will be taken up once again in Chapter 10 in the context of graphs and trees.

Property 3. There is exactly one path connecting any two nodes in a tree.

Note that the above properties are valid for any general tree. The next few properties that are going to be discussed pertain only to binary trees. As mentioned, these properties are helpful in understanding performance characteristics of some algorithms to be discussed later in this book.

Property 4. The maximum number of nodes in a binary tree of height "k" is $2^{k+1}-1$, where $k \geq 0$.

The proof is by induction on the height of the tree. When the height of the tree is zero (i.e., k = 0) then the tree contains only the root node. Thus, the property is valid when k = 0 and the induction base is proved.

Consider a tree with height k = m. The root node of the tree can have at most two children each of which is a binary tree of height less than "m". Hence, by induction hypothesis, the maximum number of nodes in each of these sub-trees can be $2^{m-1+1}-1 = 2^m-1$. The total number of nodes of the original binary tree, therefore, can not be more than $2(2^m-1)+1 = 2^{m+1}-1$. Thus, the property is proved for any binary tree.

From the above property, it can also be said that the minimum height of a binary tree with "n" nodes is $\log_2(n+1)-1$.

Property 5. Consider a non-empty binary tree with "n" nodes. Let n_i be the number of nodes with "i" children for i = 0, 1, 2. Then the following equation is valid.

$$n_2 = n_0 - 1$$

Clearly, $n = n_0 + n_1 + n_2$. The number of branches of the binary tree is (n-1) (according to Property 1). The branches emerge either from nodes with one child or from nodes with two children. In this manner, it can be seen that the total number of branches are $n_1 + 2n_2$. It follows that,

$$n-1 = n_1 + 2n_2$$

Substituting "n" by $(n_0 + n_1 + n_2)$ in the previous equation the following equation results.

$$n_0 + n_1 + n_2 - 1 = n_1 + 2n_2$$

Simple rearrangement of the terms yields the result.

Sometimes, particularly in case of search trees, it is convenient to introduce special nodes so that every node of the original tree has exactly two children. The special nodes become children of nodes with one or no child. Redrawing the tree of Figure 7.8(a) after introducing these special nodes, the tree looks like the one drawn in Figure 7.12.

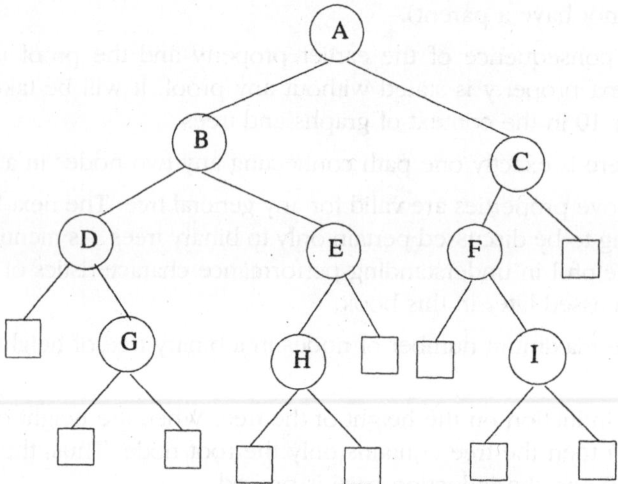

Figure 7.12 A sample binary tree after introducing special "external" nodes as shown by boxes. Every node in such a tree has either zero or two children.

The special nodes are denoted by squares in the diagram of Figure 7.12. In this case, it is important to distinguish between the original nodes of the tree and the special nodes which are added to the original tree. The original nodes of the tree are referred to as internal nodes and the special nodes are called external nodes. It may be easily verified that the external nodes are always leaf nodes and the internal nodes are always non-leaf nodes.

Property 6. A binary tree with "n" internal nodes has (n+1) external nodes.

This property can be proved by induction on the number of internal nodes of a binary tree. A binary tree with no internal node has exactly one external node. So, the property holds for n = 0 and the induction base is proved. Assume a binary tree with "m" internal nodes. Let the left sub-tree of the root contains "k" internal nodes. Then, the right sub-tree has to contain "m-k-1" internal nodes. By induction hypothesis, the said property holds for the left and the right binary trees. Therefore, the numbers of external nodes of the left and right sub-trees are (k+1) and (m-k-1+1), i.e., (m-k) respectively. Thus, the total number of external nodes of the entire binary tree becomes "k+1+m-k" = m+1. Thus, the property is proved.

Before discussing the next property, one more new terminology needs to be introduced. Define "internal path length" of a tree as the sum of the levels of all the internal nodes in a binary tree. Equivalently, internal path length can also be defined as the sum of the lengths of the paths from each node to the root. For the tree in Figure 7.12, the internal path length can be computed as

$$2*1 + 3*2 + 3*3 = 17$$

Analogously, external path length of a tree can be defined as the sum of the levels of all the external nodes of the binary tree. Therefore, the external path length of the tree of Figure 7.12 is given by

$$1*2 + 3*3 = 6*4 = 35$$

Property 7. If "E" and "I" denote the external and internal path lengths of a binary tree having "n" internal nodes then the following identity holds.

$$E = I + 2n$$

This property can also be proved by using induction on the number of internal nodes of a binary tree. If n = 1, the tree contains only one internal node which is the root node of the tree. Consequently, it has two external nodes as the left and the right sub-tree. Therefore, in this tree, I = 0, E = 2 and n = 1. Thus, the identity holds and the induction base is proved.

Consider a larger tree having "m" internal nodes in which "v" is an internal node so that both children of "v" are external nodes. Let the level of "v" be "k". Let "E" and "I" be the external and internal path lengths of the tree. Now, eliminate "v" from this tree.

The reduced tree contains (m-1) internal nodes and therefore the induction hypothesis may be assumed to be true in this reduced tree. Let E′ and I′ be the external and the internal path lengths of the reduced tree. By induction hypothesis, it can be said that

$$E' = I' + 2(m-1) \qquad .....(1)$$

Quite obviously, $I' = I - k$

The level of two external nodes, which were children of "v" in the original tree, is (k+1). These two external nodes are no longer present in the reduced tree. Therefore, the external path length of the reduced tree decreases by 2(k+1). But, since "v" is eliminated, a new external node is introduced whose level is "k". Thus,

$$E' = E - 2(k+1) + k$$

Substituting E′ and I′ in equation (1), the following equation is obtained.

$$E - 2(k+1) + k = I - k + 2(m-1)$$

i.e., $E - 2k - 2 + k = I - k + 2m - 2$

i.e., $E - 2 = I + 2m - 2$

i.e., $E = I + 2m$

Therefore, the property is proved for any binary tree.

One more interesting property regarding the height, external path length and the number of leaf nodes of a tree is explored in the exercise.

7.7.1 Counting binary trees

Consider a combinatorial problem of counting the number of distinct binary trees with "n" number of nodes. For example, if "n" is 1 then there could be only one binary tree as shown in Figure 7.13 (a). If "n" is 2 then there are two distinct binary trees as shown in Figures 7.13 (b) and (c).

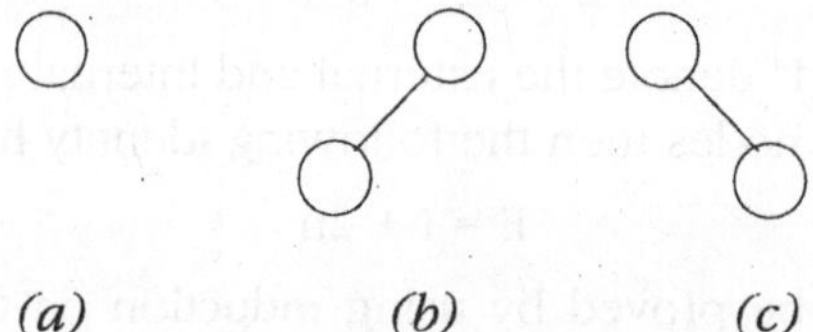

Figure 7.13 Distinct binary trees with one or two nodes.

Suppose, "n" is 3. There are five distinct binary trees which are shown in Figures 7.14 (a) to 7.14 (e).

Observe that, the information fields of the nodes are not considered as that is not relevant when structurally different binary trees are of primary concern. That is why, labels of all nodes of all trees of Figures 7.13 and 7.14 are kept empty. It is interesting to note that there is a one to one correspondence between the set of distinct binary trees with "n" nodes and the set of well formed strings of "n" left and "n" right parentheses. The idea of well formed strings consisting of "n" left and "n" right parentheses has already been discussed in the context of stacks in Chapter 4. Recall that any string of left and right parentheses is said to be well formed if the string possesses two characteristics. First, the number of right parentheses must not exceed the number of left parentheses as one scans the string from left to right.

Secondly, the number of right parentheses in the string must be equal to the number of left parentheses in the entire string.

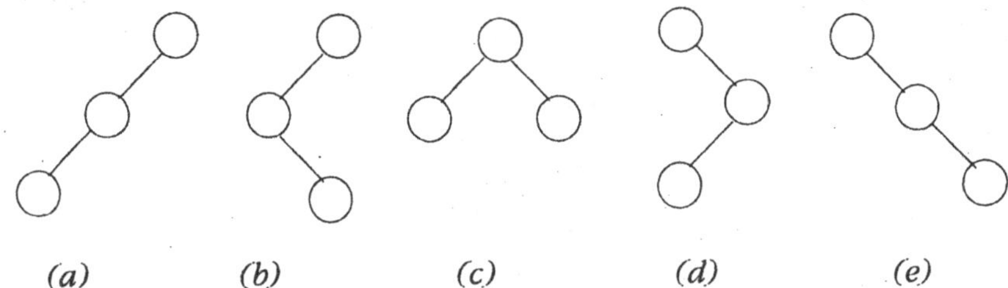

(a) (b) (c) (d) (e)

Figure 7.14 Distinct binary trees with three nodes.

To see the correspondence between the set of distinct binary trees with "n" nodes and the set of well formed strings of "n" left and "n" right parentheses, note that, a binary tree with just one node can be represented by the expression "()". Suppose that a binary tree, "T", consists of a root, a left child, "L", and a right child "R". Let the well formed strings of parentheses representing "L" and "R" are $L_{()}$ and $R_{()}$ respectively. If "L" or "R" is empty then $L_{()}$ or $R_{()}$ would also be empty. Then, the well formed string representing "T" is given by $T_{()}$ = $(L_{()})R_{()}$. As, $L_{()}$ or $R_{()}$ is well formed, T() is also well formed. The well formed expressions for the trees of Figures 7.14 (a) to (e) are given sequentially in the following.

((( ))), (( )( )) (( ))( ) ( )(( )) ( )( )( )

It is also possible to construct a binary tree given any well formed string of left and right parentheses. Suppose, the well formed string is denoted by "s". Let "s" be divided into "k" adjacent sub-strings s_1, s_2, .., s_k which are also well formed. Let u_1, u_2, .., u_k be the expressions obtained by eliminating the leftmost and the rightmost parentheses of s_1, s_2, .., s_k respectively. Then, the corresponding binary tree contains a root with a left sub-tree, which is represented by u_1 and a right sub-tree r_1. The right sub-tree of the root has a left sub-tree represented by u_2 and a right sub-tree r_2 and so on. If "k" is equal to "1" then "s" represents a tree with a root and a left sub-tree. The string representing the left sub-tree is s′ where s′ is obtained by eliminating the leftmost and the rightmost parentheses of "s". Thus, the correspondence be-ween the set of distinct binary trees having "n" nodes and the set of well formed strings of "n" left and "n" right parentheses is established. Hence, the number of distinct binary trees having "n" nodes is equal to the number of well formed strings of "n" left and "n" right parentheses.

Total number of strings containing "n" left and "n" right parentheses is the same as selecting "n" positions from possible 2n positions. This number is ${}^{2n}C_n$. From this number, the number of not well formed strings is to be excluded. One more interesting point to note is that the number of not well formed strings of "n" left and "n" right parentheses is the same as the total number of strings of (n-1) left and (n+1) right parentheses. The total number of strings of (n-1) left and (n+1) right parentheses is ${}^{2n}C_{n-1}$. Thus, the total number of well formed strings of "n" parentheses is

$$ {}^{2n}C_{n} - {}^{2n}C_{n-1} $$

To complete the proof, one has to show that the number of not well formed strings of "n" left and "n" right parentheses is the same as the total number of strings of (n -1) left and (n +1) right parentheses. This can be proved by showing that any not well formed string containing "n" left and "n" right parentheses can be converted to a string of (n-1) left and (n +1) right parentheses and vice-versa. Take a string of "n" left and "n" right parentheses which is not well formed. Scan it from left to right and stop at the k-th element of the string where the number of right parentheses encountered so far outnumbers the number of left parentheses. In the remaining part of the string, replace left parentheses by right parentheses and right parentheses by left parentheses. The resultant string contains (n-1) left parentheses and (n+1) right parentheses.

The procedure to convert a string of (n-1) left and (n +1) right parentheses to a not well formed string of "n" left and "n" right parentheses is similar. Scan the given string to find out a position "k" where the number of right parentheses encountered so far outnumbers the number of left parentheses. In the remaining part of the given string exchange left for right parentheses and right for left parentheses. The resultant string contains "n" left and "n" right parentheses and the string is not well formed.

7.8 Threaded binary tree

When a binary tree is represented using pointers then pointers to empty sub-trees are set to null. That is, the "left" pointer of a node whose left child is an empty sub-tree is normally set to NULL. Similarly, the "right" pointer of a node whose right child is an empty sub-tree is also set to NULL . Thus, a large number of pointers are set to NULL. These null pointers could be used in a different and more effective way. Assume that the "left" pointer of a node "n" is set to NULL as the left child of "n" is an empty sub-tree. Then, the "left" pointer of "n" can be set to point to the inorder predecessor of "n". Similarly, if the "right" child of a node "m" is empty then the "right" pointer of "m" can be set to point to the inorder successor of "m". In the tree of Figure 7.15, links with arrow heads indicate links leading to inorder predecessors or inorder successors while other lines denote the usual links in a binary tree. Note that the links with arrows and the normal links indicate different relationship between nodes and the links are no longer used to describe only "parent-child" relationship. Consequently, it must be understood whether the "left" or "right" link of a node "n" is leading to its children or to the inorder predecessor of "n" or to the inorder successor of "n". Two flags, "leftFlag" and "rightFlag" are to used per node to indicate the type of its "left" and "right" links. If "leftFlag" of a node is 0 then its "left" link leads to the left sub-tree of "n"; otherwise, the "left" link leads to the inorder predecessor of "n". Similarly, if "rightFlag" of a node "n" is 0 then the "right" link leads to the right sub-tree of "n"; otherwise, the "right" link leads to the in-order successor of "n". The "left" and "right" links leading to inorder predecessors or successors are called threads to distinguish them from the conventional links of a binary tree. The links are used as threads only when they would have pointed to empty sub-trees in a non-threaded binary tree.

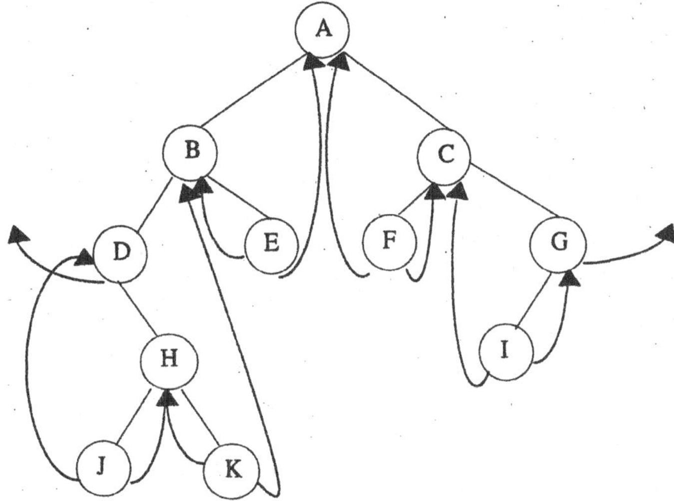

Figure 7.15 A threaded binary tree. Lines with arrows represent threads.

Every node in a threaded binary tree must contain the flags, as discussed, to indicate whether its "left" and "right" pointers are threads. Hence, the structure of a node in such trees contains two more fields in addition to the three fields: "data", "left" and "right" as shown in the following.

Left	Left Flag	Data	Right Flag	Right

The type declaration for a threaded binary tree in "C" language may be done in the following way.

```
typedef struct bThreadNode
{
```

```
    int rightFlag, leftFlag;
    char data;
    struct bThreadNode * left, * right;
} bThreadNode;
```

Consider the tree of Figure 7.15. The lines with arrows denote threads. In a non-threaded binary tree replace these lines with arrows with links to NULL. The inorder traversal sequence of the nodes of this tree is:

D, J, H, K, B, E, A, F, C, I, G

For instance, take the node "J" in the tree of Figure 7.15. Since the node "J" does not have a child, the "left and "right" pointers of this node are used as threads. The left thread is used to point to the node "D" which is the inorder predecessor of the node "J". And the right thread is used to point to the node "H" which is the inorder successor of the node "J". Consider the nodes "D" and "G" in this tree. The left and right links of these nodes are kept dangling because the node "D" does not have any inorder predecessor and the node "G" does not have any inorder successor. These pointers may be set to NULL. Another approach to get rid of such problems is to introduce a header node in a threaded binary tree as shown in the following diagram. The left and right pointers of the header node are treated as normal links (not threads) and are initialized to point to the header node itself.

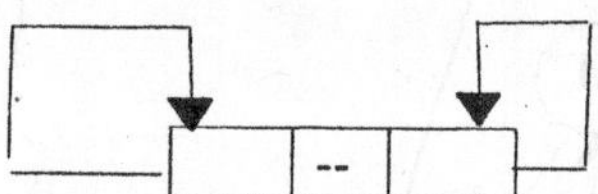

The actual tree is set to be the left child of the header node. The "left" pointer of the first node and the "right" pointer of the last node in inorder sequence are set to the header node. The pointer representation of the tree of Figure 7.15 is shown in Figure 7.16.

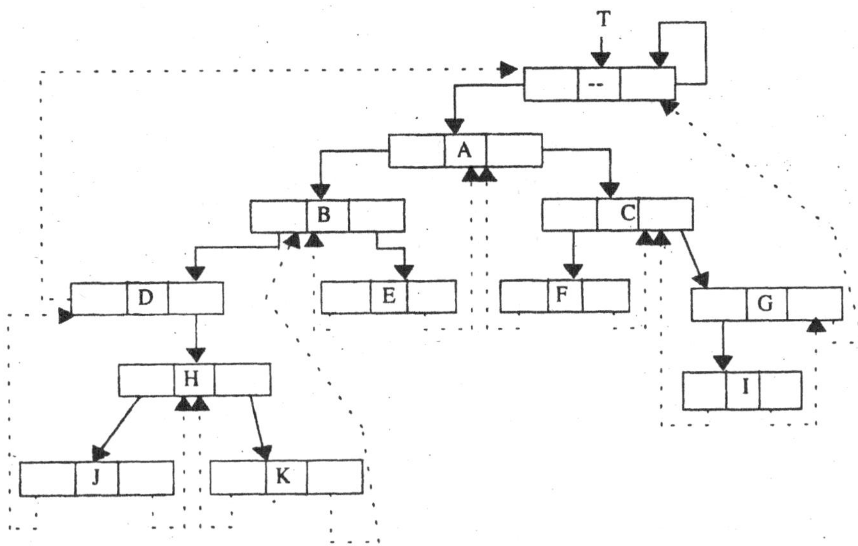

Figure 7.16 Pointer representation of a threaded binary tree including the header.

In the ensuing discussions, however, it will be assumed that the idea of the header node is not used. In stead, the left and right threads of the first and the last node in the inorder sequence are set to NULL.

It is interesting to find out how threads of all nodes can be initialized for any given unthreaded binary tree. It is also important to understand algorithms to insert a new node to a threaded binary tree or to delete a node from a threaded binary tree. Before these algorithms are described, advantages of a threaded binary tree are discussed. Observe that it becomes very easy to find out inorder successor of any node, "n", in a threaded binary tree. If the "rightFlag" of "n" is "1" then the node pointed to by its "right" pointer is the desired inorder successor. If the "rightFlag" of "n" is "0" then its inorder successor must be on the right sub-tree of "n". So, first go to the right child of "n". The first node in the inorder sequence of this sub-tree is the inorder successor of "n". The first node of the inorder sequence of any binary tree can be reached by traversing the left sub-tree from the root as long as the left sub-tree is non-empty. This leads to the following algorithm.

```
bThreadNode * inorderSuccessor(bThreadNode * n)
{
    if(n->rightFlag == 1)
            return (n->right);
    n = n->right;
    while(n->leftFlag == 0)
```

```
            n = n->left;
    return n;
}
```

A non-recursive algorithm for traversing a threaded binary tree in an inorder manner is very simple. For traversing any sub-tree rooted at "p", proceed towards left as far as possible following the "left" pointer. The last node "n" in this sequence is the first node to be visited for the tree rooted at "p". Next sub-tree to be traversed in the right child of "n" is its inorder successor "k". The algorithm just discussed to find the inorder successor of a node in a threaded binary tree can be used here to obtain "k". This step can be repeated as long as the right pointer of the node is not a thread pointng to NULL. The "C" function is presented next.

```
void inorderThreadedTree(bThreadNode * root)
{
    bThreadNode * x;
    x = root;
    while(x->leftFlag == 0)
            x = x->left;
    while(x !=NULL)
    {
            printf("%c ", x->data);
            /* The remaining part of the body of the while loop is */
            /* identical to the function "inorderSuccessor" */
            if(x->rightFlag == 1)
                    x = x->right;
            else
            {
                    x = x->right;
                    while(x->leftFlag == 0)
                            x = x->left;
            }
    }
}
```

Consider preorder traversal of a threaded binary tree. The root of the tree is visited. If there is a left child then the child is visited; otherwise, the right child is visited. This process continues until a leaf node is encountered. If the node is a leaf then we need to go back to the first node whose right sub-tree has not been traversed. This can be done by traversing through parents of the leaf node until a node is reached which has a non-empty right sub-tree. It is amazing to note that such a node may be found by merely following the in-order successors of the leaf node. This is so because, if the inorder successor of a node "n" which does not have a right child is the node "k" then "k" must have been visited before "n" in preorder. Once again, if "t" is an inorder successor of "k" and "k" does not have a right child then "t" must have been visited before "k"(i.e. also before "n") in preorder. This reasoning can be continued until the computed inorder successor has a non-empty right sub-tree. Once an inorder successor is found which does have a right child, the right sub-tree of that node has to be visited in a preorder manner. This leads us to the following "C" function.

```
void preorderThreadedTree(bThreadNode * root)
{
   bThreadNode * x;
   x = root;
   while(x !=NULL)
   {
          printf("%c", x->data);
          if(x->leftFlag == 0)
                 x = x->left;
          else if(x->rightFlag == 0)
                 x = x->right;
          else
          {
                 while(x && (x->rightFlag == 1))
                        x = x->right;
                 if (x) x = x -> right;
          }
   }
}
```

To conclude this section, it must be mentioned that traversing a threaded binary tree non-recursively in postorder fashion is also possible. However, this is more involved and explored in the exercises.

7.8.1 Insertion into a threaded binary tree

Suppose that a new node, "t", is to be inserted as the right of a node, "s", in a threaded binary tree. "s" may or may not have non-empty right sub-tree before inserting "t" as the right child of "s". This gives rise to two cases which are discussed in the following.

Case 1: "s" does not have a non-empty right sub-tree as shown in Figure 7.17

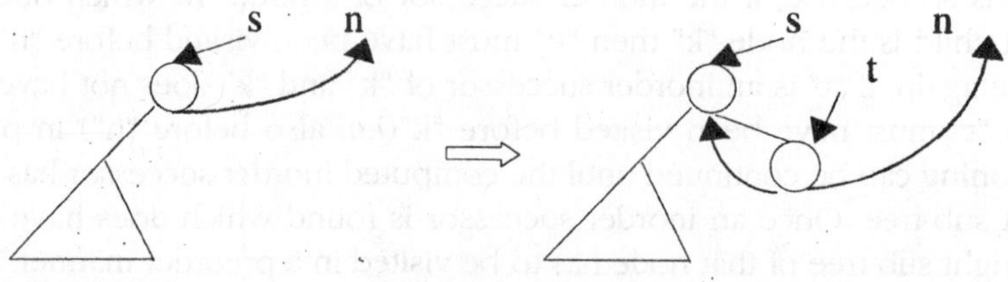

(a) Before insertion *(b) After insertion*

Figure 7.17 Illustration for insertion of a node (pointed to by "t") as the right child of a node pointed to by "s" where the right pointer of "s" is a thread before insertion. All threads are denoted by dotted arrows.

The "right" link of "s" is a thread pointing to "n" before "t" is inserted to the right of "s". After insertion, "s" becomes the inorder predecessor of "t" as both the right and left sub-trees of "t" are empty. Also, "n" becomes the inorder successor of "t".

Case 2: "s" has a non-empty right sub-tree.

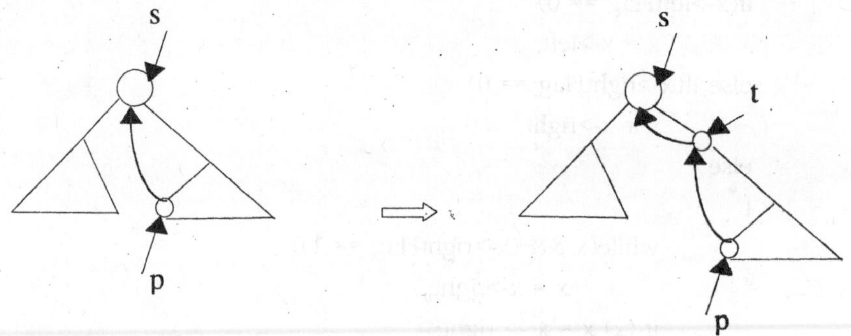

(a) Before insertion *(b) After insertion*

Figure 7.18 Illustration for insertion of a node (pointed to by "t") as the right child of a node pointed to by "s". Before insertion, "s" has a right child and "p" is the inorder successor of "s".

Then there must be a node, "p", which is the inorder successor of "s". and "p" lies on the right sub-tree of "s". The "left" link of "p" must be a thread pointing to "s" as "s" is the inorder predecessor of "p". If "t" is made a right child of "s" then the right sub-tree T of "s" must be made a right sub-tree of "t". Left sub-tree of "t" will be empty and must be made a thread pointing to "s", the inorder predecessor of "t". The inorder successor of "t" is "p". So, the "left" link of "p" has to be set to point to "t".

The "C" function for the above procedure is described in the following.

```
void insertRighThreadedTree(bThreadTree * s, bThreadTree * t)
{
    bThreadTree * x;
    t->right = s->right;
    s->right = t;
    t->rightFlag = s->rightFlag;
    t->leftFlag = 1; /* thread */
    t->left = s;
    if(t->rightFlag == 0)
    {
            x = inorderSuccessor(t);
            x->left = t;
    }
}
```

A node can similarly be inserted as a left child of a node in a threaded binary tree.

7.9 Binary Search Tree

Binary search trees form an important sub-class of binary trees. In an ordinary tree, the elements are not ordered in any way. However, data are ordered in many applications. Information in the nodes in a binary search tree is maintained in some order. Usually, the nodes in a binary search tree represent some records and these records are ordered. Records are ordered on some key properties. Therefore, the information part of a node in a binary search tree is assumed to have some key attributes. For the purpose of studying binary search trees one may just concentrate on these keys. Thus, the information field of nodes in a binary tree will be referred to as just keys.

A binary search tree is a binary tree which is either empty or in which the following criteria are satisfied.

1. All keys of the left sub-tree of the root are "less than" the key in the root.
2. All keys of the right sub-tree of the root are "greater than" the key in the root.
3. The left and right sub-trees of a binary search tree are binary search trees once again.

The definition is recursive. An example of a binary search tree is given in Figure 7.19 (a).

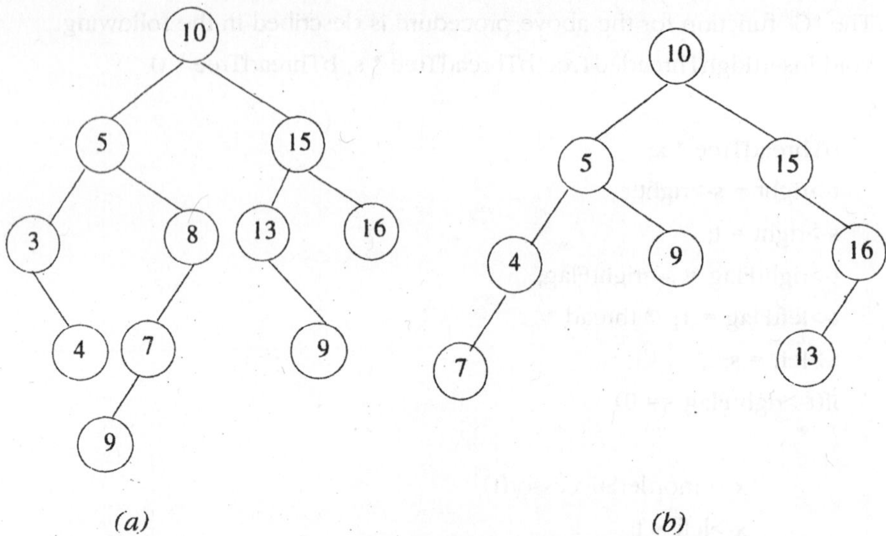

Figure 7.19 Examples of binary search trees. The tree in Figure (a) is a binary search tree while the tree in Figure (b) is not so.

However, the tree shown in Figure 7.19(b) is not a binary search tree because the sub-tree of this tree rooted at the node with key = 15 is not a binary search tree. In that sub-tree, the key at the root (i.e. 15) is not less than 13 which is the key value of a node in its right sub-tree violating the second condition of the definition of a binary search tree. Since the right sub-tree is not a binary search tree, the tree rooted at "10" is also not so according to the third condition of the definition. It must also be borne in mind that there may be different binary search trees for a given set of key values. For example, all the trees shown in Figure 7.14 (a) to (d) are binary search trees for the set of key values S = {1, 2, 3, 4, 5}.

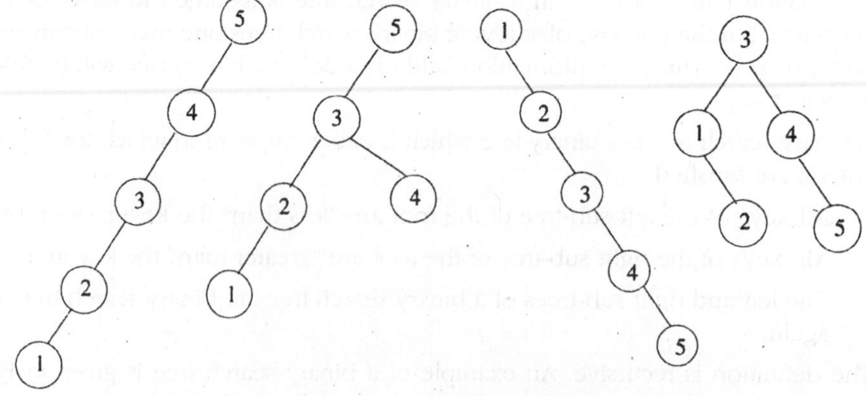

Figure 7.20 Different binary search trees for the set of key values {1, 2, 3, 4, 5}

It must be emphasized that no two nodes in a binary search tree can hold equal key values. The operations defined on a binary search tree are typically based on this property. The basic operations on a binary search tree are search, insertion and deletion. In the next sub-sections, algorithms for these operations are discussed.

7.9.1 Search in a Binary Search Tree

Searching for a key in a binary search tree can be easily defined recursively. The key is compared with the key at the root. If they are equal then "search" terminates successfully. If the given key is less than the key at the root then search is initiated only at the left sub-tree of the current root. Otherwise, the right sub-tree of the current root is to be searched. The "search" process terminates unsuccessfully when "search" is done on an empty tree. Before describing the recursive function for search, it is required to define the data type for a node in a binary tree. It is assumed that the information field in each node of the tree is an integer.

```
typedef struct bIntNode
{
    int data;
    struct bIntNode *left;
    struct bIntNode *right;
} bIntNode;


int search(bIntNode *root, int k)
{
    if(root == NULL)
            return 0;
    if(root->data == k)
            return 1;

    if(k < root->data)
            return(search(root->left, k));
    else
            return(search(root->right, k));
}
```

The function "search" returns "1", if the key "k" is found in the tree; otherwise, the function returns "0". As this function is tail recursive, it is easy to convert this function to an iterative one. The iterative equivalent of "search" function is described in the following.

```
int iterativeSearch(bIntNode * root, int k)
{
L1:if (root == NULL)
        return 0;
    else if (k == root->data)
        return 1;
    else if (k > root->data)
    {
        root = root->right;
        goto L1;
    }
    else
    {
        root = root->left;
        goto L1;
    }
}
```

The "goto" statements can be easily replaced by a while loop as shown in the following function.

```
int iterativeSearch1(bIntNode * root, int k)
{
    while((root != NULL) &&(k != root->data))
    {
        if(k < root->data)
            root = root->left;
        else
            root = root->right;
    }
    if(root == NULL)
        return 0;
    else
        return 1;
}
```

7.9.2 Insertion into a Binary Search Tree

While inserting a key into a binary search tree, the conditions mentioned in the definition of a binary search tree must be preserved, so that the tree remains a binary search tree even after insertion. Insertion of a node with key "k" in a binary search tree "T" can be defined recursively as follows. If the tree is non-empty then "k" is compared with the key of the root of "T". If the key is less than that of the root then the key is to be inserted into the left sub-tree; otherwise the key is to be inserted into the right sub-tree. If the left (or right) sub-tree is empty then the new node with key "k" is set to be the left (or right) child of the current node.

```
void insertTree(bIntNode *root, bIntNode *newNode)
{
    if(root->data > newNode->data)
    {
            if(root->left == NULL)
                    root->left = newNode;
            else
                    insertTree(root->left, newNode);
    }
    else {
            if(root->right == NULL)
                    root->right = newNode;
            else
                    insertTree(root->right, newNode);
    }
}
```

The above function should not be called for an empty tree (i.e. with NULL as the first parameter). The new node must be created with its "data" set to the target data and the left and right children of the new node must be pointing to empty trees. An iterative version of the above algorithm is easy to get as the algorithm involves tail recursion only. The iterative algorithm is described next.

```
void iterativeInsertTree(bIntNode *root, bIntNode *newNode)
{
    while (root != NULL)
    {
            if (newNode->data < root->data)
```

```
        {
            if (root->left == NULL)
            {
                root->left = newNode;
                root = NULL;
            }
            else
                root = root->left;
        }
        else
        {
            if(root->right == NULL)
            {
                root->right = newNode;
                root = NULL;
            }
            else
                root = root->right;
        }
    }
}
```

7.9.3 Deletion from a binary search tree

Deletion of a node from a binary search tree is more complicated than searching in a binary search tree or insertion of a node into a binary search tree. The node to be deleted is usually first found out in the given binary search tree employing a "search" function and then the node is deleted. The node that is to be deleted may be a leaf node or may have one child or may have two children. For example, consider the binary tree of Figure 7.21

Assume that the node with key "16" (being pointed to by "p") is to be deleted. Since it is a leaf node, the only task to be done is to reset the respective pointer of its parent (i.e., the "left" pointer of the node with key value as "18") to null. Even when the node to be deleted has only one child, the situation remains simple. Let the node to be deleted is "p" and its parent is "q". As "p" has only one child "r", deletion of "p" involves making "r" a child of "q" in place of "p". This is achieved by changing the pointer ("left" or "right") of "q" which points to "p" before deletion

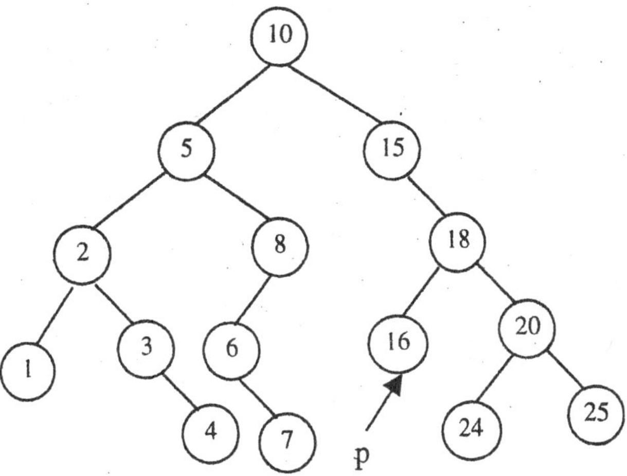

Figure 7.21

and setting that pointer of "q" to point "r". For example, if the node "p", with data "15" is to be deleted then the right child of its parent is reset to the child "p". The case where the node to be deleted, "p", has two children is a little involved. In this case, the inorder successor of "p" is to be found out. An inorder successor of a node "x" is the node "y" that comes next to "x" if the tree is traversed in an inorder manner. Inorder successor of a node which has two children can be found out by first going to its right child and then continually going to left as long as an empty sub-tree is not encountered. For example, inorder successor of the node with data "5" in Figure is the node with data "6". Now the data of the inorder successor of "p" is copied to the data part of "p" and then the inorder successor is deleted. The inorder successor of any node with two children can have at most one child because it can not have a non-empty left sub-tree. Thus, deleting the inorder successor of "p" involves deleting a node with one or zero child. This process of deleting a node with two children is further illustrated in Figure 7.22.

Note that, the steps outlined for deletion operation require two pointers: (i) a pointer to the node to be deleted and (ii) a pointer to the parent of the node to be deleted. Thus, the "delete" function has three formal parameters: a pointer to the root node of the tree, a pointer to the node to be deleted and a pointer to the parent of the node to be deleted. The assumption is that before the function "delete" is called to delete a node pointed to by "n", the parent of "n" is found out and passed as a parameter to the function. Moreover, if "n" haapens to be the root node then the parent of "n" is set to NULL before calling the function "delete".

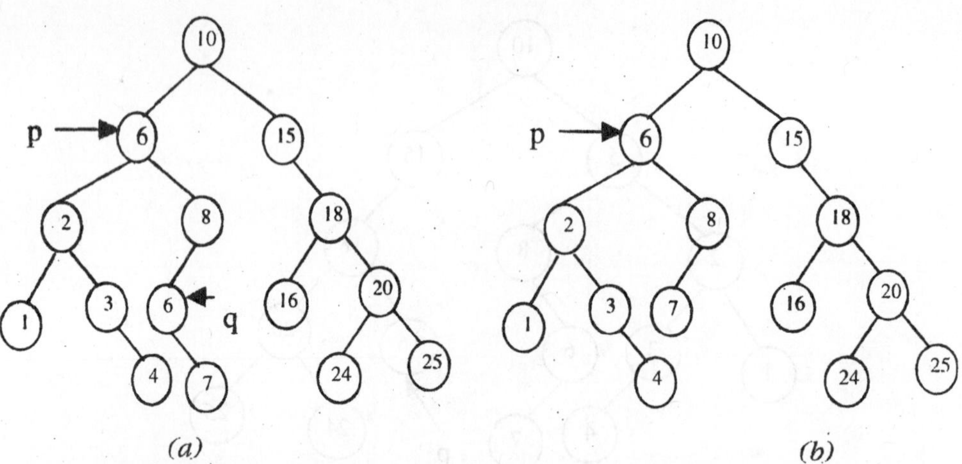

Figure 7.22. Illustration of the deletion process when the node to be deleted has two children. The node labelled "5" in the tree of Figure 7.21 is to be deleted. As a first step, the inorder successor of that node is found out. The inorder successor is pointed to by "q" in Figure (a). Then the content of "q" is copied as the content of "p". Then the node "q" is deleted. The tree after deleting "q" is shown in (b).

```
bIntNode *delete(bIntNode *root, bIntNode *n, bIntNode *parent)
{
    bIntNode *inorderSuccessor, *x;
    if((n->left != NULL) && (n->right != NULL))
    {
        parent = n;
        inorderSuccessor = n->right;
        while(inorderSuccessor->left != NULL)
        {
            parent = inorderSuccessor;
            inorderSuccessor = inorderSuccessor->left;
        }
        n->data = inorderSuccessor->data;
        n = inorderSuccessor;
    }
    if(n->left == NULL)
    {
        if(parent)
```

```
        {
                if(parent->left == n)
                        parent->left = n->right;
                else
                        parent->right = n->right;
                x = root;
        }
        else
        {
                x = n->right;
        }
    }
    if(n->right == NULL)
    {
        if(parent)
        {
                if(parent->left == n)
                        parent->left = n->left;
                else
                        parent->right = n->left;
                x = root;
        }
        else
                x = x->left;
    }
    return x;
}
```

Deletion of a node "n" with exactly two non-empty children can also be performed by first finding out the inorder predecessor of "n", copying the information of the inorder predecessor of "n" to "n" and then deleting the inorder predecessor. Thus, the resultant tree after deletion of a node is not unique.

Performance of all the algorithms for binary search trees discussed so far depend on the height of the tree. In fact a close look at any one of them reveals that the time complexity of search or insert or delete algorithms on a binary search tree is

O(h) where "h" is the height of the binary search tree. But the height of a tree with "n" nodes may be as large as (n-1) and as small as $\log_2 n$. Thus, the worst case complexity of these algorithms will be O(n) for a tree with "n" nodes. However, the best case complexity of the search algorithm is O(1) where the key to be searched is the same as the key of the root of the tree.

7.10 Representation of general trees

In previous sections, binary trees, their several representations and various operations were the main focus of discussion. A general tree, however, is not binary as any node in a general tree may have "k" number of children. Definition of a general tree has been discussed in the introductory section. This section deals with representation of a general tree and traversal algorithms to visit all nodes in such a tree.

The simplest way to represent a node in an ordered tree, "T", is to define a "struct" containing the data and a number of self-referential pointers to the same structure where each pointer points to the root of one sub-tree of "T". The problem is that different nodes in "T" have different number of children and thus a variable size record is required for such a representation. Handling variable size records is difficult. An immediate solution may be possible by keeping an array of pointers to the children for every node and setting the maximum size of the array to the degree of the tree which is the maximum number of children in any node in "T". Quite naturally, this representation tends to be too wasteful as can be seen in the following.

Let "T" be a k-ary tree (i.e. a tree of degree k) and let "T" have "n" nodes. Assume that the nodes are represented by fixed sized structures as shown below.

Data	Link to first sub-tree	....	Link to k-th sub-tree

The total number of link fields defined for "T" is (nk). However, the total number of pointers actually required is (n-1) as the root node is not pointed to by any pointer and every other node is pointed to by exactly one pointer. Therefore, the total number of unused pointers become nk-n+1 i.e. n(k-1)+1. The proportion of unused nodes grows rapidly as "k" increases. When k =3, about two third of pointers are NULL. Even in a binary tree where each node is essentially a fixed size record, the number of unused pointer fields would be almost half of the number of nodes in the tree. This was pointed out in the section on threaded binary tree. Thus, it is important to find out whether an ordered tree can be converted to a binary tree.

If an ordered tree, "T", is defined recursively as a structure which is either empty or containing a root "r" and a set, "S", of ordered trees then "T" may be denoted by,

$$T = [r, S]$$

Subsequently "S" may be defined recursively as a structure which is either empty or which is containing an ordered tree, T_1, and a set ordered trees, S'. So, "S" may be denoted by,

$$S = [T_1, S']$$

A closer look at the previous formalisms reveal that "T" contains a root, "r", the first child "T_1" and the set of other children "S'". The other children in "S'" may also be said to be brothers/sisters (i.e. siblings) of the sub-tree "T_1", a child of "T". Thus, a relationship other than parent-child relationship is found among nodes of "T". This relationship, which may be termed as "first child-next sibling", is characterized by two quantities. Consequently, each node may be represented in the way shown below.

Data	Link to the first sub-tree	Link to the next sibling

This means that each node in the tree is no longer connected to the set of its children (which are empty or non-empty sub-trees). In stead, each node in the tree is just connected to its first child and its next sibling. Consider the tree of Figure 7.23(a) and transform it to the tree of Figure 7.23(b) by redrawing the nodes of Figure 7.23(a) along the suggested line.

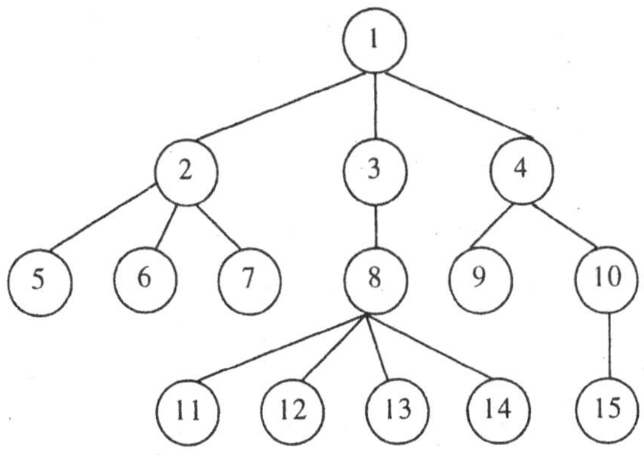

Figure 7.23 (a) A sample general tree

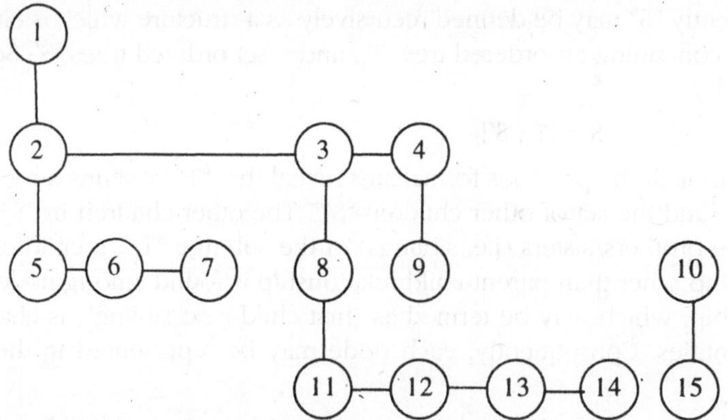

Figure 7.23 (b) The tree generated by redrawing each node of the tree of Figure 7.23(a) enforcing "first child- next sibling" relation ship.

See that each node in Figure 7.23(b) has exactly two links. The first link points to its first child and the other pointer points to its next sibling. For example, the first link of the root node, points to the node labelled "2". As the root node does not have a sibling, the other pointer of the root node is null. The node labelled "2" has two pointers: one pointing to its first child (node labelled "5") in the original tree and the other pointing to its sibling (node labelled "3") in the original tree. The tree, so obtained, does not look like a binary tree. But, if a rotation of 45° is applied to the tree in Figure 7.23(b) then the tree of Figure 7.24 is obtained, which definitely looks like a binary tree.

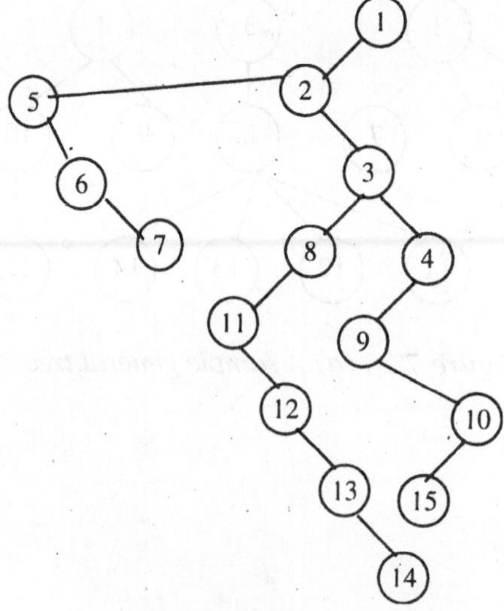

Figure 7.24. The tree of Figure 7.23(b) is rotated by 45° and redrawn.

It should be obvious that the right child of the root node is always empty as the root can not have a sibling. If a forest is defined to be a set of trees then a forest can also be transformed into a binary tree in which the root will have a right child. The right child of the root should be the next tree in a forest. Consider a forest with three trees as shown in Figure 7.25(a). Each tree in the forest is first converted to a binary tree as shown

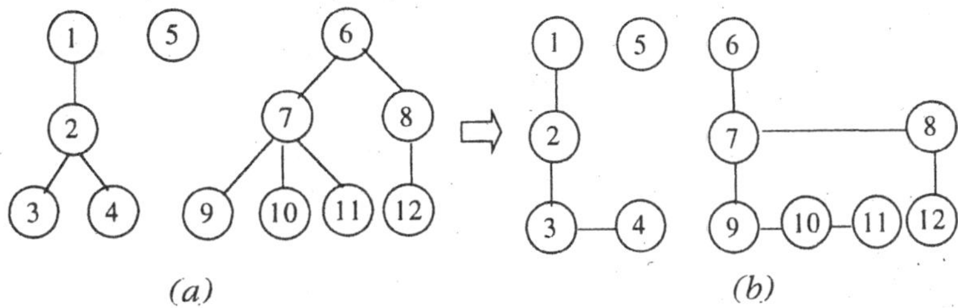

Figure 7.25(a) A forest consisting of three general trees.
(b) The trees contained in the forest are individually represented by corresponding binary trees.

in Figure 7.25(b). The tree rooted at node labelled "5" is made the right child of the root labelled "1". And the tree rooted at node labelled "6" is made the right child of the node labelled "5". After making these changes the tree looks like the one shown in Figure 7.26(a).

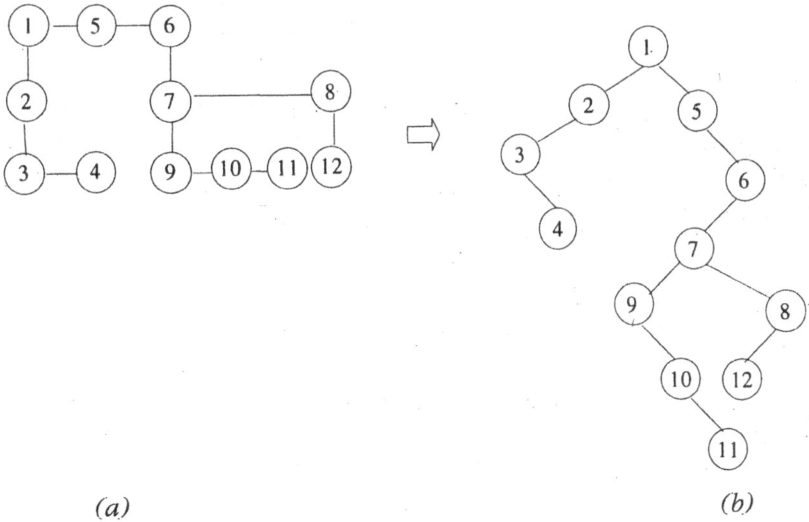

Figure 7.26(a) The trees of Figure 7.25(b) are combined as one single tree. The tree rooted at "5" is made the right child of the root of the first tree (i.e., the tree rooted at "1"). The tree rooted at "6" is made the right child of the root node of the second tree (i.e., the tree rooted at "5").
Figure 7.26(b) The tree of Figure 7.26(a) is rotated by 45° and then redrawn.

After applying a rotation of 45° to the tree of Figure 7.26(a), the tree of Figure 7.26(b) is obtained.

With this background, representation of a forest in terms of a binary tree may be formalized. Let "F" be a forest of trees $T_1, T_2, \ldots, T_m$. The binary tree representation of "F" denoted by B(F) may be defined as follows.

If F is empty then B(F) is an empty binary tree. If $F = [T_1, T_2, \ldots, T_m]$ and T_1 has a root T_{11} with sub-trees $T_{21}, T_{31}, \ldots, T_{n1}$ then B(F) is a binary tree with root "r", a left child "L" and a right child "R" so that $r = T_{11}$, $L = B(F_1)$ and $R = B(F_2)$ where T_{11} is the root of the T_1, F_1 is the forest of trees $T_{21}, T_{31}, \ldots, T_{n1}$ and $F_2 = [T_2, \ldots, T_m]$.

Like a tree, a fundamental operation on any forest is its traversal. The traversal techniques described in the context of binary trees can be generalized to a forest too. Thus, a preorder traversal on a forest "F" may be defined as follows.

1. Preorder traversal of an empty forest involves doing nothing.
2. If $F = [T_1, T_2, \ldots, T_m]$ and T_1 contains the root node T_{11} and the set of trees T_{21}, $T_{31}, \ldots, T_{n1}$ then preorder traversal of "F" would imply
   (i) visiting the root T_{11};
   (ii) traverse the forest $F = [T_{21}, T_{31}, \ldots, T_{n1}]$ in preorder;
   (iii) traverse the forest $F = [T_2, \ldots, T_m]$ in preorder;

A preorder traversal of the forest of Figure 7.26(a) visits the nodes in the sequence mentioned below.

1, 2, 3, 4, 5, 6, 7, 9, 10, 11, 8, 12

It should be evident to the reader that the nodes in a Forest, "F", visited in a preorder manner will be the same as the nodes visited in a preorder traversal of the binary tree B(F). This can be formally proved by induction on the depth, "d", of a binary tree. To prove the induction base, let "d" be 0; that is, B(F) contains only one node, the root. Then, "F" consists of only one tree with only one node in that tree. Thus, the preorder traversal of B(F) is the same as preorder traversal of "F"

Now, assume the result to be true for any B(F) whose depth is less than "d". Consider a forest "F" so that the depth of B(F) is "d". B(F) contains a root "r", a left sub-tree "L", and a right sub-tree "R", where $r = T_{11}$, $L = B(F_1)$ and $R = B(F_2)$, $F_1 = [T_{21}, T_{31}, \ldots, T_{n1}]$ and $F_2 = [T_2, T_3, \ldots, T_m]$. Depth of "L" and "R" are less than "d". Thus, preorder traversal of "L" is the same as traversing "F_1" in preorder manner and pre-order traversal of "R" is the same as traversing "F_2" in preorder manner.

Clearly, preorder traversal of "B(F)" visits the root "T_{11}", traverses "T_1" in preorder and traverses "T_2" in preorder. This sequence is also identical to visiting "T_{11}", traversing "F_1" in preorder and traversing "F_2" in preorder which is the definition of preorder traversal of "F". Thus, for a tree B(F) of depth "d", the hypothesis is true. Therefore, preorder traversal of "F" is identical to preorder traversal of its binary tree equivalent, "B(F)"

Similar to preorder traversal of a forest, an inorder traversal of a forest "F" may be defined as follows.

If "F" is empty then its inorder traversal involves doing nothing. Otherwise, inorder traversal of "F" would mean the following.

1. Traverse the trees in "F_1" in inorder;
2. Visit the root of "T_1" in "F";
3. Traverse the trees in "F_2" in inorder;

Once again, it can be proved that the inorder traversal of "F" as defined above is the same as traversing the binary tree B(F) in inorder fashion.

7.11 Data Structure for disjoint Sets as an application of tree

In many applications, "n" distinct elements are required to be grouped into a number of disjoint sets. There could be two major operations on these disjoint sets. The first one is called "find" which is used to identify the set to which a given element belongs. The other operation is making a union of two disjoint sets to create a new set. In the ensuing discussion it is not important for us to identify the actual elements but some indices to actual elements would serve our purpose. So, the elements can be assumed to be integers from "0" to "n" which could actually be indices to the real elements. Also, if {1, 3, 9} forms one set and {2, 5} forms another set then these sets are to be identified by some name. In this discussion, the sets are identified by some element of the set known as the representative. As long as the same representative is returned to identify the set, choice of a representative is not any problem. Thus, "3" could represent (or identify) the set {1, 3, 9} and "2" could represent the set {2, 5}. A data structure for manipulating disjoint sets must maintain a collection S = {S_1, S_2, … , S_m} where each S_i is a set and any two sets in "S" are disjoint. The operations supported on this data structure are as follows.

(i) createSet(x), which creates a set with a single element "x";

(ii) find(x) which identifies the set to which "x" belongs;

(iii) union(S_1, S_2) which creates a new set S_3 which is set union of S_1 and S_2. Since the data structure contains disjoint sets only, the sets S_1 and S_2 must be destroyed from the collection "S".

These sets can be conveniently represented by trees where each node contains one element and each tree represents one set. The root of such a tree is assumed to be the representative of the set. For example the set S_1= {1, 3, 9, 10} may be represented by a tree as shown in Figure 7.27.

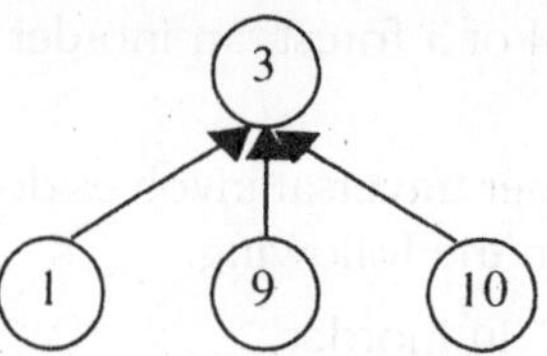

Figure 7.27 Representation of the set {1, 3, 9, 10} by a general tree.

The root of the tree of Figure 7.27 is "3". So, the set is represented (identified) by the elements 1", "9" and "10" are sub-trees of "3". Note the direction of the links. Unlike usual trees, each node contains a link to its parent. Thus, each of the calls find(1), find(3), find(9) and find(10) should return "3" indicating that the set to which "1", "3", "9" and "10" belong is identified by "3". For any given set, there is only one element acting as its representative. As already mentioned, the selection of the representative is arbitrary and immaterial as long as the same representative is returned by several calls to "find". Consider another set S_2 = {2, 5, 6} which may be represented by the tree of Figure 7.28.

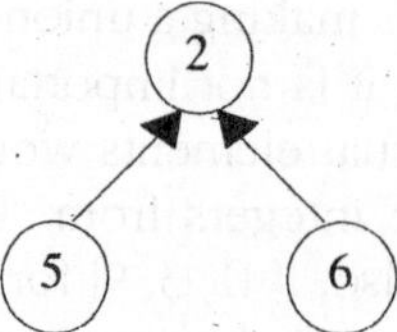

Figure 7.28 Representation of the set {2, 5, 6} by a general tree.

Now consider a "union" operation on S_1 and S_2. Clearly, if $S_3 = S_1 U S_2$ then S_3 = {1, 3, 9, 10, 2, 5, 6}. If the root of the tree of Figure 7.28 is made a new child of the root of the tree of Figure 7.27 then a new tree is generated which is shown in Figure 7.29 (a).

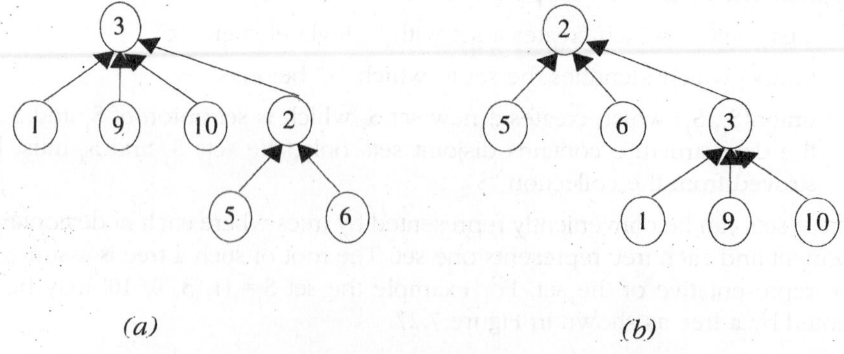

Figure 7.29 The union of the sets {3, 1, 9, 10} and {2, 5, 6} represented by trees. Two such trees are possible as shown in Figure (a) and (b).

This new tree represents S_3. The set S_3 is represented by "3", the root of the tree of Figure 7.29(a). Also note that, the root of the tree of Figure 7.27 could also be made a new child of the root of the tree of Figure 7.28 producing the tree as shown in Figure 7.29(b). This tree also represents S_3 but with a different representative.

7.11.1 Simple algorithms for union and find

First, consider the representation of the trees. The nodes in the trees described in the context of sets contain a link to its parents and the nodes are integers from "0" to "n". If eleven elements from 0 to 10 are considered then one array "parent" of "11" elements can store the links of the parents of each node. In such an array, if parent[i] is "j" then the parent of the node containing element "i" is "j". Also note that the parent of a root node can be set to the root node itself for convenience. For example, suppose that eleven elements are grouped into five sets {1, 3, 9, 10}, {2, 5, 6}, {4}, {7}, {0, 8}. The trees corresponding to the five sets are shown in Figure 7.30(a). The array "parent" representing these trees are shown in Figure 7.30(b).

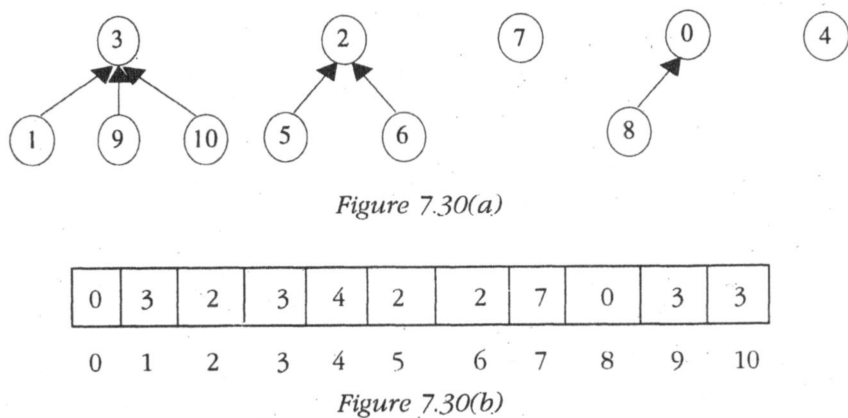

Figure 7.30(a)

0	3	2	3	4	2	2	7	0	3	3
0	1	2	3	4	5	6	7	8	9	10

Figure 7.30(b)

Figure 7.30 The sets {3, 1, 9, 10}, {2, 5, 6}, {7}, {4}, {0, 8} represented by trees as shown in (a). The array "parent" describing these trees is shown in (b).

The "C" functions for "find" and "Union" are presented next.

```
int find(int i)
{
    int t;
    t = i;
    while(parent[t] != t)
            t = parent[t];
    return t;
```

```
}
void Union(int i, int j)
{
    parent[i] = j;
}
```

For example, if Union(3, 2) is called then the "parent" array would look like the following which represents the tree of Figure 7.29(b).

0	3	2	2	4	2	2	7	0	3	3
0	1	2	3	4	5	6	7	8	9	10

If find(9) is called now then the parent of "9" which is "3" would be visited. Then, parent of "3" which is "2" would be visited. As parent[2] is "2", the "while" loop terminates. Thus, the function "Union" takes a constant time, but the time complexity of the function "find" is O(h) where "h" is the height of the tree representing the set. Suppose that "n" elements are numbered "1" to "n" and let there be "n" sets initially. These sets are denoted by S_1, S_2, ... , S_n such that

$$S_i = \{i\} \text{ for } 1 \leq i \leq n.$$

To represent the singleton sets S_i, $1 \leq i \leq n$, the elements of the array "parent" are to be initialized as parent [i] = i for all "i".

Now, consider a sequence of (n-1) "Union" and "find" operations as mentioned below.

Union(1, 2), find(1)
Union(2, 3), find(1)
Union(3, 4), find(1)

Union(n-2, n-1), find(1)
Union(n-1, n), find(1)

As a result of (n-1) "Union" operations the tree as shown in Figure 7.31 is obtained.

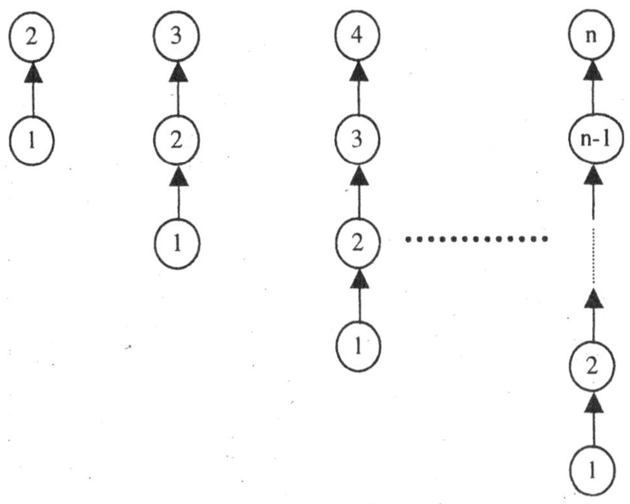

Figure 7.31 The growth of the tree due to the union operations as described in the text.

Find(1) is called (n-1) time and the total time complexity of (n-1) "find" operations is O(1+2+ ... +n-1) = O(n(n-1)/2) = O(n^2).

7.11.2 Improved versions of algorithms for Union and find operations

The time complexity of "find" operation may be improved if the height of the tree produced by a "union" operation is kept at its minimum. To explain this point further, consider the trees as shown in Figure 7.32 and assume that Union(2, 3) is called.

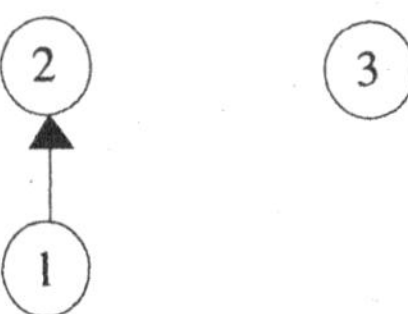

Figure 7.32 Trees representing the sets {1} and {2, 3}.

Two trees could be the result of this operation as shown below.

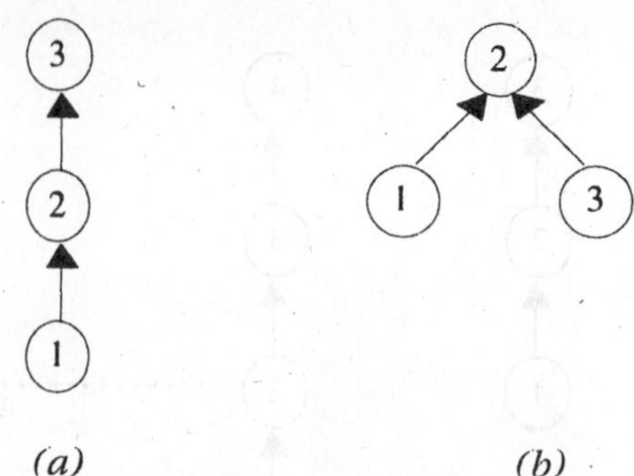

Figure 7.33 Two possible trees obtained as Union of {1}, {2,3}. The tree in (b) is better as the height of this tree is small and hence will result in efficient "find" operations.

The tree in Figure 7.33(b) is better because the height of this tree is less and therefore future "find" operations would be less expensive. Thus, an intelligent decision is to be taken in the function "Union (i, j)" before setting the parent of "i" to "j". This decision could be made based on the number of elements in the sets represented by "i" and "j". The parent of the tree with fewer nodes would be the root of the tree with larger number of elements. To implement this idea, a new array "size" is required for each root node to store the number of elements in the tree with that root. Thus, size[i] is defined if "i" is the root of some tree; otherwise, size[i] is undefined.

In this background, the "Union" function can be redefined by utilising the size information of the trees rooted at "i" and "j".

```
void union_wt(int i, int j)
{
   if(size[i] < size[j])
   {
          parent[i] = j;
          size[j] += size[i];
   }
   else
   {
          parent[j] = i;
          size[i] += size[j];
   }
}
```

Consider the same set of elements {1, 2, ... , n}. The first "n" operations performed are a sequence of creation of "n" sets S_1, ... , S_n, where S_i = {i}. Figure 7.34 depicts "n" trees representing "n" initial singleton sets, and the contents of the arrays "parent" and "size" after creation of "n" sets is complete.

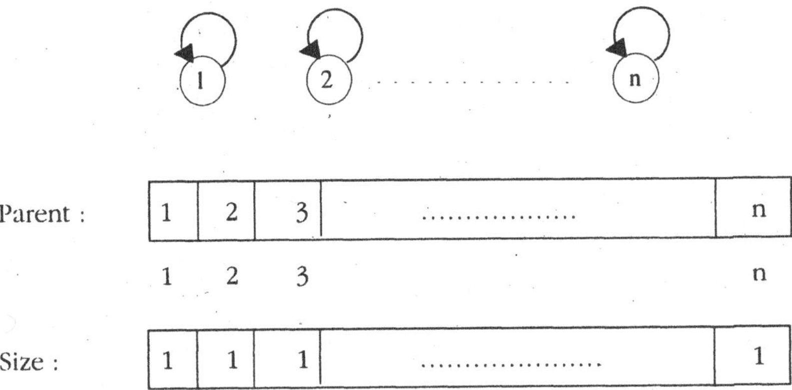

Figure 7.34 Representation of "n" singleton sets as trees shown in (a); The contents if the arrays "parent" and "size" at this stage are shown in (b) and (c) respectively.

Now, consider the sequence of operations union_wt(1, 2), union_wt(1, 3), union_wt(1, 4). First, consider union_wt(1,2). As size[1] is equal to size[2], parent[2] will be "1" and the tree representing $S_{12} = S_1 \cup S_2$ looks like the tree in Figure 7.35(a) and size[1] will be "2". Then union_wt(1, 3) may be performed.

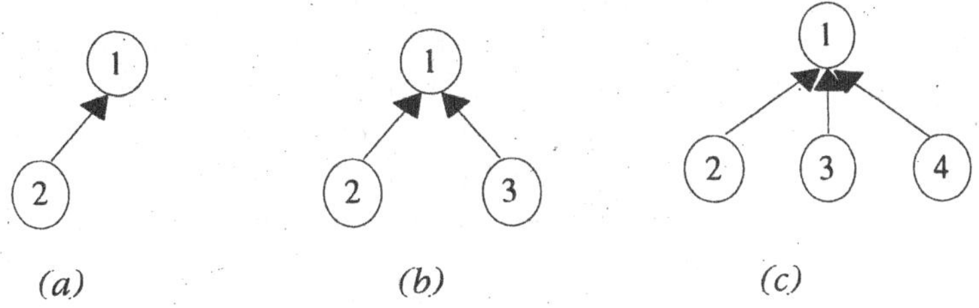

Figure 7.35 The trees generated after union_wt(1, 2), union_wt(1, 3), union_wt(1, 4) are called.

As size[1] (i.e. 2) is more than size[3] (i.e. 1), parent[3] to set to "1" signifying that "1" is made the parent of "3" which is depicted in Figure 7.35(b). Next call to union_wt(1, 4) once again resents parent of "4" to "1" producing the tree of Figure 7.35(c). Clearly, the height of the tree is restricted in this version of the union algorithm. As a result, "Find(1)" will require minimum time.

Sometimes a different metric other than "size" is selected for limiting the growth of the height of these trees. This metric is called "rank". Rank of a set with a single element is zero. When two disjoint sets S_1 and S_2 are united, the tree representing the set with less rank is made a sub-tree of the tree representing the set with higher rank. Like "size", "rank" is associated with the root node of a tree representing some set. If rank of S_1 and S_2 are the same then the tree corresponding to either of the sets is made a sub-tree of the tree for the other set. The rank of the new set which is union of two sets is made one more than its previous rank.

The new algorithm for "union" using rank values is presented as "C" function.

```
void unionRank(int i, int j)
{
if(rank[i] < rank[j])
    parent[i] = i
else
{
    parent[j] = i;
    if(rank[i] == rank[j])
            rank[j] += 1;
}
}
```

It can be proved that the height of such a tree can not be more than O(logn). The algorithm for "find" can also be used to improve the structure of the tree in which "find" is operating. Consider the tree as shown in Figure 7.36(a). If "find(m)" is called then the nodes labelled "k", "j", "i" are traversed by following the links through the "parent" array. Once "i" is found, if the tree is restructured in such a way that trees rooted at nodes "j", "k", "m" become direct sub-trees of the node "i" (as shown in Figure 7.36(b)) Then, future "find" operations become less expensive. The improvement just described is also called "collapsing" or "path compression" of a tree. The new version of "find" is presented in the following.

```
int find(int i)
{
    int j, k, t;
    j = i;
    while(parent[j] != j)
            j = parent[j];
    k = i;
    while(k != j)
    {
```

```
            t = parent[k];
            parent[k] = j;
            k = t;
    }
    return j;
}
```

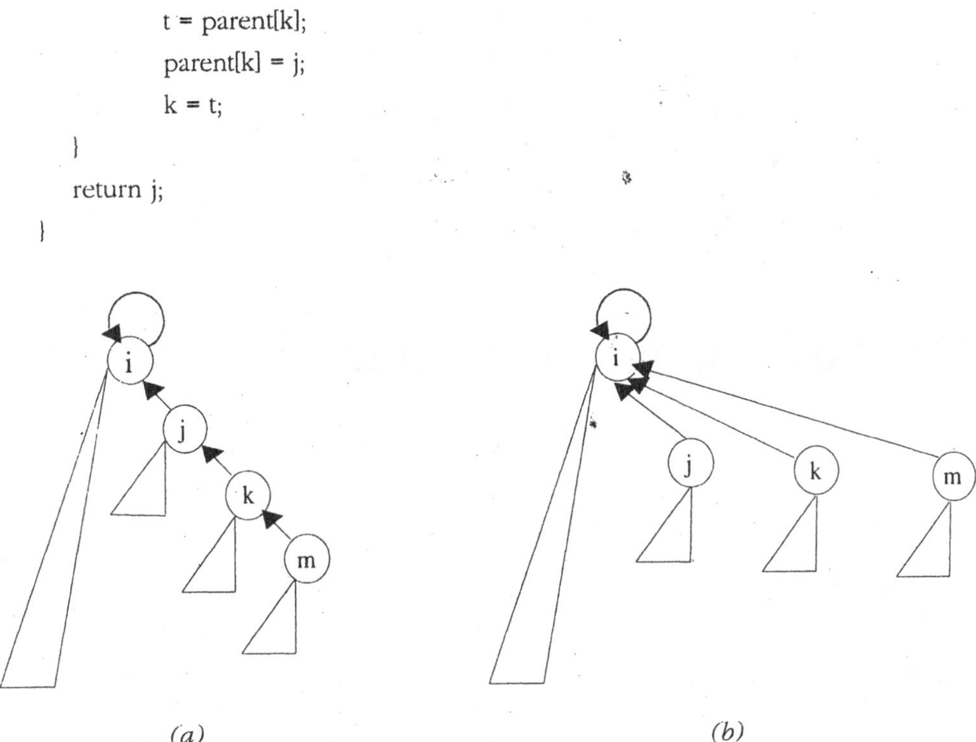

Figure 7.36 Collapsing a tree during "find" operation. The tree before "find(m)" is called is shown in Figure (a). During execution of "find(m)", the tree is collapsed and the tree in Figure (b) is produced.

It is interesting to know about the time complexities of these improved versions of "find" and "union" algorithms. Recall that a very fast growing function, Ackermann's function, has been defined in the exercises of Chapter 6. Regarding Ackermann's function, A(m, n), the following facts can be established.

(a) A(m, n+1) > A(m, n)

(b) A(m+1, n) > A(m, n)

(c) $A(3, 4) = \left.2^{2^{2^{\cdot^{\cdot^{2}}}}}\right\}$ 65,536 two's

A new function, f(m, n), closely related to the inverse of the function A(m, n) may be defined as follows.

$$f(m, n) = \min\{x \geq 1 \mid A(x, 4\lceil m/n \rceil) > \log_2 n\}$$

From the above definition of f(m, n) and the properties (a) and (b) of A(m, n) it can be proved that f(m, n) ≤ 3 whenever log n < A(3, 4). Since A(3, 4) is a very large number as can be seen from property (c) of A(m, n), f(m, n) will be less than or equal to 3 for any practical purposes. Assume T(m, n) be the worst case time required to process a sequence of "m" find operations and (n-1) union operations applied on elements of a collection of disjoint sets where $m \geq n$. Further suppose that "find" is implemented using the collapsing rule and "Union" is implemented using the "size" information of the sets to be united. Then, there exist two positive constants c_1 and c_2 so that the following inequality holds.

$c_1 mf(m, n) \leq T(m, n) \leq c_2\, mf(m, n)$

The proofs of all these properties and the proof of the time complexity of the result just stated regarding the performance of improved "find" and "Union" algorithms are quite involved and are beyond the scope of this book.

7.12 Points to be remembered

- Tree is the most important non-linear data structure where hierarchical relationship among data elements is easily represented.
- The tree data structure is defined recursively. A tree consists of a unique node called root and a number of sub-trees. The sets of nodes present in these sub-trees are mutually disjoint. These sub-trees are trees once again. Often, these sub-trees are called children of the root. A node with no children are called terminal or leaf nodes.
- Diagrammatically, each node of a tree is drawn as a circle with the children of a node drawn below the parent. The parent and its children are connected by lines which are also called edges. A tree so drawn can be horizontally partitioned into levels with a number of nodes belonging to each level.
- A binary tree is one major sub-class of general trees where every binary tree is either empty or consists of a root, a left child and a right child. These children of the root are binary trees once again. There are fundamental differences between a tree and a binary tree. For example, a binary tree may be empty whereas a tree can not be empty. The children of any node in a binary tree are ordered from "left" to "right" whereas the children of a node in a tree are unordered. The notion of level applies to binary trees as well. Height of a tree may be defined as the maximum level of a tree. A binary tree is complete if the level all leaf nodes is the same and all non-leaf nodes have exactly two non-empty children.
- A binary tree may be implemented as self-referential structures using pointers or it may be implemented using three arrays. A binary tree can also be implemented as a single one-dimensional array. This representation is wasteful except for complete or near complete binary trees.
- A fundamental operation on a binary tree is its traversal. Traversal of a binary tree implies visiting every node of that tree exactly once in some sequence. There are three standard types of tree traversal: preorder, inorder and postorder. In a preorder traversal, the root of the tree is visited first; then the left child of

the root is visited and finally the right child of the root is visited. The traversal is defined recursively fully exploiting the recursion inherent in the definition of the tree data structure. Similarly, an inorder and a postorder traversal is defined as LDR and LRD respectively where L denotes traversing the left child of the root, R denotes traversing the right child and D denotes visiting the root. All these traversals can be defined recursively as well as non-recursively.

- There are other operations applicable on a binary tree like copying a binary tree, testing equality of two binary trees etc. These are explored in the exercises. A unique binary tree can not be reconstructed from its inorder, preorder or postorder traversal alone. However, a binary tree can be uniquely reconstructed from its inorder and preorder traversals or from its inorder and postorder traversals.
- There are some important structural properties of a tree or a binary tree.
- The number of edges in a tree with "n" nodes is (n-1).
- Every node in a tree must have a unique parent and there may not be any cycles in a tree.
- The maximum number of nodes in a binary tree of height "k" is $2^{k+1}-1$.
- The number of nodes with two children in a binary tree is always one less than the number of leaf nodes.
- The number of external nodes in a binary tree is always one more than the number of its internal nodes.
- If "E" and "I," denote the external and internal path length of a binary tree of "n" nodes then E = I + 2n.
- The number of distinct binary tree with "n" nodes is the same as the number of well-formed strings of "n" left and "n" right parentheses. This number is also the same as the number of different permutations of {1, 2, 3, 4, ..., n} possible to realize by pushing these numbers into a stack in the order 1, 2, 3, 4, ..., n and popping them in all different ways. This number is well-known as n-th Catalan number.
- In a binary tree, many nodes have one child or no children. The pointers for the empty children for these nodes are set to NULL. A more effective utilization of these pointers is possible if "NULL" left pointers are set to point to the inorder predecessor of that node and "NULL" right pointers are set to point to the inorder successor of that node. These pointers, so introduced, are called threads. Threads help in writing non-recursive versions of inorder, preorder and postorder traversals.
- Binary search tree is yet another major sub-class of binary trees. In a binary search tree, the data elements present in the nodes are ordered in a particular way. Specifically, all keys of the nodes in the left child of the root of a binary

tree are less than the key of the data in the root. And all keys of the nodes in the right child of the root of a binary tree are greater than the key of the data in the root. The left and right children of the root of a binary search tree are again binary search trees.

- There are three fundamental operations on a binary search tree: search, insertion and deletion. Algorithms for all these operations can be easily written. Time complexities of all these algorithms are of the order on the height of the binary search tree. The height of a binary search tree may be as bad as the number of nodes present if the binary tree is a skew one. The minimum height of a binary tree of "n" nodes is $\log_2 n$. Thus, the worst case performance of these algorithms applied on a binary search tree of "n" nodes is O(n).
- A general tree and even a forest can be represented by a binary tree so that the preorder or inorder traversal defined on a general tree visits the same sequence of nodes in the binary tree corresponding to the general tree.
- Set is an important application of a general tree. "Find" and "Union" are two basic operations on a collection of mutually disjoint sets. Efficient algorithms may be written to implement these algorithms incorporating heuristics like size or rank and path compression.

Exercises

1. Write a "C" function to determine the height of a binary tree.
2. Construct two binary trees so that their preorder traversal sequences are the same.
3. Write a "C" function to count the number of leaf nodes in a binary tree.
4. Write a "C" function to copy a binary tree. The input to the function is a pointer to the root node of a binary tree. The tree is copied node by node to another tree (by necessarily creating new nodes). The function returns the pointer to the root node of the new binary tree constructed by the function.
5. Write a "C" function to test whether two binary trees are identical or not. The inputs to the function are two pointers to two root nodes of two trees. The function returns "1" if the trees are identical; otherwise, the function returns "0". Two binary trees are identical if their roots are the same and the left and right sub-trees of their roots are identical.
6. Write a "C" function to swap a binary tree.
7. Write a "C" function to compute the maximum number of nodes in any level of a binary tree. The maximum number of nodes in any level of a binary tree is also called the width of the tree.
8. Construct two binary trees so that their postorder traversal sequences are the same.

9. Write a "C" function to traverse a binary tree level by level. In each level, the tree is traversed from left to right.
10. Write a "C" function to find out the inorder successor of a given node in a binary tree. The inputs to the function are (i) a pointer to the root of the tree, and (ii) a pointer to a node. The function returns a pointer to the inorder successor of the given node.
11. Write a "C" function to find out the inorder predecessor of a given node in a binary tree. The inputs to the function are (i) a pointer to the root of the tree, and (ii) a pointer to a node. The function returns a pointer to the inorder predecessor of the given node.
12. Write a "C" function to compute the internal path length of a binary tree.
13. Write a "C" function to compute the external path length of a binary tree.
14. Write a non-recursive "C" function to traverse a binary tree in preorder which does not use any "goto" statement.
15. Write a non-recursive "C" function to traverse a binary tree in preorder which does not use any stack.
16. Prove that every node in a tree except the root node has a unique parent.
17. Write a "C" function to traverse a tree in inorder manner if the tree is represented by a single one-dimensional array.
18. Let "T" be a binary tree with "k" number of leaf nodes. Then, the height "h" and external path length "E" of "T" satisfy the following conditions.

$$h \geq \lceil \log_2 k \rceil$$

$$E \geq k \log_2 k$$

19. Write a "C" function to reconstruct a binary tree from its preorder and inorder traversal sequences.
20. Prove that the inorder and preorder traversal sequences of a binary tree uniquely characterize the binary tree.
21. Prove that the inorder and postorder traversal sequences of a binary tree uniquely characterize the binary tree. Write a "C" function to to reconstruct a binary tree from its postorder and inorder traversal sequences.
22. Show, by a counter example, that preorder and postorder traversal sequences of a binary tree do not uniquely characterize the binary tree.
23. Write a "C" function to traverse an inorder threaded binary tree in postorder without using stack or recursion.
24. Write a "C" function to find out (i) the minimum and (ii) the maximum element in a binary search tree.
25. Write a "C" function to delete a node from a binary search tree which ultimately

deletes the inorder predecessor of the node to be deleted if the node has exactly two non-empty children.

26. Show that the inorder predecessor of a node with two non-empty children in a binary search tree does not have a right child and the inorder successor of a node with two non-empty children in a binary search tree does not have a left child.

27. Prove that traversing a general tree in inorder produces the same sequence of nodes as obtained by traversing the corresponding binary tree in inorder.

Chapter 8

Advanced Trees

8.1 Introduction

The importance of tree data structure in organizing a huge volume of data in a hierarchical fashion has already been discussed in the previous chapter. The beauty of this organization lies in efficient searching, insertion and deletion operations on a large bulk of data. The Binary Search Tree (BST), in particular, is very useful for an efficient data organization. But even in a Binary Search Tree, the efficiency of the three fundamental operations (namely, Search, Insertion and Deletion) on a tree depends on the height of the tree. Unfortunately, the height of a Binary Search Tree is completely dependent on the sequence of insertion and deletion operations and the height of a degenerate BST having "n" nodes can be (n-1) in the worst case. The advantage of organizing data in the form of a BST becomes less and less as the BST degenerates into a linear structure. One major topic of this chapter is AVL trees where a BST is never allowed to degenerate beyond a certain limit.

Two points must also be borne in mind in this context. Firstly, the set of all possible data to be handled is usually so large that construction of a well-balanced tree storing all data is not feasible. Therefore, only useful data are stored as a tree and the actual volume of data being used constantly changes through insertion of new data and deletion of existing data. Contrast this scenario with the one where searching is done on a stable volume of data. Secondly, the data may be resident in primary memory or in secondary memory. B-trees, one of the major data structures discussed in this chapter, are suitable for organizing data in secondary memory for efficient usage.

This chapter begins with a discussion of AVL-trees and algorithms manipulating them. This is followed by describing another approach to solve the problem of degenerated BST. This approach uses general trees in the form of 2-3 trees. Then, B-trees are discussed which are generalizations of 2-3 trees. Finally, priority queue data structure is discussed which is represented by heaps.

8.2 AVL Tree

In a full binary search tree, the heights of the left and the right sub-trees of any node are equal. Such trees are ideal for efficient searching because the height of such a tree with "n" nodes is $O(\log_2 n)$. But, when insertions and deletions are performed randomly on a binary search tree, the binary tree often turns out to be far from ideal. A close approximation to an ideal binary search tree is achievable if it can be ensured that the difference between the heights of the left and the right sub-trees of any node in the tree is at most one. A binary search tree in which the difference of heights of the right and left sub-trees of any node is less than or equal to one is known as an AVL tree. The name "AVL Tree" is derived from the names of its inventors who are Adelson-Velskii and Landi.

In order to represent a node in an AVL tree, a new field must be introduced. This additional field stores the "balance factor" of a node which denotes the difference of height between the left and the right sub-trees of the tree rooted at that node. A node in an AVL tree can be defined in the following way using "C" language.

```
typedef struct AVLNode
{
   int data;
   struct AVLNode *left, *right;
   int balanceFactor;
}AVLNode;
```

Consequently, the balance factor of a node in an AVL tree can assume one of the three possible values {-1, 0, 1}. If the balance factor of a node is "0" then the heights of its left and right sub-trees are equal. If the balance factor is "1" then the height of its left sub-tree is one more than the height of its right sub-tree. If the height of the right sub-tree of a node is one more than the height of its left sub-tree then the balance factor of that node is "-1". Given any binary search tree, the balance factors of all nodes may be easily computed. If the magnitude of the balance factor of any node is found to be more than one then the given binary tree is not an AVL tree. A few trees are shown in Figure 8.1 where balance factors of all nodes are computed. These balance factors are shown inside the circles representing nodes. From the balance factors, it can be easily seen that some trees of Figure 8.1 are AVL trees and some are not.

Quite clearly, the trees of Figures 8.1(a) and 8.1(b) are not AVL trees while the trees of Figures 8.1(c) and 8.1(d) are AVL trees. Sometimes, the balance factors are pictorially denoted by the set {\, -, /}. The symbol "\" at a node represents the fact that the right sub-tree is taller than the left sub-tree by one. Similarly, the symbol "/" at a node denotes that the balance factor of that node is "1". The symbol "-" denotes that the heights of the left and the right sub-trees are equal.

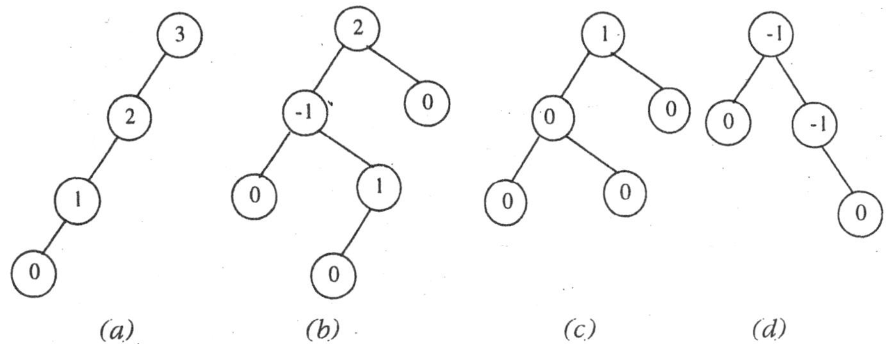

Figure 8.1 Examples of AVL and non-AVL trees

8.2.1 Insertion of a node into an AVL tree

Algorithms for three operations viz., search, insertion and deletion on AVL trees will be discussed in this section. Let us start with searching for a key value in an AVL tree. Searching for a key in an AVL tree is quite same as searching for a key in any ordinary binary search tree. This is obvious because an AVL tree, by definition, is also a binary search tree. As a consequence, the algorithm to search in an AVL tree is exactly the same as the search algorithm for a binary search tree. However, insertion of a new node to an AVL tree is a significantly different operation. The steps to insert a new node with key "k" into an AVL tree begins by comparing the key "k" with the key of the root of "T" and then inserting the new node into the left or right sub-tree depending on the result of the comparison. The recursion terminates when the left or right sub-tree to which insertion is to be done happens to be empty. In that case, the new node is attached to the current root as its child. This is the familiar scheme to insert a new node into any binary search tree. But such an insertion may spoil the balance of the AVL tree by making the magnitude of the balance factor of some node in the path from the point of insertion to the root of the tree more than one. Consider the tree in Figure 8.2(a) where the key in each node is an integer as written inside the nodes.

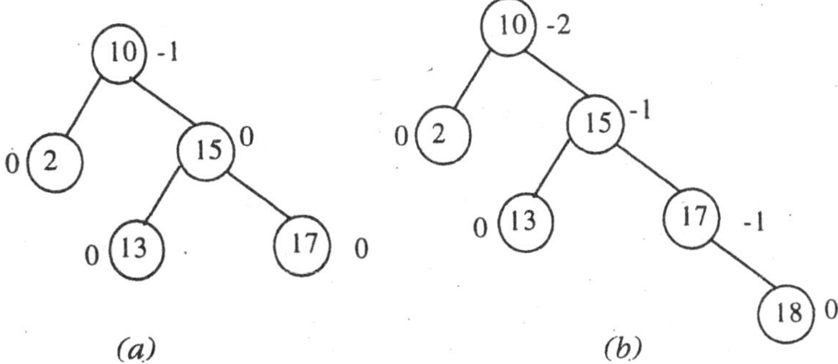

Figure 8.2 A sample AVL tree is shown in (a). If "18" is ordinarily inserted into the tree then the resultant tree is shown in (b). The tree in (b) is not an AVL tree.

The balance factor of each node is shown against the node. If a new node with key "18" is inserted in an ordinary way (i.e., in the way an insertion takes place in any binary search tree) then the tree as shown in Figure 8.2(b) will be produced. Note the balance factors mentioned against the nodes and see that the resultant tree is no longer an AVL tree. But also keep in mind that it is not necessary that ordinary insertion of a new node into an AVL tree must convert an AVL tree into a non-AVL one. For example, if a new node with key "8" is inserted into the tree of Figure 8.2(a) then the tree as shown in Figure 8.3 is produced which is also an AVL tree.

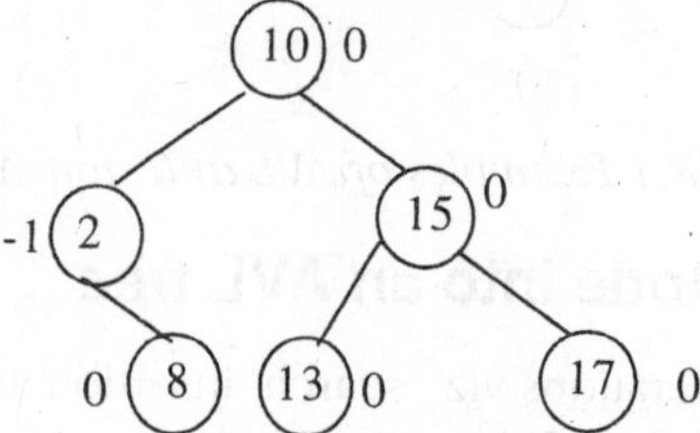

Figure 8.3 The tree obtained as a result of inserting "8" to the AVL tree of Figure 8.2(a) in an ordinary way. This tree remains an AVL tree after insertion.

In fact, if a new node is added to the shorter sub-tree of a node "n" then it may often be the case that height of that sub-tree changes without affecting the height of the tree rooted at "n". Then, the effect of insertion does not propagate above "n". When a new node is added to the taller sub-tree of a node "n" and the height of the taller sub-tree increases further resulting in an increase in the magnitude of the balance factor of "n" (which is already one) then the original tree becomes non-AVL. Assume that a key "k" is to be inserted to an AVL tree. By searching for a proper place to add the new node, we descend down from the root node and finally reach a node "x" to the right of which the new node is to be added. The node "x" does not presently have a right child. It may have no left child or at most one left child. Treat these two cases separately. First assume that the node "x" has one left child as shown in the Figure 8.4.

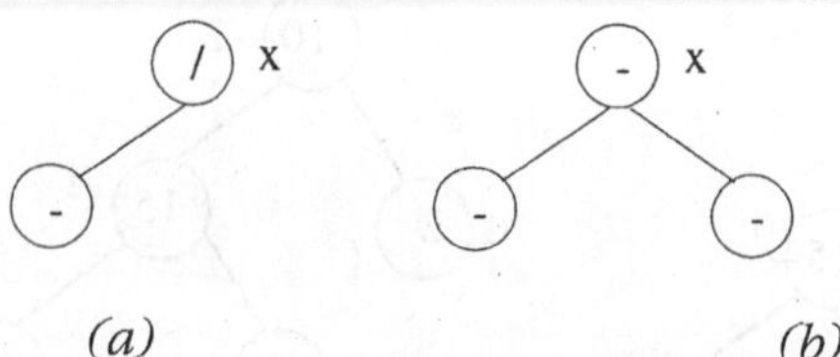

Figure 8.4(a) The balance factor of the node "x" before insertion. The node "x" does not have a right child and a new node is to be inserted as a right child of "x".

Figure 8.4(b) The sub-tree rooted at "x" after inserting a new node as its right child. The balance factor of "x" changes. But the height of the tree rooted at "x" does not change.

After insertion of the new node, the height of the tree rooted at the node "x" does not change and so the sub-tree rooted at parent of the node "x" does not change too. As it has been discussed, the insertion procedure ends there. But if the node "x" has no left child to begin with then the height of the tree rooted at "x" increases after inserting the node to the right of "x". This calls for checking the effect of this growth in the tree rooted at, "y", the parent of "x". The balance factor of "y" (before insertion) may be 0, 1, -1. These three cases are dealt with in the following.

Case 1:

Suppose that the balance factor of "y" is "-1" before insertion as shown in Figure 8.5(a). Then, the tree rooted at "y" is no longer an AVL tree as shown in Figure 8.5(b).

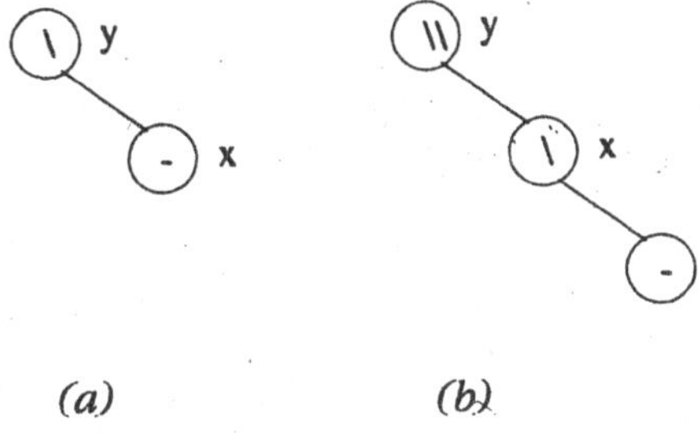

Figure 8.5 (a) "x" is a right child of "y" which does not have a left child.

(b) A new child is added as a right child of "x" changing the balance factors of "x" and "y". The resultant tree is a non-AVL tree.

If this happens then an adjustment needs to be made to make the tree rooted at "y" an AVL tree. After adjusting this sub-tree rooted at "y", if this sub-tree grows taller then the parent of "y" is to be examined again. This process continues until the root of the tree is reached or at some node, the height of the adjusted AVL tree remains the same as it was before insertion.

Case 2:

Let the balance factor of "y" be "0" before inserting the new node (as shown in Figure 8.6(a)). After insertion, the tree becomes non-AVL and the height of the tree rooted at "y" increases (see Figure 8.6(b)). Therefore, the tree rooted at "y" needs to be adjusted and may have to be examined in turn.

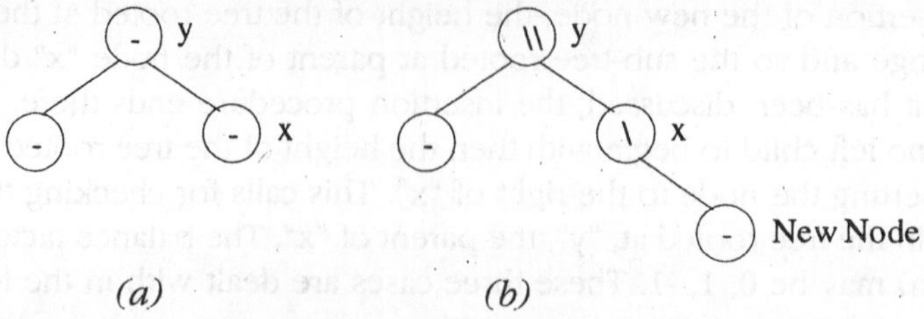

Figure 8.6 (a) "x" is a right child of "y" which also has a left child.

(b) A new child is added as a right child of "x" changing the balance factors of "x" and "y". The resultant tree is a non-AVL tree. The height of the tree rooted at "y" increases.

Case 3:

Let the balance factor of "y" be "1" before insertion. Then, the height of the tree rooted at "y" does not increase after insertion of the new node (as shown in Figure 8.7(a) and (b)).

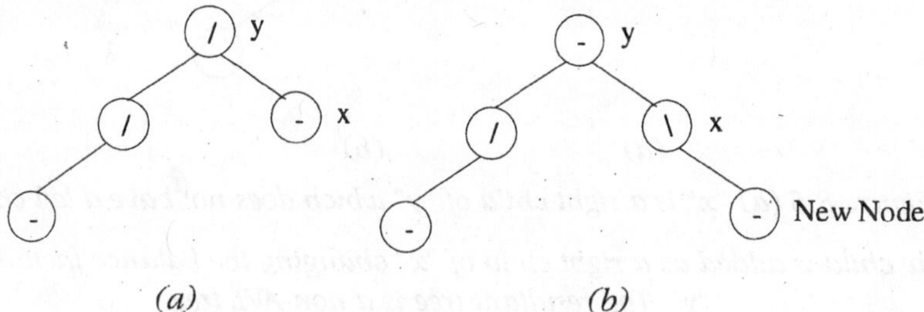

Figure 8.7 (a) "x" is a right child of "y". The left sub-tree of the tree rooted at "y" is taller.

(b) A new child is added as a right child of "x" changing the balance factors of "x" and "y". The resultant tree remains an AVL tree. The height of the tree rooted at "y" remains the same.

As the sub-tree rooted at "y" does not grow taller, the parent of "y" need not be examined and the effect of insertion does not propagate further. Thus, observe that it may be required to continually move up towards the root of the tree as long as the sub-trees rooted at nodes along the path from "x" to the root node grows taller. In the worst case, the height of the original tree may increase by one. It is also mentioned that in some cases, the sub-trees rooted at the nodes along the path from the point of insertion to the root may become non-AVL trees and a re-balancing of the tree at that point may be necessary. As mentioned earlier, this re-balancing becomes necessary if the height of a sub-tree increases due to an increase in the height of its already tall sub-tree. So, the basic step in insertion is travelling along the path from "x" to the root and to restore balance of the tree whenever the magnitude of the balance factor of a node in this path exceeds one.

Assume that a node "y" lies on the path from the point of insertion to the root. Let "y" be the first node in this path where insertion causes an imbalance of the AVL tree. Also assume that the new node is added to the right sub-tree of "y" increasing the height of the right sub-tree. If the balance factor of "y" is "1" then insertion to the right of "y" cannot pose problem as insertion is performed to the shorter sub-tree. Consider that the balance factor of "y" is (-1). Now, the balance factor of "x", the right child of "y", has to be "0" before insertion. The new node may be inserted to the right or to the left sub-tree of "x" giving rise to two cases. Consider these cases one after another.

First, assume that the balance factor of "x" is "0" before insertion takes place. The relevant part of the tree is shown in Figure 8.8(a). Heights of sub-trees T_1, T_2, T_3 are "h". If insertion of a node in T_3 increases the height of the tree rooted at "x" then balance factor of "x" and "y" becomes (-1) and (-2) respectively. This is shown in Figure 8.8(b).

A re-balancing now implies making "y" a left child of "x" and putting "T_2" as the right child of "y" as shown in Figure 8.8(c). This act of re-balancing is similar to rotate the tree to its left around "y" and is known as left rotation. The height of the resultant tree rooted at "x" does not increase due to a left rotation. The "C" function to left rotate a tree is presented in the following. The root of the sub-tree changes after a rotation is applied to its root. Therefore, the new root is passed to the caller as a return value in the function "leftRotate".

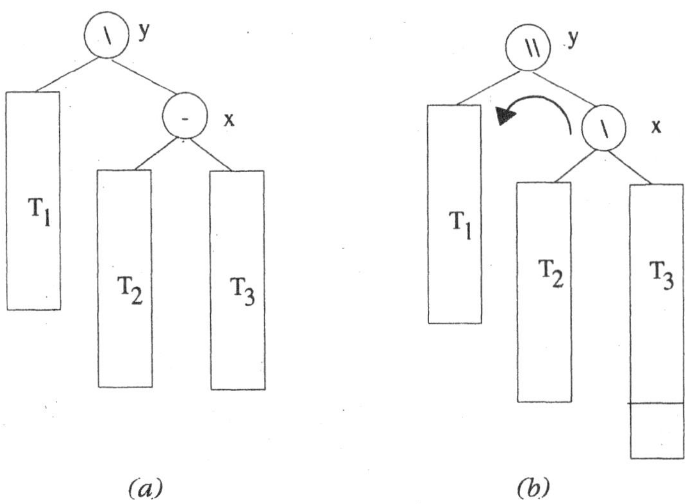

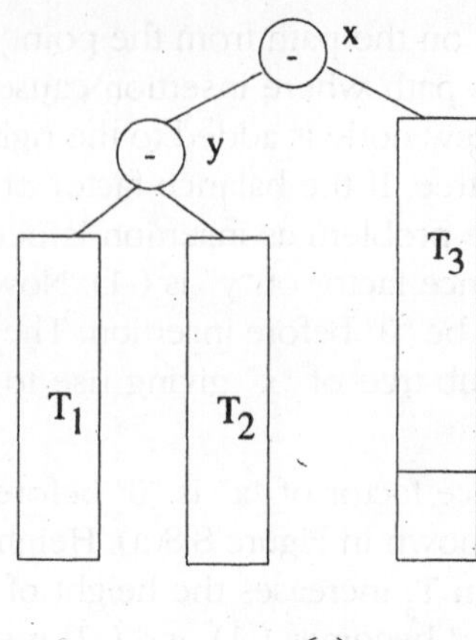

(c)

Figure 8.8(a) Before insertion, the right sub-tree of the tree rooted at "y" is taller. The right child of "x" has a balance factor zero.

(b) A new node is added to the right sub-tree of "x" due to which the balance factor of "x" has become "\". Addition of a new node is shown by the box appended to T_3 of Figure 8.8(a). The tree rooted at "y" becomes non-AVL. A left rotation has to be applied to restore balance.

(c) The resultant tree after balance is restored.

```
AVLNode *leftRotate(AVLNode *y)
{
    AVLNode *x;
    x = y->right;
    y->right = x->left;
    x->left = y;
    return x;
}
```

Next, consider the case where the height of the sub-tree rooted at "x" is increased due to an increase in its left sub-tree as shown in Figure 8.9(a).

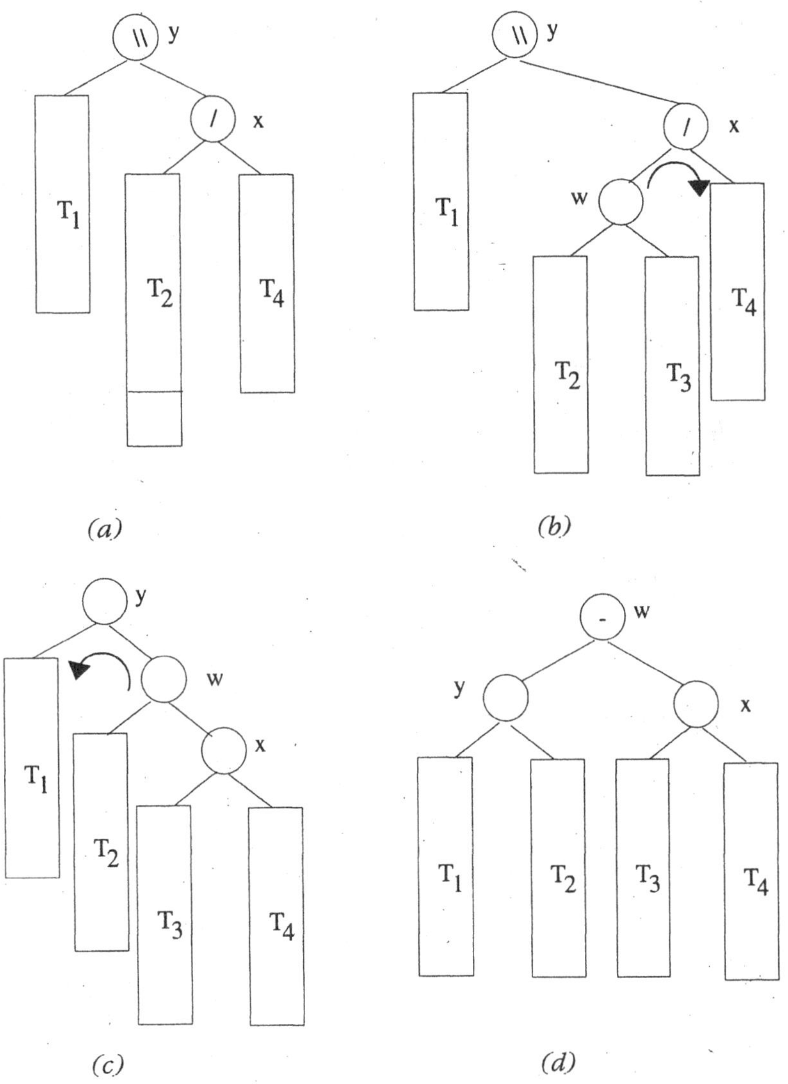

Figure 8.9(a) A new node is added to the right sub-tree of "x" due to which the balance factor of "x" has become "/". Addition of a new node is shown by the box appended to T. The tree rooted at "y" becomes non-AVL.

(b) A right rotation around "x" has to be applied first to produce the tree as shown in Figure 8.9(c).

(c) A left rotation around "y" is then applied to restore the balance completely.

(d) The resultant tree after balance is restored.

By expanding the left sub-tree of the tree rooted at "x" to one more level, the tree of Figure 8.9(b) is obtained. A re-balancing now involves first a right rotation around "x" after which the tree becomes as shown in Figure 8.9(c). Then a left rotation around "y" is applied, the effect of which is shown in Figure 8.9(d). The new balance factor of "w" is zero but the new balance factors of "x" and "y" depend on the old balance factor of "w" in the tree of Figure 8.9(b). Before the right rotation, it was only known that the height of the sub-tree rooted at "w" is (h+1). So, the heights of T and T could be "h" or (h-1) but the heights of both of them could not be (h-1). The balance factor of "w" at that stage could be –1, 0, 1. Depending on the original balance factor of "w", new balance factors of "x" and "y" can be calculated according to the following table.

Old balance factor of "w"	**New balance factors of "x"**	**New balance factors of "y"**
0	0	0
1	-1	0
-1	0	1

The operations discussed till now are required to restore the balance of a sub-tree the root of which ("y" in our discussion) has a balance factor of "-2" as a result of insertion. As it has been discussed, the balancing act is a single left rotation or a double rotation depending on the new balance factor of the right child of "y". The algorithm to rotate a tree towards right is presented next which is very similar to the function "leftRotate".

```
AVLNode *rightRotate(AVLNode *y)
{
    AVLNode *x;
    x = y->left;
    y->left = x->right;
    x->right = y;
    return x;
}
```

Next the function "rightBalance" is presented. This function helps to restore the balance of a node whenever its balance factor becomes "-2" as a result of insertion. This function also returns the new root to the balanced tree after applying appropriate rotations.

```
AVLNode *rightBalance (AVLNode *y, int *taller)
{
    AVLNode *x, *w, *z;
```

```
x = y->right;
switch (x->balanceFactor)
{
        case –1: /* right sub-tree of "x" is taller  */
                y->balanceFactor = 0;
                x->balanceFactor = 0;
                z = leftRotate (y);
                *taller = FALSE;
                break;
        case +1: /* left sub-tree of "x" is taller. */
                w = x->left;
                switch (w->balanceFactor)
                {
                        case 0:
                                y->balanceFactor = 0;
                                x->balanceFactor = 0;
                                break;
                        case 1:
                                y->balanceFactor = 0;
                                x->balanceFactor = -1;
                                break;
                        case -1:
                                y->balanceFactor = 1;
                                x->balanceFactor = 0;
                }
                w->balanceFactor = 0;
                z = rightRotate(x);
                y->right = z;
                z = rotateLeft (y);
                *taller = FALSE;
                break;
        }
        return z;
}
```

If the balance factor of "y" is "1" and the height of its left sub-tree increases because of an insertion then a symmetric situation arises. Under that circumstance, the balance factor of "y" becomes "2". As before, a single right rotation is to be applied to "y" if the balance factor of the left child of "y" is "/". If , however, the balance factor of the left child of "y" is "\" then a double rotation (a left rotation followed by a right rotation) has to be applied to "y". The function "leftBalance" restores the balance of a sub-tree if the balance factor of its root becomes two.

```
AVLNode *leftBalance (AVLNode *y, int *taller)
{
    AVLNode *x, *w, *z;
    x = y->left;
    switch (x->balanceFactor)
    {
            case -1: /* left sub-tree of "x" is taller. */
                    y->balanceFactor = 0;
                    x->balanceFactor = 0;
                    z = rightRotate (y);
                    *taller = FALSE;
                    break;
            case +1: /* right sub-tree of "x" is taller. */
                    w = x->right;
                    switch (w->balanceFactor)
                    {
                            case 0:
                                    y->balanceFactor = 0;
                                    x->balanceFactor = 0;
                                    break;
                            case 1:
                                    y->balanceFactor = -1;
                                    x->balanceFactor = 0;
                                    break;
                            case -1:
                                    y->balanceFactor = 0;
                                    x->balanceFactor = 1;
                    }
                    w->balanceFactor = 0;
```

```
            z = leftRotate(x);
            y->right = z;
            z = rightRotate(y);
            *taller = FALSE;
            break;
        }
        return z;
}
```

With this background, consider the algorithm to insert an AVLNode to an AVLTree. The procedure to insert is essentially recursive. Attempt to insertion starts at the root of the tree and continues towards either right or left sub-tree of the root. The function "InsertToAVLTree" is called recursively on either the left or the right sub-tree. Finally, "InsertToAVLTree" is called on a tree which is NULL. A new node is created with the given key, this new sub-tree becomes taller and this function returns to its caller, another instance of the "InsertToAVLTree" function with the information that the sub-tree where insertion took place has become taller. At this level, the tree rooted at the current node may need some adjustment depending on its balance factor. For instance, if the balance factor of the current node is "/" and insertion to its left sub-tree resulted in an increase in the height of the sub-tree then the tree rooted at the current node must be balanced by applying "leftBalance" function. The new height of the tree rooted at the current node must be recomputed and that information has to go back to its caller. This process continues until the first call to "InsertToAVLTree" returns. By the act of restoring balance, the root nodes of the sub-trees may change. That is why the function "InsertToAVLTree" returns a pointer to the new root at every node along the path from the point of insertion to the root.

```
AVLNode *InsertToAVLTree (AVLNode *y, int key, int *taller)
{
    int tallerSubtree;
    AVLNode *z;
    if (y == NULL)
    {
            y = (AVLNode *) malloc (sizeof(AVLNode));
            y->data = key;
            y->left = y->right = NULL;
            y->balanceFactor = 0;
            (*taller) = TRUE;
            return y;
```

```
}
if (key < y->data)        /* if inserted to the left */
{
        z = InsertToAVLTree (y->left, key, &tallerSubtree);
        y->left = z;
        z = y;
        if (!tallerSubtree)
        {
                *taller = FALSE;
                return z;
        }
        switch (y->balanceFactor)
        {
        case 0:
                y->balanceFactor = 1;
                *taller = TRUE;
                break;
        case 1 :
                z = leftBalance (y, taller);
                break;
        case (-1):
                y->balanceFactor = 0;
                *taller = FALSE;
                break;
                } /* Switch statement */
                return z;
}
z = InsertToAVLTree (y->right, key, &tallerSubtree);
y->right = z;
z = y;
if (!tallerSubtree)
{
        *taller = FALSE;
```

```
            return z;
    }
    switch (y->balanceFactor)
    {
    case 0 :
            y->balanceFactor = -1;
            *taller = TRUE;
            break;
    case 1 :
            y->balanceFactor = 0;
            *taller = FALSE;
            break;
    case -1:
            z = rightBalance (y, taller);
            break;
    }
    return z;
}
```

The function "InsertToAVLTree" traverses the path in the AVL tree from the leaf where insertion takes place to the root. At each node along this path some adjustments (including right or left balancing) are to be made. Time complexity of these adjustment operations is O(1). So the total time complexity of the function for insertion is O(h) if "h" is the height of the AVL tree. The following example illustrates the process of insertion of a node to an AVL tree. Consider the following AVL tree as shown in Figure 8.10.

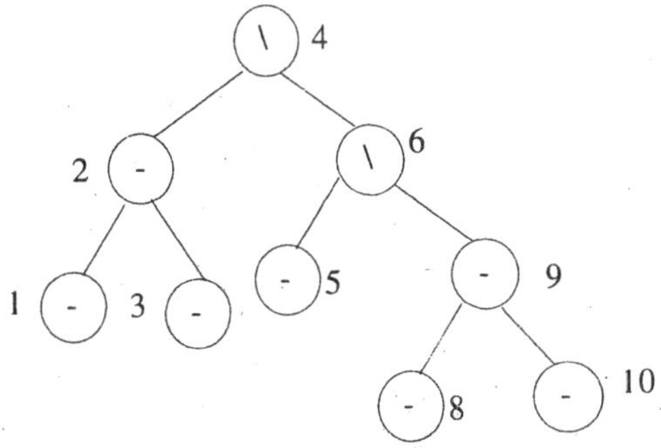

Figure 8.10 A sample AVL tree to which a new node with key "7" is added.

Try to insert an integer '7' to this tree. The first sequences of calls to Insert function will be as follows:

1. InsertToAVLTree(pointer to node containing 4, 7, address of taller)
2. InsertToAVLTree(pointer to node containing 6, 7, address of taller)
3. InsertToAVLTree(pointer to node containing 9, 7, address of teller)
4. InsertToAVLTree(pointer to node containing 8, 7, address of taller)
5. InsertToAVLTree(NULL, 7, address of taller)

The last insert function inserts a new node containing "7", marks the balance factor of the new node to "0", sets the value of "taller" to TRUE and then returns to the previous call to "Insert". The balance factor of the current root (for the call number 4, the root is the node containing the number "8") is "0". The new balance factor becomes "1", reflecting the fact that the height of its left sub-tree has increased and the value of "taller" becomes TRUE. The call at this level returns to the call number 3. The current root is the node containing "9". The new balance factor of this node is "0". As before, the new balance factor becomes "1", "taller" becomes TRUE and this call returns to its previous call. In this call (call numbered 2), the root is the node containing "6". Note that, after insertion, the height of its sub-tree (which was already the higher sub-tree) has increased further resulting in a lack of balance of the binary tree. A closer observation also reveals that the sub-tree rooted at the node "6" (as shown in Figure 8.11(a)) (with the addition of the new node) looks like the tree of Figure 8.9(b) which requires a double rotation for re-balancing. Algorithmically, the current balance factor of the current root is (–1). Therefore, the function "right balance" is called.

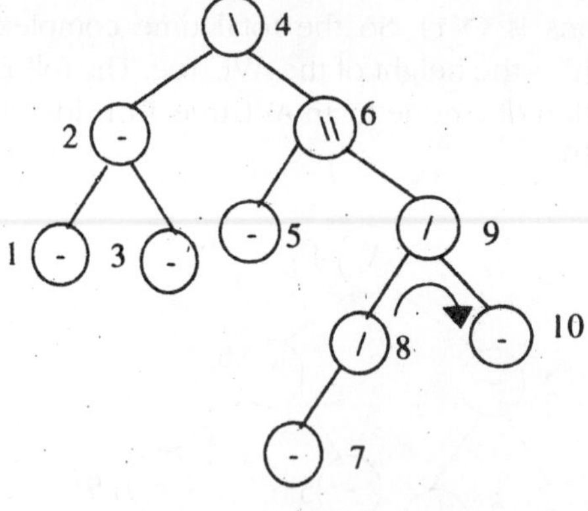

(a)

Figure 8.11 Illustration of the process of insertion of a node to an AVL tree. "7" is added to the AVL tree of Figure 8.10.

In this function, "x" points the right child of current root i.e. "x" points to the node containing "9".The balance factor of this node is "1". So, compute "w" which points to the left child of "x". That is, "w" points to the node containing "8". The balance factor of the node pointed by "w" is "1". The new balance factors of the current root and the node pointed to by "x" are computed to be "0" and "1" respectively. Then a rotation around "x" is performed as shown in 8.11(a). This is followed by a left rotation around "y" as shown in Figure 8.11(b).

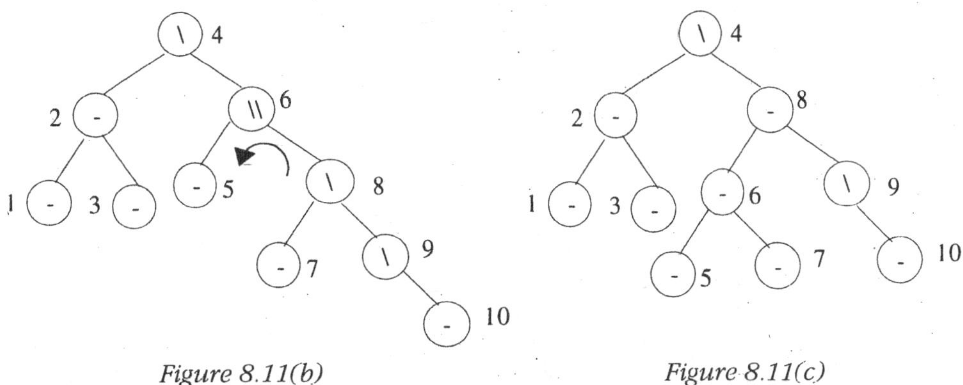

Figure 8.11(b) *Figure 8.11(c)*

Figure 8.11(b) The tree after a right rotation is applied to the tree of Figure 8.11(a).

(c) The tree after a left rotation is applied to the tree of Figure 8.11(b).

8.2.2 Deletion from an AVL Tree

Deletion of node with a given key value, say "k", from an AVL tree is the next operation to be discussed. Quite obviously, the first step in deletion is to search for the node whose key value matches with "k". It is seen that insertion to a sub-tree in an AVL tree might increase the height of that sub-tree and consequently may require a re-balancing of the AVL tree. Similarly, deletion of a node may decrease the height of a sub-tree and can potentially destroy the AVL property at a node along the path from the deleted node to the root. In case of insertion, the new node is always inserted as a left or right child of some node which does not have a corresponding child before insertion. This may not be true for deletion. The node to be deleted can have zero, one or two children. In the discussion on deletion from a binary search tree, it was pointed out that it is easy to delete a node with one child or no children. The same is also true for AVL trees. Fortunately, this can always be the case even when the node to be deleted has two children, The trick employed is the same as the trick used to delete a node with two children from a binary search tree. In such cases, the in-order predecessor of a node having two children has at most one child. See Figure 8.12.

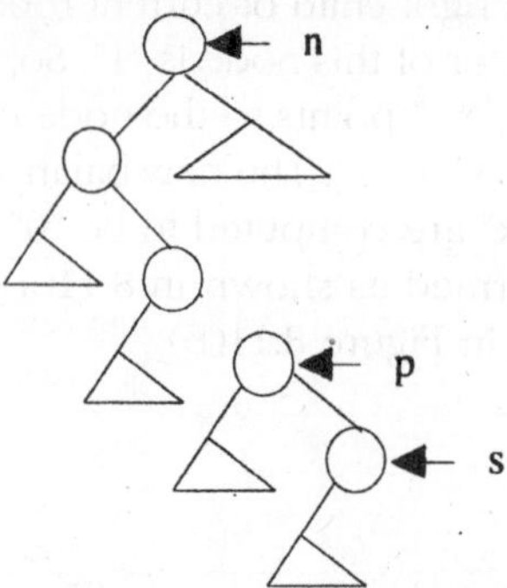

Figure 8.12 Inorder predecessor, "s", of a node "n" where "n" has two non-empty children. Note that "s" can not have a non-empty right child.

If a node "n" has two non-empty children and a node "s" is the in-order predecessor of "n" then "s" can not have a right child. Note that the key of "s" is the largest key in the left sub-tree of the node "n". Therefore, the information in node "s" can be copied to node "n" thereby deleting the original key value of node "n". Now the node "s" has to be deleted from the tree and "s" has at most one child. (Recall that the algorithm to find the in-order predecessor of a node in a binary tree is simple and is left as an exercise of the previous chapter.) In the remaining part of the discussion on deletion, it will be assumed that the node to be deleted has exactly one child. The next step in deletion is to attach the child of "s" to its parent (see Figure 8.12) "p". Now the balance factor of "p" may change. If the balance factor of "p" is already "1" then a further reduction in the height of its right sub-tree would make the tree rooted at "p" a non-AVL Tree. The schemes that are going to restore the balance are the same single and double rotations that were discussed in the case of insertion. Similar to before, the cases whenever a sub-tree gets shorter after deletion, the parent of this sub-tree needs to be re-examined for its balance factor. And if the height of shorter sub-tree of a node gets decreased then a balancing is required. Consider the cases that arise during deletion systematically.

Let "y" be a node from the point of deletion to the root. Also assume that deletion took place in the left sub-tree of "y" resulting in a reduction of the height of the left sub-tree of "y". Depending on the balance factor of "y", three cases may arise.

Case 1: Balance factor of "y" is 0. The situation is described in Figures 8.13(a) and (b). The node is deleted in T_1 of that figure so that the height of T_1 has become shorter after deletion.

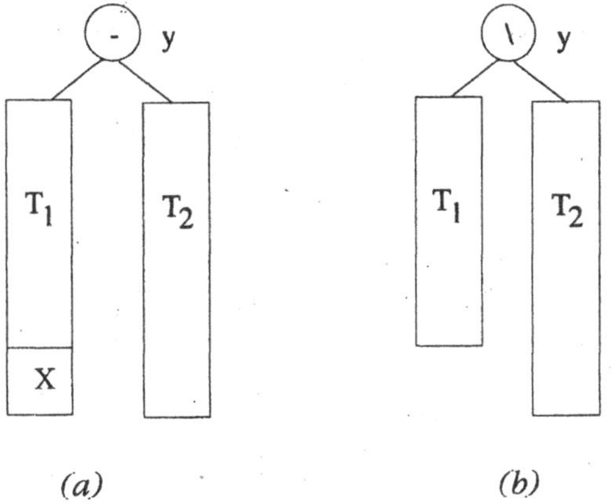

Figure 8.13(a) Deletion of a node from the left sub-tree of the tree rooted at "y". The height of the left sub-tree decreases due to deletion. The balance factor of "y" is zero before deletion.

(b) The tree rooted at "y" after deletion. The balance factor of "y" becomes "\".

After deletion, the new balance factor of the node "y" becomes (–1) but the height of the tree rooted at "y" does not change. Hence, the deletion process ends here.

Case 2: Balance factor of "y" is "1" as shown in Figure 8.14(a). As before, the height of T_1 decreases by "1" after deletion of a node in that sub-tree.

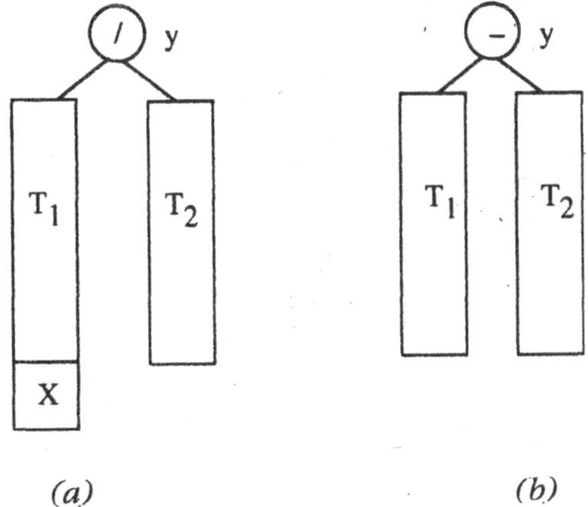

Figure 8.14(a) Deletion of a node from the left sub-tree of the tree rooted at "y". The height of the left sub-tree decreases due to deletion. The balance factor of "y" is "/" before deletion.

(b) The tree rooted at "y" after deletion. The balance factor of "y" becomes "-". The height of the tree rooted at "y" decreases.

After deletion, the new balance factor of "y" becomes zero but the height of the tree rooted at "y" decreases.

Case 3: Balance factor of "y" is (–1). Here, three more sub-cases are to be dealt with depending on the balance factor of the right child, "x", of "y".

Case 3.1: Balance factor of "x" is "0".

The situation is described in Figure 8.15(a). Heights of T_1, T_2 and T_3 must be "h", "h", "h" before deletion. After deletion, the height of T_1 becomes (h-1). A single left rotation around "y" restores the balance in this case. The new balance factors of the nodes "x" and "y" and the new tree are shown in Figure 8.15(b). The height of the tree rooted at "x" (the new root of the tree rooted at "y" before deletion) does not change.

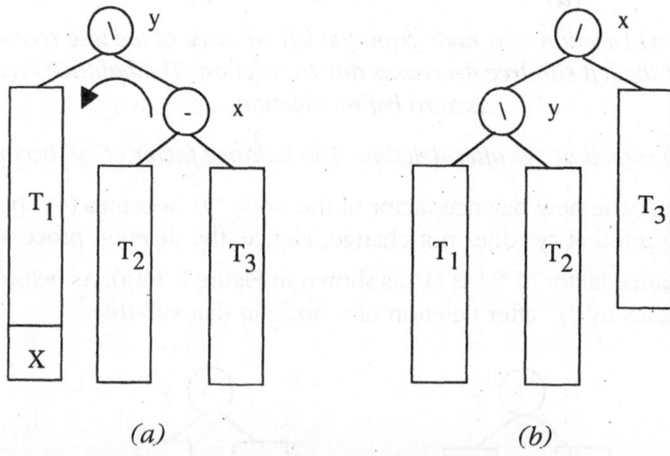

(a) (b)

Figure 8.15(a) Deletion of a node from the left sub-tree of the tree rooted at "y". The height of the left sub-tree decreases due to deletion. The balance factor of "y" is "\" before deletion. The balance factor of "x" is "-" before deletion. A left rotation is required to restore the balance.

(b) The tree after balance is restored. "x" becomes the new root. The height of the tree rooted at "y" remains unchanged.

Case 3.2: Balance factor of "x" is (-1). The heights of T_1, T_2 and T_3 in Figure 8.16(a) before deletion are "h", (h-1) and "h" respectively. After deletion, the height of T_1 decreases resulting in an imbalance at "y". A left rotation around "y" restores the balance. The new root of the tree becomes "x". The situation is identical to case 3.1 except for the new balance factors of "x" and "y".

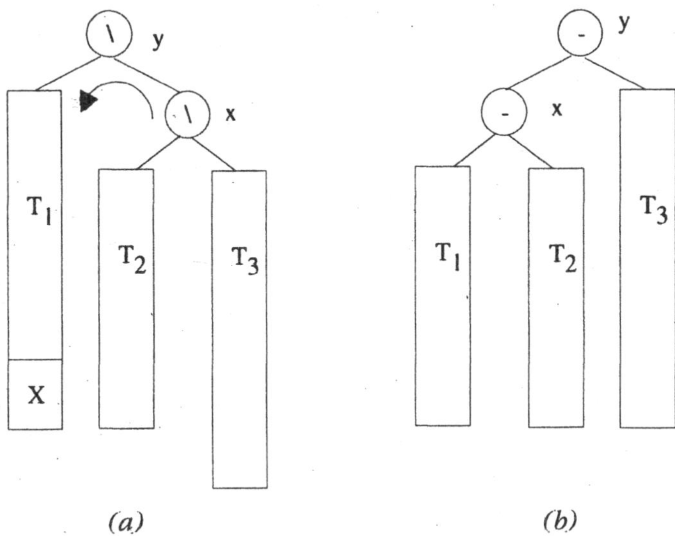

Figure 8.16(a) Deletion of a node from the left sub-tree of the tree rooted at "y". The height of the left sub-tree decreases due to deletion. The balance factor of "y" is "\" before deletion. The balance factor of "x" is "\" before deletion. A left rotation is required to restore the balance.

(b) The tree after balance is restored. "x" becomes the new root. The height of the tree rooted at "y" remains unchanged.

Case 3.3: Balance factor of "x" is "1". This is the most complex case and it is depicted in Figure 8.17(a). Before insertion, balance factors of "y" and "x" are opposite (-1 and +1 respectively). Thus, the heights of T_1 and T_4 are "h" and (h-1) respectively. The left sub-tree of "x" is further explored and let "w" be the root of the left sub-tree of "x". The height of one of T_2 and T_3 must be (h-2) and the height of the other or both is (h-1). Thus, the balance factor of "w" could be "0", "1" or (-1). To restore balance, first a right rotation around "x" is to be applied followed by a left rotation around "y". "w" becomes the root of the new tree whose new balance factor must be zero. The balance factors of "y" and "x" depend on the old balance factor of "w" according to the following table.

Original balance factor of "w"	**New balance factors of "y"**	**New balance factors of "x"**
0	0	0
1	0	-1
-1	1	0

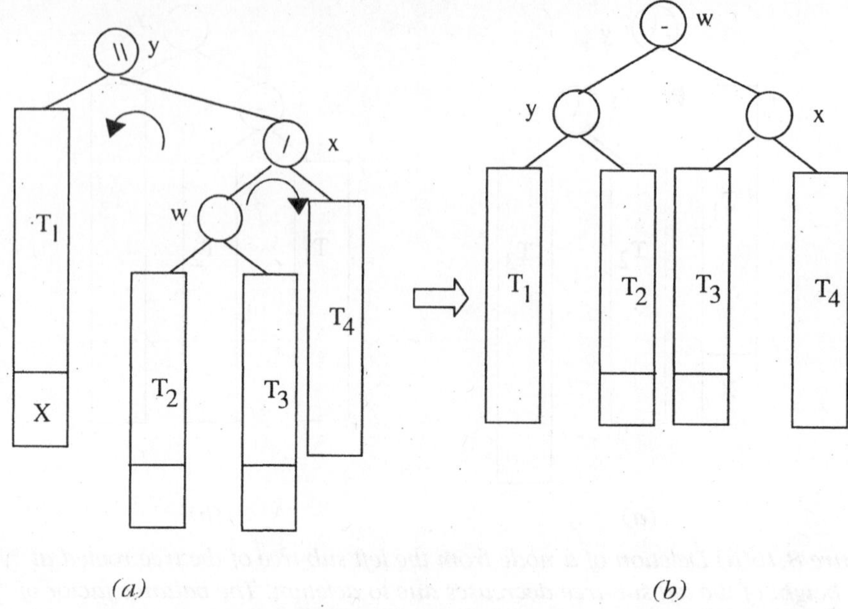

Figure 8.17(a) Deletion of a node from the left sub-tree of the tree rooted at "y". The height of the left sub-tree decreases due to deletion. The balance factor of "y" is "\" before deletion. The balance factor of "x" is "/" before deletion. A double rotation is required to restore the balance.

(b) The tree after balance is restored. "w" becomes the new root. The height of the tree rooted at "y" decreases.

If deletion takes place in the right sub-tree of "y" and as a result of deletion, the height of that sub-tree decreases then three more symmetric cases (analogous to Case 1, Case 2, Case 3) are to be considered.

Consider the AVL tree as shown in Figure 8.18(a). The node with key "3" is deleted. Once this is deleted, the algorithm proceeds from this node to the root. First the node with value "5" is visited. The height of the left sub-tree of "5" has decreased and the balance factor of the node with key "5" is "1" before deletion. This is the "case 2" as discussed in the text. Hence, the new balance factor of this node becomes "0" and the height of the sub-tree rooted at "5" decreases. So, the parent of "5", i.e., node with key "10" is examined. The sub-tree rooted at "10" resembles (See Figure 8.18(b)) the "case 3.1" and so, a left rotation is necessary. The left rotation restores the balance without changing the height. The new AVL tree is shown in Figure 8.18(c).

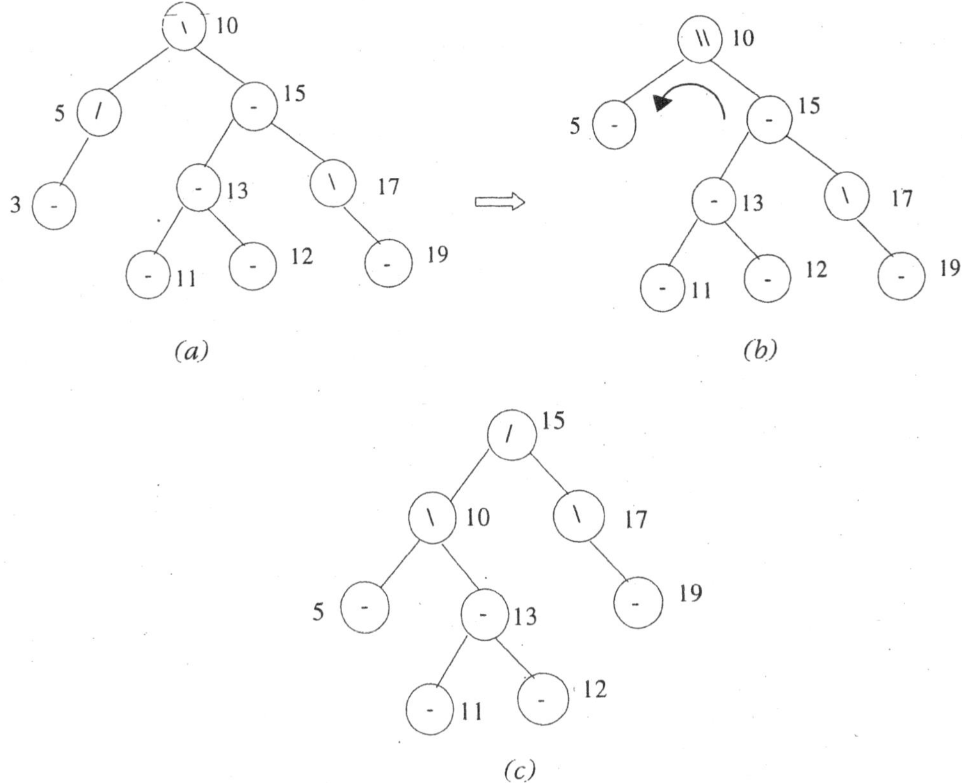

Figure 8.18(a) A sample AVL tree from which the node with key value "3' is to be deleted.

(b) The state of the AVL-tree after the adjustment of the balance factor of the node "5". To adjust the tree rooted at the node "10", a left rotation is required.

(c) The tree after applying left rotation to the tree of Figure 8.18(b).

8.2.3 Maximum height of an AVL Tree

It is very difficult to compute the height of an average AVL tree having "n" nodes. But it is fairly easy to ascertain the height of an AVL tree in the worst case. Instead of finding out the maximum height of an AVL tree having "n" nodes, one can compute the minimum number of nodes in an AVL tree of height "h". Let F_h denote the minimum number of nodes in an AVL tree of height "h". Such an AVL tree has a left child and a right child, both of which are AVL trees. The heights of these sub-trees can be (h-1) and (h-2) at the minimum. These sub-trees must contain minimum number of nodes as the tree with height "h" has minimum number of nodes. Thus, the number of nodes in the left and the right sub-trees are F_{h-1} and F_{h-2}. Since the actual tree contains these sub-trees and the root node, the following recurrence relation is obtained.

$$F_h = F_{h-1} + F_{h-2} + 1.$$

where $F_0 = 1$ and $F_1 = 2$. Such trees are also known as Fibonacci trees. In Figures 8.19(a) and (b), AVL trees having minimum number of nodes with height "2" and "3" are shown.

To solve the recurrence relation, add one to both sides of the equation to obtain the following recurrence formula.

$$F_h + 1 = (F_{h-1} + 1) + (F_{h-2} + 1)$$

Equating $F_h + 1$ to G_h, it can be easily seen that the resultant recurrence formula follows the famous Fibonacci sequence with the subscripts changed by "3". In Chapter 1, it was shown that the value of the i-th Fibonacci number is approximately equal to ϕ where ϕ is given by the following formula.

$$\phi = \frac{1}{\sqrt{5}}\left(\frac{1+\sqrt{5}}{2}\right)$$

Thus,

$$n \approx \frac{1}{\sqrt{5}}\left(\frac{1+\sqrt{5}}{2}\right)^{h+3}$$

i.e., $h \approx 1.44\log n$

Therefore, the height of the sparsest possible AVL tree of "n" nodes is of the order of $\log_2 n$. Since the worst case complexities of all algorithms discussed in this section for AVL trees of height "h" are O(h), their complexities are O(log n) in the worst case.

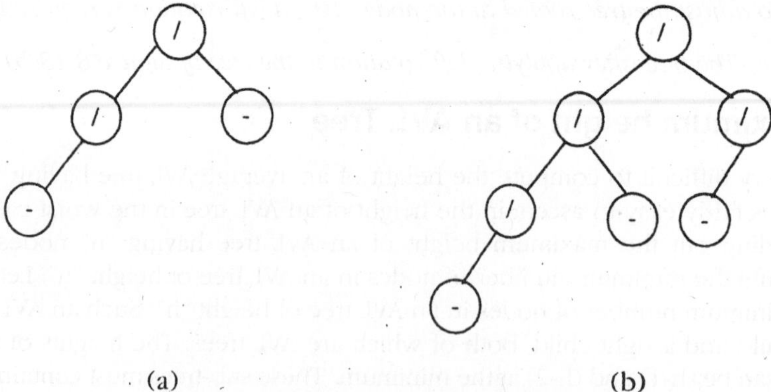

Figure 8.19(a) The sparsest possible AVL-tree having height "2".

(b) The sparsest possible AVL-tree having height "3".

8.3 2-3 Trees

One major objective of designing search trees is to organize data in such a way that any sequence of search, insertion, deletion operations can be performed in an efficient manner. It is already seen that AVL trees serve this purpose by ensuring that the trees are approximately height balanced. But, algorithms for performing these operations are very involved and difficult to understand. Moreover, the constant factor implicit in O(log n), the time complexity of search, insert or deletion operations on AVL-trees having "n" nodes, is significantly high due to the inherent complexities of rotations. A relatively different technique is employed to balance trees in another data structure known as a 2-3 trees. Algorithms for manipulating 2-3 trees are conceptually simple. A 2-3 tree is a general tree, which satisfies the following criteria.

- Each non-leaf node in a 2-3 tree must have exactly two or three non-empty children each of which is a 2-3 tree in turn.
- All leaf nodes are in the same level.
- The nodes which have two children contain exactly one key value "k". Key values of all nodes in the left child of these nodes are less than "k" and key values of all nodes in the right child of these nodes are greater than "k".
- Nodes having three children contain two key values "k" and "k", k < k. The children are ordered – left, middle and right. Key values of all nodes in the left sub-tree are less than "k"; key values of all nodes in the middle sub-tree are more than "k" but less than "k" and key values of all nodes in the right sub-tree are more than "k".

An example of a 2-3 tree is shown in Figure 8.20. It can be easily seen that the height of a 2-3 tree is always bounded by O(log n). Each non-leaf internal node in a 2-3 tree has 2 or 3 children. If all non-leaf nodes in a 2-3 tree of height "h" have three children then the total number of elements would be $(3^{h+1} - 1)$. Similarly, if each node of 2-3 tree has two children then the tree has $2^{h+1} - 1$ elements. Therefore, a 2-3 tree with "n" elements having height "h" always satisfies the following condition.

$$2^{h+1} - 1 \leq n \leq 3^{h+1} - 1$$

Consequently, $\log_2(n+1) \leq h \leq \log_3(n+1)$.

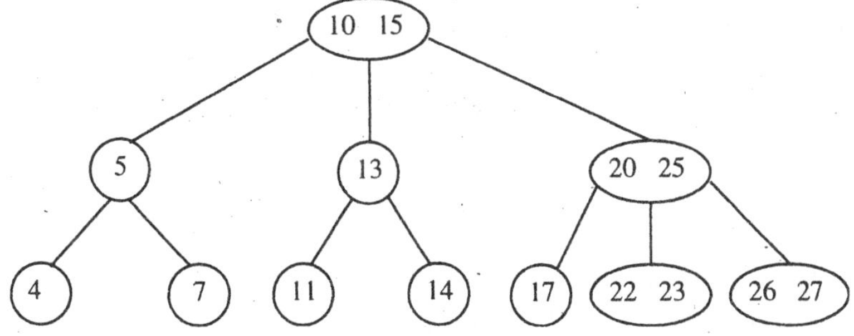

Figure 8.20 A sample 2-3 tree.

The data type of a node in a 2-3 tree can be defined in "C" language in the following way. It is assumed that the data record stored in each node contains an integer key value only.

```
typedef struct twoThreeNode
{
    int noOfKeys;
    int key[3];
    struct twoThreeNode * child[4];
}twoThreeNode;
```

It is assumed that the array "key" of two elements is always sorted in ascending order for nodes with three children.

8.3.1 Search, insertion and deletion operations on a 2-3 tree.

First, consider the algorithm to search for a key value "k" in a 2-3 tree given by "T". Start searching from the root node of "T". To search in a node with two children, compare "k" with key[0]. If "k" is less than key[0], continue the search in the sub-tree rooted at child[0]; otherwise, continue search in the sub-tree rooted at child[1]. While searching in a node with three children, if "k" is less than key[0], search in the tree rooted at child[0]. Continue the search in the tree rooted at child[1] if key[0] < k < key[1]; otherwise, search the tree rooted at child[2]. If "k" is equal to key[0] in a node having two children then search terminates successfully and the pointer to the node is returned. Similarly if "k" is equal to either key[0] or key[1] in a node with three children, search process terminates successfully. If "k" does not exist in "T" already then search process will terminate unsuccessfully at a leaf node (with two or three children).

The "C" function "searchTwoThreeTree" is presented next which searches for a key value "k" in a 2-3 tree pointed to by "T". The function returns a pointer to the node that contains the given key value, "k", for a successful search. Moreover, the function sets the value of "*found" to "True" and "*position" to "i" if key[i] is equal to "k" for a successful search. For an unsuccessful search, the function sets the value of "*found" to "False" and returns a pointer to the last node (a leaf node) which was visited during the search operation. The function also sets the value of "*position" to "i" so that key[j] > k for j>i.

```
twoThreeNode *searchTwoThreeTree(twoThreeNode *T, int k, int *position, int
*found)
{
    int i;
    for (i = 0; i < T->noOfKeys && T->key[i] < k; i ++);
    if ((i < T->noOfKeys) && (k==T->key[i]))
    {
```

```
            *found = 1;
            *position = i;
            return T;
    }
    if (T->child[i] == NULL)
    {
            *found = 0;
            *position = i;
            return T;
    }
    if (k < T->key[0])
            return(searchTwoThreeTree (T->child[0], k, position, found));
    else
    {
            if(T->noOfKeys >1)
            {
                    if(k < T->key[1])
                            return(searchTwoThreeTree (T->child[1], k, position,
                            found));
                    else
                            return(searchTwoThreeTree (T->child[2], k, position,
                            found));
            }
            else
                    return(searchTwoThreeTree (T->child[1], k, position, found));
    }
}
```

The process of inserting a key "k" into a 2-3 tree "T" begins by searching for "k" in "T". The search will become unsuccessful at a leaf node "x" where "k" is to be added. If "x" has two children, add "k" in the array "key" of "x" and increase the number of children of "x". The insertion procedure is over. If "x" is a leaf node with two key values key[0] and key[1] then "x" has to be split into two nodes "y" and "z". "y" will contain the key with the smallest value among "k", key[0], key[1]; "z" will contain the largest value among "k", key[0], key[1]. Let the middle value among "k", key[0], key[1] be "m". "m" is added to the parent node "p" of "x". If "p" has two children then its number of children would increase with the addition of one key value "m". If "x" is child[i] of "p" before insertion then "y" will become child[i] of "p"; "m" becomes key[i] of "p" and "z" would become child[i+1] of "p".. These manipulations would complete the insertion procedure in this case. If "p" has three children then "p" will be split (in the same way "x" was split) and the process continues upwards along the path from "x" to the root. In case "x" is the root then a new node with two children is created which becomes the new root with "y" as its left child and "z" as its right child.

The following example illustrates the process of insertion. Suppose that a key, "21", is to be inserted to the 2-3 tree as shown in Figure 8.20. First "21" is searched. As 10<15<21, the right child of the node (10, 15) is followed. The second node in this search procedure contains "20", "25". As 20<21<25, the middle child of the node (20, 25) is followed. This node (22, 23) is a leaf node. The key, "21", is to be added to this node. As this node already contains two key values, the node has to be split. First, "21" is inserted to the array, "key", of this node appropriately so that the array becomes (21, 22, 23) and then the node is split around its median key which is "22". As a result of the split operation two nodes (21) and (23) are created. The median "22" is pushed up to the parent node, (20, 25) for insertion (See Figure 8.21(a)). This node (20, 25) is also full and so, the new node (20, 22, 25) is split again. The new nodes are (20) and (25) and the median is pushed up to the parent which is the root node of the tree. See Figure 8.21(b). The root node is already full hence, it is split after adding "22" around the median which is "15".

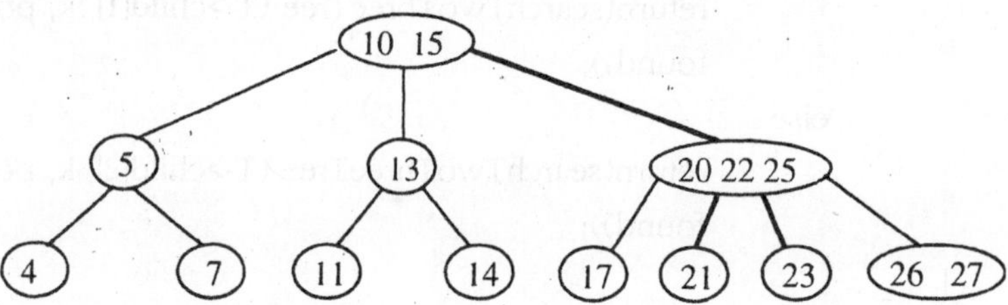

Figure 8.21(a) The tree after "21" is inserted to the leaf node (22, 23) of the tree of Figure 8.20. As a result, the node (21, 22, 23) is split and the median "22" is pushed up to the parent node (20, 25) for insertion.

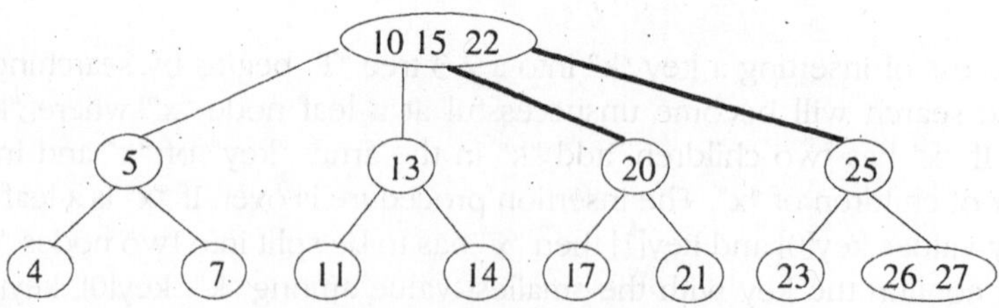

Figure 8.21(b) The tree after "22" is inserted to the node (20, 25) of the tree of Figure 8.21(a). As a result, the node (20, 22, 25) is split and the median "22" is pushed up to the parent node (10, 15) for insertion.

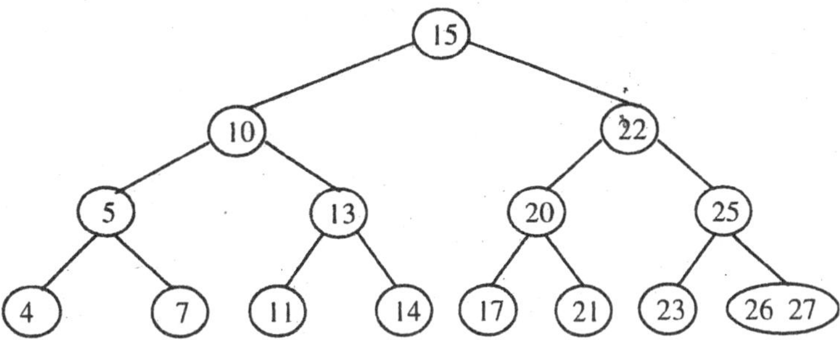

Figure 8.21(c) The tree after "22" is inserted to the node (10, 15) of the tree of Figure 8.21(b). As a result, the node (10, 15, 22) is split and the median "15" is made the new root with two children nodes (10) and (15).

The process of deletion is nearly the reverse of the process of insertion. During insertion, an already full node (i.e., a node having two keys) is split whenever another key is added to it. Similarly, during deletion, a node merges with a neighbouring node whenever a key is deleted from a node that contains the minimum number of keys (i.e., only one key). It is easier to delete a key from a leaf node. In order to delete a key, "k", from a non-leaf node, "p", first locate the leaf node, "q", which contains the immediate predecessor, "k′", of "k". Replace "k" in "p" by "k′" of "q". Then delete the key, "k′", from "q" which is a leaf node. If the leaf node, "q", contains two key values then deleting one of them causes no new problem and the deletion process is over just by removing the key value from the leaf node. If "q" contains only one key and that key is to be deleted then look for left or right sibling of "q". Suppose that the left sibling contains two key values. Then shift the maximum key of the left sibling to the parent and shift an appropriate key from the parent to "q" as illustrated in the following figure.

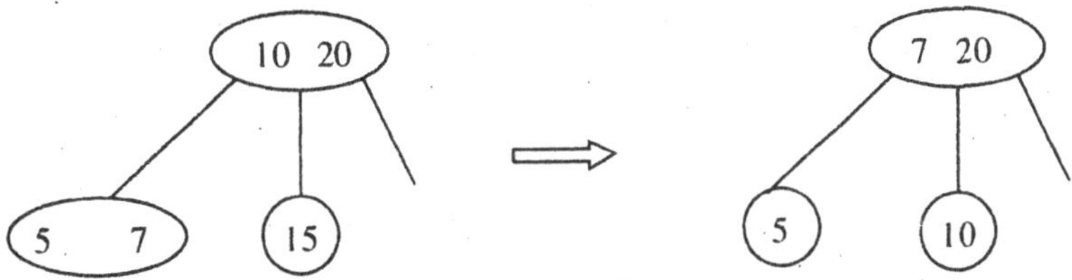

In the preceding figure, let "q" point to the leaf node containing "15". The key "15" is to be deleted. The left sibling of "q" has two key values "5" and "7". If "q" is the i-th child of its parent then the value key[i-1] ("10" in this case) is moved to "q". And, the maximum key value of the left sibling of "q" (i.e., "7") is pushed as key[i-1] of the parent of "q".

If no sibling of "q" contains more than one key then a key from the parent has to be moved to down to one sibling of "q". Due to this movement of key, the parent of "q" may now have no key value. As if, a key is deleted from the parent of "q".

Consequently, the process, as discussed, repeats at the parent node of "q". This process may propagate upwards and may even reach the root node in which case the height of the tree reduces by "1". The process of deletion is illustrated in the following example. Consider, the 2-3 tree as shown in Figure 8.20. Suppose the key, "11", is to be deleted. The only sibling of "11" is a node containing "14". Once "11" is deleted, the key "13" must move from the parent to the node (14). The new tree is shown in Figure 8.22(a). Note that the parent of "11" no longer contains any key. But one of its siblings (the right sibling) contains two keys. So, the minimum value of the keys of the right sibling (20) is moved upwards and the key, "15", in the parent is moved to the empty node producing the tree as shown in Figure 8.22(b) and the deletion process is over.

The algorithms for insertion and deletion operations on a 2-3 tree are not provided in this section. The next section presents a new data structure known as B-trees which is a generalization of the 2-3 trees. Algorithms on B-trees are provided and they are also applicable to 2-3 trees.

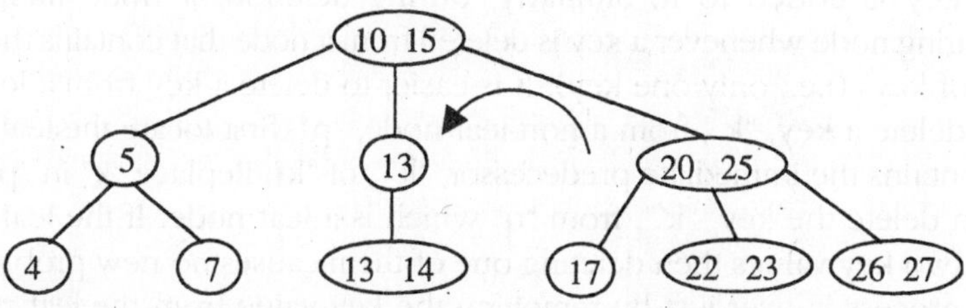

Figure 8.22(a) Illustration of the process of deletion from a 2-3 tree. The key value "11" is to be deleted from the 2-3 tree of Figure 8.20. The node containing "11" is found out. Deletion of the key leaves the node with zero number of keys. So, the right sibling (14) is merged with a key from its parent "13" to form a new node. As a result, "13" is to be deleted from the parent of the new node.

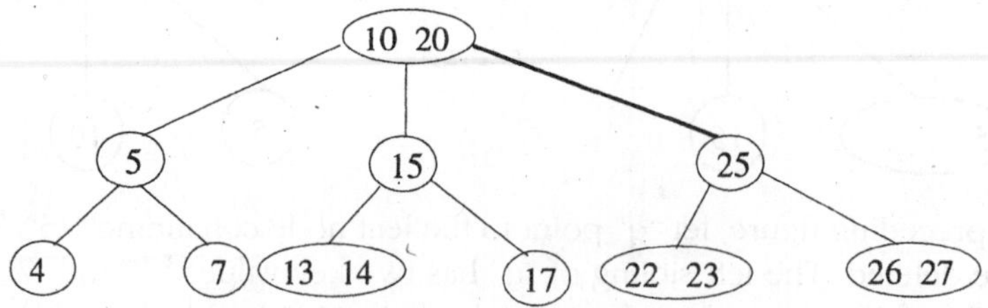

Figure 8.22(b) If "13" is deleted from the parent node of (13, 14) of Figure 8.22(a) then that node is left with no key values. Its right sibling (20, 25) contains more than one key values. So, "15" is moved to the node having no key value from its parent and the minimum key, "20" is moved from (20, 25) to its parent.

8.4 B-Trees

The nodes in binary search trees and in AVL trees typically contain only one record. The major concern has been reduction of height of the tree for efficient operations. Sometimes data which are organized as search trees are not resident in primary memory and they are stored in secondary memory such as hard disks. Time required to access secondary memory is a thousand times more than time required to access primary memory. Also, blocks (and not words) are usually accessed from secondary memory at one shot. A block may, naturally, contain a number of data records. And in operations involving secondary memory, the main reason of inefficiency is heavy access to secondary memory. An efficient data organization in these scenarios would attempt to store multiple records in one block and to make multi-way decisions to decide the next course of action. Thus, multi-way trees are more appropriate for such situations.

Multi-way trees are generalizations of binary trees. A multi-way tree of order "m" is a tree where each node may have at most "m" children. If a node has "k" number of children ($k \leq m$) then that node must have exactly (k-1) number of keys (or records). The children partition all the keys into "k" sub-sets. Some of these sub-sets may be empty in which case the corresponding children are also empty.

Definition

A B-Tree is a multi-way search tree of order "m" such that the following properties hold.

1. All non-leaf nodes except the root must have at least $\lceil m/2 \rceil$ children and at most "m" children.
2. If a node has "t" number of children then it must have (t-1) number of keys.
3. The keys of a node "x" are sorted in non-decreasing order. If a node "x" has (t-1) keys and a key is denoted by $key_i(x)$ for i = 0 to (t-2) then,
$$key_0(x) \leq key_1(x) \leq \ldots \leq key_{t-2}(x)$$
4. The keys in a node separate the ranges of keys stored in each child of that node. Let "t" children of a node "x" be denoted by $child_i(x)$ for i = 0 to (t-1) and let k_i denote any key stored in a sub-tree $child_i(x)$. Then,
$$k_0 \leq key_0(x) \leq k_1 \leq key_1(x) \leq \ldots \leq k \leq key_{t-1}$$
5. The root may have at most "m" non-empty children but may have as few as two children if the root is not itself a leaf node. If the root is also a leaf node then it may not have any child.
6. All leaf nodes are on the same level, which defines the height of the tree.

An example of a B-tree of order "4" is shown in Figure 8.23.

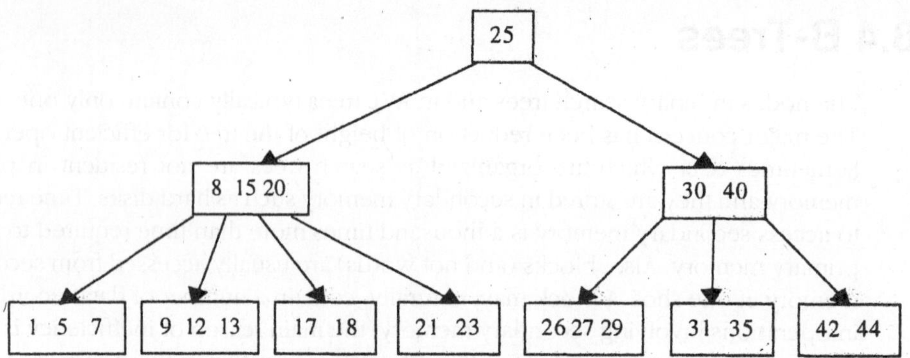

Figure 8.23 A sample B-tree of order "4".

It can be easily seen that a 2-3 tree is a B-tree of order "3". The structure required to represent one node of a B-tree of order "m" is very similar to the one defined to represent a 2-3 tree. The structure of a B-tree is presented in the following. It is assumed that the key values are integers.

```
typedef struct BTreeNode
    {
        int noOfKeys;
        struct BTreeNode *children[MAX_NO_CHILDREN + 1];
        int key[MAX_NO_CHILDREN];
        struct BTreeNode *parent;
    }BTreeNode;
```

When a variable of type BTreeNode is created, its "noOfKeys" should be initialized to 0 and all pointers of the array "children" should be initialized to NULL. The pointer "parent" is added to store the pointer to the parent node of a B-tree whenever required. This field should also be initialized to NULL.

Time complexities of most of the operations on a B-tree are proportional to its height. The following property of a B-tree analyzes the worst case height of a B-tree.

Property 1: The height, "h", of a B-tree of order "m" (m > 1) is related to the number of keys "n" stored in that B-tree according to the following inequality.

$$h \le \log_{\lceil m/2 \rceil}((n+1)/2)$$

Proof: For a m-way B-tree of height, "h", the number of its nodes are minimized if the root contains just one key and all other nodes contain exactly ($\lceil m/2 \rceil$ - 1) keys. Let "t" denote $\lceil m/2 \rceil$. In such a tree, the number of keys stored in level "0" is "1"; the number of keys stored in level "1" is (t-1)*2 = 2(t-1); the number of keys stored in level "2" = 2*t*(t-1). Thus, the minimum number of keys stored in a B-tree of height "h" is given by the following expression.

$1 + 2(t-1) + 2.t.(t-1) + 2.t.t(t-1) + \ldots + 2t^{h-1}(t-1)$

i.e., $1 + 2(t-1)\Sigma_{i=1,h}(t^{i-1})$

i.e., $1 + 2(t-1)(t^h-1)/(t-1)$

i.e., $1 + 2(t^h-1)$

i.e., $2t^h - 1$

i.e., $n \geq 2t^h - 1$

i.e., $h \leq \log_t((n+1)/2)$

This concludes the proof. This also means that as "m" increases, the height of the B-tree of order "m" decreases. The choice of a suitable value of "m" is very critical for the efficiency of several operations on a B-tree. In case of B-trees, the nodes typically contain many key values (basically indices to actual records) and these nodes are stored in secondary memory. Thus, the nodes are usually stored in one block so that a node can be entirely read from the secondary memory by one "read" operation. So, the maximum capacity of a node is often dictated by the size of a block in a particular machine.

8.4.1 Searching a B-tree

Searching in a B-tree is very similar to searching in a 2-3 tree. If a search is performed for a key "k" from the root "x" of a B-tree then the i-th child of "x" is chosen for next search if "k" is larger than all $key_j(x)$ for j = 0 to (i-1). If "i" is less than "t", the number of children of "x", then "k must also be less than $key_i(x)$. The search procedure then operates recursively on a child of "x" unless searching halts unsuccessfully at a null child or searching terminates successfully at any particular node. Thus, this procedure is a straight-forward generalization of the search procedure for a 2-3 Tree. The "C" function for searching for a key "k" in a B-tree rooted at the node "root" is presented next. The function returns a pointer to the node where the key, "k", is found in case of a successful search. In addition, the formal parameter, "*position", is set to the value of "i" so that key[i] is equal to "k". For unsuccessful search, the function returns NULL and sets "*position" to the largest value of "i" so that key[i] < k.

```
BTreeNode * BTreeSearch(BTreeNode * root, int k, int *position)
{
    int i = 0;
    while((i < root->noOfKeys) && (k < root->key[i]))
            i++;
    if((i < root->noOfKeys) && (k == root->key[i]))
    {
            *position = i;
            return root;
```

```
    }
    if (root->children[i] == NULL)
    {
        *position = i;
        return NULL;
    }
    return(BTreeSearch(root->children[i], k, position));
}
```

It is easy to convert this function to a non-recursive one. One can also easily verify that the worst case time complexity of the above function is equal to the height, "h", of the B-tree, which is always less than or equal to $\log_{\lceil m/2 \rceil}((n+1)/2)$. This also implies that the number of disk accesses required by the search algorithm is "h" in the worst case. It is assumed in the above analysis that the time for searching for a key value in a node is insignificant. However, if "m" is too large (making "h" too small) then the time complexity of searching for a key inside a node may become dominant. So, there is always a trade off. It can be shown that the time complexity of the function "BTreeSearch" decreases with increase in "m" upto a certain value of "m". Beyond that value of "m", even if "m" increases, the time required by the search function also increases.

8.4.2 Insertion of a key to a B-tree

The procedure to insert a given key in a B-tree essentially involves a search to find out the correct sub-tree to insert to. Finally, a point is reached where the key is to be inserted into a leaf node. If the leaf node is not yet full then adding another key does not create any problem and the algorithm ends there. For example, consider the B-tree of Figure 8.24(a) where a key "14" is to be inserted.

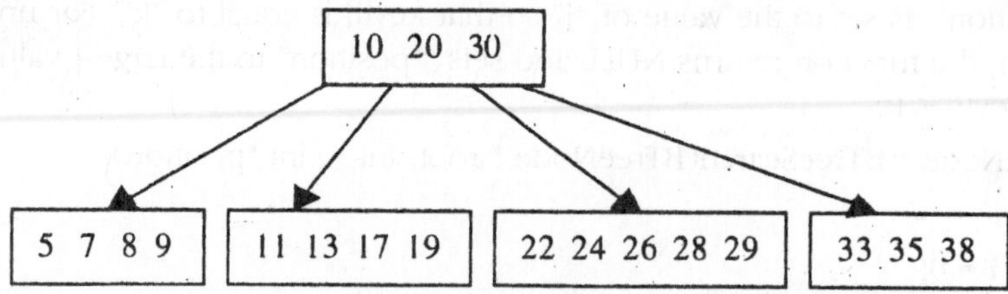

Figure 8.24(a) A sample B-tree of order "4" to which a key "14" is to be inserted.

To search for "14" from the root, it is found that the second sub-tree of the root is to be searched as $10 \leq 14 \leq 20$. Going to the second sub-tree, it is found that the node is a leaf node and hence "14" is to be inserted to this leaf node. Since the leaf node is not yet full, it is easy to put "14" in the array "key" of that node producing a B-Tree as shown in Figure 8.24(b).

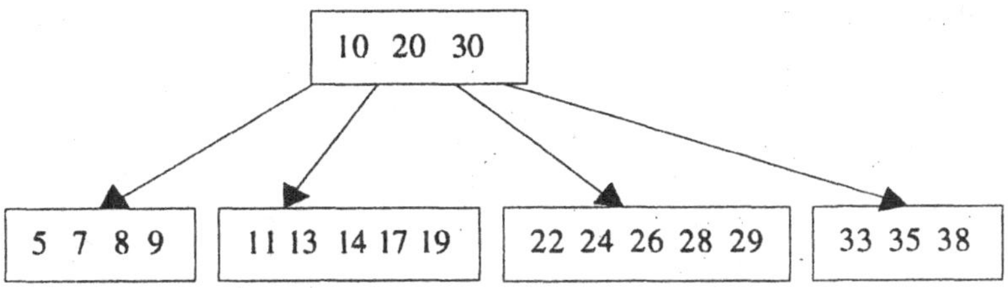

Figure 8.24(b) The B-tree after key value "14" is added to the B-tree of Figure 8.24(a).

However if "23" is to be inserted in the tree of Figure 8.24(a) then an insertion to a "full" leaf node (the 3rd child of the root) is to be done. Since, number of keys in node can not be more than "5", the leaf node must be split into two as shown in the following.

22 23 24 26 28 29 ⟹ 22 23   26 28 29

Now the middle key (say "24") is to be taken out of the left half and has to be pushed up to the root so that the left half becomes the third child of the root and the right half becomes the 4th child of the root. Thus, the new tree becomes as shown in Figure 8.24(c).

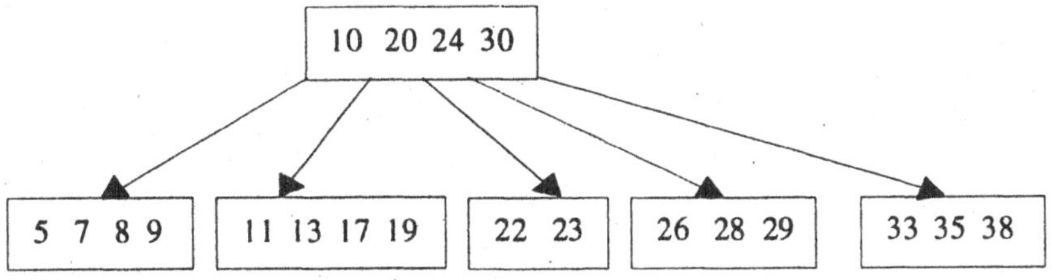

Figure 8.24(c) The B-tree after a key value "23" is added to the B-tree of Figure 8.24(a).

While trying to add "24" to the parent node, it may be found that the parent node is also full. In that case, the parent must be split again around its median key. And this process propagates upwards. The process stops either at the root or at a non-full node along the path from the point of insertion to the root. The following example elaborately illustrates the process of insertion of a key to a B-tree of degree "2". Consider a B-tree of order "4" as shown in Figure 8.25(a).

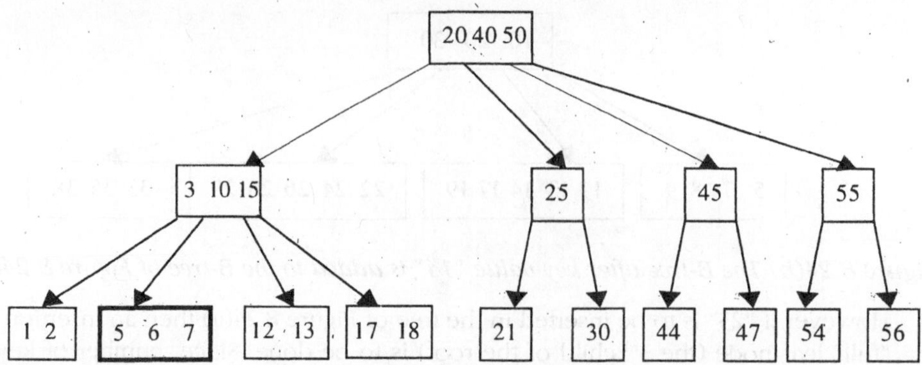

Figure 8.25(a) A sample B-tree of order "4" where "8" is to be inserted. The leaf node where insertion begins is the node (5, 6, 7), which is enclosed in a rectangle whose border is boldfaced.

Let a new key "8" be inserted to it. The first step to insertion is to find out the leaf node to which "8" is to be added. This can be accomplished by calling the function "BTreeSearch". This function will return a pointer to the leaf node and the value of "*position" would give the position where "8" is to be added in the leaf node. In this example, The rectangular node which is bordered by bold lines in Figure 8.25(a) is the node where "8" is to be added. But this node is full. So, the number of keys in this node becomes "4"after adding "8" to the array "key" of this node. As a result, the node is split after ($\lceil 4/2 \rceil$ - 1)-th (i.e., the first) key value. Thus, the original node retains the first ($\lceil m/2 \rceil$ - 1) key values and the first $\lceil m/2 \rceil$ children. A new node is created to hold the last (m- $\lceil m/2 \rceil$) key values and the last (m- $\lceil m/2 \rceil$ + 1)children. The key at index $\lceil m/2 \rceil$ is moved upwards along with a pointer to the newly created node. If these operations are applied to the leaf node in our example then the array "key" would contain the keys 5, 6, 7, 8 after inserting "8". So, the node is split. The original node contains the first ($\lceil 4/2 \rceil$ - 1) (i.e., one) element which is "5". A new node is created which would contain the last (4 - $\lceil 4/2 \rceil$) elements. So, the new node contains the keys "7" and "8". The median "6" is pushed up to be inserted into the parent of the original node. This situation is depicted in Figure 8.25(b).

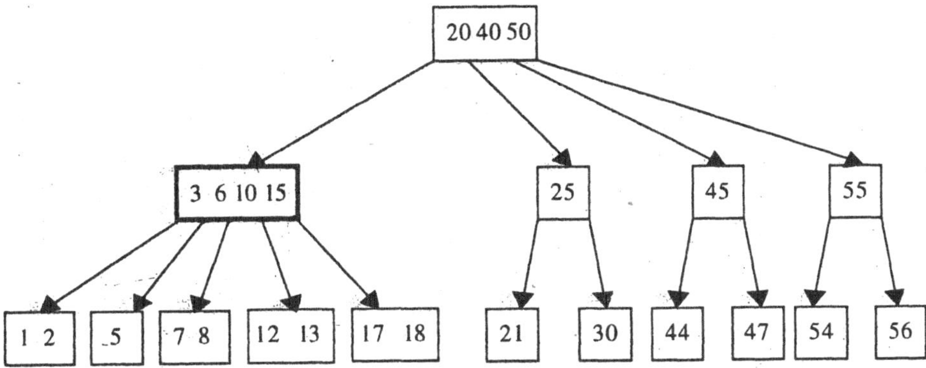

Figure 8.25(b) The B-tree after "8" is added to the node (5, 6, 7) of Figure 8.25(a). As a result, the node (5, 6, 7, 8) splits and the median "6" is pushed up o the parent for insertion.

When "6" is going to be added to the node (3, 10, 15) then "6" is added to the array "key" as mentioned before. If "6" becomes the i-th child then the original pointers children[j] for j = i+1 to "noOfKeys" are to be shifted right by one position. Moreover, children[i+1] of this node is set to the pointer of the last created node (i.e., the node (7,8) in this example). The new node now contains one more key and one more child. Now, it is once again seen that the number of keys is this node exceeds the maximum possible limit (which is "3" in this example). And hence this node is to be split. So, the original node retains one key which is "3" with two children pointing to children[0] and children[1] of the original node. A new node is created which takes the keys "10" and "15" and three children pointing to children[2], children[3] and children[4] of the original node (after inserting "6"). The median key "6" and the pointer to the new node is pushed up to the parent once again. This is shown in Figure 8.25 (c).

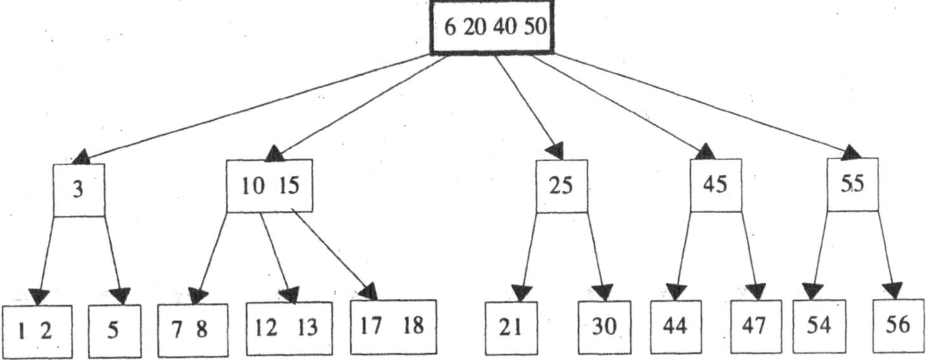

Figure 8.25(c) The B-tree after "6" is added to the node (3, 10, 15) of Figure 8.25(b) As a result, the node (3, 6, 10, 15) splits and the median "6" is pushed up o the parent for insertion.

Since the parent once again contains the maximum number of node, the same operations are applied creating a new root node as shown in Figure 8.25(d).

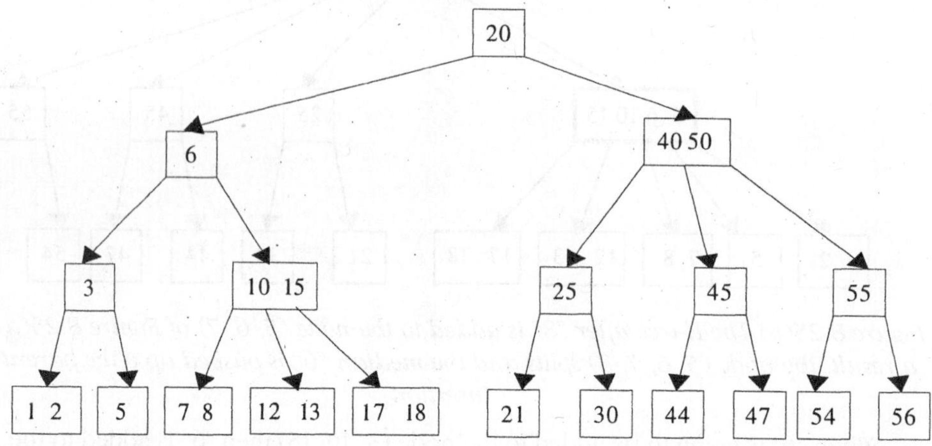

Figure 8.25(d) The B-tree after "6" is added to the node (20, 40, 50) of Figure 8.25(c). As a result, the node (6, 20, 40, 50) splits and the median "20" is made a new root.

The algorithm for insertion becomes particularly easy if is assumed that each node in the B-tree contains a pointer to its parent. Based on this assumption the following algorithm inserts a key "k" to a B-tree of order "m", which is pointed to by (*root).

```
algorithm InsertToBTree (int k, BTreeNode * *root)
{
    int i,j, pos;
    BTreeNode *x, *p, *lastCreatedNode, *t, *r;
    t = *root;
    p = BTreeSearch(t, k, &pos);
    lastCreatedNode = NULL;
    while (p != NULL)
    {
            insert "k" to the array p->key and get the position "i" where "k" is
                  inserted.
            shift p->children[j] to p->children[j+1] for j = i+1 to p->noOfKeys.
            Assign p->children[i+1] to "lastCreatedNode".
            p->noOfKeys += 1;
            if (p->noOfKeys <= (m-1))
                  return;
```

```
            create a new BTreeNode pointed to by "x".
            copy p->keys[j] to x->key[j-⌈m/2⌉] for j = ⌈m/2⌉ to (m-1);
            copy p->children[j] to x-> children [j-⌈m/2⌉] for j = ⌈m/2⌉ to "m";
            x->noOfKeys = (m- ⌈m/2⌉);
            p->noOfKeys = ⌈m/2⌉-1;
            lastCreatedNode = x;
            k = p->key[⌈m/2⌉-1];
            p = parent of "p".
    }
    create a new root node "r";
    r->noOfKeys = 1;
    r->key[0] = k;
    r->children[0] = *root;
    r->children[1] = lastCreatedNode;
    *root = r;
}
```

Writing a "C" function for the above algorithm is straight forward and hence left as an exercise. It can also be seen that the process of insertion is applied on the nodes from a leaf to the root of a B-tree once the leaf node has been found out to which insertion has to take place. In order to compute the worst case complexity of the insertion procedure, note that the function "BTreeSearch" is first applied. The function "BTreeSearch" requires "h" disk accesses to read the blocks along the path from the root to a leaf. The while-loop may continue "h" number of times in the worst case (as it was the case in our example). In each iteration, one more node may have to be created if the original node is to be split. This means that both the nodes are to be written to the disk. Thus, each iteration requires "2" disk access. Total number of disk accesses in the while-loop becomes (2h). If the root is also to be split then one more disk access would be required. Therefore, the total number of disk accesses required by the insertion procedure is (3h+1). It is assumed in this analysis that all the nodes visited by the function "BTreeSearch" may be accommodated in the primary memory. However, the number of disk access in the average case is far too low than what has been found out by the worst case analysis.

The function "BTreeSearch" may be modified a little to fill up the parent fields of the nodes from the root to the leaf where insertion begins. In the following, the modified "BTreeSearch" is written so that the parent fields of the nodes along the path of search is properly set.

```
BTreeNode * BTreeSearch(BTreeNode * root, int k, int *position)
```

```
{
    int i = 0;
    if (!root) return NULL;
    while((i < root->noOfKeys) && (k > key[i]))
    i++;
    if((i < root->noOfKeys) && (k == key[i]))
    {
        *position = i;
        return root;
    }
    if (root->children[i] == NULL)
    {
        *position = i;
        return root;
    }
    root->children[i]->parent = root;
    return(BTreeSearch(root->children[i], k, position));
}
```

The above discussions highlight the fact that it is advantageous to try to always insert a key into a non-full node. This can be ensured in a different way if the order of the B-tree is even. In fact, there are many popular versions of the definition of a B-tree. In one such version, a B-tree is defined to be a multiway search tree of degree "t" where each node (except root) may have at least "t" children and at most "2t" children. Assume that a given key "k" is being inserted into a sub-tree whose root node is "x". Also assume that "x" is non-leaf and not full. It is found that $key_i(x) < k < key_{i+1}(x)$ indicating that "k" has to be inserted in the sub-tree whose root is the i-th child of "x". Now, the node which is pointed to by $key_i(x)$ may be full or non-full. If the node children(x) is non-full, then insertion procedure may be again called from that node. But, if $children_i(x)$ is already full then there are some complications. In that case, then the node, $children_i(x)$, is split into two nodes around its median key and the median key is added to the node "x". Since "x" is non-full, this addition does not pose any problem. For example, let "x" be the node (in a B-tree of order "6") as shown in the following.

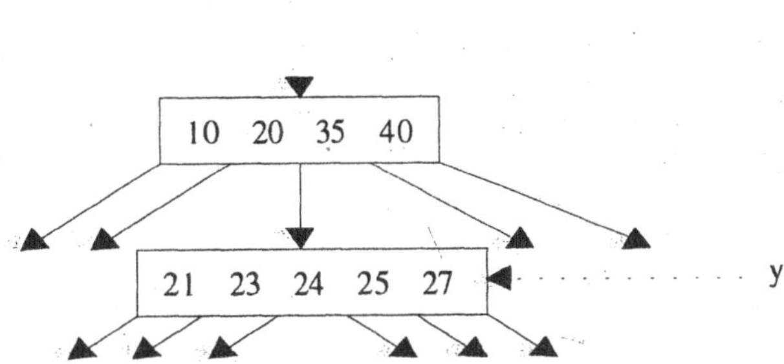

Let "k" be "26" which is to be added to "x". As $20 < 26 < 35$, "k" is to be added to the node children$_2$(x) i.e., "y". Now, "y" is already full. Consider the array "key" of "y". The median is "24". So, "y" is split around "24" into y and y as shown in the following.

Now, the median, "24" is added to "x" and y_1, y_2 are made two children of "x" as shown in the following Figure. Subsequently, "k" (i.e., 26) may be inserted to the sub-tree whose root is y_2.

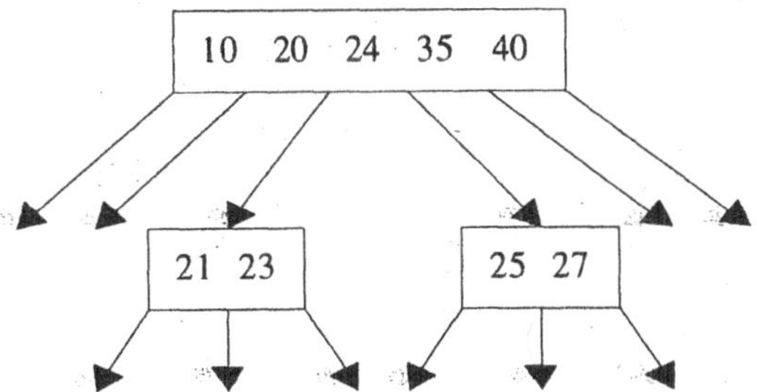

It should be clear from this discussion that splitting of a node "n_1" into "n_2" and "n" and making them the i-th and the (i+1)-th children of the parent of "n" is a fundamental operation in insertion into a B-tree of degree "t".

If the split operation is looked into closely then it may be seen that when a full node "x" is split into "x_{left}" and "x_{right}" then it is known that "x" is the i-th child of some non-full node "y". In that case, the median of "x" is separated and put into "y". x_{left} becomes the i-th child of "y" and x_{right} becomes the(i+1)-th child of "y".

The function splitFullBTreeNode is described when "x", "y" and "i" are specified as formal parameters. That is , the node "y" which is the i-th child of "x" is to be split.

```
void SplitFullBTreeNode (BTreeNode *x, BTreeNode *y, int i)
{
```

```
    int p, j, t;
    BTreeNode *z;
    z = (BTreeNode *) malloc(sizeof(BTreeNode));
    z->noOfKeys =(y->noOfKeys)/2;
    t = (y->noOfKeys)/2;
    for (j = 0; j < (t -1); j++)
    {
            z->key[j] = y->key[j + t+1];
            z->children[j] = y->children[j + t+1];
    }
    z->children[t-1] = y->children[2*t+1];
    y->noOfKeys = t;
    /* Shift(i+1)-th children and keys to last child of "y" by one
    position to right */
    p = x->noOfKeys;
    for (j = p; j > i; j—)
    {
            x->children[j+1] = x->children[j];
            x->key[j+1] =x->key[j];
    }
    x->children[i+1] = z;
    x->key[i] = y->key[t];
    x->noOfKeys +=1;
}
```

Now the stage is set to discuss the algorithm for insertion of a key to a B-tree of degree "t". The insertion procedure is never invoked on a tree whose root node is full. Thus, whenever, insertion process has to be re-initiated on a sub-tree, the root of that sub-tree (i.e. a child node of the current root) is examined to check for its fullness. If the child is "full", the node is split and only then "insertion" function is called on the appropriate child. The "C" function for the insertion procedure to non-full node is described in the following.

```
void insertIntoNonFullBTree(BTreeNode *root, int k)
{
    int i,j;
    i = root-> noOfKeys -1;
```

```
    if(root->children[0] == NULL)
    {
            /* It is a leaf node and not full by assumption. Just
            insert "k" appropriately. */
            while((i >= 0) && (k < root->key[i]))
            {
                    root->key[i+1] = root->key[i];
                    i —;
            }
            root->key[i+1] = k;
            root-> noOfKeys += 1;
            return;
    }
    while((i >= 0) && (k < root->key[i]))
            i—;
    i++;
    j = root->children[i]-> noOfKeys;
    if(j == MAX_NO_CHILDREN-1)
    {
            SplitFullBTreeNode (root, root->children[i], i);
            if(k > root->key[i])
            i ++;
            insertIntoNonFullBTree(root->children[i], k);
}
```

Finally, a call to the function "insertIntoNonFullBTree" can be made only when the "root" node is surely a non-full node. Therefore, when this function is called for the actual root of a B-tree, the root must not be full or the "root" is to be split. The following function "insertIntoBTree" serves that purpose.

```
void insertIntoBTree(BTreeNode **root, int k)
{
    int i; BTreeNode *z;
    i =(*root)->noOfKeys;
    if (i == MAX_NO_CHILDREN-1)
    {
```

```
            z = (BTreeNode*) malloc(sizeof(BTreeNode));
            z->noOfKeys = 0;
            z->children[0]=(*root);
            *root =z;
            SplitFullBTreeNode(z, z->children[0], 0);
            insertIntoNonFullBTree (z, k);
    }
    else
            insertIntoNonFullBTree(*root, k);
}
```

The example in Figure 8.26 illustrates the process of insertion of a key to a B-tree of degree "t".

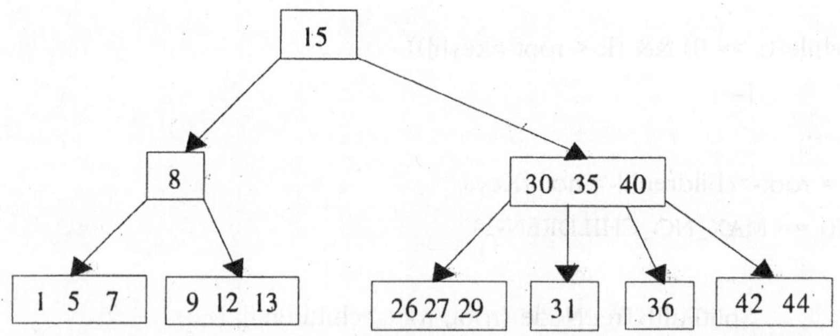

Figure 8.26(a) A sample B-tree of degree 2 (order 4) to which a new key "28" is to be added. Consequently, "28" is to be added to the sub-tree rooted at (30, 35, 40), which is a full node.

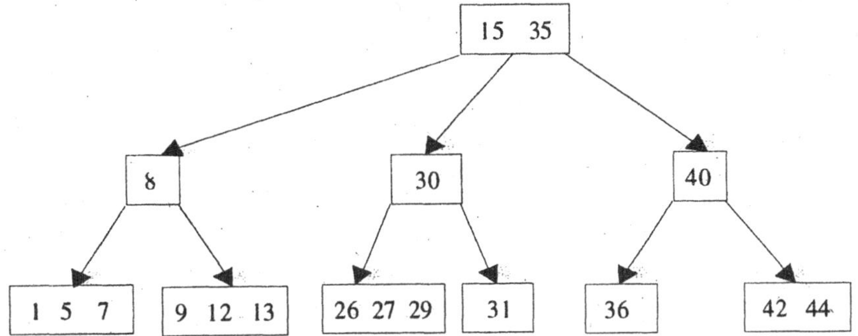

Figure 8.26(b) The node (30, 35, 40) of Figure 8.26(a) is split and the median "35" is pushed up and added to the non-full parent node. "28" is to be added to the sub-tree rooted at (30).

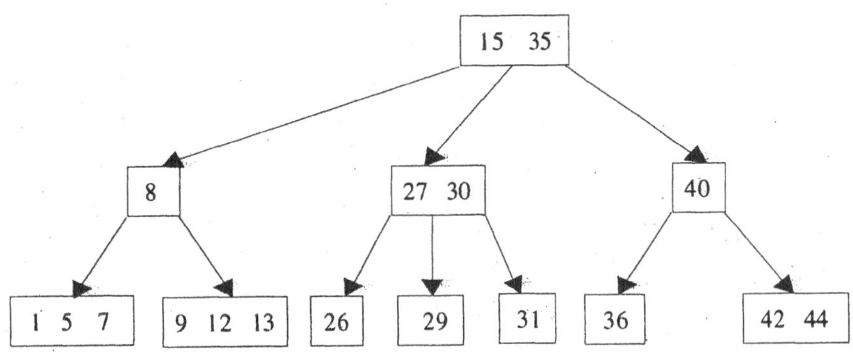

Figure 8.26(c) "28" is to be added to the left child of the node (30) of the Figure 8.26(b). Since the left child of the node (30) (i.e., (26, 27, 29)) of Figure 8.26(b) is full, it is split and the median "27" is added to the node (30).

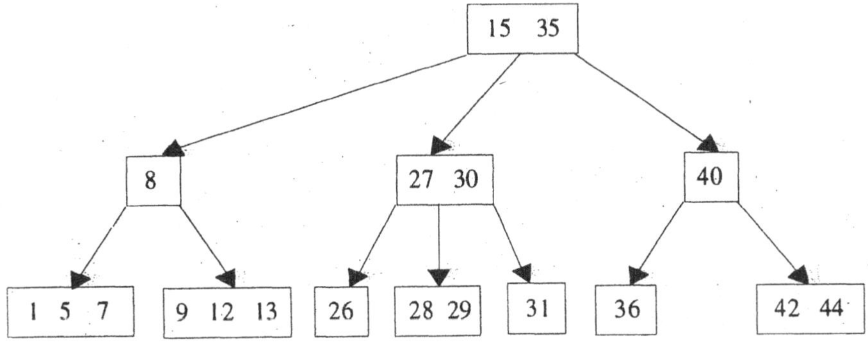

Figure 8.26(d) "28" is to be added to the middle child of the node (27, 30) of the Figure 8.26(c). Since the middle child of the node (27, 30) (i.e., (29)) of Figure 8.26(c) is non-full, "28" is simply added to that node.

8.4.3 Deletion of a key from a B-tree

Deletion of a key, "k", from a B-tree is analogous to the insertion procedure. First, "k" is to be searched in the B-tree. It was observed that insertion to a full node poses some problem. Similarly, deletion of a key from a node containing minimum number of keys is a problem. This is because, deletion in such cases destroys a necessary property that a B-tree must possess. Suppose that a key "k" is to be deleted from a leaf node, "x", of a B-tree of order "m". If "x" contains at least $\lceil m/2 \rceil$ number of keys then deleting "k" from "x" does not pose any new problem.

Suppose that "x" contains ($\lceil m/2 \rceil$ - 1) number of keys before deletion is performed. Deletion of "k" from "x" would imply that "x" no longer retains its B-tree property. Assume that "x" is the i-th child of its parent "p" (i.e., x is p->children[i]). In such case, the right sibling "y" of "x" is examined. If "y" contains at least $\lceil m/2 \rceil$ number of keys then key[i] of "p" is moved to "x" (as its maximum value) and the smallest value of "y" is moved to key[i] of "p". See the following figure.

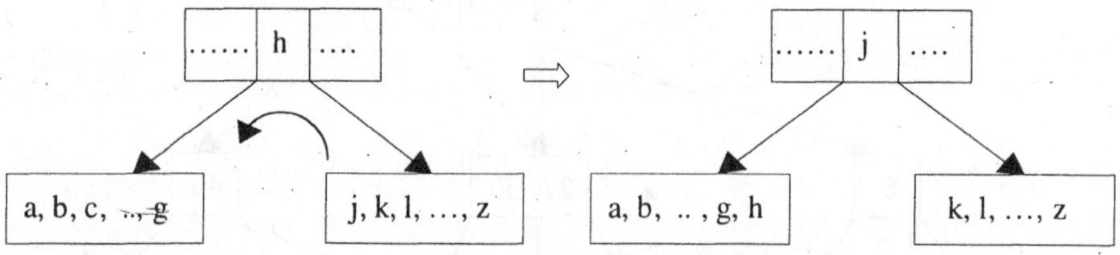

In the preceding figure, let "x" denote the node containing keys "a", "b", ... "g". Let "p" be the parent of "x" so that x = p->children[i]. Let "y" be the right sibling of "x". Suppose that some key value of "x" is to be removed and "y" contains at least $\lceil m/2 \rceil$ key values. First, key[i+1] of "p", "h", is moved as the maximum key of "x". Second, the minimum key of "y", "j", is moved to key[i] of "p". All elements of the array "key" and "children" of "y" are to be moved one unit to the left. children[0] of "y" is set to the last children of "x".

As a result, the number of keys in "p" and "x" remains the same as they were before deletion. The number of keys in "y" decreases by one. But "y" contains at least ($\lceil m/2 \rceil$-1) number of keys even after deletion. If "x" does not have a right sibling or the right sibling does not have more than ($\lceil m/2 \rceil$-1) keys then the left sibling (if any) is looked at. If the left sibling, "z", contains more than ($\lceil m/2 \rceil$-1) number of keys then key[i-1] of "p" may be shifted to "x" (as its minimum value) and the largest value of "z" can be moved to key[i-1] of "p".

Now, suppose that neither the left nor the right sibling of "x" contains more than ($\lceil m/2 \rceil$ -1) keys. Then, the left or right sibling of "x" (whichever exists) is merged with "x" along with key[i-1] or key[i] of "p". The number of keys in the merged node becomes

$$\lceil m/2 \rceil - 1 + \lceil m/2 \rceil - 2 + 1 = 2\lceil m/2 \rceil - 2 \leq (m - 1)$$

Once this is done, the key value which was taken from "p" (either key[i-1] or key[i]) must be deleted from "p". Hence, the same process as discussed must repeat from this level and may continue upto the root. The following example illustrates the process of deletion.

Suppose, "15" is to be deleted from the B-tree of order "5" as shown in Figure 8.27. Every node (except the root) in a B-tree of order "5" must have at least two keys. If "15" is deleted from the leaf node (13, 15) then this node does not have the minimum number of keys. Even its left sibling does not have one more than the minimum number of keys which may be spared to the parent so that a key may be shifted from the parent to the node "13". As a result, the left sibling is merged with the node (13) along with the key "10" of the parent to form a new node (5, 6, 10, 13). But this causes deletion of "10" from the node (3, 10). The situation is shown in Figure 8.27(b).

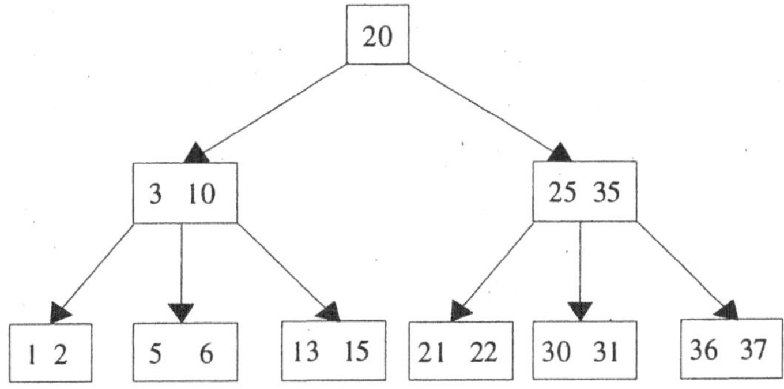

Figure 8.27 (a) A B-tree of order "5" from which the key value "15" is to be deleted. The node having the key value "15" (i.e., (13, 15)) contains the minimum number of keys. Hence, the node has to be merged with its left sibling after deletion.

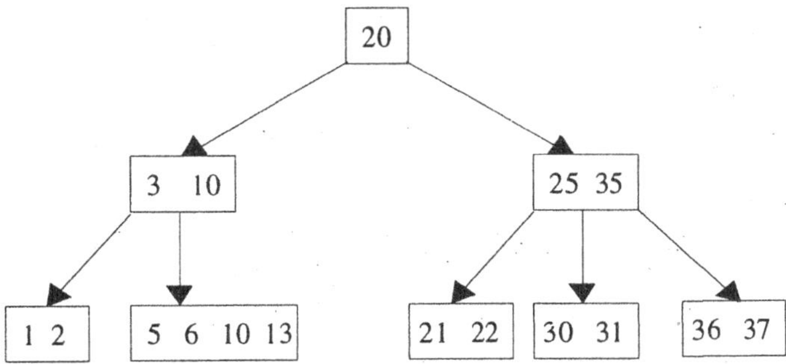

Figure 8.27(b) The node (5, 6) of Figure 8.27(a) is merged with the node (13) and a key value "10" of its parent. Now, the key value "10" is to be deleted from the node (3, 10).

At this level, the node (3, 10) becomes (3) and does not have the required minimum number of keys. Its right sibling does not have more than two keys. As before, the right sibling is merged with the node (3) and a key value of its parent to form a new node (3, 20, 25, 35) which becomes the new root. The final tree after deleting "15" is shown in Figure 8.27(c).

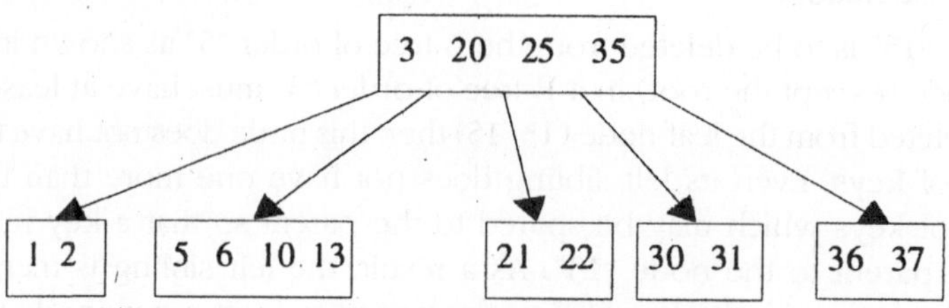

Figure 8.27(c) The tree after deleting the node (3, 10) of Figure 8.27(b).

The method for deletion can be easily translated to an algorithm as presented in the following. The algorithm "DeleteFromBTree" is based on the assumption that the key value, "k", is found out at a leaf node of the B-tree pointed to by "t".

```
void DeleteFromBTree(BTreeNode *t, int k)
{
    int pos;
    BTreeNode *left, *right, *x;
    x = BTreeSearch(t, k, &pos);
    Shift x->key[j] to x->key[j-1] for all j = pos+1 to x->noOfKeys - 1;
    Shift x->children[j] to x->children[j-1] for all j = pos+1 to x->noOfKeys;
    x->noOfKeys -= 1;
    n = x->noOfKeys;
    while ((n < (⌈m/2⌉ - 1)) && (x != t))
    {
            p = x->parent;
            if (pos < p->noOfKeys)
            {
                    right = p->children[pos+1];
                    if (right->noOfKeys > ⌈m/2⌉)
                    {
                            t = right->noOfKeys;
                            x->key[n+1] = p->key[pos+1];
                            p->key[pos+1] = right->key[0];
                            x->noOfKeys += 1;
```

```
                Shift right->key[i] to right->key[i-1] for i = 1 to t-1;
                Shift right->children[i] to right->children[i-1] for i = 1 to t;
                right->noOfKeys -= 1;
                return;
        }
        else if (pos > 0)
        {
                left = p->children[pos-1];
                if (left->noOfKeys > ⌈m/2⌉)
                {
                        t = left->noOfKeys;
                        x->key[0] = p->key[pos];
                        p->key[pos] = left->key[left->noOfKeys-1];
                        x->noOfKeys += 1;
                        left->noOfKeys -= 1;
                        return;
                }
        }
}
if (pos < p->noOfKeys)
{
        right = p->children[pos+1];
        for all j = 0 to (right->noOfKeys-1)
                right->key[j+⌈m/2⌉-1] = right->key[j];
        for all j = 0 to right->noOfKeys
                right->children[j+⌈m/2⌉-1] = right->children[j];
        for all j = 0 to x->noOfKeys-1
                right->key[j] = x->key[j];
        for all j = 0 to right->noOfKeys
                right->children[j] = x->key[j];
        right->key[⌈m/2⌉ - 2] = p->key[pos+1];
        right->noOfkeys = 2*⌈m/2⌉ - 2;
        x = p;
```

```
                pos = pos+1;
                continue;
            }
            if (pos > 0)
            {
                left = p->children[pos];
                for all j = 0 to x->noOfKeys-1
                        left->key[j + ⌈m/2⌉] = x->key[j];
                for all j = 0 to left->noOfKeys
                        left->children[j + ⌈m/2⌉ - 1] = x->chldren[j];
                left->key[⌈m/2⌉-1] = p->key[pos];
                left->noOfkeys = 2*⌈m/2⌉ - 2;
                x = p;
                continue;
            }
        }
}
```

The worst case time complexity analysis of deletion algorithm is very similar to the analysis of the insertion procedure. The number of disk accesses to delete a key from a B-tree of height "h" is (3h + 1) in the worst case.

8.5 Priority Queues

In many applications, data to be processed are not fully available. A set of records is collected, being processed and in the mean time, some more records are collected and so on. An appropriate data structure for such applications is one that supports operations to insert and delete elements efficiently. Two such data structures have already been introduced: stacks and queues. In a stack, the latest or the newest element is deleted. In a queue, the oldest element is deleted. It may also be useful to process not the oldest or the newest but the element in the current set with the highest priority. A data structure that supports efficient insertions of a new element and deletions of elements with the highest priority is known as "priority queue". In fact, a priority queue may be viewed as a generalization to "stack" or "queue" data structure. Priority queues are used for implementing job scheduling by the operating system where jobs with higher priorities are to be processed first. Another application of priority queues is simulation systems where priority might correspond to event times.

It is instructive to list down different possible operations on the priority queue data structure. Assume that the data are a set of records where each record contains a numerical value known as its priority. Then, the following operations are to be supported.

Construct a priority queue with "N" given elements.

Add a new element to a priority queue.

Remove the element with the highest priority from a priority queue.

Replace the largest element with a new element in a priority queue.

Change the priority of an element in a priority queue.

Remove a specified element.

Join two priority queues into one.

The above descriptions of various operations on a priority queue provide a good example of the definition of an abstract data type. In fact, a closer scrutiny of these operations would reveal that many of them can be defined in terms of others. For example, the "Replace" operation is equivalent to an "Add" operation followed by a "Remove" operation. The "construct" operation can be implemented by repeated use of "Add" operation. The "change" operation is actually equivalent to "Remove" operation followed by an "Add" operation. This abstract data type can be implemented in many ways. Different implementations will lead to different performance characteristics for various operations. The simplest implementation of a priority queue can be done by using an array or using an ordered list represented by an array. However, a more efficient implementation is possible by representing a priority queue using an advanced data structure known as "heap".

8.5.1 Array implementation of a priority queue

In the ensuing discussion of priority queues, elements of the priority queue are assumed to contain only their priority values and hence, the type of elements is assumed to be integer only. The most rudimentary way to implement a priority queue of "n" elements is to store these elements in an array of integers in a completely unordered manner. Suppose that the name of the array to store the elements of the priority queue be "Elements". The algorithms for the operations "Construct", "Add", "Remove" are quite straight forward in this case and are presented in the following.

The "Construct" operation assumes that the elements of the priority queue to be constructed are available in an array, "X", and the number of elements in the array "X" is "m". Thus the algorithm involves merely copying the elements of one array "X" to the elements of another array, "Elements". In all functions, the array "Elements" and the number of elements in the priority queue, "n", are assumed to be global. It is further assumed that "n" elements of the priority queue are stored from index 0 to (n-1) in the array "Elements".

```
void Construct (int X[], int m)
```

```
{
        for (n = 0; n < m; n++)
        {
                Elements[n] = X[n];
        }
}
```

The "Add" operation is equally simple and involves nothing but incrementing "n" and setting the value of Elements[n]. In the following function, "val" holds the new value to be added to the queue.

```
void add (int val)
{
    Elements[n++] = val;
}
```

The time complexities of the above two functions are optimal. But such an organization of values in a priority queue leads to a very inefficient implementation of "remove" operation. To remove the largest element in the priority queue, the largest element is to be searched and Elements[n-1] is to be exchanged with the largest element and finally "n" is to be decremented. This leads to the following function.

```
int remove( )
{
    int i, max, val;
    max = 0;
    for (i = 1; i < n; i++)
            if (Elements[i] > Elements[max])
                    max = i;
    val = Elements[max];
    Elements[max] = Elements[--n];
    return val;
}
```

The performance of the "remove" function may be improved if the elements of the priority queue are maintained in ascending or descending order of their priority values. Assuming that elements are stored in ascending order of their values, "remove" operation simply retrieves Elements[n-1], decrements "n" and then returns the retrieved value. But the modified algorithms to insert items into a priority queue or to construct a priority queue would become time consuming to support such an ordered list representation of a priority queue.

8.5.2 Heaps and Priority queues

Heap is a data structure which can be used to support the operations defined for a priority queue in an efficient way. Heaps can also be used to efficiently sort a list of elements as will be discussed in chapter 9. By definition, a heap is a complete binary tree of "n" nodes satisfying "heap property". The "heap" property is that the key value of any node must be greater then (or equal to) the key values of its children. Thus, the root node of a heap contains the largest element. A heap may be recursively defined to be a complete binary tree so that

(i) The root contains the largest element and

(ii) Both the left and the right sub-trees of the root are heaps once again.

The notion of "complete" binary trees must be clarified at this point. A "full" or "completely full" binary tree is one where all leaf nodes are at the same level and all non-leaf nodes must have two children. In a "complete" binary tree, all leaf nodes must be situated at adjacent levels, "m" and (m-1), and the nodes (if any) to the left of all non-leaf nodes at level (m-1) must have two children except the last non-leaf node from left at level (m-1) which must have exactly one left child.

It has already been discussed in Chapter 7 that complete (or near complete) binary trees may be implemented by a single one-dimensional array where the nodes of a tree are numbered level by level and form left to right in the same level. If this numbering scheme starts from index "1" then the children of the i-th node in a tree are located at "2i" and (2i+1) indices of the array. Similarly, the parent of any node at the i-th index is located in the index (i/2) of the array.

Most of the operations on priority queues would first modify the structure of the underlying heap. For instance, "add" operation on a priority queue will result in insertion of an element to the heap . Heap property of some node in the original heap may be violated due to such a modification of the heap. A restructuring is, thus, necessary to restore the tree to a heap. Take, for instance, the heap of 10 elements as shown in Figure 8.28.

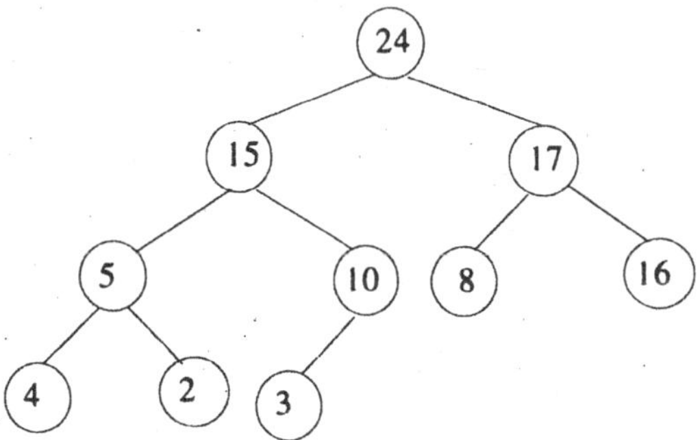

Elements:

MAX_INT	24	15	17	5	10	8	16	4	2	3	....

Figure 8.28 A priority queue and its heap representation.

Note that the elements of the heap are stored from index 1 of the array "Elements". Element[0] is a sentinel key which contains the maximum integer. This element helps in handling boundary conditions in subsequent algorithms which are explained later.

If a new element "25" is to be inserted. Elements[11] is first set to "25". But the parent of this node is Elements[5] which is "10" and the value of the parent is less than that of its child. To fix the problem, one would exchange values of the parent and the concerned child resulting in the tree of Figure 8.29(a). Even in this tree, the heap property is not satisfied for the parent of the 5th node. So, it may be required to go on restructuring along the path from one node to the root of the tree.

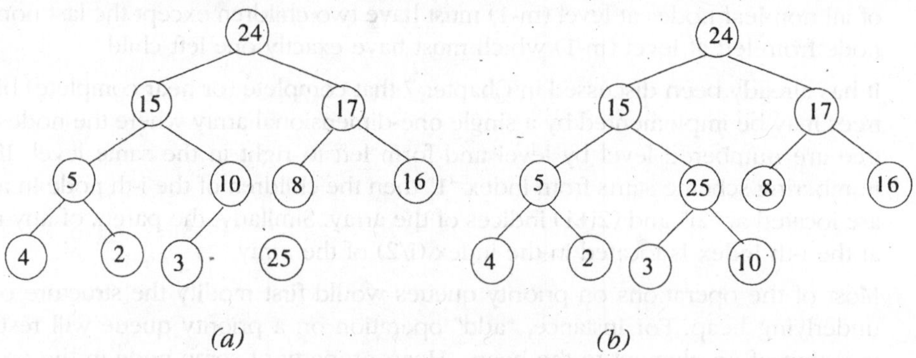

Figure 8.29(a) "25" is to be added to the priority queue. The heap property is not satisfied at the node (10).

(b) The key values of the nodes (10) and (25) of Figure 8.29(a) are exchanged. Once again the property is violated at the node (15).

The following algorithm "restoreHeapUp" serves this purpose by restoring the heap-property of all nodes along the path from the k-th node to the root.

```
void restoreHeapUp (int pos)
{
    int val;
    val = Elements[pos];
    while (Elements[pos/2] <= val)
    {
```

```
            Elements[pos] = Elements[pos/2];
            pos = pos/2;
            }
    Elements[pos] = val;
}
```

To simplify the procedure for restoring the heap, the value stored at Elements[0] is assumed to be greater than any value stored in the array from index "1" to "n". Thus, whenever, "pos" is "0" Elements[0] will be greater than "val" and the while-loop will terminate.

Adding an element to the priority queue is just adding the element to the last of the array "Elements" and restoring the heap upwards.

```
void add (int newVal)
{
    Elements[++n] = newVal;
    restoreHeapUp (n);
}
```

Next, consider the "replace" operation which would attempt to modify the priority of the largest element in the priority queue. Therefore, the value of the root node in the heap will change and it is possible that the heap property at this node is violated due to the change. For example, suppose that the value of the root node of the heap of Figure 8.28 is to be changed to "1". The values of the children of the root are "15" and "17" respectively. To restore the heap at the root, the value of the root and the largest value of its children are exchanged yielding the heap as shown in Figure 8.30(b). But the heap condition is now violated at the node with value "1". Once again, the heap is restored by exchanging value of this node with the largest value of its children as shown in Figure 8.30(c). Thus, replace operation necessitates traversing the heap downwards and restoring the heap property from the root to the leaves. The following function "restoreHeapDown" accomplishes this task from any arbitrary node whose position is given by "pos".

```
void restoreHeapDown (int pos)
{
    int i, val;
    val = Elements[pos];
    while (pos <= n/2)
    {
            i = 2*pos;
            if ((i < n) && (Elements[i] < Elements[i+1]))
```

```
            i ++;
        if (val >= Elements[i])
                break;
        Elements[pos] = Elements[i];
        pos = i;
    }
    Elements[pos] = val;
}
```

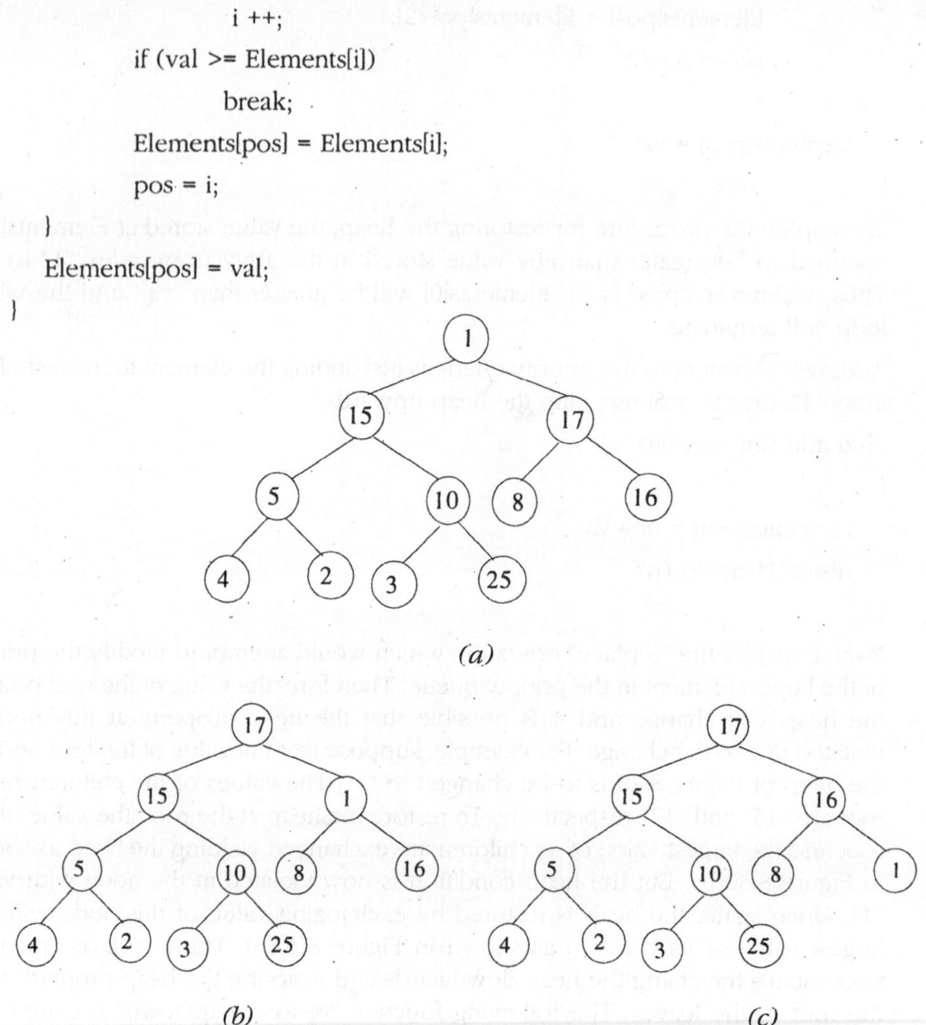

Figure 8.30(a) The value at the root of the heap of Figure 8.28 is changed to "1". Consequently, the heap property is not satisfied at the root node.

(b) The values of the root and its child with maximum value of Figure 8.30(a) are exchanged. Even then, the heap property is not satisfied at the node (1).

(c) The values of the node (1) and its child with maximum value of Figure 8.30(b) are exchanged. Now, the heap property is satisfied at all the nodes.

The "remove" operation on a priority queue may be viewed as a simple extension of "replace" operation. "Remove" operation would delete the element at index "1" of Elements array and as a result, the value of "n" must decrement. Suppose that the value of the root is replaced by the value of the element at n-th index (before removing the largest element) and then, "n" is decremented and the heap is restored. As a consequence, the "remove" operation would be implemented. This scheme is employed in the following function.

```
int remove ( )
{
    int val;
    val = Elements [1];
    Elements [1] = Elements [n—];
    restoreHeapDown (1);
    return val;
}
```

The functions "restoreHeapUp" and "restoreHeapDown" traverses the heap along a path from the root (i.e. the node at position "1") to some leaf. Thus, the time complexity of these functions can not be more than O(h) where "h" is the height of the tree. Since the heap is a near complete binary tree, $h \leq \log_2 n$. Thus, the time complexity of these two functions is $O(\log_2 n)$. The functions "add" and "remove" merely use the functions "restoreHeapUp" and "restoreHeapDown" and the complexity of additional processing in "add" and "remove" is O(1). Thus, the complexity of "add" and "remove" functions is also $O(\log_2 n)$.

8.5.3 Construction of a heap

Assume that "n" key values are stored in the array "Elements" from index 1 to "n". These key values may be represented by a tree. But the heap property may not be true in many nodes of the tree and hence the tree represented by the array "Elements" will not necessarily be a heap. For instance, let "n" be "15" and the array "Elements" look like the following.

Elements:

MAX_INT	1	2	3	4	5	6	7	8	9	10	11	12	13	14	15

The tree represented by this array is shown in Figure 8.31(a).

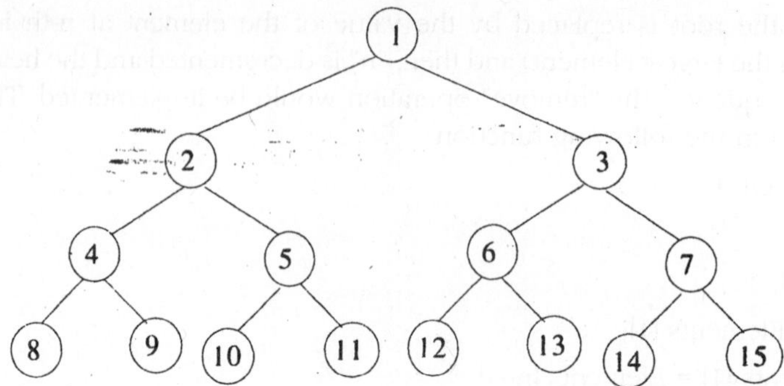

Figure 8.31(a) The initial tree represented by the array "Elements".

A heap may be constructed out of this tree in a bottom-up manner. That is, smaller heaps are being constructed from the leaves to the root so that the sub-trees rooted at any node is always a heap as the algorithm progresses. Since any leaf node is root of a tree with one node, the heap condition is always valid for a tree rooted at any leaf node. So, the algorithm starts with nodes whose level is one less than the maximum level of the tree. So, the sub-trees rooted at "7", "6", "5", "4" are taken up and these sub-trees are converted to heaps by executing "restoreHeapDown" on these sub-trees. As a result, the tree shown in Figure 8.31(b) results.

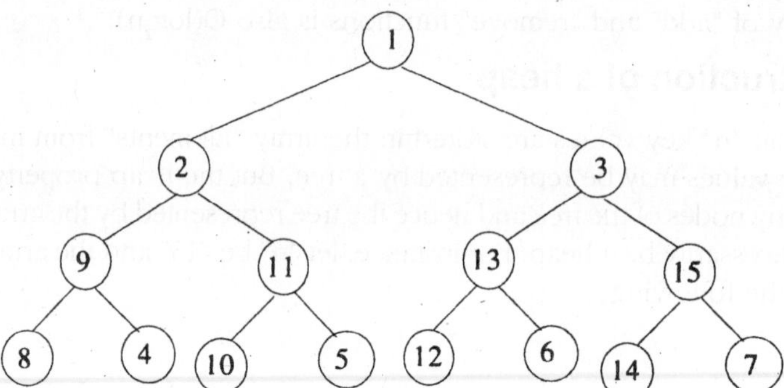

Figure 8.31(b) The trees rooted at the nodes of level "2" are made heaps.

Now, sub-trees beneath the nodes in the next lower level are taken up. That is, trees with roots at "3" and "2" are converted to heaps by running "restoreHeapDown" on trees rooted at these nodes. This transforms the tree into one shown in Figure 8.31(c).

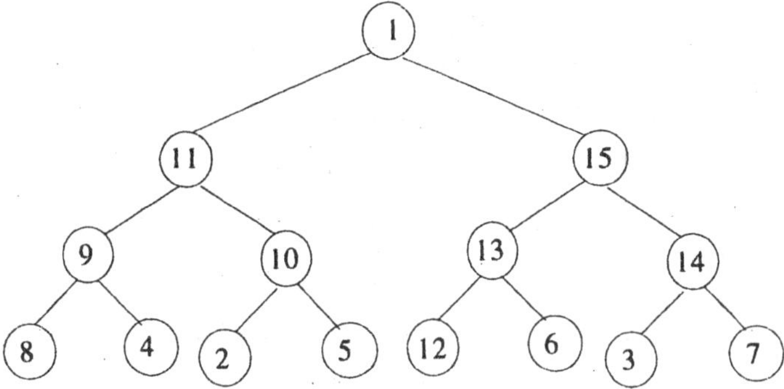

Figure 8.31(c) The trees rooted at the nodes of level "1" are made heaps.

Next, the tree below the nodes at the next lower level is taken up. In this example, there is only one node, the root, is available at that level. So, "restoreHeapDown" is run on the root and the entire tree becomes a heap as shown in Figure 8.31(d)

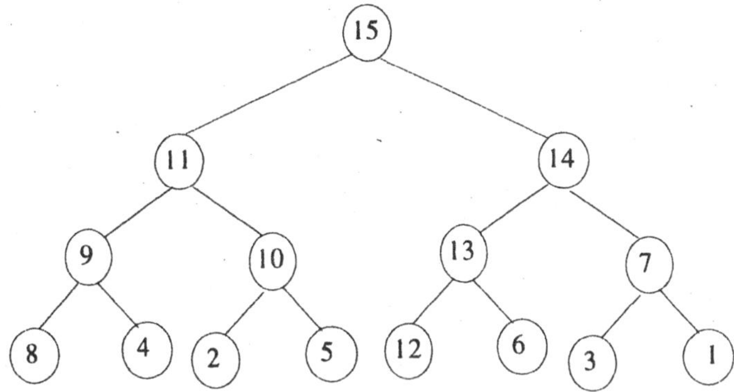

Figure 8.31(d) The heap out of initial tree of Figure 8.31(a).

Thus, the algorithm to construct a heap is very straight forward. It just calls "restoreHeapDown" for all nodes in positions from (n/2) to "1" in succession. In the following algorithm, the array "Elements" and the integer "n" are considered to be global.

```
void constructHeap ( )
{
    int i;
    for (i = n/2; i >=1; i—)
    restoreHeapDown (i)
}
```

Let n = 2^m-1. Then, there are "m" levels and in the i-th level there are 2^{i-1} number of nodes. Height of a sub-tree rooted at a node at the i-th level is (m-i). The function "restoreHeapDown" works on all sub-trees rooted at (i-1) number of nodes of height (m-1) for all levels "i". So, the total complexity of the algorithm "construct" is given by

$\Sigma_{i=1,(m-1)} O(m-i+1)\ 2^{i-1}$

$\leq k\ \Sigma_{i=1,(m-1)}\ 2^{i-1}(m-i+1)$

$\leq\ k\ ((m).2^0 + (m-1).2^1 + (m-2).2^2 + \ldots + 2^{m-1}) = O(n).$

Thus, bottom-up heap construction may be performed in linear time.

8.6 Points to be remembered

- AVL Trees are height balanced binary search trees where the difference between heights of left and right sub-trees rooted at any node can not be larger then one.
- The fundamental operations, namely search, insertion and deletion, are efficient on AVL Trees. The complexities of these operations on an AVL Tree having "n" node is O(log n) as the maximum height of an AVL Tree is also O(log n).
- The process of insertion adds a node as a left or right child of an existing node in the AVL Tree. From that point, the process retraces its path to the root through a series of parent nodes. At each node along the path, the new balance factor is computed. Whenever necessary, the tree is re-balanced using left and/or right rotations. The process stops at a node where the new height is the same as the old height or the node reached is the root node.
- Deletion process is analogous. But deletion is preferably done on a node with at most one child. This was also the case for deleting a node from a binary search tree. The same trick is applied in this case.
- A different way to construct a height balanced tree is possible if some restrictions are applied on the non-leaf nodes. This is done in a 2-3 tree where all non-leaf nodes must have either two or three children. Nodes with three children have two key values which are sorted in ascending manner. Further, the property of binary search trees also applies (in a generalized form) to 2-3 trees.
- The procedure for insertion, deletion operations on a 2-3 trees are different then those on an AVL Tree. They do not involve rotation but involves splitting a node or merging two nodes.
- A B-tree of order "m" is a m-way search tree where each node except the root must have at least $\lceil m/2 \rceil$ children and at most "m" children. The root node is allowed to have two children at the minimum.
- B-trees are particularly used to organize data in secondary memory such as hard disk. This means that the nodes of a B-tree typically reside in hard disk.

Efficient operations on data residing in secondary memory must ensure minimum access to secondary memory. Also, note that the secondary memory is accessed by blocks and not by words. This is why, the order "m" of a B-tree is chosen in such a way that a node with all its keys and pointers to its children can be accommodated in one block.

- The height of a B-tree of order "m" and having "n" nodes is not greater than

$$\log_{\lceil m/2 \rceil}(n+1)/2.$$

All operations such as search, insertion, deletion on a B-tree require O(h) number of disk accesses.

- Search, insertion and deletion operations on a B-tree are generalizations of the same operations on a 2-3 tree. It is interesting to note that B-trees grow or shrink upwards during insertions or deletions of key values. In ordinary trees, the trees grow or shrink towards the leaves during these operations.
- Priority queues are generalized versions of stacks and queues where elements are removed based on their priority values. That is, the element with the highest priority value is removed first.
- A straight forward array implementation of a priority queue is not efficient for both operations "add" and "remove". If the complexity of one of them becomes O(1) then the complexity of the other operation becomes O(n) for a priority queue of "n" elements.
- Heap is a good data structure for implementing a priority queue. A heap is a complete binary tree with a special property. This property states that the key value at any node is greater than or equal to the key values of both its children. Such a tree can be conveniently implemented by a single one-dimensional array.
- Both "add" and "remove" operations on a heap can be accomplished in O(logn) time. Moreover, construction of a heap of "n" elements can be done in linear time.

Exercises

1. Insert the following keys in that sequence into an AVL tree. Find out the number of rotations required in each case.

   (a) 1, 2, 3, 4, 5, 6, 7, 8, 9, 10, 11, 12

   (b) 12, 11, 10, 9, 8, 7, 6, 5, 4, 3, 2, 1

   (c) 6, 3, 1, 2, 4, 5, 9, 7, 8, 11, 10, 12

2. Write a "C" function to check whether a given binary search tree, "T", is an AVL tree or not.
3. Write a non-recursive "C" function to insert a node in an AVL tree.
4. Write a non-recursive "C" function to delete a node from an AVL tree.

5. Write a recursive "C" function to delete a node from an AVL tree.
6. Draw an AVL tree with 12 nodes such that the height of the AVL tree is maximum. Can you provide a sequence of 12 key values which could be inserted to the AVL tree producing an AVL tree of maximum height?
7. Write an algorithm to find the k-th smallest element in an AVL tree "T". Use of an additional field in each node of the tree may be helpful in solving this problem. Assume that each node in an AVL tree, "T" has a field which contains the number of nodes in its left sub-tree. Show that the k-th smallest element can be found in O(logn) time if there are "n" nodes in "T".
8. Write an algorithm to list all nodes of an AVL tree, "T", in ascending order of the key values. Show that the time complexity of this algorithm is O(n) if "T" has "n" nodes. What is the time complexity of a similar algorithm if it is applied on an ordinary binary search tree?
9. Write a "C" function to merge the nodes of two AVL trees "T_1" and "T_2" to obtain a new AVL tree. What is the time complexity of your algorithm?
10. Write a "C" function to split an AVL tree, "T", into two AVL trees "T_1" and "T_2" such that all keys in "T_1" are less than a given value "x" and all keys in "T_2" are greater than "x". What is the time complexity of your algorithm?
11. Insert the following keys into a B-tree of order (i) 3, (ii) 4 and (iii) 5.

    10, 24, 23, 11, 31, 16, 26, 35, 29, 20, 46, 28, 44, 54, 14, 40, 42, 43, 55, 41
12. Delete the key "16" from the tree generated as a result of solving Exercise 11. From the resultant tree, delete the key "40".
13. What is the minimum number of keys in a B-tree of order 5 and height 3?
14. Write "C" functions to find the minimum and the maximum keys stored in a B-tree of order "m".
15. Write an algorithm to print the k-th largest element in a B-Tree. Introduction of an array of integers in every node of a B-tree storing the number of nodes in each of its children might be helpful in solving this problem.
16. Assume that the keys 1, 2, 3 ... are inserted into an empty B-Tree of order 3. Which keys cause a node to split? Which keys cause the height of the tree to increase? If the keys are deleted in the same order, which keys cause nodes to be merged and which keys cause the height to decrease?
17. Write "C" functions to find the immediate predecessor and immediate successor of a given key value in a B-Tree.
18. Prove that the immediate predecessor and immediate successor of a key "k" must lie in leaf nodes if "k" is not in a leaf node.
19. Write a "C" function to insert a new key to a B-tree of order "m".
20. Write a "C" function to delete an existing key from a B-tree of order "m".

21. B^+ tree is another popular version of B-tree. In a B^+ tree the leaf nodes store data records whereas the non-leaf nodes store only key values. What are advantages and disadvantages of B^+ trees compared to B-trees? Write an algorithm to insert a new key to a B^+ tree. Also, write an algorithm to delete a key from a B^+ tree.
22. What are the minimum and the maximum number of elements in a heap of height "h"?
23. Insert the following keys to a heap in the given order:

    1, 2, 3, 4, 5, 6, 7, 8, 9, 10, 11, 12, 13, 14, 15

    Assume that the heap is initially empty.
24. Delete the keys 15, 14 in that order from the heap built after solving Exercise 22.
25. Show how one can implement stacks and queues as special cases of heaps.
26. If a heap is implemented using arrays then which element(s) of the array may contain the third largest element of the heap?
27. Write a "C" function to delete the k-th smallest element from a heap.
28. Write a recursive "C" function to accomplish the task done by the function "restoreHeapDown" described in this chapter.
29. Prove that there are at most $\lceil n/2 \rceil$ nodes of height "h" in a heap having "n" elements.
30. Write an algorithm to merge or join two given heaps. What is the time complexity of your algorithm?

Chapter 9

Searching and Sorting

9.1 Searching

Frequently, it becomes necessary to search a list of records to identify a particular record. Usually each record contains a field whose value is unique for each record. Such a field is often called the "key" field. Identifying a particular record refers to finding a record whose key value is equal to a given value. This operation is called "searching". If search results in locating the desired record then the search is said to be successful. Otherwise, the search operation is said to be unsuccessful. For simplicity, each record is assumed to consist of a key field only. Further, the type of the key field is considered to be integer.

9.1.1 Sequential Search

It was discussed in Chapter 2 that a simple way to search for a key value "k" in an array "A" is to compare the values of the elements in "A" with "k". The process starts with a comparison between the first element and "k". As long as a comparison does not result in a success, the algorithm proceeds to compare the next element of "A" and "k". The process terminates when the list is exhausted or a comparison results in a success. This method of searching is known as sequential search or linear search. The following function employs this technique to search an element whose value equal to "k" within an array "A" of "n" elements defined as A[0:n-1]. The function returns an integer which holds the index of the element of "A" in the case of a successful search. When the search is unsuccessful, the function returns (–1).

```
int sequentialSearch(int k, int A[], int n)
{
    int i = 0;
```

```
    while (i < n)
    {
            if (k == A[i])
                    break;
            else
                    i++;
    }
    if (i < n)
            return (i);
    else
            return (-1);
}
```

When the values in the array "A" are not distinct then the function will return the first index, "i", of the array "A" which is equal to "k".

The analysis of the above algorithm is based on the assumption that "A" contains distinct values. First, note that the number of comparisons required for a successful search is not fixed. It depends on the position, which "k" occupies within the array. If it is the first element then only one comparison is necessary and if it is the last element then "n" comparisons are required. In general, "i" comparisons are necessary to search the i-th element. Now if "p_i" is the probability that the i-th element will be searched then the expected number of comparisons for a successful search is given by

$$C_s = 1.p_0 + 2.p_1 + \ldots + n.p_{n-1} = \Sigma_{i=0,(n-1)} i.p_i \quad \ldots\ldots(1)$$

If it is assumed that any element is an equally likely candidate for searching then $p_0 = p_1 = \ldots = p_{n-1} = 1/n$. In this case, we have

$$C_s = (1/n).\ \Sigma_{i=1,n} i = (n + 1)/2$$

In case of an unsuccessful search, all elements must be examined unconditionally. Therefore, the expected number of comparisons in case of an unsuccessful search is given by

$$C_u = n$$

Equation (1) shows that "C_s" can be minimized if the probabilities "p_i" ($0 \leq i < n$) are known and if it is possible to organize the array in any desired order. Since $p_0 + p_1 + \ldots + .p_{n-1} = 1$, "$C_s$" is minimum when $p_0 \geq p_1 \geq p_2 \geq \ldots \geq p_{n-1}$. In other words, "$C_s$" is very small when the most frequently searched elements are placed towards the beginning of the array. This gives a basis for organizing an array to aid sequential searching.

A common experience is that in most of the cases, search is limited to the most active 20% elements of the array. If these 20% elements can be identified then the array can be better organized for linear search by placing the active elements near the beginning of the array.

9.1.2 Linear Search on a sorted array

A reduction in the expected number of comparisons required for an unsuccessful search is possible when the linear search technique is applied to a sorted array. Assuming that the values appear in ascending order, the search can be terminated as soon as an element with a value greater than or equal to "k" is found. When the array element is equal to "k" then the search is successful. When the value of an element is greater than "k", it can be concluded that "k" is not present in the array and the search ends unsuccessfully. The function to search sequentially in an array (sorted in an ascending manner) is presented in the following.

```
int searchSequentialSorted(int k, int A[], int n)
{
    int u = 0;
    int j = -1;
    while (u < n)
    {
        if (k ==A[u])
        {
            j = u;
            break;
        }
        else if (A[u] > k)
            break;
        else
            u = u + 1;
    }
    return (j);
}
```

In this case, there is no change in the expected number of comparisons for a successful search. The number of comparisons required for an unsuccessful search depends on the given value of "k". The number of comparisons for an unsuccessful search may be "1" in the best case and "n+1" in the worst case. In fact, this value may lie in any one of the (n+1) intervals created by the "n" elements. If "k" lies in any one of these intervals with equal probability, the expected number of comparisons is given by

$$C_u = (1 + 2 + .. + n + n)/(n+1) = n(n + 3)/2(n + 1)$$

$$= (n/2) + n/(n + 1) - (n/2 + 1) \text{ for large "n".}$$

This clearly justifies the intuitive expectation that there is a reduction of the expected number of comparisons required for an unsuccessful search.

If the array is assumed to be sorted, several searching techniques using the basic principle of linear search is possible. One such technique is described here. Suppose every r-th element of the array is compared with the given value, starting from the first element. The comparison proceeds until an element with greater than or equal to the given value is located or the last element of the array is reached. This enables to identify a contiguous portion of the array (not exceeding "r" elements) where the requested value is likely to be present. This portion is now linearly searched in the reverse order until a match is found or it is established that an element with the desired value is not present.

To see that the method is an improvement over the usual sequential search, the worst case behaviour of the algorithm given can be analyzed. The maximum number of comparisons required when every r-th element is examined is given by (n/r). Again, when the portion consisting of "r" or fewer elements are examined in the reverse order then the maximum number of comparisons that may be required is "r". Now, if "C" is the expected number of comparisons, then

$$C \leq n/r + r$$

Considering that the usual sequential search requires (n+1)/ 2 comparisons on an average, it may be mentioned that the present technique requires fewer comparisons when n>2r (approximately).

9.1.3 Binary Search

When the given array is sorted then a considerably better method of searching is possible. This method, known as binary search, makes a comparison between "k" and the middle element of the array. Since the array is sorted, this comparison results either in a match between "k" and the middle element of "A" or identifying the left half or the right half of the array to which the desired element may belong. In the case when the current element is not equal to the middle element of "A", the procedure is repeated on the half in which the desired element is likely to be present. Proceeding in this way, either the element is detected or the final division leads to a half consisting of no element. In this case, it is ascertained that the array does not contain "k".

This is a very efficient method of searching because each comparison enables one to eliminate half of the elements from further consideration. Because of this basic principle of elimination, the method is also known as dichotomous search.

There may be an ambiguity over the determination of the middle element of an array when the number of elements is even. In this case, there are two elements in the middle. However, an arbitrary choice of any one of these as the middle element will serve the purpose.

Suppose the array "A" consists of the following elements.

10, 25, 48, 69, 92, 101

Further, suppose that the array is searched for a given value of "25". Since the array consists of "6" elements, A[3] ("69") is chosen as the middle element. Since "25" is less than "69", it may be concluded that if "25" is at all present in "A" then it must be present in the half consisting of the first three elements. In this half, the number of elements is three. So, A[1] becomes the middle element. A comparison with this element results in the match. This algorithm leads us to the following function.

```
int binarySearch(int k, int A[], int n)
{
    int lower = 0, mid;
    int i = -1;
    int upper;
    upper = n-1;
    while (upper >= lower)
    {
          mid = (upper + lower )/2;
          if (k == A[mid])
          {
               i = mid;
               break;
          }
          else
          {
               if (k > A[mid])
                     lower = mid + 1;
               else
                     upper = mid - 1;
          }
    }
    return (i);
}
```

To analyze the performance of binary search, the maximum number of comparisons required for a successful search will be computed first. Let "j" be the smallest integer such that

$$2^j \geq (n+1) \qquad \text{.........(2)}$$

The maximum number of elements that are left after the first comparison is $2^{(j-1)} - 1$

and in general, the maximum number of elements left after "k" comparisons is $2^{(j-k)}$ - 1. The desired element will definitely be found after "j" comparisons in which case we are left with no elements to be compared. Thus, C_{max}, the maximum number of comparisons for a successful search is given by C_{max} = j where "j" is the smallest integer satisfying (2). Alternatively,

$$C_{max} = \log_2(n + 1)$$

Note that C_u, the number of comparisons required by an unsuccessful search, is equal to C_{max}. This is because, search can be declared as unsuccessful only when there are no elements to be probed.

Now, find the average number of comparisons under the assumption that each key is an equally likely candidate for a search. In other words, the probability that a particular element will be requested in a search is (1/n). For simplicity, we assume $n = 2^j - 1$ for some "j". Now, the element in the middle position requires only one comparison to be searched. Similarly, the elements in the middle positions of the two halves require two comparisons each when searched. In this way we see that the total number of comparisons required to search every array element is given by

$$C = 1.2^0 + 2.2^1 + 3.2^2 + \ldots\ldots\ldots\ldots + j.2^{j-1} \ldots\ldots\ldots\ldots (3)$$

To find an expression for "C", multiply both sides of (3) by 2 to get

$$2.C = 1.2^1 + 2.2^2 + 3.2^3 + \ldots + j.2^j \ldots\ldots\ldots (4)$$

Subtracting (3) from (4), we get

$$C = j.2^j - (2^0 + 2^1 + 2^2 + \ldots 2^{(j-1)})$$

$$= 1 + 2^j(j-1)$$

Now, C_s, the expected number of comparisons for a successful search, is given by

$$C_s = C/n = \{1 + 2^j.(j-1)\}/n$$

$$= [1 + (n + 1).\{\log_2 (n + 1) - 1\}]/n$$

$$= (n + 1).\log_2 (n + 1)/n - 1$$

$$= \log_2 n \text{ for large "n".}$$

Although the above result has been derived under the assumption that "n", the number of elements, is of the form $2^j - 1$, the approximate result is also valid for any value of "n". This is because there is no significant difference in the values of $\log_2 n$ for different values of n in the range $2^{(j-1)} \leq n \leq 2^j - 1$.

Thus, it is shown that the expected numbers of comparison for a successful as well as for an unsuccessful search are approximately given by

$$C_u = C_s = O(\log_2 n)$$

Comparison with corresponding expressions for sequential search shows that binary search is more efficient than sequential search when any element is equally likely to be searched. It must be mentioned here that binary search relies heavily on random access to the elements of the list. Thus, a binary search implementation on a liked list of record would not be efficient.

9.1.4 How fast can one search

The process of searching for "k" in an array "A" by means of comparing "k" with elements of "A" can be conveniently expressed in terms of a binary tree. Each node in such a tree represents a comparison between "k" and A[i] for some "i". These nodes may be represented by just the integer "i". Two edges emanating out of a node represent the results of the comparison which could be either ">" or "<". In case "k" is equal to A[i], the search ends at that node. If k < A[i] then the search follows the edge "<" for future operation. Similarly, if k > A[i], then the search process follows the edge ">". The process of sequentially searching for "k" in a sorted array "A" having "4" elements may be expressed by the tree of Figure 9.1(a). The tree in Figure 9.1(b) shows the sequence of comparisons required when binary search is applied to an array of "4" elements.

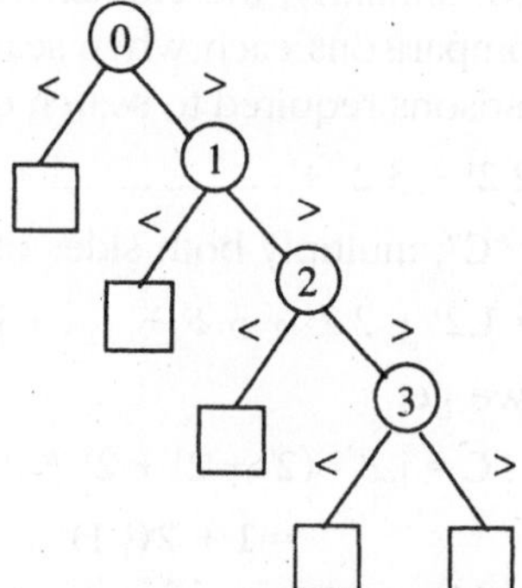

Figure 9.1(a) Comparison tree for sequential search of a sorted array of 4 elements.

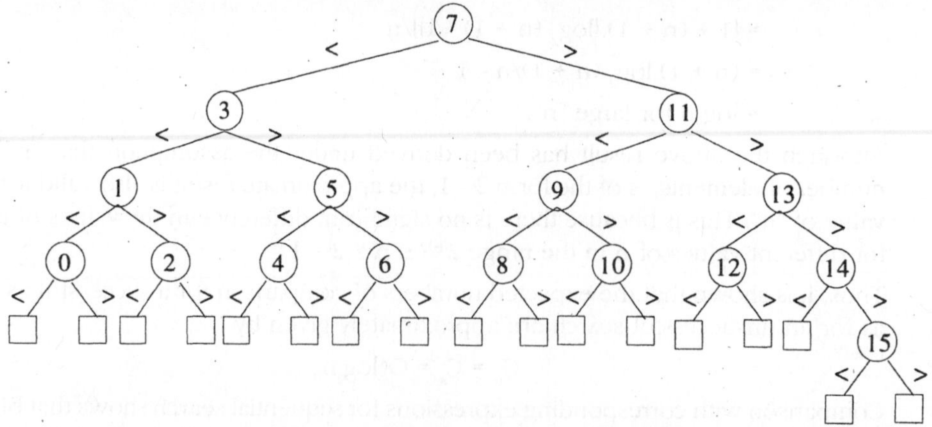

Figure 9.1(b) Comparison tree showing the sequence of comparisons when binary search is applied on an array of 16 elements of an array A[0:15]

Observe that the search starts by the comparison at the root node of the tree. A successful search terminates in some internal node while an unsuccessful search terminates in an external node. These trees are often called comparison trees. Thus, any process of searching "k" in an array of "n" elements can be represented as a comparison tree having at least "n" internal nodes. Thus, the minimum worst-case complexity of search procedure must be equal to the minimum height of all comparison trees having "n" internal nodes. But, the minimum height of a tree having "n" nodes is $\lfloor \log_2 n \rfloor$. Thus, there can not be comparison-based search algorithm where worst case complexity is less than $\lfloor \log_2 n \rfloor$.

If a successful search ending in an internal node makes "i" comparisons, then i is one plus the internal path length of that node. The average number of comparisons for a successful search would be the sum of the number of comparisons required to search successfully all the internal nodes divided by the number of internal nodes. Hence,

$$C_s = (1/n)\Sigma_{\text{all internal nodes}}(1 + \text{internal path length})$$

$= 1 + I/n$, where "I" is the total internal path length of the comparison tree.

If an unsuccessful search ending in an external node makes "i" comparisons then i is the path length of that node. Number of external nodes of a binary tree having "n" internal nodes is (n+1). Therefore, C_u, the average number of comparisons required for an unsuccessful search is given by

$$C_u = E/(n+1)$$

where "E" is the total external path length of the binary tree.

It is known that "E" and "I" are related according to the equation $E = I + 2n$. Hence,

$$C_s = ((n+1)/n)C_u - 1$$

It is easy to see that both the values of "C_u" and "C_s" become minimum when "E" and "I" are minimum. The quantities "E" and "I" are minimum when all external nodes lie on adjacent levels. Then, the values of "E" and "I" are $O(n\log_2 n)$. Thus, the average number of comparisons for successful and unsuccessful searches based on comparison-based search techniques can not be less than $O(\log_2 n)$.

9.2 Internal sorting

Sorting is an important operation and the need for sorting a list arises frequently in many applications. Sorting is formally defined on a list of elements $a_1, a_2, a_3, \ldots, a_n$ if there is a binary relation "<" defined for any two distinct elements, a_i and a_j of that list. The list $(a_1, a_2, a_3, \ldots, a_n)$ may be arranged in (n!) ways. Sorting refers to one permutation $(a_{i1}, a_{i2}, a_{i3}, \ldots, a_{in})$ of the list so that $a_{ij} < a_{ik}$ whenever $j < k$. In many occasions, the list to be sorted is small enough so that the list can be entirely accommodated in the primary memory of a computer. Sorting of such lists is referred to as internal sorting. As opposed to this, the process of sorting a list stored in a file in secondary memory (such as hard disks) is known as <u>external sorting</u>. Internal sorting is the major focus of our discussion in this chapter. Very often, the list to be sorted will be implemented by an array in the algorithms developed in this chapter. Thus, the terms "list and "array" would be freely mixed up when no confusion arises. Moreover, a list is often referred to as A[lower:upper] indicating the fact that the list is stored in an array "A" from the index "lower" to the index "upper" including both.There exists an overwhelmingly large number of sorting methods. The number is so large that we shall have to limit ourselves only to a small fraction of these. It is also true that there is no "best" method of sorting. There are several good and popular sorting methods each of which has an edge over the others in some respects. As such, it is not easy to discard a sorting method by calling it useless.

Several methods will be discussed in this chapter as applications of various data structures. It will also be shown how suitable data structures can bring improvements to algorithms for sorting.

Classification of Sorting Methods

Usually, more than one sorting method is found to employ the same basic principle. This gives rise to "families" of sorting methods. For example, there is a family of sorting methods known by the name "sorting by selection". The basic principle used in these methods is as follows. At first, the element with the smallest key is selected. The selected element is somehow discarded from the array and the smallest of the remaining elements is selected next and so on. Obviously, the elements when placed in an output array in the order of their selections form a sorted array. The individual methods of the family differ in the matter of implementation details but the basic principle remains same. Similarly, there are families like "sorting by insertion", "sorting by exchange", "sorting by merging", etc. Various sorting methods will be discussed according to such classifications. However, these families are not watertight compartments and in many cases a particular method may qualify to be included in more than one such family. In such cases, a qualitative decision is to be taken on the basis of the method's inclination towards a family.

Another classification of sorting methods is based on the manner in which the keys are handled. Many sorting methods work by comparing the key fields of the elements. The main concept in these methods is to compare the keys of two elements to determine which of these two should relatively be placed before the other in the sorted array. These methods are known as comparative sorts. Most of the sorting techniques fall in this category. An alternative approach to sorting is to distribute the elements to one or more auxiliary arrays using certain principles and then to collect them to obtain the final sorted array. The placement of an element in an auxiliary array is based on inspecting its key value. The inspection may consist of comparing the key value against some standard or it may involve computations with the key value. These methods are known as Key-value sorts or distributive sorts for obvious reasons. Some of the distributive sorts do not totally dispense with the key comparisons and use these for limited purpose only.

Factors Affecting the Applicability of Sorting Methods

Choice of an appropriate sorting method depends on the circumstances in which the method is to be applied. In order to make an intelligent and effective choice in a given situation, one must take into account the various characteristics of sorting methods. These characteristics are described in the following.

Data Sensitiveness

For some sorting methods, the order in which the elements appear in the original array has a marked effect on the time required to sort the array. Such methods are known as data sensitive methods. On the other hand, the methods which are not data sensitive, require roughly the same amount of time to sort a list of "n" elements regardless of the order in which the elements appear in the array. Data sensitive methods can benefit from the existing ordering provided this is favourable to it. Unfortunately, there is no quantitative measure for the existing ordering and the ordering which is favourable to a particular data sensitive method may not be favourable to another.

Stability

When the initial list contains elements with non-distinct keys, any sorting method will place these elements in consecutive positions of the sorted array. However, only a few of the methods will preserve the original ordering among these elements. Preserving the original ordering means that if a_r and a_t are two elements with identical keys and a_r precedes a_t in the original array then a_r should also precede a_t in the sorted array. The methods that preserve the original ordering among the elements with non-distinct keys, are known as stable methods. An unstable sorting method cannot be used in many applications and therefore, stability is an important attribute for sorting methods. A method which is inherently stable, may not remain so if proper care is not taken during implementation. Thus, stability of a sorting method implies that there is a stable implementation of that method.

Storage Requirement

Some sorting methods work by rearranging the elements within the storage space occupied by the original array. As a result, when the sorting is completed, the original array has been overwritten by the sorted array. These methods are called the minimal storage sorting methods as they do not require any extra storage space except perhaps some negligible amount of working storage. Other methods require additional storage space which is proportional to the size of the given array. Sometimes, even more storage space is required. In the case of arrays with large number of elements, the minimal storage sorts are obviously advantageous. Storage requirement can be conveniently expressed by storage ratio which is the ratio of total storage requirement to the storage space required by the input array. Storage ratio for a minimal storage sort is 1.

Efficiency

To get an idea of the amount of time required to sort an array of "n" elements by a particular method, the normal approach is to analyze the method to find the number of comparisons (or some other representative operation such as "exchange") required by it. If the method is not data sensitive then determination of this figure-of-merit is not difficult. However, most of the sorting methods are data sensitive and for them, these metrics depend heavily on the order in which the elements appear in the array. The usual practice for data sensitive methods is to analyze the method for various cases such as the "best" case, "worst" case and the "average" case. The average case behaviour of an algorithm is evaluated under the assumption that the keys are distinct and their initial distribution is random. Suppose that there are "n" elements in an array. With these "n" elements, it is possible to construct (n!) different arrays. Under the assumption that the elements are randomly distributed, the probability that any of the (n!) arrays is given for sorting is (1/n!). Thus, to find the average number of designated operations (such as exchange, comparison etc.), one can first find, Q(n!), the number of operations required to sort all the (n!) arrays. The average number is then given by (Q(n!)/n!). It is also instructive to note that the said assumption is equivalent to the assumption that any of the "n" keys can occupy any of the "n" positions of the given array with equal probability.

Evaluation of the average case complexity of a data sensitive method often involves complex analysis. Moreover, the average case analysis is of little practical interest because in many real life applications, the assumption of distinct and randomly distributed keys does not hold good. Nevertheless, such analysis is quite interesting from a theoretical standpoint and provides a considerable insight about the relative efficiency of a sorting method.

9.3 Sorting by Insertion

An important characteristic of these methods is that they do not require all elements of the given array to make a beginning. The elements may be provided sequentially one by one and these are inserted into a growing sorted array of previously encountered elements. The process starts with this growing array as empty and ends when the last element of the given array has been inserted. Some of the methods do not start with an empty array. Instead, they start with an array consisting of the first element. In most of these methods, the growing array is realized as a segment of the given array so that ultimately, the sorted array is developed without using any extra storage space. Some important insertion sorts are described in the following.

9.3.1 Shuttle Sort

When there are "n" elements in a given array, "A", shuttle sort requires (n-1) passes. By the time the i-th pass ($1 \leq i \leq n-1$) begins, the first "i" elements i.e., elements A[0] to A[i-1] have been sorted and these occupy the first "i" positions of the array. To insert the (i+1)-th element, A[i], during the i-th pass, A[i] is compared with A[i-1] and if the key of the former is found to be smaller then the two elements are exchanged. If an exchange takes place then A[i-1] and A[i-2] are compared and if necessary, they are exchanged. The process continues until either no exchange is found necessary or the beginning of the array is reached. Figure 9.2 illustrates shuttle sort with the help of an example.

Original unsorted array	**First Pass**		**Second Pass**		**Third Pass**		**Fourth Pass**		**Fifth Pass**	
	array before	**array after**	**array before**	**array after**	**array before**	**array after**	**array before**	**array after**	**array before**	**array**
15	15	8	8	8	8	8	8	8	8	8
8	8	15	15	15	15	12	12	12	12	12
17	17	17	17	17	17	15	15	15	15	15
12	12	12	12	12	12	17	17	17	17	17
38	38	38	38	38	38	38	38	38	38	19
19	19	19	19	19	19	19	19	19	19	38

Figure 9.2 Illustration of Shuttle Sort on a list of "6" elements. Numbers of exchanges in the five passes are 1, 0, 2, 0, 1 respectively.

An algorithm to sort an array "A" by shuttle sort technique is presented in the following.

```
void shuttleSort (int A[], int n)
{
   int i = 1, j;
   int T;
   while (i < n)
   {
          j = i - 1;
          while (j >= 0)
          {
                 if (A[j] > A[j+1])
                 {
                        T = A[j];
                        A[j] = A[j+1];
                        A[j+1] = T;
                        j—;
                 }
```

```
            else
            break;
        }
        i++;
    }
}
```

The comparison (j ≥ 0) in the inner while-loop is costly in the sense that this comparison most often would evaluate to "TRUE". One way to avoid the comparison is to load A[0] with a value less than the smallest key present in A[1:n-1]. That is, A[0] must have a key which is less than the smallest possible key value. Such a key is often referred to as the sentinel key.

Shuttle sort is a data sensitive method. Although (n-1) passes are always required, the number of comparisons required in a pass depends on the arrangement of the elements in the given array. The "best" case for shuttle sort arises when the given array is already sorted. In this case, every pass requires just one comparison and no exchanges which is the minimum number of comparisons that a pass can have. Thus, in the best case, (n-1) comparisons are required by shuttle sort. On the other hand, the maximum number of comparisons required in the i-th pass being "i", the upper limit for the number of comparisons necessary to complete the sort is 1 + 2 + 3 .. + (n-1) = n(n-1)/2. The "worst" case arises when the given array is sorted in the reverse order. The number of exchange operations in the worst case is also O(n).

Now, analyze the average case complexity of the shuttle sort algorithm. Consider the i-th pass (1 ≤ i ≤ n-1) of the function "shuttleSort". In this pass, A[i] is to be placed in its proper position. This position can be anything between "0" and "i" including both. Assuming that A[i] can occupy any one of these (i+1) positions with equal probability, the expected number of comparisons for the i-th pass, is given by

$$C_i = = (i+2 +..+ (i-1)+2i)/(i+1) = 1+i/2-1/(i+1)$$

Note that when the element being inserted occupies A[0], "i" comparisons are required. However, this would be (i+1), if a sentinel key were used. The current implementation does not consider a sentinel key. Therefore, the expected number of comparisons is

$$C = \Sigma_{i=1,n-1} C_i = n(n+3)/4 - \Sigma_{i=1,n}(1/i)$$

The asymptotic behaviour of the sum $\Sigma(1/i)$ can be approximated by $\log_e n$ for large "n". Therefore,

$$C = n(n+3)/4 - \log_e n$$

The above analysis shows that shuttle sort is $O(n^2)$ method. The storage ratio is "1". The method is also stable. Because of the dominant role played by exchanges, the method is also known as insertion-exchange sort.

Straight Insertion Sort

Shuttle sort can be improved considerably by replacing each of its exchange operation to a transfer operation. Note that in the i-th pass of shuttle sort, A[i] is inserted into a sorted segment A[0:i-1] producing a longer sorted segment in A[0:i]. This insertion is performed through a sequence of exchanges which places the element in A[i] to its correct position and moves all elements greater than this element to the right by one position each. The same objective can also be achieved in the following manner. In the beginning of the i-th pass, A[i] is assigned to a variable "x". Now "x" is successively compared with A[i-1], A[i-2], etc. until either an element smaller than "x" is found or the beginning of the array is reached. Elements that are found to be greater than "x", are moved right by one position each to make room for "x". When comparisons and movements are interleaved, the insertion process becomes identical to that of shuttle sort except that the sequence of exchanges becomes a sequence of transfers. In fact, insertion through transfer is more logical and efficient than insertion through exchanges.

An implementation of the straight insertion sort to sort an array A[0:n-1] is given in the following.

```
void straightInsertion (float A[], int n)
{
    int i = 1, j, k = 0;
    float x;
    while (i < n)
    {
            j = i - 1;
            x = A[j+1];
            k=i;
            while (j >= 0)
            {
                    if (x < A[j])
                    {
                            k = j;
                            j—;
                    }
                    else
                    break;
            }
            j = i;
            while (j > k)
            {
```

```
                A[j] = A[j-1];
                j--;
            }
            A[k] = x;
            i++;
        }
    }
```

As mentioned above, there is no basic difference between shuttle sort and straight insertion sort. As such, the number of comparisons and other attributes remain same. Taking into account the assignment A[i] to "x" and the placement of "x" in the correct position, the number of transfers is slightly more than the number of exchanges required for shuttle sort.

Binary Insertion Sort

Like shuttle sort or straight insertion sort, this method also inserts A[i] in its proper place in the i-th pass. However, the process of insertion is somewhat different. Binary search is applied on the first "i" elements to determine where exactly A[i] is to be inserted. Note that the first "i" elements are sorted and there is no problem in applying binary search to this segment. Suppose that binary search reveals that A[i] should be placed in the r-th position. Except when "r" is equal to (i+1), all elements stored in the r-th to the i-th positions are to be moved right by one position each to make room for the element to be inserted at the r-th position. Through the use of binary search, the number of comparisons is reduced considerably but the number of transfers remains the same as that in case of straight insertion sort. Moreover, comparisons and transfers cannot be interleaved. As such there should be two inner loops - one for the binary search and the other for the transfers. The actual implementation of the method is left as an exercise.

The number of comparisons required by binary search in the case of the i-th pass is $\log_2 i$ approximately. Thus, the sorting method requires "C" number comparisons where "C" is given by

$$C = \Sigma_{i=1,(n-1)} \log_2 i = \log_2 (n-1)! = \log_2 n! - \log_2 n$$

Approximating (n!) by Stirling's formula for large "n", we have

$$C = \log_2(\sqrt{(2\pi)} n^{(n+1/2)} e^{-n}) - \log_2 n$$

$$\approx \log_2 (\sqrt{(2\pi/n)} + n\log_2(n/e)$$

Although "C" is quite low, the time complexity of the method is still O(n) because the average number of transfers required by this method is the same as that in the case of straight insertion and is given by the expression

$$T = (n-1)(n+4) / 4$$

Binary insertion sort is not stable because when there are duplicate keys, binary insertion may place a latter key before its duplicate encountered earlier. The storage ratio is 1.

Shell Sort

This internal sorting technique is due to Donald L. Shell (1959). This method makes repeated use of straight insertion sort or shuttle sort. Shell sort operating on an array of "n" elements requires that in each pass, a number called increment be chosen. The increments must be less than "n"; they should be progressively smaller and the increment for the last pass must be equal to "1". In other words, if "p" is the number of passes then one must choose the increments d_i, $1 \le i \le p$, such that

$$n > d_1 > d_2 > \ldots > d_p = 1$$

There are various recommended ways of choosing the number of passes and the increments and that issue will be considered later. For the time being, concentrate on the function in the i-th pass of shell sort. When the i-th pass begins, let $a_0, a_1, a_2, \ldots, a_{n-1}$ be the elements occupying the positions 0, 1, 2, ..., (n-1) respectively. Also suppose that "d" is the increment chosen for this pass. During the i-th pass, the array is conceptually divided into the following "d" sublists:

$$(a_j, a_{j+d}, \ldots, a_{j+md}); \; 1 \le j \le d$$

where "m" is the largest integer such that j+md=n. Note that the sub-arrays are constructed by taking elements which stand at a distance of "d" from each other. Also note that the construction of the sub-arrays is conceptual and the elements remain in their original positions. Now, each of the "d" sub-arrays is sorted by using the straight insertion sort (or shuttle sort). Thus, at the end of the pass, elements at a distance of "d" from each other become sorted among themselves. In the last pass, the increment is "1". As such, the last pass is a straight insertion sort or a shuttle sort.

Note that as long as $d_p = 1$, sorting is ensured at the end of the last pass. The exercise in the previous passes merely aims to introduce some degree of ordering among the elements so that the last pass becomes very easy. Thus, the previous passes are preparatory passes with the objective of helping the last pass. The actual help, of course, depends on how the increments are chosen. According to the original suggestion of Shell, the increments should be as follows:

$$d_1 = n \text{ div } 2 \text{ and } d_{i+1} = d_i \text{ div } 2.$$

Figure 9.3 illustrates the working of the algorithm on an example array. Number of elements in the array is "8". In the first pass, "d" is chosen as (8/2) (i.e., 4). Consequently, the original array is divided into "4" sub-lists: (a_0, a_{0+4}), (a_1, a_{1+4}), (a_2, a_{2+4}), (a_3, a_{3+4}). Each of these lists is sorted using insertion or shuttle sort producing the list: (18, 70, 12, 43, 83, 87, 97, 51). In the second pass, the value of "d" is 2. The array produced after the first pass is divided into two sub-lists: $(a_0, a_{0+2}, a_{0+2*2}, a_{0+3*2})$ and $(a_1, a_{1+2}, a_{1+2*2}, a_{1+3*2})$. These two sub-lists are sorted using insertion sort. The resultant array produced by this pass is the input for the final pass where the entire list is sorted using insertion sort.

Original array	First Pass (d_1 =4)		Second Pass (d_2=2)		Third Pass (d=1)	
	array before	**array after**	**array before**	**array after**	**array before**	**array after**
83	83	18	18	12	12	12
87	87	70	70	43	43	18
12	12	12	12	18	18	43
51	51	43	43	51	51	51
18	18	83	83	83	83	70
70	70	87	87	70	70	83
97	97	97	97	97	97	87
43	43	51	51	87	87	97

Figure 9.3 Illustration of Shell Sort

An algorithm for Shell sort that operates on the array A[0:n-1] is given in the following. Shuttle sort is used to sort the individual sub-lists in each pass.

```
void shellSort (int A[], int n)
{
    int i, k, m, j;
    int T;
    for (m = n/2; m > 0; m /= 2)
    {
        for (j = m; j < n; j ++)
        {
            for (i = j-m; i >= 0; i -= m)
            {
                if (A[i+m] >= A[i])
                break;
                else
                {
                    T = A[i];
                    A[i] = A[i+m];
                    A[i+m] = T;
                }
            }
        }
```

    }
}

The choice of increments is the most important issue in shell sort. However, the question of finding an ideal sequence of increments is still open. The original suggestion of Shell is found to be unsatisfactory when the binary representation of "n" contains a long sequence of zeros. For example, suppose n = 2^r and the given array is

$$(2^{r-1}+ 1, 1, 2^{r-1} + 2, 2, \ldots\ldots).$$

Now, it can be easily verified that with Shell's choice of increments, not a single element will be moved in any pass other than the last one and actual sorting will take place only in the last pass. This defficiency of Shell's choice of increments was first pointed out by Frank and Lazrus (1960). They suggested that while calculating increments as per shell's formula, whenever necessary, a "1" should be added so as to make the increments odd. Hibberd (1963) proposed that the increments should be taken as

$$d_1 = 2^k\text{-}1 \text{ and } d_{i+1} = d_i \text{ div } 2 \text{ where } 2^k < n \leq 2^{k+1}$$

Several other choices of increments have been suggested in literature but, as yet, there is no "best" sequence of increments, Hibberd's sequence of increments is usually recommended for use with shell sort. Another choice of increments is as follows:

$$d_p = 1, d_{i-1} = 1 + 3^*d_i \text{ and } d_1 \leq (n/9).$$

So far, it has not been possible to evaluate the time complexity of Shell's method for an arbitrary array and for any general choice of increments. It is needless to mention that several attempts with fascinating results for specific cases have been made. In fact it can be shown that shell sort never does more than "n" comparisons when $d_p = 1$, $d_{i-1} = 1 + 3^*d_i$ and $d_1 \leq (n/9)$. There have also been several experimental studies on the method. The average performance of Shell's technique is found to be $O(n\log_2 n)$. Storage rate for shell sort is 1. The method is not stable.

9.4 Sorting by Selection

As mentioned in section 9.2, every member of this family of sorting method works by successively selecting the smallest element, the second smallest element, the third smallest element and so on. The selected elements are placed sequentially in the output array in the order of their selections. It is obvious that such a method will correctly sort a given array. A selection sort can also work by selecting the largest element, then selecting the second largest element and so on. In this case the elements are to be placed in the output array in a reverse manner. Three methods of this family are described below.

9.4.1 Simple Selection Sort

The simplest possible technique, based on the principle of repeated selection, makes use of "n" passes over a given array. In the i-th pass, the i-th smallest element is selected and it is placed in the i-th position of a separate output array. In order to ensure that an element once selected is not selected again, the position of the selected element in the original array is filled up with a value (say, "H") which exceeds any of the key values of the given array. The method is explained with a suitable example. Let an array "A" of six numbers be (40, 45, 23, 15, 18, 95). In the first pass, the smallest element is found in A[3]. The element B[0] of an output array "B" is assigned the value of A[3] and then A[3] is set to "H". In the second pass, the smallest element is searched in the array which is A[4]. B[1] gets the value of A[4] and A[4] is assigned "H". This process continues for six passes. Figure 9.4 illustrates the working of simple selection sort.

First Pass		Second Pass		Third Pass		Fourth Pass		Fifth Pass		Sixth Pass	
A	B	A	B	A	B	A	B	A	B	A	B
40	15	40	15	40	15	H	15	H	15	H	15
45		45	18	45	18	45	18	H	18	H	18
23		23		H	23	H	23	H	23	H	23
H		H		H		H	40	H	40	H	40
18		H		H		H		H	45	H	45
95		95		95		95		95		H	95

Figure 9.4 Illustration of Simple Selection Sort. The lines with arrow indicate that the value of an element from the original array is assigned to an element in the output array.

An implementation of the method is simple and is presented next. Here A[0:n-1] is the original unsorted array and B[0:n-1] is the final output sorted array. The number "100" is assumed to be the value of "H" which, in this case, exceeds any of the key values of the given array.

```
void simpleSelectionSort (float A[], float B[], int n)
{
    int i = 0, k, j;
    float T;
    T = H;
    k=0;
    while (i < n)
    {
        for (j = 0; j < n; j++)
        {
            if (A[j] < T)
            {
                T = A[j];
                k = j;
```

```
            }
        }
        A[k] = H;
        B[i] = T;
        T = H;
        i++;
    }
}
```

It may be observed that the method is not data sensitive. In every pass, the entire array is searched to find the smallest element. This requires (n-1) comparisons in each pass. Since there are "n" passes, a total of n(n-1) comparisons are required. Thus, the time complexity of the above algorithm is $O(n^2)$. In the above algorithm, the smallest element has been searched in such a way that if there exists more than one smallest element then the one that occurs first will be selected. Because of this, the method is stable. The storage ratio is 2.

9.4.2 Straight Selection Sort

This is merely an improvement of the simple selection sort. Instead of replacing the selected element by "H" in the i-th pass, the selected element is exchanged with the i-th element, A[i-1]. Thus, at the beginning of the i-th pass, the first (i-1) elements of the array are those that have been selected in the previous passes. The smallest element is now searched in the remaining (n-i+1) elements. After (n-1) passes, the sorted array is completely developed in the space occupied by the original array. The working of this method is shown in Figure 9.5. In the first pass, A[0] is swapped with "15", the smallest element in the entire array. In the second pass, A[1] is swapped with "18", the smallest element in the array A[1:5]. In the third pass, A[2] is swapped with "23", the smallest element in the array A[2:5]. In the fourth pass, A[3] is swapped with "38", the smallest element in the array A[3:5]. No more exchanges are necessary in the fifth pass.

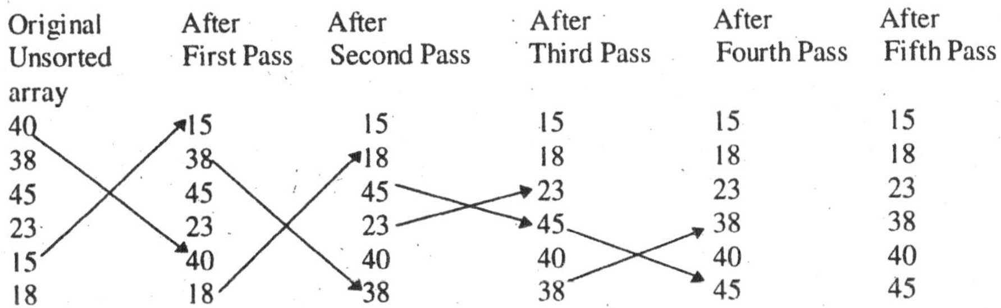

Figure 9.5 Illustration of Straight Selection Sort

An implementation of the straight selection sort is given below. Here, A[0:n-1] holds the unsorted array in the beginning and sorted array at the end.

```
void straightSelectionSort(float A[], int n)
{
    int i, k, j;
    float T;
    i = 0;
    while(i < n)
    {
        k = i;
        for(j = i+1; j < n; j++)
        {
            if (A[j] < A[k])
            k = j;
        }
        T = A[i];
        A[i] = A[k];
        A[k] = T;
        i++;
    }
}
```

This method is not data sensitive. There are "n" passes and in the i-th pass, the smallest element is searched among (n-i+1) elements. Therefore, the number of comparisons required to sort an array of "n" elements by this method is given by

$$C = \Sigma_{i=1,(n-1)}(n-i) = n(n-1)/2$$

Thus, although this method requires only half the number of comparisons required by simple selection sort, the time complexity is still $O(n^2)$. The method is stable as per the implementation given here. The storage ratio is 1.

9.4.2 Bubble Sort

Bubble sort is one of the most popular sorting methods. Bubble sort can be viewed as a selection sort because this method is also based on successively selecting the smallest element, second smallest element, etc. as in the case of any other selection sort. In order to find the successive smallest elements, the method relies heavily on the exchange of adjacent elements. Because of this, the method is often classed as "sorting by exchange".

Let "n" be the number of elements in an array "A". The first pass begins with a comparison of the keys of the n-th and (n-1)-th element. If the n-th key is smaller, the two elements are exchanged. The smaller key, now in the (n-1)-th position, is compared with the key of the (n-2)-th element and if necessary, the elements are exchanged to place the smaller one in the (n-2)-th position. Comparisons progress in this manner and the first pass ends with the comparison and possible exchange of the elements A[1] and A[0]. It is easy to observe that this exercise in the first pass will "bubble up" the smallest element to A[0]. The second pass is an exact repetition of the first pass except that this time, the pass ends with the comparison and possible exchange of A[1] and A[2]. Thus, the second pass will "bubble up" the second smallest element to A[1]. Each subsequent pass is similar to the previous pass except that it excludes one more position (in the beginning of the array) from its consideration. The sorting method terminates after (n-1) passes by which time the array is sorted. The method may even be terminated earlier if no exchange is found necessary in an earlier pass. Absence of any exchange in a pass ensures that the elements are in correct order and there is no point in continuing the method.

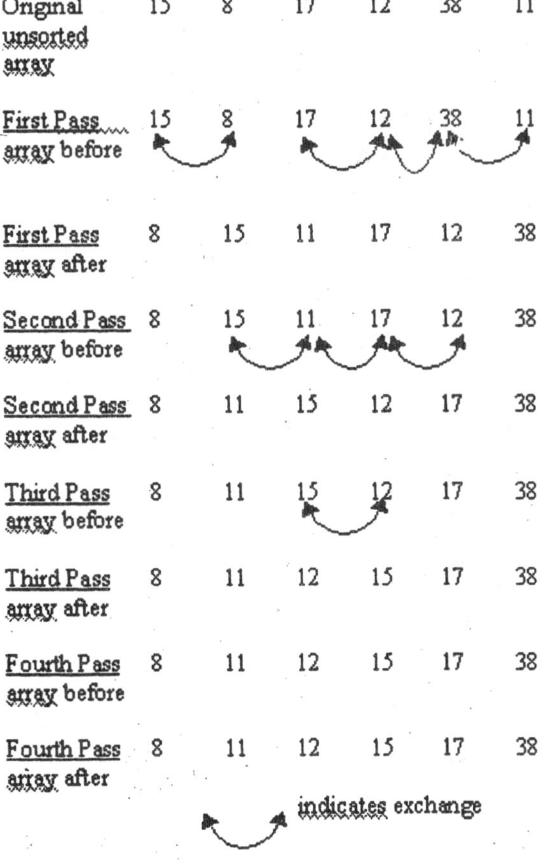

Figure 9.6 Illustration of Bubble Sort

Figure 9.6 shows an example of bubble sort with 6 elements. Note that instead of "5", only "4" passes are required because no exchange is required in the fourth pass.

The following algorithm sort the array A[0:n-1] using the bubble sort technique. The algorithm is self explanatory.

```
void bubbleSort (int A[], int n)
{
    int i, flag, j;
    int T;
    for (i =0; i < n; i++)
    {
        j = n-1;
        flag = 0;
        while (j > i)
        {
            if (A[j] < A[j-1])
            {
                T = A[j];
                A[j] = A[j-1];
                A[j-1] = T;
                flag = 1;
            }
            j --;
        }
        if (flag == 0)
        break;
    }
}
```

Bubble sort is data sensitive. The number of passes required may be anything between "1" and (n-1). However, the number of comparisons required in a pass is not dependent on data. In the case of i-th pass, (n-i) comparisons are required. In the best case for bubble sort, only one pass is required. The number of comparisons required is obviously (n-1). This case arises when the given array is sorted. In the worst case, all the passes are to be performed requiring, a total of

$$(n-1) + (n-2) + \ldots\ldots\ldots + 2 + 1 = n(n-1)/2$$

comparisons. An instance of the worst case arises when the given array is sorted in the reverse order.

The analysis of bubble sort in the average case is not trivial. To find the expected number of comparisons, one must find the expected number of passes first. Again, an extra pass is usually required in bubble sort to ensure that sorting has been completed. This is the "no exchange" pass which will be ignored for the time being. Let $(y_1, y_2, \ldots, y_n)$ be the array elements after sorting is over. Obviously, (n!) different arrays are possible with the "n" elements and any one of these can be the initial array. Now, suppose that the initial array is such that y_i occupies the i-th position and that the other elements are sorted among themselves. When j < i then sorting requires y_i to be moved left to the j-th position through exchanges. Note that a single pass of bubble sort will achieve this. On the other hand, when j > i then y_i is to be moved right to the j-th position and (j-i) passes will be necessary to do this. The reason for this is that bubble sort will only move down y_i by one position in each pass. The above discussion indicates that the maximum upward displacement of any element from its final position determines the number of passes. Let "d" denote the maximum upward displacement. Then y_n can occupy any one of the (d+1) positions from the bottom of the given list. Similarly, y_{n-1} can occupy any one of the (d+2) positions from below except the position occupied by y_n. Proceeding in this way, it can be found out that each of the (n-d) elements can be placed in the "n" positions in $(d+1)^{n-d}$ ways such that the upward displacement of any one of them does not exceed "d". The remaining, "d" elements namely, $y_1, y_2, \ldots, y_d$ can be placed in the "d" positions left unoccupied by others in (d!) ways. Note that the maximum upward displacement in the case of any one of these "d" elements must be less than "d". Therefore, the probability that "x", the upward displacement of an element, does not exceed "d" is given by

$$\text{Probability}(x \le d) = ((d+1)^{n-d}\, d!)/n!$$

Now, $\text{Probability}(x = d) = \text{Probability}(x \le d) - \text{Probability}(x \le d-1)$

$$= ((d+1)^{n-d}\, d! - d^{n-d+1}\,(d-1)!)/n!$$

The expected value of "x" is, therefore, given by

$$\begin{aligned} E(x) &= \Sigma_{d=1,n} d.\text{Probability}(x = d) \\ &= (1/n!)\Sigma_{d=1,n} d.\ ((d+1)^{n-d}\, d! - d^{n-d+1}\,(d-1)!) \\ &= n - z(n) \end{aligned}$$

where $z(n) = (1/n!)\Sigma_{d=1,n}\, d^{n-d}.d!$

Taking into account the extra "no exchange" pass required in most cases, the expected number of passes is given by

$$P = x + 1 = (n+1) - Z(n)$$

Since (n-i) comparisons are required in the i-th pass, the expected number of comparisons are

$$\begin{aligned} C &= \Sigma_{i=1,p}(n - i) \\ &= nP - P(P + 1)/2 \\ &= P(2n - P - 1)/2 \end{aligned}$$

$$= \tfrac{1}{2}\{(n + 1) - z(n)\}\{(n - 2) + z(n)\}$$

It can be shown that

$$\lim_{n \to \infty} Z(n) = \sqrt{(n\pi/2)}.$$

Thus, for large "n",

$$C = O(n^2).$$

The above analysis shows that bubble sort is no better than the selection sort discussed earlier. Its time complexity is still $O(n^2)$. However, being a data sensitive method, it may perform better provided the maximum upward displacement in the list is not large. The storage ratio is 1. The implementation discussed earlier is stable.

Variations of Bubble Sort

There can be many variations of the bubble sort technique discussed earlier. For example, instead of starting from the last element of the array, we can start from the beginning and can move to the end putting the largest element to the last position. Thus, in the i-th pass, the i-th largest element will be moved down to the (n-i)-th index. The average performance of this version of bubble sort is the same as the discussed one. However, this version will be advantageous if the maximum downward displacement is smaller than the maximum upward displacement. To make things clearer, consider the array elements as (5, 2, 4, 3, 6). The maximum upward displacement is "3" while the maximum downward displacement is "2". Therefore, a downward bubble sort will require "3" passes and "9" comparisons and an upward bubble sort will require "4" passes and "10" comparisons.

Another variation of the bubble sort is known as cocktail shaker sort or simply shaker sort. In this method, the direction of the sort is reversed in alternate passes. The idea here is to take care of the upward and downward displacements in alternate passes. In fact, it can be shown that the average number of comparisons required by this is marginally less than that of the usual bubble sort.

9.5 Quick Sort

Quick sort introduced by Hoare in 1962 is a very fast method of internal sorting. The principle of quick sort is as follows. Let A[lower : upper] be the array to be sorted. For simplicity, assume that all elements in the array "A" are distinct. In quick sort method, y = A[lower] is used as a control element which is also referred to as the "bound". The array A[lower : upper] is partitioned in such a way that

A[lower : (r-1)] contains all elements smaller than "y";

A[(r+1) : upper] contains all elements greater than "y" and "y" is placed at A[r].

"r" is called the rank of "y". Note that in this approach, the key initially at A[lower] is placed at its proper index with repect to the entire array and the task of sorting the entire array now boils down to sorting two sub-arrays as obtained after the partitioning is done. The task of partitioning can be accomplished by the use of the following technique. Two index pointers "p" and "q" are initialised in such a way that "p" refers to A[lower+1] and "q" refers to A[upper]. The pointer "p" moves towards right searching for an element greater than "y" and the pointer "q" moves towards left looking for an element smaller than "y". When these elements are found they are interchanged. Again "p" moves towards right and "q" moves to left as before and exchange is made whenever necessary. The process ends whenever the pointers "p" and "q" meet or cross over. Thus, the array A[lower : upper] is partitioned in such a way that A[lower+1 : r-1] contains all elements smaller than "y" and A[r : upper] contains elements greater than "y". Next, "y" and A[r-1] are swapped. Subsequently, the subarrays A[lower : r-2] and A[r : upper] are sorted separately by applying the same procedure. Finally, only subarrays of length one remain and the array is sorted. In the quick sort method, any element of the array can be chosen as the bound and a very similar procedure may be used to partition the array.

The above procedure is explained with the help of the following example. In this example, the first element of the array is selected as "y" which is treated as the bound. Let the array of numbers be

24	28	13	15	18	34	06	19	07	11	12	26	35	29

In the first pass, lower = 0, upper = 13 A[0] = 24 is to be properly placed. To do so, "p" and "q" are set to the indices of the second and the last elements of the array respectively as shown in the following.

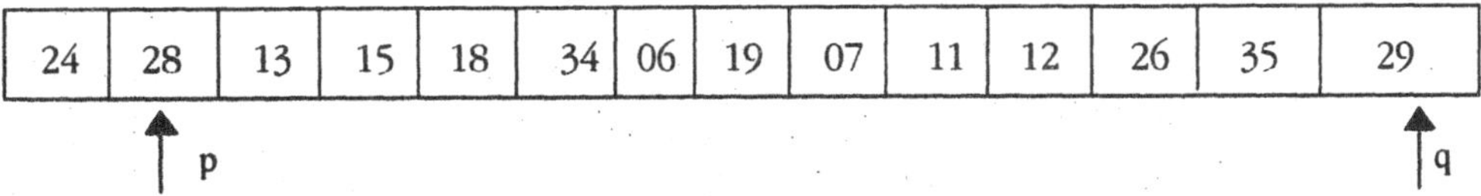

Now move "p" towards right until A[p] > 24. Hence, "p" does not move any further to the right and stops immediately as A[p] (=28) > 24. Then, move "q" towards left until A[q] < 24. So, "q" moves "3" units to the left and the situation may be described as shown in the following.

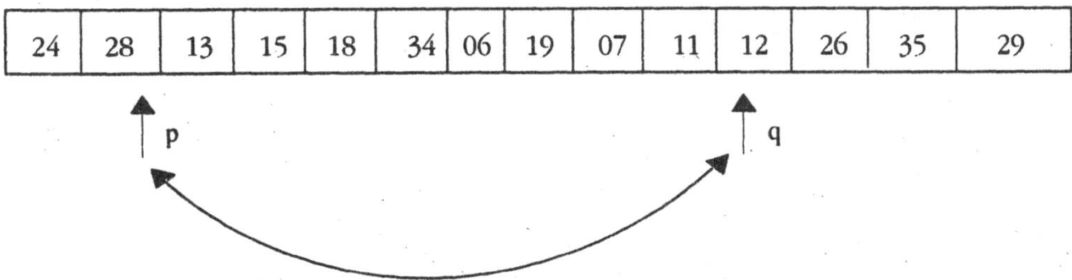

At this point, A[p] and A[q] are swapped and the movement of "p" and "q" resumes.

Now "p" moves "4" units to the right and "q" moves only once to the left as shown in the following.

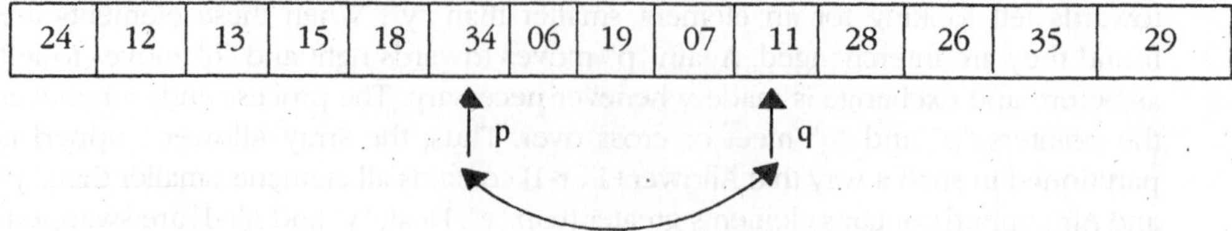

Once again A[p] and A[q] are swapped and movement of "p" and "q" resume> Now, "p" moves "4" times to the right and "q" moves once to left as shown in the following.

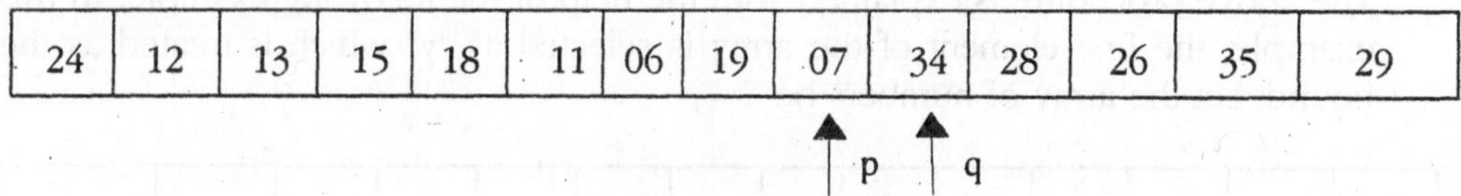

Since the index "p" becomes more then "q", the process ends after swapping A[lower] and A[q]. The resultant array looks like the following.

07	12	13	15	18	11	06	19	24	34	28	26	35	29

Note that "24" is positioned at index "8". All elements A[i], lower ≤ i < 8, are less than "24" and all elements A[i], 8 < i ≤ upper are greater than "24". Thus, "24" is properly positioned at index "8" in the array A[lower : upper] producing two smaller unsorted arrays A[lower : 8-1] and A[8+1 : upper]. The same procedure may be applied on these sub-arrays to sort them individually. In case the array "A" contains only one element then the algorithm returns without doing anything. One can easily see that the process is defined recursively and that the method essentially belongs to divide and conquer paradigm. The method outlined in this discussion is translated into the following recursive "C" function.

```
void quickSort(int A[], int lower, int upper)
{
    int i;
    if(upper > lower) /*"a" contains more than one element */
    {
        i = partition (A, lower, upper);
```

```
            quickSort(A, lower, i -1);
            quickSort(A, i+1, upper);
    }
}
```

The function "partition" is presented next.

```
int partition(int A[], int lower, int upper)
{
    int i, p, q, t;
    p = lower;
    q = upper + 1;
    i = A[lower];
    while (q >= p)
    {
            while (A[++p] < i);
            while (A[--q] > i);
            if (q > p)
            {
                    t = A[p];
                    A[p] = A[q];
                    A[q] = t;
            }
    }
    t = A[lower];
    A[lower] = A[q];
    A[q] = t;
    return q;
}
```

A small problem arises if the bound (A[lower] in our case) happens to be the maximum element. Because, in that situation, "p" will tend to more beyond "upper" as A[p] would always be less that the bound. To prevent such situations, a sentinel key having the largest possible value is needed to be stored at A[n]. Another subtle point is to be mentioned for dealing with equal keys. If a key equal to the bound is encountered through "p" or "q" then one can stop at that position or one can still increase (or decrease) "p" (or "q"). It is found that it is better to make the pointers "p", "q" stop on encountering elements equal to the bound. It seems that some additional exchanges take place as a consequence.

The function "quickSort" is tail recursive. Tail recursion may be removed very easily. Even after removing tail recursion, there would be one more recursive call remaining in the function. That recursive call may be removed by using a stack of integers to store the values of "p" and "q" at intermediate calls. The non-recursive version of quick sort algorithm is presented next.

```
void quickSortNonRecursive(int a[], int N)
{
    int i, lower, upper;
    stackOfIntegers s;
    lower = 0;
    upper = N;
    initialize (&s);
    for(; ;)
    {
            while (upper > lower)
            {
                    i = partition (a, lower, upper);
                    push(&s, lower);
                    push(&s, i -1);
                    lower = i + 1;
            }
            if (isEmpty(s))
                    break;
            upper = pop(&s);
            lower = pop(&s);
    }
}
```

In this version of non-recursive quick sort, the left half after partitioning the array is always pushed into the stack. In case this half is always larger in size (and the right half may not even contain any element), the stack grows. The size of the stack to be used becomes O(n) under these circumstances. However, one can push either half (left or right) without affecting the basic algorithm. If the smaller half is always pushed then the size of the stack can not grow beyond O(logn). This can be accomplished by changing the while-loop a little as shown in the following.

```
while (upper > lower)
```

```
{
   i = partition (a, lower, upper);
   if ((i – lower) < (upper – i))
   {
            push(&s, lower);
            push(&s, i –1);
            lower = i + 1;
   }
else {
            push(&s, i + 1);
            push(&s, upper);
            upper = i - 1;
   }
}
```

Let P(n), S(n) and C(n) denote the number of passes, exchanges and comparisons respectively required to sort an array of size "n". C(1) = C(0) = 0; S(1) = 0; and P(1) = 1. The function "partition" makes (n-1) comparisons if the function is applied on an array of "n" elements. After partitioning, the array is divided in two parts of size "r" and (n-r-1) where "r" may have any value from "0" to (n-1). If the initial array is such that it is already sorted in the ascending order then the value of "r" would be always "0". In such a case, the following recurrence relation is valid for C(n).

$$
\begin{aligned}
C(n) &= (n+1) + C(n-1) \\
&= (n+1) + n + C(n-2) \\
&= (n+1) + n + (n-1) + C(n-3) \\
&\quad . \\
&\quad . \\
&= (n+1) + n + (n-1) + \ldots + 1 \\
&= (n+1)(n+2)/2 \\
&= O(n^2).
\end{aligned}
$$

It can be easily verified that if the initial list is sorted in ascending manner then P(n) is O(n). If, however, the initial list is sorted in descending manner then the number of swaps or exchanges is maximized. In that case, the number of swap in the first pass is (n+1) and the list is partitioned into two sublists of length "0" and (n-1) respectively. In this case, The recurrence relation for S(n) is given by

$$S(n)= (n+1) + S(n-1)$$

$= O(n^2)$

To compute the average number of comparisons required by quick sort, the exact recurrence relation of C(n) needs to be analyzed. The recurrence relation of C(n) is given by

$$C(n) = (n+1) + C(r-1) + C(n-r)$$

As every element of the array A[lower+1:upper-1] is compared with A[lower], there are (n-1) comparisons. Another two comparisons take place when the two pointers cross over. The equation depends on the value of "r", which may be any integer from "1" to "n". Assuming that any value of "r" is equally likely, the expected number of C(n) may be obtained by adding C(n) for all values of "r" and then dividing the sum by "n". Thus, the expected value of C(n) is given by

$$C(n) = (n+1) + (1/n)((C(0) + C(n-1)) + (C(1) + C(n-2)) + (C(2) + C(n-3)) + \ldots + (C(n-3) + C(2)) + (C(n-2) + C(1)) + (C(n-1) + C(0)))$$

Note that the terms C(0), C(1), C(2), ..., C(n-1) occur twice in the sub-expression. Thus,

$$C(n) = (n+1) + (2/n)(C(0) + C(1) + C(2) + \ldots + C(n-1))$$

$$nC(n) = n(n+1) + 2(C(0) + C(1) + C(2) + \ldots + C(n-1))$$

Replacing "n" in the previous equation by (n-1), the following equation is obtained.

$$(n-1)C(n-1) = (n-1)n + 2\,(C(0) + C(1) + C(2) + \ldots + C(n-2))$$

Subtracting the last equation from its previous equation,

$$nC(n) - (n-1)C(n-1) = n(n+1) - (n-1)n + 2C(n-1)$$

i.e., $nC(n) = (n+1)C(n-1) + 2n$

Dividing both sides by n(n+1), the following equation is obtained.

$$C(n)/(n+1) = C(n-1)/n + 2/(n+1)$$

$$= C(n-2)/(n-1) + 2/n + 2/(n+1)$$

$$= C(2)/3 + 2/3 + 2/4 + \ldots + 2/n + 2/(n+1)$$

Now, $\Sigma_{i=3,n} (2/i) \leq 2 \int (1/x)dx = 2 \log_e n$

Hence, on the average $C(n) = 2(n+1)\,O(\log_e n)$ » $1.39n\log_e n + O(n)$

Calculation of the average number of exchange operations is rather involved and therefore the detailed calculation is omitted. The average number of exchange operation can be shown to be $0.69\ (n\log_2 n/3)$.

Selection of the k-th smallest number in an array of integers is another interesting problem which can be solved efficiently by using a procedure similar to quick sort. Note that if "k" is "1" then the problem can be solved using O(n) comparisons.

When "k" is more, the complexity of a simple solution tends to be nonlinear. Quick sort provides an interesting solution for all values of "k" and which runs in linear time on the average. Recall that quick sort partitioning method splits an array A[lower:upper-1] to place A[lower] in a position "r" such that all elements in A[lower:r-1] are less than A[r] and all elements in A[r+1:upper-1] are greater than A[r]. If "r" is equal to (lower+k-1) then A[r] is the desired k-th smallest element in the array A[lower:upper-1]. If "r" is greater than (lower+k-1) then the k-th smallest element has to be found out in the left half. If, however, "r" is less than (lower+k-1) then the k-th smallest element must be in the right half. Since, all elements in the array A[lower:r] are less than the k-th smallest element, the k-th smallest element in the entire array would be the (k-r)-th smallest element in the right half. This method immediately leads to the following recursive "C" function for selecting the k-th smallest element in the Array A[lower:upper-1]. The element A[k] would contain the k-th smallest element after the function returns.

```
void select (int A[], int lower, int upper, int k)
{
    int r;
    if (upper > lower)
    {
            r = partition (A, lower, upper);
            if (r > lower+k-1)
                    select (A, lower, r-1, k);
            if (r < lower+k-1)
                    select (A, r+1, upper, k-r);
    }
}
```

9.6 Sorting by Merging

There are several methods in this class of internal sorting. All these methods employ merging as the dominant operation to achieve sorting. Merging operation refers to combining two sorted lists into one sorted list. The complexity of this operation is linear as will be seen when a very well known method of this family will be described in detail. Subsequently, outline of another method will also be discussed.

Straight Two-way Merge Sort

In chapter 6, "divide and conquer" technique of designing algorithms has been discussed. It was also pointed out that this technique may be used to efficiently sort a list of elements. Merge sort is one such sorting method based on "divide and conquer" philosophy. Its basic action is to split an initially unsorted array A[lower :

upper] around its middle element, "mid"(where mid = (lower + upper)/2), into two unsorted arrays A[lower : mid] and A[mid+1: upper]. The algorithm is then used recursively to sort the arrays A[lower : mid] and A[mid+1 : upper] and then these two sorted sub-arrays are merged. The process of dividing the original array continues till there is only one element in the array in which case, the array is sorted. First, let us explain the method by a suitable example. Let the initial array be

(24 28 15 13 18 34 19 06)

where lower = 1, upper = 8. Hence, the value of "mid" is "4". Thus, the array is split into two halves as shown in the following.

((24 28 15 13) (18 34 19 06))

Take the first half (i.e. the list (24 28 15 13)) and sort this array. To sort this half, this list has to be divided again as shown below.

(((24 28) (15 13)) (18 34 19 06))

Once again, the list (24 28) is to be divided into two lists ((24) (28)). These arrays (24), (28) are individually sorted (because they contain one element each) and hence, the sorting method does nothing when applied to them. Now, the pending task of sorting the list (24 28) has to be resumed because the tasks of sorting the two arrays after dividing (24 28) is over. This task is to merge the sorted arrays (24) and (28) into one. On merging, the resultant list becomes (24 28).

Once this is done, the first task in sorting the list (24 28 15 13) (i.e. the task of sorting the first sub-list (24 28)) is over. Next task is to sort the list (15, 13). To do so, this list is divided into two lists (15), (13). These lists are already sorted because each of them contains only one element. Then, these lists are merged to produce (13 15). Now, the last task of sorting the list (24 28 15 13) is to be resumed. This task is to merge the already sorted lists (24 28) (13 15).

Once they are merged the new list becomes (13 15 24 28). This completes the first task of sorting the original list. The next task, now, is to sort the list (18 34 19 06). Readers are encouraged to proceed with sorting this list manually to produce the list (06 18 19 34). Once this is over, the merge operation for sorting the original list remains to be done which merges the already sorted lists (13 15 24 28) and (06 18 19 34). These two lists are merged to form the new list (06 13 15 18 19 24 28 34).

The above method discussed so far leads us to the following recursive "C" function which sorts an array A[lower : upper].

```
void mergeSort(int A[ ], int lower, int upper)
{
    int mid;
    if(upper > lower)
    {
            mid = (lower + upper)/2;
            mergeSort (A, lower, mid);
            mergeSort (A, mid+1, upper);
            merge (A, lower, mid, mid+1, upper);
    }
}
```

it should be clear by now that "merge" is a crucial operation in the context of the function "mergeSort". The "C" function for merging two arrays x=A[lower1 : upper1], y=A[lower2 : upper2] is presented in the following. The function maintains two pointers "p", "q" to mark the beginning of the two arrays. As long as the element indexed by "p" in the first array is less than or equal to the element indexed by "q" in the second array, the elements in the first array are copied to a temporary array "D" and "p" is incremented. This is followed by copying the elements indexed by "q" in the second array and incrementing "q" as long as this element is less than or equal to the element indexed by "p" in the first array. This process continues until either the first or the second array is exhausted. Then, the remaining elements are copied from one array to the temporary array "D". Finally the elements are copied back from "D" to the original array "A".

```
void merge (int A[], int lower1, int upper1, int lower2, int upper2)
{
    int p, q, j, n;
    int D[100];
    p = lower1; q = lower2; n = 0;
    while ((p <= upper1) && (q <= upper2))
    {
            D[n++] = (A[p] < A[q]) ? A[p++] : A[q++];
    }
    while (p <= upper1)
            D[n++] = A[p++];
    while (q <= upper2)
```

```
        D[n++] = A[q++];
    for (q = lower1, n = 0; q <= upper1; q++, n++)
        A[q] = D[n];
    for (q = lower2, j = n; q <= upper2; q++, j++)
        A[q] = D[j];
}
```

The function "merge" runs in O(n+m) time if the first and the second list contains "n" and "m" elements respectively. However, this operation also requires a space for temporarily storing all (n+m) elements in one single array. If T(n) denotes the time required to sort "n" elements using the function "mergeSort", then the following recursive relation is valid for T(n).

$$T(n) = T(n/2) + T(n/2) + O(n) \text{ where } n=2^m \text{ for some "m".}$$

The first two components in the right hand side of the recurrence equation arise due to the time to be taken for sorting the individual sub-lists. The recurrence relation can be solved as follows.

$$\begin{aligned}
T(n) &= T(n/2) + T(n/2) + k.n \text{ for a constant "k"}\\
&= 2T(n/2) + k.n\\
&= 2(2T(n/4) + k(n/2) + k.n\\
&= 2^2T(n/2^2) + nk(1+1)\\
&= 2^mT(n/2^m) + nk(1+1+\ldots+1)\\
&= nT(1) + nk.m\\
&= n + kn \log n\\
&= O(n\log n)
\end{aligned}$$

Thus, it is proved that the worst case time complexity of merge sort is O(nlog n). It should be clear from the above analysis that the most time consuming part of merge sort algorithm is the merging operation. Thus, the best and average case complexities of the algorithm are also the same. Since the operation "merge" is stable, the merge sort algorithm is also stable.

Bottom up merge sorting

Merge sort can also be designed in a non-recursive way. The non-recursive algorithm of merge sort works in a botom-up manner. Before the non-recursive algorithm is discussed, a term which will be constantly used in the description of this algorithm is introduced. This term is "run" and it is used to denote a sorted segment within an array. The length of a "run" is the number of elements in the "run". In literature on sorting, runs are often called strings. However, since string is also an accepted term to denote a sequence of characters, the term "string" will be avoided in this context and the term "run" will be used to mean a sorted segment. The algorithm starts by considering each element to be a run of length "1". The first pass merges pairs of runs to create runs of length "2". For this purpose, first and second runs are taken as a pair to be merged. Similarly, third and fourth runs are merged and so on. Therefore, at the end of the first pass, (n/2) runs of length "2" are created where "n" is the number of elements in the given array. The second pass consists of merging pairs of runs created in the first pass. The pairs are selected for merging in the same manner as in the case of first pass and at the end of the second pass, (n/4) runs each of length "4" are created. Successive passes are similar and in each pass the number of runs is reduced by half and the lengths of runs are doubled. Thus, if $n=2^p$ then at the end of "p" passes a single run of length "n" is created and this is the desired sorted array. An example of this straight two-way merge sort is shown in Figure 9.7. In this example, the array consists of 16 elements and 4 passes are required.

Original array	After First Pass	After Second Pass	After Third Pass	After Fourth Pass
14	14	8	8	3
39	39	14	14	8
16	8	16	16	14
8	16	39	34	16
34	34	34	37	29
46	46	37	39	34
37	37	46	46	35
53	53	53	53	37
49	3	3	3	39
3	49	35	29	42
42	35	42	35	46
35	42	49	42	49
61	61	29	49	53
89	89	57	57	57
57	29	61	61	61
29	57	89	89	89

Figure 9.7 Illustration of Straight Two-way Merge Sort. Each column stands for a pass. In each pass, the rows correspond to a "run". The original array contains "16" runs. After the first pass there are "8" runs. After the second pass, there are "4" runs and so on.

When "n" is a power of "2", there is no problem with this method. However, several problems crop up when "n" is not a power of "2". In a situation like this, we are left with an odd number of runs to be merged in a pass. To overcome the situation, the normal practice is to merge pairs of runs as usual until the last run is reached. This solitary run is copied to be considered as a merged run. This solution is not fully satisfactory because the last run will be of length different from that of the runs generated by merging. As such proper care should be taken to handle the last run.

An implementation of the straight merge sort is shown in the following. A[1:n] holds the given array. The algorithm takes the help of a function "merge" as discussed earlier.

```
void mergeSortBottomUp (int A[], int n)
{
    int i, j, k, m, r1 ,r2;
    int T;
    for (i = 1; i <= n; i += 2)
    {
        if (A[i] > A[i + 1])
        {
            T = A[i];
            A[i] = A[i + 1];
            A[i + 1] = T;
        }
    }
    for (k = 2; k < n; k = 2*k)
    {
        for (i = 1, j = k + 1, m = 1; m <= n; i += 2*k, j += 2*k, m += 2*k)
        {
            r1 = i + k – 1;
            r2 = j + k – 1;
            merge (A, i, r1, j, r2);
        }
    }
}
```

The number of passes required for the method is $\lceil \log_2 n \rceil$. The number of comparisons required in a pass is approximately "n". This is because the merging of "n" elements requires roughly "n" comparisons. Thus, the number of comparisons required by the method is given by

$$C = n\log_2 n$$

It must be noted that merge sort technique involves lots of assignments during its merge operation too. Since the height of the recursion tree is $O(\log_2 n)$ and at each level of the tree a total of $O(n)$ assignments take place during merging, the total number of assignment operations become $O(n \log_2 n)$.

The method is not data sensitive and the time complexity is $O(n\log_2 n)$ for any array of "n" elements. The storage ratio for the method is "2". The method is stable, provided identical keys are taken care of properly during the merging of runs.

Merge sort using linked lists

Out of the sorting methods discussed so far, merge sort is specially suitable to be used in linked representation of lists. In fact, when merge sort is applied to a list implemented as a linked list, the temporary storage is not required during merge operation. Suppose that merge sort is to be applied to a singly connected linked list of integers. The type of each node in such a list is declared as a self-referential structure, which contains a member "data" of type "int". The type declaration of such a node is presented in the following.

```
typedef struct node
{
    int data;
    struct node *next;
}node;
```

The merge operation merges two lists pointed to be "a" and "b" and the pointer to the merged list is returned.

```
node *merge(node *a, node *b)
{
    node *c,*d;
    if(a->data <= b->data)
    {
            c = d = a;
            a = a->next;
    }
    else
    {
            c = d = b;
            b = b-> next;
    }
```

```
    while((a != NULL) && (b != NULL))
    {
        if(a->data <= b->data)
        {
            c->next = a;
            c = a;
            a = a->next;
        }
        else
        {
            c->next = b;
            c = b;
            b = b->next;
        }
    }
    if (a)
        c->next = a;
    else
        c->next = b;
    return d;
}
```

The first task in the merge sort algorithm is to divide the input list in two approximately equal halves. This is accomplished by maintaining two pointer "a" and "b". "a" is initialized to point to the beginning of the list. "b" is set to point to the third node in the list. Subsequently, "b" is incremented twice whenever "a" is incremented once. Thus, when "b" points to NULL then "a" points to the middle of the original list. Once the splitting is done, "mergeSort" can be recursively called on the individual lists.

```
node *mergeSortList(node *c)
{
    node *a, *b;
    if (c->next != NULL)
    {
        a = c;
        b = c->next->next;
        while ((b != NULL) && (b->next != NULL))
```

```
        {
            c = c->next;
            b = b->next->next;
        }
        b = c->next;
        c->next = NULL;
        return merge(mergeSortList(a), mergeSortList(b));
        }
        return c;
}
```

Natural Merge Sort

One drawback of the merge sort algorithm is that it cannot take advantage of the existing ordering that may be present in the original array. The natural merge sort exploits the presence of natural runs in a given array. In this method, the first pass consists of discovering the runs by scanning the list sequentially from the beginning. For example, if the given array is

(13, 17, 23, 05, 50, 12, 10, 19, 35)

then the runs identified in the first pass are (13, 17, 23), (05, 50), (12) and (10, 19, 35). The subsequent passes are similar to those of ordinary merge sort except that now the runs are of variable lengths. Obviously, natural merge sort is advantageous when long runs are expected in the given array. The main disadvantage is the handling of variable length runs. This requires considerable amount of book-keeping as we must keep track of the beginning and end of each run.

Other Techniques Based on Merging

Several internal sorting techniques based on the principle of merging are in use. For example, both ordinary merge sort and natural merge sort can be easily extended to k-way merging (k > 2). As a result, longer runs are generated in each merge and fewer passes are required. Sometimes merges of different orders ("k" denotes the order of a merge) are combined in the same method. These methods are called unbalanced merge techniques as opposed to the balanced merge techniques which restrict to a fixed order merge (except perhaps in the case of last few runs). Note that ordinary merge sort as well as natural merge sort are balanced merge techniques. Unbalanced merge techniques are normally used in the case of external sorting.

9.7 Heap Sort

The notion of a "heap" has been introduced in Chapter 8. Algorithms to construct a heap from an initial list in a bottom-up manner and to remove the largest element from a heap have also been discussed. Heaps provide an elegant way to sort an array of records. On one hand, heap sort does not use any additional array for intermediate use and on the other hand, the worst case time complexity of sorting "n" records using heap sort is $O(n\log_2 n)$.

The strategy to sort using a heap is straight forward. First, a heap is constructed from an array "A" of "n" elements in linear time. If a sentinel key (key with a value that is higher than the highest key value in "A") is assumed to be stored at A[0], then A[1] is the largest key value in the list "A". Now, A[1] and A[n] may be swapped which puts the largest element of the array "A" in A[n]. Next, the heap size is reduced by "1". The new tree represented by the array A[1:n-1] may no longer be a heap due to a change in the value of A[1] (i.e., the root of the heap). The new tree is converted to a heap by using the function "restoreHeapDown" (described in Chapter 8). The resulting algorithm is very simple and is presented next.

```
int n;
int A[100];
void heapSort()
{
    int i, t, m;
    for (i = n/2; i >= 1; i—)
            restoreHeapDown(i);
    m = n;
    while(n > 1)
    {
            t = A[1];
            A[1] = A[n];
            A[n] = t;
            n = n - 1;
            restoreHeapDown(1);
    }
    n = m;
}
```

A global variable "n" is used in this function, which is set to the number of elements in the global array, "A". Note that the name of the array was chosen to be "Elements" in Chapter 8. The worst case complexity of the function "restoreHeapDown" is $O(\log_2 n)$ for a heap of size "n". Hence, the total complexity of the algorithm "heapSort" is

$$\Sigma_{i=1,n} \log_2 i = \log_2 n!$$

As it has already been seen, $\log_2 n!$ can be proved to be approximately equal to

$O(n\log_2 n)$ for large value of "n" by applying Stirling's formula. Thus, the worst case time complexity of the "heapSort" algorithm is $\Theta(n\log_2 n)$. An example of sorting an array "A" of numbers is shown in Figure 9.8.

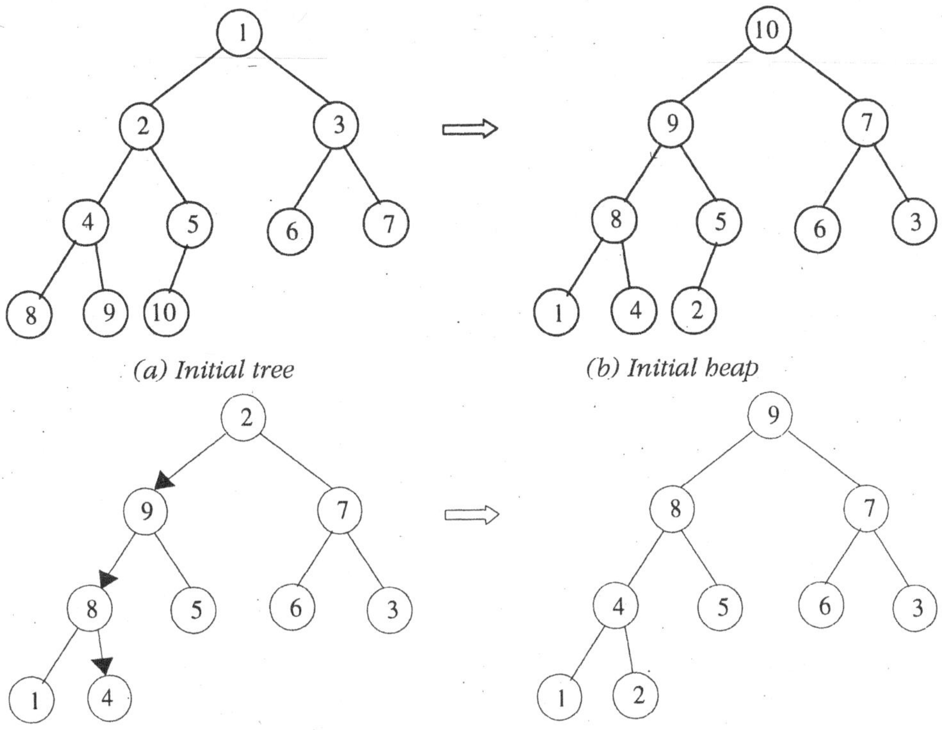

(a) Initial tree *(b) Initial heap*

(c) The tree after exchanging A[1] with A[10] (in the first iteration of the while–loop); The tree is converted to a heap by applying the function "restoreHeapDown". The lines with the arrows show the exchanges necessary for the function "restoreHeapDown".

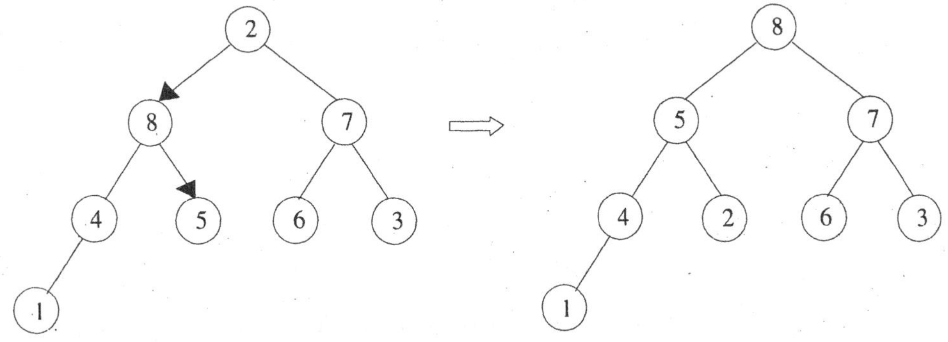

(d) The tree after exchanging A[1] with A[9] (in the second iteration of the while–loop); The tree is converted to a heap by applying the function "restoreHeapDown". The lines with the arrows show the exchanges necessary for the function "restoreHeapDown".

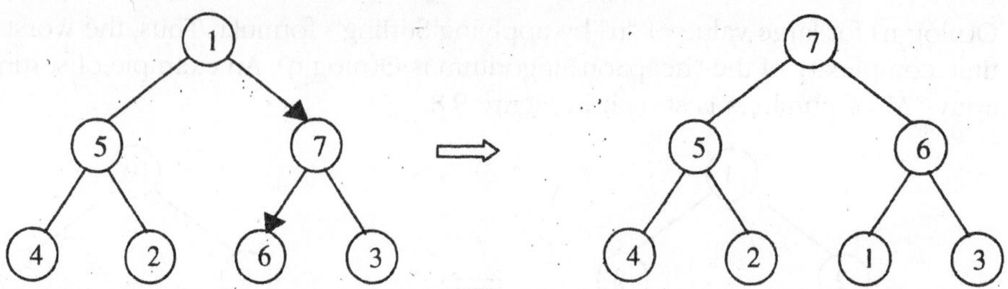

(e) The tree after exchanging A[1] with A[8] (in the third iteration of the while–loop); The tree is converted to a heap by applying the function "restoreHeapDown". The lines with the arrows show the exchanges necessary for the function "restoreHeapDown"

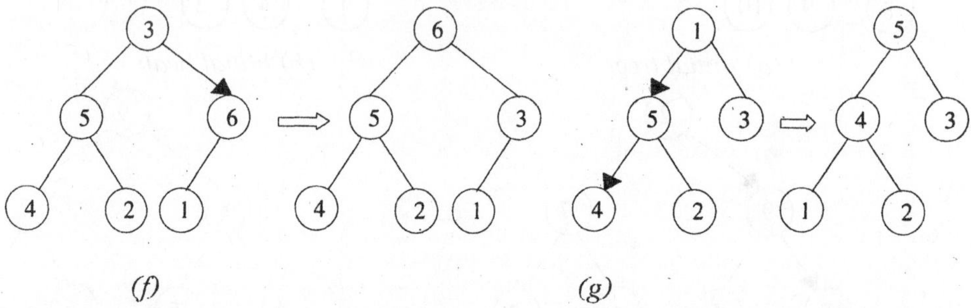

(f) *(g)*

(f) The tree after exchanging A[1] with A[7] (in the fourth iteration of the while–loop); The tree is converted to a heap by applying the function "restoreHeapDown". The lines with the arrows show the exchanges necessary for the function "restoreHeapDown".

(g) The tree after exchanging A[1] with A[6] (in the fifth iteration of the while–loop); The tree is converted to a heap by applying the function "restoreHeapDown". The lines with the arrows show the exchanges necessary for the function "restoreHeapDown"

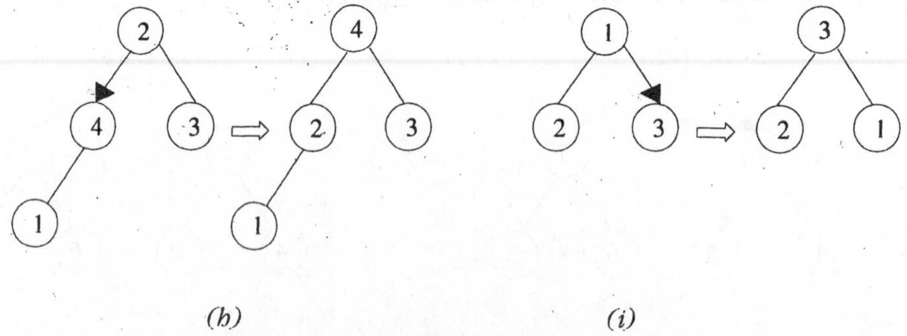

(h) *(i)*

(h) The tree after exchanging A[1] with A[5] (in the sixth iteration of the while–loop); The tree is converted to a heap by applying the function "restoreHeapDown". The lines with the arrows show the exchanges necessary for the function "restoreHeapDown"

(i) The tree after exchanging A[1] with A[4] (in the seventh iteration of the while-loop); The tree is converted to a heap by applying the function "restoreHeapDown". The lines with the arrows show the exchanges necessary for the function "restoreHeapDown".

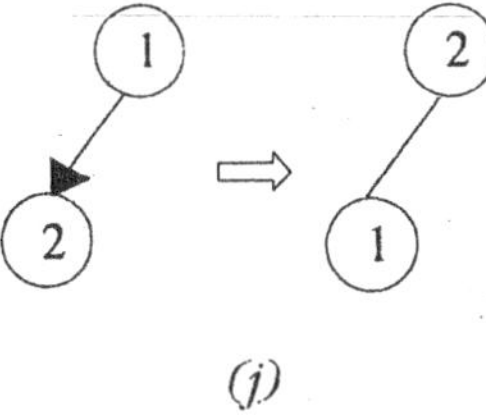

(j)

(j) The tree after exchanging A[1] with A[3] (in the eighth iteration of the while-loop); The tree is converted to a heap by applying the function "restoreHeapDown". The lines with the arrows show the exchanges necessary for the function "restoreHeapDown".

9.8 How fast can we sort?

The methods described so far use comparison as the basic mechanism for sorting. Therefore, the sequence of comparisons made by any such algorithms may be expressed in the form of a tree where each node denotes a comparison between A[i] and A[j]. These nodes are labelled by (i, j) and the two edges emerging out of this node represent the result of the comparison. These trees are slight modifications to the comparison trees discussed in the context of searching. For example, the tree of Figure 9.9 represents the sequence of comparisons made by the selection sort algorithm.

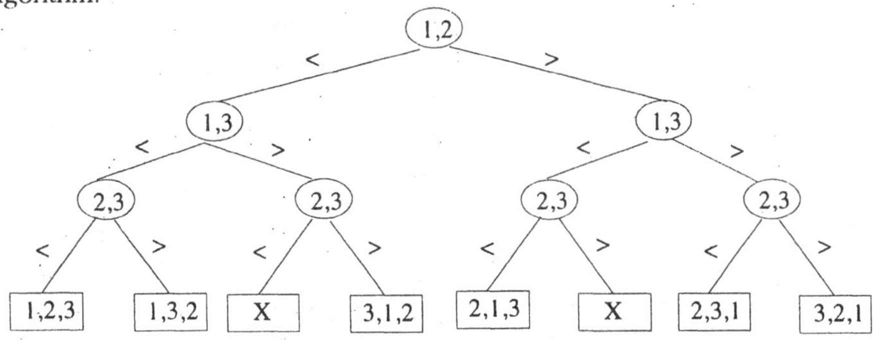

Figure 9.9 Comparison tree for sorting an array of three elements using selection sort. The elements assumed to be a, a, a. Some external nodes marked "X" reflecting the fact that the process of sorting would never visit that node.

The external (leaf) nodes in these trees represent all possible permutations of "n" elements. Assuming all elements are distinct, at least (n!) external nodes must be present in any such tree. A tree having at least (n!) external nodes must have a height of log(n!) at the least. Any sorting algorithm must traverse from the root to the leaf node. So, the worst case complexity of any sorting algorithm can not be less than O(log(n!)) which is O(nlogn).

9.9 Hashing

Sequential search or binary search techniques described earlier in this chapter are based on comparing a given key with existing key values in a list. It has been observed that there are theoretical lower bounds on the average case complexity of search methods based on comparison. Therefore, one has to delve into new paradigms in order to find out a better mechanism for searching. "Hashing" provides a conceptually different mechanism to search a table for a given key value. In hashing, the record for a key value, "k", is directly referred by calculating the address from the key value.

Consider that there are "n" elements which are to be stored in a hash table of size "M", where ($M \geq n$). An element with key value, "k", will be put in slot "j" of the hash table, if j = h (k); "h" is called the hash function. For example, h (k) may be defined as k mod M+1, where $1 \leq h(k) \leq M$ for any integer "k". Ideally, hash functions should result in a unique value when applied to any key. But, such a hash function is not practically available. So, it is quite possible that $h(k_1)$ may be the same as $h(k_2)$ for two distinct key values "k_1" and "k_2". As a result, while inserting a key "k_2" to the address given by $h(k_2)$, it is possible to find that the address is already used by another key "k_1", previously encountered. This indicates that two keys "k_1" and "k_2" collided. Often, "k_1" and "k_2" are called synonyms. Then, there has to be some collision resolution strategy to resolve this conflict.

It is easy to see that collision plays a major role in hashing methods. Thus, while the objective of a hash function is to minimize the collision, the objective of a collision resolution strategy is to locate a vacant position as efficiently as possible once collision occurs.

9.9.1 Hash Functions

The problem of finding a hash function can be stated as follows. There are "n" keys such that all key values are between "a" and "b". It is required to find a hash function f(key) that transforms a key into an address in the range "0" to (M-1). Moreover, M > n. Note that it is sufficient to map the addresses in the range "0" to (M-1). In case the storage locations start from an address "x" then the address computed by the hash function is to be added to "x" to get the effective address. The domain of the hashing function namely, the interval [a, b] is usually very wide. For example, suppose that there is an array of 800 elements and each key consists of 6 digits. If the array is housed in a storage area consisting of 1000 addresses, we have n=800 and m=1000. The domain of the hashing function is (0,999999) and its range is (0, 999).

An ideal hash function should distribute the keys uniformly over the range (0, M-1). In other words, the probability of generating an address "x" (where $0 \leq x \leq (M-1)$) for a given key "k" should be (1/M). This is considered to be an "ideal" hash function because any key can occupy any address with equal probability. As such, it is not likely for a good hash function to overburden particular address with too many keys. Consequently, the number of collisions is expected to be low for a good hash function.

There are many methods for hashing. Some of the popular hash functions are discussed in the following. In all these cases, the keys will be assumed to be numeric integers. In case of alphanumeric keys, they are to be transformed into numeric values and then hash function is to be applied on the numeric equivalent of the keys. The numeric equivalent of the alphanumeric keys can be found by taking the ASCII values of the characters forming the keys.

The Division Method

In this method, the key is divided by "M" and the remainder is taken to be the address. Thus, the hash function, "h", is given by

$$h(k) = k \bmod M$$

An advantage of this method is that it produces addresses exactly in the range "0" to (M-1). However, "M" should be chosen carefully. Certain choices of "M" are not at all satisfactory. For example, if the keys are decimal integers and "M" is chosen to be a power of "10", say 1000, then all keys having identical last three digits will hash into the same address. Again, if "M" is chosen to be an even integer then all even keys will hash into odd addresses. Obviously, keys will not be hashed uniformly in the range (0, M-1). For example, if there are more odd keys than the even ones, the method will produce more odd addresses. Any hashing method that seeks to retain the effect of the original key sequence pattern should be avoided. Experience has shown that any number which is not divisible by 2, 3, 5, 10 is usually a good choice for "M". It has also been pointed out that non-prime odd integers having no divisors less than "19" can produce very good results when chosen as the value of "M". Another good choice of "M" is a prime number. Such a choice of "M" usually removes any pattern present in the key sequence from the generated addresses. However, a prime number related to the base of the number system used for the key by some simple relation should be avoided. For example, primes such as 4999, 7001 or 7999 are related to 10 by the relations $q.10^p + 1$ or $q.10^p - 1$. Use of such prime numbers would have effects of the last p-digits of the original key on the remainders. It is easy to see that if 4999 is chosen as "M", keys such as 00234, 05233, 10232, 15231 etc. all map into the address 234. Here, the quotient of the division of the first digits by 5, when added to the last three digits produces the address.

The Mid square Method

In this method, the key is squared and a portion of the squared value is selected from the middle which is chosen as the address. Suppose that a q-digit address is to be generated from a p-digit key. To do so, the p-digit key is first squared to yield a 2p-digit value. The q-digit address, then, is selected from the middle of this 2p-digit result. For example, let p = 4, q = 3 and the key be "3271". Square of "3271" is "10699441". Since 3 digits are to be extracted from the middle, the first three and the last two digits can be removed and "994" may be selected as the address. The method can also be modified to select "699" as the address.

This mid square method has the advantage that it is a flexible method and it can be suitably modified if needed. For example, when the key is large then only a selected part of the keys may be squared. Usually, mid square method is found to produce addresses that are uniformly distributed over the range of the hashing function.

Folding

Suppose we have p-digit keys from which q-digit addresses are to be generated. In this method, the digits of a key are partitioned into groups of q-digits from the right. These groups are then added and the rightmost q-digits of the sum is selected as the address. The following example will show the working of the method. Suppose we have an 8-digit key namely, 39427829 and we have to generate a 3-digit address from it. When partitioned we have three groups as shown below.

39/427/829

Adding 39, 427 and 829, we get 1295. Selecting the last three digits we get the desired address as 295. This method is also flexible like the 'Mid square' method and can be modified as desired. In case the key is string of characters, this can be converted into a number consisting of string of ASCII values of the characters.

For example, let the key value be "DOEACC". Then taking the ASCII values of the characters we get k = 687969656767. When partitioned we have four groups as shown in the following

687/969/656/767

Now adding these groups we get 3079. Thus, the generated address becomes 79.

Analysis for an ideal Hash Function

It was mentioned earlier that an ideal hash function should distribute "n" keys uniformly into "M" addresses. Such hash functions are called uniform hash functions. Therefore, "p", the probability that a particular address "a" ($0 \leq a \leq M-1$) will be generated for a key value, "k" is given by

p = (1/M)

Call the event of generating some address "a" by one trial of the hashing function to be a "success". When the addresses for all keys have been generated then there have been "n" trials and each such trial is independent. The random variable, "X", denoting the number of success in "n" trials follows a "Binomial distribution". Therefore, p(x), the probability of "x" successes in "n" trials, is given by

$$p(x) = ({}^{n}C_{x})\, p^{x} (1 - p)^{n-x}$$

Again, Binomial distribution can be approximated by Poisson's distribution for large "n". Thus, for large "n",

$$p(x) = ((np)^{x} e^{-np})/ x!$$

$$= (\alpha^{x} e^{\alpha})/ x! \qquad \ldots.(5)$$

where $\alpha = np = n/M$. "α" is also called the load factor.

Now, p(x) can also be interpreted as the probability that "x" keys will be mapped to a single address, "a", by an ideal hash function. It is interesting to note that this probability depends only on the load factor "α". This is why, the load factor is so important in hashing.

Using (5) as a working formula, one can find certain other attributes for an ideal hash function. One such attribute is "r", the expected number of distinct addresses that will be generated. Obviously, "r" is less than "n". An expression for "r" can be computed in the following manner. The probability that the address "a" will not be generated at all is given by p(0). Therefore, (1 – p(0)) gives the probability that some address "a" will be generated at least once. This gives

$$r = (1 - p(0)).m$$

$$=(1-e^{-\alpha}).m$$

Expressions for two other attributes may be computed by using "r". These are β, the expected number of home keys expressed as percentage of "n", and γ, the expected number of synonyms expressed as percentage of "n". The home keys are the ones which are hashed to a particular slot in the hash table for the first time. Synonyms are keys which are hashed to the same address giving rise to collision.

$$\beta = 100\ (r/n) = 100\ (1 - e^{-\alpha}) / \alpha$$

$$\gamma = 100 - \beta = 100\ (\alpha + e^{-\alpha} - 1) / \alpha$$

The values of β and γ for various values of α are shown in the following table.

α	0.1	0.2	0.3	0.4	0.5	0.6	0.7	0.8	0.9	1.0
β	95.2	90.6	86.4	82.4	78.7	75.2	71.9	68.8	65.9	63.2
γ	4.8	9.4	13.6	17.6	21.3	24.8	28.1	31.2	34.1	36.8

It may be mentioned from the table that a value around 0.5 is a good choice for "α". A choice of $\alpha = 0.5$ signifies that if the number of entries of the hash table is twice the number of key values to be stored then the average number of synonyms or collisions may be restricted to the level of 21%.

Although this analysis is related directly to ideal hash functions only, it provides α method for testing the effectiveness of a given hash function. One can perform trial runs with the given hash function and can compare the number of synonyms obtained with the expected number of synonyms given by the corresponding equation obtained for an ideal hash function. A more elaborate and thorough test would be to find the distribution of the synonyms experimentally. It can now be compared with the theoretical distribution of the synonyms obtained for an ideal hash function.

9.9.2 Conflict resolution techniques

Every hash function is expected to generate the same address for distinct key values. The key values which are transformed to the same address are often referred to as synonyms. Therefore, one must know how to cope with such situations. Methods to deal with synonyms are known as collision resolution techniques. These techniques fall into two broad classes called open addressing and chaining. If a conflict occurs while inserting a key and if the conflict is resolved using "open addressing" methods then an empty position is found out within the hash table itself and the new key is inserted in that empty position. So, in "open addressing" methods, no space outside the hash table is used for storing the key values. In "chaining" methods, synonyms are placed in linked lists. Nodes of linked lists may be allocated from some space outside the hash table. There are several methods in each class. Some important and widely used methods from each class are described below.

Linear and Quadratic Probe

In this open addressing method, if the hashed address (typically an index to the hash table) is found to be already occupied by an element then the indices following the hashed index are sequentially examined to locate the first empty position. The concerned element is stored in the index so located. For the purpose of sequential examination, the hash table is considered to be circular. That is, the first index in the table is taken as the position next to the last index. Linear probe technique requires a means to identify whether a position in the hash table is empty or not.

In order to present algorithms, certain assumptions are made. As before, it is assumed that an element of the array consists only of the key field. The array, "A", is assumed to be of size "m". Another array, "T", is used to indicate whether an element of "A" is empty or not. It is assumed that if the i-th element of "T" is false then the i-th element of "A" is empty; otherwise, it is not empty. Algorithms to insert an element "k" and to search an element "k" using "linear probe" method are presented in the following.

```
int insertLinearProbe(int k)
{
    int i = 0, j;
```

```
    j = hash(k);
    do
    {
            if (T[j] == false) /* no key occupies A[j] */
            {
                    A[j] = k;
                    T[j] = true;
                    return j;
            }
            i++;
            j = (j + i)%m;
    } while (i < m);
    return (-1);
}
```

Note that the existence of a function called "hash" has been assumed. This function returns an address in the range of "0" to (m-1) for a key. If A[j] ("j" is the index generated by the hash function) already contains some key then A[j+1], A[j+2], etc. are sequentially examined to find out an empty slot in "A". To produce the wrap-around effect, modulo-m additions are performed while incrementing "j". The function returns (-1) when no space is available for insertion. The "insertLinearProbe" function stores only one element at a time. It has to be repeatedly called to store more than one element. All the elements of the array, "T", should be initialized to "false" at the beginning.

The procedure for searching looks for the presence of a key value "k" in a hash table "A". The function returns an index of "A" where "k" is found. In the case of an unsuccessful search, the function returns (-1). The function is described next.

```
int searchLinearProbe(int k)
{
    int i = 0, j;
    j = hash(k);
    do
    {
            if (A[j] == k)
                    return i;
            i++;
```

```
        j = (j + i)%m;
    } while ((T[j] == True) && (i < m));
    return –1;
}
```

Note that the search terminates either upon detection of the key or upon detection of an empty location (i.e. when "T" is false). This means that the number of keys to be stored in the array "A" must be less than "m" so that there will be at least one empty location to terminate the algorithm in the case of an unsuccessful search.

Linear probing is easy to implement but it suffers from "primary clustering". A collision at address "i" indicates that many keys are mapped to the same address "i". Linear probing would not distribute these keys in the hash table. Instead, all keys mapped to "i" will be clustered around that slot building up long runs of occupied slots. This would increase the search and insertion times. Thus, linear probing is not a good approximation to uniform hashing.

One way to reduce primary clustering is to use quadratic probing to resolve collision. Suppose, "k" is to be inserted in a hash table and h[k] = j where "h" is the hash function. If A[j] is already occupied then "k" has to be inserted at some other location. In quadratic probing, the locations "j", (j+1), (j+4), (j+9), ... are examined to find out the first empty slot where "k" may be inserted. Thus, the increment in this case is i^2 for i = 1, 2, 3, ...All additions are modulo-m where "m" is the size of the hash table. Although this technique reduces primary clustering, it does not ensure that all slots in the hash table would be examined to find out an empty slot. Thus, it is possible that a key could not be inserted even when the hash table is not full.

Double Hashing

Double hashing provides an easy way to virtually eliminate the problem of clustering. This method requires two hashing functions $f_1(k)$ and $f_2(k)$. The function $f_1(k)$ is used as a primary hash function. In case the address determined by $(1 + f_1(k))$, say "a", is already occupied by a key, the function $f_2(k)$ is evaluated. The second hash function is used to compute the increment to be added to the address obtained by the first hash function in case of collision. The resultant sum becomes the new address for search or insertion operation. Let "b" be the value of $f_2(k)$. The search for an empty location to house the new key is made successively at the addresses a + b, a + 2b, a + 3b etc. until one empty slot is found. As in the case of linear probe, the storage space is considered to be circular for the purpose of calculating addresses like a + b, a+ 2b, a+ 3b etc. Note that this increment was "1" in case of linear probe technique which gave rise to clustering. The second hash function is to be chosen carefully. While $f_1(k)$ generates an address in the range "0" to (m-1), $f_2(k)$ generates a value in the range "1" to (m-1) that is relatively prime to "m". In other words, there should not be any common factor between "m" and the values generated by

$f_2(k)$. In case "m" is a prime number, any value between "1" to (m-1) could be generated by $f_2(k)$.

The program to insert a new key "k" using double hashing is shown below. The assumptions made in the linear probe algorithm are also used here. Two hash functions "hash1" and "hash2" are assumed to be available.

```
int storeDoubleHashing(int k)
{
    int j, k, u, i = 0;
    j = hash1(k);
    u = hash2(k);
    do
    {
            if (T[j] == false)
            {
                    A[j] = k;
                    T[j] = true;
                    return i;
            }
            i++;
            j = (j + i*u)%m;
    } while (i < m);
    return -1;
}
```

The search for an element in the array should follow the same path used to store the element. The search algorithm is simple and left as an exercise.

It can be mentioned here that the division method can be used for hash functions $f_1(k)$ and $f_2(k)$. The divisor should be a prime number. Then, $f_1(k)$ and $f_2(k)$ are given by

$$f_1(k) = k \bmod m$$

$$f_2(k) = \{ k \bmod (m - 1)\} + 1$$

However, if "m" is a prime number then (m–1) is even. To avoid division method with an even divisor, $f_2(k)$ can be taken as

$$f_2(k) = \{ k \bmod (m - 2)\} + 1$$

This will generate values in the range 1 to (m–2). But, since these values are relatively prime to "m", there will not be any problem.

In all open addressing methods, deletion of a key is not straight-forward. If there are many keys, which are hashed to the same address then removal of a key from the middle implies that all synonyms must be packed. Otherwise, handling insertion and search operations would become difficult. Moreover, packing is a time-consuming operation. Another approach for deletion is that when a key is deleted the corresponding entry in the hash table is marked with a special symbol. But this approach leads to inefficient search operations.

Separate Chaining

In this method, linked lists are maintained to store all elements that hash to the same address. Let the hash table "A" contains "m" entries or slots. Each slot contains a pointer to a linked list and the list stores the elements hashed to this slot. Each node in such a list is a self-referential structure containing a key value and a pointer to the same structure. A typical "C" declaration for a node may be done in the following manner.

```
typedef struct node
{
    int key;
    struct node *next;
}node;
```

Then, the hash table "A" containing "m" pointers may be defined as follows.

```
node *A[50];
```

It is assumed that the maximum value of "m" is 50. This declaration implies that each entry in the array is a pointer to a list. For all "i", A[i] should be initialized to NULL. While inserting a key "k" using a hash function "h", first h(k) is computed. Let, h(k) be "i", $0 \le i \le m-1$. Then "k" is inserted to the list pointed to by A[i]. Therefore, each slot in the hash table maintains a separate chain (i.e., a linked list) to store all elements hashed to that slot. This is why, this method is known as "separate chaining" method. Also note that in this method, "k" is not stored in the table "A". Instead, a node is created to store "k" and that node is added to the list pointed to by A[i].

As an example, let us consider the list

L=(351, 493, 251, 71, 706, 146)

Suppose that an array A[0:6] is used as the hash table. Let the hash function used be defined as h(k) = k mod 7. The hashed addresses generated for the elements in "L" are 1, 3, 6, 1, 6, 6 respectively. If the keys are inserted in the order they appear in the list then the hash table along with the chains will be as shown in Figure 9.10.

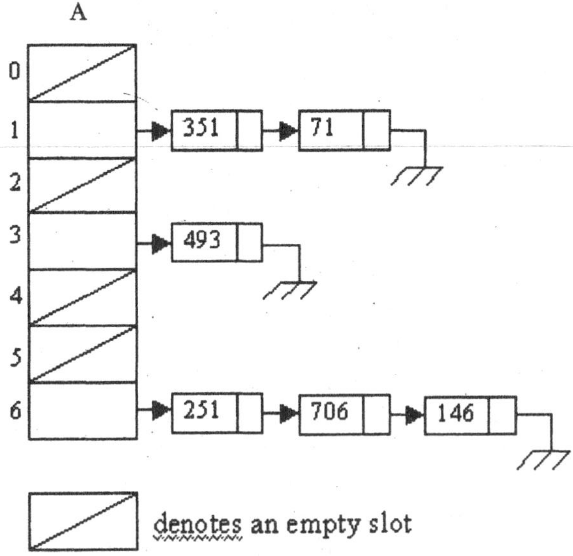

Figure 9.10 Situation of the hash table after inserting the elements in "L"

Note that since no ordering among the keys is assumed, a new key can be placed anywhere within a chain. As such the new node is appended at the end of a chain. Algorithm to insert a new key is a simple enhancement to the algorithm to append a key at the end of a singly connected linked list whose header is stored at the hashed address. Similarly, the search algorithm reduces to one that searches through a linked list. Note that in separate chaining, the load factor "α" can have a value greater than "1".

Coalesced Chaining

This technique is similar to linear probe method except that all keys that hash to the same address are linked together. Each node in the hash table should have an additional field that will either contain the address of the node holding a synonym or a "null" link. The node for a home element will contain the address of the first synonym and this node in turn will contain the address of the second synonym and so on. A null link will indicate the end of the chain. The search for a synonym is different from that in the case of linear probe. Here, a synonym is looked up by traversing the links rather than by examining the consecutive positions. It may be noted here that links will occupy the same positions as in the case of linear probe because both techniques place a synonym in the first empty position following the hashed address.

The process of placing a synonym in the first available empty position has a drawback. It is just possible that this is the address of a different element that may be loaded afterwards. Thus, some elements, which are not synonyms, are also deprived of their original positions be ·cause they are loaded later. In chaining method, such an element is also placed in the same chain in which the synonyms occupying its original position appears. The chains are, therefore, really coalesced chains containing synonyms as well as elements deprived of their home positions for the above mentioned reasons. This does not create any problem except that the chains may become longer. However, the average length of such chains is not very large.

In order to present the algorithm that an element using this technique, assume that an element consists only of the key field. The keys are stored in the array A[0: m-1] while the links are stored in link[0: m-1]. Null links are denoted by zeroes. A negative value in the link field denotes that the position is empty. In the beginning all the link fields are assumed to contain negative values (say –1).

When a key is to be inserted and a collision takes place then the coalesced chain is traversed first to find the last node of the chain. The addresses following this last node is then sequentially searched to locate an empty node. Satisfy yourself that this is actually the first empty node following the hashed address. One could also search in a straight forward manner (as done in the insert algorithm for linear probe). However, traversal of the chain is faster and this also enables one to insert the new node at the end of the chain without further examination.

9.9.3 Analysis of Collision resolution techniques

Statistical analysis of the collision resolution techniques has been carried out to find out their average case performances. The figures of merit that are chosen include the number of probes required for successful and unsuccessful search operations. There are other metrics to measure performance of the collision resolution techniques. For example, the complexity of inserting a new record or deleting an existing record is also very important. However, the search operation appears to be more important than insertion or deletion because hashing is generally used for lists that are searched frequently. Suppose that a hash table of "m" slots is used to store "n" keys. Let C_u (n, m) and C_s (n, m) denote the average number of probes required for an unsuccessful and for a successful search respectively. It is not easy to find even approximate expressions for C_u (n, m) and C_s (n, m). In some cases the calculations are quite involved. In this section, the final expressions for different metrics of several collision resolution techniques will be mostly quoted omitting the calculations for those results.

Open addressing with random probes

Given an open address hash table using an increment function that is random with a load factor α ($\alpha < 1$), the expected number of probes in an unsuccessful search, C_u (n, m), is at most $1/(1 - \alpha)$ assuming uniform hashing. Moreover, the expected number of probes in a successful search, C_s (n, m), is at most $(1/\alpha)\log(1/(1 - \alpha))$.

The expression for C_u (n, m) is easy to obtain. If the load factor is "α" then the probability that the first probe hits an occupied slot is "α". Therefore, the probability that the first probe hits an unoccupied slot is $(1 - \alpha)$. Thus, the probability that an unsuccessful search makes exactly one probe is $(1 - \alpha)$. If the slot in the first probe is occupied then the next slot (i.e., the slot located at an address equal to the address of the first slot plus some increment) needs to be examined. Assuming that the increments generated by the increment function are random and independent to one another, the probability that the slot in the second probe is unoccupied becomes $(1 - \alpha)$. The probability that the number of probes in an unsuccessful search is "2" may be given by the probability that the first probe hits an occupied slot multiplied by the probability that the second probe hits an unoccupied slot. Generalizing,

probability(number of probes in an unsuccessful search = k)

$= \alpha^{k-1} (1 - \alpha)$

Therefore, $C_u(n, m)$, the expected number of probes for an unsuccessful search is given by

$\Sigma_{k=1,\infty} k\, \alpha^{k-1} (1 - \alpha)$

$= (1 - \alpha)/(1 - \alpha)^2$

$= 1/(1 - \alpha)$

An element is inserted only if there is vacant space in the table (i.e., $\alpha < 1$). Insertion operation requires an unsuccessful search followed by placing the key in the first empty slot. Thus, inserting an element into an open address hash table with a load factor a requires at most $1/(1 - \alpha)$ probes on the average.

Linear probe

Analysis of this method shows that

$$C_u(n,m) = ½\,(1+ 1/(1 - \alpha)^2)$$

$$C_s\,(n, m) = ½\,(1+1/(1 - \alpha))$$

Where α is the load factor (i.e. $\alpha = n/m$)

Separate Chaining

Under the assumption of simple uniform hashing, any key "k" is equally likely to be hashed to any of the "m" slots. The average time for an unsuccessful search for a key "k" is the average time to search all elements in one of the "m" lists. Since a total of "n" keys are stored in "m" slots, the average number of elements in any slot is the load factor (n/m). Thus, the expected number of elements examined for an unsuccessful search is α and the total time required for this purpose (including the time to hash) is $O(1 + \alpha)$

The expected number of elements examined during a successful search for a key "k"is one more than the average number of elements examined when "k" had been inserted. Let "k" be the i-th element to be inserted. Before that insertion, there were (i-1) elements in the hash table. So, there were an average of (i-1)/m number of elements in each slot of the hash table. The expected number of elements examined to insert "k' must be (i-1)/m. Hence, the expected number of elements examined to search for "k" is 1+ (i-1)/m. But the value of "i" could be any thing from "1" to "n" Thus the expected number of elements examined for a successful search is given by

$$(1/n)\Sigma_{i=1,n}(1+(i-1)/m))$$
$$= 1 + (1/nm)\ \Sigma_{i=1,n}(i-1)$$
$$= 1 + (1/nm)\ ((n-1)n/2)$$
$$= 1 + \alpha/2 - 1/2m$$

Thus, the total time required for a successful search is $O(1 + \alpha)$.

In fact, if "α" is nearly equal to "1" then insertion operation takes O(1) time in the worst case and deletion operation also takes O(1) worst-case time provided the lists are doubly linked. Thus, all three operations can be supported in O(1) time on the average.

Coalesced Chaining

The analysis of coalesced chaining method is too involved. We shall, therefore, simply mention the results. In this case

$$C_u(n, m) = 1 + (1/4).(e^{2\alpha}\alpha - 1 - 2\alpha)$$

$$C_s(n, m) = 1 + (1/(8\alpha)).(e^{2\alpha}\alpha - 1 - 2\alpha) + (1/4).\alpha$$

Comparison of the collision resolution techniques

The expressions of the two metrics corresponding to various collision resolution techniques have been evaluated for some selected values of "α". The results are presented in the following table.

Load Factor (α)		0.5	0.6	0.7	0.8	0.9
Linear Probe	Unsuccessful	2.50	3.625	6.055	13.00	50.50
	Successful	1.50	1.75	2.167	3.00	5.50
Random Probe	Unsuccessful	2.00	2.50	3.33	5.00	10.00
	Successful	1.40	1.53	1.72	2.00	2.60
Separate Chaining	Unsuccessful	1.25	1.30	1.35	1.40	1.45
	Successful	0.50	0.60	0.70	0.80	0.90

First of all, it must be mentioned that the theoretical calculations are in unison with the results obtained through empirical study to a very good extent. It appears from the above table that the chaining methods are expected to perform better than the open addressing methods. Notice that the open addressing methods get degraded as "α" tends to unity. Moreover, separate chaining seems to be the best. In this case, the chains contain only those keys that hash to the same address. As such, these chains are definitely smaller than those in the case of coalesced chaining. This is a major reason for better performance of separate chaining. The only disadvantage of separate chaining is its requirement of extra storage space. All keys have to be stored outside the space of the hash table in the form of linked lists. However, the space required for the hash table is much less compared to other methods because only pointers are stored in the hash table. This saving is significant, as the hash table must have room for more elements than those appear actually in the list.

9.10 Points to be remembered

- Sorting and searching are fundamental operations, which are frequently used in many applications. In fact, efficient searching was a major motivation behind designs of the different search trees discussed in the previous chapters. In this chapter, however, the focus of attention has been to search in a linear list of "n" records.
- The simplest searching technique is to scan all records of a list sequentially until the desired record is found or the list is exhausted. The average number of comparisons required for a successful search using "linear search" technique is O(n/2). But the average number of comparisons required for an unsuccessful search remains a constant "n". In order to reduce the average number of comparisons for an unsuccessful search, the list is kept sorted in increasing order of their keys. With this assumption, even a linear search can detect the absence of a record in the list by making O(n/2) comparisons on the average.
- Once the list is kept sorted, a number of improved searching algorithms may be designed. Binary search, the most popular searching method, utilizes the ordering present in the list to the fullest extent. Binary search may be naturally designed as a divide and conquer recursive algorithm. The worst and average case complexity of this algorithm for successful and unsuccessful search is O(logn). It can be shown that any search algorithm based on comparison would make O(logn) number of comparisons in the worst and average case. Binary search relies heavily on random access of elements of the list. Therefore, binary search can not be efficiently implemented on linked representation of lists.
- Sorting refers to arranging a list of elements in a particular order. That is, the elements are arranged in increasing or decreasing order of their key values. There are a over-whelming number of sorting methods out of which a few popular ones have been described in this chapter. It is very difficult to compare

different sorting techniques. There are several metrics available for the purpose of comparison. Significant among them are average and worst case complexities in terms of number of comparisons between two records, the number of exchanges, transfers of records etc. Other metrics include amount of additional storage used by these sorting methods, the stability of the sorting algorithms etc.

- One important class of sorting methods works by successively inserting a new record properly in an already sorted list. Thus, these methods can be used to sort lists where records are obtained dynamically. These methods include shuttle sort, insertion sort and shell sort. Shuttle sort and insertion sort differs in the way they place the new record in the already sorted list. While shuttle sort uses exchange operations for this purpose, insertion sort uses transfers. Both the algorithms have a O(n) average and worst case complexity. If the initial list is sorted then both the methods work in O(n) time. Shell sort tries to order elements lying far apart using shuttle and insertion sort in several passes. Once this is done, shell sort boils down to a simple insertion or shuttle sort.
- Another class of sorting algorithms is based on successively selecting the smallest, second smallest, third smallest elements and putting the selected elements at the proper positions. Simple selection sort first selects the k-th smallest element in the k-th pass and puts that element at the index "k" of the array. Bubble sort, on the other hand, relies heavily on exchange of adjacent elements to push the k-th smallest element towards its correct position of the array. The average and worst case complexity of both the algorithms are O(n). But, bubble sort takes O(n) time when it works on an already sorted list. Bubble sort makes more number of exchange operations than selection sort. Selection sort makes about n/2 number of comparisons and "n" exchanges while bubble sort makes about n/2 comparisons and as many exchanges.
- Two recursive sorting algorithms break the barrier of O(n) worst-case time complexity. The first one discussed in this chapter is quick sort. First, quick sort puts one element of the array in the position where it would stay had the list been sorted. This position enables one to split the list into two halves which need to be sorted. This approach is more "conquer and divide" than "divide and conquer". The performance of quick sort heavily depends on the way the list is split. Thus, on an already sorted array, the complexity of quick sort algorithm becomes O(n). But, on the average, quick sort is very efficient and its average case complexity is O(nlogn). The average number of comparisons and exchange operations required by the quick sort algorithm are approximately 1.39 nlogn and 0.23 nlogn respectively. A non-recursive version of quick sort needs an additional space of O(logn) for maintaining the stack.
- Merge sort is a typical "divide and conquer" sorting algorithm. It divides the input list into two equal halves, sorts them and finally merges these sorted lists.

As the merge operation may be done in linear time, the worst case complexity of merge sort is O(n logn). The major shortcoming of this approach is that a simple implementation requires an O(n) additional space during the merge operation. This algorithm has a natural non-recursive version which works in a bottom-up manner. Another advantage of merge sort is that it can be conveniently implemented on linked representation of lists. The method is "stable" but data insensitive.

- Comparison between merge sort and quick sort is normal. While the average number of comparisons in merge sort is nlogn, the same for quick sort is 1.39 nlogn. Thus quick sort makes 39% more comparisons on the average. However, merge sort makes nlogn number of assignments whereas quick sort makes 0.23 nlogn number of exchanges. A machine language implementation of exchanges would take two assignments per exchange. Thus number of assignment operations required by quick sort would be more than 50% less than the same in merge sort.
- Yet another elegant approach to sorting is offered by the heap data structure. The worst case complexity of heap sort is O(nlogn). It can be proved that the worst case complexity of any comparison based sorting method cannot be less than O(nlogn).
- Since comparison based search operations can not be made better than O(logn) time complexity even on the average, a different technique to search is developed. Hashing tries to compute the address where an element is to be inserted or found in a table by applying a hash function to the given key value. If such an ideal function could be invented so that every distinct key value can be transformed to a unique address then searching could be performed in constant time. Such a function is always available if a table can be created to store all possible key values. Since the number of all possible key values is prohibitively large, such a table cannot be allocated in the computer. Thus, the hash function is almost always non-ideal in the sense that distinct keys are mapped to the same address giving rise to collision.
- Many different hash functions and collision resolution techniques are available in the literature. Some of them have been discussed in this chapter. Division method, folding etc. are some important hash functions which distribute the keys uniformly to the slots of the hash table.
- There are two broad categories of collision resolution techniques: open addressing and chaining. Important open addressing methods include linear and quadratic probing, double hashing etc. It is found that separate chaining method is superior to other methods in terms of performance.

Exercises

1. It is required to search an arbitrary array of "n" elements to find the element closer to a given number. Derive an algorithm based on the principle of linear search. Assuming that the given number is not equal to any of the array elements, find the expected number of comparisons.
2. Write a recursive "C" function to implement binary search and compute its time complexity.
3. Insertion into a sorted array can be accomplished in the following manner. Apply binary search to find the position that the new element will occupy. Move down the elements that must follow the new element by one position each. Now insert the new element in the appropriate place.
   a) Write the algorithm in the form of a "C" function.
   b) Can the movement of elements be interleaved with comparisons?
   c) What is the expected number of comparisons?
4. Given an array "A" of "n" elements, design an algorithm to produce another array "R" of "n" elements, such that the i-th element of "R" contains the rank of the i-th element of "A". Rank of an element is defined to be the position it would occupy had the list been sorted. It may be assumed that the elements are all distinct. Show that the above algorithm will not require more than n(n-1)/2 comparisons to find the ranks.
5. Write an algorithm to delete all elements in between and occupying two specified positions.
6. An array is required to be searched to determine the first occurrence of a given sub-array within it. Let "A" and "B" are two arrays of "n" and "m" elements respectively where m ≤ n. It is required to find the smallest "i"(≥1) for which A[i:i+m-1] is identical to B[i:m]. Explore the possibilities of using linear search as well as binary search in this case. Can you think of an application where such a requirement can arise?
7. Determine with the help of an example whether the initial order of elements is preserved in the case of bubble sort.
8. Find the expected number of passes, comparisons and exchanges for bubble sort when the number of elements is equal to "10". Compare these results with the actual number of operations when the given sequence is as follows.

   7, 1, 3, 4, 10, 9, 8, 6, 5, 2,
9. An array contains "n" elements of numbers. The several elements of this array may contain the same number "x". Write an algorithm to find the total number of elements which are equal to "x" and also indicate the position of the first such element in the array.
10. With the help of a suitable example show that shell sort is not stable.

11. Analyze the shell sort with the increment "h" and "i", to find the expected number of comparisons. Assume that the keys are random and "n", the number of elements, is divisible by "h". Compare this method with straight insertion sort when h = n.

12. Write a "C" function to sort a list of integers using insertion sort technique where the list is represented through links using pointers.

13. Compare bubble sort with shuttle sort and find out which one is generally preferable.

14. Show that the average number of comparisons required by the function "select", as described in this chapter, to compute the k-th smallest element of an array of "n" integers is O(n).

15. Write a non-recursive version of the function "select" to compute the k-th smallest element of an array of integers. Your function should not use any stack or any "goto" statement.

16. What is the time-complexity of the quick sort algorithm to sort a list of "n" equal elements?

17. You are to merge four sorted arrays "A", "B", "C" and "D". You can do it using any of the techniques indicated below.

    a) Apply 4-way merge.

    b) Merge A and B first. Now, merge C with the output of previous merge. Finally, merge D with the last output.

    c) Merge A with B and C with D. Now, merge the two outputs.

    Comments on the merits and demerits of the three techniques in terms of the required number of comparisons and transfers.

18. Write a "C" function to merge sort an array of numeric values in a bottom-up manner. The number of elements in the array may not be a power of "2".

19. Write a "C" function to merge sort a list of numbers in a bottom-up manner when the list is represented by a linked list using pointers.

20. Write a "C" function to find out the smallest and the second smallest numbers in an array of integers. Your algorithm should make minimum number of comparisons. How many comparisons are necessary for finding the smallest and the second smallest numbers?

21. Write a "C" function to sort a matrix row-wise and column-wise. Assume that the matrix is represented by a two dimensional array.

22. Suppose the programming language that you are going to use provides a function "rnd" that returns a random number between "0" and "1" (exclusive of both). How this function can be used to generate hash addresses? Can you make use of a good hashing function as a random number generator?

23. Show the hash table that results when the letters in

    COMPUTER SCIENCE

    are stored in the given order using the linear probe collision resolution method. Assume a hash table of size 19 and use the hash function h(k) = k mod 19 for the k-th letter of the alphabet.

24. Solve exercise 23 using double hashing with the second hashing function as h(k) = {k mod 17} + 1.

25. Do you think that with separate chaining, the maintenance of chains as ordered lists, is of any use? If so, state when and how this may be useful.

26. The elements of the list (34, 15, 53, 60, 23, 71) are to be stored, in the order of their appearances, into a hash table of size "11" using double hashing with the functions

    h(x) = x mod 11

    h(x) = (x mod 10) + 1

    Explain what happens in the case of the last element.

27. Find the length of the largest coalesced chain if the elements of the following list are stored in a hash table of size "17" using the coalesced chaining method.

    (68, 41, 18, 36, 25, 93, 52, 57, 54, 79, 71, 70, 89, 86)

    Use the hashing function h(x) = x mod 17.

28. Suppose that a hash table contains "m" entries. Show that the number of entries examined by quadratic probe collision resolution technique may be as less as (m+1)/2.

Chapter 10

Elementary Graphs

10.1 Introduction

Various "Tree" data structures have been discussed in depth in chapters 7 and 8. If a node in a tree is considered to be an entity and an edge between two nodes represent a relation between two entities then a tree can conveniently represent a one to many relation from a given set of objects to the same set. However, if the relationship is many to many then describing that relation using a tree would not be possible. Because, edges describing many to many relations would form cycles among nodes in a tree. Many problems can be best described by many to many relation among a set of objects. These problems cannot be solved by using tree data structures. This chapter introduces "graphs", a very important data structure, to deal with such problems.

Consider a classic problem known as "travelling sales person problem". A sales person has to tour a number of cities by road before coming back to the city where he started. The cities are connected by roads and the sales person has to minimize the distance to be covered by the tour. Note that some pairs of cities are directly connected. Let the cities be represented by nodes and let an edge between two cities represent that these cities are connected. Moreover, suppose that each edge is labelled with the distance between the cities connected by the edge. Suppose there are five cities. The interconnections among these cities are shown in Figure 10.1.

The diagram in Figure 10.1 consists of vertices (nodes) and edges. Such diagrams are called graphs. There are many other situations which are represented by graphs. There are many other domains of applications e.g., Electrical Engineering, Geographical Information System etc. where the problems are best represented by graphs.

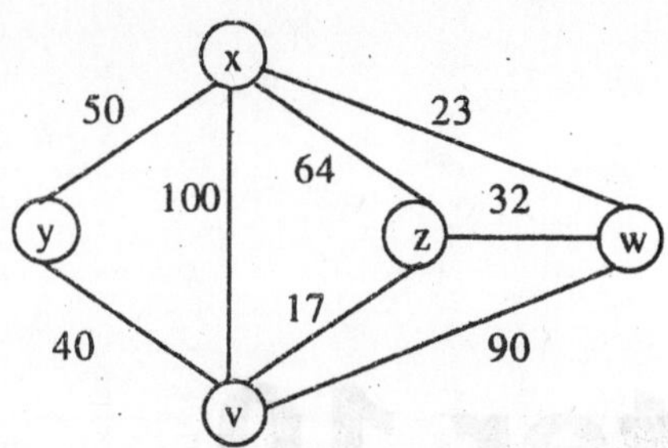

Figure 10.1 Five cities and their interconnections by road.

10.2 Basic definitions

Graphs: Undirected, Directed

A graph "G" consists of a finite non-empty set "V" of vertices and a set "E" of edges. "G" is denoted by a tuple (V, E). Vertices represent entities, which have names and other properties. An edge connects a pair of vertices. An edge represents a relationship between two objects. For instance, vertices in the graph of Figure 10.1 represent cities while an edge between two cities represent the fact that these two cities are connected by road. Each edge e_k belonging to the set "E" is identified by a pair (v_i, v_j) of vertices where both "v_i" and "v_j" belong to "V" representing the fact that the vertices "v_i" and "v_j" are related to each other. Thus, the set "E" is a subset of the cartesian product of the set "V" and "V". If the number of vertices in a graph (i.e., the cardinality of the set "V") is infinite then the graph is said to be an infinite graph; otherwise, the graph is called a finite graph. In this chapter, finite graphs are only considered. An example of a graph is shown in Figure 10.2.

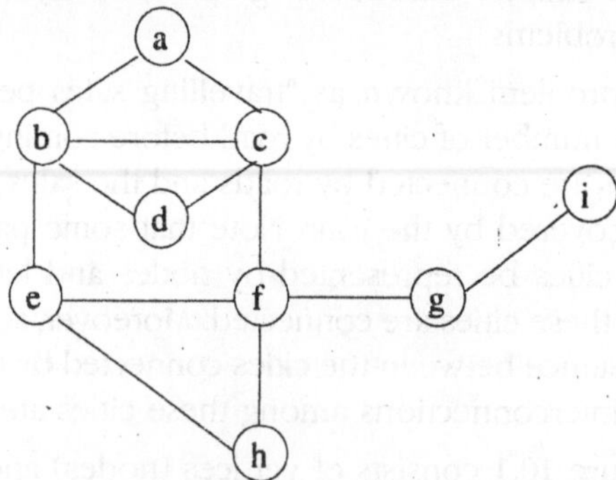

Figure 10.2. Example of an undirected graph. The set of vertices V = {a, b, c, d, e, f, g, h, i}; The set of edges E = {(a, b), (c, a), (b, c), (d, b), (b, e), (c, d), (c, f), (e, f), (e, h), (f, h), (g, f), (i, g)}.

When the edges of a graph are unordered pairs then the graph is said to be an undirected graph. Hence the pairs (v_i, v_j) and (v_j, v_i) represent the same edge connecting the vertices "v_i" and "v_j". Note that the order in which the vertices "v_i", "v_j" occur in the pair (v_i, v_j) is immaterial for describing the edge. That is why, these edges are called unordered pairs.

A graph is called a directed graph if each edge is identified by an ordered pair of vertices (v_i, v_j) . In a directed graph, the first element of the pair is called the start-vertex and the second element is called the end-vertex of the edge. The edge is said to be directed from the start-vertex to the end-vertex. Therefore, the pairs (v_i, v_j) and (v_j, v_i) represent two different edges in a directed graph. Example of a directed graph is shown in Figure 10.3.

Degree, incidence, adjacency

Let there be an edge "e_i" between two vertices "v_i" and "v_j" in an undirected graph. Then, the vertices "v_i"and "v_j" are called adjacent and the edge "e_i" is said to be incident on vertices "v_i"and "v_j". In Figure 10.2, the vertices "e" and "f" are adjacent but "a" and "g" are not. The number of edges incident of a vertex "v_i" is also known as the degree of the vertex "v_i".

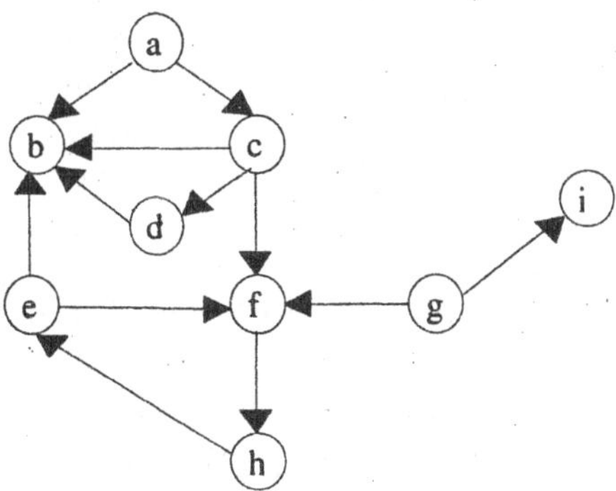

Figure 10.3 Example of a directed graph. . The set of vertices V = {a, b, c, d, e, f, g, h, i}; The set of edges E = {(a, b), (a, c), (c, b), (d, b), (e, b), (c, d), (c, f), (e, f), (h, e), (f, h), (g, f), (g, i)}.

In a directed graph, if there is an edge "e_i" from the vertex "v_i" to the vertex "v_j" then the vertex "v_i" is said to be adjacent to "v_j" and "v_j" is said to be adjacent from "v_i". The in-degree of a vertex "v_i" is the number of edges with "v_i" as their end-vertex. Similarly, the out-degree of "v_i" is the number of edges whose start-vertex is "v_i". The degree of "v_i" is the sum total of its in-degree and out-degree. In Figure 10.3, the in-degree of the vertex "f" is three; the out-degree of "f" is one; degree of "f" is "4".

A directed graph is <u>symmetric</u> if the existence of an edge from "v_i" to "v_j" implies that there must also be an edge directed from "v_j" to "v_i". The graph of Figure 10.3 is not a symmetric graph.

If an edge connects two vertices "v_i" and "v_j" where "i" is equal to "j" then, the edge is called a loop.

A graph is <u>complete</u> or completely connected if and only if every pair of vertices is connected in at least one direction. Figure 10.4 shows a complete graph of "4" vertices.

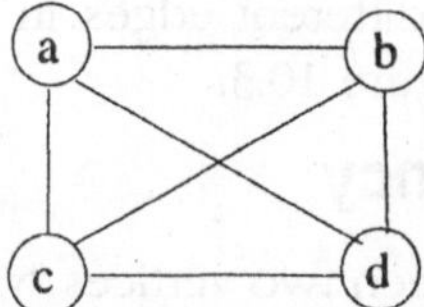

Figure 10.4 A completely connected undirected graph having four vertices.

Path, cycle, connected graph

A <u>path</u> in a graph from any vertex "x" to another vertex "y" is a sequence of vertices, $x=v_1, v_2, \ldots, v_n = y$, where "$v_i$" and "$v_{i+1}$" are adjacent. The length of such a path is the number of edges on that path. A path in which all the vertices (except possibly the first and the last) are distinct is called a simple path. In the graph of Figure 10.2, the sequence of vertices "a", "c", "f", "h", "e" is a simple path from "a" to "e". Another simple path from "a" to "e" is "a", "c", "d" "b", "e". However, the sequence "a", "c", "d" "e" is not a path as the vertices "d" and "e" are not adjacent. Consider the directed graph of Figure 10.3. Note that the sequence "a", "c", "d" "b", "e" is not a path from "a" to "e". One path from "a" to "e" is "a", "c", "f", "h", "e". A path, which contains all vertices in a graph is called a Hamiltonian path.

A <u>cycle</u> is a path in which the initial and final vertices are the same. In other words, a path from a vertex to itself is called a cycle. There are many cycles in the graph of Figure 10.2. For instance, the paths, ("a". "b" "c', "a"), ("a", "c", "d", "b", "a"), ("a", "c", "f", "h", "e", "b", "a") are cycles of different lengths in the graph of Figure 10.2. However, the graph of Figure 10.3 has only one cycle: ("e", "f", "h", "e"). A directed graph is <u>acyclic</u> if it has no cycles. A directed acyclic graph is also referred to as DAG.

A graph is said to be <u>connected</u> if there exists a path between any two vertices "v_i", "v_j"; otherwise, the graph is disconnected. For example, the graphs of Figures 10.2, 10.3, 10.4 are connected graphs. But the graph in Figure 10.5 is not connected. Observe that there is no path between the vertices "0" and "4" or between "5" and "7". In this case, the graph is said to consist of components which are connected. The graph of Figure 10.5 contains three components.

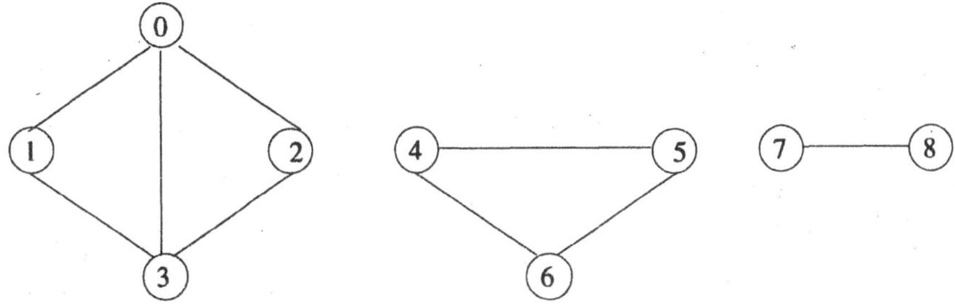

Figure 10.5 Example of a disconnected graph. V = {0, 1, 2, 3, 4, 5, 6, 7, 8} E = { (0,1), (0, 2), (0, 3), (1, 3), (2, 3), (4,5), (5, 6), (4, 6), (7, 8)}

Weighted graph, sub-graph

A weighted graph is a graph in which edges are assigned weights. This is often required to model certain physical situations by means of a graph. For example, the edges of the graph of Figure 10.1 have weights. Weights in that graph denote distances between the cities connected by the corresponding edges. Weight of an edge is also called its cost. The connotation of the weight of an edge is dependent on the situation being modelled as a graph. In case of a weighted graph, an edge is a 3-tuple (u, v, w) where "u" and "v" denote the vertices connected by the edge and "w" denotes the weight of the edge. Thus, the set "E" is a subset of VxVxW where "V" is the set of vertices and "W" is the set of all possible weights. The graph of Figure 10.6 is an example of a weighted graph.

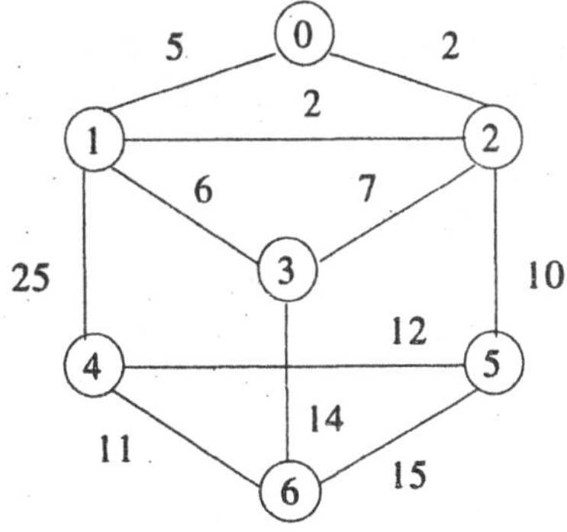

Figure 10.6 A weighted graph

A graph G′ = (V′, E′) is called a subgraph of G = (V, E) if V′ is a subset of "V" and E′ is a subset of "E". For G′ to be a subgraph of "G", all the edges and vertices of G′ should be in "G". Some subgraphs of Figure 10.2 are shown in Figure 10.7.

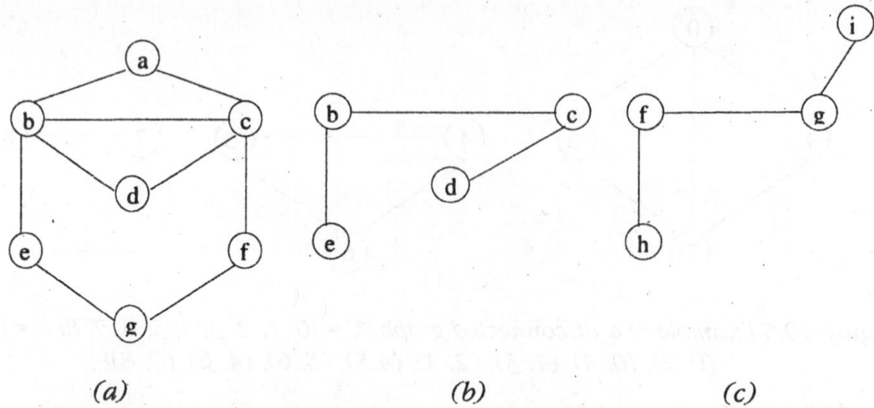

Figure 10.7 Some sub-graphs of the graph of Figure 10.2

But the graph of Figure 10.8 is not a subgraph of Figure 10.2 because the edge (d, e) does not belong to "E". So, E' is not a subset of "E".

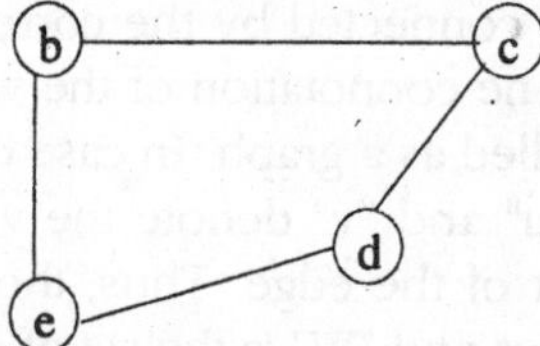

Figure 10.8 A graph which is not a subgraph of Figure 10.2.

Normally, the term <u>relation</u> is used in connection with sets. A relation "R" on a set "S" is a set of ordered pairs of elements of SxS. For example, if S = {1,2,3,4} then a relation "R" can be defined as

R = {<1,2>, <1,3>, <2,4>, <4,4>}

Any relation can be represented by a graph in which the vertices represent elements of the set "S" and edges represent pairs of the relation. The graph of Figure 10.9 depicts a set "S" and a relation "R" as mentioned earlier.

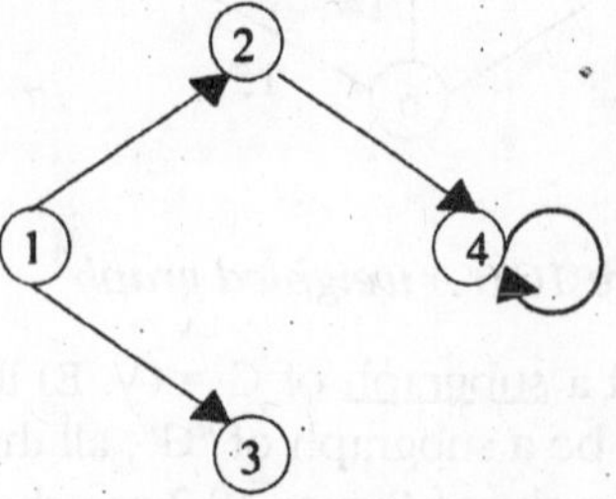

Figure 10.9 A graph showing the relation "R" = {<1,2>, <1,3>, <2,4>, <4,4>} on a set S = {1, 2, 3, 4}.

A digraph is a relation without any loop.

Trees, Spanning trees, Minimal spanning trees

Trees can be defined as special cases of graphs. A tree may be defined as a connected graph without any cycle. The graphs of Figures 10.2, 10.4 are not trees as both of them contain cycles. The graphs of Figure 10.10 are example of trees.

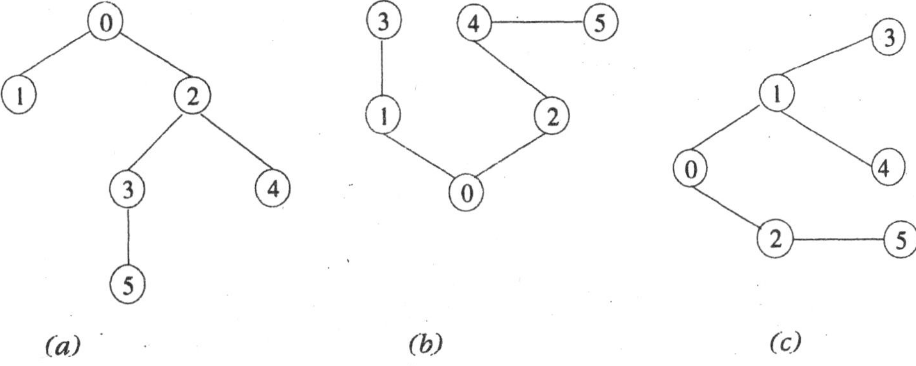

(a) *(b)* *(c)*

Figure 10.10 Example of trees

The only difference between general trees defined in Chapter 7 and trees defined here is that a tree defined as a special case of a graph does not have a special vertex called the "root". In fact any vertex may be chosen as the root.

A sub-graph of a graph G = (V, E) which is a tree containing all vertices of "V" is called a spanning tree of "G". If "G" is not connected then there is no spanning tree of "G". Similarly, there will not be a unique spanning tree of a graph "G". Two spanning trees of the graph of Figure 10.11 are shown in Figure 10.12(a), (b).

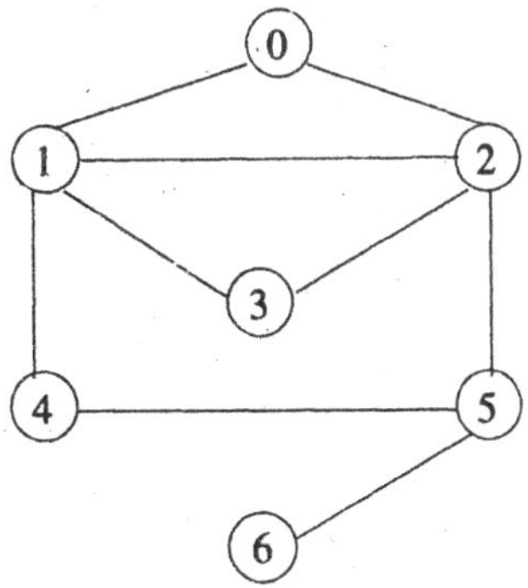

Figure 10.11 A sample graph

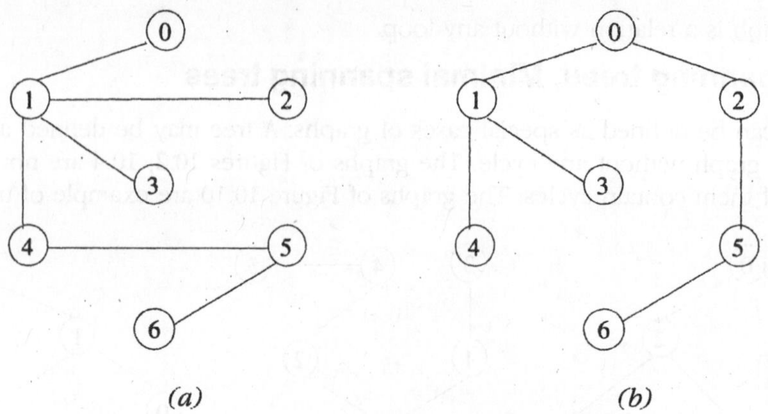

Figure 10.12 Spanning tree of the graph of Figure 10.11

If "G" is a weighted graph and "T_1", "T_2" are two spanning trees of "G" then the sum of weights of all edges of "T_1" may be different from that of "T_2". A spanning tree "T" of "G" where the sum of weights of all edges in "T" is the minimum is called the minimal cost spanning tree or the minimal spanning tree of "G". Note that the minimal spanning tree of a graph is not necessarily unique.

10.3 Representation of Graphs

10.3.1 The Adjacency Matrix

The adjacency matrix or the connectivity matrix "A" representing an undirected graph "G" is defined as follows. The rows and columns of "A" correspond to the vertices of "G". If the element "a_{ij}" of "A" is "1" then there is an edge from the vertex "v_i" to the vertex "v_j" in "G". If a_{ij} is "0" then the graph "G" does not contain an edge from "v_i" to "v_j". The adjacency matrix of the graph of Figure 10.2 is shown in the Figure 10.13.

It may be noted that if any element "a_{ij}" of "A" representing an undirected graph "G" is "1" then the element "a_{ji}" would also be "1". This is because if "a_{ij}" is "1" then there is an edge between vertices "v_i" and "v_j" of "G". Consequently, "a_{ji}" would also be "1". Therefore, an adjacency matrix of an undirected graph is always symmetric. This also means that only the upper triangular or the lower triangular matrix of "A" is sufficient for representing "G".

	a	b	c	d	e	f	g	h	i
a	0	1	1	0	0	0	0	0	0
b	1	0	1	1	1	0	0	0	0
c	1	1	0	1	0	1	0	0	0
d	0	1	1	0	0	0	0	0	0
e	0	1	0	0	0	1	0	1	0
f	0	0	1	0	1	0	1	1	0
g	0	0	0	0	0	1	0	0	1
h	0	0	0	0	1	1	0	0	0
i	0	0	0	0	0	0	1	0	0

Figure 10.13. Adjacency matrix of the graph in Figure 10.2.

Adjacency matrix representation of a directed graph is very similar. If "A" is the adjacency matrix of a directed graph "G" then the rows and columns of "A" represent the vertices of "G". An element "a_{ij}" of "A" is "1" if and only if there is an edge from a vertex "v_i" to a vertex "v_j" of "G". If there is no edge between the vertices "v_i" and "v_j" then "a_{ij}" is set to "0". The matrix of Figure 10.14 shows the adjacency matrix of the directed graph of Figure 10.3.

	a	b	c	d	e	f	g	h	i
a	0	1	1	0	0	0	0	0	0
b	0	0	0	0	0	0	0	0	0
c	0	1	0	1	0	1	0	0	0
d	0	1	0	0	0	0	0	0	0
e	0	1	0	0	0	1	0	0	0
f	0	0	0	0	0	0	0	1	0
g	0	0	0	0	0	1	0	0	1
h	0	0	0	0	1	0	0	0	0
i	0	0	0	0	0	0	0	0	0

Figure 10.14. Adjacency matrix of the directed graph of Figure 10.3.

Adjacency matrix of a graph can be represented by a simple two-dimensional array of integers in "C" language. But, in that case, the vertices of a graph must be identified by a set of integers {0, 1, 2, ..., m-1} where the number of vertices in the graph is "m". Note that the vertices of the graphs of Figures 10.2 and 10.3 are identified by small letters of the English alphabet. To get rid of this problem, the vertices of a graph having "n" vertices are identified by "n" different integers "0",

"1", "2", ..., (n-1). In many algorithms in this chapter, this fact is used. The degree of any vertex "i" of an undirected graph can be readily computed from the adjacency matrix of that graph just by counting the number of "1"s in the i-th row of the adjacency matrix. For a directed graph, the in-degree of a vertex "i" is the number of "1"s in the i-th column and the out-degree of a vertex "i" is the number of "1"s in the i-th row of the adjacency matrix. The number of non-zero elements of an adjacency matrix "A" indicate the number of edges in a directed graph represented by "A".

Adjacency matrix is also suitable to represent a weighted graph. For a weighted graph "G", the elements of its adjacency matrix "A" are not zeroes and ones but the elements may assume values corresponding to any real number. In fact an element "a_{ij}" of "A" is a real number which is equal to the weight of the edge between the vertices "v_i" and "v_j". If there is no edge between "v_i" and "v_j" then the weight of the non-existent edge is assumed to be infinity and consequently "a_{ij}" is set to infinity. "a_{ii}" may be set to "0" for all "i"'s.

Although adjacency matrix representations of graphs are conceptually simple, such representations have several drawbacks. First, this representation requires n^2 elements to represent a graph having "n" vertices. If a directed graph has "e" edges then $(n^2 - e)$ elements in the matrix would be zeroes. Thus, for graphs with very less number of edges, the matrix becomes very sparse. Second, parallel edges cannot be represented by an adjacency matrix.

It has already been mentioned that if the number of edges in a graph are very few then its adjacency matrix will be sparse. In these circumstances a different representation known as "Adjacency list" is usually more efficient.

10.3.2 Adjacency Lists

Another efficient means of representing a graph G=(V,E) uses linked lists of adjacent vertices for all vertices in "V". That is, this approach creates separate linked lists for each vertex in "V". For example, consider the undirected graph of Figure 10.11. Vertices adjacent to the vertex "0" are "1" and "2". Therefore, the linked list corresponding to vertex "0" is as shown in the following.

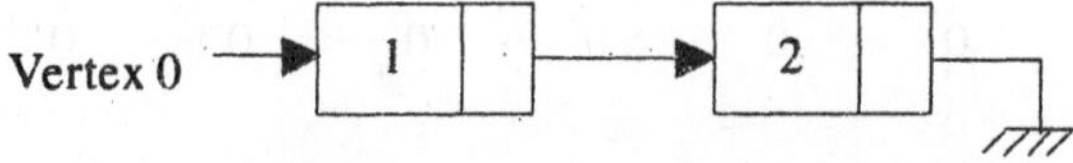

Similarly the vertices adjacent to the vertex "5" are "2", "4", and "6". The adjacency list for the vertex "5" is shown in the following.

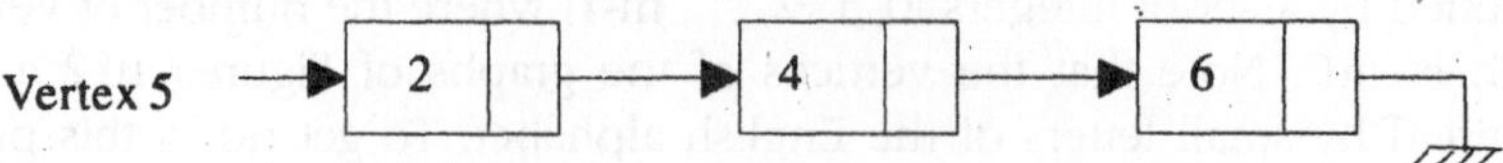

The adjacency list for the entire graph is the set of adjacency lists for each vertex in that graph. The adjacency list of the graph of Figure 10.11 is shown in Figure 10.15.

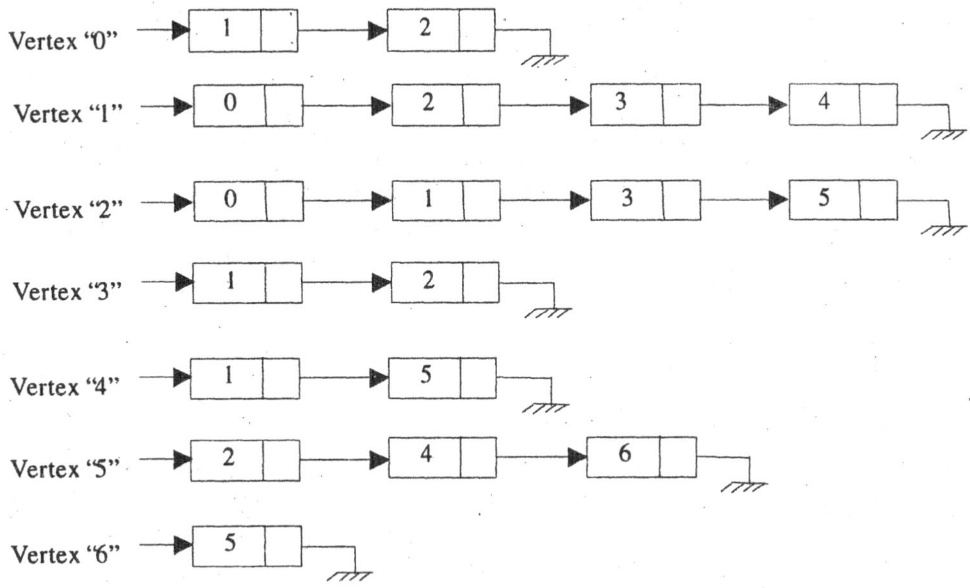

Figure 10.15. Adjacency list representation of the graph of Figure 10.11.

It generally uses less memory when a large number of vertices and a small number of edges are contained in a graph. The total number of nodes in an adjacency lists for an undirected graph with "n" vertices and "e" edges is (n+2e) and the same for a directed graph is (n+e). However, if "e" is very large then due to the overhead of maintaining pointers, adjacency list representation may become more wasteful compared to the adjacency matrix representation. Computation of the degree of a vertex in an undirected graph is the length of the list pointed to by that vertex. But, computation of in-degree of a vertex in a directed graph may require O(e) number of comparisons as all the lists pointed to by all vertices may have to be examined. Similarly, checking the existence of an edge between vertices "i" and "j" is also more time consuming.

In "C" language, the adjacency list of a graph may be represented by an array of pointers. Each pointer points to a linked list of vertices adjacent to a particular vertex. The number of elements of the array would be equal to the number of vertices present in the graph. As usual, it is assumed that the vertices are identified by a number "i", $0 \leq i \leq (n-1)$, in a graph with "n" vertices. Thus, a graph is a structure as defined in the following.

```
typedef struct graph
{
    int noOfVertices;
    adjVert *adjList[100];
}graph;
```

It is assumed that the maximum number of vertices in a graph is 100. Each node in the list pointed to by adjList[i] is a self-referential structure containing an integer identifying a vertex adjacent to the vertex numbered "i". Therefore, "adjVert" is another structure as defined in the following.

```
typedef struct adjVert
{
    int vertex;
    struct adjVert *next;
}adjVert;
```

Note that the type definition of "adjVert" must precede the type definition of "graph".

A minor modification is required to represent weighted graphs using adjacency list. In this case, a node containing information about an edge must include its weight. Thus, the type definition of "adjVert" is to be modified in the following manner.

```
typedef struct adjVert
{
    int vertex;
    float weight;
    struct adjVert *next;
}adjVert;
```

10.3.3 Incidence Matrix

Let "G" be a graph with "n" vertices, "e" edges and no self-loops. Consider an (nxe) matrix A = (a_{ij}) whose rows correspond to the "n" vertices and the columns correspond to the "e" edges as follows.

a_{ij} = 1 if "e_j" is incident to the vertex "v_i"

= 0, otherwise.

Such a matrix is known as the incidence matrix of a graph. The incidence matrix of the graph of Figure 10.11 is shown in Figure 10.16.

	(0,1)	(0,2)	(1,2)	(1,3)	(1,4)	(2,3)	(2,5)	(4,5)	(5,6)
0	1	1	0	0	0	0	0	0	0
1	1	0	1	1	1	0	0	0	0
2	0	1	1	0	0	1	1	0	0
3	0	0	0	1	0	1	0	0	0
4	0	0	0	0	1	0	0	1	0
5	0	0	0	0	0	0	1	1	1
6	0	0	0	0	0	0	0	0	1

Figure 10.16 Incidence matrix of the graph of Figure 10.11.

The elements "a_{ij}" of an incidence matrix of a directed graph is defined as follows.

a_{ij} = 1 if "e_j" is incident out of "v_i"

= -1 if "e_j" is incident into "v_i"

= 0 if "e_j" is not incident to "v_i"

Since every edge is incident to exactly two vertices, each column of "A" has two 1's for undirected graphs (exactly one "1" and one (–1) for directed graphs). The number of 1's in a row gives the out-degree and the number of (–1)'s in a row gives the in-degree of the vertex "i" in a directed graph.

Parallel edges in a graph produce identical columns in its incidence matrix. It may be recalled that an adjacency matrix cannot be used to represent a graph with parallel edges. However, incidence matrix requires more spaces than adjacency matrix as this is a (nxe) matrix and usually, e > n.

10.3.4 Adjacency multi-lists

In adjacency list representation of a graph, each edge (i, j) is included twice: once in the list for vertex "i" and another in the list for vertex "j". This drawback may be removed by including the edge (i, j) in two lists rather than in one list. Therefore, each edge must be connected to two lists and the structure of an edge (i, j) looks like the following.

i	j	Next edge in adjacency list for vertex "i"	Next edge in adjacency list for vertex "j"

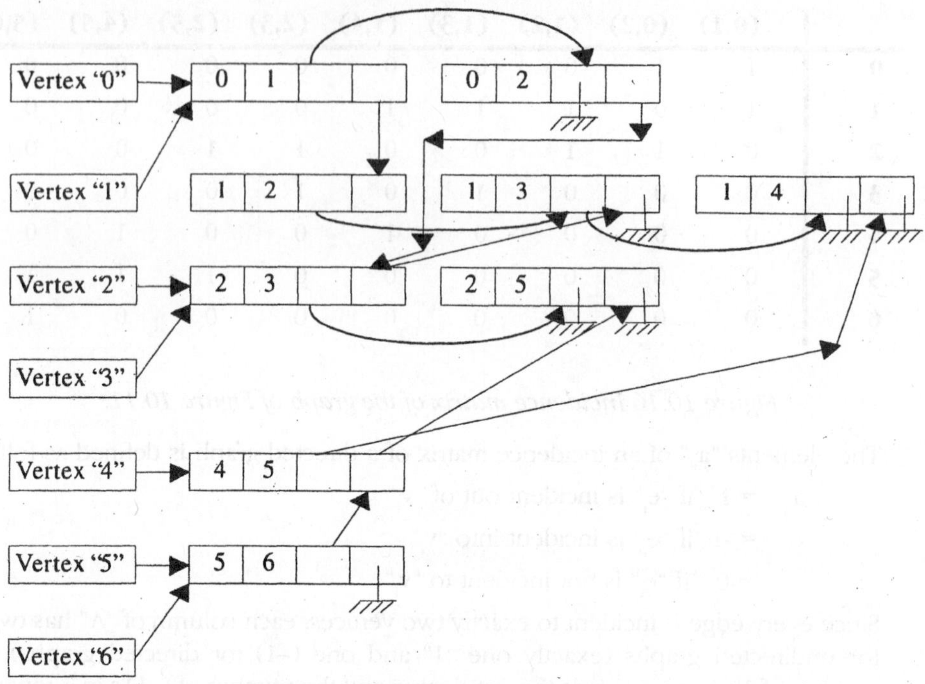

Figure 10.17 Adjacency multi-list of the graph of Figure 10.11.

Since adjacency lists are maintained in a multi-list, the representation is called adjacency multi-lists. The adjacency multi-list representation of the graph of Figure 10.11 is shown in Figure 10.17. See that the edges incident on a vertex "i" may be obtained by traversing the appropriate links of the edges pointed to by vertex "i".

10.4 Traversal of Graphs

A number of graph problems involves traversal of a graph. Traversal of a graph means visiting each of its vertices exactly once. This is accomplished by visiting the vertices in a systematic way. Two commonly used techniques of graph traversal are known as Depth-first search (DFS) and breadth-first search (BFS). These algorithms are discussed for undirected graphs unless otherwise mentioned. However, these algorithms do work for directed graphs also.

10.4.1 Depth First Search

This is one popular technique for systematically traversing the vertices of a graph. The method starts traversing the graph from a given vertex "v_0". That is "v_0" is the first vertex to be visited. The next vertex to visit is an unvisited vertex adjacent to "v_0". If "v_0" has a number of unvisited adjacent vertices then any one of them may be selected for visiting next. Once a vertex is visited, it is marked as "visited" to facilitate the task of finding unvisited adjacent vertices. Thus, from any vertex "v_i", a new adjacent unvisited vertex "v_j" is explored. Next, another new vertex adjacent to "v_j" is explored without traversing along other edges incident to "v_i". When a vertex "v_p" is reached from "v_q" and "v_p" does not have any unvisited adjacent vertex then "v_q" is re-examined to check whether it has any more unvisited adjacent vertex "v_m". Then, depth first search is initiated from the vertex "v_m". The process continues until all adjacent vertices of the starting vertex have been visited. This leads to a recursive description of the traversal technique as explained in the following.

Depth first search (DFS) from a vertex "i", would mean marking the vertex "i" as visited and initiating DFS from a vertex "j" where "j" is an unvisited adjacent vertex of the vertex "i". DFS from the vertex "i" would be complete when there is no unvisited adjacent vertex of the vertex "i". In order to write an algorithm, the information about already visited vertices must be remembered. For this purpose, an array "visited" of zeroes and ones may be kept where visited[i] = 0 means that the vertex "i" has not been visited and visited[i] = 1 means that the vertex "i" has already been visited. The array "visited" and a variable "g" of type "pointer to graph" are assumed to be global to the function "DFSearch". Moreover, the array "visited" must be initialized so that visited[i] is set to "0" for i = 0 to (g->noOfVertices-1) before calling "DFSearch". For simplicity, "g" is assumed to be a connected graph.

```
void DFSearch (int start)
{
    int v;
    adjVert *adj;
    visited[start] = 1;
    printf("%d ", start);
    adj = g->adjList[start];
    while(adj != NULL)
    {
            v = adj->vertex;
            if (!visited[v])
                    DFSearch(v);
            adj = adj->next;
    }
}
```

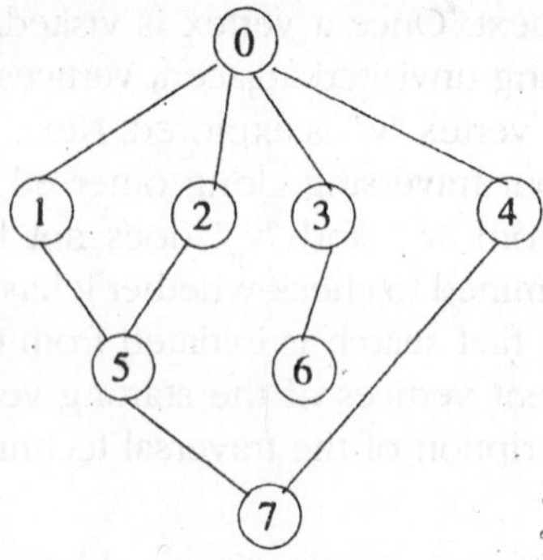

Figure 10.18(a) A sample graph

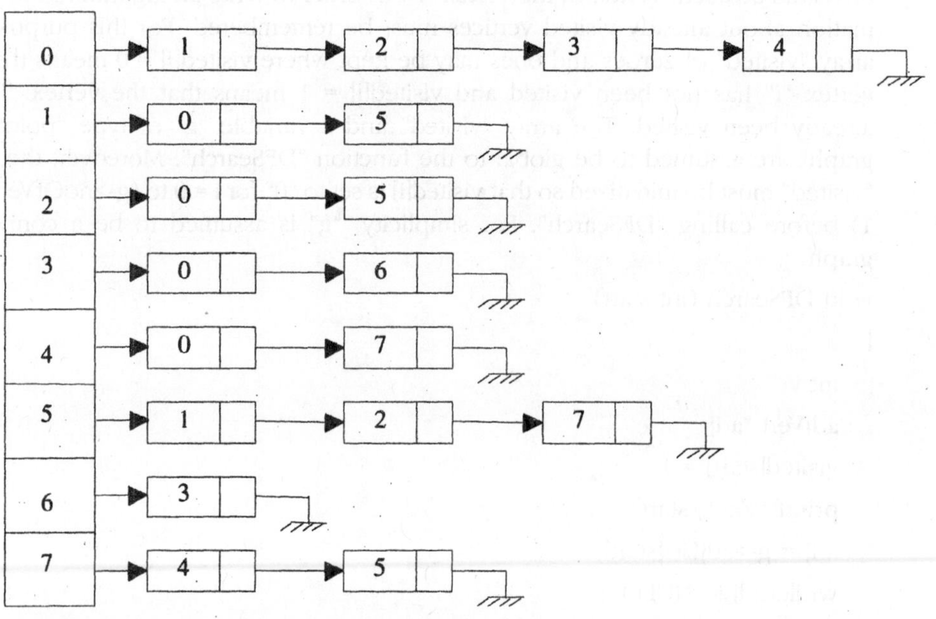

Figure 10.18(b) Adjacency list representation of graph of Figure 10.18(a)

The recursion tree obtained by applying the function "DFSearch" on the graph shown in Figure 10.18(a) is shown in Figure 10.19. The adjacency list representation as shown in Figure 10.18(b) of the graph of Figure 10.18(a) is used to find out adjacent vertices from a given vertex. Traversal starts from the vertex numbered "0". Each node in the recursion tree is labelled with the vertex number on which the function is recursively called. Along with every node in the recursion tree, the content of the array "visited" is also mentioned in Figure 10.19. The content of the array is mentioned at the time when a call to the function is made.

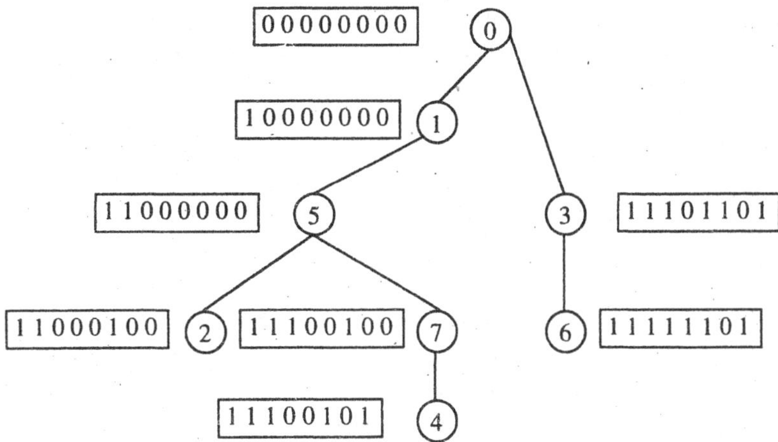

Figure 10.19 Recursion tree obtained by applying DFSearch(0) on the graph of Figure 10.18(a).

The following output will be produced as a result of the call "DFSearch(0)"

0 1 5 2 7 4 3 6

It must be mentioned that the adjacency list or adjacent matrix representation of a graph is not unique. A different numbering scheme of the vertices may yield different adjacency matrices for the same graph. Similarly, the order in which the adjacent vertices of a given vertex are stored in the list is not fixed and consequently there could be different adjacency lists representing the same graph. Due to non-uniqueness of adjacency list or adjacency matrix representation of a graph, the order in which the vertices would be traversed in a DFS is also not unique. Also note that the vertices which are traversed by the DFS are connected by edges. Thus, depth first traversal produces a spanning tree of a given connected graph. For example, the recursion tree shown in Figure 10.19 also represents a spanning tree produced by depth first traversal of the graph of Figure 10.18(a). Such spanning trees are often referred to as depth first search spanning trees.

If the graph is not connected then the resultant depth first spanning tree does not contain all vertices of the graph. In fact the tree produced by depth first search is a spanning tree for one component only. In other words, all vertices connected to the "start" vertex would be traversed by the function "DFSearch". Thus, the component of the graph of which a spanning tree will be generated depends on the "start" vertex (on which "DFSearch" is applied). To generate the forest of all spanning trees for all components, depth first search is to be called repeatedly on all vertices which are yet unvisited. The algorithm to print all connected components is discussed in section 10.4.3.

Observe that the function "DFSearch(0)" traverses adjacency list for vertex "i" only once. Thus, the total complexity of that function is O(2e) because there are (2e) number of nodes in the adjacency list of a graph. Therefore, the complexity of the function "DFSearch" is O(e) if the graph having "e" edges is represented by adjacency list. If the graph having "n" vertices is represented by adjacency matrix then finding all adjacent vertices of a vertex implies scanning a row of "n" elements. So, in that case, depth first traversal would require $O(n^2)$ time.

Removal of recursion from the algorithm "DFSearch" implies that the vertices not visited so far must be maintained in a list in such a way that the vertices encountered last are explored first. A natural option to store the unexplored vertices is to use a stack. The stack should contain only the start vertex at the beginning. At every iteration, the stack is popped to obtain the current vertex. Traversal restarts from the current vertex. All vertices adjacent to the current vertex which are not visited and which are not already stored in the stack are pushed into the stack. The information regarding whether a vertex is already visited or is already existent inside the stack is maintained in the array "visited". Since the vertices are identified by integers only, a stack of integers would serve the purpose.

```
void DFSNonRecursive(int start)
{
    int v;
    stackOfIntegers s;
    adjVert *adj;

    initialize (&s);
    push (&s, start);
    while (!isEmpty(s))
    {
            v = pop (&s);
            visited[v] = 1;
            printf ("%d  ", v);
            adj = g->adjList[v];
            while (adj != NULL)
            {
                    if (!visited[adj->vertex])
                    {
                            visited[adj->vertex]  = 1;
```

```
                push (&s, adj->vertex);
            }
            adj = adj->next;
        }
    }
}
```

As it was the case with "DFSearch", all elements of the array "visited" must be set to zero before calling "DFSNonRecursive". The functions "initialize", "push", "pop" and the type definition of "stackOfIntegers" have been described in Chapter 6.

One can easily note that the order in which the function traverses the vertices of the graph of Figure 10.18(a) (represented by the adjacency list of Figure 10.18(b)) is not the same as the order in which the vertices are visited by the recursive algorithm. First, trace the execution of the non-recursive algorithm as explained in the Figure 10.20. Note that the adjacent vertices are pushed from left to right and thus will be popped in the reverse manner. The content of the stack is shown from left to right in an open-ended rectangle where the open end corresponds to the top of the stack.

Stack content	**"visited" array**	**vertex visited**
0	00000000	-
1 2 3 4	10000000	0
1 2 3 7	11111000	4
1 2 3 5	11111001	7
1 2 3	11111101	5
1 2 6	11111111	3
1 2	11111111	6
1	11111111	2
	11111111	1

Figure 10.20 The content of the stack and the status of the array "visited" at the beginning of each iteration in the while loop. The vertex visited in each iteration of the while loop is also shown.

The algorithm for depth first traversal also works for directed graphs. However, depth first traversal may produce a forest even when applied to a connected directed graph.

10.4.2 Breadth First Search

This is another popular way to visit the vertices of a graph systematically. This method starts from a given vertex "v_0". The vertex "v_0" is marked visited. All adjacent vertices of "v_0" are visited next. Then, one of the adjacent vertices of "v_0" is taken up and its unvisited adjacent vertices are visited next. This process continues until all vertices reachable from "v_0" are visited. A breadth first search (BFS) initiated from "v_i" visits all vertices in "v_p" where "v_p" denotes the set of all unvisited adjacent vertices of "v_i". Next, the process continues from any vertex in "v_p". The method continues until all the vertices adjacent to "v_i" are fully explored. The algorithm for breadth first traversal has to maintain a list of vertices which have already been visited but whose adjacent vertices have not been explored still. The vertices whose neighbours are yet to be visited can be stored in a queue. Initially the queue contains the start vertex. In every iteration, a vertex is removed from the queue and all of its adjacent vertices, which are not encountered yet, are marked visited and then added to the queue. The algorithm terminates when the queue becomes empty.

The algorithm for BFS is described in the following. As usual, it assumes a global array "visited" to keep track of vertices already explored. Also the graph is assumed to be represented by an adjacency list and the graph is globally available as a variable "g". The algorithm depends on the availability of an implementation of a circular queue of integers. So, a type "queue" and three functions "queueInit", "addToCircq" and "deleteCircq" are to be properly defined before the function for breadth first search is defined. They can be easily defined by replacing "dataType" by "int" in the definition of "queue" and in the functions "addToCircq" and "deleteCircq" as described in Chapter 4. A function "queueInit" is to be written to set "rear" and "front" indices of the queue to zero. The function "deleteCircq" returns (-1) when the queue is empty.

```
void BFSearch (int start)
{
    int v, res;
    queue q;
    adjVert *adj;

    queueInit (&q);
    visited[start] = 1;
addToCircq(start, &q);
```

```
while ((res = deleteCircq (&v, &q)) != -1)
{
   printf("%d  ",v);
   adj = g->adjList[v];
   while (adj != NULL)
   {
           if (!visited[adj->vertex])
           {
                   visited[adj->vertex] = 1;
                   addToCircq(adj->vertex, &q);
           }
           adj = adj->next;
   }
}
}
```

The working of the algorithm is illustrated in Figure 10.21 by applying the algorithm on the graph of Figure 10.18(a). The graph is represented by the adjacency list of Figure 10.18(b). The vertex numbered "0" is assumed as the start vertex. The status of the queue and the array "visited" in the beginning of each iteration of the while loop are clearly mentioned in the figure. In addition, the vertex number, which is printed in each iteration of the loop is also mentioned. The queue is shown as a linear one where the "front" is represented by the left end and the "rear" is represented by the right end.

Each unvisited vertex is added to the queue. Thus, every vertex is added to the queue exactly once in the inner while loop. Also, a vertex is removed from the queue at the beginning of the outer while loop. If the graph of "n" vertices is represented by adjacency list then the outer while loop has a complexity of ($d_0 + d_1 + \ldots + d_{n-1}$) where "$d_i$" is the degree of a vertex "i". Thus, the complexity of the

Queue Content	Visited array	Vertex visited
0	10000000	-
1 2 3 4	11111000	0
2 3 4 5	11111100	1
3 4 5	11111100	2
4 5 6	11111110	3
5 6 7	11111111	4
6 7	11111111	5
7	11111111	6
	11111111	7

Figure 10.21 Illustration of breadth first search on the sample graph of Figure 10.18(a).

function "BFSearch" is O(e) as

$$\Sigma_{i=0,\ n-1} d_i = 2e.$$

If the graph is represented by an adjacency matrix then the complexity of breadth first traversal is $O(n^2)$ for a graph of "n" vertices.

Like depth first traversal, breadth first traversal generates a spanning tree of a connected graph. If the graph is not connected, breadth first traversal produces a forest.

10.4.3 Connected components

As mentioned in the context of depth first traversal of a graph, the traversal algorithms can be easily adapted to find out the components of a graph. This can be easily achieved by calling "DFSearch" or "BFSearch" for all vertices yet unvisited as shown in the function "printConnectComponents".

```
void printConnectedComponents()
{
```

```
    int i, count = 0;
    for (i = 0; i < g->noOfVertices; i++)
            visited[i] = 0;
    for (i = 0; i < g->noOfVertices; i++)
    {
            if (!visited[i])
            {
                    printf ("The vertices in the %d-th component\n", count);
                    count++;
                    DFSearch(i);
                    printf ("\n");
            }
    }
}
```

The array "visited" and the graph "g" are assumed to be globally defined and appropriately initialized. In the function "printConnectedComponents", one can also repeatedly call "BFSearch" in place of "DFSearch".

10.5 Shortest Path Problems

One of the fundamental problems encountered in many graph-theoretic applications is to find the shortest path (i.e. the path having the least cost) between two vertices in a weighted graph. Length of a path in a weighted graph is defined to be the sum of costs or weights of all edges in that path. In general, there could be more than one path between a pair of specified vertices, say "v_i" and "v_j", and a path with the minimum cost or weight is called a shortest path from "v_i" to "v_j". Note that the shortest path between two vertices may not be unique.

Consider the weighted undirected graph of Figure 10.6. It can be easily seen that there are more than three paths 0-1, 0-2-1, 0-2-3-1, from the vertex "0" to the vertex "1". The path with the shortest length is 0-2-1. The length of the shortest path is "4". It is apparent that the problem of finding the shortest path from "v_i" to "v_j" in a graph "G" is not well-defined if "G" contains a cycle whose length is negative. Because, in that case, each traversal of the cycle reduces the length of the traversed path by a constant amount. Hence, the length of the shortest path can be made arbitrarily low. The presence of negative edges does not ill-define the problem as long as the graph does not contain a cycle of negative length. However, negative edges are rare in practical applications. For simplicity, edges having positive weights have been considered. But, there are algorithms which successfully find the shortest path in a graph containing negative edges as well.

There are many different variations of the shortest path problem. They vary with respect to the specification of the start vertex (referred to as source) and the end vertex (referred to as destination). Some of the commonly known variants are listed in the following.

- The shortest path from a specified source vertex to a specified destination vertex.
- The shortest paths from one specified vertex to all other vertices. This problem is also known as single source shortest path problem.
- The shortest paths between all possible source and destination vertices. This problem is also known as all pairs shortest path problem.

In this section, the single-source shortest path problem is considered. Assume that the graph G = (V, E) contains "n" vertices 0, 1, 2, ..., (n-1). Let "c_{ij}" denote the cost of the edge "e_{ij}" which connects vertex "i" to vertex "j". Assume $c_{ij} > 0$ for all i, j and i ¹ j. "c_{ij}" is assumed to be infinity if "e_{ij}" does not exist. Without any loss of generality, assume that the problem is to find the shortest paths from the vertex "0" to all other vertices. Usually, shortest path problems are defined on weighted directed graphs. However, undirected graphs may be regarded as a directed graph where each edge in the undirected graph (u, v, w) has to be interpreted as two edges (u, v, w) and (v, u, w).

The following observations are helpful is ascertaining the correctness of the following algorithms for computing the shortest path of all vertices from a given vertex. Readers are encouraged to prove these properties.

- The length of the shortest path is always longer than the length of any of its sub-paths.
- Any sub-path from a vertex "m" to another vertex "n" of a shortest path from a vertex "i" to the vertex "j" must itself be a shortest path from the vertex "m" to the vertex "n".
- For any pair of vertices "i" and "j", the shortest path from the vertex "i" to the vertex "j" may contain at most (n-1) edges in a graph having "n" vertices.

10.5.1 Dantzig's Algorithm

Let V={0, 1, ..., n-1} be the "n" vertices of a graph. The problem is to find out the shortest paths from a particular vertex, say "0", to all other vertices of the graph that can be reached from this vertex. The set "V" is partitioned in two sets "S" and (V-S) where "S" contains all vertices for which the shortest paths are already known and the other set contains the remaining vertices of the graph, if there is any. The length of the shortest path from "0" to "i" is denoted by C[i]. Initially, "S" contains only the source vertex, "0", from which the shortest paths will have to be found. So, "S" will start with S={0} and C[0]=0 as the length from the vertex "0" to itself is zero. In the first iteration, we find the distances of all the vertices from "0" that are adjacent to "0". Then, choose the minimum of these distances and note the corresponding adjacent vertex. After the first iteration, "S" will include the vertex "0" and the vertex whose distance from the vertex "0" is the minimum. In the next iteration, the distances of all vertices that are adjacent to the last added vertex are recomputed. If a vertex "i" is the last vertex added to "S" then the distances of its adjacent vertices are re-calculated as

$$d_{ij} = C[i] + a_{ij}$$

Where C[i] is the shortest path length from the vertex "0" to the vertex "i" and "a_{ij}" is the length of the edge from vertex "i" to the vertex "j". Now the minimum distance is found among these newly computed distances and all the distances computed in the previous iterations for all vertices except the ones for which the shortest path is already known. Let "d_{ij}" be the minimum of all such distances for some "i" and some "j". Then, the vertex "j" is added to "S" and the shortest distance of "j", C[j] is set to "d_{ij}". This method is continued until no vertices are left which can be reached from "0". In all iterations, the values "d_{ij}" are saved and the minimum "d_{ij}" is considered for all "i" and "j" such that both "i" and "j" do not belong to "S". In a particular iteration, when a vertex "j" is included in the set "S" as "d_{ij}" is minimum then "d_{ij}" is replaced by a large value "∞" so that in the next iterations, these distances are not going to be considered. In case a vertex is not reachable from another vertex, this distance is also indicated by "∞". When "d_{ij}" is minimum and "j" is included in "S", the parent of the vertex "j" have to be remembered to maintain the shortest path. This task may be done by maintaining an array "T" and setting T[j] to "i" whenever "j" is included in "S" due to the fact that "d_{ij}" is the minimum.

The scheme discussed so far is applied on the graph of Figure 10.6 to find shortest paths from the vertex "0". The adjacency matrix is shown in Figure 10.22. The status of "S" and the status of the arrays "T" and "C" are shown for each iteration. The changes in the matrix "d" are also shown for each iteration.

	0	1	2	3	4	5	6
0	0	5	2	∞	∞	∞	∞
1	5	0	2	6	25	∞	∞
2	2	2	0	7	∞	10	∞
3	∞	6	7	0	∞	∞	14
4	∞	25	∞	∞	0	12	11
5	∞	∞	10	∞	12	0	15
6	∞	∞	∞	14	11	15	0

Figure 10.22 Adjacency matrix of the weighted graph of Figure 10.6.

At the start of the first iteration, S = {0}, C = (0, -,-, -, -, -, -), T = (-,-, -, -, -, -, -). So, d_{0i} for i = 1 to 6 are going to be recomputed using the expression $d_{0i} = C[0] + a_{0i}$

$d_{01} = C[0] + a_{01} = 0 + 5 = 5$

$d_{02} = C[0] + a_{02} = 0 + 2 = 2$

$d_{03} = C[0] + a_{03} = 0 + \infty = \infty$

$d_{04} = C[0] + a_{04} = 0 + \infty = \infty$

$d_{05} = C[0] + a_{05} = 0 + \infty = \infty$

$d_{06} = C[0] + a_{06} = 0 + \infty = \infty$

d_{02} is the minimum. So, "2" is added to "S"; C[2] is updated by d_{02} and d_{02} is updated to ∞.

At the start of the second iteration, S ={0,2}; C = (0, -, 2, -, -, -, -); T = (-,-, 0, -, -, -,). As "2" is the last vertex added to "S", d_{2i}, for i = 0 to 6 and i ∉ S are going to be recalculated using the expression $d_{2i} = C[2] + a_{2i}$.

$d_{21} = C[0] + a_{21} = 2 + 2 = 4$

$d_{23} = C[0] + a_{23} = 2 + 7 = 9$

$d_{24} = C[0] + a_{24} = 2 + \infty = \infty$

$d_{25} = C[0] + a_{25} = 2 + 10 = 12$

$d_{26} = C[0] + a_{26} = 2 + \infty = \infty$

Of all d_{ij} so far computed, d_{21} is the minimum. Hence, "1" is added to "S", C[1] is set to d_{21}. d_{21} is set to ∞ and T[1] is set to "2". d_{01} is also set to ∞.

At the start of the third iteration, S ={0,2, 1}; C = (0, 4, 2, -, -, -, -); T = (-,2, 0, -, -, , -). As "1" is the last vertex added to "S", d_{1i}, for i = 0 to 6 and i ∉ S are going to be recalculated using the expression $d_{1i} = C[1] + a_{1i}$.

$d_{13} = C[1] + a_{13} = 4 + 6 = 10$

$d_{14} = C[1] + a_{14} = 4 + 25 = 29$

$d_{15} = C[1] + a_{15} = 4 + \infty = \infty$

$d_{16} = C[1] + a_{16} = 4 + \infty = \infty$

Of all d_{ij} so far computed, d_{23} is the minimum. Hence, "3" is added to "S", C[3] is set to d_{23}. d_{23} is set to ∞ and T[3] is set to "2". d_{13} and d_{03} are also set to ∞.

At the start of the fourth iteration, S ={0, 2, 1, 3}; C = (0, 4, 2, 9, -, -, -); T = (-, 2, 0, 2, -, -, -). As "3" is the last vertex added to "S", d_{3i}, for i = 0 to 6 and i ∉ S are going to be recalculated using the expression $d_{3i} = C[3] + a_{3i}$.

$d_{34} = C[3] + a_{34} = 9 + \infty = \infty$

$d_{35} = C[3] + a_{35} = 9 + \infty = \infty$

$d_{36} = C[3] + a_{36} = 9 + 14 = 23$

Of all d_{ij} so far computed, d_{25} is the minimum. Hence, "5" is added to "S", C[5] is set to d_{25}. d_{25} is set to ∞ and T[5] is set to "2". d_{05}, d_{15}, d_{25}, d_{35} are also set to ∞.

At the start of the fifth iteration, S ={0, 2, 1, 3, 5}; C = (0, 4, 2, 9, , 12, -); T = (-, 2, 0, 2, -, 2, -). As "5" is the last vertex added to "S", d_{5i}, for i = 0 to 6 and i ∉ S are going to be recalculated using the expression d_{5i} = C[5] + a_{5i} .

$$d_{54} = C[5] + a_{54} = 12 + 12 = 24$$

$$d_{56} = C[5] + a_{56} = 12 + 15 = 27$$

Of all d_{ij} so far computed, d_{36} is the minimum. Hence, "6" is added to "S", C[6] is set to d_{36}. d_{36} is set to ∞ and T[6] is set to "3". d_{06}, d_{16}, d_{26}, d_{36}, d_{56} are also set to ∞.

At the start of the sixth iteration, S ={0, 2, 1, 3, 5, 6}; C = (0, 4, 2, 9, - , 12, 23); T = (, 2, 0, 2, -, 2, 3). As "6" is the last vertex added to "S", d_{6i}, for i = 0 to 6 and i ∉ S are going to be recalculated as d_{6i} = C[6] + a_{6i} .

$$d_{64} = C[6] + a_{64} = 23 + 11 = 34$$

Of all d_{ij} so far computed, d_{54} is the minimum. Hence, "4" is added to "S", C[4] is set to d_{54}. d_{54} is set to ∞ and T[4] is set to "5".

At the start of the seventh iteration, S ={0, 2, 1, 3, 5, 6, 4}; C = (0, 4, 2, 9, 24, 12, 23); T = (-, 2, 0, 2, 5, 2, 3). But now "S" contains all vertices of the graph. Hence no more iterations are required. The array "C" contains the shortest distances of all vertices from the vertex "0". "T" contains the implicit tree because T[i] = j implies that the parent of the vertex "i" is the vertex "j" and parent of any vertex is unique in a tree. T[0] is "-" indicating that the vertex "0" does not have a parent and hence, the vertex "0" may be considered to be the root vertex. The resultant tree obtained by inspecting "T" is shown in the Figure 10.23. Writing a "C" function implementing this algorithm is left as an exercise.

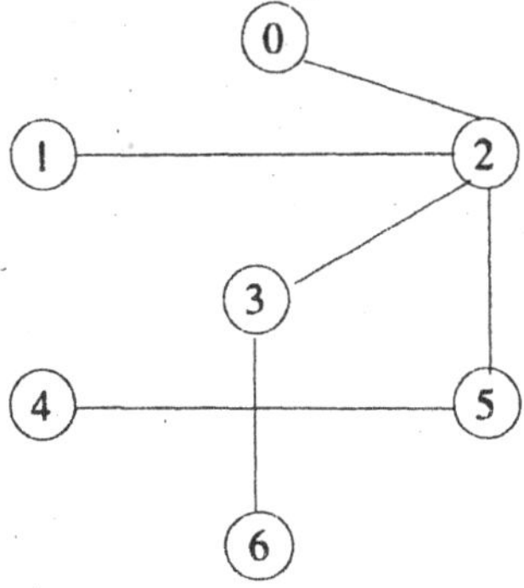

Figure 10.23 The shortest path spanning tree of the graph of Figure 10.6. The tree shows shortest paths from the vertex "0" to any other vertex of the graph.

10.5.2 Dijkstra's algorithm

Dijkstra's algorithm also works by maintaining a set "S" of vertices whose shortest paths and shortest distances from the vertex "0" is already known. At each step of the algorithm, one more vertex which does not belong to "S" is included into the set "S". To facilitate such inclusion, an array called "distance" is used to keep track of the current shortest distance of any vertex from the vertex "0". distance[i] is initialized to "c_{0i}" for all "i", $0 \le i \le (n-1)$. "S" is initialized to contain only one vertex "0". Note that, by definition of "S", distance[i] is the shortest distance between the vertices "0" and "i" provided $i \in S$. If $i \notin S$ then distance[i] is calculated as the minimum of c_{ji} + distance[j] over all "j" such that $j \in S$. Once the recalculation of all entries in the array "distance" is done, the vertex "v" is chosen such that distance[v] is minimum among all distance[i], $i \notin S$. At this point, it must be proved that distance[v] actually gives the shortest distance between vertex "0" and vertex "v". This can be proved as follows. Assume that distance[v] is not the shortest distance between vertex "0" and vertex "v" as the shortest path from vertex "0" to "v" consists of a vertex "x" which is not currently included in "S". Then, the shortest path from "0" to "v" must have one vertex "y" which is adjacent to a vertex in the set "S" and $y \notin S$. In that case, distance[y] will be computed as the shortest distance from "0" to "y". But the vertex "y" lies on a shortest path from "0" to "v". Thus, distance[y] < distance[v]. Since "v" was selected for inclusion into "S", distance[v] < distance[y]. These two facts are contradictory. Thus, distance[v] must be the shortest distance between the vertices "0" and "v".

The function "shortestPath" computes the shortest paths of all vertices from the vertex "0" of a graph "g". The graph "g" is assumed to be global. The function fills up the arrays "d" and "t". The shortest path spanning tree is implicitly constructed in the array "t". If t[i] is "j" then, the parent of the vertex "i" is the vertex "j". Whenever a vertex "v" is included to "S" due to the fact that "v" is adjacent to some vertex "w" of "S" and distance[v] is minimum among all vertices currently not belonging to "S" then t[v] is set to "w"

```
void shortestPath (int d[], int t[])
{
    int i, n, min, v, w;
    int shortestDistFound [100];
    n = g->noOfVertices;
    d[0] = 0;
    for (i = 0; i < n; i++)
    {
            shortestDistFound[i] = 0;
            d[i] = g->adjMat[0][i];
```

```
    }
    for (i = 0; i < n; i++)
    {
            min = MAX_INT;
            for (w = 0; w < n; w++)
            {
                    if ((!shortestDistFound[w]) && (d[w] < min))
                    {
                            v = w;
                            min = d[w];
                    }
            }
            shortestDistFound[v] = 1;
            for (w = 0; w < n; w++)
                    if (!shortestDistFound[w])
                            if ((min + g->adjMat[v][w]) < d[w])
                            {
                                    d[w] = min + g->adjMat[v][w];
                                    t[w] = v;
                            }
    }
}
```

The working of this algorithm on the graph of Figure 10.6 to compute the shortest paths from the vertex "0" is illustrated in Figures 10.24(a)-(f). Each figure explains an iteration of the outer "for" loop. The status of "S" before entering the loop is mentioned. The status of "d" and "t" at the end of the iteration is mentioned.

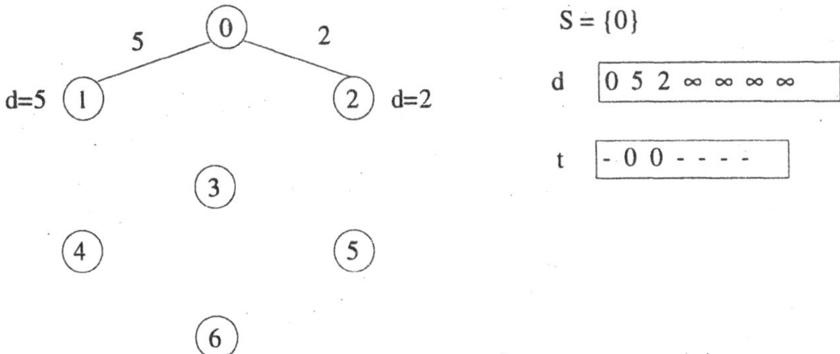

Figure 10.24(a) d[1] and d[2] are calculated. As d[2] is minimum, "2" is added to "S" in the next iteration. t[2] and t[1] are set to "0"

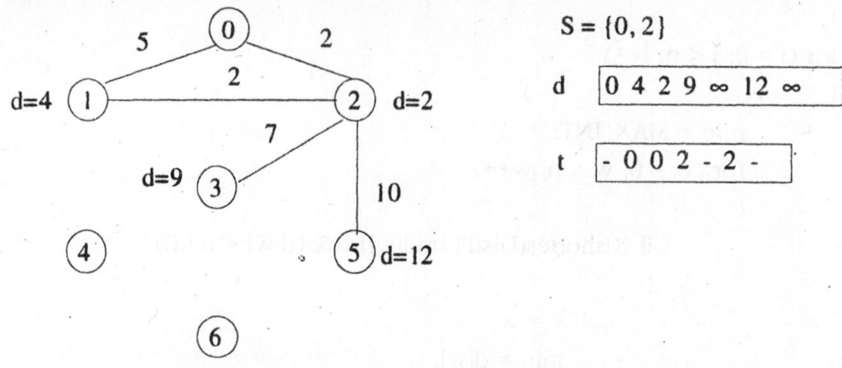

10.24(b) d[1], d[3], d[5] are recalculated as the vertices "1", "3", "5" do not belong to "S" and they are adjacent to "2", the last vertex added to "S". As d[1] is minimum among all d[i] such that "i" does not belong to "S", "1" is added to "S" and t[1], t[3], t[5] are set to "2".

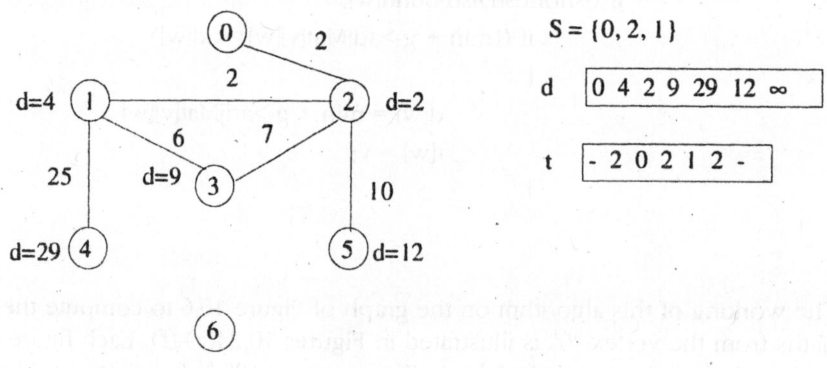

10.24(c) d[3], d[4] are reexamined as "3" and "4" do not belong to "S" and they are adjacent to "1". d[4] is updated. As d[3] is minimum among all d[i] such that "i" does not belong to "S", "3" is added to "S" and t[4] is set to "1".

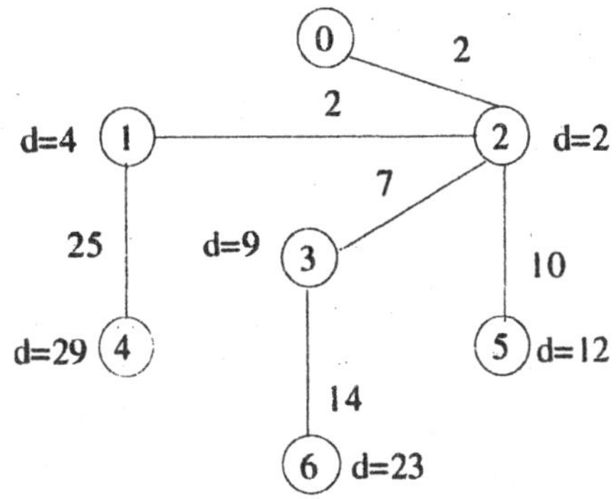

S = {0, 2, 1, 3}

d | 0 4 2 9 29 12 23 |

t | - 2 0 2 1 2 3 |

10.24(d) d[6] is reexamined as "6" does not belong to "S" and it is adjacent to "3", the last vertex added to "S". d[6] is updated. As, d[5] is minimum among all d[i] such that "i" does not belong to "S", "5" is added to "S" and t[6] is set to "3".

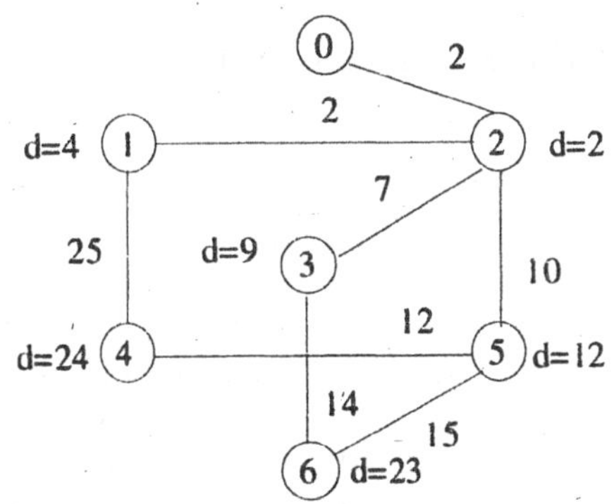

S = {0, 2, 1, 3, 5}

d | 0 4 2 9 24 12 23 |

T | - 2 0 2 5 2 3 |

10.24(e) d[6], d[4] are reexamined as vertices "6" and "4" do not belong to "S" and they are adjacent to "5", the last vertex added to "S". Only d[4] is updated. As, d[6] is minimum among all d[i] such that "i" does not belong to "S", "6" is added to "S" and t[4] is set to "5".

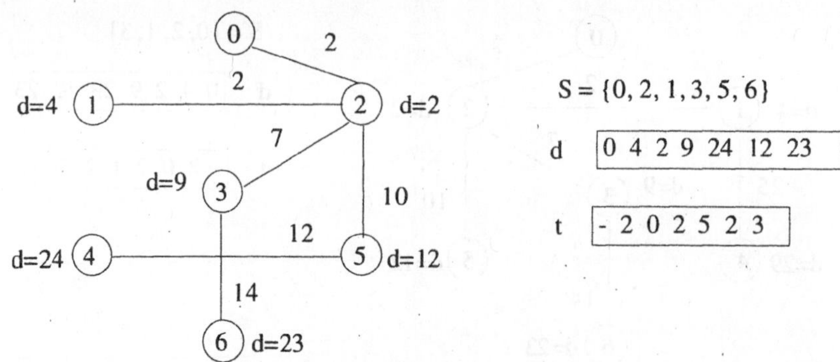

10.24(f) d[4] is reexamined as "4" does not belong to "S" and "4" is adjacent to "6", the last vertex added to "S". But, d[4] is not updated. d[4] is the minimum.

The function "shortestPath" contains two nested "for" loops each of which has a complexity of O(n). So, the total complexity of the algorithm is $O(n^2)$ if the graph has "n" vertices.

10.5.3 All pair shortest paths and transitive closure for directed graphs

Consider a more general problem of finding the shortest paths (as well as their costs) between every pair of vertices "i" and "j" of a graph. Recall that Dijkstra's algorithm computes the shortest paths from a specified vertex to all other vertices in $O(n^2)$ time for a graph having "n" vertices. This algorithm can be repeatedly applied "n" times (once for each vertex as the start-vertex) to solve the all pair shortest path problem. The resulting algorithm will have a time complexity of $O(n^3)$. However, the same problem can be solved in $O(n^3)$ time using a much simpler technique for directed graphs. One advantage of the new approach is that the actual computation involved may be less.

Assume that a directed weighted graph "G" having "n" vertices is represented by its adjacency matrix "a". Further, assume that "G" does not have any self-loop. If the vertex "j" is reached from the vertex "i" without passing through any other intermediate vertex then "a_{ij}" is the shortest distance from the vertex "i" to the vertex "j". If it is attempted to find out a possible shorter path between the vertices "i" and "j" which might include only vertex "0" then a shorter distance between vertices "i" and "j" may be discovered. More specifically, the shortest distance between vertices "i" and "j" passing possibly through the vertex "0" is the minimum of "a_{ij}" and (a_{i0} + a_{0j}). In this way, one can continue allowing more and more vertices from "0" to "k" to be used as intermediate vertices and discover even shorter paths. When "k" is equal to (n-1) then the shortest distance between the vertices "i" and "j" is found out.

This method of computation can be easily formalized. Let $A^k(i, j)$ denote the distance of the shortest path between the vertices "i" and "j" provided the path does not pass through any of the vertices "k", (k+1), (k+2), ..., (n-1). In other words, only the vertices "0", "1", ..,(k-1) may possibly occur in the shortest path between the vertices "i" and "j". Consequently, $A^{k+1}(i, j)$ may be less than $A^k(i, j)$ if there exists a shorter path between the vertices "i" and "j" through the vertex "k" which can not be found out while computing $A^k(i, j)$. If this path passes through "k" then the new cost should be computed as $A^k(i, k) + A^k(k, j)$. Therefore, $A^k(i, j)$ may be recursively defined as follows.

$$A^{k+1}(i, j) = \min \{ A^k(i, j), A^k(i, k) + A^k(k, j)\}$$

$$A^0(i, j) = a_{ij}$$

The "C" function implementing this method is presented in the following. The function accepts the adjacency matrix of a graph as a two-dimensional array "a" of integers. The shortest distance between any two pairs of vertices is computed in another two-dimensional array "x" of floating point numbers.

```
void allPairShortestDistance (int x[][10], int a[][10], int n)
{
    int i, j, k, t;
    for (i = 0; i < n; i++)
            for (j = 0; j < n; j++)
                    x[i][j] = a[i][j];
            for (k = 0; k < n; k++)
                    for (i = 0; i < n; i++)
                            for (j = 0; j < n; j++)
                            {       /* 1000 represent infinity */
                                    if ((x[i][k] == 1000) || (x[k][j] == 1000))
                                            t = 1000;
                                    else
                                            t = x[i][k] + x[k][j];
                                    x[i][j] = (x[i][j] < t) ? x[i][j] : t;
                            }
}
```

Consider the weighted directed graph of Figure 10.25. The trace of executing the function "allPirShortestDistance" on the adjacency matrix of this graph is shown in Figure 10.26. The matrices A^0, A^1, A^2, A^3, A^4 as produced after each iteration of the outer most "for" loop of the nested loop containing three "for" loops.

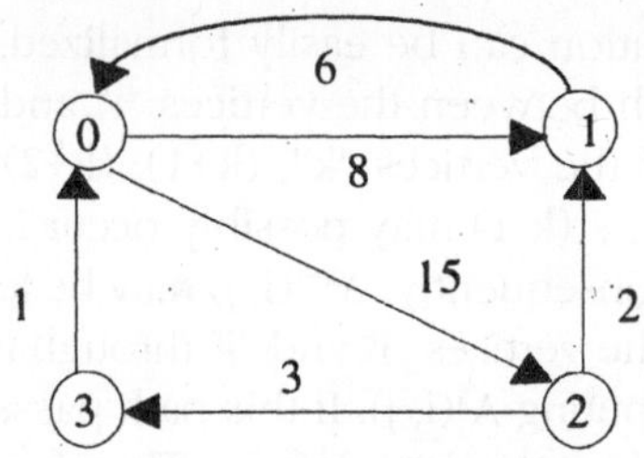

Figure 10.25 A sample weighted directed graph.

	0	1	2	3
0	0	8	15	∞
1	6	0	∞	∞
2	∞	2	0	3
3	1	∞	∞	0

Figure 10.26(a) A^0 (equal to the adjacency matrix) of the graph of Figure 10.25.

	0	1	2	3
0	0	8	15	¥
1	6	0	21	¥
2	¥	2	0	3
3	1	9	16	0

Figure 10.26(b) A^1 as computed after the first iteration of the outer most "for" loop (of the nested loop containing three "for" loops) of the function "allPairShortestDistance".

	0	1	2	3
0	0	8	15	¥
1	6	0	21	¥
2	8	2	0	3
3	1	9	16	0

Figure 10.26(c) A^2 as computed after the second iteration of the outer most "for" loop (of the nested loop containing three "for" loops) of the function "allPairShortestDistance"

	0	1	2	3
0	0	8	15	18
1	6	0	21	24
2	8	2	0	3
3	1	9	16	0

Figure 10.26(d) A^3 as computed after the third iteration of the outer most "for" loop (of the nested loop containing three "for" loops) of the function "allPairShortestDistance".

	0	1	2	3
0	0	8	15	18
1	6	0	21	24
2	4	2	0	3
3	1	9	16	0

Figure 10.26(e) A^4 as computed after the fourth iteration of the outer most "for" loop (of the nested loop containing three "for" loops) of the function "allPairShortestDistance".

Figure 10.26 Trace of execution of the function "allPairShortestDistance" when applied to the graph of Figure 10.25.

Sometimes it is required to find out whether there exists a path from a specified vertex "i" to vertex "j" in a graph. A more general version of this problem is to check whether there is a path for all pairs of vertices "i" and "j". By examining the matrix A^n of a directed graph, this question can be easily answered. Note that there is a path from the vertex "i" to the vertex "j" if and only if $A^n[i][j]$ is not infinity. Since, in this case, the existence of a path is the only concern (and not the actual cost), A^k may be regarded as a boolean matrix where the (i, j)-th entry is true if and only if there is a path from the vertex "i" to the vertex "j".

Transitive Closure matrix "T" of a graph "G" is defined to be a boolean matrix with the property that

T_{ij} = true, if there exists a path from the vertex "i" to the vertex "j".
= false, otherwise.

Now, the matrices T^k may be recursively defined as follows.

$$T^0(i, j) \begin{cases} = 1, \text{ if } a_{ij} \neq \infty \\ = 0, \text{ if } a_{ij} = \infty \end{cases}$$

where a_{ij} is the (i, j)-th entry of the adjacency matrix.

For k > 0

$$T^k(i, j) = T^{k-1}(i, j) \vee (T^{k-1}(i, j) \wedge T^{k-1}(i, j))$$

The symbols "$\vee$" and "$\wedge$" denote OR and AND operations respectively.

"T", the transitive closure matrix = $T^n(i, j)$ if the graph has "n" vertices. The operations involved in computing T^k are logical while those involved in computing A^k are arithmetic. So, the space required to store T^k's is less than that to store A^k's if bit-wise logical operations are performed and each bit represents an entry in the matrix. Similarly, the actual time required to calculate the matrices T^k's is less than that required to calculate A^k.

10.6 Algorithms for computing minimal spanning tree

The notion of minimal spanning tree of a graph has already been introduced. There are two well-known algorithms to compute minimal cost spanning tree of a weighted undirected graph. One of these algorithms was designed by J. Kruskal in 1957 and the other one is due to Prim. In this section, these algorithms will be explained.

10.6.1 Kruskal's Algorithm

This algorithm works on a list of edges of a graph and the list is sorted in order of non-decreasing cost or weight of the edges. It starts with a forest of "n" trees if the graph has "n" vertices. Each tree in the forest contains one distinct vertex of the graph and no edges. In each step of the algorithm, one edge from the sorted list is considered for connecting two forests. The edge is added only if its inclusion does not form a cycle. Once an edge is considered, the edge is deleted from the list of edges. The algorithm continues until (n-1) edges are added or the list of edges is exhausted. Once the algorithm terminates after adding (n-1) edges, a minimal spanning tree is generated. Consider the graph of Figure 10.6. There are eleven edges. An edge connecting the vertices "i" and "j" may be represented by a tuple (i, j). Then, the list of edges of the graph in Figure 10.6 sorted in non-descending order may be given by {(0, 2), (1, 2), (0, 1), (1, 3), (2, 3), (2, 5), (4, 6), (4, 5), (3, 6), (5, 6), (1, 4)}. The initial forest may be depicted by the Figure 10.27(a).

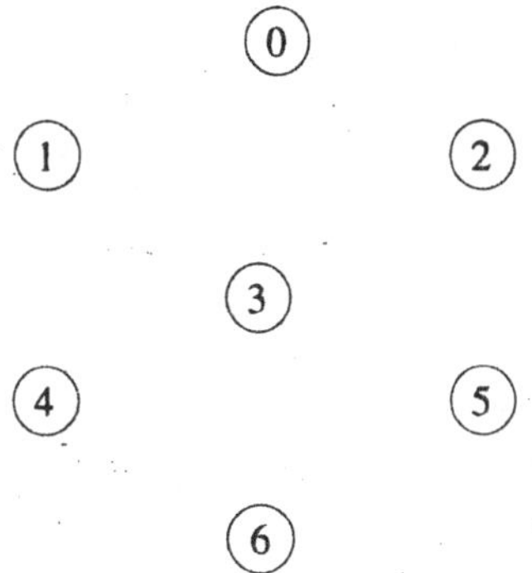

Figure 10.27(a) Initial forest of "n" trees

The first edge (0, 2) from the list of edges is considered. Since the inclusion of this edge does not form a cycle, it can be added to modify the partial minimal spanning tree resulting in the diagram of Figure 10.27(b).

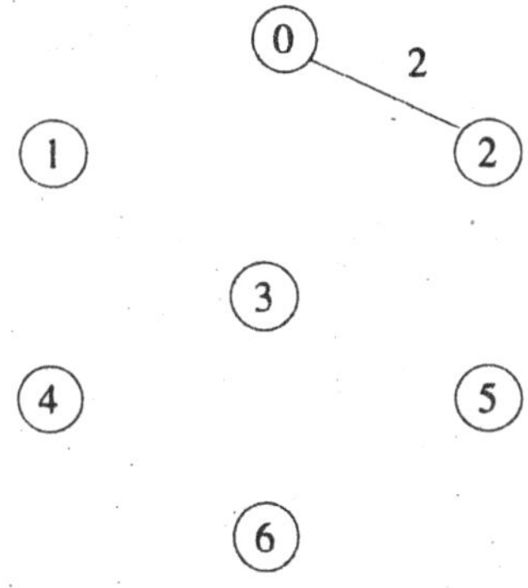

Figure 10.27(b) The edge (0, 2) is added to reduce the number of trees in the forest.

The next edge to be considered is (1, 2). Addition of this edge does not create a cycle too and hence, it will added to the partially formed minimum spanning tree of Figure 10.27(b) resulting a tree as shown in Figure 10.27(c).

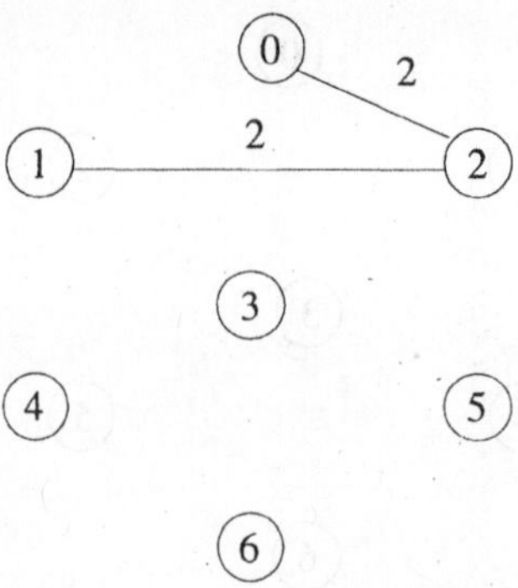

Figure 10.27 (c) The next edge (1, 2) is also added.

If the next edge (0, 1) is considered then a cycle is formed. Therefore, this edge is not added to the partially formed tree of Figure 10.27(c). And the next edge (1, 3) is chosen for consideration. Since inclusion of this edge does not form a cycle, this edge can be safely added and the partial minimal spanning tree of Figure 10.27(d) is created.

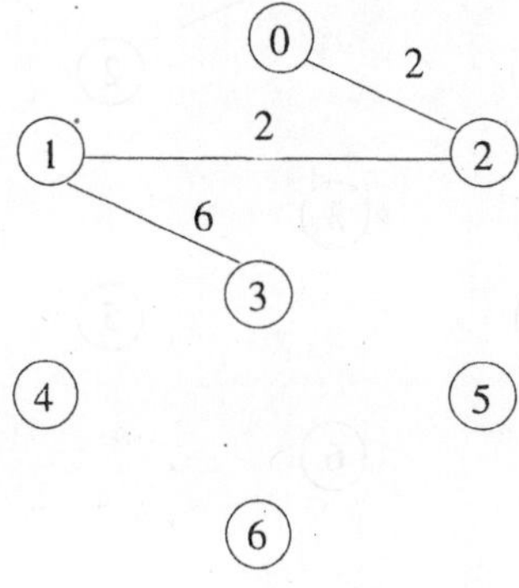

Figure 10.27(d) The edge (1, 3) is added.

If the next edge (2, 3) is added then a cycle 2-1-3-2 is formed. Therefore, this edge is not added to the partially formed tree of Figure 10.27(d). And the next edge (2, 5) is chosen. Since inclusion of this edge does not form a cycle, this edge can be safely added and the partial minimal spanning tree of Figure 10.27(e) is created.

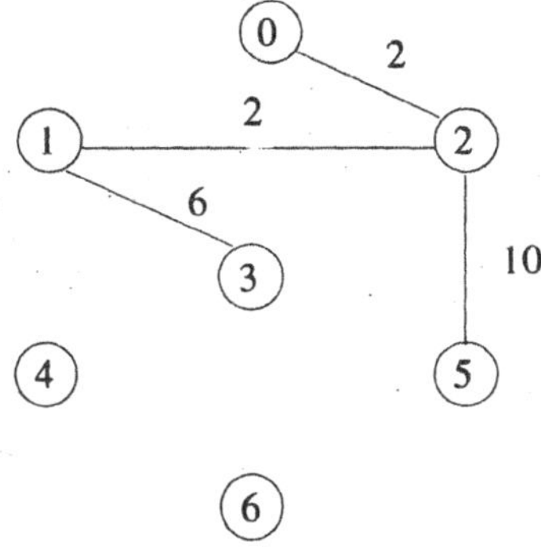

Figure 10.27(e) The edge (2, 5) is added.

Next, the edge (4, 6) is chosen. This edge can be safely added. See that the result of each step of the algorithm is not a tree but a forest. In fact, after a successful addition of an edge the number of forests decreases. See that the number of trees in the forest (shown in Figure 10.27(f)) after addition of the edge (4, 6) is 2.

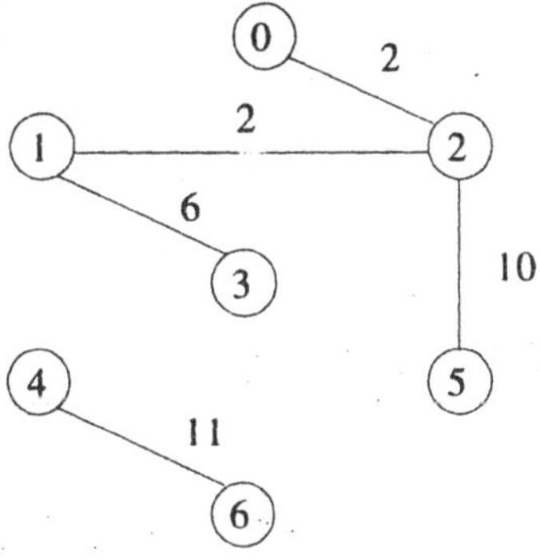

Figure 10.27(f) The edge (4, 5) is added.

The next edge in the list, (4, 5), can be added in the forest merging the two trees creating a minimal cost spanning tree, which is shown in Figure 10.27(g).

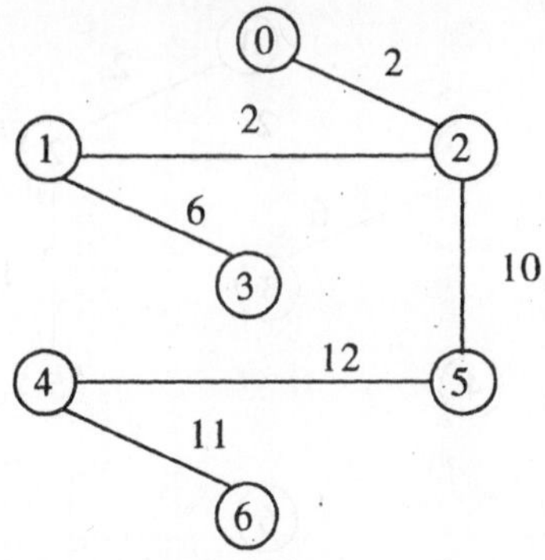

Figure 10.27(g) The edge (4, 6) is added.

Figure 10.27 Illustration of Kruskal's algorithm as applied on the graph of Figure 10.6.

Specifying Kruskal's algorithm in "C" like pseudo-code is now simple. The algorithm in C-like pseudo code is provided in the following. The input parameter of the algorithm is a list of edges sorted in non-decreasing order of their weights. Each node in such a list is a self-referential structure containing two integers representing an edge connecting the vertices identified by the integers. Such a structure is defined in the following.

```
typedef struct edgeList
{
    int u, v;
    float weight;
    struct edgeList * next;
} edgeList;
```

A list of edges can be easily computed from adjacency matrix or adjacency list of a graph. Then the list can be sorted in non-decreasing order of their weights. Once this is done, the pointer to the first node in this list may be used as input to the Kruskal's algorithm. Another input to the algorithm is "n", the number of vertices in the graph. The output of the algorithm is another list of edges which defines a tree. The graph is assumed to be connected for simplicity. If the graph is not connected then there is no spanning tree.

```
edgeList * KruskalMST(edgeList f, int n)
{
    edgeList *T;
    edgeList *e;
    int noOfEdgesAdded = 0;
```

```
    while ( (noOfEdgesAdded < (n-1)) && (f != NULL))
    {
        e = f;
        f = f->next;
        if (e does not form a cycle in T)
        {
            noOfEdgesAdded++;
            if (T == NULL)
            {
                T = e;
                r = T;
                r->next = NULL;
            }
            else
            {
                r->next = e;
                r = r->next;
                r ->next = NULL;
            }
        }
    }
    return T;
}
```

The following result establishes the fact that Kruskal's algorithm works correctly.

Result

Let a graph be G = (V, E). Suppose that "U" is a proper subset of "V" and "e" be an edge of minimum weight connecting a vertex in "U" with a vertex in (V-U). Then, "e" belongs to a minimal spanning tree "T" of the "G".

Proof:

Suppose that $e \notin T$ where "T" is any minimal spanning tree of "G". Then, add "e" to "T". Consequently, "T" will no longer remain a tree as "e" will introduce a cycle. However, as "T" is a minimal spanning tree, there must be an edge "f" other than "e" from some vertex of "U" to some vertex in (V-U). According to the condition stated, the weight of "f" is greater than or equal to that of "e". Delete "f" from the cycle and the remaining part of the graph i.e. (T+e-f) is once again a tree. The cost of this tree can not be more than that of "T". Thus, the new tree must be a minimal spanning tree contradicting the assumption that "e" does not belong to any minimal spanning tree. Hence the result is proved.

Kruskal's algorithm always connects some "U" and (V-U) by an edge with the smallest weight without introducing a cycle. Therefore, according to the previous observation, Kruskal's algorithm works properly.

Kruskal's algorithm starts by sorting all edges of a graph. The time complexity of this sorting operation is O(ElogE) if there are "E" number of edges in the graph. The "for" loop in the algorithm makes "E" number of iterations in the worst case. In each iteration, the major task is to find whether the current edge introduces a cycle. As it will be discussed, the complexity of detecting a cycle is O(logn) in the worst case if the graph contains "n" vertices. Thus, the overall time complexity of the algorithm is O(ElogE) + O(Elogn).

The only task remaining in Kruskal's algorithm is to find out whether addition of a new edge introduces a cycle in a forest. This can be done by using the Union-Find algorithms described for sets in Chapter 7. The "n" vertices of a graph may be assumed to be "n" disjoint sets where $S_i = \{i\}$, $0 \leq i < n$. Whenever an edge (i, j) is encountered, the set containing "i" and the set containing "j" are found out. If these sets are disjoint then they are united using "Union" operation. Thus, there is a path connecting all vertices in any set. If it is found that vertices "i' and "j" are contained in the same set then addition of the edge (i, j) must introduce a cycle. Thus, finding out whether incorporation of an edge "e" introduces a cycle boils down to do two "find" operations on "e.u" and "e.v". If these "find" operations return the same set then addition of edge "e" would certainly introduce a cycle and hence "e" must be rejected. However, the two sets returned by "find' are disjoint then they are to be joined by a "Union" operation to maintain the fact that now "e.u" and "e.v" belong to the same set. The modified function for Kruskal's algorithm is given in the following.

```
edgeList * KruskalMST(edgeList f, int n)
{
    edgeList *T = NULL;
    edgeList *e, *r;
    int noOfEdgesAdded = 0;
    int i;

    for (i = 0; i < n; i++)
            parent[i] = i;

    for (i = 0; i < n; i++)
            rank[i] = 0;
```

```
    while ( (noOfEdgesAdded < (n-1)) && (f != NULL))
    {
        int p1, p2;
        e = f;
        f = f->next;
        p1 = find(e->u) ;
        p2 = find(e->v);
        if (p1 != p2)
        {
            unionRank(p1, p2);
            noOfEdgesAdded++;
            if (T == NULL)
            {
                T = e;
                r = T;
                r->next = NULL;
            }
            else
            {
                r->next = e;
                r = r->next;
                r ->next = NULL;
            }
        }
    }
    return T;
}
```

The arrays "parent" and "rank" are assumed to be global so that the functions "find", "unionRank" and "KruskalMST" can refer to them. The functions "find" and "unionRank" have already been described in Chapter 7. The second version of the function "find" described in Chapter 7 should be used for efficiency. Note that the complexity of the algorithm is dominated by the time to sort the list of edges. To overcome this problem, a heap may be constructed of all edges in linear time. The heap property is to be modified to always put the minimum key at the root of any sub-tree of the heap. The key, in this case, is the weight of an edge. Then, the edge with minimum weight may be removed and added or rejected for inclusion to the minimal spanning tree. Although this modification does not improve the worst-case complexity of the algorithm but it improves the average-case time complexity.

10.6.2 Prim's Algorithm

Unlike Kruskal's algorithm, Prim's algorithm does not start with a list of edges sorted in non-decreasing order of their weights. It starts with any arbitrary vertex as the partial minimal spanning tree "T". In each iteration of the algorithm, one edge (u, v) is added to this partial tree "T" so that exactly one end of this edge belongs to the set of vertices in "T". Of all such possible edges, the edge having the least cost is selected. The algorithm continues to add (n-1) edges (if possible). Consider the same graph of Figure 10.6 and apply Prim's algorithm starting with vertex "0" The illustration of the working of Prim's algorithm is shown in Figure 10.28.

The crux in implementing Prim's algorithm is effectively choosing the successive edges. An approach suggested by Kim efficiently solves this problem. For each vertex presently not belonging to partial tree, the algorithm maintains an edge with the minimal cost so that one end of the edge is a vertex belonging to the partial tree.

Specifically, the algorithm maintains three arrays "U", "T" and "Edge". The array "U" maintains the vertices which are already included in the minimal spanning tree. The array "T" maintains the edges which form the minimal spanning tree. The array "Edge" maintains the edge with the minimum cost for each vertex not included yet in the minimal spanning tree so that one end of that edge belongs to the already formed minimal spanning tree. The array "U" initially contains the vertex "0". The array "T" is initially NULL. Type definition of the array "Edge" can be done as follows.

```
edge Edge[MAX_NO_OF_VERTICES];
```

where "edge" is a predefined type containing a tuple, (u, v, weight). "u" denotes the start vertex, "v" denotes the end vertex and "weight" denotes the weight of the edge. The type definition of "edge" is shown in the following.

```
typedef struct edge {
    int u, v;
    float weight;
} edge;
```

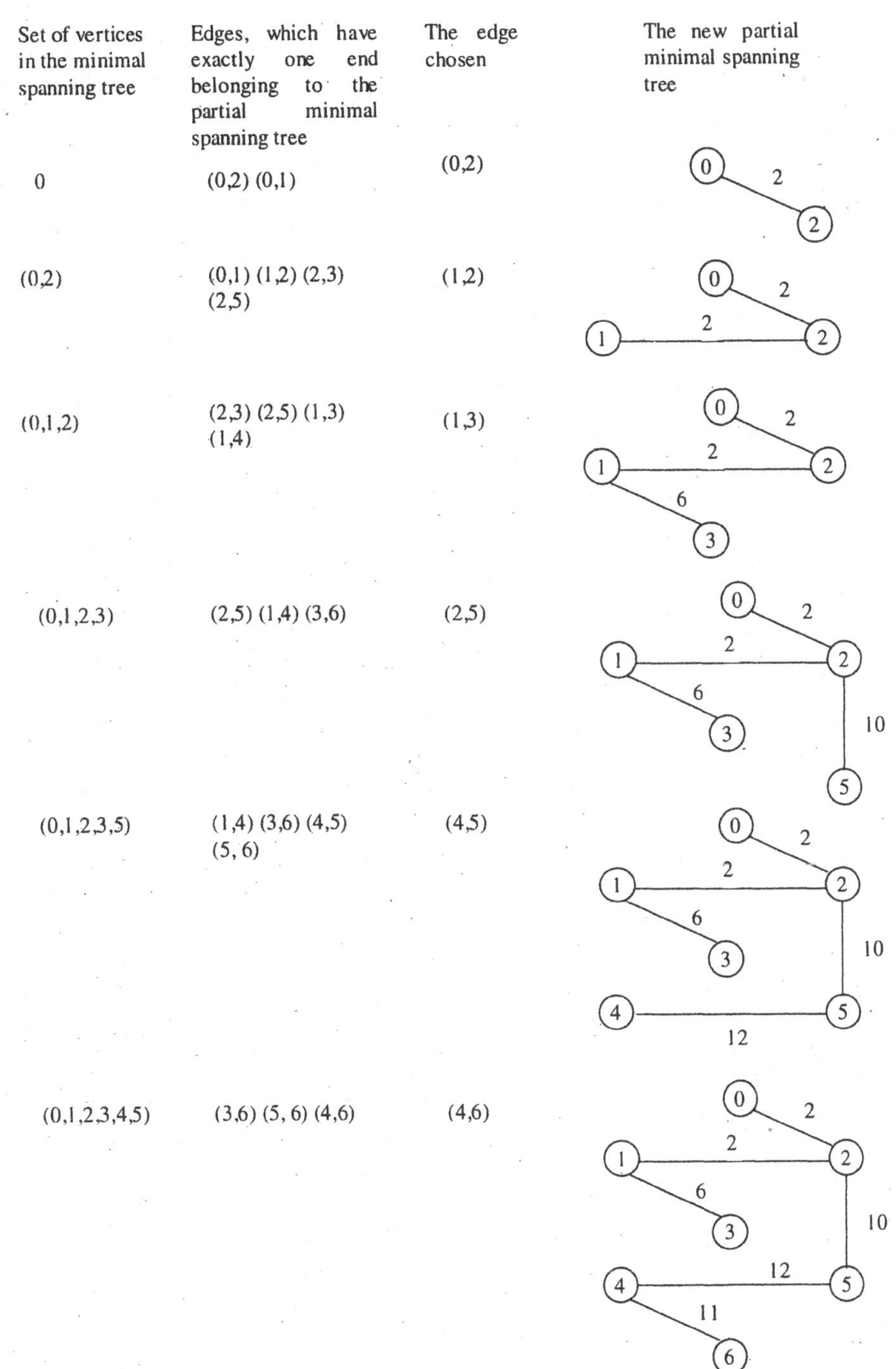

Set of vertices in the minimal spanning tree	Edges, which have exactly one end belonging to the partial minimal spanning tree	The edge chosen	The new partial minimal spanning tree
0	(0,2) (0,1)	(0,2)	
(0,2)	(0,1) (1,2) (2,3) (2,5)	(1,2)	
(0,1,2)	(2,3) (2,5) (1,3) (1,4)	(1,3)	
(0,1,2,3)	(2,5) (1,4) (3,6)	(2,5)	
(0,1,2,3,5)	(1,4) (3,6) (4,5) (5, 6)	(4,5)	
(0,1,2,3,4,5)	(3,6) (5, 6) (4,6)	(4,6)	

Figure 10.28 Illustration of Prim's algorithm by applying it to the graph of Figure 10.6.

For each vertex "i", Edge[i] is initialized as follows. Edge[i].u is set to "0"; Edge[i].v is set to "i". Edge[i].weight is set to A[0][i] where "A" is the adjacency matrix representation of the graph. In each iteration, the minimum of Edge[i] is found for all "i" such that "i" does not belong to "U". If Edge[min] is the minimum so obtained then a new "edge" (Edge[min].u, min, Edge[min].weight) is added to "T" and "min" is added to "U". Edge[i] is modified for all "i" not belonging to "U". If A[min][i] is less than Edge[i].weight then Edge[i].u becomes "min" and Edge[i].weight becomes A[min][i]. The algorithm is presented next.

```
void Prim (int A[][100], int n, edge T[])
{
    edge Edge[100];
    int i, u, v, k;
    int U[100];
    int count, j, min, minwt;

    count = 0;
    U[0] = 0;
    for ( i = 0; i < n; i++)
    {
            Edge[i].u = 0;
            Edge[i].v = i;
            Edge[i].weight = A[0][i];
    }
    for ( i = 0; i < n; i++)
    {
            min = 1;
            minwt = MAX_WT;            /* MAX_WT is a large number */
            for (j = 0; j < n; j++)
            {
                    for (k = 0; k < count + 1; k++)
                            if (U[k] == j)
                                    break;
                    if (k < count + 1)
                            continue;
                    if (Edge[j].weight < minwt)
```

```
            {
                min = j;
                minwt = Edge[j].weight
            }
        }
        T[count].u = Edge[min].u;
        T[count].v = min;
        T[count].weight = Edge[min].weight;
        count++;
        U[count] = min;
        for (j = 0; j < n; j++)
        {
            for (k = 0; k < count + 1; k++)
                if (U[k] == j)
                    break;
            if (k < count + 1)
                continue;
            if (Edge[j].weight > A[min][j])
            {
                Edge[j].u = min;
                Edge[j].weight = A[min][j];
            }
        }
    }
}
```

Prim's algorithm contains a nested loop having two "for" loops each of which has a complexity of O(n). Thus, the complexity of Prim's algorithm is $O(n^2)$ for a graph having "n" vertices. Note that the two algorithms described in this section for finding a minimal spanning tree may produce different minimal spanning trees.

10.7 Points to be remembered

- This chapter introduces graphs as more general data structure than trees in the sense that graphs are able to represent many to many relations among objects while trees can only express one to many relations among objects.

- A graph "G" consists of a set of vertices "V" and a set of edges "E". The vertices may be identified by integers "0", "1", ..., (n-1). "E" is a subset of the cartesian product of VXV. If the elements of "E" are unordered then the graph is undirected and if the elements of "E" are ordered then the graph is directed. Degree of a vertex in an undirected graph is the number of edges incident on that vertex. For a directed graph, in-degree and out-degree of a vertex is the number of edges coming in or going out of that vertex.
- A sequence of vertices connected by edges is called a path in a graph. If there is a path between every pair of vertices in a graph then the graph is called connected; otherwise, the graph is not connected. If there is an edge between every pair of vertices in a graph then the graph is called strongly connected.
- In many applications, edges are to be assigned costs or weights. Such graphs are known as weighted graphs.
- A tree may be defined as a connected graph of "n" vertices having (n-1) edges. Each connected graph has a number of sub-graphs which are trees with "n" vertices. These sub-graphs are called spanning trees. In case of a weighted graph, a spanning tree is called minimal spanning tree if the sum of weights of all edges in that tree is the minimum among that of all spanning trees.
- There are various ways of representing a graph in a computer. Adjacency matrix of a graph is a matrix representation where an element a_{ij} is one if and only if there is an edge from the vertex "i" to the vertex "j". Adjacency list of a graph is a linked list representation. In this case, there is a linked list of all adjacent vertices for every vertex in that graph. While adjacency matrix representation is suitable for dense graphs, adjacency list representation is suitable for graphs with large number of vertices and fewer edges.
- Like trees, traversal of a graph is a fundamental operation. There are two popular techniques for graph traversal: breadth first and depth first. Depth first traversal starts from a vertex and explores new vertices by initiating the same traversal from any one of the unvisited vertices adjacent to the start-vertex. The algorithm is inherently recursive. A depth first traversal of a connected undirected graph yields a spanning tree of the graph. If the graph is not connected then depth first traversal produces a forest. But for a directed graph, depth first traversal may produce a forest even if the graph is connected. Preorder traversal of a tree is a kind of its depth first traversal.
- Breadth first traversal of a graph starts at a vertex and visits all unvisited vertices adjacent to the start-vertex. Then, breadth first traversal restarts from any of the vertices adjacent to the start vertex. The breadth first traversal of a tree is similar to traversing the tree level by level.
- Depth first traversal has many important applications such as finding the components of a graph, detecting cycles in an undirected graph, determining whether a graph is bi-connected etc.

- Another important class of problem is single source shortest path problem and all pair shortest path problem. One popular algorithm for solving single source shortest path is due to Dijkstra. This algorithm is called greedy algorithm. It partitions the set of vertices "V" in to two sets "U" and (V-U). It is assumed that the shortest path to each vertex in "U" is known. The algorithm finds out a vertex from (V-U) such that the shorest distance of that vertex through some vertex in "U" is the smallest. Such a vertex from (V-U) is added to "U".
- Dijkstra's algorithm can be applied repeatedly to solve the all pair shortest path problem. But, there is a much simpler approach which computes A^0, A^1, A^2, ..., A^n where "A" is the adjacency matrix representation of a graph.
- Two famous algorithms to compute a minimal spanning tree of a weighted graph are due to Kruskal and Prim. Kruskal's algorithm works on a list of edges sorted in non decreasing order of their weights. It starts with a forest of "n" trees with each tree containing one vertex. The algorithm goes on adding the next minimum cost edge from the list without introducing a cycle in a forest so formed. The intermediate structure at different steps of the algorithm is a forest.
- Prim's algorithm starts with a vertex and goes on adding edges to an already formed partial minimal spanning tree. The edge to be added is a minimum cost edge which has exactly one end belonging to the already formed minimal spanning tree.

Exercises

1. Show that the sum of degrees of all vertices in an undirected graph is twice the number of edges.
2. Show that the number of vertices of odd degree in a finite graph is even.
3. How many edges are contained in a complete graph of "n" vertices?
4. Show that the number of spanning trees in a complete graph of "n" vertices is $2^{n-1} - 1$.
5. Prove that the edges explored by a breadth first or depth first traversal of a connected graph form a tree.
6. Show that the following definitions of a tree are equivalent:
   (a) Any connected graph with "n" vertices and (n-1) edges is a tree.
   (b) If, in a graph, there is one and only one path between every pair of vertices then the graph is a tree.
   (c) A graph is a tree if it is minimally connected.
   (d) A connected graph without any cycle is a tree.
   (e) A graph having "n" vertices, (n-1) edges and no cycle is a tree.
7. Explain how existence of a cycle in an undirected graph may be detected by traversing the graph in a depth first manner.

8. Write a "C" function to compute the in-degree and out-degree of a vertex of a directed graph when the graph is represented by
   (a) an adjacency matrix;
   (b) an adjacency list.
9. Write a "C" function to generate the incidence matrix of a graph from its adjacency matrix.
10. Write a "C" function to create a list of edges of a weighted graph in non-decreasing order of their weights if the graph is represented by
    (a) an adjacency matrix;
    (b) an adjacency list.
11. Write a "C" function that accepts the edges as tuples (start-vertex, end-vertex) from the input and creates an adjacency multi-list representation of a graph. Assume that the vertices are represented by integers from "0" to (n-1) for a graph having "n" vertices.
12. Give an example of a connected directed graph so that a depth first traversal of that graph yields a forest and not a spanning tree of the graph.
13. Rewrite the algorithms "BFSearch" and "DFSearch" so that it works on adjacency matrix representation of graphs.
14. Write a "C" function to find the shortest paths to all vertices from a given vertex using Dantzig's method.
15. Modify the function "allPairShortestDistance" so that it returns the shortest paths (not the shortest distances) between every pair of vertices in a graph. What is the time and space complexity of your function?
16. Write a "C" function to find out whether there is a path between any two vertices in a graph (i.e. to compute the transitive closure matrix of a graph).
17. Compute T^k for $k = 0, 1, 2, \ldots, n$ of the graph shown in Figure 10.25 and thus compute the transitive closure matrix of that graph.
18. Prove the following:

    Any sub-path from a vertex "m" to another vertex "n" of a shortest path from a vertex "i" to the vertex "j" must itself be a shortest path from the vertex "m" to the vertex "n".
19. Write a "C" function to delete an existing edge from a graph represented by an adjacency list.
20. Construct a weighted graph for which the minimal spanning trees produced by Kruskal's algorithm and Prim's algorithm are different.
21. Modify Kruskal's algorithm by organizing the edges of a graph as a heap as mentioned in this chapter. Also, write the functions to add an edge to and to remove an edge from the heap.

Appendix – A

In this appendix, a large number of objective type questions are given. Most of these questions have appeared in the paper "Data structure through 'C' language" in the "DOEACC" 'A' level examination in last several years. At the end of this appendix, the answers to these questions have also been provided.

1. Each question below gives a MULTIPLE CHOICE of answers. Find the most appropriate one.

1.1 f(n) is of the order of g(n) if there exist positive integers "a" and "b" such that

(a) f(n) <= a * g(n) for all n >= b

(b) f(n) <= a * g(n) for all n <= b

(c) g(n) = a * f(n) for all n >= b

(d) none of these.

1.2 A binary tree of depth "d" is an almost complete binary tree if –

(a) Each leaf in the tree is either at level "d" or at level (d-1)

(b) For any node "n" in the tree with a right descendent at level "d", all the left descendents of "n" that are leaves, are also at level "d".

(c) Both (a) & (b)

(d) none of these.

1.3 Let "q" be the queue of integers defined as follows :

```
# define MAXQ 500
struct queue {
        int items [MAXQ];
        int front, rear;
}q;
```

To insert an element in the queue, we may write operation

(a) ++q.items[q.rear] = x;

(b) q.items[q.rear]++ = x;

(c) q.items[++q.rear] = x;

(d) none of these.

1.4 Suppose that stack data structure is implemented with POP and PUSH operations along with "clearstack" and "emptystack" functions. Consider the following pseudocode, where "test" takes any integer and returns true or false.

```
clearstack (stack);
for (i =1;i <= 3;i++)
{
    if (test(i))
            putc(i);
    else
            push(stack,i);
}
while (!emptystack(stack))
{
    pop(stack,i) ;
    putc(i) ;
}
```

Which of below is not the possible output:

(a) 1 2 3

(b) 2 1 3

(c) 2 3 1

(d) none of these

1.5 Running out of memory may occur due to:

(a) non-recursive function call

(b) recursive function call

(c) because of use of more global variables

(d) none of these.

1.6 A linear collection of data elements where the linear node is given by means of pointer is called :

(a) linked list

(b) node list

(c) primitive list

(d) none of these

1.7 "p" is a pointer to the structure. A member "mem" of that structure is referenced by

(a) *p.mem

(b) (*p).mem

(c) *(p.mem)

(d) none of the above

1.8 Adjacency matrix for a digraph is

(a) unitmatrix

(b) symmetric

(c) asymmetric matrix

(d) none of the above

1.9 Which one is not correct?

(a) Pointers are used for dynamically allocated memory.

(b) Dynamic memory allocation is preferred when storage requirement is not predictable.

(c) Data access in dynamically allocated storage is faster than static allocated storage.

(d) none of these.

1.10 Which is the most appropriate?

(a) int * matrix;...;free(void *)matrix;

(b) int * matrix;...;free(matrix);

(c) int *matrix;...;if(matrix != null) free(void *)matrix;

(d) none of the above.

2. Indicate whether the following statements are TRUE or FALSE.

2.1 Heap sort is more efficient for small size of file.

2.2 In the transposition method a successfully retrieved record is interchanged with the record that immediately precedes it.

2.3 The space requirement for the quick sort method depends on the number of nested recursive calls or the size of the stack.

2.4 An ascending priority queue is a collection of items where items can be inserted arbitrarily.

2.5 One of the major drawbacks of the B-Tree is the difficulty of traversing the keys sequentially.

2.6 All primitive recursive functions can be solved iteratively.

2.7 Breadth-first search algorithm can only be used for undirected graph.

2.8 De-referencing operator * has the same effect when it is applied to a pointer, a structure or a union.

2.9 The average-case timing analysis is generally more difficult than the worst-case timing analysis.

2.10 In minimal spanning tree of the graph, we also get the shortest path between two nodes.

3. Each statement below has a BLANK space. Find the most appropriate one from the list below to fill up the blank.

a. many-to-many	b. pointer	c. file structure
d. faster	e. one-to-many	f. slower
g. doubly linked list	h. storage structure	i. list header
j. Clustering	k. Compaction	l. header node
m. stack	n. abstract data type	o. non-recursive
p. recursive	q. queue	r. global
s. band		

3.1 It is desirable to keep an extra node at the front of a list, which does not represent an item in the list, is called_________

3.2 Matrices in which the non-zero entries tend to cluster around the middle of each row are called ________ matrix.

3.3 A useful tool for specifying the logical properties of a data type is the___________

3.4 In _________, blocks of data are moved from one part of the memory to another for re-claiming sorage.

3.5 Recursion often provides elegant solution to programming task but___________ function chew up a lot of memory.

3.6 In______ data structure insertion and deletion takes place at the same end.

3.7 ____________ data structure is used to implement dynamic storage management.

3.8 Representation of data structure in memory is known as__________

3.9 Best fit approach is generally_____________ than first fit approach for memory allocation.

3.10 A graph represents______________ relationship between nodes.

4. MATCH words and phrases in Column X with the nearest in meaning of words and phrases in Column Y.

	X	Y
4.1	(n – 1) * (n – 1)	a. Bubble sort
4.2	Partition exchange sort	b. Quick sort
4.3	Extension of indexed sequential file	c. B plus tree
4.4	Sequential representation of a binary tree	d. circular list
4.5	Sequence	e. All pointers are within the array bounds
4.6	Forest	f. Ordered set of elements
4.7	Process of acquiring storage for data items at run time	g. Radix sort
4.8	To reference different but similar objects	h. dynamic allocation
4.9	Used in sparse matrix	i. Pointer
4.10	Shortest path algorithm/adjacency matrix	j. Ordered set of ordered trees
		k. dope vector
		l. graph
		m. stack allocation

5. Indicate the most appropriate answer:

5.1 If the addresses of A[1,1] and A[2,1] are 1000 and 1010 respectively and each element occupies 2 bytes then the array has been stored in________ order.

a. Row major

b. Column major

c. Compiler dependent

d. None of the above

5.2 Which of the following cannot be performed recursively?

a. Binary Search

b. Quick Sort

c. Depth First Search

d. None of the above

5.3 Which of the following data structure may give overflow error, even though the current number of elements in it, is less than its size.

a. simple queue

b. circular queue

c. stack

d. none of the above

5.4 An adjacency matrix representation of a graph cannot contain information of

a. Nodes

b. Edges

c. Direction of edges

d. Parallel edges

5.5 In the quick sort method, a desirable choice for the partitioning elements will be

a. first element of the list

b. last element of the list

c. median of the list

d. none of the above

5.6 Out of the following sort methods which method is optimum in the worst case?

a. Selection sort

b. Quick sort

c. Merge sort

d. None of the above

5.7 Quick sort is also known as

a. Merge sort

b. Heap sort

c. Bubble sort

d. None of the above

5.8 In linked list representation, a node contains at least

a. node address field, data field

b. node number, data field

c. next address field, information field

d. none of the above

5.9 Which of the following types of expressions does not require precedence rules for evaluation?

a. Fully parenthesized infix expression

b. Prefix expression

c. Partially parenthesized infix expression

d. More than one of the above

5.10 Consider the following definition of a structure.

```
struct NODE
{
    int data;
    struct NODE *lptr, *rptr;
};
```

Which of the following data structure cannot have a node of the above type NODE?

a. binary tree

b. circular queue

c. linked list

d. none of the above

6. Indicate whether the following statements are TRUE or FALSE.

6.1 Binary search performs efficiently on a linked list.

6.2 A symbol table can be constructed using binary tree.

6.3 In an empty threaded binary tree the right link of the head is a thread to itself.

6.4 Any general tree can be converted to a binary tree.

6.5 For the strings S1 and S2, S1 > S2 if length (S1) > length (S2).

6.6 The method of interpreting a bit pattern is called a data type.

6.7 The number of total elements in a queue is fixed.

6.8 O(N) (linear time) is better than O(1) (constant time).

6.9 In a circular header list, last node points back to the header node.

6.10 A pre-order and post-order traversal sequence uniquely defines a tree.

7.0 MATCH words and phrases in Column X with the nearest in meaning of words and phrases in Column Y.

X	Y
7.1 Division of array	a. Stack
7.2 Data structure as defined at logical level	b. String manipulation language
7.3 Dynamic data structure	c. Runtime memory allocation
7.4 Dynamic memory allocation	d. Isolated vertex
7.5 Static memory allocation	e. Binary Search
7.6 B-tree of order n	f. An n – (n-1)-tree
7.7 A vertex with degree 1	g. Compile time memory allocation
7.8 Vertex with no incident edges	h. Tree
7.9 SNOBOL	i. Abstract data type
7.10 Threaded	j. Pendant vertex
	k. An n – (n+1) tree
	l. Queue
	m. Sequential search

8. Each statement below has a BLANK space. Find the most appropriate one from the list below to fill up the blank.

a. one by one
b. BFS
c. 12
d. root
e. FIFO
f. 32
g. O (n)
h. n – 1
i. $\log_2 n$
j. stack
k. O (n)
l. floor ($\log_2 n$) + 1
m. n
n. floor ($\log_2(n + 1)$)

8.1 A line of cars waiting at a toll booth is an example of__________ concept.

8.2 Copying all or part of a linked list is done by taking first null list and inserting elements_______ .

8.3 Time complexity of inserting an element to a heap of "n" elements is of the order of ___________.

8.4 A B-tree of order 24 contains at least________ keys in non-root node.

8.5 A heap is the tree structure where largest/smallest element is available at the_______.

8.6 The depth of a complete binary tree with "n" nodes is _________.

8.7 A string can be reversed using a __________ of characters.

8.8 The time requirement for computing 1 + 2 + 3 + ... + n without using summation formula is__________.

8.9 _________ can be used to find the shortest distance between given two nodes in a graph.

8.10 A minimal spanning tree of a graph with n nodes will have_________ nodes.

9. Each question below gives a MULTIPLE CHOICE of answers. Fine out the most appropriate one.

9.1 Consider the following recursive "C" function to compute the n-th term in the Fibonacci sequence which is denoted by F(n).

```
int Fib (int n)
{
        if (n == 0)
                return 0;
        else if (n == 1)
                return 1;
        else return (Fib (n – 1) + Fib (n –2);
}
```

Number of additions performed by Fib (n) is :

a) F (n +1)

b) F (n +1) – 1

c) 2n

d) None of the above

9.2 A matrix, "a", is called lower triangular if and only if for all j > i, $a_{i,j}$ = 0. If such a matrix is to be sorted in a one dimensional array, A, then, $a_{i,j}$ could be mapped to the following index of A:

a) ½*i (i+1) + j

b) i + j

c) i (i+1) + j

d) None of the above

9.3 The prefix expression for the following infix expression is:

a* (b+c) / e-f

a) /*a+bc-ef

b) -/*+abcef

c) -/*a+bcef

d) None of the above

9.4 There could be two representations of a circular linked list. In the first representation the list is identified by a pointer pointing to the beginning of the list as shown below.

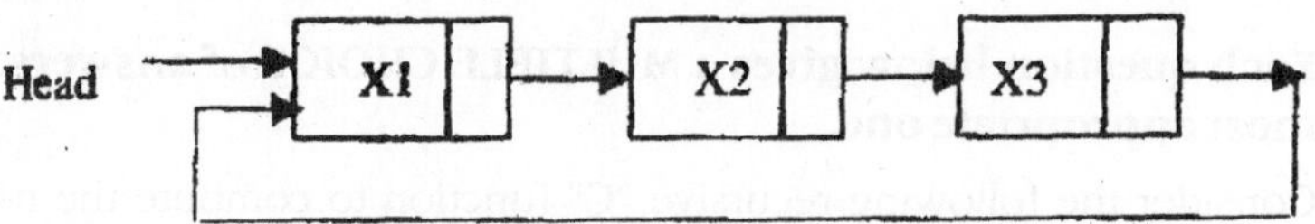

In the second representation, the list is identified by a pointer pointing to the end of the list as shown below.

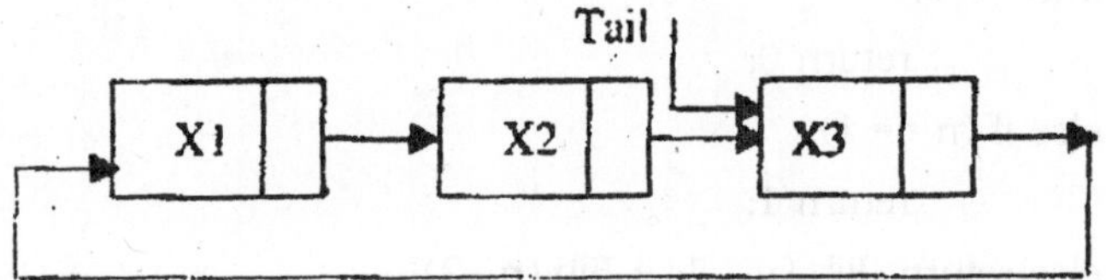

Which of the following statements is NOT true about these two representations?

a) In the first representation, insertion at the front (i.e., before the node X1) requires traversing the list.

b) In the first representation, insertion at the rear (i.e., after the node X3) requires traversing the list.

c) In the second representation, insertion only at the front (and not at the rear) does not require traversing the list.

d) In the second representation, insertion at any end (front or rear) does not require traversing the list.

9.5 In a binary tree, the number of terminal or leaf nodes is 10. The number of nodes with two children is:

(a) 9

(b) 11

(c) 15

(d) None of the above

9.6 Number of all possible binary trees with 4 nodes is:

(a) 14

(b) 34

(c) 24

(d) None of the above

9.7 The time complexity of the Depth First Search algorithm to traverse a graph of "n" vertices and "e" edges is:

(a) O (n) if the graph is represented by adjacency matrix.

(b) O (n) if the graph is represented by adjacency list.

(c) O (e) if the graph is represented by adjacency list.

(d) None of the above.

9.8 If the space occupied by two null-terminated strings "s1" and "s2" in "C" are respectively "m" and "n", the space occupied by the string obtained by concatenating "s1" and "s2" is always

(a) less than m+n

(b) equal to m+n

(c) greater than m+n

(d) none of the above

9.9 Number of nodes in a complete binary tree of depth k is:

(a) 2k

(b) 2^k

(c) 2^k -1

(d) None of the above

9.10 Which of the following is a hash function?

(a) Quadratic Probing

(b) Chaining

(c) Open addressing

(d) Folding

10. Indicate whether the following statements are TRUE or FALSE.

10.1 Merge sort is a stable sorting algorithm.

10.2 Binary tree is a tree.

10.3 If a stack is implemented as a linked list then during PUSH operation there is no chance of any overflow as long as the system has enough space for allocating a node for the stack.

10.4 A unique binary tree can be reconstructed from its pre-order and post-order traversal information.

10.5 "Linear probing" as a collection resolution technique in hashing usually leads to clustering of data.

10.6 In an undirected graph of "n" vertices and "e" edges, the sum of degrees of all vertices is 2e.

10.7 Knuth-Morris-Pratt algorithm for searching a string for a pattern scans the string from right to left.

10.8 Radix sort technique utilises "stack" data structure.

10.9 Insertion in and deletion from an array does not involve physical movement of elements of the arrays.

10.10 A tree can be implemented using arrays.

11. MATCH words and phrases in Column X with the nearest in meaning of words and phrases in Column Y.

X	Y
11.1 Collision Resolution	a. AVL Trees
11.2 External Sorting	b. k-way Merge sort
11.3 Binary Search	c. Radix sort
11.4 Height Balanced Trees	d. Breadth First Search
11.5 First In First Out	e. Stack
11.6 Static Tree Table	f. Near complete Binary Tree
11.7 Graph Representation	g. Depth First Search
11.8 Heap	h. Queue
11.9 Data Structure for backtracking	i. Adjacency Multi-list
11.10 Complexity measurement	j. Optimum Binary Search Tree
	k. Divide and Conquer
	l. Rehashing
	m. Theta Notation
	n. Memory
	o. Deque

12. Each statement below has a BLANK space. Find the most appropriate one from the list below to fill up the blank.

a. stack	b. queue	c. n*(n+1)/2
d. n	e. insertion	f. less than
g. 4*(n-1)	h. n-1	i. n/2
j. n*(n-1)/2	k. n*(n+1)	l. deque
m. $\log_2 n$	n. n/3	o. 2*n+1
p. 2*n	q. greater than	r. 4*n-3

s. greater than or equal to

12.1 The worst case time complexity to insert an element in a heap is of the order of _______.

12.2 To store a diagonal square matrix (size of the matrix is: nXn) in a one dimensional array, the minimum size of the array has to be ______.

12.3 If E and I denote the external and internal path lengths of a binary tree respectively then E – I is ______.

12.4 In a completely connected undirected graph of n vertices (where each vertex is connected with every other vertex) the number of edges is _____.

12.5 A singly linked list with a pointer pointing to the beginning of a list can be conveniently used to implement a ______ data structure.

12.6 Space required to store an adjacency matrix is ________ that to store the adjacency list of a dense graph.

12.7 It is required to extract the bottom element of a stack by using another stack. If the original stack contains "n" elements then ______ number of push and pop operations are required to perform this task so that the original stack without the last element remains the same.

12.8 In a stack number of PUSH operations must be _____ number of valid POP operations.

12.9 Minimum number of runs (sorted sub-arrays) after the first pass of merge sort algorithm applied to a list of "n" elements is __________.

12.10 A tree is a cycle free undirected graph with ________ edges.

13. Each question below gives a MULTIPLE CHOICE of answers. Find the most appropriate one.

13.1 Maximum possible height of an AVL Tree with 7 nodes is :

(a) 3

(b) 4

(c) 5

(d) none of the above

13.2 If the inorder and preorder traversal of a binary tree are D, B, F, E, G, H, A, C and A, B, D, E, F, G, H, C respectively then, the postorder traversal of that tree is:

(a) D, F, G, A, B, C, H, E

(b) F, H, D, G, E, B, C, A

(c) C, G, H, F, E, D, B, A

(d) D, F, H, G, E, B, C, A

13.3 Suppose that an undirected graph G is represented by an adjacency matrix A. Let B denote the matrix AXAXAXAXA. Which of the following is true if an element B (i, j) is non-zero?

(a) Vertex j can be reached from vertex i in exactly 5 steps.

(b) Vertex j can be reached from vertex i in atmost 5 steps.

(c) Vertex j cannot be reached from vertex i.

(d) None of the above.

13.4 "n" elements of a queue are to be reversed using another queue. The number of "ADD" and "REMOVE" operations required to do so is:

(a) 2*n

(b) 4*n

(c) n

(d) The task cannot be accomplished.

13.5 The heap (represented by an array) constructed from the list of numbers 30, 10, 80, 60, 15, 55, 17 is:

(a) 60, 80, 55, 30, 10, 17, 15

(b) 80, 55, 60, 15, 10, 30, 17

(c) 80, 60, 30, 17, 55, 15, 10

(d) None of the above

13.6 Consider the following statements:

I. An expression in prefix form is the reverse of the same expression in postfix form.

II. An expression in prefix form is the reverse of the same expression in postfix form provided all operators are binary and commutative.

III. An expression in prefix form is the reverse of the same expression in postfix form if the operators are +, * and /.

Which of the following is TRUE?

(a) All three are correct.

(b) None of the statements is correct.

(c) II is correct but I and III are incorrect.

(d) II and III are correct but I is incorrect.

13.7 Which of the following is NOT correct?

(a) $f(n) = O(f(n))$

(b) $c^*f(n) = O(f(n))$ for a constant c

(c) $O(f(n) + g(n)) = f(n) + O(g(n))$

(d) $O(f(n)^2) = O(f(n))^2$

13.8 Suppose that a linear list of "n" elements is represented by a circular linked list where "head" points to the last element of the list. If two lists of sizes "m" and "n" are represented by such circular linked lists then, complexity of concatenating them is not more than

(a) $O(m+n)$

(b) $O(1)$

(c) $O(n)$

(d) None of the above

13.9 Time complexity of insertion sort algorithm in the best case is:

(a) $O(n)$

(b) $O(n\log_2 n)$

(c) $O(n^2)$

(d) None of the above

13.10 The smallest number of keys that will force a B-Tree of order 3 to have a height 3 is:

(a) 12

(b) 10

(c) 7

(d) None of the above

14. Indicate whether the following statements are TRUE or FALSE

14.1 A B-Tree is always a binary tree.

14.2 Sequence of nodes traversed using Breadth First Traversal technique is unique for a given graph.

14.3 The adjacency matrix corresponding to a graph consisting of "n" nodes but no edges is a unit matrix.

14.4 All leaves in a heap are in adjacent levels.

14.5 A tree is also a graph.

14.6 Recursion cannot be removed without using a stack.

14.7 Number of pointers in a threaded binary tree is more than the number of pointers of the corresponding binary tree.

14.8 It is advantageous to implement a stack using a doubly connected linked list instead of using a singly connected linked list.

14.9 Deletion of a node, x, with exactly one child, T, in a Binary Search Tree may be performed by deleting x and making T the child of the parent of x.

14.10 Quick sort will be more efficient, if the table to be sorted is initially almost sorted.

15. MATCH words and phrases in Column X with the nearest in meaning of words and phrases in Column Y.

X		Y
15.1 Most Sparse AVL Tree	(a)	Binary Tree
15.2 B-Tree of order 2	(b)	Chaining
15.3 Open Addressing	(c)	Finite Automata
15.4 Number of binary trees with n nodes	(d)	Fibonacci Tree
15.5 Pattern Matching	(e)	Quick Sort
15.6 Circular List with "head" pointing to the last node.	(f)	Stack
15.7 Stable Sorting Algorithm	(g)	Adjacency List
15.8 Linear data structure where insertions and deletions are performed only at one end and the same end		
15.9 Suitable data structur or efficiently computing Adjac ices of a given vertex.	(h)	Merge Sort
15.10 Order notatio	(i)	Queue
	(j)	Quadratic Probe
	(k)	2^n

(l)	Number of permutations of 1 to n obtainable using a stack.
(m)	Adjacency matrix
(n)	Complete Binary Tree
(o)	n^2
(p)	Complexity Measurement
(q)	Time Calculation

16. Each group of statements below has a BLANK space. Choose the most appropriate words or phrases from the list below to fill up the blank

a. 2*d +1	b. 2*n	c. 2*n –1	d. n^2
e. n + 2*e	f. 3	g. $\lfloor n/2 \rfloor$	h. E/(n-1)
i. n	j. E/(n+1)	k. n+e	l. 2*d
m. log n	n. 4*n -1	o. 4*n	p. 2
q. 1	r. n + $\log_2 n$	s. n + $\lfloor \log_2 n \rfloor - 2$	

16.1 Total number of nodes required to represent an undirected graph with "n" nodes and "e" edges using adjacency list representation is ________.

16.2 Let a binary tree be such that there is exactly one leaf node in each level of the tree (except at level 1 which is the root). The number of nodes in such a tree of depth "d" is ________.

16.3 It is required to access the $(n/2^k)$-th elements of a singly connected linked list for k = 0 to $\log_2 n$ in the given order. Number of nodes to be traversed for this purpose is ______. Assume that "n" is a power of 2 for simplicity.

16.4 Number of "ADD" and "REMOVE" operations required to access n/2-th element of a queue of "n" elements so that the original queue remains the same after the access is ______. You may take help of another queue.

16.5 Number of positions where the second largest element of a heap may be stored is __________.

16.6 Complexity of an algorithm to print all "n" nodes of an AVL Tree in sorted manner is lower-bounded by order of ________.

16.7 If "E" is the total external length of a bi[illegible] tree with "n" nodes then average number of comparisons for unsuccessfu[illegible]ch is ________.

16.8 Minimum number of comparisons require[illegible] compute the largest and second largest element in an array is ________.

16.9 Worst case time complexity to search for an element in an AVL Tree is _______.

16.10 Minimum number of comparisons that may be required to search a key in a binary search tree is ________.

17. Each question below gives a MULTIPLE CHOICE of answers. Find the most appropriate one.

17.1 The following sequence of operations is performed on a stack:

push(1), push(2), pop, push(1), push(2), pop, pop, pop, push(2), pop.

The sequence of popped out values are

(a) 2, 2, 1, 2, 1

(b) 2, 2, 1, 1, 2

(c) 2, 1, 2, 2, 1

(d) 2, 1, 2, 2, 2

17.2 Which of the following expressions accesses the (i, j)th entry of a mXn matrix stored in column major form?

(a) n*(i-1) + j

(b) m*(j-1) + i

(c) m*(n-j) +j

(d) n*(m-i) +j

17.3 Sparse matrices have

(a) many zeroes entries

(b) many non numeric entries

(c) higher dimension

(d) none of these

17.4 A Stack cannot be used to

(a) evaluate an arithmetic expression in postfix form

(b) implement recursion

(c) convert infix form to postfix form of an expression

(d) allocate resources by operating system

17.5 Which of the following is not a requirement for good hashing functions?

(a) avoid collision

(b) reduce the storage space

(c) make faster retrieval

(d) none of the above

17.6 The number of swappings needed to sort the numbers 8, 22, 7, 9, 31, 19, 5, 13 in ascending order using bubble sort is

(a) 11

(b) 12

(c) 13

(d) 14

17.7 Given 2 sorted lists of size "m" and "n" respectively. The number of comparisons needed in the worst case by merge sort will be

(a) m*n

(b) Max (m, n)

(c) Min (m, n)

(d) m+n-1

17.8 Which of the following traversal techniques lists the nodes of binary search tree in ascending order?

(a) postorder

(b) inorder

(c) preorder

(d) none of these

17.9 A completely full binary tree with 10 leaves

(a) cannot have more than 19 nodes

(b) has exactly 19 nodes

(c) has exactly 17 nodes

(d) cannot have more than 17 nodes

17.10 The running time T(n) where "n" is the input size of recursive algorithm is given as follows.

$$T(n) = c + T(n-1), \quad \text{if } n > 1$$
$$= d, \quad \text{if } n \leq 1$$

The order of the algorithm is

(a) n^2

(b) n

(c) n^3

(d) n^n

18. Indicate whether the following statements are TRUE or FALSE.

18.1 Stack is useful for implementing breadth first search.

18.2 The process of accessing data stored in a tape is similar to manipulating data on a queue.

18.3 Insertion of a new element in a priority queue always occurs at the rear of the queue, irrespective of its priority.

18.4 Pointers are used for dynamically allocated memory.

18.5 Sorting is useful for responding to queries easily.

18.6 A binary tree "T" has "n" leaf nodes. The number of nodes of degree 2 in T is n-1.

18.7 A graph represents many to many relationship between nodes.

18.8 A sorting algorithm that guarantees that records with the same primary key occurs in the same order in the sorted lists as in the original unsorted list is said to be linear.

18.9 The average sequential successful search time for a sequential file having "n" records is (n+1)/2.

18.10 An algorithm is made up of 2 modules M1 and M2. If order of M1 is f(n) and M2 is g(n) then the order of the algorithm is f(n) + g(n).

19. MATCH words and phrases in Column X with the nearest in meaning of words and phrases in Column Y.

X	Y
19.1 First in last out	a. recursion
19.2 Pointer	b. depth-first
19.3 Merge sort	c. Adjacency matrix
19.4 Preorder Traversal	d. queue
19.5 Complexity	e. divide and conquer
19.6 first-fit	f. Dynamic environment
19.7 Compaction	g. one's complement
19.8 Unique representation for Zero	h. memory management
19.9 Sorted file	i. stack
19.10 graph	j. sparse matrix
	k. breadth-first
	l. combining free blocks of memory

m. two's complement

n. Algorithm

o. efficient search

20. Each statement below has a BLANK space. Choose the most appropriate words or phrases from the list below.

a. insertion sort	b. merge sort	c. radix sort	d. stack
e. queue	f. insertion	g. compaction	
h. fragmentation	i. random access	j. hash function	
k. sequential access	l. $\log_2 n$	m. $\log_2 n + 1$	
n. linked list	o. n	p. ordered set	
q. Folding	r. Mid-square		

20.1 List is an _____ of elements.

20.2 Conversion of infix arithmetic expression to postfix expression requires the use of _____.

20.3 A tree can be traversed level wise using _______.

20.4 Access to an array element is an example of _______.

20.5 The depth of complete binary tree with "n" nodes is _______.

20.6 Linked list is preferred over an array for _______ operation.

20.7 The binary search time for a sorted sequential file having "n" records is ______.

20.8 _______ is a hashing method which is performed by dividing the key into several parts and adding the parts to form a number.

20.9 The minimum number of edges in a connected cyclic graph of "n" vertices is _____.

20.10 _____ sorting can be used as an external sorting technique.

Answers

1.1	(a)	2.1	F	3.1	(i)	4.1	(a)
1.2	(c)	2.2	T	3.2	(s)	4.2	(b)
1.3	(c)	2.3	T	3.3	(n)	4.3	(c)
1.4	(b)	2.4	T	3.4	(j)	4.4	(e)
1.5	(b)	2.5	T	3.5	(p)	4.5	(f)
1.6	(a)	2.6	T	3.6	(m)	4.6	(j)
1.7	(b)	2.7	F	3.7	(g)	4.7	(h)

1.8	(c)	2.8	F	3.8	(h)	4.8	(i)
1.9	(b)	2.9	T	3.9	(f)	4.9	(d)
1.10	(c)	2.10	F	3.10	(a)	4.10	(l)
5.1	(a)	6.1	F	7.1	(e)	8.1	(e)
5.2	(d)	6.2	T	7.2	(i)	8.2	(a)
5.3	(a)	6.3	T	7.3	(h)	8.3	(i)
5.4	(d)	6.4	T	7.4	(c)	8.4	(c)
5.5	(c)	6.5	T	7.5	(g)	8.5	(d)
5.6	(c)	6.6	T	7.6	(f)	8.6	(l)
5.7	(d)	6.7	F	7.7	(j)	8.7	(j)
5.8	(c)	6.8	F	7.8	(d)	8.8	(k)
5.9	(d)	6.9	T	7.9	(b)	8.9	(b)
5.10	(b)	6.10	F	7.10	(h)	8.10	(m)
9.1	(b)	10.1	T	11.1	(l)	12.1	(m)
9.2	(a)	10.2	F	11.2	(b)	12.2	(d)
9.3	(c)	10.3	T	11.3	(k)	12.3	(p)
9.4	(c)	10.4	F	11.4	(a)	12.4	(j)
9.5	(a)	10.5	T	11.5	(h)	12.5	(a)
9.6	(a)	10.6	T	11.6	(j)	12.6	(f)
9.7	(c)	10.7	F	11.7	(i)	12.7	(r)
9.8	(a)	10.8	T	11.8	(f)	12.8	(s)
9.9	(c)	10.9	F	11.9	(e)	12.9	(i)
9.10	(d)	10.10	T	11.10	(m)	12.10	(h)
13.1	(a)	14.1	F	15.1	(d)	16.1	(e)
13.2	(d)	14.2	F	15.2	(m)	16.2	(l)
13.3	(b)	14.3	F	15.3	(a)	16.3	(b)
13.4	(d)	14.4	T	15.4	(l)	16.4	(o)
13.5	(b)	14.5	T	15.5	(c)	16.5	(p)
13.6	(c)	14.6	F	15.6	(i)	16.6	(i)
13.7	(c)	14.7	F	15.7	(h)	16.7	(j)
13.8	(c)	14.8	F	15.8	(f)	16.8	(s)
13.9	(a)	14.9	T	15.9	(m)	16.9	(m)
13.10	(c)	14.10	F	15.10	(p)	16.10	(q)

17.1	(b)	18.1	F	19.1	(i)	20.1	(p)
17.2	(b)	18.2	T	19.2	(f)	20.2	(d)
17.3	(a)	18.3	F	19.3	(e)	20.3	(e)
17.4	(d)	18.4	T	19.4	(b)	20.4	(i)
17.5	(c)	18.5	T	19.5	(n)	20.5	(m)
17.6	(d)	18.6	T	19.6	(h)	20.6	(f)
17.7	(d)	18.7	T	19.7	(l)	20.7	(l)
17.8	(b)	18.8	F	19.8	(m)	20.8	(q)
17.9	(b)	18.9	T	19.9	(o)	20.9	(o)
17.10	(b)	18.10	T	19.10	(c)	20.10	(b)

Appendix – B

B.1 Introduction

In this Appendix, two disparate topics would be discussed. The first topic, Garbage Collection, is about freeing dynamically allocated memory when not in use. In Chapter 3, generalized lists were described. Garbage collection is a sequel to generalized lists. The other topic to be discussed in this Appendix is game tree. Trees have been extensively described in Chapters 7 and 8. Game tree is an important application of general trees. Both these topics have been touched upon as these are taught in a more elaborate manner in many different courses.

B.2 Garbage Collection

Garbage collection is the process of collecting all unused nodes of a generalized list and returning them to the free pool so that the space for these nodes may become available for further use. The process of garbage collection is carried out in two logical steps. In the first step, all used nodes are marked. In the second phase, all unmarked nodes are returned to the available list. If all nodes are of equal size then the second phase becomes trivial. But, if the sizes of the nodes are different then the second phase becomes more involved. In that case, contiguous unused nodes, which are returned to the free pool should be added together to form bigger chunks of free space. This is known as compaction. In this section, algorithms for marking phase has been discussed.

B.2.1 Marking

To facilitate the process of marking, an additional "marking" bit is required to be stored in every node of the generalized list. Recall the structure of a node in a generalized list.

```
typedef struct node
{
        int flag;
        union {
```

```
            int data;
            int subList;
            } dataOrSublist;
        int next;
    }node;
```

If the "flag" of a node is set to 0 then the node contains atomic information; otherwise, the node represents a sub-list. The node structure used in the following discussion is a little different. The nodes are either atomic or they represent lists. Atomic nodes are represented by nodes with "flag" set to 0. Nodes representing lists have two links: one link, "next", to the next element in the list and the other link, "dataLink", to the content of the current element.

The modified version of the structure of each node is shown in the following.

```
    typedef struct node
    {
        int mark;
        int flag;
        union {
            int data;
            struct t_links {
                int dataLink;
                int next;
            } links;
        }atomOrList;
    }node;
```

Initially all nodes are unmarked. That is, the marking bit of each node is zero to begin with. In addition, the mark bit and the flag bit of the first node are to be set to 1 and 0 respectively. This helps in handling boundary conditions such as empty list easily. A simple marking algorithm first marks the nodes, which are directly accessible through "pointer" variables of a program. The nodes, which are reachable from the directly accessed nodes are systematically traversed. The following algorithm marks all nodes reachable from "X". The algorithm traverses all nodes, which are reachable from "X". The nodes which have not been already fully explored and currently reached are pushed in a stack of nodes. Therefore, the algorithm "SimpleMark" utilizes four functions "initializeStack", "push", "pop" and "isEmptyStack" for manipulating a stack of nodes. This algorithm is strikingly similar to any graph traversal algorithm.

```
Algorithm SimpleMark (node X)
{
        initializeStack(&s);
        push(&s, X);
        p = pop(&s);
        While (1)
        {
        while (1)
        {
                q = p.atomOrList.links.next;
                if (q.flag == 1) && (q.mark == 0))
                        push(&s, q);
                q.mark = 1;
                p = p. atomOrList.links.dataLink;
                if ((p.mark == 1) || (p.flag == 0))
                        return;
                p.mark = 1;
        }
        p.mark = 1;
        if (isEmptyStack(s))
                return;
        p = pop(&s);
    }
}
```

The computing time of this algorithm is O(m) where "m" is the number of new nodes marked by the algorithm. Thus, the algorithm is optimal as any marking algorithm must visit a node to mark it. Unfortunately, the algorithm "SimpleMark" needs a huge space to maintain the stack. But a marking algorithm would run only when the system does not have much space left. Thus, an improvement is required. The algorithm "SimpleMark" does not modify the links "next" or "dataLink" of the nodes during the execution of the algorithm. The algorithm "AdvancedMark", to be discussed, modifies the links of the nodes during its execution. However, once the algorithm halts, the link fields of the nodes are restored to their original values. The improved algorithm always traverses the nodes following the "dataLink" links before traversing the nodes reachable via "next" link. Instead of remembering the nodes reached but not further explored by means of a stack, the links of some of the nodes are changed. The algorithm "AdvancedMark" is presented next.

In this algorithm, "p" represents the current node and "t" represents the node preceding "p" in the path from "X" to "p". If "q" represents the next node for consideration then "q" is either the node "next" to "p" or "q" is the node linked through "dataLink" of "p". The node preceding "q" is the node "p". So, "p" is to be added to the path from "X". This can be done by changing the "dataLink" of "p" to denote "t" if "q" is reachable from "p" by the "dataLink" link of "p". Otherwise, "next" of "p" is modified to denote "t". All nodes from "X" to "p" should originally have their "flag" set to 1. It is also important to determine whether the "dataLink" or "next" link of "p" is modified. An extra "tag" field is introduced for this purpose. This "tag" field of "p" is also changed to signify which field (dataLink or next) of "p" is actually changed by the algorithm. Whenever, it is required to backtrack, all nodes will be traversed until "X" is reached.

```
Algorithm AdvancedMark( node X)
{
   p = X;
   t = 0;
   while (1) {
           q = p. atomOrList.links.dataLink;
           if ((q.mark == 0) && q.flag == 1)) {
                   q.mark = 1;
                   p.tag = 0;
                   p. atomOrList.links.dataLink = t;
                   t = p;
                   p = q;
           }
           else {
                   q.mark = 1;
           L1:     q = p. atomOrList.links.next;
                   if ((q.mark == 0) &&(q.flag == 1)) {
                           q.mark = 1;
                           p.tag = 1;
                           p. atomOrList.links.next = t;
                           t = p;
```

```
                    p = q;
                }
                else {
                    q.mark = 1;
                    while (t != 0) {
                        q = t;
                        if (q.tag == 0){
                            t = q. atomOrList.links.dataLink;
                            q. atomOrList.links.dataLink = p;
                            q.flag = 1;
                            p = q;
                            goto L1;
                        }
                        t = q. atomOrList.links.next;
                        q. atomOrList.links.next = p;
                        p = q;
                    }
                }
            }
        if (t == 0)
            break;
    }
}
```

The time complexity of the algorithm "AdvancedMark" is O(m) where "m" is the number of nodes marked and this algorithm does not require any extra space to maintain a stack.

B.3 Game Tree

Game tree is an interesting application of trees. Playing of games like tic-tac-toe, chess, nim etc. can be elegantly modelled as trees. For example, consider the game "nim" which is played by two players. The game is described by a board that contains "n" number of sticks. Each player has his turn to remove 1 or 2 or 3 sticks from the board. However, a player can not remove more than the number of sticks that are present in the board. Players A and B take their turns alternately. The player who removes the last stick looses the game and the other person wins it. To model it as a game tree, the game is to be viewed as consisting of a number of states or configurations. For example, in the game of "nim", a configuration of the game may be denoted by the number of sticks in the board. In the game of chess, its state is the position of all pieces in the chessboard. Each game must have an initial state or configuration. In the game of "nim", it is the number "n". In chess, the initial state of the game is the standard initial configuration of the pieces in a chessboard. The state of the game changes by moves applied by the players. In a game tree, the state of a game becomes a node of a tree. The initial state of the game determines the root node of the tree. If a player can take "n" number of moves when the state of the game is "X" then the node for that state will have "n" number of children each representing the state of the game after applying a move from the state "X". The game tree for "nim" is shown in the following where the number of sticks in the board is initially 4.

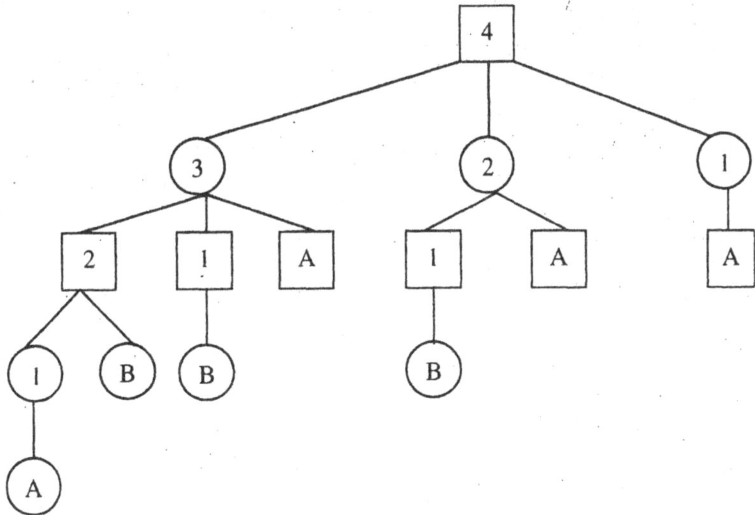

Figure B.1: A complete game tree for 'nim' with n = 4

The tree for the game "nim" is a finite one. The tree for the game tic-tac-toe is also finite. But the tree for chess would grow infinitely. In the figure B.1, there are two types of nodes: square and circular. Square nodes denote that state of the game when it is Player A's turn to make a move. Similarly, circular nodes denote that it is player B's turn to make a move. All terminals nodes in the figure are labelled by "A" or "B". Terminal nodes with label "A" indicate that the Player A has won. In the game of nim there is no configuration for a draw. However, in real games there could be states for draw conditions.

Game trees are useful in determining the next move that should be applied by a player (say player A). Suppose that the state of the game at the point of that move is described by the node 'n' of the game tree. In order to find out an appropriate move for player A, the tree of the game rooted at 'n' must be fully constructed. Further, an evaluation function, E, is to be formulated for every node of the game tree. The evaluation function should measure the value of a move for a player so that if E(X) is higher for a node "X" then player A has a higher chance of winning the game. If "q" and "r" are two children of the node "n" and E(q) is greater than E(r) then the player should make a move which would take the state of the game to "q". For the leaf nodes, computing E(X) is simple. E(X) may be 1 for a leaf node "X" if "X" is a winning node for "A", For leaf nodes, "X", which are losing configurations for player A, E(X) is –1. Now suppose that "X" is not a leaf node. So, the node "X" has "d" number of children, which are $x_1, x_2, x_3, \ldots, x_d$. Then, E(X) is defined as follows.

$$E(X) = \max_{1 \leq i \leq d} \{E(x_i)\} \text{ if "X" is a square node;}$$

$$E(X) = \min_{1 \leq i \leq d} \{E(x_i)\} \text{ if "X" is a circular node;}$$

This is because if "X" is a square node then it is player A's turn and A will chose to move to a child with the highest E value as A wants to win. Similarly, when "X" denotes a circular node then it is player B's turn and B will move to a child with least E value as B wants to win (i.e., A has to lose in that case). This procedure is known as "minimax" procedure for a game tree. Minimax procedure is illustrated on the game tree of Figure B.2. The game tree is for the game of "nim" as shown in Figure B.1. The labels of the nodes indicate their E values.

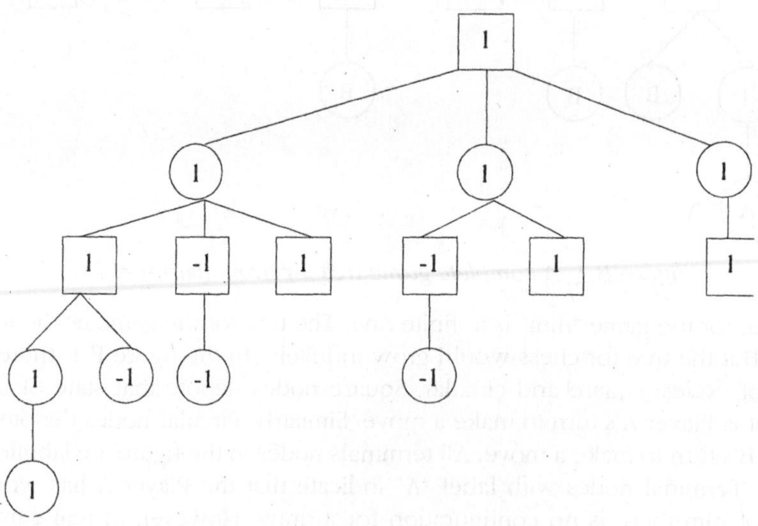

Figure B.2 The minimax procedure as applied on the tree of Figure B.1

For games like "nim" it is possible to construct the entire game tree and therefore it is possible to precisely specify the moves for a player. But for game trees, which are either infinite or enormously large, it is not possible to actually construct the entire tree from a node to find out the best move. In such cases, only a small portion of the tree is constructed from a node and the leaves are given E values based on some estimation procedures. In these cases, E values of the leaf nodes are not just 1 or -1.

Appendix - C

DOEACC

1. THE DOEACC SCHEME

1.1 The rapid spread of Information Technology (IT), in the late eighties, generated ample career opportunities. To fill this escalating demand for computer professionals, a large number of private institutions mushroomed, with varying degrees of excellence from very good to abysmally bad; the latter charging exorbitant fees without extending commensurate training to their students.

1.2 In this environment, the Ministry of Information Technology (erstwhile Department of Electronics) formulated a comprehensive policy to encourage and accelerate software export. Included, in this epoch making document, was Software Development and Training to generate Quality manpower by capitalizing on the resources existent with the computer training institutes in the Private Sector, thereby casting the net wider for computer education.

1.3 The Department of Electronics Accreditation of Computer Courses (DOEACC) was a fall out of this policy. The Scheme is under the aegis of the All India Council for Technical Education (AICTE), the statutory body for Technical Education in India, with the MIT being charged with its implementation.

1.4 **Aim.** The Scheme has a dual objective, as described below:

1.4.1 First: In the interest of the public at large, protecting them against exploitation, to set standards for the conduct of computer training, by institutes, in the private sector, at four levels O, A, B and C, spanning a Foundation Certificate Level of skill to a Post Graduate standard of knowledge in Information Technology (IT).

1.4.2 Second: To open the non-formal sector to develop IT manpower meeting an apprehended shortage of competent manpower.

1.5 **Operational Parameters**

1.5.1 Apart from administration of the Scheme, there are three functional areas of Accreditation, Examination & Registration, briefly described in this section and enlarged at Section 4 onwards.

1.5.2 Accreditation is the process of granting permission to an institution applying for it, to conduct a DOEACC course after a rigorous screening of its capabilities.

1.5.3 Registration is, an obligatory requirement for a candidate to appear at a DOEACC Society examination.

1.5.4 Examinations are held under the Scheme twice a year, all over India and test, not only the candidates, but also the institutes conducting accredited courses; the latter as determined by the number of candidates who take the examinations through respective institutes and the percentage that pass.

1.6 Calendar of Events

1.6.1 Dates for the various activities connected with examinations will be announced through newspapers, well in advance of the examinations.

1.6.2 The time schedule indicated below is for guidance of students.

	Examinations	
	January	**July**
A. Sale of Exam Application Forms		
i. Commencement date	1st Sep.	1st Mar.
ii. Closing date		
- from the office of the DOEACC Society through post/courier	15th Oct.	15th Apr.
- from the DOEACC Counselling Centres	27th Oct.	27th Apr.
- from DOEACC Society counter at New Delhi	31st Oct.	30th Apr.
B. Closing date for receipt of filled forms at DOEACC Society	31st Oct.	30th Apr.
C. Commencement of exams	2nd Sat. in January	2nd Sat. in July

NOTE

A. Application forms will be available at selected outlets, apart from the counter at DOEACC Society at Electronics Niketan, details of which will be advertised from time to time.

B. Bank of India has agreed to accept cash, through special challans, as examination fees for Modules/Papers opted for at all Levels. Candidates must send the counter foils in lieu of Demand Drafts, to DOEACC, along with completed application forms.

2. SYLLABUS

2.1 The syllabus of 'A' Level has been diversified. Examination based on the diversified framework are being held with effect from January 2000 onwards. The diversified syllabus consists of 8 compulsory papers and 2 elective papers. The structure of the diversified 'A' Level syllabus including the minimum number of contact hours for each of the papers is indicated below:

Paper Code	Name		Minimum number of hours
A1	Personal Computer Software		120
A2	Elective I (one of the following two subjects to be chosen)		
	A2.1	Business Systems	120
	A2.2	ERP Fundamentals	120
A3	Computer Organization and System Software		120
A4	Programming and Problem Solving through C Language		120
A5	System Analysis, Design and MIS		120
A6	Data Structure through C Language		120
A7	Data Base Management Systems		120
A8	Computer Graphics		120
A9	Data Communication and Network		120
A10	Elective II (one of the following four subjects to be chosen)		
	A10.1	Unix and Shell Programming	120
	A10.2	Introduction to Object Oriented Programming and C++ / Visual C++	120
	A10.3	Programming in JAVA	120
	A10.4	Introduction to Object Oriented Programming and Visual Basic	120

2.2 A project is to be completed by the candidates taking the 'A' Level examination. Details are given under the head PROJECT.

2.3 In the diversified syllabus, new subjects have been added as electives and certain amendments have been made to the syllabus on 'Personal Computer Software', 'Business Systems', 'Introduction to Object Oriented Programming and C++ / Visual C++'. All the subjects prior to diversification have been retained on diversification in the syllabus, with the amendments mentioned above.

2.4 Candidates are allowed a maximum of ten consecutive examinations, reckoned from the examination which a candidate is eligible to take as indicated in the letter of allotment of registration number to the candidate, for completing successfully the 'A' Level examination.

2.5 Three modules of O Level syllabus, prior to diversification were common to that of A Level and A Level, as a whole is a sub-set of B Level. Under the diversified O Level syllabus, if a candidate, in addition to the compulsory module of Personal Computer Software chooses the modules on Business Systems and Programming and Problem Solving through C Language and successfully completes all the four modules of O Level, the candidate is entitled to exemption from the three papers of Personal Computer Software, Business Systems and Programming and Problem Solving through C Language while taking A Level examination under the diversified syllabus.

3. REGISTRATION

3.1 Registration is compulsory and can be done throughout the year; except that, for a particular examination, there is a cut off date to register. Registration does not automatically confer the right to appear at an examination; the candidate must apply for the examination through the prescribed application form for that examination.

3.2 Some points to note in registration:

- is permitted at one level only at any point of time and appearing for examinations, at any other level, is not allowed;
- validity is for ten chances for O/A Levels and twelve chances at B/C Levels, commencing from the next eligible examination, as endorsed in the letter intimating registration;
- if a candidate qualifies at the lower level and wishes to continue in the Scheme, he/she must register at the higher level.
- in case a candidate qualifies in certain modules/papers, at a level and appears for the remaining modules/papers at that level and pending the announcement of results, registers at a higher level, in anticipation of passing, the candidate will forfeit the changes of appearing in the modules/papers in which the candidates is unsuccessful at the lower level.
- registration is to be applied for, using the form at Appendix A; clear photocopies can be used; instructions, comprehensively inscribed on the form, must be strictly followed, to avoid rejection; consult also, eligibility norms at Appendix B;
- it is advisable to register early; too close to the cut off date will invariably cause problems.

4. EXAMINATION

4.1 Only registered candidates with the DOEACC who fulfils the eligibility criteria given below should apply for the Exams.

4.2 Eligibility Criteria for appearing in 'A' Level Examination

A. **Students from an Accredited Institutes:**

Level 'O'/Government recognised polytechnic engineering diploma after class 10, followed in each case, by an accredited 'A' Level course (no concurrency).

or

A Government recognised polytechnic engineering diploma after 10+2/Graduate and an accredited 'A' Level course in each case (May be concurrent). +

B. **Direct Applicants :**

Level 'O'/Government recognised polytechnic engineering diploma/ Graduate, followed in each case, by one year relevant experience. *

\+ The 'A' Level diploma will be awarded only after successful completion of the academic stream i.e. polytechnic engineering diploma after 10+2 or degree.

* Relevant experience connotes job experience in IT, including teaching in a recognised institution as a faculty member, excludes coaching.

4.3 Work experience after completion of the minimum qualification is taken for eligibility of direct candidates. Present employment details must be entered in the Examination Application Form and the same should be certified by the head of the organization whose name and designation must be mentioned in the given space in the examination application form, legibly. Previous relevant experience (if any) must also be entered in the Examination Application Form. Attested certificates must be enclosed for prior experience cases, failure to which no credit will be granted and the examination application form may be rejected.

4.4 The responsibility to ensure that a candidate is eligible for appearing in the examination, as per the eligibility criteria given above will be that of the candidate. The decision of the examination authority in this regard will be final and binding on the candidate.

4.5 A candidate using unfair means at the Examination Hall is liable to be debarred, for a specific period, from appearing in the examinations or other action may be deemed fit by the Examination Authority.

4.6 SC/ST candidates may claim for the refund of examination fees after they clear all the papers of 'O' Level examination. Such candidates should apply along with attested photocopies of

a) Proof of their belonging to SC/ST,

b) Result Sheet (s) of DOEACC examination(s).

4.7 WARNING:

4.7.1 It has been noticed that candidates sometimes furnish teaching experience certificate from non-recognized, non-accredited training institutes. Please note that such candidates are **<u>NOT</u>** eligible.

4.7.2 Any dispute arising regarding Examination will be subject to the Jurisdiction of Delhi.

5. ACCREDITATION

5.1 Initially provisional accreditation for the conduct of a DOEACC course is granted to the institutes for a specified period within which the institute is obliged to meet certain performance criteria, which is determined by the number of candidates who take the examination through respective institutes and the percentage that pass. Failure to meet the performance criteria will lead to de-accreditation of that institute i.e. the accreditation granted to that institute to conduct DOEACC courses would be withdrawn.

5.2 On accreditation, institutes receive a letter assigning a Provisional/Full accreditation number (PROV No./FULL No.) and clear do's and don't's. A certificate, in a distinctly coloured background is given to the Institute by DOEACC, which the institute is required to display prominently as proof of having achieved that status.

5.3 It is the DOEACC course, run by that Institute that is accredited and NOT that institute or any other course run by it; NOR does this accreditation confer the status, to linked Institutes like its Franchise, Head Office, Branch, second site or extension etc.

5.4 Accreditation is for conduct of the specified DOEACC course by that Institute at the specified location ONLY and at no other location.

5.5 The institute has to name the course as "DOEACC **X** Level", as directed, in the letter of accreditation.

5.6 It is desirable that certain malpractices by unscrupulous training institutions be widely known in public interest to protect against exploitation.

5.6.1 Having been accreditation for one level, advertising that this applies to all other levels;

5.6.2 Having been accredited, discontinuing that course, and misusing the fact to run other courses;

5.6.3 Fielding outside candidates at examination as their own, giving false certificates in the examination application forms. Even candidates from their unaccredited branches are considered as outsiders;

5.6.4 Issuing DOEACC passed certificates on their own

5.7 Accreditation is a continuous process; new institutions get added from time to time; further, accreditation to existing institutes may be withdrawn if they fail to meet the specified norms.

5.8 Accreditation is PROVISIONAL initially, which is upgraded to FULL status if the performance criteria specified are satisfied by the Institute.

6. PROJECTS

6.1 Projects, in the DOEACC Scheme, are an integral part of the curriculum, to qualify for a certificate/diploma.

6.2 There is one project at 'A' Level. The project is to be submitted to the Society with documentation and fees.

6.3 SALIENT FEATURES OF THE PROJECT

6.3.1 Will be individual effort only

6.3.2 Carries 100 marks

6.3.3 The Society will arrange for an expert to conduct the viva-voce.

6.4 GUIDELINES FOR THE PROJECT

6.4.1 The project should have been carried out, during the course, over a duration of three months (full time) or six months (part time). Every candidate should do a project individually and no grouping is allowed.

6.4.2 The project will be carried out, under the guidance of the institute if he/she is through the institute conducting an accredited course. The direct candidate, in any case, will be doing a project in an organization. In that case he/she will carry out the project under the guidance of experts/professionals.

6.4.3 Reports in fulfilment of any other examination/context will not be entertained.

6.4.4 The project report should have a certificate as per the proforma given in para 6.4.6 by the candidate and one of the following :-

i) the institute where the candidate is undergoing an accredited course or

ii) the expert-guide in the case of a direct candidate.

6.4.5 The Society will arrange for viva voce of candidate relating to the project

6.4.6 **PROFORMA FOR CERTIFICATE FOR PROJECT**

This is to certify that this is a bonafide record of the project work done satisfactorily at ____________________ by Mr./Ms. ____________________________ (DOEACC Registration No. __________________) in partial fulfilment of 'A' Level examination.

This report or a similar report on the topic has not been submitted for any other examination and does not form part of any other course undergone by the candidate.

SIGNATURE OF CANDIDATE

SIGNATURE

Name :

PLACE: Designation:

DATE : Address :

Name & Seal of the Institution (with APROV. No./Organisation)

7. RECOGNITION

7.1 Recognition of DOEACC qualifications by Ministry of Human Resource Development, Government of India for employment purposes is reproduced for information at Appendix C.

7.2 Many private, public, government organizations and companies have accepted DOEACC qualifications for jobs at appropriate levels.

For further information on the DOEACC Scheme, please contact:

DOEACC Society

(An Autonomous body of Ministry of Information Technology, Government of India)

Electronics Niketan, 6, CGO Complex, New Delhi – 110 003

Tel: 011-4363330-2 (3 Lines) Fax: 011-4363335

Web Site: http://www.doeacc.org.in E-mail: doeacc@doe.ernet.in

Annexure - 1

DOEACC : AN AICTE - DOE (GOVT. OF INDIA) SCHEME
FORM FOR REGISTRATION FOR DOEACC O/A/B/C LEVEL EXAMINATION OR TRANSFER OF LEVEL

FOR OFFICIAL USE ONLY **LOT REF. NO.**

1.	PHOTO ATTESTED			Y	N	
2.	DD	I	C	P	N	INITIAL & DATE
3.	DOEACC ON DD			Y	N	
4.	DD AMOUNT		L	OK	M	
5.	EDN. CERT ATT			Y	N	
6.	EDN. QLN. OK			Y	N	REGISTRATION NO.

STN.	LOT	SRL. NO.

INITIAL & DATE

The Executive Director
DOEACC Society
Electronics Niketan, 6, CGO Complex, New Delhi-110 003

Photograph
5x4 Cms.

Attested by a
Gazetted Officer
Panchayat/
Bank Officer

Sir,

I WISH TO REGISTER FOR ☐ LEVEL EXAMINATION

WHETHER PREVIOUSLY REGISTERED YES ☐ NO ☐ (Place X)

If Yes, indicate Level ☐ and Registration No. ☐☐☐☐☐☐

1. NAME (Use Block Letters Only; Leave one blank between words)

2. FATHER'S NAME (Use Block Letters Only; Leave one blank between words)

3. PERSONAL ADDRESS (For Mailing; Please ensure correctness and keep it updated) (DO NOT REPEAT NAME)

TOWN 4. STATE

5. PIN CODE

6. AGE AND DATE OF BIRTH (in Christian era) :

AGE

DATE OF BIRTH

(DD) (MM) (YY)

7. SEX

MALE FEMALE

(Place X)

8. WHETHER UNDERGOING DOEACC COMPUTER COURSE ACCREDITED UNDER DOEACC

YES NO

(Place X)

If yes indicate name of the Institute and Place

ACCR No. of the Institute

9. EDUCATIONAL QUALIFICATION : (Write year of passing in the relevant box)

1	2	3	4	5
10+ITI Certificate (one year)	10+Govt. recognised Polytech. Engg. Diploma	10+2	10+2+Govt. recognised Polytech: Engg. Diploma	Undergoing Govt. recognised Polytech. Engg. Diploma

6	7	8	9	10
Undergoing Graduation	Govt. Recognised PPDCA	Govt. recognised PGDCA	Graduate	Post Graduate
11	12			
Doctorate	GATE (Computer)			

10. DOEACC QUALIFIED YES [ ] NO [ ] (Place X) IF YES O A B C [ ] (Place X) MM [ ] YY [ ]

11. MARITAL STATUS (Place X) SINGLE [ ] MARRIED [ ] WIDOW/WIDOWER [ ] DIVORCED [ ]

12. SCHEDULED CASTE YES [ ] NO [ ] (Place X) 13. SCHEDULED TRIBE YES [ ] NO [ ] (Place X)

14. EX-SERVICEMAN [ ] [ ] 15. HANDICAPPED [ ] [ ]

16. I enclose, herewith, Bank Draft No. .... Dated .... for Rs .... drawn on .... in favour of 'DOEACC', New Delhi as one time Non refundable Registration Fee.

Witness my hand the .... day of .... 19 ....

Signature of the Applicant ....

INSTRUCTIONS TO APPLICANTS

i) ELIGIBILITY : Given in concerned Prospectus or write-up supplied with this form.

ii) LEVEL : At any point of time registration can be only for one level.

iii) ADDRESS CHANGE : Inform immediately quoting Registration No.

iv) REGISTRATION FEE : With effect from July 2001 Examination registration fee for 'O' Level is Rs. 100/-, 'A' Level Rs. 150/-, 'B' Level Rs. 200/-, 'C' Level Rs. 300/-. Payment should not be clubbed with requests for other documents, like Prospectus, Syllabus etc. In addition to registration fees a candidate has to pay Rs. 100/- for the issue of DOEACC News letter for a period of one year from the date of registration and one time issue of a Student Guide and list of institutions authorized to conduct accredited course(s). All remittances shall be only by crossed BANK DRAFT; drawn in favour of'DOEACC', payable at New Delhi. Demand Draft, the validity period of which is to expire shortly, should not be sent with the registration form. Write your name & address on the reverse side of the DRAFT.

v) Differences in registration fee only need be paid 'if level change is due to passing the lower level & moving to immediate higher level. vi) Wherever (Place X) is indicated mark X in the box applicable.

vii) Attach attested photocopies of certificates of educational/DOEACC qualifications (only mark sheet not sufficient).

viii) Candidates undergoing 'A' Level accredited course during the pendency of graduation or Govt. recognised Polytechnic Engineering Diploma after 10+2 should send proof of the same from the respective College/Polytechnic and the institute where 'A' Level Accredited course is being undertaken.

ix) Proof of equivalence in terms of Indian Universities should be sent in case registration is sought based on foreign qualifications.

x) If a candidate registered at one level, wants to register at another level and is so registered, pending successful completion of the examination at the original level, he/she will be allowed to take the examination at the level at which he/she is subsequently registered only and will not be allowed to complete the examination at the original level in case of failure in any of the modules/papers at the original level of examination.

xi) Candidates denied registration should not refer to the attested photocopies of certificates of educational/DOEACC qualifications or other documents sent within the earlier registration form, while seeking registration again, with the submission of a fresh registration form, which should be complete in all respects, including all relevant enclosures.

Annexure 2

ELIGIBILITY CRITERIA

ELIGIBILITY CRITERIA FOR APPEARING AT EXAMINATIONS TO BE HELD AT VARIOUS LEVELS

A. Students from Institutes conducting accredited courses :

'O' Level: 10+2 or ITI Certificate (One Year) after class 10, followed in each case, by an accredited 'O' Level course.

or

Successful completion of the second year of a Government recognised polytechnic engineering diploma course after class 10, followed by an accredited 'O' Level course concurrently during the third year of the said polytechnic engineering diploma course. ¢

'A' Level: Level 'O'/Government recognised polytechnic engineering diploma after class 10, followed in each case, by an accredited 'A' Level course (no concurrency).

or

A Government recognised polytechnic engineering diploma after 10+2/ Graduate and an accredited 'A' Level course in each case (May be concurrent).+

'B' Level: Level 'A'/Government recognised PPDCA/Government recognised PGDCA/ Government recognised polytechnic engineering diploma/ Graduate followed in each case, by an accredited 'B' Level course (First two semesters are exempted for those who pass 'A' Level in full. Candidates having Government recognised PPDCA/Government recognised PGDCA will also be eligible for exemption of some subjects depending on the courses they had undergone, on a case by case basis).

'C' Level: Level 'B'/B.Tech./BE/MCA/M.Sc./Master's Degree in Mathematics/ Statistics/

Operations Research/MBA (or equivalent) with B.Sc./B.A. (Mathematics/ Statistics), GATE(Computer), followed in each case, by an accredited 'C' Level course.

B. Students-at-large (Direct Applicants)

'O' Level: 10+2 or ITI Certificate (One Year) after class 10, followed in each case, by one year relevant experience.*

or

a pass in the NCVT-DP&CS (Data Preparation & Computer Software) Examination, conducted by DGE&T (Govt. of India).

'A' Level: Level 'O'/Government recognised polytechnic engineering diploma/ Graduate, followed in each case, by one year relevant experience.*

'B' Level: Level 'A'/Government recognised PPDCA/Government recognised PGDCA followed in each case, by two years relevant experience.* (First two semesters are exempted for those who pass 'A' Level in full. Candidates having Government recognised PPDCA/Government recognised PGDCA will also be eligible for exemption of some subjects depending on the courses, they had undergone, on a case by case basis).

or

Graduate/Government recognised polytechnic engineering diploma, followed in each case by three years relevant experience.*

'C' Level: Level 'B'/B.Tech./BE/MCA/M.Sc./Master's Degree in Mathematics/ Statistics/ Operations Research/MBA (or equivalent) with B.Sc./B.A. (Mathematics/ Statistics), GATE (Computer), followed in each case, by one and half year relevant experience.*

¢ The 'O' Level certificate will be awarded only after successful completion of the polytechnic engineering diploma.

\+ The 'A' Level diploma will be awarded only after successful completion of the academic stream i.e. polytechnic engineering diploma after 10+2 or degree.

* Relevant experience connotes job experience in IT, including teaching in a recognised institution as a faculty member, excludes coaching.

Annexure 3

MHRD RECOGNITION NOTIFICATIONS

1. Government of India, Ministry of Human Resource Development, (Department of Education) in its Notification (43) dated 1st March 1995, states

   "No.F.18-23/92-TD.V/Ts-IV(.) On the recommendation of the Board of Assessment for Educational Qualifications, the Government of India has decided to recognize the 'O' Level and 'A' Level examinations conducted by the Computer Society of India (CSI) under the Department of Electronics Accreditation of Computer Courses (DOEACC) scheme as equivalent to Foundation course and Advanced Diploma level course, respectively, for the purpose of employment to posts and services under the Central Government."

2. This was amended by the same Department in its Notification (49) dated 10-4-96 stating

   "No.F.18-23/92-TD.V/TS.IV. In partial modification of Notification(43) of even number dated 1st March 1996, on the recommendations of the Board of Assessment for Educational Qualifications, the Government of India have resolved to recognize, with effect from July 1995, the change in the name of the Examination-conducting/awarding-body for 'O' Level and 'A' Level courses from Computer Society of India to the Department of Electronics of Computer Courses (DOEACC) Society."

3. No. F. 2/6/97 - T.S. III A(.)54 - On the recommendation of the High Level Committee for Educational Qualifications, the Government of India have decided to recognise the 'B' Level Computer Examination being conducted by the Department of Electronics Accreditation of Computer Courses (DOEACC) Society for the purpose of employment under the Central Government where M.C.A. is the desired qualification.

4. The Draft Notifications, to be published in Part-I Section-1 of the Gazette of India, forwarded by the Board of Assessment for Educational Qualifications, were also copied to -

   - All State Govt. and Union Territories (Education Deptt).
   - All Regional Offices of the Ministry of Human Resources Development (Department of Education)
   - All Directors of Technical Education
   - Union Public Services Commission, Dholpur House, Shahjahan Road, New Delhi.

- Staff Selection Commission, Lok Nayak Bhawan, Khan Market, New Delhi.
- All State Public Service Commissions
- Association of Indian Universities, 16 Kotla Marg, New Delhi.
- D.P.O.O (Ministry of Human Resource Development)
- All Board of Apprenticeship Training
- All Ministries and Deptts. of Government of India.
- Ministry of Information Technology, Electronics Niketan, 6, CGO Complex, New Delhi.

REFERENCES

Aho A. V., Hopcroft J. E., Ullman J. D., Data Structures and Algorithms, Addison-Wesley, 1983.

Baase S., Computer Algorithms : Introduction to Design and Analysis, Addison-Wesley, 1978.

Banachowski Lech, Kreczmar Antoni, Rytter Wojciech, Analysis of Algorithms and Data Structures, Addison-Wesley, 1991.

Berztiss A. T., Data Structures, Theory and Practice, 2nd Ed., Academic Press, 1977.

Collins W. J., Data Structures, An Object-Oriented Approach, Addison-Wesley, 1992.

Cormen Thomas H., Leiserson Charles E., Rivest Ronald L., Introduction to Algorithms, Prentice Hall of India, 1990.

Gonnet G. H., Baeza-Yates R., Handbook of Algorithms and Data Structures in Pascal and C, 2nd Ed., Addison-Wesley, 1991.

Goodman S.E., S. T. Hedetniemi, Introduction to the Design and Analysis of Algorithms, McGraw-Hill, 1977.

Horowitz E., Sahni S., Algorithms: Design and Analysis, Computer Science Press, 1977.

Horowitz E., Sahni S., Fundamentals of Data Structures in Pascal, Computer Science Press, 1984.

Kernighan Brian W., Ritchie Dennis M., The C Programming Language, 2nd Ed., Prentice Hall of India, 1989.

Knuth D. E., The Art of Computer Programming, Vols. 1-3, Addison-Wesley, 1973.

Kruse R. L., Data Structures and Program Design, 2nd Ed., Prentice Hall of India, 1992.

Lorin H., Sorting and Sortt Systems, Addison-Wesley, 1975.

Nievergelt J., Farrar J. C., Reingold E. M., Computer Approaches to Mathematical Problems, Prentice Hall, 1974.

Nilsson N., Problem Solving Methods in Artificial Intelligence, McGraw-Hill, 1971.

Reingold E. M., Hansen W. J., Data Structures, Little Brown & Co., 1986.

Roy M. K., Ghosh Dastidar D., Computer Sorting Techniques, Roy and Choudhury, 1976.

Sedgewick R., Algorithms in C, Addison-Wesley, 1990.

Standish T. A., Data Structures Techniques, Addison-Wesley, 1980.

Tenenbaum A. M., Langsam Y., Augenstein M. J., Data Structures using C and C++, 2nd Ed., Prentice-Hall, 1996.

Tremblay J. P., Sorenson P. G., An Introduction to Data Structures with Applications, McGraw-Hill, 1976.

Wirth N., Algorithms + Data Structures = Programs, Prentice-Hall, 1976.

Index

A

B

C

D

E

F

G

H

O

P

Q

R

S